A
HISTORY
OF
MENTAL
RETARDATION

A
HISTORY
OF
MENTAL
RETARDATION

R. C. Scheerenberger, Ph.D.

·P·A·U·L·H·
BROOKES
PUBLISHING C⁰

Baltimore • London

Paul H. Brookes Publishing Co.
Post Office Box 10624
Baltimore, MD 21204

Copyright 1983 by Paul H. Brookes Publishing Co., Inc.
All rights reserved.

Typeset by The Composing Room of Michigan,
Grand Rapids, Michigan.
Manufactured in the United States of America by
Universal Lithographers, Inc., Cockeysville, Maryland.

Library of Congress Cataloging in Publication Data
Scheerenberger, R. C.
  A history of mental retardation.

  Includes bibliographical references and index.
  1. Mental deficiency—History. 2. Mentally handicapped—
Services for—History. I. Title.
RC570.S25   1982   362.3′09   82-9489
ISBN 0-933716-27-3   AACR2

Contents

FIGURES

TABLES

PREFACE

P REPARING A HISTORICAL STATEMENT on any subject represents a complex, arduous task, requiring months (in this instance, years) of collecting, examining, analyzing, collating, integrating, and reintegrating the contents of numerous documents and publications. To compound the difficulty, mental retardation is primarily a problem of the common people whose activities have rarely drawn the attention of historians throughout the ages and who, in turn, have left few documents of their own.

The challenge, however, was intriguing for a variety of reasons. First, and not surprisingly, the author has held a long-standing interest in both mental retardation and history. Second, and of much greater consequence, there does not exist an extensive historical overview of mental retardation, its recognition, acceptance, and programming. This does not mean to imply that the field has not had its documentarians. Edgar and Edward Doll, J. E. Wallace Wallin, Arthur Whitney, Marie Skodak Crissey, Robert Haskell, Wolf Wolfensberger, and others have, at one time or other, prepared historical papers. Such presentations, however, either have offered a brief treatment of the field in general or were time/theme limited. Even the best known history—Leo Kanner's *A History of the Care and Study of the Mentally Retarded,* published in 1964—is quite restricted in scope. Third, some historical theses, like Procrustes's treatment of his guests, have tended to manipulate events and assign motives to "fit a theoretical bed." Fourth, several early leaders in the field have suffered greatly from what Voltaire called the "tricks that the living play on the dead." Walter Fernald is a prime example of this phenomenon. Given to the hyperbolic expression, Fernald in his earlier years rendered highly negative judgments concerning mentally retarded persons which are often quoted today. Rarely noted are his many achievements in promoting progressive thinking and community services. Fifth, a number of persons who made substantial contributions to the field remain relatively unknown. While Itard and Seguin are widely recognized, few people know of the tremendous contributions of such persons as Elizabeth Farrell, Charles Bernstein, or Charles Vaux. Finally, there is always the question of progress. In this regard, and in the parlance of the behaviorist, history provides the baseline data.

Histories are written for many purposes: to instruct, to caution against repeating the errors of the past, to prognosticate the future, or merely to shed additional light on a preceding period. This history on mental retardation is intended simply to inform, that is, to lay before the reader some of the major events and personages that have influenced the development of programs and services for mentally retarded persons. While trends and general social conditions are set forth, there has been no attempt either to prescribe individual motivations or to render sweeping generalizations concerning society as a whole, such as "Society rejects the mentally retarded."

This relatively conservative approach reflects two historical certainties. First, history tends to be reinterpreted by each generation according to contemporary ideology and needs. In doing so, historical events are often modified either in occurrence or interpretation to satisfy current expectancies. Second, it is almost impossible to know with certainty why someone acted as he or she did at a given moment in time. No less a historian than Arthur Schlesinger noted after his very close association with the administration of President John F. Kennedy, "Nothing in my own recent experience has been more chastening than the attempt to penetrate into the process of decision. I shudder a little when I think how confidently I have analyzed decisions in the ages of Jackson and Roosevelt, traced influences, assigned motives, evaluated roles, allocated responsibilities and, in short, transformed a dishevelled and murky evolution into a tidy and ordered transaction. The sad fact is that, in many cases, the basic evidence for the historian's reconstruction of the really hard cases does not exist—and the evidence that does exist is often incomplete, misleading or erroneous" (Schlesinger, 1963, p. 493).

In addition to the question of intent, historical texts are obliged to account for their sources of information. This history on mental retardation is based primarily on the written word, and every effort was made to acquire original documents. Fortunately, the massive library system(s) of the University of Wisconsin and its inter-university library loan program as well as the services of the State (Wisconsin) Historical Society proved to be invaluable. Documents and journals hundreds of years old were readily available. In addition, various organizations and people around the country dug into their archives to provide information. Secondary resources were used sparingly and primarily to fill in some of the missing gaps. Such resources were used only when their authors possessed well-established reputations for accuracy and relative freedom from bias. The three most commonly cited historians from secondary sources were Albert Duetsch, Gregory Zilboorg, and Leo Kanner.

Every effort has been made to render this presentation as objective and factual as possible. This, in turn, was not readily accomplished. Events do not record themselves; they are noted and passed forward by participants or observers of the day who are rarely neutral in judgment or opinion. Also, what is set down in writing need not reflect accurately that which was practiced. Great caution has been exercised to separate the desirable from the actual, whenever possible.

The text is divided into two parts: 1) Western European history as it relates to mental retardation until the twentieth century, and 2) U.S. history from the days of our Puritan forefathers to 1959. Western European influences affecting American programming during the twentieth century are integrated with the U.S. history for that period. The closing chapter highlights some of the major events and trends in the United States from 1960 through 1979 and offers a few final observations and comments.

The early chapters in both sections tend to treat the subject in rather broad terms owing to a relative paucity of information. Beginning with the nineteenth century, however, each chapter refers to understanding and social care and treatment, including residential services and special education. Thus, the reader has the option of either considering the subject as a whole or following a particular line of interest. Each chapter is prefaced with a brief historical statement in order to reacquaint the reader with the general conditions of the times. All too often we are inclined to interpret yesterday's events in the light of today's experiences—an interesting, but dangerous practice.

As regards style, the text has been written to allow for enjoyable reading, but, at the same time, it does retain a number of quotations not only to ensure accuracy but also to lend further flavor to the times and to the thinking of the field's leaders. For readers wishing to pursue a particular subject in greater detail, a supplemental reading list of readily available materials has been included.

Regrettably, it is impossible to acknowledge all persons who have, directly or indirectly, contributed to this history. I would, however, like to express particular gratitude to: John Toussaint, M.D., Stephen Jones, Ph.D., and Otto Puls, R.Ph., for their advice in specialty areas; John Hedrick, S.A.C., for both his participation in the abortive effort to locate the Bishop of Myra and for his excellent translations of Felix Platter's archaic Latin; Harold Schultz, Keith

Hoffman, Stephen Stidinger, Geraldine Matthews, Ph.D., Mary Moffatt, and Dianne Molvig for their assistance in locating or providing critical information; Sabra Stiemke, Darlene Harms, and especially Mary Celentani for their dedicated work and immeasurable talent in preparing the various drafts of the book; Kathy Reiner for her frequent encouragement to complete the text and for her excellent proofreading skills; Nancy Turcotte and Richard McVicar for their photographic reproductions; and the American Association on Mental Deficiency, the Association for Retarded Citizens of the United States, and the Council for Exceptional Children for their cooperation. I gratefully acknowledge the tremendous patience of my wife Emilie and her willingness to live in an environment surrounded by books, notes, papers, cards, and boxes, frequently strewn at random throughout the house. Finally, I wish to thank Paul Brookes for his interest in the book and its publication.

ABOUT THE AUTHOR

D URING HIS DISTINGUISHED CAREER, Dr. R. C. Scheerenberger has received more than 20 awards and honors for his work in the field of mental retardation, has been published more than 100 times, and has held eight editorships. University lecturer, special educator, and administrator, Dr. Scheerenberger is currently Director of the Central Wisconsin Center for the Developmentally Disabled (Madison), a lecturer and Advisory Committee member to the School of Education, University of Wisconsin-Madison, a member of the Waisman Center UAF Advisory Committee (University of Wisconsin-Madison), a member of the National Program Services Committee of the Association for Retarded Citizens, and Associate Editor of the AAMD journal *Mental Retardation*. Dr. Scheerenberger has also served as president of the American Association on Mental Deficiency and of the National Association of Superintendents of Public Residential Facilities for the Mentally Retarded.

To my wife, Emilie;
my parents, Matt and Senta Scheerenberger;
and in fond memory of
my grandfather, Andrew P. Estergard.

A
HISTORY
OF
MENTAL
RETARDATION

Part

I

WESTERN EUROPE
UNTIL THE
TWENTIETH CENTURY

Chapter

1

IN THE BEGINNING
(4,000,000 B.C.–A.D. 476)

MENTAL RETARDATION IS primarily a socioculturally determined phenomenon that undoubtedly has been apparent since the dawn of man. Any given society, including the earliest tribes, unquestionably contained members who were more capable and less capable than average. The impact of debility has, however, varied with the needs of the society, its expectancies and social consciousness.

OUR PREHISTORIC ANCESTORS

Man and his hominoid ancestors have lived, loved, raised children, worked, warred, and communalized for at least 4 million years.* *Homo sapiens*—those two-legged walking creatures with intellect—have been with us for approximately 600,000 years. Though much of their existence and their cultures remains a mystery, they must have been remarkable people, even majestic in their own way: "*Homo sapiens* managed to survive 600,000 years of slow and undisturbed existence without writing, chemistry, or machines . . . there have been four ice ages and three temperate periods during the past 600,000 years so men have already managed to survive terrors of cold, lasting up to 100,000 years on four separate

occasions, each time without the help of modern science."[1] Also, the estimated 1 million prehistoric persons roamed throughout all of Africa and the lands that compose our Western civilization. Nor were they in any way superior to modern man with regard to physical attributes: "The prehistoric individual was a sickly man. Indeed, he must have been, his mind and body wasted by sleeping on the cold, mud-tainted ground . . . by lack of food, by trauma, fears and stresses. Fossils and carved stones of that period indicated that the prehistoric man, like every man, suffered the same diseases and disorders as affect modern man, including alterations in growth and metabolism, tumors, traumas, and infections."[2]

In spite of the hardships and susceptibility to all forms of disease and injury—or perhaps because of them—our prehistoric relatives were not without skill, culture, and compassion. They had reached considerable heights prior to the arrival of modern man in approximately 12,000 B.C. They must have been tremendous hunters of exceptional talent, considering their limited hunting implements and modes of transportation. Yet, the male was capable of providing food for his family and probably other members of his communal ar-

---

Man is used in its generic sense which includes reference to both men and women.

3

rangement. Man, in fact, has a long history of social living as the result of the need for group hunting, gathering, and collective defense.

Around 12,000 B.C., man went through an inexplicable but remarkable transformation. He passed from the age of nomadic hunting to that of agriculture, symbolic reasoning, verbal communication, and rural/urban living. During this Neolithic period, man laid the foundations for the rapid development of various cultures, which, in turn, would provide the basis for our early civilizations in Mesopotamia and Egypt.

Many reasons have been advanced for these remarkable quantitative and qualitative changes in man. Noted scientist Carl Sagan speculates that this critical point in man's development involved a combination of increased brain mass, increased ratio of brain to body weight, the development of higher reasoning centers (e.g., enlarged frontal and temporal lobes), and an increased number of neural synapses.[3] The weather became temperate, and grain was discovered in the Mediterranean area. Whatever the reasons, or interactions thereof, modern man was born; and he began to congregate in small villages, abandoning a nomadic way of life.

After 7,000 B.C., man pursued responses to injury other than the natural tendencies of sucking, washing, and binding wounds. Treatment for physical and mental disorders was provided by two groups of individuals: the empirical practitioner and the shaman, or medicine man. Neolithic man, probably with some historical precedents, believed firmly in animism, that is, the existence of spirits that could do evil. Thus, if one were to become ill, he would call upon the shaman to exorcise the evil spirits. The shaman, in turn, relied heavily on magic or special rituals, including provisions for such defensive mechanisms as fetishes (objects with magical powers), amulets (protective objects against black magic), and talismans (good luck objects). More formal treatment also existed; medical practitioners applied such techniques as massages, baths, extractions, vegetable drugs, and blood-letting. They also engaged in trephination (i.e.,

removing small circular sections of cranial bone from the top of the skull) to expel demons from among persons with mental disorders and epilepsy. The pieces of removed cranial bones (called "rondelles"), in turn, were taken from the living (and some individuals did survive), strung on necklaces, and worn as amulets.

What may one assume about those who were mentally retarded among our early ancestors? First, it is highly probable that the more seriously affected did not survive birth. Second, individuals with severe orthopedic handicaps that prevented their becoming hunters or keeping up with the nomadic requirements of earlier man probably were destroyed. Infanticide was commonly practiced; as described by Will Durant:

> Most nature-people permitted the killing of the newborn child if it was deformed, or diseased, or a bastard, or its mother had died in giving it birth. As if any reason would be good in the task of limiting population to the available means of subsistence, many tribes killed infants whom they considered to have been born under unlucky circumstances. . . . The practice of infanticide was particularly prevalent among nomads who found children a problem on their long marches. . . . When famine conditions existed or threatened, most tribes strangled the newborn, and some tribes ate them. Usually, it was a girl who was most subject to infanticides; occasionally she was tortured to death with a view of inducing the soul to appear, in its next incarnation, in the form of a boy. Infanticide was practiced without cruelty and without remorse; for in the first moments after delivery, apparently, the mother felt no instinctive love for the child. Once the child had been permitted to live a few days, it was safe against infanticide; soon parental love was evoked by its helpless simplicity, and in most cases, it was treated more affectionately by its primitive parent than the average child of higher races.[4]

Infanticide would continue to be practiced the world over throughout the course of history, reasons for which ranged from necessity to egotism. Female infants and the grossly deformed were most often destroyed. As indicated, nomadic tribes often limited the number of members in the group; quite frequently, women of such groups could only tend one child at a time. Superstition (e.g., being born under the wrong sign on an inappropriate day, or during a storm), famine, illegitimacy, twin births, and incest were all reasons for infanticide. The most severe practice was that of the inhabitants of the New Hebrides who not only killed the malformed child but the mother as well.[5]

As regards our prehistoric relatives, however, the notion of brutishness and innate aggressiveness as propounded by many authorities on human behavior, including Freud and Lorenz, is being challenged by today's anthropologists and paleontologists. Recent evidence, especially that produced by the Leakey family, indicates that hominid or pre-*sapien* man who lived 2 million years ago represented a hunter-gatherer society, one which could readily provide for at least those less severely mentally retarded (however that may have been expressed).[6] As a hunter-gatherer society, women and children picked fruits and berries while the men hunted small animals (sheep, wild cattle, pigs, and land tortoises), which could easily be captured or run off the side of a cliff. There is no evidence to suggest that the various species became extinct as a result of war or murder.

In addition to speculation, interpretation, and theory, specific examples of care and affection were demonstrated by our prehistoric ancestors. Perhaps the most outstanding instance was reported by Solecki, based on his discovery in the early 1950s of the remains of several Neanderthal people near the little village of Shanidar in northern Iraq. It should be recognized that the commonly held stereotype of the Neanderthal man as a gruesome, hunched over, ape-like figure grunting and clubbing his way through life is quite erroneous. Though he possessed exaggerated cranial features by today's standards, in all other physical aspects he was quite like modern man. Nor, parenthetically, is Neanderthal man currently considered to be a direct ancestor of *Homo sapiens*. Nevertheless, he showed extreme compassion for his neighbors as is well illustrated by Shanidar I, the first remains to be discovered. Estimated to have lived 45,000 years ago, Shanidar I, a male, had an underdeveloped right shoulder blade, collarbone,

and upper right arm bone. It is believed that he was crippled with a useless right arm, which had been amputated in life just below the elbow. A thorough analysis of the skeletal remains revealed that Shanidar I was

> an individual who lived to the relatively old age of forty years, a very old man for a Neanderthal—equivalent to a man of about eighty today. He was plagued by arthritis, which seems to have been a rather common ailment among Neanderthals—and no wonder, considering the kind of life they led. As a case of rehabilitation, Shanidar I was a prime example. Not only did he possess a disability from the day he was born, but he must have been blind in the left eye . . . examinations disclosed that the right arm, collarbone, and shoulder blade had never fully grown from birth. Furthermore, there was extensive bone scar tissue on the left side of his face. And as if this were not enough, there is evidence that the top right side of his skull had received some damage which had healed well before the time of death. In short, Shanidar I—or "Nandy," as we called him around the dinner table—was at a distinct disadvantage in an environment where even men in the best of condition had a hard time. He could barely forage and fend for himself, and we must assume that he was accepted and supported by his people up to the day he died. Any manpower must have been an asset to this ancient little community, especially since it undoubtedly took group activity to hunt the gregarious beasts of the wild. That "Nandy" made himself useful around the hearth (two hearths were found very close to him) is evidenced by the unusual wear on his front teeth. It presumably indicates that in lieu of a right arm, he used his jaws for grasping, while manipulating with his good left arm and hand. The stone heap over his remains, and the mammal food remains, show that even in death his person was an object of some esteem, if not respect, born out of close association against a hostile outside.[7]

In brief, it would appear that Shanidar I's tribe favored him, protected him from undue harm, and found a productive place for him in their society. A seemingly perfect realization of our often unfulfilled twentieth century goals.

Other archeological evidence from graves has shown that a number of tribes or groups maintained and protected crippled infants, children, and adults, even though they must have represented quite a burden during times of travel. Skull fragments also were recently discovered on the Danish peninsula of Jutland, indicating that trephination had been performed on a hydrocephalic infant.[8]

While many of the more seriously affected, physically and mentally, were destroyed or died at an early age, it is probable that many of the mildly retarded not only survived but contributed to their primitive society. Though survival undoubtedly depended upon perceptual acuity, physical strength, and psychomotor coordination, demands for verbal learning did not exist. As observed by Kanner in 1949:

> In less complex, less intellectually centered societies, the mentally retarded would have no trouble in obtaining and retaining a quality of realizable ambitions. Some might even be capable of gaining superiority by virtue of assets other than those measured by the intelligence test. They could make successful peasants, hunters, fishermen, tribal dancers. They can, in our own society, achieve proficiency as farm hands, factory workers, miners, waitresses . . . their principal shortcoming is a greater or lesser degree of inability to comply with the intellectual requirements of their society. In other respects, they may be as mature or immature, stable or unstable, secure or insecure, placid or moody, aggressive or submissive, as any other member of the human species. Their "deficiency" is an *ethnologically determined phenomena* relative to the local standards and even within those standards, relative to the educational postulates, vocational ambitions, and family expectancies. They are "subcultural" in our society but may not be even that in a different, less sophisticated setting.[9]

In 1947, the late Robert Redfield, then head of the Department of Anthropology at the University of Chicago, wrote a provocative article on the social nature of prehistoric tribes. Though he recognized that such groups varied considerably, he also contended that they shared a number of common characteristics. Each tribe represented a small, very personal society. People held common interests and performed similar jobs; their associations were for life. In such a small community, each member was treated as a person, not as a "number" or "thing."[10] If Redfield's interpretation is correct, the prehistoric society may have been relatively ideal for its slower members.

The legacy of this period is most interesting.

It is obvious that some forms of mental retardation and epilepsy were evident and that some effort was made to treat these conditions. The notion that epilepsy and mental deviations were a result of evil spirits requiring spiritual healing would persist well into the seventeenth century. Trephination, at least for epilepsy and insanity, continued to be practiced until the turn of the twentieth century.[11]

Our Near Eastern Heritage

The eastern oriental countries of Mesopotamia/Babylonia, Egypt, and Palestine laid the broad foundations for the development of our Western civilization. Yet, these peoples simply adopted and expanded upon many of the precepts and practices of their predecessors. In spite of their respective advances, at least with regard to their mentally retarded members, they were more similar than different.

MESOPOTAMIA/BABYLONIA

The golden age of Mesopotamia extended from 1700 to 560 B.C., starting with Hammurabi and ending with King Nebuchadnezzar. Mesopotamia, which before the flood was described as one of the most beautiful areas in the world, brought forth the first recognized political structure, a major codification of laws, and influenced, directly and indirectly, the development of several major religions. Mesopotamia, which in many respects is well described in the Old Testament, consisted of fabulous cities; irrigation canals; soaring towers, including the Tower of Babylon; hanging gardens; and innumerable caravans with cargoes of gold, spices, and incense.

Mesopotamian society, which was developed by the Samarians and Semites, was creative, producing a complex oral and written language, and inventing such mechanical devices as the wheel, the pulley, the screw, the wedge, and the inclined plane. Politically, it was a theocratic democracy that relied heavily upon a slavery-based economy.

All citizens were required to labor at the

canals in peacetime and to soldier in wartime. The need for manpower was always great.

Disease and mental disorder were viewed as a punishment by God or a possession by evil spirits or the devil. Diseases, both mental and physical, were considered impure or taboo. While Mesopotamia generated a highly specialized series of medical practitioners, including surgeons, internalists, herb doctors, and "spell doctors," the average citizen usually placed his confidence in natural deities since he strongly believed that all illnesses were the result of sin. To compound the magnitude of such problems, sin was defined very broadly and could result from such behaviors as spitting into a canal, the dipping of feet into unclean water, and the unnecessary handling of the sick.

Hammurabi, the greatest leader of Mesopotamia, was the sixth king of the First Dynasty of Babylon and reigned for 55 years around 2500 B.C. A number of historical documents describe him as a most able administrator. He was a great soldier and a pious, god-fearing king, who destroyed his enemies and gave his people peace and security. Today, Hammurabi is known primarily for his codification of laws. Regrettably, many references to the Hammurabi Code simply dismiss it as the first elaborate systemization of law characterized by extremely harsh judgments. Yet, in many ways, the Code, which was carved on an 8-foot block of black diorite and discovered in 1902, represented a tremendous advance in societal thinking and responsibility. Not only did it place a high value on people (including slaves), but it was intended to protect women and children and to acknowledge society's responsibility to the individual. The Code was predicated on Hammurabi's belief that the duty of a king, as he admonished future leaders of Mesopotamia, was to "rightly rule his Black-Head people; let him pronounce judgments for them and render for them decisions! Let him rule out the wicked and evil doer from his land! Let him promote the welfare of his people!"[12]

Because of its significance, let us examine some of the Code's 282 laws and related judgments. First, in certain areas the Code was harsh—very harsh:

> If one man break a man's bone, they shall break his bone.
> If a man strike a man's daughter and bring about a miscarriage, he shall pay ten sheckles of silver for her miscarriage. If that woman die, they shall put his daughter to death.
> If a physician operate on a man for a severe wound with a bronze lancet and cause the man's death; or open an abscess (in the eye) of a man with a bronze lancet and destroy the man's eye, they shall cut off his fingers.

Yet, most early codes were of similar character:

> And thine eye shall not pity; but life shall go for life, eye for eye, tooth for tooth, hand for hand, foot for foot (Deut. 19:21).
> As for the thief, both male and female, cut off their hands. It is the reward of their own deeds—an exemplary punishment from Allah (Koran 5:38).

In spite of the Code's strong reprisals against what must have been deemed major crimes, it was also a Code of compassion with great legal concern for both women and children. As regards children:

> If an artisan take a son for adoption and teach him his handicraft, one may not bring claim for him. If he do not teach him his handicraft, that adopted son may return to his father's house.
> If a man, who has taken a young child as his son and reared him, establish his own home and acquire children, and set his face to cut off the adopted son, that son shall not go his way. The father who reared him shall give to him his goods one-third portion of a son and he shall go.

Thus, at least during Hammurabi's reign, children were valued, and foster or adoptive placement was both encouraged and protected. Regrettably, this societal mandate would not be sustained throughout history.

Though there is no specific reference in the Code to mentally retarded or other handicapped individuals, it is difficult to conclude that Hammurabi did not have in mind a very responsive society. Conversely, there is no indication that the disabled were excluded from any of the Code's provisions.

Hammurabi's great commitment to protect children may well have reflected upon the traditions of the Babylonians, who were also noted for their kindness to children. According to Abt, the famed medical historian, "Babylonian pediatrics was, in fact, mainly concerned . . . with prognostication. Any abnormality or monstrosity in an infant or an animal at birth was prognostic of its future welfare. An unusually large organ pointed to extension, to power, to success; an abnormally small one to weakness, disease, and failure."[13] Fetomancy (prophecy by means of fetuses) and teratoscopy (divination based on examination of abnormal births) were prevelant practices among the Babylonians. Records of "monsterology" have been found inscribed in clay tablets dating back to about 2800 B.C. Accordingly, there were three traditional subclasses: *monstres par excés* (excess size or number, e.g., hydrocephaly or six fingers), *monstres par défaut* (smallness in size or appendices, e.g., microcephaly), and *monstres doubles* (hermaphrodism). Thus, in the instance of the *monstres par excés*, "When a woman gives birth to an infant who has six toes on each foot, the people of the world will be injured."[14] In spite of this, Abt concludes that while such prognostications suggest a motive for infanticide, "it seems probable, given the Babylonians' regard for the inexorable and irrevocable in law as accomplished fact that infanticide in itself was not regarded as releasing the land or the individual from the ineluctable contained in the specific omen."[15] Thus, even some of the most severely affected might have been treated rather well, or at least not intentionally destroyed.

One can speculate that the treatment of mentally retarded persons in these societies was variable. Since there were frequent wars, the need for manpower was always great. Many of the poor did menial jobs and were drafted into canal-building or into the army. Many of the unfortunate were reduced to begging or left to fend for themselves. Again, the grossly defective probably died at birth with the mildly retarded not being visible within their subcultures. On the other hand, many mentally retarded offspring of wealthy families probably were loved by anxious, concerned parents who

went to a variety of priests and magicians to cure their children's dullness: "Medicine flourished, and had a specific panacea for every disease; but it was still bound up with theology, admittedly sickness being due to possession by evil spirits could never be cured except by the exorcising of these demons."[16]

Hopefully, some mentally retarded girls, especially those who may not have been particularly attractive, benefited from the Babylonian practice of marriage auctions. According to Herodotus, on a particular day of the year all marriageable girls were gathered at one place, and an auctioneer or crier bid them out for marriage. Each was auctioned in turn, and the most beautiful was usually the first to be sold and naturally brought the most money. Then came the second most beautiful and on down the line to perhaps the least attractive. Proceeds for each bidding were placed in a chest, and those marrying the less attractive girls received a handsome bonus.

EGYPT

Though people had lived on the banks of the Nile for thousands of years, scholars are inclined to set the initial date for Egypt's amazing history at 2850 B.C., with the advent of Menes, the first king of the First Dynasty. The advances of the Egyptians during their 3,000 years of ancient history are well known and too numerous to list in detail. Among their most notable achievements were a significant improvement in agriculture, industry, and engineering, and the probable invention of glass, linen, paper, and ink, as well as the calendar and clock. Egyptian leadership provided moments of orderly and peaceful government and initiated such governmental structures as the post office and an elaborate management structure with all the benefits and foibles of a bureaucratic structure. They also experienced what was probably the first strike in recorded history when a group of pyramid builders refused to work until they received adequate provisions. The establishment of primary and secondary schools resulted in more creative forms of writing and literature and advanced the course of medicine. Monogamy and mono-theism were an integral part of their way of life.

Many of the grandeurs of Egypt remain with us and illustrate a culture of extreme ability and an artistry and craftsmanship that rarely has been exceeded. Yet, for the vast majority of people, life in Egypt was hard: "The state of the common man in the ancient world must have been wretched in the extreme. Those tremendous works that have survived through thousands of years were achieved at a cost in human suffering and death which was never conceived of as a cost in anything of value. Nothing so cheap as human life in Egypt. . . ."[17]

The Egyptians, like the Babylonians, were extremely kind to their children. While there is some indication that human sacrifice was prac-ticed in the early Egyptian civilization, there is little evidence of either infanticide or any form of maltreatment of children. Aristotle wrote explicitly that Egyptian women bore many children and that all children born into life were well brought up. Diodorus Siculus (first cen-tury B.C.) noted that the children of ancient Egypt were clothed and reared at a frightening expense. Interestingly, parents who did kill their children were not executed; rather, they were condemned to hug their offspring con-tinually in their arms for three days and three nights in order to experience their "full des-serts of horror and remorse."[18] The tendering of deformed infants and adults is documented by one of the artistic treasures discovered in King Tutankhamen's tomb: an ornamental fu-nerary boat with a female achrondoplastic dwarf at the stern.

Egyptian society—politically, spiritually, and culturally—was dominated by priests. Its unusual preoccupation with death may well have reflected the combination of a hard life and feelings of temporal worthlessness. It is not surprising, therefore, that spiritual healing and an overwhelming belief in demons and evil spirits were to persist. The selling of amulets and charms as well as the mumbling of incanta-tions and performing of various rites were

Egyptian funerary boat.

primarily in the purview of the priests. The following prayer, taken from the *Book of the Dead,* illustrates not only the type of treatment employed but also the eternal, universal love and devotion of an anxious mother:

> Run out; thou who comest in darkness who enter-eth in stealth. . . . Comest now to kiss this child? I will not let thee kiss him . . . comest thou to take him away? I will not let thee take him away from me. I have made his protection against thee out of Efet-herb which makes pain; out of honey which is sweet to the living and bitter to the dead; out of evil parts of the Ebdu-fish; out of the backbone of the perch.[19]

While spiritual healing remained a dominant force throughout the course of ancient Egypt, medicine also made remarkable advances. It has been estimated that one-third of the drugs applied today were identified by the physicians of Egypt.

In 1862, two medical papyri were dis-covered in a tomb in Thebes (Luxor), Egypt. These documents were most interesting, not only in their understanding but in their misunderstanding. The first and oldest is the *Papyrus Ebers*, named after the German Egyptologist Georg Ebers, who acquired the manuscript in 1872.[20] This document, compiled around 1500 B.C., is believed to be the so-called Papyrus of Thebes often quoted in histories on mental retardation. It represents a collection of ancient recipes for the physician covering innumerable human ailments, ranging from "Aids to Delivery, Abortion, and Lactation" to "Tumors, innocent and malignant." Reference to mental retardation, however, is at best oblique, primarily because of difficulties associated with translation:

> As to "ndbdh of the mind": this means that the mind bt3 in the heart; another lection: it means that the mind b3b3 in the heart, which goes up and falls down, after it has reached his s3t (throat?); his mind is suffering from wj3t (debility?).[21]

Epilepsy, as well as the "perishing of mind and forgetfullness," however, were clearly a consequence of "priestly recitations."[22]

The other document, known as the *Edwin Smith Surgical Papyrus*, was intended for the Sachmet priest rather than for the physician and is much more specific. Though purchased by Smith in 1862, the Surgical Papyrus was not fully translated until the early part of the twentieth century. It outlines the diagnosis, treatment, and prognosis for 48 different types of wounds, probably based on experiences of injured soldiers. Of the 48 cases, 27 dealt specifically with head injuries; the remainder were concerned with wounds and injuries in descending body order, such as throat and neck, shoulder, and spinal column. In essence, the unknown author first identified the brain (as it was so labeled) and recognized that injury to it would be manifested in a series of motor disorders, such as gait disturbances. Though most of the case studies emphasized physical treatment, magical incantations were not entirely averted.

These papyri reflect a practice that was to continue until the seventeenth century. While wounds arising from external sources were studied in terms of cause and effect, symptoms without a wound were usually attributed to a common physiological cause or to the spirits or gods. In other words, "all diseases regardless of symptoms arose from some common disturbance of the body."[23] This attitude severely hampered not only the advance of medical science but also the understanding of mental retardation and its associated causes.

The Egyptian family represented a stable element in that society, and, as previously observed, surviving children were often treated with love and affection though, reportedly, disciplined rather strictly. The need for manpower was always great: there were battles to fight, fields to tend, fish to catch, and pyramids to build. Thus, one can assume that many of the less seriously retarded persons fulfilled a variety of roles in the Egyptian society, and the high degree of illiteracy among the lower classes rendered their disability less visible or significant.

Harms also proposed that mentally retarded or disabled children may have been protected in Egypt by the followers of Osiris, the most enduring of all Egyptian gods.[24] According to Egyptian mythology, Osiris, who was believed to have given Egypt its civilization, was a very beloved ruler whose brother Seth slew him out of jealousy. Osiris, however, was resurrected through the perseverance of his wife, Isis, who roamed the earth in search of the dismembered parts of his body until she collected them all. Their son, Horus, later avenged his father's murder by vanquishing Seth and winning from him the rule of the earth. Osiris became the god of the Egyptian mortuary religion. Accordingly, when a person died, Osiris would judge him against his earthly conduct: "Do justice whilst thou endurest upon earth. A man remains over after death, and his deeds are placed on him in heaps. However, existence yonder is for eternity, and . . . for him who reaches it without wrongdoing, he shall exist yonder like a god."[25]

There remains one curious aspect of Egyptian life with relevance to mental retardation. It was common for brothers and sisters to marry. In fact, prior to the second century A.D., three-fourths of Egyptian marriages in one area of the country involved a brother-sister combination. If consanguinity resulted in a high incidence of deformed or otherwise disabled children, there is no record of such a fact.

PALESTINE

Palestine, a small country serving as the crossroads of the Near East, was in the days of antiquity rich in rain and soil, truly a land "flowing with milk and honey." Its fishermen, farmers, and herdsmen produced no great works of art, no magnificant buildings (with perhaps the exception of Solomon's Temple), no fine pottery, no delicate linens, and no world conquests of the magnitude of Caesar or Alexander. Yet, its ultimate influence on the Western world was to exceed that of Mesopotamia, Egypt, Greece, and Rome, for out of its knowledge and experience arose three of the world's great religions: Judaism, Christianity, and Mohammedanism.

Future generations of the original Hebrew herdsmen who migrated from Arabia to Judea between 1400 and 1200 B.C. were, through Moses, to receive a moral and legal code that, in many ways, differed significantly from all similar efforts of earlier cultures. As Biblical scholars record, "In general, the Oriental legal codes dealt with legal matters only, leaving morals and religious exhortations to other branches of literature. In the Biblical *tora,* legal, moral, and religious prescriptions form one inseparable unit."[26]

The Ten Commandments and the 613 precepts contained in the tora, or Pentateuch, which are estimated to have been collated between 400 and 500 B.C., blanketed nearly every aspect of individual and collective human existence, including diet, medicine, hygiene, public sanitation, sexual conduct, and worship. Of particular interest to us is the sensitivity of these laws to handicapped and poor persons, of whom there were many:

Thou shalt not curse the deaf, nor put a stumbling block before the blind (Lev. 14:14).
Cursed be he that maketh the blind to wander out of the way (Deut. 27:18).
Ye shall not afflict any widow, or fatherless child (Exod. 22:22).
If there be among you a poor man of one of thy brethren within thy gates in thy land which

the Lord thy God giveth thee, thou shalt not harden thine heart, nor shut thine hand from thy poor brother: but thou shalt open thine hand wide unto him, and shalt surely lend him sufficient for his need, in that which he wanteth (Deut. 15:7–8).

The degree to which these edicts actually affected the lives of mentally retarded persons at that time is unknown, except that the patriarchal family became the source of strength and stability of the Hebrew people; abortion, infanticide, celibacy, and other means of limiting the population were held in ill repute. Children, male and female, however, could be sold into bondage.

GREECE AND ROME

The next major phase of our historical journey (1300 B.C.–A.D. 476) involves the remarkable cultures and civilizations of Greece and Rome. Inasmuch as the general history of these two societies is well known, attention will be limited primarily to some of the practices and possibilities concerning the treatment of mentally retarded persons.

GREECE

Greece, in the words of Bowra, required "its inhabitants to be rough, active, enterprising, and intelligent."[27] Therefore, it is not surprising that the Greeks were to perpetuate a cult of physical beauty and health, as well as to advocate for the four cardinal virtues of courage, temperance, justice, and wisdom.

The importance of intelligence, physical strength, and beauty were to be expressed continually throughout the course of the Greek experience. In the Homeric period (1300–1100 B.C.), Odysseus observed that a "bad man is not one that drinks too much, murders, and betrays; he is one that is cowardly, stupid, or weak."[28] Plato (427?–347 B.C.), who lived during the disintegrating phase of early Greek history, reconfirmed the opinion that the mentally retarded and weak had little place in society:

Why, I said, the principle has already been laid

down that the best of either sex should be united with the best as often, and the inferior with the inferior, as seldom as possible; and that they should rear the offspring of the one sort of union, but not of the other, if the flock is to be maintained in first rate condition. . . . The proper officers will take the offspring of the good parents to the pen or fold, and then they will deposit them with certain nurses who will dwell in a separate quarter; but the offspring of the inferior, or of the better when they chance to be deformed, will be put away. . . .[29]

Similarly, Aristotle (384–322 b.c.), in his *Politics,* wrote, "As to the exposure and rearing of children, let there be a law that no *deformed* child shall live."[30]

In spite of the many contributions of ancient Greece to the subsequent development of the Western world, it possessed a "narrow and egotistical morality, with little conception of what we call humanity."[31] Children, slaves, and the poor were particularly susceptible to ill treatment at various times.

Sparta

Sparta, more than any other city-state, raised the culture of physical strength and aggressive behavior to unparalleled heights. It was only natural that a society of that cultural persuasion should place heavy emphasis on eugenics and infanticide. Only the strongest and brightest of its citizens were to have children; husbands were encouraged to lend their wives to exceptional men; older or weak men were discouraged from having children. A bright, strong male marrying a less capable woman was subject to a fine and strong social disapproval.

The practice of infanticide was considered essential to controlling the nature of the Spartan population. Not only was each newly born infant faced with the father's right to terminate life, but the same infant had to be brought before a state council of inspectors. Any child that appeared or was suspected to be defective was thrown from a cliff of Mat Taygetus to die on the jagged rocks below.

The prospects for a happy life among those retarded children who lived beyond these early decisions were indeed dismal. The uncom-

promising physical demands placed on children, male and female, to survive extreme discomfort and exposure must have resulted in an exceptionally high mortality rate.

When boys reached the age of seven, they were removed from their homes; placed in a barracks-style living environment; and subjected to a rigid, physically demanding, military-type education for the remainder of their youth and adolescence. The curriculum reflected the virtues of strength, military life, and the Spartan way: "The power and pride of Sparta was above all in its army, for in the courage, discipline, and skill of these troops it found its security and its ideal. Every citizen was training for war, and was liable to military service from his twentieth to his sixtieth year."[32] Book-learning was deemed of little or no value.

The more capable students were made captains over the other children with authority to direct their activities and to render discipline when necessary. It is not too difficult to imagine that under such a system a slightly slower or physically weaker youngster was placed under tremendous pressure from the kind of teasing and meanness that only children exhibit.

Contrary to what one might expect of a society such as this, however, Spartans were not unduly cruel for their times. They did not, for example, kill the children of offending adults as did the Persians by burying them alive. Herodotus's tale about 10 Spartan soldiers clearly indicates the human side of their character. The soldiers had been sent to a home for the purpose of killing a little boy whom an oracle had declared would grow up and destroy the city:

The mother, thinking it a friendly visit, brought her son when they asked to see him, and put him in the arms of one of them. Now they had agreed on the way there that whoever first received the child should dash it to the ground. But it happened that the baby smiled at the man who took it and so he was unable to kill it and handed it to another. Thus it passed through the hands of all the ten and no one of them would kill it. Then they gave it back to the mother and went away and began to blame each other, but especially him who had first held the child.[33]

In spite of the fact that Sparta offered a hard and difficult life, it can be assumed that at least some of its more mildly retarded citizens survived the ordeals of infancy, youth, and adolescence and found acceptance in their community.

Athens

Athens began its rise as a powerful city-state with the advent of Solon, the outstanding humane leader, in 594 B.C. Athens was significant in its emphasizing, at least during its formative and golden years, a democratic system of government, individual freedom, enterprise, and thought. Unfortunately, it could not avert the numerous wars that ultimately would lay waste all of Greece.

Though children were highly prized and cherished, Athens, like other city-states, practiced infanticide. The nature and degree of this practice varied considerably over the years. In the beginning and during the golden years, infanticide was primarily limited to the weak or deformed. Even here, however, the practice varied from that of the Spartans. Newly born infants were placed in a large earthen jar which was set by a temple in the event that someone might wish to adopt the child. It is highly possible that some of the less seriously affected may have been adopted in this manner.

As Athens grew in affluence and its social values changed, infanticide became a common practice. By the third century B.C., most baby girls were automatically destroyed; only one family in a hundred had more than one girl. The lower classes killed so many of their children that the death rate exceeded the birth rate. "The whole of Greece," wrote Polybius in 150 B.C., "has been subject to a low birth rate and a general decrease of the population owing to which cities have become deserted and the land has ceased to yield fruit."[34]

Any decision concerning infanticide had to be made shortly after birth. If the infant was not destroyed before he was 10 days old, he was given his father's name, which at least insured survival and some degree of protection. On the other hand, in the early days of the Greek experience, minor sons and unwed daughters could be sold into slavery. Later, only their labor could be sold.

The selling of such labor frequently resulted in extreme hardship for both boys and girls. Boys frequently were committed to working in the mines or other similar jobs that took a high toll of human life. Many girls were assigned to a grinding mill which proved a most difficult and fatiguing job. Fortunate was the girl who became a personal maid or housekeeper. In essence, a youngster failing to measure up to the Greek notion of the "complete man" was particularly vulnerable to being sold.

Athenian boys of wealth attended schools where they pursued various academic subjects as well as music and gymnastics. In contrast, girls were cloistered at home, being offered little in the way of either education or community exposure. Their limited training emphasized marital duties as well as the social amenities of Greek society. Not surprisingly, they grew up inexperienced and shy.

Under such circumstances, one again can assume that the less capable young men of noble families received the same rebukes in school as have the mentally retarded throughout time. Mildly retarded girls, on the other hand, may have been in a better position to satisfy the requirements of Greek society.

In *Alcibades II*, a document of unknown origin but written in the style of Plato, different kinds of "unsoundness of mind" were defined: "Those who are afflicted by it in the highest degree are called mad. Those in whom it is less pronounced are called wrong-headed, crotchety, or—as persons fond of smooth words would say—enthusiastic or excitable. Others are eccentric, others are known as innocents, incapables, dummies. . . . All these kinds of unsoundness of the mind differ from one another as diseases of the body do."[35]

Astrology continued to play an important role and was universally accepted for centuries. Nearly every aspect of human ability, actions, and destiny was attributed to some astrological phenomenon. As the great Pliny noted in A.D. 70, both "learned and simple believed that a man's destiny was determined by the star under which he was born. They argued plausibly that vegetation, and perhaps the mating season in animals, depend upon factors themselves determined by the sun; and that individual character and faith, like those general phenomena, are the result of celestial conditions inadequately known."[36]

Hippocrates Among the remarkable men of Greece who were to have a profound influence on the practice of medicine until the seventeenth century was Hippocrates (460–370? B.C.), who established one of the great medical schools on the Island of Cos where he had been born, raised, and trained. Yet, in spite of his great impact, little is actually known about him, including his year of death. Some authorities conjecture that he may have lived to be one hundred.

While Hippocrates (or his school) did not significantly advance medicine in terms of innovative techniques or procedures, he was an outstanding encyclopedist, collating a tremendous amount of knowledge (and guesswork) into a series of volumes, referred to as the *Hippocratic Collection.*

Among his most famous writings was a volume entitled *Aphorisms,* which ushered forth a concern for children and a separation of their illnesses from those of adults. According to Marti-Ibanez, Hippocrates' "writings on children's diseases, injuries of the head, fractures, and articulations were masterful; his aphorisms and precepts . . . responded to the humanism and love of man that characterized the noblest of the Greeks."[37] Several of his aphorisms dealt with epilepsy and "puny" children:

> If the winter be austral and rainy, but otherwise calm, and the spring dry and boreal, women who expect to bring forth in the spring, miscarry from the slightest causes; and even those who go their full time, bring forth weak and sickly children, who either immediately perish or linger on, through life, infirm and emaciated.
> The diseases which attend on excessive rains are . . . epilepsy.
> Those who are attached with epilepsy before the age of puberty, have a chance of cure; but when the disorder comes on after the twenty-fifth year, it ceases only with life.

Hippocrates.

> Epilepsy in children is removed by changes, especially by those of age, climate, and mode of living.[38]

Typical of the Greeks, Hippocrates believed that health involved the balance or the harmonious relationship of basic body substances, in this case, four humors: "blood, phlegm, yellow bile, and black bile. These are the things that make up its constitution and cause its pain and health. Health is primarily that state in which these constituent substances are in correct proportion to each other, both in strength and quantity, and are well mixed."[39] Each of these substances had a specific location: in the heart, liver, spleen, and brain, respectively. Medical authors of subsequent years would relate mental illness and occasionally mental retardation to the lack of balance due to "sluggish" black bile.

Hippocrates was a firm believer in the healing powers of nature. As he admonished, "Whoever would study medicine right must learn of the following subjects. First he must consider the effect of each of the seasons of the year and the differences between them. Secondly, he must study the warm and the cold winds, both those which are common to every country and those peculiar to a particular locality. Lastly, the effect of water on the health must not be forgotten. Just as it varies in taste and quality, so does its effect on the body vary as well."[40] It is interesting to note that as late as 1845, Esquirol would list "sun, water, and air" as etiological factors associated with mental retardation.

Hippocrates struck a forceful note against the quasi-religious and superstitious aura surrounding epilepsy when he wrote: "I am about to discuss the disease called sacred (epilepsy). It is not in my opinion any more divine or more sacred than other diseases, but has a natural cause, and its supposed divine origin is due to man's inexperience and to their wonder at its peculiar character."[41] This statement, as well as his entire thesis that nature was the great healer, aided in placing medicine and health care in the hands of man rather than gods.

Hippocrates believed that epilepsy was the result of numerous causes, including blockage of the normal passage of phlegm from the brain; cold phlegm being discharged into warm blood; and sitting too long in the sun, which resulted in unequal heat distribution in the brain. Though Hippocrates' concept of the brain was very limited, he did recognize that the brain "is the seat of this disease [epilepsy], as it is of other very violent diseases."[42] With regard to curing epilepsy, "a man with a knowledge of how to produce by means of a regimen dryness and moisture, cold and heat in the human body, could cure this disease too, provided that he distinguish the right moment for the application of the remedies. He would not need to resort to purification and magic spells."[43]

The notion of dryness and moisture was not original with Hippocrates. Heraclitus (535–465 B.C.), for example, taught that reason depended upon "the fire with man: the drier the fire, the wiser the soul, or reason, or judgment; the more humid the soul, the closer it is to being ill—an extreme excess of humidity will bring on imbecility or madness."[44]

Despite Hippocrates' emphasis on the role of the brain, he did not ascribe to it independent, inherent psychological qualities. Rather, breath (or *pneuma*) was the source of intelligence and feeling. The *pneuma* reached the brain through the mouth and was then distributed to the various parts of the body: "I believe the brain to be the most potent organ in the body. So long as it is healthy, it is the interpreter which enables us to draw anything from the air. Consciousness is caused by air. The eyes, ears, tongue, hands and feet perform actions which are planned by the brain, for there is a measure of conscious thought throughout the body proportionate to the amount of air which it receives. The brain is also the organ of comprehension, for when a man draws a breath it reaches the brain first, and then is disbursed into the rest of the body having left behind in the brain its vigor and whatever pertains to consciousness and intelligence."[45]

As witnessed by his aphorisms, Hippocrates placed considerable emphasis on climate, suggesting changes of it for persons with epilepsy. Favorite treatments included exercise, massage, baths, diet, and drugs. He did not, however, favor the extensive use of drugs but preferred honey instead. It is highly probable that epileptic and mentally retarded persons were subjected to those forms of healing intended to help nature fulfill its role.

Finally, Hippocrates raised the practice of medicine to its highest ethical level: "I will use treatment to help the sick according to my ability and judgment, but I will never use it to injure or wrong them. I will not give poison to anyone though asked to do so, nor will I suggest such a plan. Similarly, I will not give a pessary to a woman to cause abortion. But in purity and in holiness I will guard my life and my art. . . . Into whatsoever house I enter, I will do so to help the sick, keeping myself free from all intentional wrongdoing and harm. . ." (from the *Hippocratic Oath*).

The failure of Hippocrates to expound on mental retardation does not mean that he was unaware of the phenomenon; in fact, he described both microcephaly and craniostenosis. For many centuries to come, however, physicians were concerned primarily with bodily ills and pain. Man was considered to possess a dual nature—the body, and the mind or soul. While the body was within the realm of medical practice, the mind or soul, as aptly expressed by Avicenna, was best left to philosophers.

ROME

Ancient Rome spanned a period of approximately 1300 years, from 800 B.C. till the successful invasions of Germanic tribes in A.D. 476. Its history is a kaleidoscope of contrasts and excesses. Politically, Rome underwent nearly every form of government known to man, including monarchies, aristocracies, oligarchies, democracies, revolutionary governments, and dictatorships. Its great moments of statesmanship, innovative architecture, worldwide conquests, and advances in the sciences and literature were more than frequently offset by unbridled debauchery and bestiality.

It is impossible to represent adequately all the experiences of mentally retarded persons throughout these times. The period is too expansive, and history is quite negligent in reviewing the life and times of common people. Rather, it tends to be a sequential collection of exceptional events and personages. Even then, it falls short of its goal. As Durant noted, little was known of Anconius Pius, one of the later rulers of Rome, "for he had almost no faults and committed no crimes."[46] There exist, however, historical anecdotes sufficient to indicate that mentally retarded persons were subject to highly variable living circumstances and treatment.

During the early days of the Republic (508–30 B.C.), many of the traditions found in Greece were observed in Rome. Birth of children, especially sons, constituted a major event in a family's life. Deformed infants were permitted to die, but only during the first 8 days of life. The child was raised in a strong, patriarchal family, where the father held the power of life, death, and sale into bondage or slavery. The power of the Roman father over the lives of his children (*patria potestas*) has no parallel in any other society. He could kill them, multilate them, or sell them. This power

was used, since in Rome, like Greece, the "young were never thought of except as the property of adults, whose interests always come first."[47]

Yet, in Rome's early days, close family ties were established, marriage was compulsory, and a high birth rate was encouraged. This relationship reflected a strong self-sustaining family with a considerable need for manual labor. Developing agrarian societies as well as those with a proclivity toward war always place a premium on new births.

The educated Roman of that period was loyal, sober, severe, and practical. Frequent wars and manners led to a society of men who killed without compunction or remorse. Early Romans were not by training or predisposition charitable.

Healing and medicine were primarily a matter of herbs, magic, and prayer. The few physicians in Rome at the time, and well into the future, were primarily from Greece.

While all but a few more seriously defective mentally retarded individuals probably found some role in the Republic, this was no longer true by the first century A.D. By this time, Rome had become an empire, but an empire torn by a century of strife and civil war. Slavery and massive poverty resulted in children being viewed as liabilities instead of assets. Childbirth rates dropped significantly and infanticide became prevalent. As was to reoccur many times throughout history, children had become luxuries only the poor could afford.

In this time of crisis, Rome was to yield up its greatest statesman, one whose social conscientiousness and sensitivity were matched only by those of his wife. Gaius Julius Caesar Octavianus—better known as Augustus—ruled Rome from 27 B.C. to A.D. 14. He attempted once again to restore Rome to peace and dignity, emphasizing social reforms, a strong sense of family unity, and governmental assistance to those in need. At one time, over 50 percent of the population was receiving some form of governmental assistance, usually in the form of food. His efforts, however, were frowned upon by many, donor and recipient alike. His wife, Liva, must have been a remarkably compassionate person in her own right, devoting herself to charity, helping parents of large families, providing dowries for poor daughters, and maintaining many orphanages at her own expense. Augustus, the humanitarian, ruled successfully for 44 years; when he died, he was immortalized by the citizens, rich and poor. Unfortunately, although his memory survived, his philosophy of government did not.

Infanticide again became prevalent, although direct exposure and death were not always practiced. During the first century A.D., many unwanted infants were placed at the base of Columna Lactaria, where the state provided wet nurses to feed and save the infants found there. Even under these circumstances, however, the eventual treatment of mentally retarded and other infants left at Lactaria was unfortunate. Many were horribly mutilated to increase their value as beggars. This is attested to in the elder Seneca's account of a debate that addressed the question whether those who mutilated exposed children had done wrong by the state. F. Claudius, one of the debaters, summarized the situation succinctly: "Many individuals rid themselves of misformed children defective in some part of their body or because the children are born under evil auspices. Someone else picks them up out of commiseration and, in order to defray the expenses of bringing the child up, cuts off one of its limbs. Today, when they are demanding charity, that life that they owe to the pity of one, they are sustaining at the expense and through the pity of all."[48] A description of the pathetic situation surrounding this practice was provided by Cassius Severs when he wrote, "Let us view the entire miserable family shivering, trembling, blind, mutilated, perishing from hunger—in fact, already half dead. Let us go to the origin of all these ills—a laboratory for the manufacture of human wrecks—a cavern filled with the limbs torn from living children—each has a different profession, a different mutilation has given each a different occupation."[49] The practice of mutilating children for the purpose of begging continued for many centuries. Parenthetically, the debate concluded

that since "rescued" abandoned children were, in essence, slaves, no damage was done the State.

In A.D. 54, Nero, Rome's *enfant terrible,* became emperor. Though Nero was a man of many talents with a kindly disposition toward the poor and a murderous attitude toward his political rivals, our primary concern is with his sometimes mentor and friend, Lucius Annaeus Seneca (5 B.C.–A.D. 65). Seneca, Rome's greatest Stoic philosopher and lawyer, offers one of the few direct observations concerning a mentally retarded person in Rome. In a letter to Lucilius, he wrote:

> You know that Herpaste, my wife's fool, was left on my hands as a hereditary charge, for I have a natural aversion to these monsters; and if I have a mind to laugh at a fool, I need not seek him far, I can laugh at myself. This fool has suddenly lost her sight. I am telling you a strange but true story. She is not aware that she is blind and constantly urges her keeper to take her out because she says my house is dark.[50]

Like a true Stoic philosopher, Seneca took hemlock in the tradition of Socrates when requested to commit suicide by his former student.

Greatness has many ancestries as witnessed by the rise and accomplishments of Vespasian (A.D. 9–79). In contrast to the brilliant genius of Julius Caesar and the remarkable statesmanship of Augustus, this old soldier assumed responsibility as emperor when he was 60 years of age. Of modest birth and with no signs of exceptional political talents, it was he who established the first system of state education in classical antiquity, opened schools of medicine, and fostered the development of hospitals (initially private). Both men and women were encouraged to become physicians, and many were appointed to treat the poor at state expense. Though magic and superstition still reigned as primary medical treatment modalities, especially among the poor classes (the bulk of Roman society at any time), many specialties were developed, including urology, gynecology, obstetrics, ophthalmology, and dentistry.

Yet, even Vespasian, a leader of strong will

and practical intelligence, could not stem the tide of overpopulation and impermeable class distinctions. Troubled, dehumanizing conditions persisted.

In addition to the medical advances described, Rome contributed several major medical theorists and practitioners to the field, two of whom were of particular import. First was Claudius Galen (A.D. 138–201)—brilliant, ambitious, half-philosopher, half-scientist, collector of large fees, and possessor of limited modesty: "Whoever seeks fame need only become familiar with all that I have achieved."[51] He was also a prolific writer, contributing more than 500 works on nearly every then known aspect of medical science and practice. Though he theoretically adhered to the beliefs of Hippocrates, his basic approach to medicine was through anatomical research. Though humans, live or dead, could not be used for experimental purposes, Galen conducted extensive neuroanatomical research on pigs. As a result, he was to declare that Plato, Aristotle, and Hippocrates were wrong. The brain is the seat of many intellectual functions, he observed, and it functions on the basis of the degree of dryness or softness of the nerve tissue, rather than *pneuma* or some spirit. Also, when impressions (i.e., stimuli) strike the soft part of the brain, one feels; when they strike a harder part of the brain, one moves.

He created cerebral and spinal lesions to trace nerve pathways, accurately described the cranial bones, identified a neurological cause of aphasia, and ascertained that damage to one side of the brain would be manifest in bodily disorders on the opposite side.

With regard to intelligence, Galen was quite perceptive, contending that "Not only the quantity of brain substance but also its quality is important. The keenness of the mind depends upon the fineness of the brain substance. Slow thinking is due to its heaviness. . . . Its firmness and stability produce the faculty of memory. Imbecility results from the rarefaction and diminution in quality of the animal spirits and from the coldness and humidity of the brain."[52]

Galen is considered by many to be the father of experimental neurology. His texts, like those of Hippocrates, influenced medical thinking for centuries.

Less flamboyant than Galen was Soranus of Ephesus, who settled in Rome between A.D. 110 and 130. Other than what remains of his medical dissertations, little is known about his personal life. The father of gynecology and pediatrics, Soranus was vitally concerned with the embryo, its development, the nature of the uterus and womb, and special obstetrical equipment. He was equally dedicated to the rearing of healthy infants, emphasizing parental responsibilities, proper locomotion, and the importance of posture and nutrition. Soranus was interested in both the mentally retarded and the mentally ill, violently opposing their current treatment:

> They [physicians] prescribe placing all patients in darkness without ascertaining whether the absence of light is in some cases irritating, without ascertaining whether or not this measure adds another burden to the affected head. . . . Rather than being themselves disposed to cure their patients, they seem to be in a state of delirium; they compare their patients to ferocious beasts whom they would subdue by the deprivation of food and by the torments of thirst. Misled without doubt by this error, they advise that patients be cruelly chained, forgetting that their limbs might be injured or broken and that it is more suitable and much easier to restrain the sick by the hands of men than by the weights of often harmful iron. They even advise bodily violence, like the use of the whip, as if such measures could force a return to reason; such treatment is deplorable and only aggravates the patient's condition; it stains the body and limbs with blood—a sad spectacle indeed for the patient to contemplate when he regains his senses. . . . They have the patients fall asleep by the use of the poppy; but this provokes a drowsiness or morbid torpor instead of good sleep; they rub the patient's head with oil of rose, wild thyme or castor oil, thus exciting the very organ which they are trying to quiet down; they use cold applications, ignorant of how often this acts as an exciting agent; often and with so little measure they use irritant clysters and by means of these more or less acid injections they produce no other results than dysentery.[53]

Soranus, in his hospital setting, provided humane treatment for mentally ill persons, among whom there were probably some mentally retarded individuals. Rest, sympathy, reading, and participation in dramatic performances were encouraged.

Soranus's concern with the mentally disabled was shared by an earlier colleague, Ascelpiades of Prusa. Ascelpiades, who was popular with both Julius Caesar and Mark Antony, was one of the first physicians to be recognized for his sensitive treatment and handling of the mentally disturbed, which presumably included mentally retarded and epileptic individuals. He not only disagreed with the use of bloodletting with mentally affected persons, he did so with a wry sense of humor: "While bloodletting might be successful in Athens, it was more likely to be injurious in Rome, because the Romans were already worn out with debauchery."[54]

Finally, in the medical area, Aurelius Cornelius Celsus (first century A.D.), one of Rome's more brilliant aristocrats, used the term *imbecillus* in *De Medicina,* the only portion of his multifaceted encyclopedia to survive through time. In this document, written around A.D. 30, *imbecillus* denoted a general weakness or any form of debility; its reference to a limited degree of mental retardation would not be discovered until many years later. Similarly, the term *idios,* in its original Greek form, simply meant a private person, that is, one who did not engage in some form of public life and probably did not become applied to the mentally retarded until the Renaissance. The word *fatuity,* however, was used by the Greeks and Romans to denote someone who was "witless" or mentally retarded.

While Celsus was a highly competent writer, his attitudes toward the mentally afflicted, especially the more disruptive types, were quite negative. He emphasized—for almost any minor infraction—the "fright hypothesis," which in one form or another was to be practiced until well into the twentieth century: "When he [the patient] has said or done anything wrong, he must be chastised by hunger, chains and fetters. He must be made to attend and to learn something that he may remember, for thus it will happen that by degrees he will be led to consider what he is doing."[55]

Some mentally retarded and epileptic persons undoubtedly received the fright treatment and/or were placed in dark cellars, with or without chains. Other cures for epilepsy included wearing a talisman, such as the liver of a dead athlete. By inference, Caelius Aurelianus indicated that some epileptic persons were castrated because, as he emphatically reminded the practitioner, eunuchism did not relieve one of epilepsy.[56]

Some defective infants may have found their way into one of the various charitable facilities initiated as early as A.D. 97. During the brief reign of Nerva, for example, there was an attempt to diminish the exposure and drowning of infants by founding colonies for poor families and assisting indigent parents. This philanthropy was furthered by Trajan, and in A.D. 100, some 5,000 children were cared for by the state. Hadrian (A.D. 117–138) deported a father who killed his son, and compelled parents to rear their children instead of exposing them. Though the mutilation of exposed slave children in order to make them objects of charity was a great abuse at the time, it was justified by philosophers as "better than letting them die."[57]

By the second century A.D., Roman tastes had degenerated to the point that any type of defective person became a popular source of household amusement. According to Durant, a special market was established in Rome where one might purchase "legless, armless, or three-eyed men, giants, dwarfs, or hermaphrodites."[58]

By the fourth century A.D., Christianity was beginning to exercise its influence. Edicts against infanticide and the selling of children into slavery were issued by Roman emperors Constantine (in A.D. 315 and 321); Valentinian, Valens, and Gratian (A.D. 367); Valentinian, Theodosius, and Arcadius (A.D. 391); Honorius and Theodosius (A.D. 409); Theodosius II (A.D. 438); and Valentinian III (A.D. 451). The edicts reflected a position long advanced by the church. Barnabas, a contemporary of the Apostles, the founders of Christianity, established that infanticide, by exposure or otherwise, was a heinous crime. In a series of bold, vigorous pronouncements addressed directly to the people, church fathers denounced both infanticide and abortion. For several reasons, the practice of Christianity was to have a tremendous impact on attitudes toward children, the disabled, and the ill. Even the unborn child had a soul; those who were disabled, weak, or in pain were closer to God; and to help the afflicted became a sign of strength instead of weakness.[59]

In A.D. 314, the Council of Ancyra decreed that a woman who killed her offspring should not be permitted to enter a church for the rest of her life. The Council of Nicae (A.D. 325) decreed that in each Christian village a hostelry for the sick, poor, and vagrant should be established. Some of these became asylums for children. The Council of Vaison (A.D. 442) provided that an abandoned child should find sanctuary in a church for 10 days and that its parents must be found.

The epitome of Roman achievement was its law, which today provides the foundation of many legal codes. Among its principles were:

No one is compelled to defend a cause against his will.
No one suffers a penalty for what he thinks.
No one may be forcibly removed from his own house.
The burden of proof is upon the party affirming, not on the party denying.
In inflicting penalties, the age and inexperience of the guilty party must be taken into account.[60]

The law also included the provision that none but the deformed or seriously diseased infant could be exposed. Regrettably, the revised Roman laws did not include an earlier law attributed to the legendary leader Romulus. Accordingly, as described by Dionysius, parents could expose a lame and "monstrous" infant provided they first showed the child "to five of their neighbors and these also approved of it, and besides other penalties he [Romulus] punished those who disobeyed this law with the confiscation of half their fortunes."[61]

Justinian (A.D. 483–565), who ruled Rome from Constantinople, is credited with the formation of the comprehensive legal code that summarized all Roman law. He indicated that mentally disabled persons should not suffer the same penalties as others and, in some cases, would require guardians. He also ordered institutions for the poor and infirm to provide care for those such individuals who could not fend for themselves.

What can one surmise from these historical notes? First, many mildly mentally retarded persons, especially those among the slaves and masses of the poor, probably went relatively unnoticed, sharing a common bond of poverty, manual labor, and illiteracy. Others, especially those of wealthy families, undoubtedly received some form of medical treatment and probably were accepted as close members of the family, barring serious accompanying handicaps. Most severely deformed infants, on the other hand, were probably exposed except during those periods when persons with deformities were valued as family fools. Some mentally retarded persons were sold into slavery or bondage to work in the mines, pits, or any variety of undesirable, endless tasks; and a few probably suffered the horrors of the games. In other words, the lives of mentally retarded persons were affected by many influences, including parentage, class, and existing culture.

Individual people as well as governments, however, determine human conduct, and as indicated previously, excesses were obvious. Compare, for example, the attitude of the Stoic philosopher Seneca to that of the Stoic philosopher Epictetus (A.D. 60–120) who married late in life simply to provide a mother for an infant saved from exposure. Or compare the decency of Augustus and Justinian, rulers of Rome, to that of Emperor Commodus (A.D. 161–192), who gathered together the crippled and individually shot them with bow and arrow. Such were the times—such were the people!

THE GENTLE VOICES

While civilization advanced, frequently on the shoulders of slaves with talents and strength, and men waged war for nearly every conceivable reason—fame, glory, riches, revenge, religion, women, and social expectancy—there ranged throughout the world a number of quiet voices, voices which countermanded man's inhumanity to man, his insensitivity, brutality, and cruelty. While these voices were rarely heeded in their own time, each of them, to varying degrees and at varying times, was to have an impact; and each was to elevate a few men to the level of humanity to which all pretend. Among these voices were those of Zoroaster, Buddha, Confucius, Jesus, and Mohammed.

ZOROASTER

Zoroaster, whose existence as an actual person remains in doubt, reportedly lived some time between the sixth and tenth centuries B.C. His life, according to legend, paralleled that of Jesus in a number of ways. He was to have lived in the wilderness, was tempted by the devil to no avail, and was both ridiculed and persecuted. Unlike Jesus, he lived to an old age and rose to heaven on a beam of light. Zoroaster believed in one divine and invisible god whose primary mandate to man was "to make him who is an enemy a friend, to make him who is wicked righteous, and to make him who is ignorant learned."[62] Concern for others was a cardinal principle.

BUDDHA

Siddhartha Gautama, who was to become known as Buddha (the Enlightened), was born in 563 B.C. in what is now known as Nepal, India. His father was a rajah from the Kshatriya caste, the second highest in Indian society. Buddha gave up his palace and inheritance at age 29 to search for truth, a truth which would aid people in resolving both physical and mental problems. After 6 years of endless soul-searching and frustrating wandering throughout India, he found his moment of insight while sitting under a tree. Though he was somewhat of a skeptic of human life—"More tears have floated upon this earth than there is water in the oceans"—he laid down five vital moral precepts: "No one shall kill a living creature. No

one should take that which is not given to him. No one should lie. No one should get drunk. No one should be unchaste."[63] His message was one of love and a turning away from those desires for pleasure which produce only suffering. Both he and his followers practiced self-control, humility, generosity, and mercy. Within the context of his teachings, love was expressed through helpfulness, charity, and generosity. Buddha is believed to have died in approximately 483 B.C.

CONFUCIUS

Unlike Buddha, Confucius was born to a poor but very respectable family in the province of Lu in about 551 B.C. Confucius (in Chinese, K'ung Fu-tzu), who married at 19 and became divorced at 23, was to become one of the world's greatest philosophers. Wandering through the various provinces of China, he was constantly concerned with corrupt governments. Underlying all, he believed and instructed that the key to an orderly world and a peaceful life involved the decent behavior of the individual. He attempted to develop a moral sense of responsibility toward others, to be gentle, to be kind, and to help those of "weak mind." Though he taught for 50 years, he died practically unknown in or about 479 B.C.

JESUS

While the preceding philosophers were spreading their message in their respective countries, Jeremiah, Ezekial, and Isaiah were preaching the coming of the Messiah and giving body and substance to the Old Testament. In the eyes of many, Jesus represented the fulfillment of the prophecies and promises. Jesus preached a new way of life—one based on love and mercy. His marked concern and sensitivity to children was expressed on a number of occasions. One response to his inquiring disciples has been interpreted as the "Principle of the Least," frequently quoted with regard to those who are mentally retarded: "An argument started among the disciples as to which of them would be the greatest. Jesus, knowing their thoughts, took a little child and had him stand beside him. Then he said to them, whoever welcomes this little child in my name welcomes me; and whoever welcomes me welcomes the one who sent me. For he who is least among you all—he is the greatest" (Luke 9:46).

Later in a letter to the Thessalonians, the Apostle Paul wrote, "Now we exhort you, brethren, warn them that are unruly, comfort the feebleminded, be patient toward *all* men" (1 Thessalonians, 5, 14).

Jesus' mission frequently involved the healing of the blind, the deaf, the crippled, the demoniac, the epileptic, the dumb, and the paralytic. Such healing was based on faith and the dispelling or exorcism of demoniac influences. His teachings and his healings, with their implication of evil spirits and the devil, were to have a tremendous influence on the future course of many attitudes and social development. At times, Jesus' gentle teachings held prominence; at others, the notion that the disabled were possessed by the devil held forth. Each would have its own effect upon the treatment of mentally retarded and other disabled persons.

MOHAMMED

Mohammed (A.D. 569–622) was born into a poor but distinguished family. Though illiterate, with the assistance of an amanuensis he composed the *Qur'an* (Koran), the most famous book in the Arabic language. At age 25, he married Khadi ja, a wealthy widow of 40 who would be his most cherished wife. He was described as nervous, impressionable, given to melancholy, and seldom laughed, though he reportedly had a keen sense of humor.

According to tradition, Mohammed was visited by Gabriel who told him, "Oh, Mohammed! Thou art the Messenger of Allah, and I am Gabriel."[64] Gradually Gabriel revealed to Mohammed the entire text of the Koran. Over the next few years, Mohammed announced himself openly as the prophet of Allah with the mission of leading the Arab people (and other believers) to a heightened sense of morality and

a monotheistic faith. Through times of rejection, war, and acceptance, he provided confident leadership until he was 60 years of age.

The Koran, which contains 114 chapters (*Suras*), consistently proclaims one omnipotent god—Allah—who tempers power and justice with mercy. The Koran put an end to the practice of infanticide: "Kill not the old man who cannot fight, nor the young children, nor women." Also of importance to mentally retarded people, "Give not unto those who are weak of understanding the substance which God hath appointed you to preserve for them; but maintain them thereout, and clothe them, and speak kindly unto them."

With the exception of holy wars against those who would attack the followers of Allah, war was outlawed. In essence, religion was defined in a manner quite similar to that of the Judeo-Christian tradition:

> Whosoever, for the love of God, giveth his wealth unto his kindred, unto orphans, and the poor, and the wayfarer, and to the beggar, and for the release of captives . . . and who are patient in adversity and hardship and in the time of violence: these are the righteous, these are they who believe in the Lord.[65]

Based on this belief and the tenets of the Koran, both mentally retarded and mentally ill people were considered innocents of God. As a result, the Arabs, in many respects, were reportedly more humane and socially advanced in the treatment of the mentally deviant than was western Europe during its infancy.

Each of these religious leaders expressed precepts that in no manner would bring harm to mentally retarded persons or others with afflictions.

Though we have just begun our historical venture, one can easily discern that mentally retarded and other persons of disadvantage were readily caught up in webs of highly variable political, sociolegal, and professional thought. On the one hand, we saw the very best in the concern of the Shanidars and in the enlightened thinking of some early physicians. On the other hand, we saw exposure, mutilation, and incarceration in dark cells accompanied by harsh treatment. We also witnessed at least one government that viewed its responsibilities toward the citizenry in a very positive light, while others—most others—were often devoid of any hint of humanitarianism. As we will see, the highly variable treatment of mentally retarded persons noted during these early years would persist for centuries.

Chapter

2

FROM ANTIQUITY TO ENLIGHTENMENT

(A.D. 476–1799)

I N THIS CHAPTER we examine the course of history as it relates to mental retardation from A.D. 476 to the nineteenth century, dividing the period into two major time frames: 1) The Middle Ages, Renaissance, and Reformation and 2) the seventeenth and eighteenth centuries. These years witnessed a gradual "increase in population, an increase in the acreage of land placed under the plow, and the growth of a number of communities in which it was accepted that individuals had rights as well as duties."[1] In spite of many gains, the vast majority of people were confronted with a life that was short, hard, and often cruel—cruel by the hand of nature and by the hand of man. The times were vigorous, and often violent.

THE MIDDLE AGES, RENAISSANCE, AND REFORMATION

The Middle Ages spanned a period of approximately 1,000 years, from the conquest of Rome in A.D. 476 by Germanic tribes until the Renaissance. This period encompassed the great age of the Byzantian world and the frequently troubled struggles of western Europe to attain maturity and enlightenment.

During the declining years of the Roman Empire, there again arose a militarily and politically gifted leader, Constantine I. By the year A.D. 323, Constantine had defeated his rivals and made two important decisions in an effort to unite his Empire. First, he gave legal sanction and status to Christianity; second, he moved the capitol from Rome, a scene of treachery, treason, and interminable conspiracies, to Constantinople.

Constantinople, which would survive for 1,100 years before being sacked by the Turks in 1453, provided a bridge between classical Greek and Roman cultures and the modern world. It not only retained Roman law and organization, with some modifications arising from Christian tenets, but its scholars advanced the knowledge of medicine and preserved classical literature. Higher education was encouraged; major universities were established in Alexandria, Athens, Constantinople, and Antioch; and students pursued the study of medicine, philosophy, literature, and rhetoric in these settings. Yet, all social classes continued to believe fervently in magic, astrology, divination, sorcery, witchcraft, and miraculous amulets.[2]

Charitable works by individuals, the Church, and the State were common. Each was interested in providing for the less fortunate based on the precept that "having created all things and made order and harmony reign in the world, God engraved the Law with His own finger on the Tables, and set it forth for all to see that it might prevent by happy discipline the member of the human family from hurling themselves one upon the other and the stronger from crushing the weaker. . ." (from the *Book of the Perfect,* issued about A.D. 900).[3] Many hospitals and orphanages were established. One hospital complex included 7,000 beds, providing a military hospital, an orphanage, and a home for the blind. Foundling hospitals as well as homes for the aged were also constructed throughout the Byzantian world.

The Germanic tribes that pervaded all Europe consisted of robust, energetic, and semi-civilized men and women willing to wage war against all those they encountered. By the fifth century, their invasions had split the Roman Empire into numerous kingdoms, and many Germanic tribes were beginning to settle into small villages. Much that was the glory of Rome was forgotten, including education, science, and the arts. Superstition and tribal custom replaced Roman law; trial by one's peers became trial by ordeal.

During the transition from those small villages to Charlemagne's Carolingian Empire, from feudal states to the crowded and unhealthy towns of the twelfth century, and, finally, from the city-states of the thirteenth century to the larger kingdoms of the fourteenth and fifteenth centuries, the Roman Catholic Church frequently was the unifying force and often the sole charitable institution. In the later years of the Middle Ages, humanism began to replace religious dogma, and the use of vernacular languages, rather than Latin, ushered in a new age of literacy and communication, especially after the invention of the movable printing press in 1440. The turning away from a singular preoccupation with religion set the stage for the great Renaissance that spread through Europe during the fifteenth and sixteenth centuries.

Though the Middle Ages witnessed many creative moments in the writings of Augustine, Abelard, Chaucer, and Dante; in the rise of the great Gothic cathedrals in Paris and England; in the establishment of over 800 universities, including Oxford in 1249 and Cambridge in 1284, life, as indicated previously, was difficult. With the exception of a few wealthy persons, some clerics and other religious personnel, merchants, and craftsmen, most of the people worked long hours in the field, tilling and toiling with primitive tools. Fear and superstition abounded, for life posed many threats.

Wars and plagues, which periodically decimated the population, naturally fostered an intense belief in all-knowing gods, healing through faith and miracles, and the promise of a rewarding afterlife. Less than half the population survived to maturity. Effects of the plagues, for example, were so devastating that in order to procreate, women in England, according to the *Polychronicon,* "took any kind of husbands, strangers, the feeble and imbeciles alike, and without shame mated their inferiors."[4] Boys were men at 16, and men of 25 were middle age; longevity, success, and riches were afforded to few.

The Renaissance began in Italy during the 1300s and spread throughout Europe over the next few centuries. In many respects, the Renaissance was primarily an Italian experience—an experience which saw a renewed interest in man as man, individuality, learning, and the secular arts. While religion remained a major influence, people became less preoccupied with the spiritual and more with worldly matters. The arts, science, and worldwide exploration all flourished. The family constellation remained strong, peasants became freer, educational and vocational opportunities expanded, city life became more attractive, and the factory system was initiated. Bows and lances gave way to guns and cannons as the media of wars and feuds, of which there were many.

A renewed interest in the human body and anatomy led to the development of surgery; and medical care, in general, improved. Divinity, witchcraft, spells, and amulets, however, still held a high priority in the treatment of diseases and disorders.

The effects of the Reformation, the starting date of which is usually cited as October 31, 1517, when Martin Luther nailed his 95 theses on church abuse to the church door in Wittenburg, took many forms. As the authority of the Roman Catholic Church diminished, a substantial number of established charitable institutions and monasteries were either closed or taken over by the state. Subsequently, many persons lost their sole source of employment, and the poor and misfortunate no longer found a ready refuge. Cities grew, as did poverty, the mother of mental retardation. The outskirts of London were described as "filled up with a comparatively poor and vicious class, dwelling in meanest tenements, and living in parts by theft and beggary."[5]

As indicated, the state assumed priority in affairs that, until that time, had primarily fallen within the purview of the church. The actions of Queen Elizabeth, for example, were of significance not only in meeting the needs of the mentally retarded persons of her day but also in influencing the thinking and decisions of our American forefathers. In an effort to respond to the needs of the poor (and there were many) and growing unrest, Queen Elizabeth supported the Statute of Apprentices in 1563 and a series of relatively humane Poor Laws enacted between 1563 and 1601. The last and most significant one required the state to take care of the poor: each parish had to levy a tax to provide for the unemployable poor and to support almshouses for the aged poor and workhouses for vagrants who refused to work. This law, frequently called the Elizabethan Poor Law, remained in force until the nineteenth century.

Each of these actions assigned government a growing responsibility for meeting the needs of the poor and disadvantaged. Some mentally retarded persons undoubtedly were affected by both the Statute of Apprentices and the Poor Laws. Regrettably, however, many ended up in almshouses and work houses where, as we shall see, the conditions at best were deplorable and dehumanizing.

UNDERSTANDING OF MENTAL RETARDATION

A greater, but very limited, understanding of mental retardation developed during this period from antiquity to the Enlightenment. For centuries, religious doctrine precluded the conducting of human research essential to the advancement of medical science. Many early Greek and Roman medical theses were buried in monastary libraries and perused only occasionally by monks who lacked the knowledge to understand their contents. The traditions of Hippocrates and Galen persisted, however, and were advanced primarily by Arabian physicians.

Avicenna

The most notable physician during the early Middle Ages was Abu Ali al-Husayn ibn Sina (A.D. 980–1037), better known as Avicenna. This brilliant "Prince of Physicians" was born near Bukhara (now part of Russia) to the family of a Persian tax collector. At the age of 20 he was recognized as the most learned man of his time. His medical writings influenced both Arab nations and western Europe for centuries. His major text, the *Canon of Medicine,* was used in most universities through the sixteenth century and frequently cited by subsequent medical authors, especially those engaged in the study of pediatrics. In addition to his medical writings, Avicenna also wrote 68 books on theology and philosophy, 11 on astronomy and science, and four of poetry. According to Mazhar H. Shah, his translator and biographer, Avicenna "loved wine and pleasure almost as much as intellectual work and committed many excesses which culminated in shortening his valuable life. Just before his end, he freed his slaves, gave his wealth to the poor and listened to the reading of the Koran. He died in 1037 of colic, of which he had been a specialist. . . ."[6]

The *Canon of Medicine* provides a comprehensive, systematized presentation of medical knowledge up to that time. Typical of most writings of that era, it drew heavily upon Hippocrates. Avicenna, however, proposed treatments for various childhood diseases and disorders, including meningitis and hydrocephalus. He readily recognized and defined various levels of intellectual functioning, and knew that brain injury could affect memory and speech.

Avicenna placed little confidence in the humor theory. Instead, he preferred to emphasize three primary faculties: the *physical faculty,* which is responsible for nutrition and growth and was centered in the liver; the *nervous faculty,* which provides sensation and movement and is centered in the brain; and the *vital faculty,* which is the prerequisite for the life and activity of every organ or tissue. Underlying these three faculties was the vital force—*rooh*—which provides the "innate heat" or vital energy for the entire system. Variances in the level of vital energy would affect one's intellectual functioning. In essence, much of what are referred to as faculties and vital energies would, in contemporary medicine, be considered as neurological or biochemical in nature.

In contrast, Maimonides (1135–1204), the last of the great Arab physicians, devoted considerable attention to the humor theory and related it to intellectual functioning. He contended that the brain of the "phlegmatic" man, which was too humid, produced mental retardation. At the same time, however, he was careful to state that "phlegmatic" persons, if properly instructed, could make some intellectual progress, even though such learning would be very difficult.[7]

Though, as indicated, Avicenna recognized mental retardation, as had Hippocrates and Galen, he did not, with the exception of those cases involving a physical abnormality, pursue this area in terms of treatment. Medical problems deemed untreatable were relatively ignored. He did, however, caution against applying cupping-glasses against the forehead, for "it impairs the activity of the intellect, making the offspring dull and forgetful, with poor reasoning powers and permanent infirmity."[8]

A quote concerning hydrocephaly from Batholomaeus Metlinger's *Ein Regiment der Jungen Kinder,* published in Germany in 1497,

illustrates both the acknowledged authority of Avicenna and his kindly but futile attempts to treat hydrocephaly:

Avicenna calls this disease a watery swelling of the head which affects children at times while in the mother's body, however, seldom. . . . The reason why children develop such a head only seven days after the birth is that all hereditary diseases are postponed until the age in which conditions for this are suitable as one notes in smallpox and in eruptions and so is it also in this disease. As long as the fetus is in the mother's body the heat of the mother and the subtility of the covering of the brain destroy the vapor, which is not the case after the child is born.

It is advised that the wetnurse be cleaned with medicine and be forbidden all irritating food and things which inflate the stomach. Sage in a little sac should be put in the bath and when the child is being bathed it should be placed on the head. It should be bathed fasting and after the bath should be annointed with bitter almond oil and dill oil should be put up the nostril with a little feather and then the child should be allowed to sleep before it is fed. The wetnurse should be given white lily water or marjoram water and the child should also be given a little to drink. The head should be kept warm. When these things do not help, one should make a plaster out of scrapiron, sarcocol, gum, almonds and white incense and apply it like a cap. If this does not help one should make a broth of garlic corns packed in hot ashes and mixed until it is a white mousse and mix it with a half ounce of incense and lay it on the child for some days so that the head may take its natural form. After that one should make a nasal suppository out of wolf's gall and brains with myrrh and for two months this should be shoved in the nose every eight days while the child is fasting and let it stay for a half hour.[9]

Epilepsy, which, as we have seen, had been recognized from time immemorial, received considerable attention during the Middle Ages, as testified by its inclusion in nearly every medical dissertation concerning children. Paulus Bagellardus, for example, in the first known text on children's diseases published in 1472, observed:

Epilepsy is a disease which restrains the animate members by loss of consciousness and checks movements almost entirely on account of the obstruction which occurs in the ventricles of the cerebrum and in the courses of the sensory and motor currents. Now, such a disease is due to some fear or noise or the like. Moreover, it happens to infants in earliest life either after birth or at birth.

If it happen from birth, it is not to be cured, or scarcely ever, unless by the change of age or locality or seasons. Hippocrates testifies to this. Avicenna testifies to this as do nearly all the authorities. If they are not cured by such a change, they die with it.[10]

Metlinger speculated that epilepsy, or "falling sickness," was the result of "immoral conduct in the life of the mother while she carries the child so that she leaves her room for desires, either for good or bad, or imbecility in the head of the fetus which originates under the influence of the stars."[11] The moral conduct of a pregnant woman was frequently suspect in cases involving mental retardation.

Paracelsus

During the sixteenth century, several physicians rendered observations concerning mental retardation. Of these, the most renowned was the cynical, irascible Swiss physician Aureolus Theophrastus Bombastus von Hohenheim, better known as Paracelsus (1493–1541). Rarely has any person been of such character as to raise controversy concerning both personal and professional contributions for hundreds of years into the future. The Royal Society of Medicine noted on the 400th anniversary of his death that he was "a rude, circuitous obscurantist, not a harbinger of light, knowledge, and progress."[12] To other physicians, such as Haggard, Paracelsus had "the spirit of the modern doctor, the spirit of truth, progress, observation, independence, and self-reliance."[13] So the controversy continues.

Nevertheless, prior to his premature death as the result of a bar room brawl, Paracelsus, while professor of surgery at the University of Basel (1526–1528), observed that cretinism was associated with mental retardation. He was highly interested in both mental retardation and mental illness, and distinguished between the two conditions, noting the high degree of variability within each: "Many are those who are ill who are not thought to be mentally sick. For as fools (simpletons, feeble-minded) are of many kinds, so also are there many kinds of

crazy people not of one sort nor in one way, but in many ways, of many sorts, in many patterns and forms."[14] The "feeble-minded" behaved in the "ways of a healthy animal, but the psychopathic in the manner of an irrational animal."[15]

Felix Platter

Equally remarkable but less known was Felix Platter (1536–1614). This sensitive, dedicated Swiss physician, who obtained his medical degree from the then renowned medical school of Montpelier, took a particular interest in "mental alienation," which included both mental illness and mental retardation. The notion of "mental alienation" was to persist into the early years of the twentieth century, with physicians and others interested in the practice of psychiatry being known as "alienists."

Platter was one of the first to offer a multilevel description of mental retardation (identified as *Stulitia originalis*) and to note the existence of endemic cretinism:

Now we see many (foolish or simple from the beginning) who even in infancy showed signs of simplicity in their movements and laughter, who

Felix Platter.

did not pay attention easily, or who are docile and yet they do not learn. If anyone asks them to do any kind of task, they laugh and joke, they cajole, and they make mischief. They take great delight and seem satisfied in the habit of these simple actions, and so they are taught in their homes.

We have known others who are less foolish, who correctly attend to many tasks of life, who are able to perform certain skills. Yet they show their dullness, in that they long to be praised, and at the same time they say and do foolish things.[16]

As regards endemic cretinism:

There are also some simple (*stultus*) people, who are known to have dullness from before birth along with certain defects in their nature; some of these occur at random, but the more common ones are found in certain regions: Thus in a canton of Valesia called Bremis, I saw many sitting about the streets, some of whom were brought to me . . . on the chance that I might be able to offer some help to these persons. Such persons had deformed heads, or they spoke with a large and swollen tongue and at the same time with a tumorous throat, or they were deformed in their general appearance.[17]

Ambroise Paré

Finally, there was the unusual text, *Monstres et Prodiges,* by Ambroise Paré and published in 1573. Paré (1510–1590), the famous French surgeon who raised surgery from a trade to a skilled craft and science, offered a list of 13 causes for such conditions as two-headed girls, "goat-boys," and hairy girls:

1. God's glory
2. God's wrath
3. Too much semen
4. Too little semen
5. Imagination
6. The narrowness or smallness of the womb
7. The unbecoming position of the mother, who, while pregnant remains seated too long with her thighs crossed or pressed against her stomach
8. A fall or blows struck against the stomach of the mother during pregnancy
9. The rotting or the corruption of the semen
10. Heredity or accidental illnesses
11. The mingling or mixture of seed
12. The artifice of wandering beggars
13. The influence of demons or devils

While Paré's text was rejected by most physicians, often because he was a surgeon, a medical branch frowned upon by other medical specialties, it was widely read and accepted by the general public. A second glance at the list will reveal that it was more correct than incorrect.

The sixteenth century saw numerous gains in identifying and differentiating childhood diseases, including whooping cough, smallpox, chickenpox, measles, and scarlet fever. The fact that none of these diseases was related prognostically to mental retardation was probably due to the high mortality rate.

The works of such physicians as Paracelsus, Platter, and Paré illustrate that mental retardation was well recognized by physicians during these times, but was apparently considered unimprovable due to a variety of causes, ranging from the physical to the astrological. Heredity was acknowledged but not studied.

While many physicians seemed somewhat hesitant to treat mental retardation, others were not. Most medical care, at least for the less fortunate during the Middle Ages and Renaissance, was provided by the clergy, as witnessed by Giraldus of Wales, born in 1147: "For the sick, if medicine was required, there was none to be had except in the monastery; and in this country, at all events, the monks were the only medical practitioners."[18] It also should be noted that Christianity during this period in history was a mixture of scripture, doctrine, myth, legend, superstition, and custom.

This was reflected in some of the attempted treatments. Epileptic persons, for example, were subject to a wide range of treatments, including the consumption of "the brain of a mountain goat drawn through a golden ring"; the dust of a burnt prickly pig; theriaca magna mixed with women's milk with a touch of sugar of roses;* "the gall still warm from a dog who

---

*Theriaca magna consisted of 57 substances, chief of which was the flesh of poisonous snakes.

should have been killed the moment the epileptic fell in the fit.''[19] Thomas Phaer, the father of English pediatrics, wrote in 1584, ''Saphires, smaragades, redde coral, piony, mysteltow of the oke take in the moneth of March, and the moone decreasynge, tyme, savein, dylle, and the stone that is founde in the bellye of a yong swallow being the first brood of the dame. These or one of them, hanged about the necke of the child, saveth and preserveth it, from the sayd sickeness.''[20] The Scots suggested that the sacrifice of a live cock would benefit one with epilepsy: ''On the spot where the patient falls, the black cock is buried alive, along with a lock of the patient's hair and some parings of his nails.''[21]

Nor were mentally retarded persons exempt from such treatments: ''For idiocy and folly: Put into ale cassia, and lupins, bishopwort, alexander, githrife, fieldmore and holy water; then let him drink.''[22] Similarly, Gerade's *Herbal* recommended that black helebore of the Christmas rose ''purgeth all melancholy humors, yet not without trouble and difficultie, therefore it is not to be given but to robustious and strong bodies. . . . It is good for mad and furious men, for melancholy, dull and heavy persons, and for those that are troubled with the falling sickness [epilepsy].''[23]

SOCIAL CARE AND TREATMENT

Practices concerning mentally retarded persons varied according to country and its current attitude toward them. The economy of all nations during the Middle Ages relied heavily on agricultural pursuits. The need for manual labor combined with a high mortality rate rendered all children desirable; infanticide was also rarely practiced, since it was officially frowned upon throughout this entire period of history. Charlemagne, for example, decreed that exposed children should become the slaves of those who rescued them. A Council at Rouen during the eighth century encouraged women who had secretly borne children to leave them at a church. These infants were provided for and frequently became serfs on ecclesiastical estates. Such practices gave rise to the many foundling homes and orphanages that were established throughout Europe during the Middle Ages.

During the Dark Ages, however, thousands of children were exposed, abandoned, or sold into slavery by the impoverished inhabitants of Gaul, Germany, and Britain. Not only did those wanderers sell their own offspring and expose infants they had picked up, they even stole children from the well-to-do for this traffic. Some of this misery was alleviated by holy men who purchased these children outright as chattels of the church. In these early years, however, some countries held that retarded people were innocents and children of God, being well received by all religious sects. As one of Scotland's Doric poets wrote:

Nor is there ane amang ye but the best
  Wi' him wad share;
Ye mauna skaith the feckless!
  They're God's peculiar care.[24]

Many mentally retarded offspring were served in various church or state-sponsored foundling homes, orphanages, or hospitals. In A.D. 787, Datheus, archbishop of Milan, founded the first asylum for abandoned infants, wishing that ''as soon as the child is exposed at the door of the church, it will be received in the hospital and confided to the care of those who will be paid to look after them.''[25] Though today it is difficult to believe that some effort was not made to educate these youngsters, the record indicates that such facilities were intended primarily to provide basic protection and care. Unfortunately, the care was often inadequate and most children died.

Two significant changes occurred during the late Middle Ages concerning the Roman Catholic Church's attitude toward the mentally affected. One converted the mentally retarded from children of innocence and of God to products of sin and the devil. In 1150, Gratian's *Decretum,* which was unofficially accepted by the Church, declared that ''Every human being who is conceived by the coition of a man with a woman is born with original sin, subject to impiety and death, and therefore a child of wrath.''[26] The preaching of this doctrine resulted in many medieval Christians feeling a deep sense of inborn impurity, depravity, and guilt. For centuries, this concept, which received further emphasis during the Reformation, produced untold agony among parents of disabled children.

The second major change was the Inquisition and its correlates. Though the first heretics were burned at Orleans by King Robert of France in 1022, witch-hunting and the Inquisition did not reach its full fervor until the middle of the fifteenth century, and the last witch was not burned until 1793.[27] Religion, politics, greed, and superstition all lent their weight to this dreaded experience. Only England escaped widescale persecution.

According to the infamous book by the monks Johann Sprenger and Heinrich Kraemer, entitled *Malleus Maleficarum* (The Witches' Hammer) and written in 1487, no mentally different person was excluded from being considered a witch: "If the patient can be relieved by no drugs, but rather, seems to be aggravated by them, then the disease is caused by the devil. . . ."[28] There is little question that many naive, confused mentally retarded and epileptic women, men, and children suffered this fate. Samuel Harsnett, archbishop of York, wrote in 1599, those burned as witches had ". . . their brains baited and their fancies distempered with the imaginations and apprehensions of witches, conjurors and fairies, and all that lymphatic chimera, I find to be marshalled in one of these five ranks: children, fools, women, cowards, sick or black melancholic discomposed wits."[29] Women were more commonly persecuted, since they constituted the "weaker vessel"; the entire witch-hunting experience carried numerous sexual overtones.

Similarly, Reginald Scot in his pamphlet, *The Discovery of Witchcraft*, published in 1584, also lends credence to the fact that some mentally retarded persons, as well as epileptics, were treated unmercifully during the Inquisition. As stated on the title page, it was the "poor, miserable, and ignorant people who are frequently arraigned, condemned, and ex-

ecuted for *Witches* and *Wizzards*."[30] Paracelsus was one of the few physicians to ridicule publicly the notion of demoniacal possession: "Mental diseases have nothing to do with evil spirits or devils. . . ."[31]

Dahmus's summary of this episode casts an interesting light not only upon the Inquisition but also on the times. "The bitter criticism which the medieval Inquisition has evolved in modern times is not wholly justified. In all respects, in the principles upon which it justified its action, in the procedures it followed, even in the use of torture to expedite confessions, it introduced nothing which was not in conformity with the times. Both state and society demanded the suppression of heresy, and both anticipated the church in insisting upon capital punishment."[32]

The Reformation movement offered little new hope to mentally retarded persons, especially the more severely affected. Luther's attitude toward the latter was singularly harsh:

> Eight years ago, there was one at Dessau whom I, Martinus Luther, saw and grappled with. He was twelve years old, had the use of his eyes and all his senses, so that one might think that he was a normal child. But he did nothing but gorge himself as much as four peasants or threshers. He ate, defecated and drooled and, if anyone tackled him, he screamed. If things didn't go well, he wept. So I said to the Prince of Anhalt: "If I were the Prince, I should take this child to the Moldau River which flows near Dessau and drown him." But the Prince of Anhalt and the Prince of Saxony, who happened to be present, refused to follow my advice. Thereupon I said: "Well, then the Christians shall order the Lord's Prayer to be said in church and pray that the dear Lord take the Devil away." This was done daily in Dessau and the changeling died in the following year. When Luther was asked why he had made such a recommendation, he replied that he was firmly of the opinion that such changelings were merely a mass of flesh, a *massa carnis*, with no soul. For it is in the Devil's power that he corrupts people who have reason and souls when he possesses them. The Devil sits in such changelings where their soul should have been![33]

Though Luther strongly believed in witches, goblins, and demons, his remarks are still somewhat surprising, as he enjoyed an excellent reputation as a father, not only to his own six children, but to his 11 orphaned nieces and nephews as well.

As indicated previously, practices concerning mentally retarded persons varied throughout this age. In 1376, Hamburg confined them in a tower in the city wall called the "Idiot's Cage."[34] A century later, in 1497, the Town Council of Frankfurt-am-Main required that guardians be appointed for the idiots to keep them harmless: "Idiots were not only to be kept, but confined by their friends; and when means failed them, then only did municipal authorities intervene, though they occasionally assisted the families with sums of money."[35] It should be noted that the latter practice was favored by our Puritan forefathers.

In most rural areas, mentally retarded persons probably toiled long hours alongside their parents, responding to the demands of their lord or nobleman to wage combat at varying intervals. Many undoubtedly died at an early age due to disease or pestilence. Some may have participated in the Crusades. The village idiot was common, and mentally retarded persons of mild temperament were allowed to roam the countryside unmolested, receiving aid and comfort from neighbors. Thus, on an individual basis, they became somewhat of a public responsibility.

Mentally retarded persons in the city were retained in their own homes or became laborers (if fortunate) or, under less favorable circumstances, were placed in some residential facility or became beggars. The extreme poverty of the day accompanied by limited job opportunities (or idleness) gave rise to massive numbers of beggars throughout Europe. It has been reported, for example, that over 20,000 beggars practiced their trade at the funeral of one wealthy Englishman.[36] The fact that the mentally retarded were reduced to this state was confirmed by William Langland when, in 1393, he recorded that among the many beggars were the insane and idiots as well as those whose "church are brew-houses."[37] As he wrote in *Visions of Piers the Plowman,*

"Village idiot."

Moneyless they walke
With a good wil, witless, meny wyde contreys
Rught as Peter date and Paul, save that they
  preche nat.

During various periods of the Middle Ages and Renaissance, some mentally retarded persons were procured for amusement or other home purposes. Tycho Brahe (1546–1601), for example, the first modern astronomer, had a retarded companion. This brilliant scholar, who lost his nose in a duel as a rambunctious young man, kept a dwarf named Zep, who, according to legend, was "an imbecile to whose mutterings the great astronomer listened as to a divine revelation."[38] Hibbert, in his fascinating account of the rise and fall of the house of Medici, offered the following description of Pope Leo X's dinners: "The Pope's own dinners were noted for their rare delicacies . . . and for their jocularity, for such surprises as nightingales flying out of pies or little, naked children emerging from puddings. Buffoons and jesters were nearly always to be

found at his table where the guests were encouraged to laugh at their antics and at the cruel
jokes which were played on them—as when,
for instance, some half-witted, hungry dwarf
was seen guzzling a plate of carrion covered in
a strong sauce under the impression that he was
being privileged to consume the finest fare."[39]

At various times throughout the course of
history, little people were brought into the
home or into government for various reasons.
They had served in an advisory capacity to
several pharaohs during the days of ancient
Egypt and again became quite popular in Spain
during the seventeenth century as evidenced by
their frequent appearance in paintings by
Velasquez. As late as the twentieth century, it
is reported that Colonel Nasser of Egypt retained a midget in a personal advisory
capacity.[40]

Residential Services

Mentally retarded and mentally ill persons in
need of residential protection were tended in
one of a wide variety of institutions—monasteries, hospitals, charitable facilities, prisons,
almshouses, pesthouses, workhouses, ware-
houses, and other buildings most of which had
lost their original usefulness. There were few
instances of exemplary residential programs;
many, if not most, were less than respectable.
Two of the finest were Cairo's Mansur Hospital and the family-care approach used by the
citizens of Gheel, Belgium. The Mansur Hospital, which was built during the early years of
the Middle Ages, cooled its fever wards with
fountains, contained lecture halls, a library,
chapels, and a dispensary. There were two
nurses or attendants for each resident, reciters
of the Koran, musicians to lull patients to sleep;
and storytellers, actors, and dancers were employed to provide diversion and distraction.
Upon discharge, patients were given five gold
coins to tide them over until they could find
other means of support. For some unknown

reason, this model was not replicated in western Europe or other Islamic lands.*[41]

The program at Gheel took centuries to
develop and is still in effect. During the Middle
Ages, many pilgrims with mental or physical
afflictions traveled miles to a shrine in search
of a miraculous cure. One of the best known
such shrines was dedicated to Dympna. According to legend, when Dympna's mother
died, her father, the king, became obsessed
with finding another woman who looked like
his wife. Only Dympna bore such a resemblance, and when she rebuked his advances, he had her beheaded in Gheel. Several
mentally ill persons who observed this tragic
act became lucid and sane. Thus, Gheel became a refuge and haven for the mentally
affected beginning in the seventh century.
Though a small mental hospital was eventually
built, the primary focus was on family care. As
one nineteenth century commentator observed:

> The patients were treated as members of the
> families in whose homes they had lived. They had
> their own bedrooms, ate meals with the family,
> and engaged in all family activities. Many were
> given responsibilities, such as babysitting and
> other family chores.
>
> Many were employed in the town and on farms.
> If they could handle their own money they were
> given other valuables—tobacco, snuff, eggs,
> beer, and gingerbread. They could use all the
> community facilities, such as cafes and communi-
> ty halls, were able to attend community dances
> and fairs and attended all religious ceremonies.
> Many of them were fond of music, and they were
> encouraged to play their chosen instruments or
> listen to selected music. Painting, drawing, and
> gardening were encouraged, and many patients
> had gardens of their own. A change of scene was
> viewed as beneficial, so picnics and other outings
> were organized.[43]

In spite of the positive features of this approach, it was not readily accepted by others.
Experts who visited the program during the
eighteenth and early nineteenth centuries concurred that while it represented "a very good

---

*The nature of the prescribed treatment as well as the quality of such residential programs were to survive for
generations. In 1856, Dorothea Dix wrote, "The insane of Constantinople are in *far better condition* than those of Rome or
Trieste. . . . The hospital was founded by Solyman the Magnificent, and the provisions for the comfort and pleasure of
the patients, including music, quite astonished me. I had substantially little to suggest and nothing to urge!"[42]

situation for the quiet, harmless, and incurable insane," it was not "a good curative arrangement, and not a suitable place for those who were highly excited and violent, or who required medical treatment."[44] Chains were in evidence. Esquirol, for example, observed residents "whose flesh was lacerated by the chains they had worn, and noticed in the houses at Gheel, near the chimnies and the beds, iron rings with chains attached."[45] Others, such as Burdett, had grave concerns about this approach because it was impossible to prevent "communication between the sexes" and large amounts of alcoholic beverages were readily accessible.[46] Thus, the model was not adopted by other European countries until the late nineteenth century when Germany, Scotland, Switzerland, France, Ireland, and England all introduced similar programs of family care.[47] The first attempt at such a venture for the mentally retarded in the United States was by Charles Vaux, during the 1930s. Though Gheel's foster family program remains in existence today, industrialization and higher wages seriously threaten its future.[48]

Before continuing to review the conditions found in most residential facilities during this period, comment should be made of the oft-cited reference to the Bishop of Myra. A number of texts on mental retardation with an introductory section on history indicate that this good bishop offered a residential service for the retarded. Wallin, for example, wrote that "although the Bishop of Myra (the "Saint Nicholas" of that age) initiated charitable efforts for their [the mentally retarded] cure and protection as early as the fourth century, no effort was made to train or educate them during this period. They were, at best, merely protected, housed, clothed and fed."[49] While this may be true, no other historical sources verify the existence of the Bishop's program.

Most mentally retarded and mentally ill persons during this period were served either by monks in monasteries or in a variety of less attractive settings, such as prisons. In Prussia, for example, mentally affected persons were put in jail during the twelfth century. Such action probably reflected the sentiments of the day, for as a Prussian law declared: "Be a man laden with sick women, children, brothers, sisters, or domestics, or be he sick himself, then let them be where they lie, and we praise him too if he would burn himself or the feeble person."[50]

In his well-documented account of the rise of mental hospitals, Henry notes that a number of them were developed throughout Europe during the period of history under consideration. This included facilities in Byzantium (fourth century),* Jerusalem (A.D. 491),* Fez (seventh century), Metz (1100), Bagdad (1173), Valencia (1408), and Toledo (1483). In 1369, King Edward III issued a license to "an hospitall, in the parish of Baking Church, founded by Robert Denton, Chaplen, for the sustentation of poor priests and others, men and women . . . who were to remain till they were perfectly whole, and restored to good memory."[51] Many mentally retarded persons, especially those who were abandoned or who displayed less than quiescent behavior, were placed in such facilities. Persons either mentally ill or mentally retarded were considered victims of intellectual or reasoning deficits; these conditions would not be clearly differentiated in the minds of most persons for many years.

In 1247, the sheriff of London gave his estate and all his land to the Bishop and Church of Bethlem for the purpose of building a hospital for persons associated with the Order of St. Mary of Bethlem. Bethlem Hospital, which is believed to be the oldest providing continuous service in Europe, was converted to a mental asylum in 1377. Its first mentally ill and mentally retarded patients were transferred from an old store house which was located much too close to the King's palace. Bethlem soon earned the title "Bedlum," and for good reasons: an inventory in 1398 revealed four pairs of manacles, 11 chains of irons, six locks and

---

*Some authors question the authenticity of these two facilities.

keys, and two stocks . . . for 20 patients! Less violent patients were allowed to roam around the streets of London begging.

The various facilities used to accommodate mentally retarded and mentally ill persons during those days were judged rather harshly. In 1968, for example, Gail indicated that during the Middle Ages, leper hospitals, facilities for the incurable and epileptics, and almshouses for the old and infirm poor were characterized by "indifferent attendants and no resident doctor."[52] More historically appropriate, *A Compendious Rygment or a Dyetry of Helth,* published in 1542, recommended that "every man the whiche is madde or lunatycke or frantycke or demonyacke, to be kepte in safegarde in some close house or chamber where thee is lytell light; and that we have a keeper the whiche the madde man do feare."[53] In his study of the mentally affected, Felix Platter "went directly into the dungeons and dark cellars where the mentally ill and idiots were kept."[54] Violent remedies, according to Tuke, were "always popular and easy of application, equally efficacious, whether regarded as punishment for violent acts, or as a means of thrashing out the supposed demon lurking in the body."[55] Thus, while hopefully some mentally retarded persons found sanctuary in a sympathetic, well-run monastery or similar setting, the chances are great that they did not.

One final contribution of this period was the official and legal recognition of mentally retarded and mentally ill persons during the thirteenth century. Prior to that time, custody of the idiot and his lands was entrusted to the feudal lord; however, because of frequent abuses, King Edward I, who, in the judgment of British historian Jane Murray was a great king and soldier, transferred that responsibility to the Crown. Although, unfortunately, the original act has been lost, King Edward II, who was neither a great king nor a great soldier according to Murray, reconfirmed it in 1324.[56] The act read: "The King shall have the custody of the lands of natural fools, taking the profits of them without waste or destruction, and shall find them their necessaries, of whose fee soever the lands be holden. And after the death

of such idiots he shall render them to the right heirs; so that by such idiots no alienation shall be made, nor shall their heirs be disinherited."[57] The act also included a provision for those who were mentally ill: the Crown "shall provide for the safekeeping of the lands of lunatics (*isiota a causa et infirmities*) so that the lands might be *restored to them on recovery* or to their representatives on their death."[58]

Idiocy was defined as a congenital condition (*idiota a nativitate*) with a continuing lack of mental capacity, while the lunatic was potentially able to regain his faculties. Since this law dealt only with the rich, its actual application was limited. Further, since the Crown took all the profits of an idiot's estate, relatives usually sought to have them classified as lunatics in order to retain control over their assets.[59] Thus, the King's act probably was rarely used with mentally retarded persons.

Since mental retardation was now legally recognized, it was only natural that some effort was made to assess intelligence. In the *New Natura Brevium* published in 1534, Sir Anthony Fitzherbert offered the following primitive intelligence test: "And he who shall be said to be a sot and idiot from his birth, is such a person who cannot account or number twenty pence, nor can tell who was his father or mother, nor how old he is, etc., so as it may appear that he hath no understanding of reason what shall be for his profit, nor what for his loss. But if he hath such understanding, that he know and understand his letters, and do read by teaching or information of another man, then it seemeth he is not a sot nor a natural idiot."[60] In 1591, Swineburne expanded the procedure by adding such items as measuring a yard of cloth and naming the days of the week.

SEVENTEENTH AND EIGHTEENTH CENTURIES

The seventeenth and eighteenth centuries, which represent the historical periods of "Reason" and "Enlightenment," served as a bridge between Renaissance thinking and the sudden awareness of mental retardation as an entity in itself and the tremendous contributions of Itard and Seguin during the nineteenth century. These were times of remarkable contrast: unrivaled elegance and extreme deprivation. Voltaire, Mozart, the salons of Paris, Meissen china, and baroque design against unbelievable poverty and cruelty to the less fortunate.

Modern Europe had its origins during the seventeenth century. Many of the changes initiated during the preceding centuries, especially during the Reformation, came to fruition or conclusion. The Treaty of Westphalia (1648), which ended the Thirty Years' War, clearly sanctioned the conception of national, secular, fully sovereign states theoretically equal in status. Industry grew; shipping and related commercial interests became major economic activities, including colonial expansion by England, France, and Spain; international trading of luxury items became both fashionable and expensive. Farming continued as the major economic activity, with many former peasants and serfs now owning small parcels of land. Serfdom in Europe, but not in Russia, was gradually dying.

The rise of the middle class and the expansion of world trade and industry was paralleled by an increased interest in the practice of capitalism, which Hamilton defined as "the system by which wealth other than land is used for the definite purpose of securing an income."[61] The Industrial Revolution, which was to make its appearance first in England, ushered in a new, prolonged period of hardship for many men, women, and children. Large plants grew up overnight with employees losing their sense of personal identification with management and becoming merely one part of the entire mechanical production process. Wages were kept deliberately low. By 1788, textile mills alone employed 59,000 women and 48,000 children. Long hours (12 hours per day for children), a 6-day work week, and insensitive management were all indigenous to this inhumane venture. By the turn of the eighteenth century, employees were no further ahead financially than were their ancestors in 1700. The effects on youth were obvious:

In this village, where many mills were in active operation, he [Pestalozzi] first witnessed the contrast between extreme wealth and abject poverty. He saw the children of the village playing before the school-house, with eyes sparkling with pleasure and innocence, contented and happy, even in their rags; but when he compared them with those of more mature age, the victims of overwork and manifold vices, with hollowed cheeks and sunken eyes, and with the appearance of constant misery upon their faces, his young soul was incensed against the selfishness of wealth built upon such ruins of health and happiness.[62]

Both the seventeenth and eighteenth centuries were periods of constant conflict and war with massive armies moving back and forth through Europe, leaving destruction and a variety of diseases and epidemics in their wake. Plagues (e.g., England, 1603, 1662, and 1664) and famines (e.g., France, 1662 and 1693) were common. Scurvy affected many; malaria killed 40,000 in Italy and more in England during the first half of the 1600s; and smallpox, diphtheria, typhus, and typhoid all ravaged the European population during the seventeenth century. The eighteenth century witnessed more of the same: "the bubonic plague killed 300,000 in Prussia in 1709; 30,000 French died of exanthematous typhus in 1741; malaria, diphtheria and pertussis took heavy tolls; in 1723 yellow fever appeared for the first time in Europe."[63]

Big government, large armies, colonization, and interminable wars required increasing amounts of money, and taxes were to rise to exorbitant heights in most countries. The accumulative effects of wars, diseases, famines, and high taxes produced a life of hardship and poverty among the masses of people, regardless of whether they lived in the country or in town. Begging increased substantially in all major European cities. During the Thirty Years' War, for example, there were over 100,000 beggars in Paris alone.

During the seventeenth century, begging reintroduced the barbaric practice of deliberately mutilating young children. "Professional" beggars would purchase youngsters from a foundling home or orphanage for 8 pence apiece and proceed to break their legs, or in some other way maim them, so that they could fetch more alms. When the youngsters had outgrown their usefulness, they were left on their own; naturally, many died.[64] It was such practices as these that motivated Vincent de Paul to pursue his eleemosynary programs.

UNDERSTANDING OF MENTAL RETARDATION

During the seventeenth and eighteenth centuries, medicine in general made several significant strides forward, each of which would play its own role in mental retardation in subsequent generations. William Harvey proved that blood circulated through the body (1616); Marcello Malpighi demonstrated that capillaries join the arteries to the veins (1664); Thomas Willis produced an extensive text on the nervous system (1664); Anton van Leeuwenhoek, an amateur scientist, saw germs (unidentified) in his newly devised microscope during the seventeenth century; Casper Friedrich Wolff established the scientific study of embryology (1759); and in 1798, Edward Jenner discovered a successful method of vaccination against smallpox, though he did not understand its underlying mechanisms. Many scientific societies were established, including the *Academy of Science* in France, which was to play so important a role in assessing the efforts of Itard.

With regard to mental retardation and epilepsy, however, advances were less evident. Francis Glisson (1597–1677), a famous lecturer on anatomy and leader in the understanding of rickets, was one of the few physicians granted permission to perform dissections under the reign of Queen Elizabeth. In his book *De Rachitide Sive Morbo Puerill*, published in 1650, he identified the true source of hydrocephaly: "In some bodies that we have dissected between the Dura and the Pia Mater, and in the very ventricles of the Brain, we have found wheyish and waterish humors: from whence it is manifest, That this affect is complicated with the Hydrocephalus."[65]

Robert Pemell (?–1653) not only wrote a fine pediatric text concerning the chief internal diseases of the head but published it in his natural tongue rather than Latin. He included in his discussion a lengthy review of epilepsy, proposing 45 possible treatments, which in the estimation of Ruhräh were as appropriate as any employed during the 1920s. His text was prefaced with a poem, a common practice in 1653, which clearly indicated that he appreciated the significance of the brain:

> The Head, the Heaven of man's Body is;
> 　The Mind's high Palace, wherein it doth raign;
> The Fountain, whence all motion takes its rise,
> 　The Harbour, where the Senses do remain.
> As many stars i'th the Sky conjoyned shine;
> 　So rare endowments in the head abound;
> Life, Health, Strength, Reason, Wit, do there combine,
> 　And the best Organs of the Soul are found.
> If mudless be the Spring, and silver-cleer;
> 　As Silver-cleer, the Streams will also flow;
> From muddy Fountains, muddy streams appear;
> 　And like the Fountain, do the Waters go.
> Man's health doth much depend upon his head;
> 　If that be sound, th' whole body is at ease;
> If that, will illness, be distempered,
> 　On other parts some weakness soon doth seize.[66]

Francis Sylvius (1614–1672) not only was a brilliant anatomist specializing in the brain but also took a special interest in children. His name is most familiar among those who have even an introductory knowledge as to the structure of the brain, for he is identified at least five times: the fissure of Sylvius, the aqueduct of Sylvius, the ventricle of Sylvius, the fossa of Sylvius, and Sylvian artery. In 1674, he published a miniature text on pediatrics entitled *Praceous Medica liber Quartus*, which contained a unique description of epilepsy, attributing mental retardation to repetitive seizures.

Antiquated ideas still persisted, however, as evidenced in a text by an unknown author, simply identified as "J. S." The volume, entitled *Children's Diseases, both Inward and Outward*, was published in 1661. It again noted the influence of witchcraft; for instance, "If the Child is bewitcht, a Saphir or Carbuncle hung about the Child's Neck is conceived good; so is Hartshorn hung in the House, and many more which I omit as superstitious or false."[67] Paralysis and palsy (an incomplete state of paralysis), J. S. wrote, were produced by a pituitous humor which by coldness and moistness thickens and obstructs the nerves, so that they cannot receive the animal spirits; Hippocrates was never far from the reasoning of medical practitioners, even in the seventeenth and eighteenth centuries.

Walter Harris (1647–1732) was one of the first pediatricians and medical practitioners to urge that one examine the question of heredity:

There is no one who will deny, that there are hereditary Diseases proceeding either from one or other of the Parents; or question but the Gout, Epilepsy, Stone, Consumption, etc., sometimes flow from the Parent to the Children. Whole Families proceeding from the same Stock, often end their Lives by the same Kind of Disease. For the prolific Seed often so rivets the morbid disposition into the Foetus, that it can never afterwards be removed by any Art of Industry whatsoever. But let those who prefer a strong, vigorous and healthy Offspring before Money, take care to avoid epileptic, scrophulous, and leprous Mothers (from *De Marbis Acutis Infantum*).[68]

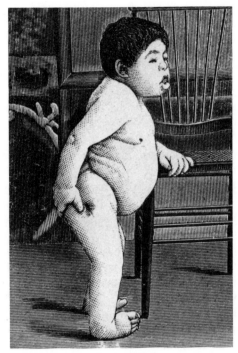

Cretin child.

He also indicated that acids may underlie many children's diseases, and warned that the drinking of any alcoholic beverages was to be avoided by children, as it could result in reduced intellectual functioning.

Wolfgang Hoefer (1614–1681), court physician in Vienna, is a relatively unknown figure in medical history. His only known publication, *Hercules Medicus, Sive Locorum Communium Medicorum Tomus Unicus,* published in 1657, was of particular importance to the field of mental retardation because it offered the first extensive description of cretinism. Of all clinical forms of mental retardation, cretinism, which was endemic to Switzerland, received considerable attention and was, as we shall discuss, important in the development of institutional programs. Hoefer contended that this condition and its mental retardation could be attributed primarily to food and education: "For this is a class of people, who delight in foods which supply much excrement, but little aliment; they are displeased with the opposites; on this account they are voracious, yet never full, except to the point of bursting when the abdomen bends. Their children, in this manner stuffed at least four times a day, they deposit near the oven, and instruct them neither in letters nor in morals nor in labors, frequently they pay no attention to their [children's] entreaties, so that, when their food also aids their melancholy and gloomy spirits, they are necessarily made *stupid* and *foolish.*"[69]

In 1702, Phillippus Jacobus Duttel submitted the first scientific monograph on birth defects, entitled *Fetal Death in the Maternal Uterus.* In the preface, he wrote, "So wretched and miserable is the condition of mankind that not only are men tormented by innumerable ills throughout their lives, but foetuses also are not free from evils and sicknesses while they are still shut up within the prison of the womb, and before they breathe with joy the vital air and look upon the light. . . ."[70] Though the significance of this thesis was not recognized in its day, Duttel's attitude was indicative of the new age of scientific thought.

Robert Whytt (1714–1766), in *Observations on the Dropsy of the Brain* published in 1768, offered the most elaborate description of hydrocephalus to that time. His 48-page description is credited with stimulating great interest in this area. Unfortunately, after studying and treating 20 cases, he could only conclude, "I freely own that I have never been so lucky as to cure one patient who had those symptoms which with certainty denote this disease."[71]

These publications clearly indicate that over the 200-year period under consideration, man's knowledge of the brain, epilepsy, and hydrocephalus had expanded. Yet, the etiology and pathology of the latter two conditions remained a mystery. Heredity had been drawn to the attention of the medical community, and one more clinical form of mental retardation was clearly identified: cretinism. Perhaps the best way to summarize the knowledge of mental retardation by 1800 is to review briefly Pinel's *A Treatise on Insanity,* published in 1801. Pinel distributed mental illness into five main categories:

1. Melancholia, or delirium
2. Mania without delirium
3. Mania with delirium
4. Dementia, or the abolition of the thinking facility
5. Ideotism, or obliteration of the intellectual faculties and affections

Ideotism was defined as

a defective perception and recognizance of objects, is a partial or total abolition of the intellectual and active faculties. This disorder may originate in a variety of causes, such as excessive and enervating pleasures; the abuse of spirituous liquors; violent blows on the head; deeply impressed terror; profound sorrow; intense study; tumors within the cavity of the cranium; apoplexy; excessive use of the lancet in the treatment of active mania. The greatest number of ideots are either destitute of speech or are confined to the utterance of some inarticulate sounds. Their looks are without animation; their senses stupified; and their motions heavy and mechanical.

The only real distinction that existed between dementia and idiocy was that "the latter condition involved the loss of both intellect and *affective* behavior."[72] In many instances, the differentiation was at best rather superficial, and there always remained in Pinel's mind the commonality between dementia and idiocy. Therefore, it is not surprising that Pinel would indicate that "the most numerous class of patients at lunatic hospitals is undoubtedly that of ideots; who, when viewed collectively, exhibit every degree and form of stupidity."[73] He did, however, distinguish between congenital and acquired forms of idiocy and recognized various levels of functioning. An extreme degree of idiocy was illustrated in his extensive review of the cretins of Switzerland.

Pinel's general impression was that, with rare exception, neither the idiot nor the demented person was susceptible to education or similar treatment. As regards mental retardation:

To be an idiot, it is almost leveled with an automaton; to be deprived of speech or to retain the power merely of pronouncing inarticulate sounds: to be obedient only to the instinct of one, and sometimes to be insensible even to that: to be incapable of feeling, attending to or gratifying without assistance the appetite for food, to remain motionless in the same place and position for several days together, without discovering one single expression either of thought or expression, to be at other times subject to sudden, furious and evanescent transports of passion. Such are the circumstances characteristic of ideotism. . . . Humane attention to their physical wants and comforts is in general the utmost that can be devised and done for those unfortunate beings. . . . Though education would not be appropriate owing to the natural indolence and stupidity of idiots, they might be engaged in manual occupations, suitable to their capacities.[74]

Though, as indicated by the preceding discussion, "ideocy" had become the commonly accepted scientific term of mental retardation, another label—"dunce"—became increasingly popular, especially among educators and laypersons. This negative connotation had its origins with the activities of John Duns Scotus, the scholar born in Scotland in 1265. In 1303, he argued against the King of France's proposal to tax the Roman Catholic Church in order to finance a war with England. In response, the Pope excommunicated the King of France, and Duns Scotus, in punishment for supporting the Pope, was banished from France.

Two centuries later, the term "dunce" was coined by Renaissance humanists and Reformation leaders who took issue with Duns Scotus's defense of the Papacy: any follower of Duns Scotus's teachings—a "Duns man" or "dunce"—was considered a dull witted person, incapable of scholarship.

Philosophy

Perhaps the greatest contribution of the seventeenth and eighteenth centuries as regards mentally retarded persons and the efforts of early pioneers in the field involved the significant and drastic changes in human thinking. Philosophers and scientists alike concurred with Alexander Pope's (1688–1744) declaration "The proper study of mankind is man."

The great legacy of this period, however, had its origins in the thirteenth century with the teachings and writings of Roger Bacon (1214–1292). This highly respected teacher at Oxford believed strongly that philosophical teachings must be verified with the facts of experience and experimentation, denying "frail and unworthy authority, long-established custom, the sense of the ignorant crowd, and the hiding of one's ignorance under the show of wisdom."[75]

Four hundred years later, Francis Bacon (1561–1626) published his famous *Novum Organum,* which, in many respects, contained ideas and concepts similar to those of Roger Bacon: knowledge about the world is acquired through sensory experience. Similarly, discovery, investigation, and explanation of "Forms" (the properties of substances) could be accomplished only by controlled observation and experimentation.

In his *Discourse on Method,* René Descartes (1596–1650) proclaimed that true understanding of the natural world would come through the proper application of mathematical principles and deductive reasoning. Thomas Hobbes (1588–1679), who occasionally served as an amanuensis to Francis Bacon, indicated in *De Corpora* that philosophy and science were practically synonymous; that is, the purpose of philosophy was the determined cause and effect relationships. In current parlance, he urged

the application of the hypothetical-deductive method of science.

The *tour de force,* however, was John Locke's (1632–1704) *An Essay Concerning Human Understanding* published in 1690. His empirical theory of knowledge played a critically important role in the development of psychology in general and in providing an encouraging basis for the treatment and training of mentally retarded persons. In essence, Locke maintained that at birth the mind is a blank table (a *tabula rasa*); that is, no one is born with innate ideas. All ideas come from experience, either from sensation or reflection. Sensation provides one with the ideas of simple substance and qualities, while reflection enables one to acquire such abstract concepts as thinking, willing, and doubting. In essence, Locke "gave the empirical approach an appealing and challenging quality which greatly contributed to its strength and influence."[76]

Locke's influence was felt in other ways, as well. He firmly believed that man was rational and that a humane, enlightened social order was possible. This positive concept of man and society would be well received by many. Parenthetically, in 1690, Locke also recognized the difference between mental retardation and mental illness: "Herein seems to lie the difference between idiots and madmen, That madmen put wrong ideas together and reason from them, but idiots make very few or no propositions and reason scarce at all."[77]

In summary, these philosophers and scientists advanced four essential concepts: 1) absolute authority of any doctrine or dogma was invalid, 2) one is not born with innate ideas, 3) man learns through his senses and reflective thinking, and 4) the experimented method, accompanied by either deductive or inductive reasoning, is critical to the validation of opinion and speculation.

Jean Jacques Rousseau Our discussion of the influence of Enlightenment philosophy on the future course of mental retardation would be incomplete without considering Jean Jacques Rousseau (1712–1778), the Swiss-French moralist and philosopher. As the most eloquent of the great rational thinkers and one of the finest writers of his day, his impact on philosophy, social consciousness, the French Revolution, and future generations of educators and other reformers is inestimable.

Rousseau was poor, sickly, extremely self-conscious, paranoiac, and, in general, rejected and berated by his society and times. His tremendous success, with the exception of *La Nouvelle Heloise,* was to occur only after his death.

In 1762, he published his two great works that were to establish him forever as a great philosopher and educator: *Du Contrat Social* and *Emilé.* The opening line from the *Social Contract* is known by every schoolboy: "Man is born free, and he is everywhere in chains." Our concern, however, is with the latter book, *Emilé,* which led to Rousseau's downfall and banishment from French society, primarily because of his attack on contemporary fundamentals of Christianity. Both he and his book were banned; and, for the remainder of his life, he moved from one country to another as a fugitive.

The opening line of *Emilé* sets the tone for the entire treatise: "God makes all things good; man meddles with them and they become evil." Rousseau's fundamental principle involved the unfolding of man according to the laws of nature rather than to those of society. Emilé is provided with a tutor who assists the boy to traverse three main educational periods: the purely physical and sensory up to the age of 12, the intellectual from 12 to 15, and the moral from 15 upward.

Rousseau's affirmation of the primary role of the senses in the formation of the mind was entirely consistent with Locke's earlier interpretations in his essay on human understanding. Rousseau stated:

> We are born capable of learning, but knowing nothing, perceiving nothing and sense experiences are the raw material of thought; they should, therefore, be presented to him [Emilé] in a fitting order, so that memory may at a future time present them in the same order to his understanding; but as he only attends to his sensations it is enough, at first, to show him clearly the connections between these sensations and the things which cause them. . . . He wants to touch and handle every-

thing; do not check these movements which teach him invaluable lessons. Thus he learns to perceive the heat, cold, hardness, softness, weight, or lightness of bodies, to judge by their size and shape and all their physical properties, by looking, feeling, listening, and above all, by comparing sight and touch, by judging with the eye what sensations they would cause to his hand.[78]

The impact of this book on all education has been unequaled by any other similar contribution. The notion of the natural child, self-direction, and the importance of sensory training and experiences directly influenced Pestalozzi and Froebel, as well as Itard, Seguin, and Montessori.

It is interesting to note, however, that while many persons have utilized Rousseau's ideas in educating mentally retarded youngsters, he himself "would not undertake the care of a feeble, sickly child, should he live to four score years. I want no pupil who is useless alike for himself and others, one whose sole business is to keep himself alive, one whose body is always a hindrance to the training of his mind. . . . A feeble body makes a feeble mind. . . . Let another tend this weakling for me; I am quite willing, I approve this charity, but I myself have no gift for such a task."[79]

SOCIAL CARE AND TREATMENT

Most of the practices affecting mentally retarded persons developed during the preceding century continued into the seventeenth and eighteenth centuries. While many retarded persons undoubtedly were retained at home and received whatever help and support they could from their parents, others continued to receive some form of either mystic or residential treatment. In the early 1600s, for example, one Alexander Drummond claimed to have cured 40 persons "visseit with frenacies, madness, falling evil (epilepsy), persones distractit in their wittis, and with feirful apparitiones, etc., and utherisis uncouth diseases; all done be sorcerie, incantation, devellische charmeing."[80] After reviewing the case, the court determined that Mr. Drummond should be strangled and burned for being too familiar with Satan. He was!

The Industrial Revolution of the eighteenth century produced a great demand for child labor. The condition of child mill-workers, of whom many were mentally retarded, was pitiable in all the industrial centers. As recorded by Pintner, "An interesting reference to the feebleminded appears in the custom, prevalent in England in the eighteenth century, of binding out pauper children to the mill owners. The parish authorities, in order to get rid of imbeciles, often bargained that the mill-owners take one idiot with every 20 children. What became of the idiots is not known, but in most cases they did not last long and mysteriously disappeared.[81] This practice led to one of the great industrial thefts of the day. John Astbury, pretending to be an idiot employee with the Elers brothers' pottery factory, stole their secrets for making quality china, mass produced the dishes, and made a fortune.

Residential Services

Mentally retarded persons who could not be maintained at home were no longer subject to infanticide, at least not legally; however, abandonment of such children became increasingly frequent. With those, and especially the poor among them, who were placed in a foundling home, hospital, prison, mental hospital or other such facility, treatment, in general, was considered to be worse than in preceding centuries. The death rate among children placed in either charitable or publicly supported retreats or hospitals was extremely, even unbelievably, high. Of 2,000 infants moved to the Foundling's Hospital of Paris in 1670, 75 percent had died within 3 months.[82] Nor did this situation improve over the next century; for example, "Of 10,272 infants admitted to the Dublin Foundling Hospital during 21 years (1775–1796), only 45 survived, a mortality rate of 99.6 percent. Of 31,951 infants admitted to the Paris Foundling Asylum during 1771–1777, 25,476 (80 percent) died before the end of their first year."[83]

As already witnessed by Pinel's comments, idiocy and dementia were deemed incurable disorders. Thus, many felt that, regardless of where they were placed, nothing could be done

and that neither the idiot nor the mentally ill person was sensitive to cold, heat, hunger, and pain. As summarized by Gay, "The prisons, crowded and disease-ridden, were a lucrative business for jailers. Prisoners with any money had to pay for food and lodgings. Juvenile offenders, petty thieves and debtors were packed together with murderers and the insane. In a day when public hangings at Tyburn drew enthusiastic crowds and when heads of traitors were left to rot in the public view, barbarity was common among jailers."[84] With regard to Bethlem, "Bedlam's patients elicited little compassion. . . . Thus they were ill-fed, ill-clothed, and cruelly treated."[85]

The Hôtel Dieu, the largest and most famous hospital in Paris, which in 1606 was ordered by the King to tend all mentally ill and idiot people, was described in the following words:

The patients were herded together in rooms crowded with miserable beds in which they were put without distinction of disease; there were two, four, six, and even twelve people bedded together in various positions; one can easily imagine how sanitary this was! Owing to the conditions of the times, the medical assistance was limited, as was the religious assistance despite the large number of priests and nuns; half of the priests were busy with the church and office work; half of the nuns were so absorbed in their devotions that they overlooked their work, while the other half were too busy to take care of the spiritual needs of the sick.[86]

Tuke, in his definitive review of Bethlem, in which he readily concedes there were many idiots, stated that chains were commonly employed to treat those who acted out or to restrain those who might hurt themselves. Dark cells were common and sexes mixed. Staff were few in number, many were satisfying prison sentences, and their quality left much to be desired. Samples from the series of original reports quoted by Tuke illustrate the nature of the services and conditions: "I stepped into Bedlam, where I saw several poor miserable creatures in chains. The men and women in old Bethlem were huddled together in the same ward. Patients are ordered to be bled about the latter end of May, according to the weather; and after they have been bled, they take vomits, once a week for a certain number of weeks; after that we purge all the patients.'' Here, as in many facilities in England, and presumably other countries, visitations were often restricted. According to one grievant, Tuke reported, ''Patients often cannot be found out, because the master lets them bear some fictitious names in the house; and if fortunately discovered by a friend, the master, or his servants, will endeavor to elude his search and defect his humane intentions by saying *they have strict orders to permit no person to see the patient.*''[87]

The practice of letting mildly mentally retarded persons and non-aggressively disturbed persons beg on the streets of Paris was discontinued in 1675. Their success had encouraged other beggars to emulate their efforts and created a public nuisance.

Until 1770, Bethlem was one of London's favorite tourist spots. People entered the ''penny gates'' and were allowed to roam the yards and to be entertained or shocked according to their personal taste and expectations. Monies for the penny gate were used to offset expenses. One such visitor, Sir Thomas More, was disturbed, as he revealed in his *De Quator Novissimis:* ''For thou shalt in Bedlum see one laugh at the knocking of his own head against a post, and yet there is little pleasure therein.''

During the seventeenth century, public support of charitable institutions was initiated with mixed reactions. For example, Henry claimed that religious residential facilities, because of ignorance and superstition, were ''barbarous.''[88] On the other hand, Tuke declared that the transition from religious organizations to state or locally operated ''houses'' of various descriptions was worse:

And there was, of course, as the primary treatment, seclusion in a dark room and fetters. . . . They were too often under the charge of brutal keepers, were chained to the wall or in their beds, where they lay in dirty straw, and frequently, in the depth of winter, without a rag to cover them. It is difficult to understand why and how they continued to live; why their caretakers did not, except in the case of profitable patients kill them outright; and why, failing this—which would have been a kindness compared with the prolonged tortures to

which they were subjected—death did not come sooner to their relief.[89]

Mentally retarded persons were often abused. Pinel, addressing himself to reformed facilities, specifically cautioned that mentally retarded persons' ''passive obedience and degradation expose them to inattention, and frequently to cruel treatment on the part of the keepers and servants.''[90]

Vincent de Paul   Perhaps the most remarkable person to serve the needy, including the mentally ill and retarded, during the seventeenth century was Vincent de Paul (1581–1660).

Born into poor circumstances, he was ''an ex-herder of pigs, one of six children who always remained poor. . . .''[91] Ordained as a priest on September 23, 1600, he spent several years (1605–1607) in bondage in Africa following capture by pirates along the Barbary Coast. His impoverished background plus his experiences in slavery made him especially sensitive to the plight of the downtrodden. Ultimately, he served as priest to both galley slave and queen (Anne of Austria). He was a remarkable reformer within the church; but above all, he was to prove to be one of the world's foremost leaders of men and women in meeting the needs of the less fortunate.

Relying primarily on lay rather than ecclesiastical help, de Paul established such groups as the first Confraternity of Charity and the Daughters of Charity, who provided innumerable hours of service to the poor, the foundling, and the ill. In spite of the times and current thinking, St. Vincent de Paul and his associates, primarily women, firmly maintained that mentally ill and mentally retarded persons were not witches—''mental disease is no different from bodily disease. Christianity demands of the humane and the powerful to protect and of the skillful to relieve the one as well as the other.''[92]

In 1632, de Paul was given the Parisian priory of Saint-Lazure, which historically had been a leprosarium. At the time he assumed responsibility for this facility, it consisted of a church, prison, penitentiary, stables, a mill, the lodgings of the Austanian monks who took care of the foundation, and a sanitorium for the sick. Through his dedicated labor and inspirational leadership, Saint-Lazure not only gradually became the heart of the religious revival of Paris and France, but it housed within its walls missionaries, ecclesiastics, orphans, novices, seminarians, wayward youths, insane persons, mentally retarded individuals, and lepers. There were also priests and learned men, while others were engaged in distributing food, clothes, books, and money to the poor, who often numbered 600 a day. Ultimately, this facility would become the Bicêtre, which, in turn, was to provide for the enlightened programming for the mentally retarded of the nineteenth century.

In 1877, Ireland wrote, "In the seventeenth century, St. Vincent de Paul, among his many works of benevolence, gathered together a few idiots in the priory of Saint-Lazure, took charge of them in person, and attempted to teach them; but his labors, though continued for years, do not seem to have been successful."[93] Vincent de Paul's sensitive approach was a rarity for its day and represents the most sterling example of humane treatment until the appearance of Pinel and Tuke in the eighteenth century.

Philipe Pinel   In 1793, one of the most dramatic events to involve a residential treatment center occurred. Philipe Pinel struck the chains from some male patients at Bicêtre.

Born to a country physician, and after briefly considering entering divinity school, Pinel (1745–1826) chose medicine and the natural sciences as his career. He became interested in mental illness when a very close friend went insane, was locked up, escaped, and was found dead, partly eaten by wolves.[94]

He came to Paris as a young physician 11 years before the French Revolution and served as physician-in-chief at the Bicêtre and the Salpétrière during the Revolution and its aftermath. He was described by a contemporary as a "conservative man, warm hearted yet detached, elastic, adaptable, but courageous."[95] Being studious and highly learned, he was familiar with early Greek and Latin literature,

Philipe Pinel.

including Soranus's writings. For several years after his arrival in Paris, he translated classical medical documents and contributed a few articles of his own concerning mental diseases. His ability to survive the French Revolution and the subsequent Reign of Terror, even though he was a leading personage in Paris, was attributed to his sincerity, intellectual honesty, and single-minded concern for the welfare of the insane rather than to any political machinations.

He was appointed to Bicêtre on August 25, 1793, and assumed a similar responsibility for the Salpétrière 3 years later. His first reaction to Bicêtre was one of shock and disbelief: "It is impossible to pass over in silence that which they called the cell service, where 600 mentally sick were massed together without order and left to the rapacity and ineptness of subalterns. It was a picture of disorder and confusion."[96]

In the late 1700s, mentally affected persons were initially admitted to the Hôtel Dieu. If they did not respond to treatment (baths, bleeding, and medications) in a short period of time, men were transferred to Bicêtre and women to Salpétrière. Conditions in both facilities prior to Pinel's administration must represent the nadir of human consideration. Salpétrière housed 7,000 women, all dressed in burlap sack. Five women slept in a bed; the daily diet consisted of one mug of gruel, one ounce of meat, and three slices of bread; and the stench was overwhelming. Over 1,000 mentally disturbed women—"those deprived of their reason"—were crowded into one wing of the facility, "in the most deplorable condition when their insanity is the sort that divests them of their instinctive cleanliness. Though the rooms are washed twice a day, these poor souls live in indescribable filth and are like the lowest animals. Mad women subject to fits are chained like dogs to the door of a kennel and separated from the attendants or visitors by a long corridor shielded by grillwork. Food is passed to them through the grillwork, and straw for their bedding. Rakes are used to remove part of the waste that surrounds them."[97]

Conditions at Bicêtre, "the beggars' Bastille," were worse: one felt queasy "at the entrance from the strong odor emitted by this receptacle for the vilest, foulest dregs of society . . . vicious persons of every kind, swindlers, defaulters, pickpockets, thieves, forgers, pederasts, etc. It is distressing to see them side by side with vagrants, epileptics, imbeciles, lunatics, the aged, and the infirm—known as the 'good poor.' Five or six hundred inmates are packed together there, a tenth of whom are dying. You cannot enter even to bring them food except behind the tip of a bayonet."[98]

Prior to releasing any male patients from their chains or other bonds at Bicêtre, Pinel had to obtain the approval of the Commune. He addressed the Commune in person and was there confronted with the revolutionary Couthon. Couthon's first response to Pinel's plea was, "Woe to you, if you deceive me and if you hide enemies of the people among your

insane." Following further dialogue, Couthon finally approved, with the following observation: "You may do what you please, but I am afraid that you are a victim of your presumptions."[99] Pinel released a few patients, one of whom, a drunken athlete named Chevigne, later saved his life from a public lynching.*

Pinel's contributions are many, including his text on classifications of mental diseases, his development of individual case histories and systematic records, and his emphasis on providing vocational and work experience for the insane. He is considered by many to be the father of occupational therapy. His greatest contributions, however, involved his perspective of management's responsibilities and organization of a mental hospital. In particular, his contention that brutality and chains and mere supervision should be eliminated in favor of "moral" management deserves great praise. Moral management involved a treatment-oriented approach; a calm retreat for disturbed persons; a system of humane vigilance; the elimination of physical abuse and chains; freedom from indignities by staff; gentle treatment on a regular, schematic basis; and the provision of entertaining books and conversation, music, and employment in various agricultural pursuits.

By today's standards, there is nothing new or startling in Pinel's concept of moral treatment; however, it was a most radical departure from the treatment of the day. Until Pinel's pronouncements, the dominant theme in treating mentally ill or mentally retarded persons was to gain ascendency over the individual. Those who treated were the masters, and those who were treated were to be rendered subservient and obedient by almost any means. In contrast, moral treatment emphasized the broad array of medical, psychological, and educational services proffered in a humane living environment. Activity and productivity

---

*Though Pinel justifiably deserves credit for institutional reform and moral treatment, similar efforts had been implemented by others at an earlier date. The Italian Vincenzo Chiarugi removed the chains from his patients 20 years earlier in 1774. His administrative orders specifically charged that "it is a supreme moral duty and medical obligation to respect the insane individual as a person."[100] A close friend of Pinel, Joseph Daquin, also introduced humanitarian reforms at the hospital at Chambery in 1787.[101]

William Tuke.

Mr. Tuke was a man for whom religion and morality were practical virtues, and in whose eyes neither riches nor poverty, imbecility nor genius, ought in the slightest degree to affect the bonds which unite all men together in common. He thought, with reason, that justice and force ought to be evinced, not by shouts and menaces, but by gentleness of character and calmness of mind, in order that the influence of these qualities might make themselves felt upon all, even when excited by anger, intoxication, and madness. The traditions of this friend of humanity are preserved in the house which he founded. Everything, even down to the patients, is silent and peaceful in this asylum. . . . Those admitted . . . whatever even their habits may have been, influenced by the tranquility of the place and the force of example, find repose in this house, which much more resembles a convent of Trappists than a mad-house; and if one's heart is saddened at the sight of this terrible malady, we experience emotions of pleasure in witnessing all that an ingenious benevolence has been able to devise to cure or alleviate it. . . .[105]

were encouraged; firmness was to be tempered with kindness, and control was possible without abuse. It called upon the participation of the individual in the treatment program with a hope for cure and release.[102]

William Tuke Another key reformer of the day was William Tuke. In 1792, a Quaker woman mysteriously died in the York Asylum, England. No explanation of this death was provided; nor were her relatives permitted to visit her prior to her death. In response to this incident, William Tuke, a merchant, petitioned the Society of Friends in the same year to establish a mental hospital of their own where "a milder and more appropriate system of treatment than that usually practiced might be adopted."[103]

Tuke was described by a contemporary as a person who "hardly reached the middle size, but was erect, portly, and of a firm step. He had a noble forehead, an eagle eye, a commanding voice, and his mien was dignified and patriarchal."[104] In 1826, Ferrus, physician to Napoleon I, visited Tuke's Retreat in York and wrote:

The Retreat at York was one of excellence, providing for both mentally ill and mentally retarded people, regardless of religious affiliation.

The horrible conditions in most institutions did not go unnoticed by some members of England's Parliament. In 1773, a bill passed the House of Commons for the "Regulation of Private Mad-houses" but failed in the House of Lords. In reaction to this rejection, a frustrated Daniel O'Connell raised the immortal political question, "If it took 20 years to do nothing, how long would it take to do anything?"[106]

Special Education

European education during this period was intended primarily for the wealthy and was offered through private schools and tutorage. For the poor, however, the picture was quite dismal. Schools were conducted in whatever space was available, and teachers were appointed for a variety of reasons, none of which seriously considered their ability to teach. To illustrate:

He [Pastor Stouber] was taken to a miserable cottage where a number of children were crowded together without any occupation, and in so wild and noisy a state that he could with difficulty get a reply to his inquiries for the master. "There he is," said one of them, pointing to a withered old man who lay on a bed in one corner of the room. "Are you the schoolmaster, my good friend?" inquired Stouber. "Yes, sir." "And what do you teach the children?" "Nothing, sir." "Why, then, were you made the schoolmaster?" "Why, sir, I had been taking care of the pigs for the countryside for many years, and when I got too old and feeble for that, they sent me here to take care of the children."[107]

From this description, it is not difficult to understand why not much attention was devoted to educating the mentally retarded. During the eighteenth century, however, several major events occurred which would radically alter education for both normal and mentally retarded students. New educational doctrines were advanced by Pestalozzi and Froebel, and significant gains were made in educating the visually and auditorily handicapped, especially the latter.

Johann Pestalozzi Johann Pestalozzi (1746–1827) was one of those unusual persons who, though repeatedly a failure in life, was to have an inordinate influence on events following his death. Pestalozzi, whose physician father died when he was 5 years old, was raised by an oversolicitous mother and nurse who emphasized his affectionate, emotional, sensitive, and generous behavior. "They appealed to his sentiments and devotion rather than to his reason and masculinity . . . puny from birth and from always living indoors, deprived of a father's influence and out of contact with boys of his own age, and all outdoor games and interests, Pestalozzi remained small and weak and awkward, impressionable and quixotic. . . . The school failed to correct the one-sided influence of the home; unfortunately, it further accentuated the character he had been forming. In his relationships with other students, he developed no power of assertion, no discernment of character nor the ability to understand the actual conditions of life, and to distinguish his own impractical notions from the world of stern reality."[108]

Pestalozzi himself described his school experiences: "From my childhood I have been everybody's plaything. . . . The day of the earthquake at Zurich [December 19, 1777], when masters and boys rushed pell-mell downstairs and nobody would venture back into the class-room, it was I who went to fetch the caps and books, but in spite of all this, there was no intimacy between my companion, and myself. . . . And so I could not take it amiss that they dubbed me Harry Oddity of Foolborough."[109]

As an adult, Pestalozzi remained physically small, unattractive, sickly, slovenly, and highly excitable. His nervousness and mannerisms were unacceptable to many of his colleagues and persons of authority. Subsequently, in spite of his promising ideas, neither he nor they were generally accepted during his lifetime.

After completing college, he attempted the ministry until he broke down during his trial sermon, and, after having given up thoughts of entering politics, he finally settled on becoming a farmer on a place called Neuhof. After 30 years of frustration and bitter disappointment, his farming efforts failed. For a brief time he converted the farm home (all that he had left) into an orphanage, which also failed. After he was well beyond 50 years of age, he became vitally concerned with education and started to produce a series of publications that ultimately won him great respect, admiration, and emulation. His greatest success came from his experiences at the Institute of Burgdorf, from 1800 to 1804, and a similar one at Yverdum, from 1805 to 1825. Both facilities were boarding schools for boys where Pestalozzi, his wife, and the unmarried teachers lived and conducted the schools as well-ordered families. Pestalozzi's theory, interests, and practice came from his intense desire to significantly change the miserable conditions of the common people. His educational principles emphasized that development must be harmonious, and that the three aspects of human behavior, the intellectual, the ethical, and the executive or constructive, must be developed in unison. Like Rousseau, he advocated that a general education, which included such aspects as nature study, geography, arithmetic, knowledge of the country, drawing, reading and language, singing, and religion, must precede the vocational. Also like Rousseau, he believed that a child is an organism which unfolds according to definite, orderly laws, and that schools should be run as a family setting. Children's powers burgeon spontaneously from within in repetitive exposure to proper experiences; they are not simply the product of an outer environment. His instructional approaches always began with the practical, the tangible, and what was real in one's life. Discipline was a function of the mutual goodwill and cooperation between pupil and teacher. Teachers' preparation was critical, and each educator was to acquire a fundamental understanding of the study of education as a science.

In 1825, the school at Yverdum failed and was closed. The remaining two years of Pestalozzi's life were filled with bitterness and sorrow.

Friedrich Froebel In contrast to Pestalozzi, Friedrich Froebel (1782–1852) was highly respected in his time. His great suffering as a child at the hands of a stepmother who, considering him to be stupid, denied him an education, led him to his lifelong concern for the proper raising of children. Following a brief session of formal training at the University of Jena, Froebel was requested to instruct drawing classes in Gruner's Normal School, which stimulated his interest in education. His most unique experiences, however, happened between 1807 and 1810 when he was responsible for training three young boys at the school of Pestalozzi in Yverdum. In 1810, he declared, "I soon saw much that was imperfect. . . . The powerful, indefinable, stirring and uplifting affect produced by Pestalozzi set one's soul on fire for a higher, nobler life, although he had not made clear or sure the exact ways towards it, nor indicated the means whereby to obtain it."[110] Following further university training and a brief stint with the army against Napoleon, he opened a school for boys at Keilhau in 1817. After starting several such schools, he became intensely interested in preschool education and finally opened a school (kindergarten) in an old mill in the mountain village of Blankenburg. Here he formulated his great principles of preschool edu-

cation that were accepted by most but rejected by the Prussian government, which considered them too radical.

Like Pestalozzi, Froebel believed in the organic unity of an individual—whose development was contingent on training the entire person rather than concentrating on separate faculties. Man's body, abilities, will, and mind unfold like a young plant. Froebel's basic principle of education involved the law of action, reaction, and integration. Like Rousseau, each infant was born good and only the perversion or suppression of the normal unfolding process would result in undesired values and behaviors.

Froebel contended that a person developed according to stages: infancy, childhood, boyhood (or girlhood), youth, and maturity. The successful completion of one stage is critical to the proper development of the next. Further, each child is a dynamic interactor with his environment, rather than simply a receptor of events: "The purpose of teaching and instruction is to bring evermore *out* of man rather than to put more and more *into* man. The child is replete with potentiality: all he is ever to be and become, lies in the child, and can be attained only through development from within outward. . . . Therefore, education, instruction, and training, originally and in its principles, should necessarily be *passive, following* (only guarding and protecting), not *prescriptive, categorical*, and *interfering*."[111] Froebel was adamant against "negative" education, or the interference in the normal unfolding process.

As stated previously, the principles and concepts of education espoused by Pestalozzi and Froebel were of marked influence on early pioneers working with the mentally retarded. Their contributions, not only to the education of the disabled child, but to all children, are monumental.

Schools for Deaf and Blind Youth While no known efforts were made during these two centuries to provide systematic instruction to mentally retarded children, gains were made in other areas of exceptionality, especially for those who were deaf and blind.

Jacob Rodriguez Pereira (1715–1780), a

Jew of Portuguese birth and Spanish ancestry, was forced to leave Portugal for France because of religious persecution. Here he became well known for his innovative techniques in teaching the deaf-mute to speak. Following his successful effort at teaching his own deaf sister to speak, he assumed the responsibility for educating a 16-year-old boy of a noble family. His repeated successes brought him to the attention of King Louis XV, who honored him with a pension. In 1753, Pereira opened his school, and in 1760 he was elected to the Royal Society.

Though Pereira was very secretive, Seguin was able, through study and interviews with former students, to surmise his basic technique: "Speech was taught by imitation with vision as a guide to the internal positions in the mouth and the external muscles of the face and neck; and, for the first known time, with touch the conductor and monitor of the innermost positions and of the organic vibrations that together produce the emission of articulated sounds. By this method, the deaf-mute of ordinary capacity could learn to speak in twelve to fifteen months."[112]

Pereira's knowledge and assumption that all the senses accomplish their functions by virtue of a more or less modified sense of touch provided the basis for the neurophysiological hypothesis underlying Seguin's marked concern for the training of the hand and the sense of touch. Pereira's approach also influenced Itard.

In the same year that Pereira was initiated into the Royal Society, the first public school in the world for handicapped children opened its door. This was the Institution Nationale des Sourds-Muets in Paris, started by Charles Michel, l'abbé de L'Epée. This school not only served the deaf but was intended for poor children. De L'Epée promoted the manual system of communication of the deaf; in Germany, Samuel Heinike advocated the oral method. Owing to Heinike's haughty attitude and refusal to debate openly, the relative merits of the oral method versus the manual system

were never thoroughly reviewed and de L'Epée's system of manual communication was universally adopted.

Though Louis IX (St. Louis) is credited with opening the first facility for the blind in A.D. 1260 to serve 300 soldiers so injured during the Crusades, little was done to educate blind children. It was not until 1651 that Harsdorffer produced a wax tablet for the blind to write on that opened the entire question of creating special devices for blind persons.

Valentin Haüy was the first to adopt embossed print and the first to claim that blind persons could be educated. He proved his contention by opening the Institution Nationale des Jeunes Aveugles in Paris in 1784. Though the school was closed for a brief time by the National Assembly, it reopened in a few years, enrolling its most famous student and, later, teacher, Louis Braille. The success of these efforts for deaf and blind people lent impetus to those interested in educating mentally retarded children.

Taken collectively, the events and gains—political, philosophical, social, and scientific—during the 1,300 years covered in this discussion are numerous and often dramatic. From the knowledge of Greece and Rome, to the ignorance and ferocity of the Middle Ages, to the faith and rekindled interest in man of the Renaissance and Reformation, and up to the nineteenth century and its era of progress, man gradually—very gradually—evolved into an increasingly caring social being. Though humanitarianism as it is known today would not emerge until the middle of the nineteenth century, attitudes toward and a heightened interest in mental retardation, as well as the revised concepts of treatment demonstrated during the eighteenth century, served as a prelude to the many changes of the nineteenth century. As concerns the care and treatment of mentally retarded persons throughout these years, however, fortunate was the youngster or adult who had a loving family capable of tending to his needs at home.

Chapter

3

THE AGE OF PROGRESS

(1800–1899)

NINETEENTH CENTURY EUROPE saw an end to many traditions and the start of many more. It was an age of mechanical progress, inventive genius, social reform, and magnificent art in all its forms. Times and circumstances changed so rapidly that, as one historian observed, it was impossible to define precisely "the normal state" of any country.[1]

England enjoyed an unparalleled 100 years of progress and international status. Her population, like that of other countries, expanded rapidly as a result of improved medicines, increased life expectancy, better sanitation, quality hospitals, finer medical care for mothers, more appropriate diets, and an official policy of "keeping people alive."[2] Innumerable reform bills were passed, including the Factory Act of 1833; the Slavery Abolition Act of 1833; the Reform Acts of 1834, 1867, and 1844 that extended enfranchisement to the majority of British citizens; and a national education act of 1870. Queen Victoria, who ascended the throne in 1837, gave the English people peace, prosperity, and expansion through colonization for most of the century.

France did not enjoy the political stability of England. From the meteoric rise of Napoleon Bonaparte at the turn of the century through the early years of the Third Republic, established in 1875, France underwent considerable political turmoil. Most reforms were slowly and painfully won by a frustrated, under-represented class of poor citizens.

Both Germany and Italy became nations during this century. Severe economic depressions and rising socialism led (or forced) Bismarck to introduce and sanction a series of social security–type acts during the 1880s, including insurance against sickness (1883), accident (1884), and old age (1889). By the turn of the century, Germany also passed laws regulating nearly every aspect of industrial life, including wages, hours, time off, grievance procedures, and safety measures.

Independent of national affiliation, however, the nineteenth century saw many gains and signs of genuine progress. Medicine advanced on all fronts: Louis Pasteur, bacteriologist, and Robert Koch, physician, firmly established the germ theory, which led to immunization and elimination of many epidemics that had cursed Europe for countless centuries; the Curies discovered radium in 1889; Ignaz Semmelweis and Joseph Lister successfully applied the germ theory to sterilization and effective sanitary hospital care; Thomas Addison described adrenal gland disorders; and Rudolf Virchow identified the function of cells. In 1868, Gregor

Johann Mendel published the results of his experiments in his cloistered garden, which were to provide the basis for the scientific study of heredity.

On November 18, 1895, by pure chance, Wilhelm Roentgen discovered the X ray. In spite of its many advantages as a diagnostic tool, at least one professional was sorely disappointed, since he had hoped "to penetrate the thick skulls of dull students and project knowledge directly into their brains."[3]

With regard to intellectual functioning and the brain, Santiago Ramon y Cajal and Camillo Golgi wrote complex histological studies of the nervous system; Francois Magendie, founder of experimental physiology, distinguished between the motor and sensory portions of the peripheral nerves; Paul Broca provided an atlas of the brain; Freud, Charcot, and Kraepelin significantly advanced the study of mental illness.

Amid the grandeur of industry, the greatness of science, and the glory of the arts, as exemplified by the music of Tchaikovsky, the writings of Dickens, and the paintings of Renoir, there rested a large population of rural and urban people suffering from extreme deprivation. Although poverty was not new, poverty in a society capable of producing enormous wealth was "the great riddle of the Age of Progress. The inadequate living standards of great masses of people marked the marvelous advances of science and industry, and troubled the social water of Europe throughout the nineteenth century."[4] Not surprisingly, uprisings among the poor plagued Europe until the 1880s when unions became accepted and many of the reform acts previously described were enacted. In many instances, however, the combined effects were minimal; in others, they simply provided the direction for future social reforms in the twentieth century.

Intellectually, the single most epochal and equally controversial publication of the era was Darwin's *Origin of the Species,* 1859. Based on years of observation and study, Darwin's thesis emphasized three points: 1) organisms do not reproduce identical replicas of their kind, but rather produce variations, many of which are hereditary, 2) nature allows the survival of only those organisms that can adapt to their environment, and 3) all organisms, therefore, undergo a struggle for existence. His theory lent great impetus to the study of man, the individual, and the effects of environment. Its impact on psychology was immeasurable; it "did as much as any single factor to shape the science as it exists today. Psychology was certain to become consistently more biological; mental processes tended more and more to be stated in terms of functions served in the task of adjusting to the world," observed G. Murphy in his *Historical Introduction to Modern Psychology,* 1949.[5]

UNDERSTANDING OF MENTAL RETARDATION

Consistent with the age, considerable progress was made with respect to understanding mental retardation and in identifying clinical forms associated with this condition. These forms included von Recklinghausen's disease (neurofibromatosis), 1863; Laurence-Moon syndrome (cataracts, optic atrophy, hypogonadism, and polydactyly), 1866; Sturge-Weber syndrome (port-wine stain), 1879; Bourneville's disease (tuberous sclerosis), 1880; Tay-Sachs disease (amaurotic familial idiocy), 1881; Gaucher's disease (cerebroside lipidoses), 1882; Pelizaeus-Merzbacher's syndrome (familial diffuse degeneration of cerebral white matter), 1885; and Marfan's disease (skeletal and connected disorder with structural eye problems), 1896. Owing to the efforts of Thomas Curling in 1860 and Charles Fagge in 1870, cretinism was identified as related to hypothyroidism. The English physician George Murray developed the first thyroid treatment in 1891. In general, however, etiological and pathological subtleties remained unknown or unappreciated; advancement in this area required the sophisticated diagnostic techniques of the twentieth century accompanied with a better understanding of biochemistry.

At mid century, W. J. Little—Senior Physician to the London Hospital, founder of the

Royal Orthopaedic Hospital, and visiting physician to the Asylum for Idiots in Earlswood—rendered an invaluable contribution to the understanding of both mental retardation and cerebral palsy. He drew critical attention to the potential deleterious effects of premature birth, difficult labor, mechanical injuries during parturition to head and neck, and hypoxia. Such injuries could result in "the slightest impairment which the parent unwillingly acknowledges or fails to perceive up to entire imbecility."[6] His well-researched case studies and frequent contributions to the literature played an important role in sensitizing the medical community to the importance of proper prenatal and perinatal care. Cerebral palsy today is often identified as Little's disease.

One of the more innovative and provocative theories developed at the turn of the nineteenth century, and one that had a far-reaching effect on the diagnosis and treatment of mental retardation, was phrenology. Though today one thinks of phrenology alongside palmistry as a questionable means of foretelling the future, it had a noble origin. Phrenology, or craniology as it was originally called, was conceived by Franz Joseph Gall (1758–1828), a highly respected brain anatomist.

Underlying the science of craniology were a number of principles: 1) the brain is the organ of the mind, 2) the mind consists of innate, independent, and autonomous faculties, 3) each faculty or center is connected with a separate fragment of brain tissue, 4) the centers were expansions of lower nervous mechanisms, and, although independent, they were able to interact with each other, 5) there exists a direct relationship between size of each fragment and strength of its correlated faculty, 6) the contour of the skull conforms to the hypothesized variations in the size of the underlying segments of brain tissue.[7] Also, intellectual functioning was affected by physical health and vice versa.

As the theory developed, various areas of the brain were associated with affective propensities (e.g., adhesiveness, destructiveness, and secretiveness) and sentiments (e.g., self-esteem, benevolence, veneration), and with per-

ceptive intelligence (e.g., individuality, form, and size) and reflective intelligence (comparison and causality). In all, there were 39 distinct areas of the brain identified with specific affective or intellectual functions or faculties.[8]

Unfortunately, Gall also postulated that measurements of the skull allowed one to deduce moral, personality, and intellectual characteristics, since the shape of the skull is modified by the underlying brain. This hypothesis laid the foundation for phrenology. When phrenology fell into disrepute, many of Gall's original contributions became suspect and often were rejected. His teachings, however, were the foundation of modern psychology: "It is almost correct to say," observed the eminent psychologist Edwin G. Boring in 1929, "that scientific psychology was born of phrenology out of wedlock with science."[9]

Gall cited as proof of his theory the smaller-sized heads of mentally retarded people as compared with those of normal or gifted persons. For example, following his examination of the cranium of Itard's famous student Victor, he wrote: "He is an imbecile to a high degree, his forehead is very little extended on the sides and highly compressed on the top, his eyes are small and quite sunken, his cerebellum is little developed."[10] In response to Gall's notion, a number of physicians—Georget, Esquirol, Lelut, Calmeil, and Prichard—spent years measuring and weighing the heads of living and deceased idiots, finally arriving at the conclusion that "no constant relation exists between the general development of the cranium and the degree of intelligence."[11]

A measure of phrenology's popularity during the first half of the nineteenth century is illustrated by the fact that in England alone there were 29 journals devoted exclusively to this subject. As will be discussed, phrenology was well received and accepted by a number of leaders and reformers in the United States, including the influential Samuel Gridley Howe.

Neither Seguin nor Ireland, however, was very impressed with this form of research. Both felt that studies of this nature contributed little to understanding mental retardation and nothing to improving treatment or education.

As discussed previously, Pinel's observations concerning mental retardation or idiocy were commonly accepted at the beginning of the nineteenth century. Idiocy was considered a condition unamenable to education; persons so affected required lifelong custodial care of a humane and gentle kind. New concepts and classifications, however, were advanced by Esquirol, Seguin, Down, Ireland, and others.

ESQUIROL'S CONCEPT

The first substantial change in concept, though limited, was advanced by Jean Etienne Dominique Esquirol (1782–1840). A fellow student of Itard under Pinel, Esquirol was the physician-in-chief of the Maison Royale des Aliéné de Charenton. In his *Mental Maladies: A Treatise on Insanity* published in 1845, mental retardation was divided into two levels: the imbecile and the idiot, recognizing degrees of variance within each category.

Imbeciles were defined as "generally well formed, and their organization is nearly normal. They enjoy the use of the intellectual and affective facilities, but in less degree than the perfect man, and they can be developed only to a certain extent. Whatever education they may receive, imbeciles never reach the degree of reason, nor the extent and solidity of knowledge, to which their age, education, and social relations, would otherwise enable them to attain. Placed in the same circumstances with other men, they do not make a like use of their understanding. . . ."[12] According to current nomenclatures, Esquirol's concept of imbecility would include mildly mentally retarded and perhaps some higher-functioning individuals in the moderate range.

Idiots were painted in grimmer colors: "We have at least reached the utmost limit of human degradation. Here, the intellectual and moral faculties are almost null; not that they have been destroyed, but never developed. Their senses, strangers to the external world, are incapable of exercising a corrective influence over each other; nor can education prove a substitute to so many disadvantages. . . . Incapable of attention, idiots can not control their

Jean Etienne Dominique Esquirol.

senses. They hear, but do not understand; they see but do not regard. Having no ideas, and thinking not, they have nothing to desire; therefore have no need of signs, or of speech."[13]

Esquirol differentiated clearly between mental retardation (amentia) and mental illness (dementia). Amentia was defined as "a cerebral affection, usually chronic and unattended by fever, and characterized by a weakening of the sensibility, understanding and will. Incoherence of ideas, and a want of intellectual and moral spontaneity, are signs of this affection. Man in a state of dementia, has lost the faculty of perceiving objects correctly, of seizing upon their relations, comparing them, and producing a distinct remembrance of them."[14] Dementia involved a great lost degree of intellectual functioning that amentia never possessed.

Though Esquirol's classification was not necessarily sophisticated even for its day, it did provide some consistency in terminology. At that time, mental retardation was identified by an infinite number of terms, including *sau-*

vages, amentia, imbecillatas, ingenii, fatuitas, morosis, and *innate dementia.*

Esquirol's suggested etiological influences are somewhat reminiscent of Hippocrates: sun, water, and air; manner of living among mothers (i.e., "lively moral affection during pregnancy"); hereditary predisposition; and geographical location. Like many of his colleagues, women's behavior and moral character were of marked importance in the incidence of mental retardation.

SEGUIN'S PERSPECTIVE

Edouard Seguin, whose life and professional contributions are reviewed later, demonstrated the most knowledge of mental retardation during the first 50 years of the nineteenth century. He employed the then commonly used term—idiocy—to describe mental retardation generically and as a sub-category. In 1846, Seguin defined idiocy as "an infirmity of the nervous system which has for its radical effect the separation of all or part of the child's organs and faculties from the regular control of his will, which frees him to his instincts and separates him from the world. The typical idiot is an individual who knows nothing, thinks of nothing, wills nothing, and each idiot approaches more or less the summum of incapacity."[15]

In spite of the implied severity of this concept, Seguin divided idiocy into four broad categories:

1. Idiocy, which probably included moderately, severely, and profoundly mentally retarded individuals
2. Imbecility, usually a mildly retarded person showing severe defects in moral (social) development
3. Backwardness or feeblemindedness
4. Simpleness or superficial retardation evidenced by the slowing down of development

His concepts were further delineated in the course of his discussions: idiocy "incapacitates mostly the functions which give rise to the reflex, instinctive, and conscious phenomena of life; consequently, the idiot moves, feels, understands, wills, but imperfectly; does nothing, thinks of nothing, cares for nothing (extreme cases), he is a minor legally irresponsible, isolated, without association, a soul shut up in imperfect organs, and innocent";[16] further, "the greater number of idiots can not count three. . . ."[17] One thing is certain: Seguin was quite conversant with the more severely affected retarded person, which is important when one considers that he nevertheless advocated training opportunities for them.

The imbecile, "who, whatever may be the origin of his infirmative, is generally mistaken for an idiot," is

rarely affected with muscular or sensorial disorders, unless from accessory causes, such as chorea, or hemiplegia, or made worse by self-abuse; his affection is more referable to the condition of the nervous centres, and is of an intellectual caste, bearing on attention, memory, reason, and so forth. He has arrived at that condition of mental degeneration by any of the circumstances which produce deficiency of nutrition, and cause idiocy in early life, and imbecility in subsequent years. The imbecile having, previously to the rest of his development, acquired experiences of things and persons, and gathered, consequentially, instinctive and social feelings; the same cause which leaves, at the outset of life, the idiot incapable, ignorant and innocent, leaves, later, the imbecile self-confident, half-witted, and ready to receive immoral impressions, satisfactory to his intense egotism. Hence, we see again coming forward, with an ungainly aspect, making show of his trinkets and offering them for trade; he can read, more or less; speaks confusedly, and recites verses with pouting emphasis and sprinkling of saliva. He might do some kind of work which may be accomplished by the repetition of simple movements, if his mind could be steadied to any employment. He delights in the company of street boys, who joke, cheat, and abuse him. These tastes and habits educate him to boasting, lying, cruelty, artifice, jealousy, and even to plotting robbery and arson, with a strong dose of hatred for those who advise him to take a better course. Later, these moral depravities make a lodgment in his brain, in the shape of false reminiscences or spurious images of impossible facts; he mistakes his best friend for his foe; does not feel safe; has seen eyes following him in the night, or a suspicious light crosses his room; he hears threats behind him; he knows the fellow, and will break his neck. The next we hear of him he will be in prison, or an insane asylum, or involved by sharpers in a law-suit; today he is an imbecile, tomorrow he may be a criminal.[18]

This negative perspective of mental retardation in terms of social responsibility and personal conduct reflected the prevalent notion of the "moral imbecile," as will be discussed.

Seguin carefully distinguished between the idiot and individuals who were backward or feebleminded. With regard to the "backward child," or the *enfant arriéré,*

> his character may be better delineated by comparison with the idiot, who presents even in superficial cases, an arrest of development, while the feeble-minded child is only retarded in his . . . the backward child is free from any distorted activity, uses his hands naturally, but with very little effectiveness, walks without defect, without firmness or elasticity, presents no sensorial anomalies, but does not much use his senses to quicken his sluggish comprehension; when the idiot does not seem to make any progress, and when the ordinary child improves in the ratio of ten, the backward child improves only in that of one, two, three, or five. This child may be, and is in fact, actually educated with the confirmed idiot; and there is no inconvenience, but advantage, in their being treated alike.[19]

Thus, in contradiction to what one occasionally reads, Seguin was extremely sensitive to the varying levels of functional behavior among mentally retarded persons and was clearly concerned with the more seriously affected individual. Underlying all of his efforts in terms of psychological and educational principles was the very firm conviction that

> most idiots, and children proximate to them, may be relieved in more or less complete measure of their disabilities by the physiological method of education . . . idiots have been improved, educated, and even cured; not one in 1,000 has been entirely retractory to treatment; not one in 100 who has not been made more happy and healthy; more than 40 percent have become capable of the ordinary transactions of life under friendly control, of understanding moral and social abstractions, of working like two-thirds of man; and twenty-five to thirty percent come nearer and nearer to the standard of manhood, until some of them will defy the scrutiny of good judges when compared with ordinary young men and women.[20]

As regards etiology, Seguin realized that factors associated with retardation are "endemic, hereditary, parental, or accidental." He was also sensitive to the fact that sensory deprivation, such as blindness and deafness, would result in retardation and that environmental factors and neglect could have a very negative effect on intellectual development. Seguin, however, was more concerned with programming than etiology or pathology.

DOWN'S ETHNIC CLASSIFICATION

J. (John) Langdon (Hayden) Down (1826–1896) also advanced the cause of mental retardation and the need for treatment and special education and, unbeknownst to him, provided the first major separate classification and comprehensive description of the Mongoloid individual. Down was appointed medical superintendent of the Asylum for Idiots at Earlswood, England, in 1858, a position he held until 1868. Later he opened a private home for the mentally retarded youngsters of wealthy families.

One of Down's most significant contributions to the field of mental retardation was his ethnic classification first proposed in 1866 and included in his text *Mental Affections of Children and Youth,* published in 1887. He classified idiocy (a term he violently disliked because it upset parents) into three etiological categories: Congenital (idiots); Accidental (idiots and feeble-minded); and Developmental (feeble-minded). He only used the labels "idiots" and "feeble-minded," believing "imbecile" should be limited to the mentally ill.

The origins of persons falling within these three categories varied. Disorders within the congenital group, for which Down developed his unusual ethnic classificatory system, were primarily hereditary in origin. Accidental cases were the result of traumatic lesions, inadequate prenatal care, unwise use of forceps, prolonged delivery, medications, and inflammatory disease. The developmentally arrested youngster was a product of disturbed mothers, parents who were inebriated at the time of conception, over-excitement during babyhood, and over-

J. Langdon Down.

bones, prominent eyes, puffy lips, wooly hair, and retreating chin

The *Malay* variety: soft, black, curly hair; prominent upper jaws, and capacious mouths

The *Negroid* variety: shortened forehead, prominent cheeks, deep-set eyes, and slightly apish nose

The *Aztec* variety: small head

The *Mongolian* variety: brownish, straight, and scanty hair; flat and broad face; roundish cheeks which extend laterally; obliquely placed eyes; large, thick lips; long, thick, and roughened tongue; small nose; dirty-yellowish skin tinge''*[21]

In spite of Down's good intentions, his classification was not widely adopted, as many physicians simply did not concur with ethnic similarities, while others rejected the notion of any ethnic classification. The American Hervey Wilbur, in his discussion of the classification of idiocy, for example, rejected Down's classificatory system in the following words, ''I find little constant resemblance to the Mongolian race and these degenerate beings, anymore than in the case of Albinos to any other race. The form of their skulls is rather incidental than racial.''[23] The classification ''Mongolism'' was to remain, however, and in recent years has been relabeled as *Down's syndrome*.

It should be observed that Mongolism had been noted by previous physicians but was frequently considered a variety of cretinism. In his 1866 text, for example, Seguin probably meant to identify the Down's syndrome youngster under the category of ''furfuraceous cretinism.'' Down also acknowledged cretinism and cited the mystery surrounding its origins, reporting that many believed it was due to malaria.

Classifying mental retardation represented but one of Down's interests. He was equally concerned with the prevention of mental retardation by the temperate use of alcohol, promot-

pressure at school at the time of second dentition and puberty. In spite of the fact that Down's clients were from poverty-stricken metropolitan areas, he did not conceive of cultural factors as producing developmental degrees of mental retardation.

Down's rather unique approach to classifying the congenital idiot according to ethnic similarities was not intended as a negative view of any given race. Rather, he had hoped that the classification system would imply that the origin of idiocy existed before birth and was universal in character, thereby averting parental guilt or avoiding the blaming of others for the child's condition (e.g., ''the nurse who might be accused of giving the infant too much opiate medication''). In addition to the large ''Caucasian Family,'' Down defined several ethnic categories:

The *Ethiopian* variety: characteristic malar

---

*Interestingly, there was neither immediate reaction nor follow-up to Down's category of Mongolism until 1876, when Fraser and Mitchell published a report describing the Down's syndrome person as a Kalmuk idiot. Apparently these authors were unfamiliar with Down's earlier reports.

ing good mental and physical health among parents, sound practices of prenatal care, and proper rearing of children at home and in school . . . "sons to be temperate and daughters to be self-possessed."[24]

As evidenced by such leading authorities in the field of mental retardation as Seguin, Esquirol, Down, and Ireland, there was great concern about the emotional health of women. Down noted, "in no fewer than in 32 percent of my cases was there a well-founded history of great physical disturbance in the mother by fright, intense anxiety, or great emotional excitement."[25] This observation represented a commonly held medical opinion of that day. Subsequently, when discussing obstetrical aspects of idiocy, Down repetitively emphasized the need to maintain the child-bearing woman in a most equitable state, "to shield her as much as possible from all causes which would disturb unduly her emotional life, and to maintain her in that hopeful spirit and placid calm which is so much to be desired both for the woman herself as well as for the infant she is incubating. These data teach us how important it is that for women generally the emotions should not be cultivated at the sacrifice of their judgment and self-control."[26]

Since Down placed considerable value on women's judgment, and in marked contrast to the general opinion of the day, he, as well as Seguin, advocated for women's rights:

> There is one subject of great interest at the present time which is made the topic of addresses from presidential chairs as well as of numerous articles and periodical literature. I mean the higher education of women . . . there can be no reason why the faculties which they possess should not be cultivated so as to make them not only fit to be "mothers of men" but also companions and helpers of men. In all events, let the trial be made without prejudice, and let us welcome the advent of a time when women shall not be the mere frivolous toys of the hour but have and enjoy the privileges and rights of which it is absurd to deprive them."[27]

Down also encouraged the education of mentally retarded persons, emphasizing their need for early training. He was extremely critical of his medical colleagues who advised

parents that their child would outgrow the condition as well as those physicians who counseled parents that their mentally retarded offspring should be educated with normal youngsters. Down, like most experts of the nineteenth century, was not an advocate of "mainstreaming."

IRELAND'S NOMENCLATURE

William Wetherspoon Ireland (1832–1909) was a man of many talents. The son of a publisher and a lineal descendent of John Knox, he attained his degree in medicine in 1855. In 1856, he was appointed assistant surgeon by the East India Company and assigned to the Bengal horse artillery. During the battle of Delhi, he was shot in both the head and shoulder and for a period of time was listed as killed in action. Because of his military injuries, he retired from service with a special pension in 1858. For the next 10 years he traveled throughout Europe and wrote a number of books, including *A History of the Siege of Delhi by an Officer Who Served There* (1861), *Randolph Methyl: A Story of Anglo-Indian Life* (1863), and *Studies of a Wandering Observer* (1867). On his return to England, he was appointed medical superintendent of the Scottish National Institution of Imbecile Children at Larbert, Scotland. He served in that capacity from 1869 through 1879; in 1880, he opened the first of three private schools for mentally retarded children. During the last 25 years of his life, he also continued writing and produced five additional books, one of which was concerned with the history of psychology. In addition to speaking French, German, Italian, Spanish, Norse, and Hindustani, he frequently contributed essays on such as Auguste Comte and Friedrich Nietzsche to the *Journal of Mental Science*. In spite of his many interests, he devoted himself wholeheartedly to mental retardation.[28]

In 1887, Ireland published the first genuinely comprehensive text on mental retardation, which included such topics as definition, etiology, incidence, education, and the law. Accordingly, he recognized two levels of intellectual functioning: 1) idiocy, which is "mental deficiency, or extreme stupidity, depending upon malnutrition or disease before birth or before the evaluation of the mental faculties in childhood" and 2) imbecility, which is "generally used to denote a less decided degree of mental incapacity. Thus, when a man distinguishes between an idiot and an imbecile, he means that the mental capacity of the former is inferior to that of the latter." Further, "imbeciles are generally credulous. . . . They may have a poor judgment, a weak memory, a feeble power of comparison, a beggarly imagination, a fitfull attention; but they do possess judgment, memory, comparison, imagination, and attention, in varying, though in meager proportions; and all these can be educated and increased by exercise."[29]

Like Seguin, Ireland drew a careful distinction between idiocy (generically applied) and dementia: "Idiocy cannot be readily confounded with any form of insanity. Dementia begins with average intelligence, which gradually diminishes; idiocy begins with a low amount of intelligence, which gradually increases."[30]

Ireland's 10-category classification of mental retardation was based primarily on physical considerations and cause (known and unknown), as follows: 1) Genetous (congenital) idiocy, which included prematurity, syphilis, and unknown causes and was evident at birth, such as the "Mongolian idiot" and "Cretinoid idiot,"* 2) Microcephalic idiocy, which Ireland was the first to define as "all heads below 17 inches in circumference; but on a point like this, it is difficult to bring observers to one rule,"† 3) Eclamptic idiocy, 4) Epileptic (grand mal and petit mal) idiocy, 5) Hydrocephalic idiocy, 6) Paralytic idiocy, 7) Cretinism (included twice by Ireland in his classi-

cation because he believed some forms were hereditary, some acquired), 8) Traumatic idiocy, which included "direct injury which the brain experiences from contusion, incision, division of the nervous tissue, or depression of the skull", 9) Inflammatory idiocy, and 10) Idiocy by deprivation.[31]

With regard to the category of Traumatic idiocy, Ireland was vitally concerned with current obstetrical practices, voicing strong opposition to the unwarranted use of forceps and suspended animation. He was also very bothered about the artificial deformation of the head, a practice apparently common in a few French locales. Ireland also suggested that heredity and brain injury may interact to produce mental retardation: "Sometimes the injury to the mental power is permanent, sometimes it disappears more or less slowly; in some cases a trifling injury causes grave disorder, in others what appears to be a great injury leaves no visible effect behind. Hereditary predisposition has, no doubt, much to do with this."[34]

As regards Idiocy by deprivation, Ireland included both physical factors (the loss or severe weakening of two or more of the principal senses such as sight and hearing) and environmental factors. Improving the latter, Ireland extensively reviewed the unusual case of Kaspar Hauser.

Kaspar Hauser

Though Victor, the wild boy of Aveyron, is known by every student of mental retardation, Kaspar Hauser is not. Yet, Hauser has been of continuous interest to historians, educators, spiritualists, and others. Since his first appearance, there have been over 2,000 books, essays, articles, reports, letters, plays, films, and novels concerning this young man.

Born on Michaelmas Day, September 29,

---

*Ireland adhered to Down's ethnic classification acknowledging cases of the American Indian type, the Ethiopian, and Malay varieties. He even suggested that a new class be introduced—the Grecian category, in which the forehead and nose run upward in an almost uninterrupted slope.[32]

†Ireland's discussion of microcephalic idiocy included a brief description of the unusual Bird-Man reported earlier by Professor Cesare Lombroso. The Bird-Man "was rather tall, and his limbs were well proportioned. . . . The head was smaller than that of an infant. . . . He chirped, he leaped on one leg, and before putting himself in motion he stretched out his two arms like wings. He used to hide his head under his armpit, and chirped strongly when frightened, or at the sight of a stranger."[33]

Kaspar Hauser.

1812, he is believed to have been taken from his mother when about three years of age and placed in solitary confinement until May 26, 1828, when he first appeared on the streets of Nuremberg. A little more than five and one-half years later, on December 14, 1833, he was mortally wounded by the dagger thrust of an unknown assailant and died three days later. Let us first review Ireland's description of Kaspar and his unfortunate circumstances and then consider the reason for their significance.

In the sad and mysterious case of Kaspar Hauser we have an instance of superficial idiocy produced, not by loss of the senses, but by deprivation of the power of exercising them. On the 26th of May 1828 a young man was observed tottering about near the Hallergate of Nuremberg. On examination it was found that he could only speak a few words, meaning, "I will be a trooper, as my father was;" and that he was scarcely able either to stand upright or to direct the motion of his legs. In fact his appearance was like that of child learning to walk. The soles of his feet were found to be as soft as the palms of his hands, and covered with blisters, while the condition of his knees seemed to indicate that they were seldom flexed. He was found unable to speak and perfectly igno-

rant of the outer world, rejecting meat, but apparently relishing bread and water. On a piece of paper being placed before him, he took the pen and traced the words Kaspar Hauser. A letter was found in his possession, but apparently it was only intended to deceive. He was believed to have been born in 1812. This mysterious affair naturally excited great curiosity, and was the subject of a careful official inquiry. Professor Daumer took the young man to his own house to educate him, and soon made out that he possessed good faculties, but that they never had been brought out from the artificial isolation in which he had lived.

When he was able to record his recollections, he said that he never remembered to have been anywhere save in a small vaulted chamber, where he sat leaning against the wall. A man occasionally visited him who never spoke. Bread and water were left by him when he was asleep. It was believed that he was occasionally washed during his sleep, his nails cut, and his clothes changed, and he recognized the taste of opium as having been now and then mixed with his water. Some toys were given him to play with, but he never remembered to have seen either rat or mouse, or any living thing save the man who at last taught him the few words he could repeat, made him practice writing his own name, and finally brought him to the place where he was found—at the gate of Nuremberg. . . .

Daumer's observations upon Hauser's condition, when first committed to his care, are exactly what might have been expected from his situation: He could say nothing but the two phrases which the man had taught him. He had the mind of a child, spoke of himself in the third person, mistook inanimate for living things, and natural productions for things made by the hand, and did not distinguish between jest and earnest. Daumer gives a number of instances of his wonderful power of seeing in the dark. At first he did not attend to sounds, but was soon deeply stirred by music. He was very sensitive to odours. Ideas accumulated in his mind with extraordinary rapidity. His memory was wonderfully accurate, especially in recalling particulars to which ordinary people pay little attention, such as how often he had eaten this or that thing. On the fourth month after his apparition he became ill, apparently from the intense working of his mind, and the rapid course of his education had for a time to be suspended. The delicacy of his senses and rapidity of his acquisitions gradually ceased, which Daumer somewhat fancifully attributed to his use of flesh meat, and at the time of his death did not seem to differ much from other young men. An examination of his brain was made after the murder. The liver was found enlarged. The skull was somewhat thicker than usual, and the brain rather small, not quite overlapping the cerebullum, which was larger in proportion to the cerebrum. The tissue was found healthy, but the convolutions were broader and simpler than usual.

"In this case," writes Dr. Heidenreich, "the mental development was not hindered by the deficient growth of the brain, but the brain was retarded in its development by the want of all mental activity and excitement."[35]

The mystery surrounding Kaspar Hauser involved his noble birth. Scholars today believe that he was the rightful crown prince of Baden, son of the Grand Duchess Stephanie Beauharnis, adopted daughter of Napoleon Bonaparte and niece of Empress Josephine. If this is true, and if he had been allowed to live his life normally, then he, as the ruling prince of Baden, and not William I of the House of Hohenzollern, would have been Bismarck's collaborator; given these circumstances, the subsequent history of Germany might well have been different.

Ireland studiously reviewed the literature on current theories of heredity and alcoholism. With regard to heredity, he agreed that "idiots frequently are born in families in which there is a decided neurotic tendency, as manifested by the appearance of insanity, imbecility, or epilepsy, amongst the members."[36] Ireland included as an appendix to his text the genealogies collected by the Norwegian scientist Dahl that indicated that all forms of developmental disabilities and insanity were found among the many branches of a family with a common ancestor. Like others, Ireland also believed that epileptics frequently had defective offspring.

Unlike many of his associates, Ireland did not believe that mentally retarded children were the product of intemperate parents: "The children of drunken parents in many cases have an unhealthy nervous system; they are weak, unsteady, and excitable, but, in my opinion, idiocy is not the ordinary legacy which drunkards leave to their children"; but, "Drunkenness generally brings other debasing influences along with it, such as poverty, disgrace, and disappointment, and thus a drunk father may lower the whole tone of health of his family. That alcoholic intoxication has a lowering effect upon the constitution which may lay the foundation of idiocy or neurotic diseases, bringing idiocy in their train, is what probably none will deny."[37]

Ireland also examined the question of scrofula and its relation to mental retardation. Scrofula was very common during this period of history, and many authorities held that scrofulous parents were prone to produce mentally retarded children. Though uncertain, Ireland did indicate that scrofula "seems to favor, or at least accompany, the production of idiocy."[*38]

By the turn of the twentieth century, a number of medically oriented classifications had been developed. Bourneville's nomenclature, which was widely accepted in both Europe and America, identified the following eight major categories of anatomo-pathological forms of mental retardation:

1. Hydrocephalic idiocy
2. Microcephalic idiocy
3. Idiocy from arrested development of the convolutions
4. Idiocy from congenital malformation of the brain (parencephalous, absence of the hard matter, etc.)
5. Idiocy from hypertrophied or tuberous sclerosis
6. Idiocy from atrophied sclerosis
   a. Sclerosis of one hemisphere, or of two hemispheres
   b. Sclerosis of one lobe of the brain
   c. Sclerosis of isolated convolutions
   d. Mortified sclerosis of the brain
7. Idiocy from meningitis or from chronic meningo-encephalitis
8. Idiocy from pachydermical cachexia or myxoedamatous idiocy combined with the absence of the thyroid gland[39]

Today, the French-born neurologist D. M.

---

*Scrofula is primary tuberculosis of the cervical lymph nodes; it may be accompanied by slowly suppurating abscesses and fistulous passages (scrofuloderma), the inflamed structures being subject to cheesy degeneration.[40]

Bourneville is recognized almost exclusively for his identification of tuberous sclerosis and anatomical research. Yet, he was a most remarkable physician who devoted his professional career to the betterment of mentally retarded persons. Serving at the institution Bicêtre, he developed a model "Medico-Pedagogical Institute," which emphasized education and training as well as physical care. He also was responsible for the republication of Itard's and Seguin's books at a time when they were completely forgotten in France.[41]

DUNCAN AND MILLARD'S BEHAVIORALLY ORIENTED CLASSIFICATION

Unlike the previous nomenclatures, which were primarily medical in orientation, P. M. Duncan and W. Millard proposed a behaviorally oriented classification. Both Duncan, the honorary consulting surgeon to the Eastern Counties Asylum for Idiots and Imbeciles, and Millard, superintendent of the Asylum, had for a number of years contributed articles on mental retardation to various scientific journals. Their collaborative effort, entitled *A Manual for the Classification, Training, and Education of the Feeble-Minded, Imbecile, and Idiotic* and published in 1866, rapidly became a classic in the field and was cited frequently in early educational literature. They strongly believed that through proper physical care and education, a mentally retarded person could be rendered more capable.

Their classification included eight levels of functioning, divided equally according to "Congenital Idiots" and "Non-congenital Imbeciles." Each class was interpreted in terms of educational implications, including the most severely affected: "Class 1. True and profound idiots; solitaries." Training experiences were offered to each class with a full expectancy of improvement. To illustrate, "Class 4. 'Feeble-minded' children, adolescents, and adults" included many individuals "born in Class 1, and by growth and training emerged into this Class."[42]

WEST'S CONCEPTS

The ideas and nomenclatures discussed represent the philosophies and concepts of professionals working directly with mentally retarded individuals and, as such, probably were read by a rather limited audience. Nonspecialists, however, were beginning to take interest in or at least acknowledge the existence of mental retardation. Among the most famous and frequently cited physicians of the day was Charles West. His comments offer a view of mental retardation commonly accepted in the general medical community.

Physician to the Hospital for Sick Children in Lambeth, England, and medical scholar, Charles West devoted considerable attention to mental illness among children and mental retardation. In his text *Diseases of Infancy and Childhood,* published in 1868, West offered a most unique discussion of mental retardation. After discussing emotional disturbances among children, he observed, "*Idiocy* is unquestionably of much more frequent occurrence in childhood than are those affections of the mind which have hereto engaged out attention. The term idiocy, however, is a very wide one, including conditions differing remarkably from each other, both in kind and in degree, while not seldom it is misapplied to cases in which there is more backwardness of the intellectual powers." His distinction between backwardness, the idiot, and the poor was exceptionally perceptive: "When the time comes for positive instruction, their [backward children's] slowness almost wears out everyone's patience; and among the poor, indeed, the attempt at teaching such children is at length given up in despair, and growing up in absolute ignorance, it is no wonder that they should be regarded as idiots. Still, dull as such children may be, and duller still they must needs become if allowed to grow up untaught to manhood, there is a difference between them and idiots. . . ."[43]

He cautioned against the premature judgment of mental retardation. Physicians were admonished to check hearing, speech defects, recent illnesses, or any other factor that might result in poor intellectual performance or the appearance of mental retardation. This was especially true among infants and young children.

Regrettably, however, West ended his discussion on a less than positive note. Since the two most notable characteristics of idiocy were indolence and a lack of attentive ability, the only place to educate such children, he wrote, was in an institution. Further, "many of his moral powers . . . cannot be brought out except in the society of other children of his own age, and not differing too widely from him in mental power."[44] He did caution, however, that the idiot should not be placed with the mentally ill, and that "children of very different degrees of mental capacity should not be thrown together at their work, nor even, without much care and oversight, in their amusements."[45] West ended his lecture on a note of professional humility: "I can wish for nothing better than that before long the labors of others shall render these observations of mine as superfluous as I know them to be imperfect."[46]

Though most physicians knowledgeable about mental retardation emphasized good basic health care and education, new and popular techniques were constantly attempted. Hypnosis was tried (unsuccessfully) with some imbeciles.[47] The introduction of electricity during the early part of the nineteenth century produced new theories of mental illness and treatment techniques. "Insanity," proclaimed the French physician Leopold Turck in 1847, "is invariably to be ascribed to an abnormal accumulation of electricity in the electro-negative organs, and especially in the skin."[48] DuBois Reymond's application of the induction coil for muscle stimulation in 1849 led to its use with epileptic and paralytic idiots. "Electricity ought to be tried," suggested Ireland, "though I cannot say that I have ever been able to trace any very decided benefit from its use."[49]

ASSESSMENT OF INTELLIGENCE

As evidenced by the preceding discussion, mental retardation or idiocy was no longer viewed as a simple, single phenomenon. By the end of the nineteenth century, mentally retarded persons were classified according to at least two levels of intellectual functioning, clinical categories, and etiological influences. Since there were no standardized tests of intelligence, practitioners relied primarily on an evaluation of speech and language. In 1838, for example, Esquirol divided mental retardation into the two main categories of imbecile and idiot with subcategories based on speech and language:

Imbecile level 1: speech is free and easy
Imbecile level 2: speech is less easy and vocabulary more circumscribed
Idiocy level 1: uses merely words and short phrases
Idiocy level 2: uses only monosyllables or certain cries
Idiocy level 3: no speech[50]

But Ireland shrewdly anticipated the future. He proposed that a more perfect system of classification would involve different items of intellectual performance based on a comparison with normal persons at different age levels. This was exactly the course of action to be pursued by Binet and Simon during the closing years of the nineteenth century.

The question of human ability and its measurement did not rest solely in the hands of those working with mentally retarded persons, however. Other scientists were vitally concerned with human functioning, both physical and psychological. As early as the eighteenth century, Albrecht von Haller (1708–1777), the famed German physiologist, adopted the empirical approach previously applied only to the physical sciences to the study of life processes. At the turn of the nineteenth century, Sir Charles Bell (1774–1842) of England differentiated between the sensory and the motor nerves. Experimental psychology received its early start with E. H. Weber (1795–1878), Gustav Fechner (1801–1887), Johannes Mueller (1801–1858), and Herman Helmholtz (1821–1894). These forefathers of experimental psychology were highly concerned with the principles of sensation and perception, emphasizing the relationship between physiological and psychological components. Though E. H. Weber is not as well known as the other scientists mentioned, it was he who clearly promoted the principle that man's behavior could be measured.

Though early experimental psychologists, such as Weber and Fechner, were aware of individual differences in performance, they did not study these differences but concentrated, rather, on the basic fundamental principles underlying the process under study. Sir Francis Galton (1822–1911), half-cousin to Charles Darwin, was the first scientist to study individual differences and similarities in a systematic manner.

His book, *Hereditary Genius,* published in 1869, demonstrated that individual greatness followed family lines with a frequency sufficient to justify the conclusion that "a man's natural abilities are derived by inheritance under exactly the same limitations as are the form and physical features of the whole organic world."[51] These results, which were consistent with Darwin's theory of evolution, led to the concept of racial improvement, the field of eugenics, and a great concern over the alleged deterioration of human intelligence due to the mating practices of intellectually inferior people. The pedigree method used in the study was later adopted by Dugsdale and Goddard with serious consequences for mentally retarded persons.

Galton's direct contributions to the field of individual testing included the examination of individual differences; the development of various testing devices and techniques, including the Galton whistle; the study of mental imagery; the first extensive use of the questionnaire; and the first application of correlational statistics to the measurement of human behavior.

Though it was not a major area of his inquiry, Galton did conduct some research with mentally retarded subjects. In notes to Jacob's 1887 study of memory, Galton indicated that using the same technique, he found idiots to have a more limited average retention span than did normal children.[52]

Though Binet and his colleagues were to play the key role in the development of individual tests of intelligence, their early interests and efforts were shared by others. Munsterberg described in 1891 a series of tests used with school children but did not report the results. The tests included: 1) reading aloud as rapidly as possible, 2) stating as quickly as possible the colors of 10 objects whose names are written on a sheet, as "white" for "snow," 3) repeating 10 given names of animals, plants, or minerals, and giving as quickly as possible the classification of each, 4) doing the same for names of cloth, of food, and of parts of the body, 5) giving as quickly as possible, when the objects were seen, the names of 10 simple designs and of 10 squares of color, 6) adding 10 single-digit numbers, 7) giving as quickly as possible the number of angles in 10 different irregular polygons, 8) naming three different perfumes or odors, 9) finding the number of digits and of letters retained by the subject after a single presentation, 10) bisecting a distance of 80 centimeters, 11) judging how many times one length is contained in another, 12) reproducing a perceived length after 5 seconds, 13) locating a sound, and finally 14) constructing a square and an equilateral triangle.[53]

A few years later, Oehrn and Krapelin published the results of what probably constitutes the earliest actual experiments in mental correlation. Their tests of adults included perception, memory, association, and motor functions. In 1897, Ebbinghaus developed the completion test for school children that is still used in intelligence testing procedures.

Binet and Henri in 1895 reviewed the concept of individual psychology and explored some of the various tests that had been used to date. In their article, they identified rather early some of the types of tests that ultimately would be incorporated into their presentations, including tests of memory, images, imagination, attention, comprehension, suggestibility, esthetic appreciation, moral sentiment, muscular force and force of will, motor skills, and the judgment of visual space. In this same article, Binet and Henri set forth the first discussion and identification of what was to become known as the field of "individual psychology."[54] Since Alfred Binet's work had its greatest impact during the twentieth century, further discussion of his contribution is postponed.

In spite of these early efforts to assess intelligence scientifically, most "mentally retarded" children were so classified on the basis of five criteria:

1. Physiognomy ("You need only look at him to see that he is bright [or stupid]")
2. Use of age ("He acts like a 2-year-old")
3. Quality of school work
4. Physical coordination (He's slow and clumsy)
5. Physical signs, such as premature aging (or, "he's a funny-looking kid")

These would change substantially in a few years.

SOCIAL CARE AND TREATMENT

Conditions for mentally retarded persons during the nineteenth century in western Europe were quite similar to those of the eighteenth century except for the increasing harshness of life for many mentally retarded persons living in urban areas and experiencing an expanding, oppressive industrial movement. Villages still had their fools, and some retarded persons were allowed to roam at will. A description by Tuke equally applies to mentally retarded persons: "Hardly a parish of any considerable extent in which there might not be found some unfortunate human creature, who, if his ill-treatment had made him 'frenetic,' was chained in the cellar or garret of a workhouse, fastened to the leg of a table, tied to a post in an outhouse, or perhaps shut up in an uninhabited ruin; or, if his lunacy were inoffensive, was left to ramble, half-naked and half-starved, through the streets and highways, teased by the rabble, and made the jest of the vulgar, ignorant, and unfeeling."[55]

Mentally retarded persons on the farm continued to work long hours in poverty with their parents. In the cities, pauper children who could not work in the industrial setting or were not accepted into an apprentice program frequently ran the streets as beggars or thieves. Those who could not be tended at home or who were picked up by the police frequently were placed in almshouses, workhouses, jails, or mental hospitals where conditions continued to be deplorable by any humane standards. Though fictional, there is little question as to the accuracy of Dickens' famous description of Oliver Twist's experiences in a late-century English workhouse:

> For the next eight or ten months, Oliver was the victim of a systematic course of treachery and deception. He was brought up by hand. The hungry and destitute situation of an infant orphan was duly reported by the workhouse authorities to the parish authorities. The parish authorities inquired with dignity of the workhouse authorities, whether there was no female then domiciled in 'the house' who was in a situation to impart to Oliver Twist, the consolation and nourishment of which he stood in need. The workhouse authorities replied with humility, that there was not. Upon this, the parish authorities magnanimously and humanely resolved, that Oliver should be 'farmed,' or, in other words, that he should be dispatched to a branch-workhouse some three miles off, where twenty or thirty other juvenile offenders against the poor-laws, rolled about the floor all day, without the inconvenience of too much food or too much clothing.[56]

Wealthy parents tended to keep their mentally retarded children at home, occasionally providing tutors for their education. According to Down, many of these children were kept in secret and great effort was made to hide them from public view.

Yet, centralized governments continued to assume increasing responsibility for mentally retarded persons. To illustrate, in 1811 Napoleon Bonaparte ordered a census of cretins to be taken in the Swiss canton of Wallis. Later, King Charles Albert of Sardinia established a commission to ascertain the numbers of cretins in his realm and to visit the affected regions.

In the same year, Napoleon also issued an imperial decree proclaiming that foundlings, abandoned children, and poor orphans were to be entrusted to public charities. As regards mentally retarded children, the Napoleonic Decree provided that "those infants who cannot be put to board, the crippled and the infirm, will be raised in the hospitals. They will be occupied in the workhouses at those employments that are not below their age."[57] In 1838, all such institutions came under the direct supervision of the French government.

Similarly, England passed a number of laws throughout the nineteenth century in an effort to provide more adequately for its "idiots and imbeciles." Included was the Poor Law Amendment Act of 1834, which provided the detention in any workhouse of any "*dangerous* lunatic, insane person or *idiot* for a longer period than 14 days" unless the "medical officer of the workhouse certified that such a person is a proper person to be kept in a workhouse, nor unless the accommodation in the workhouse is sufficient for his reception."[58] The Poor Law Act of 1844 provided that local government boards could combine county parishes in the school districts for the management of any class or classes of infant poor not above 16 years of age; every idiot and imbecile who could not be provided for by his family was entitled to a suitable provision at the public charge. The Lunatic Asylum Act of 1853 authorized the local government board to establish asylums for the sick, insane, and infirm at public costs, and "lunatic" included "idiots and every person of unsound mind."[59] The Elementary Education Act of 1870 declared that school boards were bound to provide for the education of all children, not excluding idiots, with all the necessary teachers and appliances. Finally, the Idiots Act of 1886 made general provisions for asylums for the care, education, and training of idiots and imbeciles "from birth or from an early age."[60] Even though a special idiots act was passed, in all other respects, the idiot continued to be defined under the category of the lunatic. Nevertheless, these acts, which, to one degree or the other, were emulated throughout western Europe, indicated the progression in public responsibility for the mentally retarded population, primarily in the areas of residential programs and education.

Not surprisingly, as cities grew and societies became increasing complex, as a consequence of governmental laws and regulations, the courts were called upon with increasing frequency to render judgments. As Ireland sympathetically observed, "As long as idiots had no property, or did not offend the law, or fall upon the poor-rates the old code [lunacy laws] took very little notice of them. They were very rarely shut up in lunatic asylums and were left very much to the mercy of their relatives or guardians, legal or accidental, but when they became to be treated as lunatics, they began to suffer from the thoughtlessness or ignorance of our legislators."[61]

As society developed its laws, mentally retarded persons lost many of the rights and freedoms they had enjoyed throughout the years. Ireland noted in 1877 that the idiot in England no longer had civil rights, could not convey property, could not appear by an attorney (i.e., be represented when absent), could not vote, could not be a member of Parliament, and could not appear as a witness; and any marriage could be annulled. Yet, "in a case of rape the protection accorded to female children is not extended to adult female idiots, for there is the probability of consent, and indeed a possibility of solicitation which can not be admitted in little girls."[62]

In spite of all of these denials and the frequent recognition that the mentally retarded person was in fact mentally retarded, legal judgments were often severe, especially in criminal cases. Isaac Ray, a physician who devoted over 50 years of his career to the study of jurisprudence of insanity, which regrettably included mental retardation, cited numerous instances where mentally retarded persons, regardless of understanding, were convicted of murder and subsequently executed. Marriages were frequently annulled by the courts.

In contrast, juries were reluctant to declare mentally retarded persons incompetent and unable to manage their affairs. Down was particularly upset when a "jury supported the doctrine of the liberty of the subject, and the poor congenital imbecile was allowed to go his own way to destruction, with the result of becoming speedily bankrupt in fortune, ruined in health, and a scandal to an honored ancestral name." Though Down was called upon too late to provide expert testimony, there was little question in his mind that since the young man had a cleft palate, he was also mentally retarded: "granted any suspicion of defective mental power, the deformation of the mouth, with its vaulted palate, was the strongest corroborative proof, a proof too of the congenital origin of his condition."[63]

Physicians such as Down, Ireland, and Ray vigorously opposed the inclusion of mentally retarded persons under the lunacy law and the court's simple reliance on the "right and wrong" test, which, in essence, required that "it must be clearly proved that at the time of committing the act, the party accused was laboring under such a defective reason from disease of the mind as not to know he was doing what was wrong."[64] The "right and wrong" test which had been used for years as a matter of tradition became the rule of law following the famous McNaughton case in 1843.

These physicians basically contended that to make a mentally retarded person "responsible for his actions to the same degree as one enjoying the full vigor and soundness of the higher faculties is . . . manifestly unjust; because an essential element of responsibility is the power to refrain from evil-doing, which power is furnished by the exercise of those faculties that are but imperfectly developed, if at all, in the imbecile."[65]

Underlying that position, however, was the ignoble concept of the "moral imbecile." Though the origin of moral imbecility is unknown, it was clearly part of Ray's authoritative text in 1831. In defining this condition, Ray relied primarily on the experiences of others. He was most impressed with Georget's observations that in hospitals for the insane,

> there is always a certain number of imbeciles who do the coarser work of the house, or serve as domestics and assistants to the regular officers. . . . But they have no idea, or a very imperfect one, of society, laws, morality, courts and trials; and though they may have the idea of property, they have no conception of the consequence of theft. They may have been taught to refrain from injuring others, but they are ignorant of what has been done to them if guilty of incendiarism or murder. Indeed, it is well known how common theft is among idiots and imbeciles, and for a very obvious reason. . . . Some of them have no conception of property . . . others have some notions of property, but neither a sense of morality, nor a fear of punishment furnishes a motive sufficiently powerful to prevent them from stealing. . . . Many of them for want of some powerfully restraining motive, indulge in drinking, and become lazy, drunken, and dissipated, and finally fall into the hands of justice in greater numbers than is generally expected."[66]

Ray accepted this description and was firmly convinced of the reality of the moral imbecile based on physiological reasons. An adherent or phrenology, he felt that the moral faculty was significantly impaired. The physiological basis underlying moral imbecility received considerable support in later years from the outstanding pioneer in criminology, Cesare Lombroso (1835–1909). Lombroso devoted his career to studying the anatomical components of criminality and presented his oft-cited epileptoid model of delinquency and criminology in 1896. The five levels included the criminal epileptic; the criminal moral imbecile; the born criminal; criminaloids, or the occasional criminal; and criminals by passion.[67] Other anthropological scientists, such as Virchow, supported this theory. Unlike many misconceptions of mental retardation which were relatively short lived, the notion of "moral imbecile" proved highly deleterious to the interests of mentally retarded persons in both Europe and the United States into the twentieth century.

RESIDENTIAL SERVICES

In spite of the ideals and examples set forth by Chiarugi, Pinel, and Tuke, most mental hospitals in Europe continued to be wholly inadequate and brutal. In 1818, Esquirol reviewed a number of facilities serving mentally ill and mentally retarded people and reported that the residents "were more frequently than not either naked or covered with rags, placed in narrow, dark, damp cells, having stone floors, with no bedding except a little straw, which was seldom or never changed. . . . The patients were usually without fresh air, without light, without water to allay their thirst under the dominion of gaolers who were frequently criminals of the worse type, and chained in caves which would not have been thought good enough for wild beasts. The general employment of chains was revolting; the patients had collars and belts of iron, and fetters on their hands and feet. Some were fastened to the wall by a chain a foot and one-half long, and this method was extolled as being peculiarly calming. Chains were universally preferred to straight-waist coats, because they were less expensive. There was no medical treatment directed to the medical care of the malady, and rude attendants employed seclusion, baths of surprise,* and occasional floggings at will."[68] Countless testimonies of this nature filled many pages of historical documents throughout the nineteenth century in spite of some of the reform movements (to be described). Enlightened programming for mentally ill and other persons in mental hospitals would not, in general, be realized until the twentieth century.

It should be noted that of those admitted to mental hospitals, the proportion of persons believed to be incurable because of idiocy was quite high. In 1801, Pinel, for example, reported that 30 percent of his population were idiots. Esquirol observed that from 1804 to 1813 he "received during that period 1800 insane women, of whom 795 were regarded as incurable, in consequence of the age, or because they were imbeciles, epileptics, or paralytics."[69] There is no question that a large number of poor, mentally retarded persons were inflicted with the horrible conditions common to mental hospitals of the day.

Circumstances for the mentally retarded, however, would show substantial gains during the latter half of the nineteenth century. The stimulus for this movement was provided by Seguin, Saegert, and Guggenbühl.

Edouard Seguin

While Edouard Seguin (1812–1880) is known primarily as the father of special education for the mentally retarded, he, rather than Pinel or Tuke, was really the great reformer of institutional programming for mentally retarded persons. Seguin was born in Clemancy, France, on January 20, 1812, to upper-class parents. Like many of his ancestors, he pursued his medical training at the college at Auxerre and at St. Louis in Paris. During his training, Itard served as his preceptor, and he was to become familiar with Esquirol, who, at that time, was considered the leading psychologist and psychiatrist. As a result of these experiences and his strong commitment to the philosophy of Saint-Simon, Seguin decided to dedicate his life to mentally retarded people, pursuing the psycho-educational aspects of their behavior and development.

In 1837, Seguin started a private school for mentally retarded youngsters, perhaps serving only one such child. In 1842, an aging Itard and Esquirol made arrangements for Seguin to test some of his ideas at the Bicêtre, the conditions of which prior to Seguin's arrival had been described by Brockett as characterized by "filth and degradation."[70] Seguin worked with the mentally retarded inmates at the Bicêtre for one year, during which he produced several pamphlets on mental retardation and acquired the experiences underlying his classic text, *Traitment moral, hygiène, et éducation des idiots et des autres enfants arriérés* published in 1846.

Following a disagreement with management, Seguin left the Bicêtre and once again established a private school. This would be the pattern of his life; apparently he was very sensitive and often found it difficult to relate to others, both as a colleague and later as an administrator.

Like many early leaders in the field of mental retardation, Seguin was a man of many

---

*"Baths of surprise" refers to dropping an unsuspecting patient in a barrel of cold water. An alternative approach was projecting a stream of cold water with great force down the spine of the patient.

Edouard Seguin.

interests and talents. He served as an art critic for one of the leading journals of Paris, was a friend and associate of Victor Hugo, and wrote many tracts on political and social economic issues. Of importance, he was firmly committed to the tenets of Saint-Simonism.

Claude Henri de Rouvroy Saint-Simon (1760–1825) had reacted against both the French Revolution and the militarism of Napoleon. He held that an industrial state should be directed by modern science; universal association would suppress war; and society should be organized for the productive labor of the most capable men, who would, in turn, be duly rewarded. The aim of society should be to produce things useful to life. Improving the quality of life among the poor served as the major theme of his *Nouveau Christianisme* published in 1825: "The whole of society ought to strive toward the amelioration of the moral and physical existence of the poorest class; society ought to organize itself in the way best adapted for attaining this end."[71] Though "Saint-Simonism" as a movement was re-

cently described by the French historian Manceron as "partly socialist, partly women's lib, and largely disorganized," it nevertheless impressed and excited many reformers of the day.[72]

Seguin, along with other Saint-Simonians and social discontents, became associated with a group of brilliant young men (including Victor Hugo) who gave support, tone, and character to the revolution of 1848. Anticipating that the revolution would fail, that social and political conditions would not improve, and fearing possible political retribution, Seguin, his wife, and his son migrated to the United States in 1848.

Upon arriving in the United States, he assisted in the development of a number of early institutions, including Howe's program, the Institution for Feeble-minded Youth at Barre, Massachusetts, and the experimental school at Albany. Following a brief and unsuccessful episode as a private practicing physician, he returned to assisting institutions in Connecticut, Ohio, and Pennsylvania. For a few months, he served as superintendent of the facility in Pennsylvania but was terminated.

In addition to his intense interest in mentally retarded people and the welfare of children in general, he produced several significant works on thermometry and developed the first physiological thermometer using zero to denote normal temperature. He also was very active in promoting the universal adoption of the metric system.

In his later years, he and his second wife established a day training school in New York City: the Seguin Physiological School for Feeble-minded Children, intended for mentally retarded youngsters who could remain at home. Never a robust man, one who occasionally suffered periods of "depressing disease," Seguin succumbed to acute dysentery on October 12, 1880 at his home in New York. Following his death, his wife continued to oversee the school they had established.

Seguin was described as a gentle person, one who had no traditional alliance to any religion but was a man of religious principles: "He was not a doe-face, not in any sense a weak or easily-molded man; and these decided and positive traits in his character only made his gentleness the more admirable.''[73] The historical record would indicate that indeed Seguin was not "easily molded," and, as indicated, had difficulties working with others, including Howe and Richards.

One final contribution of Seguin was to encourage the establishment of the first American association devoted solely to mentally retarded persons. In 1866, he called upon his fellow superintendents to meet annually to share their experiences, a call which ultimately would be realized in the formation of what is now known as the American Association on Mental Deficiency.

As he outlined it in his 1866 text entitled *Idiocy and Its Treatment by the Physiological Method,* Seguin conceived of an institution as an instrument for educating mentally retarded children too severely affected to profit from a normal classroom setting. Since an institution was an educational facility, it was expected that most of the students would return to their homes; however, in the event that some of the youngsters failed to make adequate gains or had no home, Seguin proposed that asylums be established for their long-term care. One should not underestimate the importance of this decision or the determination with which it was made. With perhaps the exception of Itard, no one, including Pinel and Esquirol, believed that idiots could be trained. The current definition of idiocy as contained in the *Dictionaire de Medicine* of 1837 read: "Idiocy is an absence of mental and affective faculties and an almost complete nullity of the cerebral functions. . . . It is useless to attempt to combat *idiotism.* In order that the intellectual exercise might be established, it would be necessary to change the conformation of organs which are beyond the reach of all modification.''[74]

Seguin believed that institutions should be located within the community from which it receives its students: "The institution is never so far from a city that its inmates can not be admitted to the sites of civilization and wonder. We must beware of too much isolating the naturally isolated idiot. By sending him, as

soon as he behaves, to church, to the museum, meetings, shows, and even theaters, we do not so much create in him a taste for those things, as a desire of mingling with yonder world; pregnant curiosity, which is of itself one of the mainsprings of life.''[75]

Institutions should serve few residents since before "going to breakfast the children are reviewed, one and all by the superintendent. The attendants must report to him the verbal report they made to the Matron about the night, and give the particulars about what may have transpired since they arose.''[76]

An institution should engage in research: "Among the *raisons de' être* of idiocy, the most urgent, the most neglected arises from the light to be thrown on all branches of anthropology by sound and complete observation of idiots from the cradle to the slab.''[77]

Finally, the institution should provide outreach services to young children who should remain at home with their parents. One hundred years later, these concepts would influence the future development of residential facilities throughout the world.

Guggenbühl and the Abendberg

Johann Jakob Guggenbühl (1816–1863), the Swiss physician, was perhaps the most tragic figure to cross our historical stage. Of all those who devoted their lives to mentally retarded persons, he paid most dearly.

According to Kanner, Guggenbühl's best-known biographer in the United States, when the young physician was 20 years old, "he was stirred by the sight of a dwarfed, crippled cretin of stupid appearance mumbling the Lord's Prayer at a wayside cross." When discussing the man with his mother, Guggenbühl found that she had been unable to afford any form of education for her cretin son and was unhappily resigned to watching him deteriorate from year to year.[78]

After reviewing all the literature he could locate about cretinism, which tended to be concerned only with symptomatology and etiology, Guggenbühl decided to devote his life to the "cure and prophylaxis" of the condition. He initially established a private

Johann Jakob Guggenbühl.

good diets, baths, massages, and physical exercises. He tried various forms of medication, and introduced set routines, sensory training, memory activities, and various language programs. Millard wrote about these early efforts in glowing terms:

> When the late Dr. Guggenbühl carried on his work efficiently at the Abendberg, he employed a Sister of Mercy for every three pupils, besides having a skilled male teacher. Idiots require to be taught cleanly in their habits, to wash and dress themselves, to use a spoon, and afterwards a knife and fork. Speech has to be evoked or improved, their senses to be aroused, the use of their limbs, and especially the use of their fingers to be developed; their faculties of attention and imitation to be cultivated; elementary instruction to be imparted in an interesting manner, without producing weariness, the teacher's mind dropping, as it were, into the minds of the pupils; good manners have to be engendered and bad habits counteracted. Their confidence has to be won by kindness, and then their wills can be guided by tact and firmness; their moral and religious sense has to be awakened, and some Scriptural knowledge to be conveyed, so as to excite, with God's help, simple faith in Him as their Father, Jesus as their Saviour, and heaven as their home.[79]

Guggenbühl's reforms were soon recognized and his efforts were hailed throughout the world. He received many honors, and the Abendberg was visited by innumerable persons interested in mental retardation, among whom was Samuel Gridley Howe who proclaimed, "The holy mount it should be called!"[80]

Two events occurred in the 1850s that led to the closing of the Abendberg as a residential facility for mentally retarded persons. First, many persons became suspicious of Guggenbühl's claims to be able to cure cretinism or mental retardation. Ireland was assured by "the teachers of several training schools visited by me in Switzerland, that cretins do not seem to improve under training any faster than idiots of other classes."[81]

Second, as Guggenbühl became famous, he took to extended lecture tours throughout Europe, leaving the Abendberg to the general supervision of his stepfather. This proved to be a fatal decision, for the conditions of the facility deteriorated rapidly.

Down dejectedly wrote that in 1842 much

practice in the Kleinthal of Glarus, an area with a high concentration of cretins. His experiences led him to believe that residential care for such affected individuals in a suitable environment was critical. Believing that God had chosen him for this endeavor, he sent forth a number of appeals for assistance. His plan finally caught the attention of Karl Kasthofer, a Swiss forester, who put at Guggenbühl's disposal 40 acres located on the Abendberg, near Interlaken, in the canton of Berne, Switzerland. This land was 4,000 feet above sea level, which was considered important since many authorities believed that cretinism was caused by some factor (unknown) associated with the lowlands. On this mountain summit, Guggenbühl opened his institution in 1842, the first recognized residential facility for mentally retarded persons.

Guggenbühl fully believed that his charges could be cured through proper health programming and training. He provided mountain air,

Abendberg.

attention was directed toward Dr. Guggenbühl "who entered on his work with true enthusiasm,—an enthusiasm which one regrets was quenched by the flattery of English drawing-rooms. I shall never forget the feelings of disappointment and chagrin when, on reaching the summit of the Abendberg, which I had mounted as a pilgrim to a shrine, I found the pupils in a state of physical and mental neglect while the patron saint was enervated by the Capua-like influence of the West End of London. Fortunately for the pupils the Commune stepped in and closed what had become a parody of philanthropic effort."[82]

On April 13, 1858, Gordon, the British minister to Berne, decided to call upon the Abendberg in order to visit the few English children enrolled. He found "the children in a most neglected condition and the whole institution (which the guide at first refused to show him) in disgusting disorder."[83] Gordon's report to the government of the canton resulted in an official investigation. The findings of the investigation team, as prepared by two physicians, Vogt and Verdat, were extremely negative:

1. Guggenbühl was guilty of deceiving people in his country and elsewhere by indicating he was serving the cretin. At most, only one-third of the residents were cretins.
2. Not a single cretin had ever been cured.
3. While Guggenbühl originally claimed to serve only infants, he took persons up to 23 years of age and none less than five years of age.
4. There was no medical supervision.
5. While at first, well-trained instructors were employed, the Abendberg had been without an educator for several years.
6. Heating, nutrition, water supply, and other aspects of the physical plant were inadequate.
7. Clothing was insufficient.
8. There were no records concerning the donations received for the institution.
9. No records were maintained concerning resident progress.[84]

As a result of this report, the Swiss Association of Natural Sciences withdrew its sponsorship and support. Though the Abendberg would not be closed until 1867, Guggenbühl withdrew to Montreaux, scorned and labeled a swindler, quack, charlatan, embezzler, and bigot. When he died on February 2, 1863, at the age of 47, he had been unable to reclaim any of his former prestige.

Reverend Heinrich Matthias Sengelmann best summarized Guggenbühl's work in the following words: "Not to sit in judgment of the man, the bow string was strained beyond its strength. Too much had been promised. To those who insisted on seeing the fulfillment of all promises, it was necessary to present parade horses, and this procedure could not satisfy those observers who penetrated into the character of it. The incense of adulation weakened his sober judgment. To this must be added that during his frequent absences from the Abendberg, abuses crept in which he could not at once detect or correct. Later, once suspicion was aroused, his religious tendencies, which had at first been tolerated, were made to appear as the source of these abuses, and he was unjustly stamped as a hypocrite."[85]

Carl Wilhelm Saegert

Little is known of Carl Saegert's program for mentally retarded persons other than that he provided for them in connection with the Institution of Deaf-Mutes in Berlin, of which he was director. Unable to accept them into the deaf program, he first tutored a mentally retarded youngster successfully, and later received permission (but not funding) to start a small school. In 1848 approximately 50 students were enrolled. Later, this growing institution was transferred to Neustadt-Eberswalde near Berlin. Records, however, show that his program was visited by many and was held in high regard. Tuke, in writing of Herr Saegert, remarked, "He assured us when we visited his school, in 1853, that he had indubitable cases of idiocy in which the head was small and malformed, yet in which the results of education were so triumphant that they were ultimately able to mix with the world without being recognized as idiots."[86]

The efforts of Guggenbühl, Seguin, and Saegert were to be realized in the proliferation of residential programs throughout Europe

over the next 50 years: Saxony, 1845; England, 1846; Scotland, 1853; the Netherlands, 1855; Denmark, 1855; Berlin, 1860; Sweden, 1863; Austria, 1864; Ireland, 1869; Hungary, 1875; and Norway, 1877. Some of these facilities were publicly sponsored, while others were under private auspices. Ireland reported that in 1887 there were 55 European residential facilities providing services specifically for mentally retarded persons. These institutions were small in comparison with today's facilities. Although the largest (Earlswood, England) served 594 residents, most served less than 100. Russia had two facilities: one at St. Petersburg (20 residents) and one at Riga (10).[87]

The early institutions, at least in England, had variable admission practices that reflected level of mental retardation, economic circumstances, and in some instances, chronological age. One facility accepted idiots and imbeciles above the pauper class; another, idiots and imbeciles, both private and pauper cases; another, idiots and imbeciles belonging to the lower and higher middle classes; and another, youthful idiots and imbeciles under 15 years of age. Some facilities would not admit paralytic, incurably hydrocephalic, or blind or deaf mentally retarded children.[88]

The treatment of the residents in many of these facilities was substantially less than adequate and often brutal. Attendant personnel were often poorly trained, illiterate, and uncaring. In one year alone, Tuke reported that 88 male attendants had been dismissed from service: 53 for drunkenness, insubordination, or neglect of duties, and 35 for assaults on patients. Though a number of residents had been killed by the attendants, it was not until 1870 that any were convicted. In that year, two attendants were convicted of manslaughter based on the testimony of another resident and were sentenced to 7 years' penal servitude. It would be many years before the quality of residential staff would appreciably improve.[89]

As indicated previously, Down opened a private residential facility for wealthy children. According to Brown's description of the facility following a visit during the early 1880s, it must have offered a fine home for many youngsters and adults of both sexes. Located on 20 wooded acres, the ground included ornamental shrubs, croquet, lawn tennis, cricket ground, and a variety of outdoor entertainment opportunities. The residents received many training opportunities and slept in attractively wallpapered bedrooms accommodating not more than five people. Both young adults and infants were admitted, wrote Brown; "the youngest, hardly three years old, was a veritable baby, evidently no more developed, except in size, than an ordinary infant of a few months. Handsomely dressed in white, he sat in the lap of a nurse, seeming to notice very little of his surroundings. The whole air of the room was cheerful and refined."[90] This was in stark contrast to the public facility "where three rows of adult females and a few small boys, forty, perhaps, in all, were seated idly on raised benches with two women to keep them in place."[91] This verbally painted scene would typify the average dayroom for tens of thousands of mentally retarded persons in residential facilities throughout the world for generations to come.

SPECIAL EDUCATION

A new world awaited many mentally retarded individuals during the nineteenth century; dedicated, sensitive, and talented men would open up new vistas through education. Without a doubt, the foremost leaders in this area were Itard and Seguin.

Itard and Victor

Jean-Marc-Gaspard Itard (1774–1838) was born in Oraison Provence to an upper–middle class family. His father, a merchant and master carpenter, could afford to provide Itard with better educational opportunities than most families had at that time. Consequently, Itard attended school for a number of years studying the classics and science. If it were not for the French Revolution, he undoubtedly would have become a banker; however, to avoid military conscription, he became an assistant surgeon (though he had no formal medical training) in the military services. Apparently finding this a satisfying field of endeavor, he

completed his medical training in 1800. Shortly after completing his training, he successfully treated Abbé Sicard, Director of the National Institute for Deaf-Mutes, who, later in the year (December 31, 1800), created the post of physician at the Institute and hired Itard specifically to work with Victor, the wild boy of Aveyron.

By the time Victor came under the tutelage of Itard, he was already well known throughout France and had, in fact, been somewhat of a *cause célèbre*. Victor apparently was first noticed in 1797 when peasants in the region of Lacaune in south central France spied him fleeing through the woods. In 1798 he was again seen by woodsmen and captured, despite his violent resistance. He was put on public display but subsequently escaped again to the forest. For the next 15 months, he was seen on a number of occasions digging up potatoes and turnips or seeking acorns to eat. On July 25, 1799, three hunters spotted him in the same woods and captured him. He was brought back to Lacaune and entrusted to the care of an elderly widow. After 8 days, he again succeeded in escaping. This time he did not return

Jean-Marc-Gaspard Itard.

Victor, the Wild Boy of Aveyron.

round chin; an agreeable visage; and a pleasant smile. His whole body is covered with scars, of which the greater parts seem to have been produced by burns. There is one on the right eyebrow; another in the middle of the cheek on the same side; another on the chin; and another on the left cheek. . . . If these numerous scars are not an irrefutable proof of the bad treatment he suffered and of the attempts made to destroy him, they prove at least that he had no garments while he lived in the forest. He was not deformed in any way and the absence of deep calluses of the knees would indicate that he walked upright. His speech was limited to guttural sounds; he disliked company; was very insensitive to visual or auditory stimuli which did not relate to his immediate needs, which usually meant feeding; and his affections were limited. He gave no indication of loving anyone nor being attached to anyone, including those with whom he had contact.[92]

As regards intelligence, Bonnaterre continued,

All these details and many others that we could add established that this child is not totally without intelligence, reflection, or reasoning; however, we are obliged to say that in all those cases where it is not a matter of meeting his natural needs or of satisfying his appetite, we find only purely animal function. . . . I have not, however, detected any clear sign of idiocy in this young man; I have found only the profound shadowy ignorance of a simple soul, who no doubt appears stupid next to a Parisian of the same age, well-brought-up and sharp-witted. I believe, moreover, that it may prove impossible, even for the renowned Sicard, to remove completely this inertia in the mind of the boy.[93]

On Bastille Day in 1800, Victor was transferred to Paris where he was enrolled in the Institute for Deaf-Mutes. During his trip, he contracted smallpox, but no visible signs remained.

Pinel, who had been Itard's teacher, also conducted an extensive evaluation of Victor and reported his observations to the Society of Observers on Man. Following review and interpretation of Victor's state in terms of organic functions and intellectual faculties, and comparing him with other affected children and adults, Pinel reached the following conclusion: "We know the other details of his life from the time he entered society—his judgment always limited to the objects of his basic needs; his

to his original forest but climbed the mountains and traveled across the broad plateau of the Department of Aveyron. For some unknown reason, he approached the workshop of the Dyer Vidal. The government commissioner for St. Sernin, Constans-St. Esteve, took charge of the boy, and on the following day, he sent Victor to an orphanage at Saint-Affrique. According to various descriptions of Victor at that time, he appeared to be congenitally deaf and mute, 12 years of age, nice looking, and intensely concerned with escaping. On several occasions he escaped from Saint-Affrique but was recaptured. The boy's story appeared in newspapers throughout France, bringing him to the attention of the Abbé Pierre-Joseph Bonnaterre, Professor of Natural History at the Central School of Aveyron.

Bonnaterre studied Victor intensely, and later published a paper entitled, "The Historical Notice on the Savage of Aveyron and on Several Other Individuals Found in the Forest at the Various Times." Bonnaterre reported that:

Victor was 4-1/2 feet tall; approximately 12 or 13 years old; light complexion; round face, dark deep-set eyes; long eyelashes; brown hair; a long, somewhat pointed nose; an average mouth; a attention captured solely by the sight of food, or by means of living independently, a strongly acquired habit; the total absence of subsequent development of his intellectual faculties with regard to every other subject. Do these not assert that the child ought to be categorized among the children suffering from idiocy and insanity and that there is no hope whatever of attaining some measure of success through systematic and continued instruction?"[94]

Itard, however, did not hold this point of view. His judgment or thinking was more influenced by the writings of Condillac than the conclusions of his medical colleagues.

Etienne Bonnet de Condillac (1750–1780), an influential French philosopher, a man of the cloth, and a director of a monastery, was very interested in the empiricism of Locke, and wrote extensively on learning through the senses. According to Condillac, man could become a highly rational person solely on the basis of his sensory experiences and without relying on Locke's hypothetical need for reflection.

In essence, Itard did not believe that Victor was a born idiot; rather, his intellectual deficiencies were a consequence of the absence of appropriate sensory experiences in a socialized environment. Thus, Itard, perhaps viewing both Locke and Condillac in a relatively superficial manner, contended that Victor would show substantial intellectual development through an adequate program of training.

In addition to his genuine concern for Victor, Itard undertook this educational experiment for another reason, as well. A number of feral children had been found throughout the years; yet, none had been scientifically studied.* Therefore, even if the training efforts

with Victor were to fail, "there would be found in this age of observation someone who, *carefully collecting the history of so surprising a creature, would determine what he is and would deduce from what he lacks the hitherto uncalculated sum of knowledge and ideas which man owes to his education.*"[97]

Victor's Education Itard's educational legacy exists in his brief text *L'Enfant Sauvage,* usually interpreted as *The Wild Boy of Aveyron.* "Sauvage," a term frequently used by Itard, meant simply an uncivilized person. *The Wild Boy of Aveyron* is actually a compilation of two reports, the first of which was published as a separate work in 1801, and the second a report submitted on request to the Minister of the Interior and dated 1806. In the Foreword, Itard makes reference to Condillac and his theories concerning the effects of isolation on human development and the importance of the senses. Itard's five aims for Victor's education were as follows:

1. To interest him in social life by rendering it more pleasant to him than the one he was just leaving, and above all more like the life which he had just left.

2. To awaken his nervous sensibility by the most energetic stimulation, and occasionally by intense emotion.

3. To extend the range of his ideas by giving him new needs and by increasing his social contact.

4. To lead him to the use of speech by inducing the exercise of imitation through the imperious law of necessity.

5. To make him exercise the simplest mental operations upon the objects of his physical needs over a period of time, afterwards

---

*Esquirol summarized his impressions of the noble savage in the following words: "Do savages exist? If we understand by this term, men endowed with intelligence, living alone, isolated, strangers to all civilization, without education, and having never had communication with others of their species, doubtless they do not exist . . . men, found in the woods, towards whom the eloquence of the philosophers of the last century awakened the interest of the civilized world; whom they exhibited, with a degree of affectation, to public curiosity, as perfect men, superior even to Newton and Bossuet; only wanted education. Those wretched beings were not savages, but idiots; abandoned and fugitive imbeciles; whom the instinct of self-preservation, and a thousand fortuitous circumstances had preserved from death."[95] Ireland was somewhat more conservative: "I therefore proceed to put together some of the best authenticated cases of wolf children, without, however, presuming myself to pronounce any opinion, either adverse or favourable."[96]

inducing the application of these mental processes to the objects of instruction.

In collaboration with Madame Guerin, who assumed the maternal and housekeeping responsibilities for Victor, Itard engaged his student in a wide range of very carefully conceived educational activities. The sequence of his efforts were: 1) development of the functions of the senses, 2) development of the intellectual functions, and 3) development of emotional faculties.

Regrettably, it is impossible to describe Itard's methods in any detail. Perhaps a brief comment on how Victor got his name will at least illustrate the intensity with which Itard pursued his responsibility:

At the beginning of December, I made a most interesting observation. One day when he was in the kitchen occupied with cooking potatoes two people had a sharp dispute behind him, without his appearing to pay the least attention. A third arrived unexpectedly, who, joining in the discussion, commenced all his replies with these words,—"Oh, that is different." I noticed that every time that this person let his favorite "Oh!" escape, the *Savage of Aveyron* quickly turned his head. That evening when he went to bed I made some experiments upon this sound and obtained almost the same results. I went over all the other simple sounds known as vowels but without any success. This preference for "O" obliged me to give him a name which terminated with this vowel. I chose Victor. This name remains his and when it is called he rarely fails to turn his head or to run up.[98]

In spite of Itard's ingenuity and affection, Victor's progress was frustratingly slow, and at times, the experience was most difficult for both teacher and student. When Victor could not cope with a new effort or became anxious, he also tended to become violent.

After 5 years of dedicated work, Itard decided to terminate the program. This was a difficult decision and a most disappointing time for Itard because he had hoped that when Victor reached puberty his educational gains would increase significantly. Victor, however, because of a lack of maturity or inadequate training (or both), simply could not relate effectively with women, and as a result, he became highly agitated, restless, and unhappy. These personal problems seriously impeded his educational progress.

Madame Guerin, the real heroine of this epic, was allocated 150 francs a year by the Ministry to attend to Victor in a nearby house belonging to the institute. Victor died in that house, in his forties, in 1828. Regrettably, the naturalist Virey reported after visiting Victor in later years that he was "fearful, half-wild, and unable to learn to speak, despite all the efforts that were made."[99]

In his 1806 report to the Minister of the Interior, Itard succinctly summarized Victor's progress after 5 years of training:

1. That by reason of the almost complete apathy of the organs of hearing and speech, the education of this young man is still incomplete and must always remain so;

2. That by reason of their long inaction the intellectual faculties are developing slowly and painfully, and that this development, which in children growing up in civilized surroundings is a natural fruit of the time and circumstances, is here the slow and laborious result of a very active education in which the most powerful methods are used to obtain most insignificant results;

3. That the emotional faculties, equally slow in emerging from their long torpor, are subordinated to an utter selfishness and that his puberty, which was very strongly marked and which usually sets up a great emotional expansion, seems only to prove that if there exists in human beings a relation between the needs of the senses and the affections of the heart, this sympathetic agreement is, like the majority of great and generous emotions, the happy fruit of education.

However:

1. That the improvement of his sight and touch and the new gratification of his sense of taste have, by multiplying the sensation and ideas of our sauvage, contributed powerfully to the development of his intellectual faculties;

2. When one considers the full extent of this development, among other real improvements, he will be found to have both a knowledge of the conventional value of the symbols of thought and the power of applying it by naming objects, their qualities, and their action.

3. That in spite of his immoderate taste for the

freedom of open country and his indifference to most of the pleasures of social life, Victor shows himself sensible of the care taken of him.[100]

Many authorities in the field of mental retardation have observed that Itard considered himself a failure with regard to Victor. While in many ways the boy's progress fell far short of initial expectancies, Itard's final comments concerning Victor were not those of a defeated person:

> To be judged fairly, this young man must only be compared with himself. Put beside another adolescent of the same age, he is only an ill-favored creature, an outcast of nature as he was of society. But if one limits oneself to the two terms of comparison offered by the past and present states of young Victor, one is astonished at the immense space which separates them; and one can question whether Victor is not more unlike the *Wild Boy of Aveyron* arriving at Paris, than he is unlike other individuals of his same age and species.[101]

While Victor was to spend his remaining years with Madame Guerin, Itard, already well known and respected throughout Europe for his educational experiment, was to gain further recognition and fame for his outstanding contributions to the deaf. Much of the knowledge gained in working with Victor was transferred by Itard to educating the deaf, advancing significantly the techniques of oral communication. After years of experimenting with oral communication, Itard devised a classification of hearing losses with direct relevance to the acquisition of language. These efforts, which culminated in the publication of the *Physiological Training of the Ear*, were applied throughout Europe and officially recognized by the French Academy of Sciences. His *Treatise on Disease of Ear and Hearing* is a classic in medical literature and marks the beginning of otology.

During the last year of his life, Itard, now a very sick person living in constant pain, was once again requested to take on the education of some retarded youngsters. He indicated that he could not but that if an appropriate student could be found, he would supervise his activities. That student, as noted, was Edouard Seguin.

Edouard Seguin and the Physiological Method

Though many educational and psychological theories have been introduced pertaining to the education and training of mentally retarded children during the twentieth century, none has had the impact of Seguin's physiological method. It was his philosophy and educational approach that encouraged many persons in both Europe and the United States to undertake the education of mentally retarded persons.

The primary psychophysiological principle underlying Seguin's theory was presented in his 1866 text, *Idiocy and Its Treatment by the Physiological Method:*

> Our method, to be really physiological, must adapt itself in principles as well as in its means and instruments, to the healthy development and usage of functions, particularly of those of the life or relation: the apposition to be true must leave no gap, suffer no discrepancy. Man being a unit, is artificially analyzed, for study's sake, into his three prominent vital expressions, activity, intelligence, and will. We consider the idiot as a man infirm in the expressions of his trinity; and we understand the method of training idiots, or mankind, as the philosophical agency by which the unity of manhood can be reached as far as practicable in our day, through the trinary analysis.
>
> According to this Trinitarian hypothesis, we shall have to educate the activity, the intelligence, the will, three functions of the unit man, not three entities antagonistic one of the other. We shall have to educate them, not with a serial object in view (favorite theory of A. Comte), but with a sense of their unity in the one being.
>
> Activity, besides its unconscious and organic functions, divides into contractility and sensibility, with their specific tendencies; Intelligence branches into many sub-functions, and Will into its protean expressions, from love to hatred.
>
> The predominance of any of these functions constitutes a disease; their perversion leads to insanity; their notable deficiency at birth constitutes idiocy, afterwards imbecility, later yet dementia.
>
> Physiological education, including hygienic and moral training, restores the harmony of these functions in the young, as far as practicable, separating them abstractedly, to restore them practically in their unity.
>
> This is the psycho-physiological principle of the method.[102]

As indicated previously, Seguin assumed that there was a definite neurophysical relationship between sensory activity and higher levels of thinking. Therefore, he stressed the systematic training of the senses of sight, hearing, taste, and smell and of eye-hand coordination. As illustrated in his articles "The Psycho-Physiological Training of an Idiotic Hand" and "The Psycho-Educational Training of an Idiotic Eye" (1880), no detail or minor imperfection was too small to ignore.

His approach involved five steps: 1) training the muscular system, 2) training the nervous system, 3) educating the senses, 4) acquiring general ideas, and 5) developing the ability to think in abstract terms and acquiring a strong understanding and practice of moral (social) precepts. In developing his methodology, he readily adapted "materials and techniques from Pereira, Sicard, Itard, and Amoros; utilized motivational techniques from Rollin and Rousseau; employed physiological theories from Lecat and Rochoux; and adopted medical techniques from Pinel, Esquirol, and Belhomme."[103]

Seguin's theory of education and its application was encompassing, ranging from passive exercises for the nonambulatory child through academic training and vocational placement for the more capable individual. His curriculum was quite contemporary in nature: learning involved perception, imitation, coordination, memory, and generalization.

Many of his techniques are commonly used today, including positive reinforcement procedures and modeling. Physical punishment was to be applied sparingly and only with those youngsters who knew beforehand that they were doing wrong.

Seguin was equally sensitive to the environmental components of the learning experience:

The surrounding circumstances are to be equally instrumental to our purpose: light or darkness, solitude or multitude, movement or immobility, silence or sound, and so forth, are to be chosen or prepared in view of their moral influence on the actions demanded of the idiot. We must remember that our teaching how to do a thing, is to him of no practical value if we do not place him in the best circumstances to accomplish it; as to put him

among other children doing the same thing; to let him see them do it without attempting to do it himself; to make him imitate the nearest thing to the one wished of him; to let him desire what we desire him to do.[104]

His theory encouraged active interaction with the environment at all times. His concentration on the role of imitation, the importance of play activities, and the need for opportunities to experience and test what one has learned is remarkably similar to the cardinal concepts of Piaget.

Seguin placed considerable emphasis on "moral treatment" in addition to the more academic aspects of education. As he felt a very strong moral obligation in his own life toward others, he fully expected the idiot to attain a similar standard of conduct:

That the idiot is endowed with a moral nature, no one who has had the happiness administering to him will deny . . . he is sensible to the eulogy, reproach, command, menace, even to imaginary punishment. He sympathizes with the pains he can understand; he loves those who love him; he tries to please those who please him; his sense of duty and propriety is limited, but perfect in its kind; his egotism is moderate; his possessive and retentive propensities sufficient; his courage, if not Samsonian, is not aggressive, and may easily be cultivated. As a collective body, idiotic children are, in their institutions, equal in order and decency, and true lovingness, if not in loveliness, to any collection of children in the land.[105]

In essence, the moral aspects of education involved developing, whenever possible, a strong sense of values, obedience and participation, duty, and responsibility for work. Education without the moral component was unacceptable.

It cannot be overemphasized that Seguin was convinced that the physiological method and moral treatment was applicable to all retarded youngsters regardless of their level of retardation. Much of his energy was devoted to those more severely retarded. This is well illustrated in the 1866 text in which he includes as an appendix a brief description of various youngsters he or his followers had diagnosed and/or treated. One case illustrates not only his interest in the education of the severely mentally retarded youngster but also his interminable patience: "Five-year-old Charles, seems not to hear, look, taste, or smell. . . . He does not masticate; digests badly; is careless; salivates constantly; does not blow his nose, weep, nor perspire, his head gives out a fetid odor. His sleep is sound; generally, it ends in the morning with an epileptic attack. . . . Charles presents not a trace of intellectual operations."[106] Seguin concluded that Charles was an "idiot, in the full meaning of the term; but much more than idiot, since epilepsy prostrates him 10 to 20 times a day; I have never seen, even in the *hospices,* a subject offering a more complete type of these two infirmities." Yet, Seguin wrote, "During his short stay I had only time to study him, and favorable prognosis has not resulted from such study; nevertheless, it would have been necessary to have tried to treat him at least one year, to affirm that he was *incurable,* or that his condition could not be *anekuirated.*"[107]

This case, combined with his reported educational studies with hydrocephalic children, proves unequivocally that he was intensely interested in providing for all mentally retarded children. It also reflects the tremendous faith he had in his own approach to meeting their developmental needs.

While it is neither possible to review Seguin's education methodology in detail nor offer a description of the many supplemental educational materials he developed, a glimpse of a single school day at the Bicêtre will demonstrate that he took education very seriously:

5:00 AM	Students rise and have one-half hour to wash, groom, and dress
5:30 AM	Morning hymn and first breakfast, consisting of a simple piece of bread
6:30 AM	Sensory training activities (smelling, tasting, hearing, eye-hand coordination, etc.)
8:15 AM	Arithmetic (all classes were graded according to the students' abilities)
9:00 AM	Second breakfast, a bowl of soup, and a plate of meat
10:30 AM	Reading classes
11:15 AM	Writing classes
12:00 PM	Gymnastics
12:30 PM	Music
1:00 PM	An afternoon of labor (all students engaged in some form of manual activity, ranging from shoemaking to the simple tilling of the ground)
4:30 PM	Dining and play
7:00 PM	Meet with teachers and read to each other or hold conversations to enhance reflective thinking (two evenings a week at this time were allocated to a concert or dance)
8:15 PM	Evening hymn and retirement[108]

Today's educational community no longer accepts Seguin's neurophysiological premises, places less emphasis on sensory training per se, offers less regimented classroom schedules, and employs less mechanical processes. Nevertheless, many of his learning principles and specially adapted educational materials are being used successfully in classrooms throughout the world. His educational concepts, in combination with those of Itard, influenced the thinking of future educational leaders, especially Maria Montessori. Mentally retarded persons, knowingly or unknowingly, will always owe a debt to Seguin.

Other Educators and Their Concepts

Though Itard and Seguin provided the stimulus and means for educating mentally retarded persons and were to have the greatest impact on educational programming, others, too, were concerned with this area. Several short-lived educational attempts preceded Seguin's program at the Bicêtre (e.g., Guggenmoos established such a school in 1828 in Salzberg, Austria; Haldenwang attempted a similar operation in Wildberg for cretins; Ferret had started a classroom for mentally retarded residents at the Bicêtre as early as 1828). As discussed previously, both Guggenbühl and Saegert introduced educational programs with varying degrees of success.

Felix Voisin   Another early school was started by Felix Voisin (1794–1872), a physician who constantly appears in the background of early educational programs at the Bicêtre. In 1826, Voisin published a text, *Des Causes Morales et Physiques des Maladies Mentale,* in which he expressed concern specifically for the education and medical treatment of four categories of children with special needs: 1) the feebleminded, those intermediate in grade between idiocy and normality, 2) those born normal but who were failing because of an inappropriate education, 3) those showing character abnormalities from birth (e.g., uncontrolled passions and "evil propensitie"), and 4) those born of insane parents and therefore predisposed to nervous or mental disorders. For each group, Voisin had a special education program that combined the medical and the educational into what he termed "orthophrenic treatment." This method required that each case be viewed on an individual basis and that treatment (medical and educational) should attempt to expand the youngster's intellectual sphere, repress or develop faculties, and foster the morals and standards essential to living in social harmony. He started a private school at Issy for all four groups of youngsters in 1837. The "Orthophrenic Institution," however, closed after a few years for lack of financial support, and Voisin was appointed physician to the Bicêtre annex, where he was at least partially responsible for hiring Seguin and was his immediate supervisor. When Seguin left the Bicêtre, Voisin continued to supervise the educational programs for its mentally retarded inmates.[109]

J. Langdon Down and William Wetherspoon Ireland Both Ireland and Down had definite ideas concerning education, and in one very critical respect—the importance of speech and language—they were in accord. Both also advocated that the institution was the proper place to educate mentally retarded children in order to free them from isolation. For example, in 1877, Down wrote, "The most successful training is effected with the child's equals; in this way a healthy emulation is established. Intelligent children will not take part in the amusements and games of feeble-minded ones, moreover, there is no community of feeling or

of interest. The outcome of an attempt to train the feeble-minded child with others more intelligent than himself is infallibly to make his life *solitary . . .* association with their superiors condemns them to a life of isolation which renders nugatory all efforts for their improvement."[110]

Down also contended that all treatment must have a broad medical orientation to ensure that proper health measures are taken, including proper diet, bathing, and skin care, because he believed health was important to intellectual functioning. An appropriate training program should include a variety of physical activities to ensure strength and coordination. Intellectual training required a cultivation of the senses, basic self-care skills, elimination of defective speech, use and value of money, gardening, and vocational training; of these areas, speech and language were viewed as primary to reflective thinking. Moral training was critical: "he has to be taught to subordinate his will to that of another. He has to learn obedience; that right-doing brings pleasure, and that wrong-doing is followed by its deprivation."[111] Like Seguin and Ireland, Down placed considerable emphasis on obedience training, but both corporal punishment and denial of food for behavior management were strictly forbidden.

Like most conscientious physicians and administrators of that day, Ireland devoted considerable attention to methods of educating idiots and imbeciles. As with Down, his treatment emphasized both the mental and physical aspects of education, an area in which he drew upon the experiences of Pestalozzi, Itard, and Seguin.

Teaching, he felt, should begin with very simple exercises; education should begin at approximately 7 years of age, since it was seldom advisable to remove an idiot child from his home, if he had any mother at all, before this time. Ireland found that idiots and imbeciles admitted between 12 and 18 years of age improved more than those admitted at an earlier period of life.

Again, cultivation of the senses was an integral part of the educational program. Ireland also stressed the importance of physical exercise. Such programs should be developed in a sequential manner, and attention should be paid to the "importance of drill and open air exercise . . . in correcting automatic and spasmodic motions, and strengthening the frame, and giving the pupil a more perfect command of his muscles."[112] He encouraged range-of-motion activities and outlined a series of corrective-type exercises, such as treading upon footsteps marked on the floor, using balancing beams, catching and throwing exercises, and keeping time with musical instruments.

Of great consequence, in Ireland's judgment, was the need to develop language and speech: "Language itself is well-nigh an indispensable element in education; sometimes it may impede thought, but generally supports it. Words represent and recall definitions and generalizations, and little progress can be made in education unless the pupil has a language of one kind or another."[113] Thus, Ireland devoted many pages of his text to the development of language and speech skills among mentally retarded persons.

Academic subjects (reading, writing, and arithmetic) were vitally important as were their practical application. Ireland's teaching techniques were modeled after those developed by Pestalozzi. Moral and religious tuition and the teaching of trades rounded out a person's education.

With regard to self-support, Ireland noted that there were "a good many instances recorded in reports of training-schools of imbeciles who have learned to support themselves. This in general is after a long apprenticeship, of 10 to 12 years. In any case, it is no easy matter to bring about such results, as trades are taught in the ordinary institutions for idiots, where they are very often withdrawn either before they are strong enough to commence any handicraft, either to be totally neglected or to get under less advantageous circumstances the additional instruction which they require."[114]

Since Ireland believed that mentally retarded persons could be trained to become employable, he was concerned that he could not retain a student past 18 years of age. He noted that

institutions in Europe placed much greater emphasis on vocational preparation than did American facilities, which devoted a proportionately larger amount of time to education.

One other person should be cited in connection with education since he put forth the notion of "happiness" that was to influence certain educators in the future. John Charles Bucknill, who collaborated with Tuke on several publications dealing with insanity and idiocy, wrote: "If the happiness of a community, even a community of idiots, be secured, the paths of goodness and of usefulness will not be left untrod."[115] Happiness of the idiot was effected by: 1) teaching him the senses and use of his muscles, 2) teaching him to speak and converse, if possible, 3) teaching him to love and trust, not to hate and fear, and 4) training him to engage in wholesome, useful, and agreeable activities. Although Bucknill placed "happiness" in the context of a total educational program, there were those who misinterpreted him and believed that the primary function of special education and the school was simply to keep the mentally retarded child happy.

P. M. Duncan and W. Millard   As indicated previously, Duncan and Millard strongly believed that through proper physical care and education, a mentally retarded person could be rendered more capable. Formal training followed restoration of health and well-being plus the elimination of bad habits. A theme of tenderness and respect ran throughout all Duncan's and Millard's recommendations: "freedom from unkind remarks, brutality, and derision, is usually followed by a speedy improvement in the temper; and as the idiot reflects, more than other children, the temper and disposition of its teachers and associates, so supreme care should be taken to give it a good example, and to exercise great forebearance."[116]

Their text took into full consideration that many mentally retarded children would never be served in an institutional setting (nor was residential placement encouraged) and was written in the style of a "home adviser." The detail of their recommended ministrations, their recognition of the home setting, and their deep concern for even the most severely mentally retarded person (i.e., Class I) was exceptional, not only for their day but for ours as well. The authors provided a very detailed educational prescription for each of the eight levels of intellectual functioning previously mentioned, taking into consideration clothing; diet; bathing and washing; drill and gymnastic exercises; speaking lessons; toys, pastimes, and useful employment; mental training (academics); the prevention of bad habits; proper morals; control of temper; and religion. Respect as well as tender love and care (e.g., no one should wear hand-me-down clothes) permeated their entire thesis, regardless of level of retardation or chronological age. (Anyone serving the severely or profoundly mentally retarded child would be well advised to read Duncan and Millard's text.)

The Auxiliary School Though Johann Traugott Weise (1793–1859), a German educator, wrote a pamphlet entitled "Thoughts about Feeble-minded Children, with Regard to Varieties, Basic Causes, Manifestations, and Ways of Getting at Them Easily by Means of Education" in 1820, it was not until 1859 that the first special class, or auxiliary school, was established.[117] Weise's publication went relatively unnoticed and probably would be unknown today had it not been reproduced 91 years later; today, Weise is given credit for the first educational publication specifically concerned with mentally retarded students.

The first special class (*Hifsklassen*) or auxiliary school (*Hifsschule*) for mentally retarded students was established in 1859 at Halle in Saxony (Germany) in response to the recommendations of Haupp, a school principal. He specifically requested the "formation of a separate or special class for defective pupils (now numbering 17), providing for about two hours of instruction daily."[118] This class predated a similar effort in the United States by approximately 40 years.

In the beginning, special education was opposed for several reasons. In Germany, special education encountered some opposition from the regular *Volkschule* teachers, who believed that all children committed to their attention could be taught successfully—an unusually challenging task, since a primary school teacher, for example, was responsible for 70 to 80 students. Others opposed special classes because they felt that special education should remain within the purview of the institution as it did in England. Fortunately, this attitude was not commonly held in Europe.

In spite of the opposition, the first auxiliary school (which included both the special class and separate school) was established, and the movement gradually spread throughout Germany by the turn of the century: Dresden, 1867; Gera and Elberfield in the 1870s; Leipzig, 1881, Königsberg and Krefeld, 1885; Frankfurt, 1889; Hamburg, 1892; Karlsruhe, 1896; and Berlin, 1898. A number of other European countries followed Germany's lead: Norway, 1874; Switzerland, 1888; Prussia, 1892; Austria, 1895; and England, 1898. Denmark, Holland, and Belgium all started special programs in 1900, joined shortly by Sweden in 1904. Though Italy did not formally adopt the auxiliary school plan until after 1900, backward children had been grouped together and taught by women teachers. Dr. de Sanctis also established in 1899 an independent "asylum school," a day school and home for 40 mentally retarded children of poor parents in Rome. In spite of considerable interest, France did not initiate its first special class until 1909.[119]

There were several very significant differences between early European and American efforts. First, mentally retarded youngsters (and adults) in Europe were not viewed as negatively as they were in the United States. Mentally retarded students were simply youngsters with unusual needs, who, with an appropriate education, would become substantial citizens and adults, regardless of their socioeconomic background: "Many times the parents are in very poor circumstances; but in spite of this, they manage somehow to keep themselves and their children (often numerous) with assistance from either public or private charities. In other cases—and there are many such—the parents are addicted to strong drink, dislike work, lead immoral lives, or have come into frequent touch with the strong arm of the law."[120]

Second, most European leaders, in marked contrast to those in the United States, did not consider institutions appropriate settings for the less severely affected; institutions were to serve only those who were "entirely helpless or imbecile."[121] According to Maennel, "schools were not anxious at all to have their youngsters placed or transferred to an institution. Any persons who have ever attempted to bring [such a] proposal to the attention of the authorities can testify to the difficulties involved in placing the child in [an] institution."[122]

Subsequently, the goal of European special education was identical to that of all students: "to become useful members of society." The special educator was expected to make his students "as independent as possible, in order to keep them from making mistakes in later life."[123] By contrast, early special programs in the United States were considered a primary step toward institutionalization.

Great caution was exercised in all countries to avoid the indiscriminate placement of backward children into special classes for mentally retarded children. Most European countries established a supplemental program for those students who required a little more concentrated work in order to catch up with their normal peers. After touring several European countries at the turn of the century, Fernald provided a comparative description of special class students he saw in auxiliary classes in England: "In the schools that I examined, the pupils seemed distinctly inferior, both mentally and physically, to the pupils found in the school departments of the American institutional school for feeble-minded. I saw very few pupils of the same degree of intelligence as the brighter school classes at Elwyn, Syracuse, and Columbus; and the standards of nutrition and bodily vigor were decidely below that of pupils in American institutions or in the En-

glish institutions."[124] It is thus quite evident that the auxiliary school provided for a substantial number of both moderately and mildly retarded individuals.

B. Maennel, the outstanding early German special educator, identified five basic rules governing special class studies, at least in Germany:

1. The day study should be arranged to meet the demands of mental energy required for each.
2. The first lesson of the day should not always make the heaviest demand upon the child.
3. If a lesson has especially aroused and stimulated one side of the child's nature, the next lesson should appeal to another phase which has not yet been stimulated.
4. The same subject should be taught in every class at the same time.*
5. The auxiliary school should have no afternoon session. This demand, so recently urged in connection with regular schools in our larger cities, has a special significance for the auxiliary school. As a rule, auxiliary school pupils are forced to travel considerable distances to and from schools, and occasionally these long walks cause suffering to delicate children.[125]

The nine major areas of study in Germany were: 1) religion, 2) observation, speaking, reading, and writing, 3) history, 4) drawing, 5) manual training, 6) singing and gymnastics, 7) home geography and general geography, 8) arithmetic, and 9) natural history and nature study. Considerable attention was also devoted to preparing students for a meaningful job in the community.

The auxiliary schools were often assisted in their efforts by various community associations. For example, the Association for the Care and Training of Mentally Deficient Children in Berlin undertook at the turn of the century such tasks as providing care, food, clothing for retarded youngsters in need; establishing day homes for mentally retarded youngsters; and monitoring the appointment of proper caretakers and professional assistants to watch over the children. Following a student's

---

*The notion that the same subject should be taught in every class at the same time was a relatively standard approach to education employed throughout Europe for all students, regardless of intelligence.

completion of school, the Association advised parents and teachers concerning appropriate vocations, recommended reliable employees, established evening classes for technical training, and provided various forms of aid and assistance that the young adult required.[126]

In addition, teacher organizations and a number of special education journals appeared prior to the turn of the century. In 1866, Stolzner and Kern started the first society for the study of the educational advancement of mentally deficient children in Hanover; however, their effort was relatively short lived. It was not until 1898 that the National Association of Auxiliary Schools was formed. *Kinderfehler* and the *Hischule,* two journals devoted to the auxiliary school movement and the science and treatment of abnormal children, were widely read.

In Italy, mentally retarded people were attended to primarily in institutions, insane asylums, and poorhouses. There were several notable exceptions, however. In Aosta, the Sisters of Mercy had an educational facility for both children and adult cretins. Cretinism in that area was most prevalent, and the Sisters were successful in facilitating the cretins' ability to express themselves verbally and contribute to manual labor.[127] Then, at the turn of the century, Italy produced an outstanding educator.

Maria Montessori Maria Montessori (1870–1952) was born at Chiaravalle, Italy, of parentage descended from a noble Bolognese family. After considering various professions, Montessori settled on medicine, somewhat to her father's chagrin. Nevertheless, she became Italy's first female medical student and first female doctor of medicine upon completing her degree in 1896.

Soon after graduating, Montessori was appointed assistant doctor at the Psychiatric Clinic in the University of Rome. Her duties required visitation to asylums for the insane in Rome, and in this way, she became exposed to many mentally retarded persons who, in Rome as in other cities, were housed with the mentally ill. According to E. M. Standing, her collaborator and biographer, one of her early

Maria Montessori.

experiences gave rise to her ultimate dedication and concern:

> In one of the lunatic asylums she came across a number of these unhappy children herded together like prisoners in a prisonlike room. The woman who looked after them did not attempt to conceal the disgust with which she regarded them. Montessori asked her why she held them in such contempt. "Because," the woman replied, "as soon as their meals are finished they throw themselves on the floor to search for crumbs." Montessori looked around the room and saw that the children had no toys or materials of any kind—that the room was in fact entirely bare. There were literally no objects in their environment which the children could hold and manipulate with their fingers. Montessori saw in the children's behaviour a craving of a very different and higher kind than for mere food. There existed for these poor creatures, she realized, one path and one only towards intelligence, and that was through their hands. Instinctively the poor deficient mites had sought after that path by the only means in their reach.

The more Montessori came in contact with these defective children—studying them, meditating over their condition, longing to help them—the more strongly did she come to differ from the generally accepted views with regard to them. It became increasingly apparent to her that mental deficiency was a pedagogical problem rather than a medical one. She came to believe that, with special educational treatment, their mental condition could be immensely ameliorated, a view she found to be shared by the French doctors Jean Itard and Edouard Seguin, and a few others.

She says, "That form of creation which was necessary for these unfortunate beings, so as to enable them to reenter human society, to take their place in the civilized world and render them independent of the help of others—placing human dignity within their grasp—was a work which appealed so strongly to my heart that I remained in it for years."[128]

In view of her interest, she travelled to London and Paris to study the methods of Itard and Seguin. At a pedagogical conference in Turin in 1899, Montessori gave public expression to her growing concern for and knowledge of educating mentally retarded children. As a result of her presentation, which emphasized that "defective children were not extra-social beings, but were entitled to the benefits of education as much as—if not more than—normal ones," she was invited to organize the Orthophrenic School for the Cure of the Feeble-minded. She accepted the challenge and served as director for two years from 1899 to 1901.[129]

For her times, Montessori held many unusual views on children. She believed, for example, that youngsters had an amazing ability to concentrate, that they preferred repetition, order, freedom of choice, work over play, and silence. Also, even they had a strong sense of personal dignity.

Montessori's cardinal principle of education, however, was her concept of spontaneity: the young child is "at a period of creation and expansion, and it is enough to open the door. Indeed that which he is creating, which from not being is passing into existence, and from potentiality to actuality, at the moment it comes forth from nothing cannot be complicated . . . and there can be no difficulty in its manifestation. Thus by preparing a free environment, an environment suited to this moment of life, natural manifestations of the child's psyche and hence revelation of his secret should come about spontaneously."[130] Thus, "education is not what the teacher gives;

education is a natural process spontaneously carried out by the human individual, and is acquired not by listening to words but by experiences upon the environment."[131] A structured environment and sensory motor development utilizing many of the ideas set forth by Seguin and self-teaching didactic materials were essential to the educational experience.

Her experiences with the program for mentally retarded youngsters was highly successful. As she observed:

I succeeded in teaching a number of the idiots from the asylums both to read and to write so well that I was able to present them at a public school for an examination together with normal children. And they passed the examination successfully. . . . While everyone was admiring the progress of my idiots, I was searching for the reasons which could keep the happy healthy children of the common schools on so low a plane that they could be equalled in tests of intelligence by my unfortunate pupils![132]

Her enthusiastic evaluation and personal surprise was well documented by others. Based on such experiences, she believed that similar methods could be applied to normal children, a pursuit she was to follow successfully, starting in 1906.

Between 1901 and 1906, Montessori combined teaching, studying, and writing, primarily along medical lines. During this time, she held a university chair of anthropology and released her first major publication, *Pedagogical Anthropology.*

In 1906, she once again approached the problem of education, this time in establishing the first *Casa dei Bambini,* a program for children from the slum district of Rome known as the San Lorenzo quarter. Like her preceding effort, the *Casa dei Bambini* and its programs were highly successful. Upon publication of her first educational book, *The Method of Scientific Pedagogy as Applied to Infant Education and the Children's Houses* in 1909, her reputation spread throughout the world.

Over the next 30 years, Montessori schools were established not only throughout Europe but in Africa, Asia, Japan, Latin America, and Canada. Her reception in the United States was the most mixed. She visited the United States on several occasions, and, while she was positively received, her educational approach was criticized severely by two of the outstanding educational leaders of the day, William Kilpatrick and John Dewey. Kilpatrick reviewed her method and criticized it on a number of sensitive issues, including the absence of adequate social cooperation, restrictive didactic apparatuses, and its failure to fit into the total educational scheme. He felt that her concept of "autoeducation" (i.e., self-education) was "more a wish than a fact."[133] Dewey was equally critical because, in his opinion, while the youngsters were allowed to select didactic materials in a very structured environment, "there [was] no freedom allowed the child to create. He [was] free to choose which apparatus he will use, but never to choose his own ends, never to bend the materials to his own plans. For the material is limited to a fixed number of things which must be handled in a certain way."[134] The impact of these judgments by two of the country's most respected educators was quite severe, and Montessori schools did not begin to develop in the United States until the late 1950s. Nevertheless, when she died in May of 1952 in Noordwijk, Holland, her reputation as a physician, feminist, and educator was well established throughout the world. Though many of her ideas are now no longer accepted in their entirety, many of her principles and materials are in current use with both mentally retarded and normal youngsters.

From the preceding discussion, it can be ascertained that not only were special education classes established for mentally retarded persons, but also that such programs introduced many ideas and materials currently in use. The relative importance of sensory training versus the acquisition of language is still debated among various schools of educational thought. In other words, much of that which is vital in contemporary special education had its origins during the latter half of the nineteenth century.

In summary, the century reviewed witnessed an exponential increase in the interest in, concern for, and knowledge of mental retardation. New clinical forms of mental retardation were identified, but etiological influences remained shrouded in a veil of uncertainty and moral conviction. Mental retardation had become clearly differentiated from mental illness, and much attention was devoted to the physical care and education of mentally retarded persons. Governments assumed a greater role in meeting their needs, and efforts were made to support special education and improve the quality of residential services. Much, however, remained to be accomplished in all areas.

Part

II

THE UNITED STATES

Chapter

4

THE
FORMATIVE YEARS
(1620–1849)

T HOUGH COLUMBUS DISCOVERED America in 1492, there was no immediate rush
to occupy the newly found lands. With the
exception of an occasional explorer, no serious
attempt was made to colonize until Sir
Humphrey Gilbert and Sir Walter Raleigh ventured forth in 1578 and 1584, respectively. The
crew and passengers of the *Mayflower* (most of
whom were not Pilgrims) did not land in
Provincetown harbor until 1620. Over the next
50 years, most of the Atlantic coastal region
was settled, and by 1650 there were 50,000
persons of foreign origin in the United States,
settled primarily in Massachusetts and Virginia. By 1850, the population had grown to 38
million.

These years saw the United States grow from
a few scattered settlements to an established
new nation. Many changes were wrought,
many reforms were initiated, and much remained the same. Let us begin by examining
the colonial years from 1620 to 1799.

THE COLONIAL YEARS

America was "a transplanted Europe" rather
than a fresh beginning. It was, in the words of
philosopher George Santayana, "a rebirth of
Europeans among greater opportunities."[1]

Thus, the three dynamic sociological forces of
early American history that were to become
deeply ingrained traditions—Protestantism,
nationalism, and capitalism—were propensities transferred from England.

Each of these was well expressed by our
Puritan forefathers. Of all early American
communities, that of the Puritans is best known
but frequently the least understood. Although
the Puritans lived a God-fearing, difficult life,
they were, by English standards, political reformers and radicals. As Edward Channing
observed, Puritanism was "an attitude of mind
rather than a system of theology—it was idealism applied to the solution of contemporary
problems. . . . In society it assumed the shape
of a desire to elevate private morals, which
were shockingly low [in England at that time].
In politics it stood for a new movement in
national life which required the extirpation of
the relics of feudalism and the recognition of
the people as a power in the state."[2] Puritans
were not only rebels of their day, they were
among the world's best farmers.

Mental retardation was acknowledged from
the very beginning of the American experience. This is evident by John Winthrop's
(1587–1649) *Modell of Christian Charity*,
which he drafted on his way to America in 1630

91

aboard the *Arbella*. A lawyer by training and a Puritan by conviction, Winthrop served as the first governor of Massachusetts. Though his portraits and his grave, measured prose present him as a rather sober individual, he possessed a kindly disposition. As governor, he was noted for his pragmatic administration, having on at least one occasion been rebuked by the church elders for his leniency.

His *Modell of Christian Charity* reflected the very essence of Puritanism, and as regards mentally retarded persons:

> God Almighty in his most holy and wise providence has so disposed of the condition of mankind as at all time some must be rich, some poor, some high and eminent in power and dignity, others mean and in subjection. Reason: First, to hold conformity with the rest of his works, being delighted to show forth the glory of his wisdom in the variety and difference of the creatures and the glory of his power, in ordering all these differences for the preservation and the good of the whole.
>
> Reason: Secondly, that he might have the more occasion to manifest the work of his spirit. First, upon the wicked in moderating and restraining them, so that the rich and mighty should not eat up the poor, nor the poor and despised rise up against their superiors and shake off their yolk. Secondly, in the regenerant in exercising his graces in them, as in the great ones, their love, mercy, gentleness, temperance, and so forth in the poor and inferior sort, their faith, patience, obedience, and so forth.
>
> Reason: Thirdly, that every man must have need of other, and from hence they might be all knit more nearly together in the bond of brotherly affection.[3]

It is quite evident that Winthrop's Puritan conception of God and His love recognized differences in abilities. Further, those with more talents or goods had a responsibility to those less fortunate.

Similarly, early laws and regulations governing the new citizen bodies in America acknowledged mental retardation. The *Body of Liber-*

ties, this country's first code of laws and adopted by the Massachusetts General Court in December, 1641, included:

> No man shall be pressed in person to any office, worke, warres, or other publique service, that is necessarily and suffitiently exempted by any naturall or personall impediment, as by want of yeares, greatnes of age, defect of minde, fayling of sences, or impotencie of Lymbes.
>
> Children, Idiots, Distracted persons, and all that are strangers, or new comers to our plantation, shall have such allowances and dispensations in any cause whether Criminal or other as religion and reason require.[4]

Not only was mental retardation recognized, but it could prove important. Like most sets of laws developed during that period, the *Body of Liberties* was a combination of the civil and ecclesiastical: thus, a person could be put to death for worshipping an untrue god, being a witch, blaspheming the name of God, willful murder, killing in anger or cruelty of passion, copulating with a beast or animal, homosexual activities, adultery, theft, false witness, and any form of rebellion or encouragement thereof against the Commonwealth. Mental retardation could mean the difference between life and death.

Though the Puritan society in the Massachusetts Bay area reflected many liberal ideas, a rigid religious orthodoxy became the law of the land, and church and state were inseparable. It was a society in which people were constantly under the pressure of impending evil, condemnation, and a perpetual fear of God and the devil. Children were brought up strictly; it was not their role to challenge their parents, and if they did, the law provided the death penalty for such unforgivable behavior: "Rebellious children, whether they continue in riott or drunkenese, after due correction from their parents, or whether they curse or smite their parents, to be put to death."[5]*

---

*Severe laws concerning the potential punishment of youngsters when they disregarded the wishes of their parents remained popular until the middle of the nineteenth century. For example: in 1819, the state of Illinois approved "An Act Respecting Crimes and Punishment," which read in part: "*Disobedience of children and servants.*—Be it further enacted, That if any children or servants shall, contrary to the obedience due to their parents or masters, resist or refuse to obey their lawful commands, upon complaint thereof to any justice of the peace, it shall be lawful for such justice of the peace to send him or them so offending to the jail or house of correction, there to remain until they shall humble themselves to the said parents or masters' satisfaction: and if any child or servant shall, contrary to his bounden duty, presume to assault or strike his parent or master, upon complaint or conviction thereof before two or more justices of the peace, the offender shall be whipped not exceeding ten stripes."[6]

In spite of the severe nature of this law, rarely, if ever, was it put into practice. Certainly the death penalty was never invoked and only once, in fact, was it brought before the courts as a possibility. The *Plymouth Colony Records* note that in 1679, "Edward Bumpus for stricking and abusing his parents, was whipt at the post; his punishment was alleviated in regard hee was crasey brained, otherwise hee had bine put to death or otherwise sharply punished."[7]

Though public flogging, as well as branding or shaming in stocks and pillars was relatively common, it is highly improbable that many mentally retarded persons were so treated. First, the Church tended to rely primarily on excommunication rather than severe types of punishment. As stated in *The Cambridge Platform of 1644,* which defined the essentials of Puritan church organization: "In dealing with an offender, great care is to be taken that we be neither over strict or rigorous, nor too indulgent or remiss; our proceeding herein ought to be with the spirit of meekness, considering ourselves, lest we also be tempted; and that the best of us have need of much forgiveness from the Lord. On some have compassion, others save with fear."[8]

Nor, according to the records of the Dorchester Church between 1659 and 1779, was the Church ignorant of the variances in human abilities, especially among the young. Cotton Mather exemplified this position in his address to Dorchester Church on March 31, 1660: "children of the church [should] look at themselves as to expect the benefit and privilege of church watchfulness and that they would so carry themselves as such as must give an account in case of defect according as their age or capacity would permit."[9]

Early elementary schools, however, were dominated by fear, discipline, and ruthless flogging, a practice that continued well into the nineteenth century. As Handlin and Handlin observed in their history of youth facing life, "In the school William Wells opened in Cambridge, Massachusetts in 1830, there was never a half day without a good deal of flogging. Terror disheartened the boys slow to learn; and one such youngster spent weeks and

weeks upon a few pages of Latin grammar which he blottened with tears and blackened with his fingers until they were hardly legible."[10]

In spite of the recognition of mental retardation in both law and practice, the birth of a defective or abnormal child was always suspect. Such an event reflected upon either God's wrath or the devil. Both Governors Braddock and Winthrop had the bodies of still-born children examined for evidence of witchcraft.

There is evidence that mentally retarded persons were among those accused of witchcraft in Salem during the hysterical summer of 1692. During the preceding 40 years, only 10 persons had been convicted of witchcraft; but during that summer, 19 people were hung and one was pressed to death; 55 others had confessed to witchcraft; and another 150 were awaiting trial when Governor Phips indignantly dismissed the Puritan court after his wife had been accused of witchcraft because she had pardoned an offender. Erickson indicated that many of those accused and condemned were "witless persons with scarcely a clue as to what happened to them."[11] An eye-witness at the time wrote that of three accused persons reviewed by Governor Phips, two "were the most senseless and ignorant creatures that could be found."[12] Later study of the witchcraft experience by psychiatrists in 1848 led to the conclusion that of "those who pretended that they had been bewitched by persons whom they accused, perhaps a few were some deranged in mind, but more frequently they were hysterical and extremely nervous and weak-minded women and children, or wicked imposters and perjured villains."[13]

The first half of the eighteenth century witnessed an exponential increase in immigration as a result of European conflicts, religious persecution, poverty, and the promise of a new start and riches. Immigrants came from many countries, including England, Scotland, Germany, Holland, Switzerland, Finland, Sweden, and Africa. By 1750, the population along the entire Atlantic coast had multiplied many times, with the northern areas retaining both their popularity and influence.

Those who immigrated to the colonies, however, did not represent a cross-section of European society. The noble, the wealthy, and the well educated remained; it was the "middling and the poor that immigrated . . . the aggrieved middle classes and the impoverished who found themselves, voluntarily or involuntarily, becoming Americans."[14] Many persons came under indenture contracts, and many were petty criminals.

The need for dependable labor was critical during these early years. Since land was cheap and readily available, many persons remained on jobs for short periods of time. This situation led to a heightened interest in slavery, indenture, and the public auction. At public auctions, which were common, "the head of the household could buy orphans or the children of the poor or incompetent, to be held until the age of 21, or he could buy indentured servants for a term of years, or he could buy African or Irish slaves—they and their progeny to be his property forever."[15] Deutsch, Richards, and other early writers in the field all attest that mentally retarded persons were commonly indentured or placed in bondage.[16]

Apprenticeship programs were also common in America, another tradition transferred from Europe. Unlike Europe, however, there was neither laws nor guilds to supervise these programs, and what should have been an instructional experience under the benevolent, paternal influence of a master frequently resulted in the apprentice simply becoming another laborer, working long hours and being treated poorly. Mentally retarded persons were often sought as apprentices.

In its youth, America was a restless country. Young people left home at the ages of 14 or 15 to strike out on their own. The family tradition of heavily populated Europe could not be sustained; it simply could not compete with the wide-open spaces that afforded an unparalleled opportunity for young people to better themselves. Self-sufficiency and strength, not dependency and weakness, were the order of the day and garnered respect—a most difficult, if not impossible, situation for many mentally retarded persons.

As indicated previously, the well-educated and wealthy of Europe did not migrate to America; consequently, self-sufficiency became an individual matter. With the absence of physicians, medical treatment was frequently prescribed by religious leaders, civil officers, barbers, and plantation owners. Persons with epilepsy continued to be treated with antiquated recipes inherited from Europe, including the moss from the skull of a dead man unburied who had died a violent death, blood letting, thirty drops of spirits, pulverized brains of a young man, and the traditional administration of hellebore. Dr. Jackson of Boston recommended that epilepsy be cured by starvation.[17] Astrological considerations also remained popular.

In general, mentally retarded persons received no special treatment. Early settlers from England based their social programs on the Elizabethan Poor Laws. This, in turn, introduced three lasting principles: local responsibility for the poor, the requirement that people provide support to their poor relatives, and the idea that towns were liable only for and to their own residents.[18] In 1647, for example, Rhode Island passed into law the very essentials of the Elizabethan Poor Laws of 1601. Towns were enjoined to "provide carefully for the reliefe of the poore, to maintayne the impotent . . . and [to] appoint an overseer for the same purpose. . . ."[19] Similarly, in 1661, the commissioners of Surrey County, Virginia, contracted with Robert House to board John Deanne, an "Iddiott," to provide him with food and clothing. In some cases, the town fathers reimbursed parents or relatives for maintaining the mentally retarded individual.

While in the beginning, such efforts may well have been charitable and noble in intent, mentally retarded persons soon were viewed as innately inferior and without rights and dignity and, in general, were treated with contempt rather than sympathy or compassion. Any problems arising from mental retardation were usually handled under laws intended for paupers: the "sick poor, old poor, able-bodied poor, infant poor, insane, and feeble-minded—all were grouped together under the same stigmatizing labels, paupers, and all were treated in very much the same manner."[20]

Though the first almshouse was built in Boston in 1660, the first workhouse in Philadelphia in 1771, and the first poorhouse in Philadelphia in 1773, such facilities were not used extensively for mentally retarded persons or others until the nineteenth century, when cities became cities instead of towns and villages. When mentally ill or mentally retarded persons could not participate in a work or apprentice program, and/or their heritage was one of poverty, they were either placed in jail if a public nuisance or "placed out." In 1727, Connecticut authorized the first house of corrections, which, clearly, was intended to serve mentally retarded persons: "all rogues, vagabonds and idle persons going about in town or country begging, or persons . . . feigning themselves to have knowledge in physiognomy, palmistry, or pretending that they can tell fortunes, or discover where lost or stolen goods may be found, common pipers, fiddlers, runaways . . . common drunkards, common nightwalkers, pilferers, wanton and lascivious persons . . . common railers or brawlers . . . as also persons under distraction and unfit to go at large, whose friends do not take care for their safe confinement."[21]

"Placing out" was a program by which the town would financially support a person or family to provide for a mentally retarded dependent. In 1756, for example, the General Assembly of Connecticut County charged:

There is now at Wallingford a strolling woman that has been sometime wandering from town to town, calling herself Susannah Roberts of Pennsylvania, who is so disordered in her reason and understanding that she passeth from place to place naked, without any regard for the laws and rules of decency. . . . The Assembly ordered the selectmen of Wallingford to clothe the insane woman and to commit her to the care of some discreet person that she may labour for her support . . . and agreed to pay the difference between her earning and the cost of her keep.[22]

Following the Revolutionary War, communities grew in size, and more efficient means of production significantly increased the importance of indenture and apprenticeship programs. Reliance was placed more on institutional than family support programs. The exception was Kentucky, which in 1793 passed an "act providing that where an idiot or lunatic was unable to support himself and had no estate, the court could grant him a sum of money to be paid out of the state treasury."[23] This eleemosynary effort, as will be discussed, was to come under considerable attack by Dorothea Dix and others during the nineteenth century.

The first hospital to establish a separate section for mentally ill and mentally retarded persons was not approved until 1751. The leadership for that program, like so many others during the colonial period, was provided by the ubiquitous Benjamin Franklin. In 1752, the Pennsylvania Hospital admitted its first mentally disturbed residents; by 1756, when the hospital was finished, the cellar had been set aside for the mentally affected. Unfortunately, both management and programs at the Philadelphia Hospital were closer to those of Bedlum than to Tuke's Retreat at York, ("John Cresson, blacksmith, against ye hospital, 1 pair of handcuffs, 1 legg locks, 1 large rings and 1 large staples, 5 links and 2 large rings and 2 swifells for legg chains").[24] The offensive practice of placing residents on public display for a slight fee from the townspeople was also introduced. Moral treatment and other reforms were not introduced until the advent of Dr. Benjamin Rush, whose accomplishments will be reviewed.

The first American hospital or institution intended solely for mentally ill and mentally retarded persons had its beginning in 1766 when the governor of the Virginia Colony, Francis Fauquier, made an earnest appeal that such a facility be developed with the idea that "a legal Confinement and proper Provision ought to be appointed for these miserable Objects, who can not help themselves."[25] Though the House of Burgesses at that time was concentrating on the freedom speeches of Patrick Henry and possible revolution, the governor persisted. It was not until 1769, however, that the legislature finally passed an act "To make Provision for the Support and Maintenance of Idiots, Lunatics, and other persons of unsound minds."[26] The hospital officially

opened on October 12, 1773. Interestingly, no
similar facility was to be built for another 50
years; the second mental hospital in the United
States opened in Lexington, Kentucky, in
1824. Though no record remains of the treatment protocol of the Williamsburg asylum,
knowledgeable historians indicate that it probably was quite similar to that of Philadelphia
Hospital. As will be discussed, reforms were
initiated in the latter facility by Benjamin
Rush.

BENJAMIN RUSH

"Taut, elegant, long-white-hair flowing,"
Benjamin Rush (1745–1813) was one of the
great men of the new republic, and in many
ways his achievements were equal to those of
Washington, Jefferson, John Adams, and
Franklin. A co-signer of the Declaration of
Independence, Rush had been instrumental in
encouraging Thomas Paine to write *Common
Sense*. During the Revolutionary War, he
served for several years as the physician gener-
al of the Medical Department of the Army. His
text *Directions for Preserving the Health of the
Soldiers* became a classic in military medicine.
It was used up to and during the Civil War, and
was republished as late as 1908 in the journal
Military Surgery.

After the Revolutionary War, Rush became
an advocate of many causes and was a physician to the poor, for whom he also founded the
first free dispensary in American history. He
served as president of the Society for the Abolition of Slavery and was an indefatigable champion of free public education for the poor and
higher education for women. He is also recognized as the founder of American psychiatry.

Rush's dedication to medicine and most
significant contributions to the field were not
realized until his later years. His foremost
interest was politics, and he chose medicine as
a career only through the process of elimination
and recommendation. Selecting an appropriate
professional field to pursue was difficult. Having no interest in business or family connec-
tions to facilitate a future in it, he was basically
left with one of three typical choices of the day:

Benjamin Rush.

the church, law, or medicine. Owing to his
skills as an orator, Rush initially believed he
should enter the school of law, the "babbla-
tive" art. He was soon convinced by an associate to abandon this idea, however, since the
practice of law was held in ill repute. The
Fundamental Constitutions of Carolina, for
example, specifically called it a "base and vile
thing to plead for money or reward."[27] Rush
finally entered the field of medicine because of
its social and financial status. Though he was
successful and creative, prior to 1799 his commitment "was more practical than passionate."[28] He is credited with being the first
physician to relate smoking to cancer and tried
desperately to introduce golf to the United
States in the belief that the fresh air, exercise,
and general physical activity would tend to
prolong a person's life and reduce many of the
physical discomforts thereby associated. In
this sense, he was probably the world's first
advocate for "wellness" programs.

It was not until his political fortunes changed
as a result of his compulsive talking, puritanical attitudes, and humorless disposition, that

Rush actively pursued medicine, especially the area of mental health. In 1787, he had assumed responsibility as physician and teacher at the Pennsylvania Hospital and the University of Pennsylvania. He supervised the hospital section devoted to mentally ill and mentally retarded residents, the conditions of which were recorded by Manasseh Cutler:

> From the men's ward Rush walked down to the basement, where the lunatics were housed in cells. "These cells are about ten feet square, made as strong as a prison," Manasseh Cutler wrote after Rush had shown them to him in 1787. He added: "On the back part is a long entry, from which a door opens into each of them; in each door is a hole, large enough to give them food, etc., which is closed with a little door secured with strong bolts. On the opposite side is a window, and large iron gates within to prevent their breaking the glass. They can be darkened at pleasure. Here were both men and women, between twenty and thirty in number. Some of them have beds; most of them clean straw. Some of them were extremely fierce and raving, nearly or quite naked; some singing and dancing; some in despair, some were dumb and would not open their mouths; others incessantly talking. It was curious indeed to see in what different strains their distraction raged. This would have been a melancholy scene indeed, had it not been that there was every possible relief afforded them in the power of man. Everything about them, notwithstanding the labor and trouble it must have required, was neat and clean.[29]

Rush's treatment approaches were a curious mixture of enlightenment and tradition. On the one hand, "he protested against the cold cells and lack of occupation for patients. He wanted them to be taught to spin, or turn a wheel to grind corn, or dig in the garden, and he fought for new, separate quarters to house them in."[30] His sympathetic approach to mentally ill people was understandable, since both his brother and his favorite son were severely disturbed and spent most of their lives in a mental hospital. On the other hand, if a resident was upset or aggressive, Rush did not hesitate to order blood-letting and/or the use of various mechan-

The tranquilizer chair.

ical contraptions to cool their spirits. One of his inventions, the "gyrator," was a device he adapted from an earlier design by England's Dr. Cox.* The idea behind this machine, which spun at a terrific rate, was that persons suffering from "torpid madness" would be exhilarated—and they were!

Another of Rush's inventions was the tranquilizer chair. An upset or hyperactive resident, mentally ill or mentally retarded, would sit in this chair and be strapped hand, foot, and head, in order to reduce muscular action and motor activity.

In spite of these unusual modalities of treatment, Rush was successful in promoting a humane concept of programming for mentally ill and mentally retarded patients. This was not an easy task in the days of untrained nurses and

*Cox had previously designed a four-chair gyrator which turned at more than 100 revolutions per minute. Instead of curing his mentally ill patients, they became violently ill; therefore, he gave the gyrator to the "idiots" for recreational purposes. According to Burdett in 1891, they found it to be great fun.[31]

illiterate attendants. He introduced moral treatment, required clean rooms, and insisted that residents be provided warm water for bathing, an unheard of provision in his day.

An observant and great recorder of individual cases, he was able to produce his last and greatest work, *Medical Inquiries and Observations Upon the Diseases of the Mind,* in 1812. Though his discussion of mental illness contained many innovative concepts, his views on mental retardation (labeled as "fatuity") were relatively superficial even for the times. Fatuity was defined as an affection of the mind that "consists in a total absence of understanding and memory. It has different grades, from the lowest degree of manalgia, down to that which discovers itself in the vacuity of the eye and countenance, in silence and garrulity, slobbering, lolling of the tongue, ludicrous gestures of the head and limbs."[32] Interestingly, however, he was quick to point out that the characteristics of the mentally retarded or the fatuitous varied considerably. For example, one could find among this population very active passions or the total absence of them. They were either innocent or extremely vicious. The passions that most commonly appeared in idiots were anger, fear, and love. They sometimes felt "an inordinate degree of sexual appetite and [were] generally great feeders."[33] Like Pinel, Rush viewed fatuity as a reduction in intellectual functioning regardless of cause or age of onset. Surprisingly, he did not advocate training or any other form of behavioral or medical treatment for mentally retarded persons. Nevertheless, Rush's contribution was great, because he brought the condition of mental retardation to the attention of the American medical community at a relatively early date.

A year after publishing his *Medical Inquiries,* Rush died. In a letter to John Adams, Jefferson said of him, "Another of our friends of seventy-six is gone my dear Sir. Another of the co-signers of the Independence of our country. And a better man than Rush could not have left us, more benevolent, more learned, or finer genius, no more honest."[34] Rush, however, described himself in more moderate terms . . . obstinate and occasionally "hasty, and tinder like."

THE NEW NATION: 1800–1849

The dawn of the nineteenth century saw the country still mourning the death of George Washington on December 14, 1799. John Adams was completing his final year as president, and by the end of the year, Thomas Jefferson would be elected the third president of the United States. Like Europe, nineteenth century America was the scene of progress, reform, and tragedy.

The early 1800s saw the rapid expansion of the cotton industry in the northeastern section of the country. Many women and children were employed in this industry which represented "light work." Children earned 33 to 67 cents a week. Boston, like other northeastern cities, saw the rise of numerous, similar factories that relied heavily on the labor of women and children. Some industries adopted the "Waltham System," which hired unmarried women, paid them a respectable wage ($2–$3 per week), and provided a supervised living arrangement free of charge.

All worked long hours. Even 10-year-old children tended their looms from 4:15 A.M. to 7:45 P.M. Though by today's standards such practices would be considered extremely harsh, they were not so viewed in their day: "A society accustomed to seeing the children of even fairly well-to-do farmers put to work full-time in the field was not shocked by the sight of children working all day in mills."[35*]

By 1850, the United States led the world in the production of those items and goods requiring the use of precision instruments, and industry was well on the way to mass production methods. American clocks, pistols, rifles, and

---

*The long work-week was not simply a working condition of the nineteenth century. The 12-hour work day, and the 7-day work week did not officially end in the steel industry until 1923.[37]

locks were outstanding. A continual stream of new inventions, such as the screw-making machine, the friction match, the lead pencil, interchangeable parts, and the Bessemer technique for making steel, all led to industrial units becoming larger, more specialized, and more mechanized. While productivity increased, the quality of craftsmanship, job variety, and pride in manual labor suffered grievously.

Both working and social conditions changed dramatically during the two decades preceding the Civil War. The tremendous influx of immigrants—500,000 during the 1840s and 1.5 million during the 1850s—created a large pool of unskilled laborers willing to work for very low wages. Women's wages, for example, dropped from $3.00 per week to 12 cents.[36]

Education during the nineteenth century made gains, but very slowly. Until the 1830s and 1840s, education remained primarily in the hands of the church and private individuals.

The nineteenth century also saw the Supreme Court become a genuine power and authority in the affairs of the country. Under the leadership of John Marshall, who possessed little legal training and no judicial experience, the Supreme Court began to function in a highly competent, assertive manner, willing to overturn legislative decisions in conflict with constitutional provisions.

The first recognized residential service intended specifically for mentally retarded persons in the United States was initiated in 1818. At that time and for several years, the American Asylum for the Deaf and Dumb in Hartford, Connecticut, made an effort to instruct idiot children. Though the measure of success was rather limited, the youngsters' physical condition improved, and a few of those who were mute were taught to converse in sign language. This program, however, was the exception; and after 1820, all but the smallest of communities placed a greater reliance on the almshouse and its derivatives, as well as the mental hospital. The results were less than positive.

America was developing a social conscience, however. An increasing number of persons began to react against many social policies and practices, including those affecting mentally retarded individuals: "Hardly any institution in American life escaped the scrutiny of some group determined to change it. There were campaigns for the abolition of slavery, for penal reform, for better care of the insane, for temperance, for communal living, for industrial socialism, and for many other schemes to improve the status quo."[38]

MID-CENTURY REFORM AND REFORMISTS

Among the major leaders who contributed significantly to mentally retarded persons were Samuel Gridley Howe, Charles Sumner, Horace Mann, and Dorothea Dix. While each pursued his or her individual area of interest, at times they collaborated. First, let us consider their concerns.

Many of the traditional ways of resolving "problems" of poor and mentally affected people that had been developed during the preceding two centuries were reconfirmed during the early years of the nineteenth. Mentally retarded persons of wealth who were attended at home, regardless of training or social visibility, and those who were lovingly accepted within a family less financially fortunate had at least some reasonable chance for an enjoyable life. When these conditions did not exist, however, the mentally retarded person's future was indeed grim. As indicated previously, most were treated under poor laws—laws "meant to deter, to make poverty unpalatable, to make relief come bitter and dear."[39]

Prior to the 1820s, the major emphasis of state and local governments was to provide "outdoor relief" (i.e., financial support to parents or relatives to retain the individual in the home) or auctioning (bidding out) a person to another individual to provide care and maintenance. Supporting the individual in his home was extensively practiced in Kentucky. In some instances, families no doubt were very concerned about their mentally retarded dependents and genuinely needed financial support, such as the older couple reported by Deutsch who requested financial help to enable them to continue to provide for their four retarded adult offspring, ages 26 to 30.[40] Dorothea Dix and other reformers, however, objected to this practice based on their experiences. For example, Dix reported:

> In Kentucky I found one epileptic girl subject to the most brutal treatment, and many insane in perpetual confinement. Of the *idiots* alone, supported by the State at a cost of $17,500.62, in indigent private families, and of which class there were in 1845 four hundred and fifty, many were exposed to the severest treatment and heavy blows from day to day, and from year to year. In a dreary block-house was confined for many years a man whose insanity took the form of mania. Often the most furious paroxysms prevented rest for several days and nights in succession. No alleviation reached this unhappy being; without clothes, without fire, without care or kindness, his existence was protracted amidst every horror incident to such circumstances. *Chains in common use.*[41]

Bidding out and contracting were at best inhumane solutions to human problems. In essence, the pauper and the mentally retarded person were sold to someone who would cheaply provide their care and maintenance. In 1845, Emaley Wiley bought all the paupers of Fulton County, Illinois, for $594.[42] In the Indiana territory, poor, mentally retarded, and mentally ill persons were bid out annually on the first of May. Such practices led to exploitation and very low standards of care. Fields summarized these practices as "offering a reward to the avarice and inhumanity of the man who would consent to neglect them more flagrantly and to inflict upon them a worse abuse than any other man in town could be induced to practice. It was useless to resolve that only the bids of good men should be taken, and that overseers should visit them from time to time, and that bonds should be required from the successful bidders for their proper treatment. Then as now, a bad man was often a good politician. . . ."[43]

The long-standing practice of "warning out" continued to be used, that is, informing a newcomer that the town would not be responsible for his misfortunes, then or in the future. Communities did not want to add to their financial obligations any unwarranted paupers or persons in need. "Passing on" also became popular; a town representative would load mentally retarded and mentally ill people into a cart, transport them to another town, and leave them there. That town, in turn, would reject these social outcasts and repeat the process. Consequently, some mentally retarded and mentally ill persons were perpetually shuffled from one community to another.

During the 1820s, many states and local governments determined that bidding out, contracting, and even passing on were too expensive and decided to build almhouses, poorhouses, and county homes instead. These facilities rapidly became filled with the sick, insane, and mentally retarded, as evidenced by a report to the Massachusetts legislature after 10 years' experience with the Boston House of Industry built in 1823:

> When this establishment was commenced, it was intended for the reception and employment of the able-bodied poor, who should claim the charity of this city; hence it was called the House of Industry. . . . Instead of being a House of Industry, the institution has become at once, a general Infirmary—an Asylum for the insane, and refuge for the deserted and most destitute children of the city. So great is the proportion of the aged and infirm, of the sick insane, idiots and helpless children in it, that nearly all the effective labor of the females, and much of that of the males, is required for the care of those who cannot take care of themselves.[44]

The creation of these alternative care facilities did not improve the quality of life for most mentally retarded and other affected persons. The miserable care provided in almshouses and jails and through the various bidding-out practices was the focal point of Dorothea Dix's campaign. In her report to the Massachusetts legislature, she outlined the deplorable conditions in cryptic terms:

> *Medford:* One idiotic chained, and one in a close stall for 17 years.
> *Bridgewater:* Three idiots; never removed from one room.
> *Cohasset:* One idiot, one insane; most miserable conditions.
> *Plympton:* One insane, three idiots; conditions wretched.
> *Ipswich* (jail): Immediately adjacent to this stall was one occupied by a *simple* girl, who was "put there to be out of harm's way."[45]

In other reports, she provided more detailed descriptions:

> My second visit to the alms-house, produced new distrusts of the management of the lunatic department, and confirmed first opinions. I found in the men's ward, a poor man in a "tranquilizing chair," whose countenance wore an expression of agonized suffering I can never forget. His limbs were tightly bound, his legs, body, arms, shoulders, all were closely confined, *and his head also*. Feeble efforts to move were broken down by this inexorable machine. Upon his head, sustained by the apparatus, which confined the movements of the neck, was a quantity of broken ice. This, as it gradually melted, flowed over his person, which however, was in some degree protected from the wet by a stiff cape, either of canvass or leather. It was a very hot day, but he was deadly cold, and oh, how suffering! To suffer would have been his lot, perhaps, under any circumstances; but this treatment, "employed *to keep him still,*" was a fearful aggravation of inconceivable misery. I asked how long he had been under this restraint. "Four days!" What, day and night? "No, at night we take him off and strap him upon the bed." How long will you keep him so? "Till he is quiet." How long have you ever kept the patients in this condition? "Nine days, I believe, is the longest." . . . Why the alms-house alone, of the numberous public charities of Philadelphia, should show a condition so adverse to the objects it proposes to accomplish, is a problem I cannot resolve.[46]

Dix was not alone in expressing indignation over the conditions of these homes. A report to the New York legislature in 1838 was equally terse—one chamber had 10 beds occupied by 19 persons of all ages and conditions, namely, "two married men and their wives, and one aged colored woman, two male idiots, one very old man, and eleven children."[47] In 1841, following his visit to a physically attractive lunatic asylum still in the process of being built, Charles Dickens wrote:

> everything had a lounging, listless, madhouse air, which was very painful. The moping idiot, cowering down with long dishevelled hair; the gibbering maniac, with his hideous laugh and pointed finger; the vacant eye, the fierce wild face, the gloomy picking of the hands and lips, and munching of the nails: there they were all, without disguise, in naked ugliness and horror. In the dining-room, a bare, dull, dreary place, with nothing for the eye to rest on but the empty walls,

a woman was locked up alone. She was bent, they told me, on committing suicide. If anything could have strengthened her in her resolution, it would certainly have been the insupportable monotony of such an existence.[48]

Though there are few records of that time to indicate how mentally retarded persons in the community were treated, Samuel Gridley Howe offers at least a glimpse in his 1847 report following his travels around Massachusetts:

> In some towns, we found the idiots, who were under the charge of kind-hearted, but ignorant persons, to be entirely idle, given over to disgusting and degrading habits, and presenting the sad and demoralizing spectacle of men, made in God's image, whom neither their own reason, nor the reason of others, lifted up above the level of the brutes.
>
> In other towns, idiots, who, to all appearance, had no more capacity than those just mentioned, were under the charge of more intelligent persons, and they presented a different spectacle—they were healthy, cleanly and industrious.
>
> We found some, of a very low grade of intellect, at work in the fields, under the direction of attendants; and they seemed not only to be free from depraving habits, but to be happy and useful.[49]

From these descriptions, it is quite obvious that those concerned with reforming programs for mentally retarded persons were not without justification. As regards mentally retarded persons, Howe himself was in the forefront.

Samuel Gridley Howe

Probably no person in the history of the United States was more concerned about people in need, more effective in realizing appropriate programs for them, or more personally sacrificing than Samuel Gridley Howe (1801–1876). As Edward Everett Hale observed after Howe's death, "He found idiots chattering, taunted, and ridiculed by each village fool, and he left them cheerful and happy. He found the insane shut up in their wretched cells, miserable, starving, cold, and dying, and he left them happy, hopeful, and brave. He found the blind sitting in darkness, and he left them glad in the sunshine in the love of God."[50]

Though Howe's father was a wealthy rope-

Samuel Gridley Howe.

maker, his politics and attitudes were democratic. Samuel acquired the positive thinking of
his father, which at times was to prove a great
inconvenience. While attending Brown
School, a private facility primarily for children
of wealthy merchants, his liberal attitudes created such consternation among his fellow students that they threw him down the stairs. As a
student, he was frequently in difficulty and on
at least one occasion was suspended for mischief, which, in this case, involved leaving the
president's horse on the fourth floor of the
school.

A handsome young man, Howe decided to
pursue the field of medicine and entered the
Harvard Medical School in 1821. At that time,
the Harvard Medical School included 60 students, three professors, two lecturers, and one
librarian. Like his fellow students, Howe on
occasion resorted to grave robbing in order to
obtain a cadaver.

Upon completion of his degree in 1824, the
newly licensed physician went to Greece to
assist the country in their revolt against four
generations of Turkish domination. For the
next 6 years, he was, in one way or the other, to
participate in this cause. For 4 years, he was
intensely active in Greece, wrote a popular

book on the history of the war, and became a
celebrated hero. In 1828, he came home to
raise funds for the Greek cause and became
well known through his public speaking. He
again returned to Greece and attempted to
establish a series of public work projects,
schools, a hospital, and a colony for displaced
refugees, a project which proved only partially
successful. In 1830, he left Greece and traveled
throughout Europe.

In 1831, he returned to Boston, uncertain as
to his future but knowing that he did not want to
go into private practice. His entering the field
of the blind was initiated by accident when a
college friend, John D. Fischer, asked him to
help finalize plans for an asylum for blind
persons and become its first director. Howe
responded positively and decided to tour Europe visiting various schools for the blind.
While so engaged, he was requested to assist in
distributing relief funds for Polish refugees
who had fled to Prussia. When Howe complained bitterly about their treatment, he was
put in solitary confinement. After 5 weeks, he
was released from prison, finished his tour, and
returned to the United States in 1832 to begin
his life's work.

While the Massachusetts legislature agreed
to fund the care and education of 30 blind
students, it provided no building. Fortunately,
however, Howe's father agreed to let him use
his home for this purpose. Howe then searched
throughout Massachusetts for blind children
and started his efforts with two young sisters,
Abby and Sophia Carter, successfully using
Haüy's embossed materials technique. The
number of blind students served in the Howe
home soon became too many, and Colonel
Thomas Perkins offered his estate and gardens
for the school on the condition that $50,000
could be raised toward its support. Money was
raised, and Howe transferred the program to
what would be known as the Perkins Institute
and Massachusetts School for the Blind. Here
he was to train his most famous student, Laura
Bridgeman, a blind deaf-mute. Being extremely gifted, Laura learned to communicate
effectively with those around her.

Elizabeth Peabody's note concerning Howe

in 1833 provides an interesting commentary on the man and his character:

> When we first became acquainted with Mr. Mann, he took Mary (afterwards Mrs. Mann) and me to a small house in Hollis Street [Miss Peabody's memory fails her here; it was in Pleasant Street] where, in the simplest surroundings, we found Dr. Howe, with a half-dozen first pupils he had picked up in the highways and byways. He had then been about six months at work, and had invented and laboriously executed some books with raised letters, to teach them to read, some geographical maps, and the geometrical diagrams necessary for instruction in mathematics. He had gummed twine, I think, upon cardboards, an enormous labour, to form the letters of the alphabet. I shall not, in all time, forget the impression made upon me by seeing the hero of the Greek Revolution, who had narrowly missed being that of the Polish Revolution also; to see this hero, I say, wholly absorbed, and applying all the energies of his genius to this apparently humble work, and doing it as Christ did, without money and without price.[51]

Like many of his contemporaries (e.g., Walt Whitman, Horace Greeley, and Horace Mann), Samuel Howe was extremely influenced by phrenology. As Julia Ward Howe later recalled, her husband made an applicant for domestic service in his household remove her bonnet so that he could judge her suitability.*[52]

Again, it is difficult today to realize the tremendous impact that phrenology had on the treatment of not only developmentally disabled persons but also those considered mentally ill. Its influence upon Howe took two forms. First, phrenology emphasized that through training, individual faculties could be strengthened. This was an important consideration when working with blind, deaf, and mentally retarded persons.

Second, the Scottish philosopher, George Combe, had expanded Gall's original thinking about phrenology into a broad social policy. His philosophy, best described in the *Constitution of Man* (1851), was based on the concept that natural laws govern man's behavior and are vital to his development, physically, intellectually, and morally. Education was emphasized, as was the need for man to have time and opportunity to develop his potential. Combe was bitterly opposed to long working hours because they were so physically fatiguing that man could not develop his intellectual and spiritual nature. It was a very positive philosophy, one which made it incumbent upon the individual to respond to his potentialities and society to structure itself in such a manner as to enable the daily exercise of each person's inherent nature and faculties. In many respects, phrenology as a series of separate faculties was almost incidental to Combe's social theory.

In 1839, Howe accepted into the school a blind idiot, whom he successfully trained. A little later, he accepted two more such affected youngsters. As the result of his positive experiences with these youngsters plus a genuine concern for mentally retarded people, he began to urge that a special facility be established for their training. Some of Howe's concern may well have reflected rejection of the mentally retarded students by other blind residents. Even Laura Bridgeman complained, "I should be so happy to be much more pleasantly established with the whole house if they could prescribe the Idiots not to have our rooms."[53]

Inspired by Howe, Judge Horatio Boyington moved the House of Representatives in 1846 to appoint a committee to determine the extent of the problem and what future directions the State should take in meeting the needs of mentally retarded persons. A three-man committee was appointed—Judge Boyington, Dr. Howe, and Gilman Kimball. The committee visited over 60 cities within the Commonwealth of Massachusetts and personally examined 574 individuals considered mentally retarded. On February 26, 1848, the commissioners submitted their report; it read, in part:

> The benefits to be derived from the establishment of a school for this class of persons, upon humane

---

*In 1843, Samuel Howe married Julia Ward, 20 years his junior. It was a case of an older, demanding nineteenth century man marrying a younger, highly creative and gifted twentieth century woman. The union brought moments of anguish to both.

and scientific principles would be very great. Not only would all the idiots who should be received into it be improved in their bodily and mental condition, but all the others in the State and the country would be indirectly benefitted. The school, if conducted by persons of skill and ability, would be a model for others. Valuable information would be disseminated through the country; it would be demonstrated that no idiot need be confined or restrained by force; that the young can be trained for industry, order, and self-respect; that they can be redeemed from odious and filthy habits, and there is not one of any age who may not be made more of a man and less of a brute by patience and kindness directed by energy and skill.[54]

As a result of this cogent appeal, the legislature, though skeptical about the idea of educating mentally retarded people, nevertheless consented to provide $2,500 for a 3-year experimental school for 10 idiot children. On October 1, 1848, a wing of the Perkins school was opened to provide for this experimental school.

After a year's trial, Howe reported that the "result thus far seems to be most gratifying and encouraging. . . . They [the pupils] have improved in personal appearance and habits, in general health, in vigour, and in activity of the body. Almost all of them have improved in the understanding and the use of speech. But what is most important, they have *made a start forward*. They have begun to give their attention to things; to observe qualities, and to exercise thought. The mental machinery has been put in operation, and it will go on more easily and more rapidly in future. . . ."[55] After two years, he observed:

A great change has come over them. They have improved in health, strength, and activity of body. They are cleanly and decent in their habits. They dress themselves, and for the most part sit at table and feed themselves. They are gentle, docile, and obedient. They can be governed without a blow or an unkind word. *They begin to use speech*, and take great delight in repeating the words of simple sentences which they have mastered. They have learned their letters, and some of them, *who were speechless as brutes*, can read easy sentences and short stories. They are gentle and affectionate with each other; and the school and the household are orderly, quiet, and well regulated, in all respects.[56]

It should be noted that one of the persistent historical myths about Howe and other early American institutional leaders is that they intended to "cure" mental retardation; yet, there is no historical evidence to support that contention. In fact, Howe talked of improvement only, not cure. In his initial report of 1846, *The Condition and Capabilities of Idiots in Massachusetts,* he clearly stated: "Confining our attention to the cases of real idiots . . . it is found that 188 are under 25 years of age. Of these, 172 seem capable of improvement; they present proper cases for attempts at instruction, and the formation of regular, industrious, and cleanly habits. Only 16 seem incapable of improvement. Of those over 25 years of age, there are 73 who seem capable of little or no improvement in mental condition."[57]

In 1851, the Joint Committee on Public Charitable Institutions visited the school and found the results very promising. They observed, "The experiment seems to have succeeded entirely. The capacity of this unfortunate class for improvements seems to be proved beyond question."[58] As a result, Howe's beginning efforts were, in 1855, realized in the establishments in south Boston of the Massachusetts School for Idiots and Feeble-Minded Youth.

In later life, Howe continued to work on behalf of blind and mentally retarded persons. In 1867, he again went to Greece, to help with the short-lived Cretan revolt. Nine years later, an aging and ailing Howe suffered a fatal stroke while on his daily walk to the Perkins school.

Charles Sumner and Horace Mann

Many of Howe's efforts to improve conditions for the disabled and disadvantaged received considerable support from both Charles Sumner and Horace Mann. Quite often they collaborated.

Charles Sumner (1811–1874) played an important role in assisting in the establishment and development of the first publicly sponsored residential program for mentally retarded persons. This tall (6'4") U.S. senator had long been an advocate of social reform. Many years before the Civil War, he vigorously opposed the exclusion of black children from school and condemned laws prohibiting intermarriage between blacks and whites. Before entering the Senate in 1851, he had also spoken against the Mexican War Bill of 1835.

Though a trained lawyer, he was not a legislator in the sense of drafting and proposing new bills. Rather, he was the outspoken critic of current social practices, playing "the role of an ancient Hebrew prophet, engendering moral enthusiasm, inspiring courage and hope, and assailing injustice."[59] He also served as Howe's "alter ego."

Charles Sumner's brother George also played a key role. In 1847, he visited Seguin's school at the Bicêtre and wrote a glowing report of the program and the students' progress. His correspondence was quoted frequently by Howe in promoting the development of residential services.

Horace Mann (1796–1859), a brilliant scholar, lawyer, and educator, served in the Massachusetts legislature from 1827 to 1837. As noted previously, while president of the Senate, he signed the epic-making mandatory education bill that became law on April 30, 1837. He subsequently served as secretary of the State Board of Education, a position he held for 12 years. Having given up a promising law practice and a promising political future, Horace Mann devoted his energies to the status and quality of free schools, normal school training of teachers, and editing the first state education journal. He also was intensely concerned with the well-being of the mentally ill and mentally retarded population and effectively supported Howe on a number of occasions. He was a living example of his own dictum delivered in his last commencement address as president of Antioch College, Ohio: "Be ashamed to die until you have won some victory for humanity."

Julia Ward Howe's rhyme concerning her husbands activities nicely recapitulates the common bond of these three men:

Rero, rero, riddlety rad;
This morning my baby caught sight of her Dad.
Quoth she, "O Daddy, where have you been?"

"With Mann and Sumner, a-putting down sin!"[60]

In addition to these reformers, the Association of Medical Superintendents of American Institutions for the Insane also supported the idea that separate facilities should be established for mentally retarded persons. In 1848, the association reported that it had repeatedly "called attention of our readers to the deplorable and neglected condition of the Idiotic and Imbecile, and the urgent necessity of establishing asylums and schools for their comfort and improvement."[61]

Dorothea Lynde Dix

Dorothea Lynde Dix (1802–1877) was a dynamic force in promoting better environments and programs for many of the less fortunate citizens of the United States. At 12 years of age, she ran away from an unhappy home situation to spend her growing years with her Boston grandfater, Dr. Elijah Dix, who instilled in her a strong sense of public spirit and a high level of energy. Her own father has been described as a "feeble character and a religious fanatic."[62]

Dix's youthful years were devoted to training children, including those of the Reverend William Channing family, with whom she traveled to the West Indies. Upon returning to the United States, she wrote a number of books for children and established a school. In 1838, "nervous, overstrained, and delicate with insipient lung trouble," she closed her school.[63] Several years later, she undertook a Sunday school program in the East Cambridge (Massachusetts) House of Correction. Here she found the conditions deplorable, with insane women being kept in an unheated room. As a result, she spent the next 2 years quietly visiting jails, almshouses, and various houses of correction throughout Massachusetts recording lengthy lists of observations and grievances in her ever-handy notebook.

This remarkable, wily, and certainly indefatigable woman visited many jails, almshouses, poor houses, and mental hospitals. In 1850, she traveled over 10,000 miles. Her crusade led her to address many legislative

Dorothea Lynde Dix.

bodies, including those of Massachusetts (1843), New York (1844), New Jersey (1845), Pennsylvania (1845), Kentucky (1846), Tennessee (1847), North Carolina (1848), Mississippi (1850), and Maryland (1852).

In 1848, she addressed the 30th Congress of the United States, making a passionate plea for it to set aside 5 million acres of land in order to provide proper construction and farming sites to accommodate the "wards of the Nation," that is, mentally ill, epileptic, and mentally retarded persons, into the then 30 states. Though this bill passed both houses of Congress, it was vetoed by President Pierce in 1845 because "if Congress had power to make provision for the indigent insane *without the limits of this district* [District of Columbia], it has the same power to provide for the indigent who are not insane, and thus the transfer to the Federal Government the charge *of all the poor in the states.*"[64]

Her appeal to the Massachusetts legislature was perhaps most significant, since it was her first attempt to call upon a state to assume responsibility for its mentally ill and mentally retarded residents:

> I shall be obliged to speak with a great plainness, and to reveal many things revolting to the taste, and from which my woman's nature shrinks with peculiar sensitiveness. But the truth is the highest consideration. *I tell what I have seen*—painful and shocking as the details often are—that from them you may feel more deeply the imperative obligation which lies upon you to prevent the possibility of a repetition of continuance of such outrages upon humanity. If I inflict pain upon you, and move you to horror, it is to acquaint you with sufferings which you have the power to alleviate, and make you hasten to the relief of the victims of legalized barbarity.[65]

In this appeal and in other matters, Dix solicited the help of Samuel Howe, recently elected to the state legislature. Though he was initially reluctant to join with Dix because she was a maiden lady who had recently been quite ill, after examining her notes and visiting the Cambridge Hospital, he supported her effort entirely. In those days it was inconceivable that any woman would address a governmental body; thus, Dix's original speech was presented by Samuel Gridley Howe and strongly supported by George Sumner, who wrote: "The correctness with which Miss Dix has described the four almshouses I have seen leads me to place entire confidence in her report."[66] In addition, Howe wrote several exposés for the Boston press based on her statements and documents.

Dorothea Dix's basic approach, with ample documentation and vignettes of horror, was that the states, as opposed to county and local jurisdictions, had a primary responsibility for establishing mental hospitals. She strongly advocated that mental hospitals serve mentally ill, epileptic, and mentally retarded people. She did not, however, request separate facilities for mentally retarded persons; nor did she advocate their education and return to the community. She viewed mental retardation primarily as a consequence of depravity and intemperate parents: "The increased number of idiots during seventeen years seems to have exceeded the proportion usually computed, allowing for the increase of population. I ascribe this in part, and in large part, to the intemperance of parents. The fact that habits of intoxication induces partial or entire imbecility in children, in frequent instances, is too well established to require proof here."[67]

Some of her ideas would not hold favor today. She violently disagreed with mentally ill or retarded persons being retained in their homes or substitute settings. For example, she stated the "indiscriminate association of idiots and families with other children, has often been observed to have injurious influences: on the contrary, these unfortunates are more carefully and kindly looked after by parents than by strangers. But I think there can arise no question as to the greater fitness of gathering these often helpless creatures into an Asylum in which they may be surrounded with every needed care."[68]

Like so many others of her day, she placed great emphasis on the negative aspects of immigration: "There is less insanity in the southern, than in the northern states, proportional to the inhabitants of each; for this disparity several causes may be assigned: there is, in the former, comparatively but a small influx of foreigners, while they throng every district of the latter."[69]

This fascinating woman had an immeasurable impact in arousing states to recognize and accept their responsibility for mentally affected persons. She was a curious mixture of quietness and dignity; yet, when necessary, she could approach her audience with great passion and missionary zeal:

> In the province of God, I am the voice of the maniac whose piercing cries from the dreary dungeons of your jails penetrate not your Halls of Legislation. I am the Hope of the poor crazed beings who pine in the cells, and stalls, and cages, and waste rooms of your poor houses. I am the Revelation of hundreds of wailing, suffering creatures, hidden in your private dwellings and in pens

and cabins—shut off, cut off from all healing influences, from all mind-restoring cares.[70]

By the advent of the Civil War, the once "shy, uncertain recluse" had become poised, confident, and aggressive. She was, in the words of one admirer, a "moral autocrat," while, in the words of another, "she was a kind old soul, but very queer and arbitrary."[71] While such characteristics were well suited to a militant advocate, they were ill suited to her role as Superintendent of Women Nurses during the war between the states. Her inability to relate effectively with others in the service and her prudishness—no attractive women between 18 and 30 years of age could serve as nurses during the war—resulted in a most unsatisfactory experience for all concerned. In her own perceptive words, her Civil War experiences were "not the work I would have my life judged by."[72]

Dorothea Dix died quietly in her bed on July 17, 1877, and was eulogized by Dr. Charles H. Nichols in the following words: "Thus has died and been laid to rest, in the most quiet and unostentatious way, the most useful and distinguished woman America has yet produced."[73]

The efforts of Dorothea Dix, Samuel Gridley Howe, and other reformers signaled a new day in programming for mentally retarded persons, especially those emerging from economically disadvantaged circumstances—the day of the specialized institution. This marked a significant departure from the personalized commitment of our Puritan forefathers. Over the years, many small parochial communities became large heterogeneous population centers in which city fathers lost a sense of individuality as costs rose and immigrants appeared. Governments, state and local, relied more and more on the external, institutional setting.

Chapter

5

STRIFE, RECONSTRUCTION, AND THE GILDED AGE

(1850–1899)

M ID-CENTURY AMERICA saw a country divided followed by a bloody Civil War (1861–1864), a very troubled period of reconstruction, and the Gilded Age—the age of Carnegie, Vanderbilt, Gould, Drew, Fisk, Rockefeller, and Morgan. The latters' accumulation of power and wealth was frequently accompanied by depressing circumstances for those who produced the wealth. Public spirit among these magnates varied significantly. Carnegie declared that the concentration of wealth was necessary, but that those with money must use it "in a manner which is best calculated to produce the most beneficial results for the community. The rich man was merely a trustee for his poor brethren, to bring to their services superior wisdom, experience, and ability to administer."[1] While many argued with Carnegie's methods during his lifetime, his ultimate philanthropy has touched nearly every American. His attitude was in marked contrast with that of Vanderbilt, whose philosophy was expressed quite simply: "The public be damned."[2] And it often was!

The 1870s and 1880s were peak periods of immigration—with 2.5 million and 5.0 million immigrants per decade, respectively—and many settled in large cities, cities unable to accommodate them humanely. The foreign-born population of Chicago in 1890 almost equaled its total population in 1880, and four out of five residents in New York City were either foreign-born or children of immigrants.[3] The results often were drastic. Many a dream was shattered and many an immigrant was "indigent and helpless, often left to starve among strangers."[4]

The nation's boundaries were extended from sea to sea through purchases, war, and the exploitation of native Americans. The country was opened via the construction of roads and canals, the advent of power-generated ships, and the completion of a transcontinental railroad.

Sectional differences that existed prior to and following the Civil War, combined with problems of immigration, fear, and greed, all contributed to a growing, vicious cycle of prejudice and hostility. "Black men, red men, or white; aboriginal inhabitants or recent arrival; savage, husbandman, or city worker—anyone who blocked the ambitions of his more powerful fellows received short shrift in post–Civil War America."[5]

Education during the latter half of the nineteenth century made continued gains but, again, most slowly. Through the dynamic leadership of Horace Mann, Massachusetts became the first state in 1852 to require children between the ages of 8 and 14 to attend school for 12 weeks a year. Even that proved too much in many cases, and the law was poorly enforced. Though the federal government established the Department of Education in 1867, as late as 1876, less than 35 percent of children between 5 and 17 years of age were enrolled in school.[6] In predominantly rural America, 3 or 4 short years in the "little red school house" represented the sum total of formal educational experiences.

Though approximately 500 colleges and universities were established during the 1800s, many were finishing schools and homes for delinquent wealthy adolescents or young adults. As late as 1871, the renowned educational reformer, Charles W. Elliott, president of Harvard University, complained, "the ignorance and general incompetence of the average [medical] graduate was horrible to contemplate."[7] It was not until the later years of the century that institutions of higher learning began to pursue their scholastic and research responsibilities in a serious manner.

Understanding of Mental Retardation

As indicated previously, general understanding and comprehension of mental retardation during the early years of the century remained approximately at the level of the eighteenth century until the advent of institutional programs. Rush's text was frequently cited but not replaced.

This situation changed dramatically during the latter half of the nineteenth century. More Americans, primarily physicians, became actively interested in mental retardation, professional organizations were formed, journals published, and international communications on mental retardation established. Professional

journals, books, pamphlets, international visits and conferences, as well as personal correspondence all contributed to a commonality of understanding. Articles appearing in the early journals of the American Association on Mental Deficiency frequently cited the contributions of Ireland and Down and included papers by Shuttleworth of England and Bourneville of France.

DEFINITION AND CLASSIFICATION

Definitions of mental retardation during the latter half of the nineteenth century were quite similar to those developed in the twentieth: "Mental deficiency, depending upon imperfect development, or disease of the nervous system, dating from birth or from early infancy, previous to the evolution of the mental faculties. Imbecility is a milder form of mental incapacity."[8] According to Wilmarth (1906), the first definition of mental retardation "formulated and endorsed" by the American Association on Mental Deficiency in 1877 read:

> Idiocy and imbecility are conditions in which there is a want of natural or harmonious development of the mental, active, and moral powers of the individual affected, usually associated with some visible defect or infirmity of the physical organization and functional anomalies, expressed in various forms and degrees of disordered vital action, in defect or absence of one or more of the special sense, in irregular or uncertain volition, in dullness, or absence of sensibility and perception.[9]

The three broad categories of intellectual functioning—idiot, imbecile, and feeble-minded—were commonly used then much in the same manner as they are today. No generic term applicable to mental retardation, independent of a subclass label had been adopted. Subsequently, "idiocy" continued to be applied not only to the most limited range of intellectual abilities but to the entire class. By the turn of the century, however, the label "feeble-mindedness" tended to be applied with equal frequency.

Kerlin's classification of 1884 included a fourth major category, the moral imbecile, which he defined as one who lacks the "will-power to be other than they are, or to do otherwise than they do."[10] Further, "these moral monstrosities are often conceived and born in the best of families; inheriting graces of body and precocious in accomplishments, there is an inherent failure to recognize the claims of others, which is the foundation of duty, truth, respect for property, prudence, discretion, and all the primary virtues of civilized societies: in this declension consists the essence of moral insanity and imbecility."[11] According to Rogers, the moral sense was "lacking or very weak, while the intellectual faculties are sufficiently active to suggest great possibilities for evil."[12]

Moral imbecility, variously labeled as juvenile insanity, moral insanity, physical epilepsy, and moral paranoia, was an encompassing concept, ranging from relatively minor behavior problems (frequently sexual in nature) to serious aggressiveness. Representatives from Wisconsin even went so far as to state that "the recognition in the kindergarten and in the primary schools of *congenital moral imbeciles* is believed to be possible. Such children, although often precocious in the power to acquire school learning, should be withdrawn from the community before they reach crime age, and are best cared for under the discipline of institutions for the idiotic and feeble-minded."[13] Interestingly, some superintendents believed they had many such residents, while others felt they had none: *moral imbecility* was a concept subject to considerable interpretation.

ASSESSMENT OF INTELLIGENCE

While the rudiments of standardized testing were being formulated in Europe, a number of Americans were also interested in the area of individual differences and their measurement. Most notable was James McKeen Cattell, professor of psychology at the University of Pennsylvania. Cattell, who had received his doctorate in Germany and had served for a brief period as an assistant to the famous Wundt at Leipzig, explored a variety of individual traits and characteristics, primarily among college students. His investigations included such aspects as reaction time, perceptual processes, classification methods as related to association, span of attention, color perception, and perception of letters and words. Cattell introduced the concept of "mental tests" to the United States as early as 1890 and, through a wide range of publications, that of individual differences.

In 1897, Johnson conducted a study utilizing Cattell's association approach and reported that the responses of mentally retarded boys involved a simple objective association rather than more complicated logical ones. Not only did the association tend to be more simple, but the average number of associations for any given item tended to be made at a much lower rate by mentally retarded persons than by normal boys.[14]

While Cattell was introducing the notions of mental tests and individual differences and a few studies such as Johnson's were being published, their total impact on the diagnosis of mental retardation was at best minimal. Persons working with mentally retarded individuals and those suspected of being mentally retarded relied primarily on subjective summations of such aspects as physiognomy ("You need only to look at him to see that he is stupid"), age ("He acts like a 5-year-old instead of 10"), number of years behind regular school grade, and general coordination ("Was he awkward, slow, or clumsy?"). Variance in the interpretation of mental retardation under such circumstances was quite remarkable.

While the literature did not reflect the new dimensions of testing as related to mentally retarded individuals, three students who were completing their doctorates at Clark University were to have a significant impact upon the field: Henry Goddard, Lewis Terman, and Fred Kuhlmann. Interestingly, these doctoral candidates all studied under the direction of the famed child psychologist G. Stanley Hall, who vigorously opposed their pursuing the field of mental measurement.

Regrettably, early cautions about assessment tended to be ignored when intelligence testing did become popular. In 1884, Kerlin had expressed sensitivity to the prospects of an erroneous diagnosis: "So, in social and governmental dealings with the defective classes it is all-important that a right interpretation be made upon observed phenomena; for, if a mistake be made in the premises, the sequences of the relief or correction administered may be detrimental."[15] Wilbur, too, was concerned about the measurement of intelligence: "It is hardly necessary to say that the test of normal intelligence is not a uniform one. Allowance must be made for the surroundings of those submitted to it; in other words, for the occasions and modes of exercise of their faculties and powers. Allowance must be made for heredity, racial, and family influences. The same is true in the case of those deprived of the use of one or more of their senses."[16]

PREVALENCE

The United States Government made its first attempt to estimate the number of mentally retarded and mentally ill persons in 1840. The results were: white insane *and* idiotic, 14,508; colored insane *and* idiotic; 2,926; a total of 17,434.[17] This initial report created considerable confusion because mentally ill and mentally retarded persons were treated together. In 1850, however, and for four subsequent decennial surveys, the two categories were separated with the following results:

Year	Number of Mentally Retarded Persons
1850	15,706
1860	18,865
1870	24,527
1880	76,895
1890	95,571

The 1890 census also noted that 5,254 mentally retarded persons were in a special institution for the mentally retarded (public or private), 2,469 were in asylums for the insane, and 7,811 were inmates of an almshouse.[18]

In spite of the recognized limitations and errors in collection and interpretation, these statistics were often cited. Some people used them to demonstrate that the rapid increase of idiocy in the United States could be attributed only to immigration and/or heredity. Others used the data to urge construction of more institutions.

In addition to these national surveys, various state studies were conducted, the most interesting being reported by Kerlin for the state of Pennsylvania in 1871. He found a total of 3,500 feebleminded persons, the distribution of whom reflected upon family status, location, and relation to institutionalization:

717 in families of substance—at home or private institutions.

604 in moderate-income families—could not pay more than one-half costs.

1619 poor families "who were quite unable to pay for support away from home, yet absolutely unwilling to relieve themselves of a painful burden by casting their children on the county."

560 in homes of the most degraded character or at public expense in almshouses.[19]

Note the fiscal implications. Public institutions for mentally retarded persons were intended for the economically disadvantaged.

ETIOLOGY

Americans, like their European counterparts, were cognizant of various clinical types, but were equally in the dark and frequently in error concerning causation. Etiology was still studied and discussed in broad categories, as evidenced by the 1886 report of the Committee on Provisions for Idiotic and Feeble-Minded Persons of the American Association on Mental Deficiency. The report also included an interesting commentary on the various conditions:

Finally, your committee cannot close this report without a brief reference to an examination into the *causes of idiocy*, as presented by a special study of some hundreds of cases.

1. As a very large proportion of imbecile children are first-born, and as a very large proportion of imbeciles are said to have been delicate in their infancy before any imbecility was noticed, may not the skill and attention of the physician be exercised more directly

for the instruction of young mothers in the intelligent care of their babes, especially in families where hereditary tendency to mental and other disorders is known to exist?

2. It will be seen by our tables that in ten families of each hundred there have been infelicities and antipathies arising from unsuitableness of the parties in contract to live with each other, and of a character so unfortunate that the parents have been willing to state these as the supposed cause of their children's congenital blight. Is there not in this a suggestion that a better race will be developed when women shall regard a shameful and unfortunate marriage as more shameful than dying unwedded, and when all shall grant a difference of nobility in favor of a cultured and useful unmarried woman over an unsuccessful wife and unfit mother?

3. If in twenty-five per cent. of idiocy there is a maternal anxiety and over-tax sufficient to enter as a direct or accessory cause of the child's infirmity, may we not urge as a rule that, during the whole gestative period, safety to the body and brain of the embryo demands exemption of the mother from exhaustive duties and hyperexaltation of the nerve centres either in housework or in frivolity, particularly in families of neurotic and consumptive disorders?

4. That fifty-six per cent. of idiocy should descend from strumous and consumptive families impels the conclusion that any prudent man or woman would avoid intermarriage with this diathesis, if through such union he or she intensifies this condition in a line of children of feeble bodies and frequently defective minds.

5. That in thirty-four per cent. of idiocy there should be the family history of alcoholism, with cases of epilepsy, nervous disease, and crime in the same inheritance, is an argument for the restraint of alcoholic inebriety.

6. That the children of epileptics should inherit so frequently the same dread disease, or its co-relations of chorea, insanity, and idiocy, should deter marital union of those afflicted with epilepsy.

7. That in twenty-seven per cent. of cases of idiocy, we find as a concurrence imbecility and insanity begetting idiocy, introduces a very serious question for the law of the State to settle; namely, whether marriage of the evidently unfit shall be tolerated, and whether pauper imbeciles shall continue to entail on the community a burden of woe and expense that heaps up in misery the further it descends.[20]

Scrofula, a very common condition during the eighteenth and nineteenth centuries, was a suspected cause of retardation.[21] Emotional prenatal trauma among mothers also remained a prime consideration as an etiological factor. In 1886, Greene, for example, reported at length about a defective boy born to a mother who had undergone severe emotional shock during the Civil War. Though the event had occurred approximately 20 years prior to conception, it was still contended that the emotional problems arising from the husband's absence from the home were to blame.[22]

The question of intemperance was debated continuously. Interestingly, many looked more closely at the problem of alcohol among fathers than mothers, Seguin being perhaps the sole exception. He proposed that if the father were drunk at the time of conception, the male child would be affected, and if the mother were drunk, then the female offspring would be affected. In 1866, Shuttleworth approached the subject more scientifically; after reviewing many statistics, he raised two questions:

First, are an unusually large proportion of the immediate progenitors of idiot children intemperate people? Secondly, are an unusually large proportion of the children of drunkards idiots? In the light of such British statistics as we possess, and judging from personal observation of a large number of parents afflicted with idiot children, I should hesitate to answer in the affirmative the first question. With regard to the second an affirmative answer will, I think, only apply when the subject is considered *broadly*. Congenital idiocy is probably not, as a rule, the *immediate* legacy of the drunkard to his offspring. Doubtless, however, physical and mental degeneracy in diverse but correlated forms is the *entailed inheritance* of the drunkard's prosperity, scrofulous disease, epilepsy, nervous instability, and more obliquity being perhaps the more direct bequest.[23]

Though Down's syndrome was recognized and divorced from cretinism, the degree of differentiation was fragile. Wilbur, for example, referred to Down's syndrome as "that modified form of cretinism quite common in this country and in Great Britain. . . ."[24] Though the underlying cause of Down's syndrome was not to be defined with any degree of specificity until the mid-twentieth century, in

1889, Wilmarth, the ever-observant physician and noted pathologist, came close: Mongoloids were of a similar causative influence of prenatal origin, which was active during the formative stages of fetal existence and which created an abnormal nutritive condition.[25]

During the latter years of the nineteenth century, a number of studies were conducted in an effort to treat cretinism and which relied primarily on various thyroid extracts. Cretins were reported to respond positively with notable changes in physical features, growth, temperament, and manners, but not necessarily intelligence. Ultimately, thyroid treatment proved highly successful, thus giving rise to the hope that "endocrine therapy" would eliminate most mental retardation.

Microcephaly, as noted, had been well recognized for centuries and probably from the dawn of man. During the late nineteenth century, however, an effort was made to relieve this condition through linear craniotomy. This surgical technique, first used by Lannelongue at the Bicêtre under the assumption that microcephaly was caused by the premature closing of the sutures and fontanelles, involved incising the skull to permit the cortical area to develop. This technique was hailed as a miracle cure by the public media, but some physicians, such as Keen, questioned parental motives: "I have in several cases had a pretty strong suspicion that parents brought children to me with a distinct hope that they would die, and in such cases I have uniformly declined to operate."[26]

Both Europeans and Americans debated the merits of this surgical procedure. It finally was abandoned as being unsuccessful—an expensive lesson since the mortality rate of 15 percent was relatively high.[27] In 1898, Rogers cautioned against extensive use of brain surgery with mentally retarded people since in many cases the surgery results in further deterioration: "The performance of a fruitless operation and useless danger to a human life is always to be deplored."[28]

Surgery, which was coming into its own, was also used in an attempt to control epilepsy and to manage behavior. Desexualization was done with reported success in facilitating compliant behavior; only the failure of states to sanction such surgery prohibited a greater application of this behavior management technique.

Epilepsy represented a constant major concern to persons providing services to affected individuals. Up to 60 percent of mentally retarded persons in institutions during the latter half of the century were epileptic, with varying degrees of intelligence. The origins of epilepsy as well as its pathology remained unknown and confused, as Kerlin's comments of 1882 illustrate:

> Our records supply many illustrations to prove the epileptic change as developing slowly and surely from causes acute and transient in their action, and operating at long intervals,—worms in the alimentary canal, excitement with the Fourth of July, an indigestible supper after fatigue; any one of many such causes may give the first impulse to the development of an epileptic centre; repetitional impulses through the unrestrained life of the child finally add to the sum total, to create a chronic epilepsy for which we have no radical cure.[29]

In 1894, Dr. Sweringen was much closer to the truth. In response to the question "Do you think the lesion is in the brain?" he responded:

> In all those cases, you may call it a hyper-sensibility or loss of the power of the brain to control the impressions that it receives or to dispose of them properly—I don't know how to make it clear exactly. If we come upon something unexpectedly we dodge it, long before the brain can convey the will so to do. It is a purely reflex affair. The brain has not the power of inhibiting it. When a nerve center is paralyzed the inhibiting power is paralyzed. In strychnine poisoning when Setchenow's center is paralyzed the reflex runs riot, a breath of air only being sufficient to precipitate a spasm. In the administration of atropine if the inhibiting power of the heart is paralyzed the heart runs riot. The nervous mechanism is continually holding it down. If you cut the vagus how rapidly the heart runs. So in reflex epilepsy, according to my idea, the power of inhibiting the results of these peripheral stimuli is lost.[30]

Treatment of epilepsy was highly variable, with little or no success. Diet, exercise, mixed bromides (a prescription originally recommended by Seguin), morphine, caffeine, digitalis, chloroform, arsenic, bleeding, "horse nettles," hypophosphites of the alkaline earth, and cephalic galvinization were all tried.[31]

Heredity

Though an increased knowledge of etiological factors associated with mental retardation was evident, nothing was more misrepresented than heredity. It was viewed very broadly, implying a wide range of ancestrial, prenatal, perinatal and early postnatal experiences. Nineteenth century scientists and physicians alike considered heredity almost as a mystical transmission of parental vices and moral transgressions: "There seems to be a correlation of causation, symptomology, and results under treatment of insane and imbecile children in our asylums for the feebleminded; of the incorrigible child in the reformatory; and of the insane adult in the hospital. All these, with rare exceptions, are the victims of similarly violated physiological laws."[32]

Much of the constant emphasis on moral behavior reflected a deeply ingrained social attitude at the time as well as a fundamental misunderstanding of mental retardation and heredity itself. Compounding the problem was the frequent misinterpretation, consciously or unconsciously, of Richard Dugdale's study of the "Jukes."

Richard L. Dugdale and the "Jukes"
Richard L. Dugdale (1841–1883) was born in Paris and immigrated to the United States in 1851. As described by Estabrook, Dugdale was a "modest man of frail physique. . . . He was unpretentious but efficient, and gave all his life to altruistic work."[33]

In 1868, Dugdale was appointed to the Executive Committee of the Prison Association of New York; while on a tour of inspection of 13 county jails in New York in July, 1874, he found in one jail members of four interrelated families. Curiosity led him to the discovery that other members of the families throughout the years had high records of incarceration. Stimulated by these results and encouraged by Elisha Harris, Dugdale undertook the study of this family, which he fictitiously named the "Jukes."

The family origins were traced back to pre-Revolutionary days and, for the purposes of the genealogical study, started with the birth of Max sometime between 1720 and 1740. A descendant of early Dutch settlers, Max was described as "a hunter and fisher, a hard drinker, jolly and companionable, averse to steady toil."[34] Max had a large number of youngsters, legitimate and illegitimate. Two of his sons married two of six sisters (the "Juke" girls). One of the six sisters disappeared rather early, and Dugdale was left with the task of studying the lineage of the Juke family of the five sisters—Aida, Bell, Clara, Deila, and Effie—through six generations. At the end of six generations, he found 540 relatives directly related by blood to the Jukes and 169 by marriage or cohabitation. Though the total number of descendants was 1,200 persons, only 709 were studied.

In brief, Dugdale found a preponderance of pauperism, harlotry, illegitimate children, syphilis, deformed youngsters, and a higher crime rate among the offspring of those with Juke blood as compared with the 169 descendants as a result of marriage or cohabitation. He did not, however, interpret his findings in terms of "hereditary criminality" or "hereditary degeneracy." Rather, he emphasized environmental influences:

Where the organization is structurally modified, as in idiocy and insanity, or organically weak as in many diseases, the heredity is the preponderating factor in determining the career; but it is, even then, capable of marked modification for better or worse by the character of the environment. . . . Environment tends to produce habits which may become hereditary, especially so in pauperism and licentiousness, if it should be sufficiently constant to produce modification of cerebral tissue . . . environment is the ultimate controlling factor in determining careers, placing heredity itself as an organized result of invariable environment. The permanence of ancestral types is only another demonstration of the fixity of the environment within limits which necessitate the development of typal characteristics.[35]

In spite of Dugdale's repetitive statements concerning the impact of a never-changing backwoods environment upon the behavior of the Jukes, his conclusions were ignored by most authorities. As Giddings observed, in 1910,

Dugdale "was intent on discovering the truth, whatever it might turn out to be, and presenting it completely, clearly and simply. His readers have not always been so ingenuous, certainly not always so cautious."[36]

Many leaders in the field of mental retardation simply assumed that the Juke girls were mentally retarded. These leaders also tended to agree with Wilbur's assumption that "where idiocy exists, there is an underlying physical defect or default as a prime cause of the mental state so defined."[37] Under such circumstances, one need not explore other possibilities too seriously.

Not all physicians working with mentally retarded persons, however, held this position. Broomall advanced a more reasonable position and asked the pertinent question, "Over our antecedents we have no control but we can to some extent escape the influence of our surroundings. That far our actions are our own, and that far and no farther our responsibility extends. Where is the dividing-line? Where does the effect of heredity cease?"[38] L. Blake, a young physician with only 6 months' experience at the Elwyn Training School, seriously challenged the thinking of his older, more experienced colleagues at a convention of the superintendents: "Heredity has long been a convenient, and, perhaps, the most common makeshift to dispose of causes in the majority of mental alienations, and yet the ablest authorities differ materially in the scientific definition of the term."[39] There is no record of his colleagues' response.

Other suspected etiological determinants soon proved to be in error, including a "button in the nose," rheumatism, masturbation, fright, a blow to the chest, nervousness, and adenoiditis. Nor were mentally retarded residents driven insane by too much excitement or stimulation.[40]

In addition to the general etiological dimensions of mental retardation, a number of studies were initiated during the late 1890s concerning the more specific physical and psychological characteristics of mentally retarded individuals. Extensive studies of their teeth and jaws, physical reflex actions, and height and weight were conducted. Attention, memory, and motor ability were also investigated.[41] As was to be demonstrated repeatedly during the twentieth century, mentally retarded individuals revealed deficits in each of these areas.

Prevention and Control

By the 1880s, mentally retarded persons were no longer viewed as "unfortunates" or "innocents" who, with proper training, could fill a positive role in the home and/or community. As a class, they had become undesirable, frequently viewed as a great evil of humanity: the social parasite, criminal, prostitute, and pauper. Anyone remotely connected with the possibility of transmitting mental retardation was viciously attacked, including the immigrant:

> We must move on the general government to shut down the flood-gates through which rushes upon us the torrent of impure blood from the east and from the west. If we are to remain the dumping-ground of all nations, we can not build prisons, insane hospitals, and retreats for the defective classes fast enough to supply the demand.[42]

the epileptic:

> The hopeless epileptic is not a thing to smile at and when we contemplate that, though not always, but frequently, they are the offspring of those who were themselves the possessors of an unhealthy nervous organization and that these epileptics are permitted, unchallenged, to marry and still further pollute the springs of life, the subject assumes a seriousness that cannot be portrayed in words.[43]

and the mentally retarded person:

> Is it because there are in the United States an army of perhaps half a million tramps, cranks and peripatetic beggars crawling like human parasites over our body politic, and feasting upon the rich juices of productive labor? Many of these human parasites have committed no crime and are guilty *per se* of no wrong, unless it is a crime and a wrong to be brought, without one's volition, into this world, burdened with the accumulated inherent sins of a vitiated and depraved ancestry; to be bred in filth, to be born in squalor and to be raised in an atmosphere tainted of course with crime. Many of these wretches are what they are because they are what they were made, not what they have made themselves. Handicapped by the vices of their inheritance they are simply not strong enough to keep up to the social, civil and moral

ethics of the age, and as an inevitable consequence, just as water seeks its level, they drop back by degrees to become in turn deficient, delinquent, defective and dependent.[44]

By 1891, those who condemned the immigrant as being a major source of social ills were victorious, for the Fifty-first Congress of the United States amended the Immigration Act to exclude "all idiots, insane persons, paupers or persons likely to become a public charge, persons suffering from a loathsome or a dangerous contagious disease, persons who have been convicted of a felony or other infamous crime or misdemeanor involving moral turpitude, polygamists. . . ."[45]

The fact that most mentally retarded children emanate from poverty was well recognized and documented:

Here is an ever increasing army of incompetents becoming as they breed, still more incompetent and irresponsible, still more destructive; ever more and more debasing and depressing alike upon the body politic. . . . Walk any of our large cities and you touch arms with all sorts of mental abnormalities, some harmless, some harmful, but all pitiable, and betrayed by the eccentric gait, the neuropathic eye and the other signs, which you as specialists may read even as you run. Mental blights linked to the intensifying influences of poverty and physical distress skulk threateningly in the rear, while in your path you brush by many slumbering mental volcanoes that only wait some peculiarly exciting stimulus to make them burst forth their murderous, ruinous fires.[46]

A study by an organization of 175 young society women interested in investigating the condition of feebleminded children in New York City in 1892 documented these contentions: "Children feeble in mind, mentally deficient or diseased, or both, abound in the homes of the poor, swarm the slums, wander the streets and obtrude upon the legitimate work of the public schools."[47]

As is readily understandable from the tenor of the preceding comments, prevention was viewed primarily in terms of prolonged institutionalization, prohibition of marriage, and desexualization. Rogers truculently proclaimed, "One step farther we propose—To keep those whom we can not cure and equip for life in custody until they are past the reproducing age,

and stamp out hereditary imbecility and epilepsy right here and now."[48] Similarly, Martin Barr, one of the early presidents of the American Association on Mental Deficiency, supported desexualization with the laconic statement, "The surgeon's knife in place of sentimentality, and a nurse instead of a keeper."[49]

Only Mrs. Brown, one of the few early pioneers to maintain a positive attitude toward mentally retarded people throughout the nineteenth century, viewed prevention from a broader, more humane perspective: "Risking the appelation of materialist, I deem the first need of men and women of this generation to be, not higher education, nor the higher spiritual life, e'en, but healthy bodies, strong, and active muscles, blood free from poisonous humors, brains with no vicious heredities, bodies fit to receive the apostolic title, Temples of the Holy Ghost."[50] Ultimately, she hoped "to see Hospitals for Incurables supplanted by the lecture-room of the medical scientist, and prevention of disease rather than cure to be the theme of his eloquence."[51]

Before considering society's response to the needs of mentally retarded persons, it should be noted that mentally retarded men served their country admirably during the Civil War. In spite of the federal government's position that persons manifesting "mental imbecility" should be rejected from military service (approximately four out of every thousand individuals examined were so rejected), many mentally retarded men fought and died.[52] Seguin acknowledged three of them:

_____ remained in our school six years, devoting a part of each year to manual labor on the farm, in the stable or shop; learning in each department to make himself useful . . . when the war broke out (1861) he entered the Navy as gunner's mate on board the *Ossipee*; was afterwards transferred to the *Cumberland* and thence to *Brooklyn*, on which he served during the remainder of the war.

_____ formerly from the Pennsylvania Training School, an apprentice to the shoemaking business, entered the Army, performed good service as a soldier, was captured in General Grant's move through the wilderness, and died at the Anderson prison-pens.

_____ served for two years in the Army; at

Gettysburg, where his bravery was acknowledged by his officers, and in the Battle of the Wilderness, where he was severely wounded; on that occasion he is reported to have run away from the hospital to join his comrades in the Army of the James. And lastly, transferred to Shenandoah Valley, he was fatally wounded at Fisher's Hill, and now sleeps at Winchester.[53]

SOCIAL CARE AND TREATMENT

As in all ages, mentally retarded persons were treated differentially according to circumstances. In predominantly rural America, probably all but the most severely mentally retarded persons worked from sunup to sundown with their parents. In small communities, the picture painted by Howe in the 1840s persisted throughout the century. In the rapidly developing ghettos of immigrants in metropolitan areas, the younger mentally retarded population may or may not have attended school, worked in a variety of menial or oppressive job settings, or ran the streets, soon attracting the attention of the local police.

Mentally retarded persons brought before the courts tended to fare better in the United States than in Britain. Though Abraham Prescott was tried, convicted, and executed in New Hampshire in 1834 for the murder of Mrs. Sally Cochran, such decisions were the exception rather than the rule.[54] In many cases, mentally retarded people were considered inculpable, regardless of the "right or wrong" test.

Marriages involving mentally retarded persons were occasionally annulled; however, most judges supported the 1852 *Wood* v. *Dulaney* decision that such marriages not be annulled if the mentally retarded person(s) understood what was involved.[55] Their right to make a will, which, parenthetically, was contained in the *Body of Liberties*, was also supported by a number of court cases: "Mere feebleness of intellect, short of what might by many be supposed to amount to idiocy, is insufficient to render a will void," decided Judge Gibson in *Dornick* v. *Reichenback*, 1889.[56] At that time,

every mentally retarded person had a constitutional right to vote.

On a less positive note, and in spite of reform efforts and pleas to legislative bodies as well as the addition of residential facilities specifically for mentally retarded persons, bidding-out, jails, almshouses, and other such programs and facilities continued to be used frequently throughout the nineteenth century. Little improvement was noted. In Ohio:

What is to be done with them? Think of their surroundings. The raving of the maniac, the frightful contortions of the epileptick, the driveling and senseless sputtering of the idiot, the garrulous temper of the decrepit, neglected old age, the peevishness of the infirm, the accumulated filth of all these; then add the moral degeneracy of [those who] from idleness of dissipation, seek a refuge from honest toil in the tithed industry of the country, and you have a faint outline of the surroundings of these little boys and girls. This is home to them. Here their first and most enduring impressions of life are formed.[57]

In Illinois:

The conditions were almost too shocking to describe . . . nakedness, filth, starvation, vice, and utter wretchedness, which a very slight exercise of common sense and of humanity might have entirely prevented.[58]

In New York:

They [boys housed in the institution's laundry] were intermingled with the inmates of the wash-house, around the cauldrons where the dirty clothes were being boiled. Here was an insane woman raving and uttering wild gibberings, a half-crazy man was sardonically grinning, and an overgrown idiotic boy of malicious disposition was teasing, I might say torturing, one of the little boys. There were several other adults of low types of humanity. The apartment . . . overhead was used for a sleeping room, and the floor was being scrubbed at the same time by one of the not overcareful inmates; it was worn, and the dirty water came through the cracks in continuous droppings upon the heads of the little ones, who did not seem to regard it as a serious annoyance.[59]

Unfortunately, these brief descriptions typified alternative care facilities provided by government throughout the United States. Equally unfortunate was that in spite of the advent of public residential facilities, a large number of mentally retarded persons continued to be served in almshouses. As late as 1910, a United States census indicated that while 20,731 mentally retarded persons were being served in a special residential facility, 13,238 were in almshouses.[60]

Dorothea Dix's objections to Kentucky's family support system went unheeded. In 1892, Stewart, commenting on Kentucky's effort, observed, "I know that a large number of children who are receiving from the State this stipend could be taught some useful trade, but their families prefer the money to any sort of mental improvement."[61]

Given such circumstances, legislative bodies of populous states lent their authority and state revenues to the construction of specialized institutions. Motivations for their actions, however, changed during this period: "Hope through education" during the 1850s became "control and prevention" by the middle 1880s. The American Association on Mental Deficiency, in part, played a role in fostering this change.

THE AMERICAN ASSOCIATION ON MENTAL DEFICIENCY

Edouard Seguin had, for a number of years, urged institutional superintendents to meet occasionally to share experiences and ideas. In conjunction with the Centennial Exposition of the United States held in Philadelphia in 1876, Isaac Kerlin issued an invitation to superintendents from around the country to meet in Media, Pennsylvania. On June 6, 1876, six men—E. Seguin, H. B. Wilbur, G. A. Doren, C. T. Wilbur, H. Knight, and I. Kerlin—met in the parlor at the Pennsylvania Training School and drafted the purposes and structure of a national organization. The following day, "The Association of Medical Officers of American Institutions for Idiots and Feeble-minded Persons" was established. The organization's title was undoubtedly suggested by that of the "Association of Medical Superintendents of American Institutions for the Insane," the oldest American medical society, founded in 1844.

The primary purpose of the newly created association as stipulated in its constitution was "the discussion of all questions relating to the causes, conditions, and statistics of idiocy, and to the management, training, and education of idiots and feeble-minded persons; it will also lend its influence to the establishment and fostering of institutions for this purpose."[62]

On June 8, 1876, 10 superintendents were declared active members, and all those not in attendance were designated honorary members. In addition to the superintendents, four of their wives were also elected active members based on a rather unique resolution for its day: active membership was offered to "ladies [who] have been identified with our work. . . ."[63]

Though Seguin was elected the Association's first president, neither he nor others, such as Samuel Gridley Howe, provided leadership. Rather, the mantle of authority passed to Isaac Kerlin, a dynamic motivating force, who strongly advocated for the proliferation of institutions.

As the concerns and interests of the Association changed throughout the years, so did its official title. In 1907, it became "The American Association for the Study of the Feeble-minded"; since 1933, it has been known as "The American Association on Mental Deficiency." Similarly, its official publication, which started simply with the Association's convention proceedings, was expanded in 1896 and retitled the *Journal of Psycho-Asthenics;* in 1940 this was renamed the *American Journal of Mental Deficiency.* For purposes of convenience and clarity, only the Association's current title will be used throughout this text.

RESIDENTIAL SERVICES

The advent of the first public residential facility has been described. Howe's 10-bed experimental unit, however, was preceded by the opening of the first private facility in Barre, Massachusetts, in July, 1848. The initiator of this effort and its first administrator was Hervey B. Wilbur.

Hervey B. Wilbur

Hervey B. Wilbur (1820–1883) was a remarkable person, physician, and pioneer who remained active in the field until his death. He was one of the founders and early contributors to the activities of the American Association on Mental Deficiency as well as the short-lived National Association for the Protection of the Insane and the Prevention of Insanity in the 1880s. He also participated in the founding of Syracuse University.

Wilbur was described as one whose "sympathies embraced the wide field of humanity, and no human being was too lowly or degraded for his notice. To him the humblest of his neighbors came for advice and aid in their petty troubles, sure that he would accord them both."[64] An anecdote provided by Seguin perhaps best illustrates Wilbur's concern for the youngsters:

> In selecting residents for a new public facility at Syracuse, New York, which Dr. Wilbur was to

Hervey B. Wilbur.

assume responsibility for in 1851, he selected several youngsters from New York City, neither of whom could speak, nor appear to hear or understand, and could only follow a few simple commands expressed by gesture. Upon arriving at his facility, Dr. Wilbur hurried them into the bathing-room, and brushed, and combed, and aproned them after their journey, before they could be seen by the teachers. . . .[65]

Wilbur first became involved with mental retardation when he accepted into his home in 1847 the 7-year-old, mentally retarded son of a distinguished lawyer. Out of this initial act quickly grew a private institution for feeble-minded children, one intended to provide for "the management and education of all children who by reason of mental infirmity are not fit subjects for ordinary school instruction."[66]

From the beginning, Wilbur, like Howe, expressed no intent to cure mental retardation; the early founders clearly understood the challenge and the limits of their task:

> We do not propose to create or supply faculties absolutely wanting, nor to bring all grades of idiocy to the same standard of development or discipline, nor to make them all capable of sustaining creditably all the relations of a social and moral life; but rather to give to dormant faculties their greatest possible development, and to apply those awakened faculties to a useful purpose under the control of an aroused and disciplined will. At the base of all our efforts lies the principle, that the human attributes of intelligence, sensitivities, and will are not absolutely wanting in an idiot, but dormant and undeveloped.[67]

Wilbur aggressively pursued a training program based on the philosophy and principles of Edouard Seguin. Again in agreement with Howe, Wilbur persisted in his "prejudice against large asylums for any purpose."[68]

In 1851, Wilbur became the first superintendent of what was to become known as the Syracuse Institution for the Feeble-minded. His selected replacements for Barre were Dr. and Mrs. George Brown, both of whom contributed to the field of mental retardation for many years. Mrs. Katherine (Wood) Brown (1827–1907) assumed a more visible role in the American Association on Mental Deficiency than did her scholarly, somewhat retiring husband. A "dignified and cordial" person,

Institution at Barre, Massachusetts.

she tenaciously clung throughout the century to the concepts of education, intermixing of sexes, and the need for small institutions to retain a homelike atmosphere.

Pennsylvania joined its sister states in 1852, when a private residential facility was established in Germantown under the direction of J. B. Richards, an educator. In a few years, this facility was relocated to Media, becoming the Pennsylvania Training School for Feeble-minded Children; today it is known as the Elwyn Institute.

J. B. Richards

J. B. Richards (1817–1886), son of an American missionary family, was born in Ceylon but as a young child came to the United States with his father, who died shortly thereafter. Richards never saw his mother again, and following a brief youth with his "stern, pious" uncle, he became an educator . . . "an educator of excellent repute, waging a constant war against the scholasticism of the day." In addition to being an adamant abolitionist, Richards believed and often proclaimed that the "lowest idiot and criminal could be reached and humanized, if only enough love were spent on him."[69]

As a result of his remarkable success teaching "unrulies" in Chauncy Hall, New York, Richards was recommended by Horace Mann to Samuel Gridley Howe as a possible teacher for his new program for mentally retarded youngsters. Shortly after joining Howe's staff, Richards was sent to France to study Seguin's methods. He was unimpressed: the visit "proved indeed that there was little or nothing to be learnt there about the practical part of the work, that would not have been arrived at here, by any intelligent person, who started with correct views of the principle which underlies the whole subject. It was something, however, to know that."[70] Little wonder that these sensitive gentlemen encountered difficulties at a later date.

Richards's educational approach emphasized object-teaching, imitation, variety, repetition, constant review, sanitary conditions, and physical exercise. Teachers were admonished to be firm but affectionate: "get on the

J. B. Richards.

floor—get down where the child is, right down there . . . become one with your student.''[71]

Owing to a variety of administrative problems (not all of his doing), the institution nearly failed, and Richards left in 1856. The remainder of his life was, in the words of Reverend Williams, ''one of sorrows and disappointments.''[72] While trying to establish a new family training home for mentally retarded youth, he was stricken with a fatal illness and died on February 14, 1886.

Isaac N. Kerlin

In 1863, Isaac Newton Kerlin (1834–1893) assumed responsibility for the Pennsylvania Training School and played an unparalleled, dominant role in the field of mental retardation for nearly 3 decades. Born in Burlington, New Jersey, he graduated from the University of Pennsylvania School of Medicine in 1856. Following his residency, he became the assistant superintendent of the Pennsylvania Training School, a position he held until 1862,

when he enlisted as a medical officer in the Army of the Potomac. Having served a little over a year in the army, he returned to the Pennsylvania Training School where he served as superintendent from 1863 until his death in 1893.

W. Fish, a former medical associate and later a superintendent in his own right, described Kerlin in the following words: ''Doubtless many of you recall his appearance . . . the stout compact figure, the mobile and expressive face with its smooth shaven upper lip, full beard, just beginning to be streaked with gray, the dome like head, scantily covered with hair, the kindly eyes sparkling with merriment, which at times could blaze with righteous indignation.''[73]

Kerlin was a brilliant, forceful, puritanical, but benevolent autocrat. His control over the institution as well as his other activities is well documented. In acknowledging Kerlin's influential role in the American Association on Mental Deficiency, Osborne, in his presidential address, said: ''So long as he lived no one

Isaac N. Kerlin.

perhaps would have thought to challenge his relation to the work or to question the correctness of his leadership, for even those who sometimes differed with him or were made to feel the strength of his opposition, recognized his inherent force of character, his marvelous skill in organizing, his suave diplomacy and his tireless zeal. He was essentially a strong man and it is because of this quality the Association became largely what he made it."[74]

Kerlin led the movement to expand residential programs. As with most philosophers at any given time, his presumptions were both correct and incorrect. In 1876, he strongly urged the development of institutions in the belief that mentally retarded persons should not be placed and neglected in insane asylums, penal institutions, or almshouses. On the other hand, he contended that mentally retarded persons "could not with advantage, be placed in ordinary school with other children," and that "in a great majority of instances they are better and more successfully treated in well organized institutions, than is possible at their homes."[75]

Apparently a devoutly religious man, Kerlin believed in the "Fatherhood of God, and Brotherhood of Man," which may, in part, explain his negative observations and judgments concerning the mentally retarded as a class but apparent tenderness toward them as individuals. Thus, while he stated with galling frequency that mentally retarded persons were doomed to a life of crime, pauperism, and prostitution and, therefore, needed lifelong institutionalization, he described his residents in affectionate terms:

A warm-hearted mother enters our school-room, with the preconceived and popular impressions, that all the inmates are necessarily objects of disgust. Beckie, our little mute girl, trips up to our lady visitor. A sweet expression rests on her countenance, and her cheeks quickly change color, with the varying emotions that swell her little bosom; and her eyes dance with intelligent delight, as the tiny hands of the infant, which rests in the arms of the mother, are thrown out to meet her.[76]

Kerlin tolerated no ill-treatment: "It is distinctly and positively enjoined that our rule of government is one of kindness, and that no severities or meanness towards the children will be tolerated . . . attendants and others are positively prohibited carrying switches, sticks, canes, etc. . . . the position of attendant is a sacred one. Its requirements are to improve and cheer the most helpless of earth's unfortunates . . . to teach them to be kind, obliging, and respectful, you must be so yourself."[77] In other words, "modeling" was essential.

As noted previously, one of Kerlin's crowning achievements was the establishment of the American Association on Mental Deficiency. Though he was not elected president until the year of his death, Kerlin served as its secretary from the time of its inception and thus was in a good position to guide its growth and development.

He and other early leaders were highly successful in promoting institutions as the best means for meeting the needs of mentally retarded persons. By 1880, there were 15 publicly supported institutions in the United States serving 4,216 mentally retarded persons. As would be anticipated, the primary concentration of such facilities was in the northeastern states; however, other states (even those recently formed) were represented: California, Connecticut, Illinois, Indiana, Iowa, Kansas, Kentucky, Massachusetts, Minnesota, Nebraska, New Jersey, New York, Ohio, and Pennsylvania.[78]

Purposes and Programs

While institutions for mentally retarded persons were viewed as beneficial by many authorities of the day, their purpose, programs, and administration changed dramatically by the 1880s for a variety of reasons, genuine and ignoble. The small, homelike educational establishment was replaced by the large, overcrowded, and underfinanced multipurpose facility that would typify institutions for generations to come.

Initially, institutional programs were educational, intended to serve school-age (CA 6–16 or 18) mentally retarded youngsters and adolescents. Most of the facilities started during the 1850s and early 1860s had a single, simple admission criterion: "by deficient intellect is rendered unable to acquire an education in the common schools."[79] Some institutions excluded epileptic youngsters; all refused admission to hydrocephalic children.

In a few years, however, most of these fledgling programs were confronted with several genuine problems: what to do, for example, with residents when they attained the legally established upper age limit for education. Historically, even as it related to Howe's first 10-bed unit, most mentally retarded residents were "either orphans or the offspring of indigent parents."[80] Many had no homes or their parents refused to welcome their return. In 1856, Howe lamented, "There is the greatest reluctance on the part of the parents and guardians to remove those pupils whose terms have expired, partly because they think they are better here, and partly because they dislike to resume the care and responsibility. This is especially true of the most unfortunate children—of the lowest idiots."[81]

Left with little choice other than sending older residents to county homes, almshouses, and other such less dedicated operations, administrators requested permission to retain residents into their adult years. The problem was succinctly described by Knight in 1886: "The only provision made outside of state institutions for the education and custodial care of the feeble-minded is to be found in the county poorhouses, where they are subject to every possible form of neglect. . . . I could horrify this audience by a recital of facts that have come under my personal observation in this regard. . . . When girls are discharged from the institutions, we have no place to send them but to the county infirmaries."[82]

The unavailability of a family, a job, or other forms of necessary support in the community, plus the inadequacy of alternative residential provisions, led to the ultimate elimination of upper age limits. Further support for the retention of adults in institutions—especially women—resulted from growing negative attitudes toward mentally retarded persons.

The concern over adult mentally retarded women "reproducing their kind" became an obsession with many institutional administrators, planners, and legislators. In 1878, the legislature of New York authorized the establishment of the Asylum for Adult Imbecile Women at Newark solely for "the care, protection, and safe-keeping of adult idiotic and feeble-minded females." Knight saluted this effort: "New York, in providing special care and protection for her adult girls, has taken a step forward whose influence, even considered simply as a preventive measure, we cannot overestimate; for we owe it not only to the adult imbecile herself, but to humanity and the world at large, to guard in every possible way against the abuse and increase of this class."[83]

Others, however, such as Katherine Wood Brown, seriously questioned this practice. Even Kerlin (perhaps motivated by his wife) disagreed: "All of us who have visited it [the Newark facility] and are studying the outcome of it, agree with Mrs. Kerlin that it is a palpable mistake."[84]

This obsession was reflected throughout the country. For years the teacher's association in Wisconsin had lobbied for an institution for mentally retarded persons, one that would "be inaugurated as a SCHOOL."[85] When the first institution finally opened on June 16, 1897, there were no school provisions, for its purpose was to provide custodial care for "those feeble-minded persons who were a danger to the community, especially women of childbearing age, who, because of mental and emotional limitations, easily fell into immorality."[86]

Commensurate with the developing concern for the adult resident was the problem of meeting the needs of the more severely affected population. In 1886, Powell summarized the situation in the following words:

> The members of the "low grade" or asylum division merit our warmest sympathy; their utter helplessness, together with their habits, subject them to possible neglect. What shall we do with them? The day of the "survival of the fittest" is past. . . . I believe it to be the duty of those having charge of institutions to continue to urge the claims of this class before the public, until special provision may be made for them, adapted to their helpless natures.[87]

In discussing this matter, institutional administrators obviously were sensitive to parental concerns and the effects of having a severely mentally retarded person in the home. Kerlin, for example, noted that "the wear and tear of an excitable idiot baby of from two to ten years has wrecked many a family, and sent others down to pauperism."[88] Similarly, administrators wanted to provide an answer to the aged parents' question, "Who will care for and guide my afflicted child in the future?"

How best to provide for the more severely mentally retarded person was debated for years. In the end, it was decided that most residential facilities would provide both a "school" section and an "asylum" section, rather than have distinctly separate institutions.

A similar issue was raised concerning the epileptic individual: Should they have their own facility or be admitted to a multipurpose institution? Though New York, Ohio, and Massachusetts did build separate facilities for epileptics, most states simply broadened their admission requirement to include both feebleminded and epileptic persons.[89]

The ever-expanding role of public institutions resulted in an equally expanded political and bureaucratic interest and involvement. The day of the "noble experiment" with a few mentally retarded school-age children was over. Institutions now affected many constituents as well as politicians and represented a sizable line item in state budgets. These new "facts of life" were bemoaned by many administrators:

In the beginning we had trouble to get politicians to accept our work; to appreciate its necessities or to contribute public funds to its support. Politicians were the last to be convinced that establishments for the feeble-minded should exist. The scales have turned however. Now these institutions have become so popular that politicians begin to consider them their legitimate prey, and our chief danger seems to lie in our apparent inability to prevent them from appropriating the work bodily. They have learned the political value of institution patronage and the facility with which the public will divert its funds to a merciful cause. These funds make nice pickings for partisan cormorants.[90]

Nor was the state bureaucracy to be ignored. In 1891, Mott, representing the state of Minnesota, had a "few words" for the superintendents: "You are the superintendents of the institutions which you represent. . . . Let the State authorities build and equip the nests and you adapt yourselves to them as best you may."[91]

Changes in attitude, philosophy, and governmental practices of the magnitude described naturally resulted in a tremendous modification of services offered. As indicated, the primary goal of early institutions was educational in that they sought to improve the quality of intellectual functioning, moral character, and general community acceptance of mentally retarded youngsters. By the mid 1880s, the significance of education was challenged, because in the minds of at least some administrators, the purpose of institutions no longer reflected increased independence and community acceptance: "We have no desire," wrote Johnson in 1897, "to make our child self-directing as he must always be under the direction of the institution. What we *do* wish is, to make him as nearly self-supporting as possible in the institution."[92] Similarly, Butler contended, "An idiot awakened to his condition is a miserable one."[93]

Fortunately, other institutional leaders rejected such pessimism. In 1892, for example, Fernald was first (with the exception of Seguin) to advocate training experiences for the more severely affected, probably referring to the moderately mentally retarded. Sense training, play, walks, physical activities, music, and imitation programs were all beneficial: "Indeed, books, slates, and the conventional curriculum of the school room are not for these low grade children. Yet, all of this training is education in the truest sense."[94]

The Working Resident Though educational programs were continued, primarily for mildly mentally retarded persons, institutions placed a growing emphasis on vocational training. The need for early and extended vocational experience was essential since, in reality, residents became responsible for many of the institution's basic operations. Residents worked long hours, performing a wide range of skilled and unskilled tasks:

There is no occupation so suitable for the middle grade imbecile as the care of the low grade idiot.[95]

Our carpenter boys did all the carpenter work, under the direction of their teachers, making the doors, putting in the windows, laying the floors, wainscoting the rooms, and finishing them so far as they were able, leaving undone the plastering and painting. . . .[96]

We have been employing our pupils at mechanical pursuits more than in former years. Our brush shops are tolerably successful. We have been making some mats in our mat-shop. In our laundry and bakery some work has been done, and certainly in the department of female industries we have accomplished more than ever. Our little girls have done a great deal of new work and mending.[97]

Many residents, but not all, worked for little or no money, and by 1890 the question of resident reimbursement was a major topic of deliberation among superintendents, for their experiences varied widely. Some administrators found that reimbursement led to the natural consequence that the resident employee wanted more money: "We had a very good driver who had been with us a few years; some suggested that we pay him ten cents a week; in the course of a month or two he thought he should receive twenty-five cents, then he wanted fifty cents, and so on to exorbitant ideas of his value, and such stretches of discipline and disobedience, that the only way to get him back to his tracks again was to put him back in the ranks."[98]

Others, such as Fish and Powell, reimbursed residents who would be returning to the community, but not others. This program was intended to enable community-bound youngsters and adults "to care for themselves [and to] learn the value of money."[99]

Kerlin paid many of his residents a small amount of money and provided a canteen. Interestingly, a number of superintendents, including Kerlin, Powell, and Stewart, discharged a few of the more capable residents and hired them into such positions as direct care workers, painters, and drivers. In general, however, most institutions relied heavily on resident labor, free of charge.

This emphasis on work was not solely for mercenary reasons, though economical considerations were important. Most institutions were not well supported financially; they frequently were in conflict with other forms of institutions also undergoing reform and expansion, and all were considered "charitable" at a time when charity was not popular. Legislators expected institutions to operate as economically as possible, and so did most administrators. Some superintendents fervently tried through their industrial programs to operate at no cost to the state, though those who were relatively successful did not believe the state should earn a profit from this venture. Of all "institutional industries," farming was one of the most important, since it provided the bulk of an institution's food supply; enthusiasm for this program was well expressed by Doran of Ohio: "If the State would give him one thousand acres of land, they could take care of all their custodial cases free of further expense."[100]

It should be remembered, however, that asking young people as well as adults to labor for long hours was consistent with the work ethic of the day. It was fully expected that each person in a family contribute to the welfare of that family as well as to his own support. Also, most administrators believed firmly that "a busy child is a happy child" and that work was a therapeutic experience consistent with Pinel's earlier thesis.[101]

The heavy work requirements of the institution did not go unnoticed by reform-minded persons in the community. On occasion, such practices were criticized severely. In defense, Kerlin retorted: "To rob the superintendent of the garden and farm life of his boys is the same as to deprive the surgeon of his best instruments; to limit him to the avocation and direction of the school-room is to wither his right arm; to confine him to medical practice is to forget his broader relations to his patients in all their varying psychical moods and higher moral life; to restrict or abridge in the slightest his free movement of men, women, and material is to ignore the many-sided aspects of his professional duty."[102]

Another topic of frequent concern was appropriate disciplinary measures. Some facilities relied heavily on physical forms of discipline; others rejected any form of corporal punishment. Fish's position (1889) was one of the more humane in that he viewed corporal punishment as "the extreme measure, which should not be tried until all else had failed"; and only he or his assistant could execute such disciplinary action. Fish preferred contracting: "With our more intelligent boys and girls I have bridged over many hard places by kindly reasoning in the quiet of my office. Several of our former notoriously "bad boys" have pledges of good behavior, signed, sealed, and witnessed with due formality, on file in my office, promising obedience for a specified time; and these pledges are often voluntarily reviewed."[103]

Though there was a decreasing emphasis on returning adults to the community and a growing need for resident manpower, not all adults were retained. Some administrators still believed and could demonstrate that community placement for some was both desirable and feasible. As reported by Fish in 1892, "The experience of the past thirty years proves that, of the feeble-minded who are received and trained in institutions, ten to twenty per cent. are so improved as to be able to enter life as bread-winners; that from thirty to forty per cent. are returned to their families so improved as to be self-helpful, or at least much less burdensome to their people. . . ."[104]

In addition to training, work experience, and discipline, providing adequate physical care and health maintenance presented almost insurmountable problems and heartbreak. Shuttleworth's mortality rate figures for mentally retarded persons in England were similar to those reported in the United States. Of mentally retarded persons 5 to 10 years of age, approximately 50 percent died, compared with 6.1 percent for normal youngsters (a ratio of 8:1); of those 10 to 15 years of age, 33.9 percent, compared with 3.4 percent (10:1); and of late adolescents, ages 15 to 20, 45.1 percent, compared with 4.8 percent of the normal population (9:1).[105]

Primary causes of death were infectious diseases and tuberculosis. In 1886, Brown reported that of the 41 deaths of mentally retarded individuals for that year, 51 percent died of lung diseases and 32 percent to various epidemics.[106] The high rate of death from tuberculosis and other lung diseases could be readily understood, since the most commonly applied treatment, according to Fish, was cod liver oil.[107] Similarly, Wilmarth reported that of 58 cases of severely retarded residents who had contracted rubella, 10 died.[108] As Down sympathetically observed, "Nothing is more remarkable than the readiness with which feeble-minded children succumb to acute disease of any form."[109] At that time, even a simple tool like the thermometer was a major medical advance. Most treatment consisted simply of fresh air, clean surroundings, and good nutrition.

The "Colony" Plan

By 1890, the school facilities of the 1850s evolved into the large institutions intended to serve four groups of residents on the "colony" plan:

First, the teachable portion of a school-attending age; second, the helpless, deformed, epileptic, and those practically unteachable; third, the male adult portion who have passed the school-age and are not self-supporting, whose friends are unable or unwilling to provide for them, and who, in many instances, are friendless and homeless; and fourth, for reasons too sadly and too widely known, the adult female portion, all of whom should be kept under the careful custody of the State unless they can be released under exceptionally favorable and well-guarded surroundings.[110]

The colony plan, adopted throughout the country, included a training school as well as an industrial, custodial, and farm department. This approach provided "the cheapest as well as the wisest method, utilizing, as it does, the labor a class whose work would command absolutely nothing if brought into competition with even the most unskilled labor of persons of normal mind."[111]

Many of the facilities designed during the late 1800s (and well into the twentieth century) followed a pattern similar to that recommended by Kerlin:

The grades of specific idiocy and imbecility presuppose a wide classification, so that at the commencement this should be planned for somewhat as follows:

1. Central building for the school and industrial departments. Near at hand should be located the shops.
2. Separate buildings for the care of cases of paralysis and profound idiocy, with special arrangement of dormitory and day-room as the infirm character of the inmates may require.
3. Other remote buildings for the custodial and epileptic departments, with accessories for both care and training.
4. Provision should eventually be made for colonizing lads, as they grow into manhood, in properly-arranged houses, as farmers, gardeners, dairy-help, etc.[112]

Such institutions, according to Kerlin, "should be in the country, about one mile from a postal town, and easily accessible at all seasons."[113] Wilmarth was a little more cautious—"close but not too close": "I think it will be universally conceded that a site not too far from some large commercial center is preferable. If too near, the institution is subject to so many visitations as to interfere seriously with the household work. If too far off from any large city, transportation becomes so costly as to increase very materially the running expenses of the institution. A distance of from twenty to fifty miles should be reasonably free from either of these objections, and at this distance land is cheaper than it is too near a large city."[114]

In spite of the growing size and rural setting of the institutions, a homelike atmosphere was still encouraged and sought by most authorities—but not all:

We must dismiss from our minds and from our vocabularies the thoughts and the words which seem to imply that the healthy, trained, adult imbecile is a patient, or a pupil, or a prisoner. He is neither, but he is a laborer, either a skilled mechanic, or an unskilled worker, and usually of the commonest class. He does not need sumptuous appointments nor do they make him happy. He is happiest when he lives with his feet near the ground. A plain building suits him better than a palace. A log hut would be his ideal. He does not need constant medical care, nor high-priced tuition, nor hospital buildings, nor detention within iron bars. He needs outdoor or indoor work and plenty of it, outdoor preferred. He needs plain food and the simplest and plainest clothing.[115]

The irony of the situation was that when Howe first proposed the concept of residential programs, his thoughts and precepts became the law of the land; but when he urged constraint and reevaluation, his observations were ignored:

Now the danger of misdirection in this pious and benevolent work is, that two false principles may be incorporated with the projected institutions which will be as rotten piles in the foundations and make the future establishments deplorably defective and mischievous. These are, first, close congregation; and, second, the life-long association of a large number of idiots; whereas, the true, sound principles are: separation of idiots from each other; and then diffusion among the normal population. . . . For these and other reasons it is unwise to organize establishments for teaching and training idiotic children, upon such principles as will tend to make them become asylums for life. . . . *Even idiots have rights* which should be carefully considered! At any rate let us try for something which shall not imply segregating the wards in classes, removing them from our sight and knowledge, ridding ourselves of our responsibility as neighbors, and leaving the wards closely packed in establishments where the spirit of pauperism is surely engendered, and the morbid peculiarities of each are intensified by constant and close association of others of his class.[116]

Not Howe's concern but Kerlin's dream and vision of the future—his "cities of refuge"— won the day:

The future of this work contemplates far more than the gathering into training schools of a few hundred imperfect children. . . . The correlation of idiocy, insanity, pauperism, and crime will be understood, as it is not now. There will be fewer almshouses, but more workhouses. Jails, criminal courts, and grog-shops will correspondingly decrease; and here and there, scattered over the country, may be "villages of the simple, made up of warped, twisted, and incorrigible, happily contributing to their own and the support of those more lowly,—"cities of refuge," in truth; havens in which all shall live contentedly, because no longer misunderstood nor taxed with exactions beyond their mental or moral capacity. They "shall go out no more" and "they shall neither marry nor be given in marriage" in those havens dedicated to incompetency.[117]

While it is easy to criticize the tremendous emphasis placed on institutionalization, it must be kept in mind that the times were insensitive to the needs of mentally retarded persons and the poor. Many youngsters were placed in almshouses: children who were paupers, delinquents, neglected, abandoned, "children who swarm the streets, prowl about docks and wharves, and are almost sure to take up crime as a trade, orphans who have no one to provide or care for them, and all vagrant and abandoned children."[118] During the last quarter of the century, reformers began to realize that almshouses were not appropriate places for children who, as described by Abbott, "were consigned to live with the aged, the insane, the feebleminded, and the diseased. They were usually cared for by the older inmates and taught, if at all, by ignorant employees; their physical needs were neglected, and the mortality was very high. Those who survived knew only the life and routine of a pauper institution."[119] In 1879, the Massachusetts legislature passed the first reform bill intended to stop almshouse placements and to develop orphanages for unfortunate children. This bill, developed and supported by Samuel Gridley Howe and Frank B. Sanborn, specifically *excluded* those who were mentally retarded:

> It shall be unlawful to retain in any almshouse any such child, that can be cared for as above directed, without inordinate expense: *provided*, that nothing herein contained shall apply to any child, that has no legal settlement in the state, nor any child, that is idiotic or otherwise so defective bodily or mentally as to make such a child's retention in an almshouse desirable, nor to any child under the age of eight whose mother is an inmate in the almshouse, and a suitable person to aid in taking care of such a child.[120]

In 1879, Illinois established by legislative mandate industrial schools for girls, which were "to provide a home and proper training"; however, "no imbecile or idiotic girl, or one incapacitated for labor, or any girl having any infectious, contagious, or incurable disease shall be committed or received. . . ."[121]

One of the most unique programs to assist children from poverty areas was the "Orphan Train" sponsored by Children's Aid Society of New York. From 1853 to 1929, over 100,000 children were transported from New York and other eastern cities and placed with foster parents in midwestern states. According to Charles Loring Brace, founder of the Children's Aid Society, "the best of all asylums for the outcast child is the *farmer's home* [where] children are a blessing, and the mere feeding of a young boy or girl is not considered at all. . . ."[122] Again, some mentally retarded children were rejected, returned, and institutionalized:

> Two little girls of 3 and 5 years, were taken into the home of one of the leading citizens of the city. They were supposed to be sisters, but the foster parents became convinced that they had at least different fathers. Since the children continually talked about "little Lucy," another sister, the foster parents decided to send to the New York society for this child and take her into their home, in order that the three sisters might be brought up together. . . . It soon developed, however, that not only was Lucy mentally deficient but also one of the other little girls. The foster parents found that they were unable to train these two children at all, although they made every effort to do so. These children therefore were returned to the New York society and at the time of inquiry were in a colony for the feeble-minded.[123]

It is easy to see that even those who had assumed a reforming posture for many children simply did not consider mentally retarded youngsters in the same worthy light. It was either the almshouse or the institution, the latter being by far the lesser of two evils.

SPECIAL EDUCATION

It is difficult to determine precisely when the first public school special education program for mentally retarded students was initiated in the United States. Credit for establishing the first special class is usually given to the public school system of Providence, Rhode Island. According to Rhoda A. Esten, supervisor of special schools for Providence, an auxiliary school (Burnside) for 15 mentally retarded students opened in December, 1896.[124] There is some indication, however, that the Cleveland school system may have established such a class 20 years earlier. In 1918, Charlotte

Steinbach provided the following anecdote:

> According to our local history, the first special class in the United States was organized in Cleveland in 1875. Perhaps one reason why Cleveland is not known to boast about this particular achievement is because it came to a tragic end at the close of the school year. The story as told to me by a school official who knew firsthand the facts, is as follows: About 14 of the most serious cases of imbecility in the most congested quarters of the town were gathered together and a superior, conscientious teacher placed in charge. The good folk responsible for this inauguration were united in their belief that pupils would soon become as normal children, once they were properly taught. The teacher heroically attacked the problem, but before the close of the year, all were aware that the experiment was doomed to failure. At the close of the term, the class was disbanded—the imbeciles returned to their homes, probably not much worse for their 'schooling,' but the poor teacher suffered a mental collapse which necessitated a sojourn at our state hospital.[125]

By 1898, the city of Providence had established three auxiliary schools and one special classroom for 50 "backward" children and others requiring "special discipline and instruction." In spite of this progress, however, at least 100 additional students required services, for it "would be impracticable and unwise to retain the pupils longer in the regular schools for association with children with whom they are not able to compete will discourage them, and being unable to comprehend the subjects taught, their already feeble power of attention will be lost, their interest destroyed, and the result will be that they will soon become apathetic, rendering it almost impossible for the special teacher to rouse them to activity if they are ever placed under favorable conditions for development."[126]

Other cities soon followed Providence's example: Chicago (1898), Boston (1899), Philadelphia (1899), and New York (1899). By the turn of the century, special education provisions for mentally retarded students were generally accepted, though not always implemented, in most large cities throughout the country.

It is highly probable that the experience of New York was typical of most cities starting programs prior to the turn of the century or soon thereafter. According to E. E. Farrell, inspector of ungraded schools in New York, "It is interesting to know that this class, which was to demonstrate the need for further classification of children in public schools, was not the result of any theory. It grew out of conditions in a neighborhood which furnished many and serious problems in truancy and discipline. The first class was made up of the odds and ends of a large school. There were over-age children, so-called naughty children, and the dull and stupid children. The ages ranged from eight to sixteen years. They were the children who could not get along in school."[127]

Purposes and Eligibility

The alleged purposes of special education programs were highly variable during the period of 1850 to 1900, and there was little consensus. Many early educators and institutional administrators contended that the primary purpose of public school classes was to prepare mentally retarded youngsters for institutional life. Some, such as Esten, believed that the goal of such education was to raise "these children to a standard of useful, self-supporting, self-controlling citizenship, rather than to support them and their progeny in almshouses and prisons."[128] Few, however, agreed with C. M. Lawrence, who wrote that the "line between feeble-mindedness is not a fixed affair; that feeble-mindedness is a relative state or condition; that there is as much difference between two feeble-minded children as there is between two children in the grades; that the connecting link between these two varying classes is another varying class we call the dullards."[129] Education might well reduce these disparities.

By all standards of the day, educational services offered in the public school setting were intended primarily—though not exclusively—for the mildly retarded students. A large number of mentally retarded and other developmentally disabled children were excluded from school. Not surprisingly, some parents petitioned the courts for relief as early as 1874.[130] The courts, however, consistently left the establishment of eligibility to local school boards and administrators. This was made eminently clear in *Alvord* v. *Inhabitants of the Town of Chester* (Massachusetts, 1901): "The right given every child by statute to attend public school is not unqualified, but is subject to such reasonable regulations as to numbers and qualifications of pupils as the school committee shall from time to time prescribe."[131]

Early Training Programs

Esten's presentation concerning the first special education classes in Providence offers an excellent overview of early curricular conceptions:

> The education of these children must include the elements taught in our regular schools, combined with a course of physical training that will arouse to activity their dormant energies, strengthen their weak muscular and nervous powers, cultivate their weak wills, increase their feeble power of attention and train and educate their special senses. Their affection must be nursed, wrong habits corrected and ideas of obedience and moral rights implanted and nourished. . . .
>
> A graded course of physical exercises, beginning with the kindergarten and embracing calisthenics and industrial training adapted to the special needs of each child in order that every side of the child's nature may be developed.
>
> Advancing hand in hand with the above must be imparted the instruction given in our regular schools, beginning with a modified course of kindergarten work. The teaching must be direct, simple, practical and concrete. The objects used for illustrating the subjects taught and those to be handled by the pupil must be larger than those in the ordinary school. Object teaching in its broadest must be a prominent feature. Size and age of pupils must be lost sight of for the time as these children are suffering from prolonged infancy and must be trained according to their degree of development. New principles must be imparted slowly and clearly and the lesson repeated until it is clearly understood, assimilated and thoroughly connected with and made a part of their previous knowledge. Care must be taken that the lessons in any department are not too long thereby producing exhaustion and defeating the end for which they were given.
>
> Nature study should have an important place in the daily program. Lessons on living animals and plants interest and hold the attention of these children for a greater length of time than those on

any other subject; they are real, live and concrete. Excursions for the study of nature should be made monthly and would well repay the cost. Instruction on living objects will implant in the minds of these children the lesson of love and helpfulness for each other. The discipline should be mild, gentle and firm, and in no case should corporal punishment be used. Medical supervision is also necessary for the success of the work and the medical director should prescribe and tabulate the physical exercises necessary for each child. Parents' meetings should be held at least once a month for talks on the special need of these children in regard to diet, sleep, baths, and suggestions given for the home care and training.[132]

Esten's comments reflect the essential ingredients found in most early training programs:

1. A strong emphasis on sense training consistent with Seguin's teachings
2. Basic academic subjects slightly modified
3. Manual or industrial training
4. Nature study

Other educators of the day would have added "play," both as a subject area and as an educational technique. In 1897, for example, one educator wrote, "Teachers of these children have naturally reduced much of their school instruction to the form of games, and with great advantage. . . . If an interest for games, a real play enthusiasm could be awakened in these children, it would be of greatest value."[133] As implied by Esten and as supported by nearly all educators engaged in meeting the needs of mentally retarded persons, great emphasis was placed on concrete learning experiences.

Physical education was also stressed by most educators, referring back to Seguin's concept of educating the mind through the perceptions instead of prearranged reasonings. At the turn of the century, Gulick described an elaborate physical education program that embodied many of the ideas and activities later expressed in a popular developmental theory of the mid twentieth century. The youngster's physical activities were to be consistent with the "organization of nerve centers, those of the trunk being followed by those of the shoulder, elbow, thigh, knee, wrist, ankle, fingers, face, tongue, and so on." By such activities as walking a balance beam or a carpet seam and tracking objects tossed in the air, "considerable portions of the brain . . . are directly trained."[134]

Curiously, however, not all education experts of the day agreed with the need for or desirability of teaching academics to even the more mildly affected. For example, G. E. Johnson, a fellow in pedagogy at Clark University, observed in 1897: "Reading, simply as an accomplishment, should not be taught the feeble-minded. . . . Reading and writing are tasks as unsuited to a feeble mind as precise work is to baby fingers."[135]

Regardless of philosophical differences, many innovative approaches were initiated prior to 1900 in an attempt to meet the needs of mentally retarded students. In 1898, the "Baltimore plan" was introduced; this provided different programs for normal, bright, and dull children. In the same year, the "Batavia [New York] plan" was adopted, which added a second teacher to the regular classroom to assist in providing individual instruction to slower students.[136] In other words, many current techniques—the team teacher, the resource person, and dual tracking—were all evident before the turn of the century.

Teacher Recruitment and Training

Though there were no formal training programs for special educators before 1896, teachers were selected very carefully. Esten placed great emphasis on the competence of the individual teacher as critical to a successful special education program. She specifically sought out those who satisfied the following criteria:

> Teachers who have carefully studied and understand the reciprocal influence of body upon mind and mind upon body and are able to apply that knowledge in their work; who are comparatively young and possessed of good physical health, original in devising ways and means, versatile in presenting subjects, gentle and patient in the constant repetitions necessary to fix ideas in the minds of their pupils, and above all, having an enduring love in their hearts for their pupils, a devotion to their vocation and faith that their efforts will be crowned with success.[137]

Nationally, it was most common to recruit teachers with an elementary school background augmented by a few months' exposure to mentally retarded persons in a residential setting. Lightner Witmer's program at the University of Pennsylvania, however, was distinctly different. On July 6, 1896, Witmer introduced the first university laboratory course on the education of retarded children. The 3-week program entitled "Methods and Results of Child Psychology" included four areas of interest: characteristics of defective children, special methods of training, class and individual experiments, and visits to institutions.[138]

Lightner Witmer

Born in Philadelphia, Lightner Witmer (1857–1956) attended the Episcopal Academy and graduated in 1888 from the University of Pennsylvania, where he served as assistant to the famed psychologist James McKeen Cattell. From his close association with Cattell, Witmer developed an intense interest in individual psychology. After a 2-year period of teaching English, he embarked upon the study of law but returned to his first interest—psychology—receiving his master's degree from the University of Pennsylvania in 1891 and his doctorate, under Wilhelm Wundt, at the University of Leipzig in 1892. Upon returning to this country, he soon succeeded Cattell as director of the Laboratory of Psychology at the University of Pennsylvania.

Witmer was an intelligent, analytical, iconoclastic, and athletic man, knowledgeable in a number of areas, including science, art, literature, and history. He was serious, dedicated, and somewhat reserved. As a close friend noted, "Witmer owes his adornments to his mother and his limitations to his father. The former were largely in the field of intellect, the latter in the affect. Psychoanalysts would call him an introvert."[139]

Witmer was not merely an administrator but a uniquely creative person, introducing and advancing the field of clinical psychology (so named by him) in the United States. He defined the role of clinical psychology in the develop-

Lightner Witmer.

ment of personality in a single word, "person-eering." In analyzing the problem of human conduct, he emphasized the "corrective," "preventative," "directive," and "creative" phases in the "production of preferred patterns of human behavior," or personality. This attitude of individuality is well illustrated by the six functions of his psychological clinic:

1. To make an analysis of individual reaction patterns and capacities;
2. To discover the etiology of these patterns and capacities;
3. To interpret the integration of the inter-organization and individual behavior;
4. To study the adjustment of the individual on the basis of the above;
5. To outline methods . . . for readjustment;
6. To recommend, assist with, or, on occasion, to direct the application of these methods.[140]

From March, 1896, when Witmer first worked with a child who could not learn to spell, until the end of his career, he remained interested in the area of diagnostic and remedial work with the intellectually and educationally deviating child. He firmly believed

that his special laboratory could be of great value in this area in four ways: "(1) the examination of the physical and mental conditions of school children; (2) the study of defective children; (3) the establishment of a psychological museum with a collection of specimens of work done by defective children and of the instruments, apparatus, results of investigations on normal and defective children; and (4) the establishment of an experimental training school for the remedial treatment of deviates."[141] The purpose of the clinical psychologist was to discover the relation between cause and effect in applying the various pedagogical remedies to a child who is suffering from general or special retardation.

Because of the magnitude of the problem, which automatically required both medical and behavioral evaluations, Witmer required an interdisciplinary approach to any problem. This he identified as "orthogenic treatment," which simply meant the involvement of "any agency known to science likely to develop, preserve, or restore personal competency."[142]

Witmer rejected current psychological theories of the day; insisted on the evaluation of the individual in terms of total life experiences, including his home and communal environment; and demanded individualized, prescriptive teaching. He also approached the subject of mental retardation circumspectly:

Mental retardation must not be considered as the equivalent of mental defect. In many cases, doubtless, retardation rests upon an effect of the brain or some other physical defect, the result of heredity, accident or disease, but in some cases the retardation is purely functional and may be a consequence of disuse through neglect. The normal child of six years is possessed of a group of mental and moral qualities characteristic of his age and sex. These qualities change into others through the acquisition of new or the loss of old qualities and through modification due to growth. The normal child of nine years of age differs from the normal child of six. If a child who was entirely normal at the age of six remains in possession of the same mental and moral qualities when he reaches the age of nine, he represents the condition of retardation. This retardation may involve one or more, possibly the entire group of qualities. A single quality may have a potent influence upon the course of intellectual development. Thus, the central mental process determining the course of intellectual evolution is attention. The development of concentrated attention results partly from the genetic process alone—that is, it is a growth from within—and partly from the environment in the form of school training and home discipline. Through neglect of proper training, the young man of twenty-one may find his powers of attention inadequate for the proper fulfillment of the requirements of a college course and more appropriate to a child of eight or ten. He is suffering from a partial arrest of development, the result of neglect. An arrest in the development of attention will carry with it an arrested development of the intellectual processes. [143]

Though Witmer did not believe that the mentally retarded person's intelligence per se would be affected by proper instruction, his performance would be.

Before his death in 1956 at the age of 89, Witmer's accomplishments were many. His special laboratory realized most of its goals; he helped establish similar programs at Bryn Mawr College in 1896 and Lehigh University in 1903; he became a psychologist at the Pennsylvania Training School for Feeble-minded Children in 1896; and, in 1907, he began publication of a new psychological journal, *The Psychological Clinic*. Finally, in 1920, he started the Witmer School for mentally retarded youngsters, which was in operation at the time of his death.

The Educational Setting

One area of controversy surrounding the early efforts at special education was evident: Where should the mentally retarded youngster be educated? As already acknowledged, many professionals continued to believe that the institution was "the best place in which to shape the [educational] environment to meet the peculiarities of these feeble-minded children." [144]

Esten, however, preferred the auxiliary or special school setting:

For the better training and development of our pupils already under special instruction and for those for whom we ought to provide, I would respectfully recommend that a suitable building be secured in some control location large enough to accommodate all, and that these children be placed there under an experienced, well-trained,

competent principal and a sufficient number of assistants. This would mean, of course, the transportation of the pupils living at a distance at the expense of the city, but, as these pupils who ought to be provided for are living in different sections of the city, nearly all remote from the schools already established, to properly provide for them in their own districts would require the establishment, equipment and maintenance of seven additional schools at, I think, a greater cost to the city than that of transportation; besides, the best work that could be done in these separate schools would be necessarily inferior to that which could be accomplished by concentration. . . . [Further] The teaching of these unfortunates is peculiarly exhausting and often discouraging, hence, teachers having them in charge need to be associated for mutual help and encouragement. . . . By bringing these children together they could be classified according to capacity and similar needs and much valuable time saved in teaching. They also would be able to profit by the mistakes of each other and be stimulated to a healthy rivalry. . . . It would cost less to equip and maintain one large school than several small ones. [145]

Esten quickly added that, in her opinion, such special schools would not stigmatize the children: "Such a conclusion would be possible only to the ignorant who should be properly instructed, or to those unfortunates who have an arrested moral development. The condition of a feeble-minded child is more degrading than that of a child with a weak heart, weak lungs, or defective hearing. In each case the child is not responsible and should, therefore, awaken not only our pity, but should call forth our tenderest care and best efforts for his development. These are God's little ones, entrusted to our care—let us see to it that we are not found 'wanting' in our duty." [146]

Others preferred the "ungraded" class in the regular school. E. E. Farrell from the New York Public School System set forth this preference:

The ungraded class is always part and parcel of the regular school. It is not in a separate building. I need not justify this I am sure. By having the class a part of a regular school we avoid the stigma that might attach to any child attending it; we get a relation between the ungraded class children and others which is most desirable. As you know, these children frequently excel in some of the manual arts. An exhibition of this kind of work for the benefit of all the grades brings to the ungraded class child a recognition which up to this time he has not received. It also gives encouragement to the parent. At an exhibition of work held recently in a public school the parents were surprised at the work done in chair-caning, carpentry, and basketry. Many parents asked when their child would get in that class so as to learn something useful.[147]

In the final analysis, all systems were used, but most mentally retarded students remained in the regular classroom without special attention.

In summary, the nation had become alert to mentally retarded persons and through state and local actions had begun to develop services in two areas: institutionalization and special education. For most of this period, primary attention was devoted to the provision of residential services, which went through the discouraging transformation from education and independence to custody and dependence. By 1890, the die had been cast: state-sponsored institutions would serve a highly heterogeneous population in terms of intelligence, age, and medical condition on the colony plan. While related decisions were frequently justified on the basis of need and the absence of suitable alternatives, there is little question that mentally retarded persons were often held in ill regard. The advent of special education held new promise and introduced many of the controversies which, with some variation, are still being debated by educators, including, what to teach, how to teach, and where to teach.

Chapter

6

THE PROGRESSIVE ERA
(1900–1919)

THE PERIOD BETWEEN the Spanish-American War and World War I is often designated by historians as the "Progressive Era," and as such, it introduced fundamental changes in the American way of life. By the turn of the century, the Gilded Age had produced a handful of private, wealthy citizens who wielded immense power; their organizations controlled much of the country's wealth and all that went to produce it at great cost and sacrifice to millions of people.[1] Though many persons wanted change, there was no single progressive group or party seeking a single goal; rather, the "progressives were essentially middle-class moralists seeking to arouse the conscience of 'the people' in order to purify American life. Local, state, and national government [was to] be made more responsive to the will of the unorganized mass of decent citizens who stood for all the traditional values."[2]

Targets for reform were numerous, including the need to 1) exercise some control over the practices of big business, 2) eliminate horrendous slum conditions, 3) change working conditions affecting 1.5 million children under age 16 who worked 13 hours a day for a pittance, 4) upgrade salaries of the working adults, many of whom worked 59 hours per week for less than 10 dollars, 5) provide safe working conditions, accident insurance, and pensions, and 6) improve the lot of the American poor, of whom there were over 50 million.

Added to those who sought political reform, business reform, and human services reform were those who advocated with equal fervor for women's rights and prohibition.

In brief, many people sought political innovations to attain a system which would be more humane and responsive to the needs of all the people. Yet, they desired neither to destroy capitalism nor to introduce any major change in governmental structure and organization. Nor were they particularly sympathetic toward blacks, and though interested in improving living conditions in the slums, progressives remained both suspicious and intolerant of the country's 10 million immigrants. While they struggled for better working conditions and salaries, employees organizations were not favored. It was, as aptly phrased by May, "a movement to remake America in a homogeneous, classless and virtuous image"—a society agreeable to middle-class standards and expectancies.[3] It was concerned with "needs" rather than "rights." Consequently, progressives promoted a paternalistic governmental system for the protection and often the coercion of those considered less fortunate.

The movement found its political champion in Theodore Roosevelt when he assumed the presidency in September, 1901. There was no question in his mind that there was a major role for the federal government in regulating agencies that affected the lives of many:

Unquestionably . . . the great development of industrialism means that there must be an increase in the supervision exercised by the Government over business enterprises. . . . Neither this people nor any other free people will permanently tolerate the use of the vast power conferred by vast wealth, and especially by wealth in its corporate form without lodging somewhere in the Government the still higher power of seeing that this power, in addition to being used in the interest of the individual or individuals possessing it, is also used for and not against the interest of the people as a whole. . . . No final satisfactory result can be expected from merely State action. The action must come through the Federal Government.[4]

Thus, the stage was set, and the federal government became increasingly involved in a broad spectrum of activities affecting the daily affairs of its citizens. In 1913, the Sixteenth Amendment to the Constitution was ratified, authorizing the federal government to collect income taxes, thereby producing the financial means with which to execute its newly assumed responsibilities.

In 1909, President Theodore Roosevelt called together the first White House conference on children, which was concerned particularly with the care of dependent youngsters. Mental retardation was not a visible topic of concern; however, when President Wilson called a similar conference in 1919 to celebrate "Children's Year," Walter Fernald prepared an important paper on "A State Program for the Care of the Mentally Defective," which became part of the proceedings on protective standards for children with special needs. The contents of that paper are reviewed later.

As an outgrowth of the first White House conference, the Children's Bureau was established in 1912 to "investigate and report upon all matters pertaining to the welfare of children."[5] Its early efforts included the study of mentally and physically disabled children in the District of Columbia (1912) and in Delaware (1917 and 1919). Other segments of the federal government were also concerned with mentally retarded persons. The U.S. Department of Commerce continued its national census studies, and the U.S. Public Health Service took a particular interest in mental retardation

among developing school children in rural communities.

Clifford Whittingham Beers published *The Mind That Found Itself* in 1908. This book reflected the deplorable conditions in mental hospitals during his 3-year confinement between 1900 and 1903. It received national attention and led to a broad-based mental hygiene movement that extended services to mentally retarded as well as to mentally ill persons.

The notion of a pure, virtuous middle-class society was to have a tremendous impact on mentally retarded persons. This philosophy pervaded nearly every aspect of social programming for the developmentally disabled for years to come.

UNDERSTANDING OF MENTAL RETARDATION

The first decades of the twentieth century represented the nadir of professional sensitivity toward mentally retarded persons, at least as a class or subpopulation. The negativism of the past century reached its zenith between the year 1900 and World War I, and its impact on sociopolitical attitudes and decisions was severe and often uncompromising. In other words, the negative professional debates of the nineteenth century became the social reality of the twentieth, with grave consequences for those deemed or suspected to be mentally retarded. At the same time, however, attitudes underwent change, and many of the seeds for the future development of a broad spectrum of services were planted, setting forth concepts and models yet to be fully realized.

DEFINITION AND CLASSIFICATION

The three essential components of a definition of mental retardation were well recognized by the turn of the century: 1) early onset, 2) reduced intellectual functioning due to a developmental disorder, and 3) an inability to adapt to the full demands of society. In 1910, the United States government, for example, announced that "Feeble-mindedness has been broadly defined as comprising all degrees of mental defect due to arrested or imperfect mental development as a result of which the person so affected is incapable of competing on equal terms with his normal fellows, or of managing himself or his affairs with ordinary prudence."[6] While such definitions generically identified mentally retarded persons, they lacked reasonable parameters. Thus, anyone who was illiterate, poor, "ill bred," orphaned, or of foreign birth could be classified as mentally retarded if they did not perform to the diagnostician's personal expectancy for normal social participation or the "prudent" conduct of one's affairs.

The introduction of standardized tests of intelligence in the United States by Goddard, Kuhlmann, Terman, and others altered this situation to some degree. The notion that a mentally retarded person would perform at a mental level of 12 years or less, or would have an IQ score less than 75 to 80 helped restrict the interpretation of mental retardation. Nevertheless, many persons "functioning as mentally retarded," regardless of their ability or circumstance, or perhaps because of the latter, continued to be labeled mentally retarded, and many spent a significant portion of their life in a public institution for the feebleminded and epileptic.

In 1910, the Committee on Classification of Feeble-minded of the American Association on Mental Deficiency issued its definition and level of retardation classification, incorporating Goddard's term "moron":

> The term feeble-minded is used generically to include all degrees of mental defect due to arrested or imperfect development as a result of which the person so affected is incapable of competing on equal terms with his normal fellows or managing himself or his affairs with ordinary prudence.
>
> The tripartite classification of mental retardation included:
>
> Idiots: Those so deeply defective that their mental development does not exceed that of a normal child of about 2 years.

> Imbeciles: Those whose mental development is higher than that of an idiot but does not exceed that of a normal child of about 7 years.
>
> Morons: Those whose mental development is above that of an imbecile but does not exceed that of a child of about 12 years.[7]

Adoption of the term "moron" which, according to Goddard (1910) originated with the Greek term "moronia" meaning foolish in the sense of deficient judgment, ended the cumbersome practice of using the term "feebleminded" generically and specifically.

With regard to level of retardation and programmatic possibilities, Barr's scheme, an extension of Fernald's work, was commonly accepted and frequently quoted[8] (see Table 1).

ASSESSMENT OF INTELLIGENCE

Though intelligence testing was not to receive its primary impetus until Goddard adopted the Binet-Simon scale in 1908, Kelly (1903) and Norsworthy (1906, 1907) continued to study Cattell's physical attributes and association ideas among normal and mentally retarded individuals. The tests included such aspects as height, weight, pulse, temperature, memory of unrelated words, part-whole tests, and opposite tests. The conclusion reached by both researchers was that while mentally retarded persons did distinctly less well than normal, there was a fairly even transition from lowest to highest scores. Norsworthy also recorded that feebleminded persons were not a "species" and that it was extremely difficult to distinguish between the more intelligent among them and the normal, a problem which was to persist, as we shall see, even after the introduction and extensive use of the Binet-Simon test.[9]

With the advent of special education, the need to standardize the psychological protocol became quite evident, and in 1901, the Committee on Psychological Research of the American Association on Mental Deficiency provided a format for an appropriate psychological examination. Categories of consideration in-

Table 1.   Barr's educational classification of the feeble-minded

		IDIOT.	
	Profound.	{ Apathetic. } { Excitable. }	Unimprovable.
Asylum Care.	Superficial.	{ Apathetic. } { Excitable. }	Improvable in self-help only.

IDIO-IMBECILE.
Improvable in self-help and helpfulness.
Trainable in very limited degree to assist others.

MORAL IMBECILE.

*Custodial Life
and Perpetual
Guardianship.*

Mentally and morally deficient.
Low Grade: Trainable in industrial occupations; temperament bestial.
Middle Grade: Trainable in industrial and manual occupations; a plotter
   of mischief.
High Grade: Trainable in manual and intellectual arts; with a genius
   for evil.

IMBECILE.

*Long Apprentice-
ship and Colony
Life Under
Protection.*

Mentally deficient.
Low Grade: Trainable in industrial and simplest manual occupations.
Middle Grade: Trainable in manual arts and simplest mental
   requirements.
High Grade: Trainable in manual and intellectual arts.

BACKWARD OR MENTALLY FEEBLE.

*Training for a
Place in the
World.*

Mental processes normal, but slow and requiring special training and
   environment to prevent deterioration; defect imminent under slightest
   provocation, such as excitement, over-stimulation or illness.

Source: Barr, 1904, p. 90.

cluded anthropological measurements (e.g., age, height, head measurements, hereditary conditions, stigmata of degeneracy); sensation, including such perversions as nystagmus and color-blindness; perception; memory; emotions; instincts, including nutrition, fears, affections, curiosities, feeling of pride, as well as love, sex, and masturbation; volition; association of ideas; attention; judgment; reasoning (deductive and inductive); imagination; special talents (music, mechanical, memory of places and dates); and a definitive school record, including reference to reading, writing, numbers, and mechanical abilities.[10]

The need and interest was evident, and only Goddard's interpretation of the 1905 Binet-Simon test in 1908 was required to open the gates of unparalleled activity in the area of individual differences and intelligence testing.

Alfred Binet

Born in Nice, France, the only child of a physician father and an artist mother, Alfred Binet (1857–1911) was to leave an indelible imprint on the study and measurement of individual differences. Following receipt of his law degree in 1878, Binet immediately enrolled in the Sorbonne to pursue the natural sciences, completing his doctoral studies in 1897.

Binet's interest in psychology, however, had already been well established by the time he received his doctorate degree. As early as 1880, he published an article concerning the fusion of similar sensations; in 1891, he joined Henri Beaunis at the Laboratory of Physiological Psychology at the Sorbonne. Upon Beaunis's retirement in 1895, Binet became the director and held that position until his death.

Alfred Binet.

Independently wealthy, not bound by the ties and responsibilities of a professorship, and with an entirely free hand as administrator of the laboratory, Binet had great opportunity to pursue his many interests. A uniquely curious and industrious person, like so many other gifted persons who have contributed to the field of mental retardation, Binet held a wide array of interests, including micro-organisms and insects; writing plays concerning abnormal behavior; hypnotism; mental fatigue; graphology; and cephalometry. By nature somewhat introverted, he was, nevertheless, a prodigious, demanding worker, one who frequently offended his collaborators and colleagues (with the apparent exception of Theodore Simon) with his domineering attitude. Nor was he averse to taking advantage of an opportunity—though his dislike of student assistants was well known, he was initially attracted to Simon because the latter served as psychiatrist to the colony at Perray-Vaucluse and, therefore, had ready access to 300 mentally retarded male subjects.

On occasion, Binet could be a harsh critic. In

1907, he graciously acknowledged that Seguin showed how one might "by dint of much ingenuity and patience, increase the intelligence and improve the character of some of these unfortunate children" but added, his "work must not be examined too closely; those who praise it have certainly not read it. Seguin impresses us as empiric, endowed with great personal talent, which he has succeeded in embodying clearly in his works. These contain some pages of good sense, with many obscurities, and many absurdities."[11]

Perhaps Binet's most distinguishing characteristic was his insatiable curiosity and perpetual willingness to expand his horizons and modify his concepts. Throughout the course of his professional development, he was never intellectually content; at the time of his death, he was seriously pursuing further changes in the measurement of intelligence.

Among his other contributions, in addition to his measurement of intelligence, he co-developed the *L'Année psychologique* in 1895. In 1900, he was instrumental in organizing the *Société libre pour l'Étude psychologique de l'Enfant*, a society composed of psychologists, school teachers, and school principals concerned with the practical problems in the schools.

Though Binet's initial intelligence test, co-developed with his student Theodore Simon, did not appear until 1905, many of the basic ideas and concepts underlying the test were formulated through his extensive experiences working in the school systems during the 1890s as well as studying mental retardation in the schools of Paris and in the colony at Perray-Vaucluse.

In collaboration with several colleagues, Binet investigated intensely many facets of children's behavior, including memory, suggestibility, descriptions of objects and pictures, attention, and adaptation. These as well as many other studies of children's performances involved mentally retarded, normal, and gifted students in public school settings. For example, in 1899, he observed that "less intelligent" school children failed to adapt to new tasks as rapidly as did "more intelligent" students.[12] In addition, and in a manner quite similar to that of Jean Piaget, he conducted a number of observational studies of his two daughters, Alice and Madeleine, in such areas as movement, perception, visual illusions, and visual memory reference. He also was concerned with fears among children and thresholds of sensation.

Simon also undertook several studies with mentally retarded persons at the colony of Perray-Vaucluse. In one study, he found that the more severely retarded residents were beyond suggestibility. In another, he recorded anthropometric measurements of mentally retarded boys and found some indication that slower students revealed a general lack of physical development, rather than any major defects of a particular kind. A modification of this study served as the basis for his doctoral dissertation (in medicine).

In addition to their studies related to the measurement of intelligence, both Binet and Simon continued physical studies of mentally retarded persons until as late as 1910, when they concluded that "nothing is more deceiving than physical appearance."[13] Thus, by the time they published their first intelligence scale, both scientists had extensive experience in studying behavior. Binet alone or in collaboration with others had published over 200 articles and books.

Binet-Simon Individual Tests of Intelligence

The first such test appeared in 1905, constructed as it was in response to an emergency situation that had arisen in the Paris school system. In the early fall of 1904, the minister of public instruction appointed a commission to study measures to be taken to provide appropriate educational experiences for subnormal children in Paris. It had been decided that youngsters who could not benefit from the regular curriculum because of intellectual inadequacies would be instructed in special classes. To accomplish this goal as objectively as possible, the commission was appointed with much of the responsibility falling to Binet in view of his extensive work with tests and children, including mentally retarded children.

The 1905 version, a "metrical scale of intelligence," was intended to distinguish between subnormal and normal school-age children. The 30 items included visual coordination, prehension, cognizance of food, execution of simple orders, imitation of gestures, verbal knowledge of objects, reproduction of a series of three digits immediately after oral presentation, weight discrimination, definitions of familiar objects, and distinctions between abstract terms.[14]

The first scale was not divided according to age levels but was interpreted in terms of the three levels of mental retardation: idiocy, imbecility, and moronity. The levels were determined by the number of items an individual successfully passed in the hierarchy of intellectual functioning. Idiots would not proceed beyond Test 6; imbeciles, beyond Test 15. Determination of moronity, however, presented difficulties. In general, morons would not proceed beyond Tests 23 and 24, though occasionally they might pass one of the tests at a higher level. According to Binet, the primary distinguishing factor between moronity and normalcy involved judgment; thus, while morons could pass many basic items, they would have difficulty with those involving abstractions. In general, the authors estimated that morons functioned at the 12-year level of intelligence.

From their educational and psychological studies, Binet and Simon posited educational definitions of idiocy, imbecility, and moronity:

> An idiot is any child who never learns to communicate with his kind by speech—that is to say, one who can neither express his thoughts verbally nor understand the verbally expressed thoughts of others, this inability being due solely to defective intelligence, and not to any disturbance of hearing, nor to any affectation of the organs of phonation.
>
> An imbecile is any child who fails to learn how to communicate with his kind by means of writing—that is to say, one who can neither express his thoughts in writing, nor read writing or print, or correctly understand what he reads, this failure being due to defective intelligence, and not to any defect of vision or any paralysis of the arms which would explain his inability.

A moron is one who can communicate with his kind by speech or writing, but who shows a retardation of two or three years . . . in his school studies, this retardation not being due to insufficient or irregular attendance.[15]

Binet believed he was successful in defining levels of retardation more precisely based on the combination of test scores and educational history. He had long been concerned about the classifications rendered by medical personnel which "looked as if they had been drawn by chance out of a sack."[16]

Two more versions (1908 and 1911) were published before his death. These included the distribution of items by age level.

Of great consequence was Binet's genuine concern that intelligence tests as devised play an important role in instructional matters. He was thoroughly convinced that intelligence could be enhanced, and in his most theoretical statement, *Les Ideés Modernes Sur les Enfants*, published in 1909, he spoke out strongly against the "brutal pessimism" of persons who believed that intelligence was a fixed quantity that could not be increased.[17] Though Binet never posited a definition of intelligence or proposed an elaborate theory of intellectual functioning, he did observe:

Now if one considers that intelligence is not a single, indivisible function with a particular essence of its own but that it is formed by the combination of all the minor functions of discrimination, observation, and retention, all of which have been proved to be plastic and subject to increase, it will seem incontestable that the same law governs the ensemble and its elements, and that consequently the intelligence of anyone is susceptible of development. With practice, enthusiasm, and especially with method one can succeed in increasing one's attention, memory, and judgment, and in becoming literally more intelligent than before; and this progress will go on until one reaches one's limit. And . . . what is important in order to act intelligently is not so much the force of the faculties as the manner of using them; that is to say, as the *art* of intelligence, which is necessarily capable of being refined by practice.[18]

This belief in the educability of intelligence was reflected in his special educational methods: "Having on our hands children who did not know how to listen, to pay attention, to keep quiet, we pictured our first duty as being not to teach them the facts that we thought would be most useful, but *to teach them how to learn*. We have therefore devised . . . what we call exercises of mental orthopedics. The word is expressive and has come into favor. One can guess its meaning. In the same way that physical orthopedics straightens a crooked spine, mental orthopedics strengthens, cultivates, and fortifies attention, memory, perception, judgment, and will."[19]

Though Binet died before he had accomplished many of his personal goals, his testing efforts were pursued aggressively by others, but not in France. Simon did not feel sufficiently capable to continue the work, since, as a physician, he lacked the research background. Rather, he spent most of his remaining years serving as psychiatrist and doctor-in-chief of several large mental hospitals in Paris. Interestingly, in an interview with Theta Wolf in 1959, he expressed his strong objection to the addition of the IQ to intelligence testing.

For some unexplainable reason, while the Binet-Simon test was eagerly sought in many parts of the world, it did not receive favor in France. It was used only by Simon until the 1920s. Interest in furthering the study of intelligence and its measurement transferred to the United States.

As indicated, Goddard, who had been introduced to Binet's work by the famed Belgian educator-physician Ovide Decroly, translated the Binet-Simon test and became its most fervent advocate. According to Florence Goodenough, a later leader in the field of mental testing, like "the apostle of old, he proclaimed his beliefs in all possible quarters. He gave public lectures, demonstrated the method of testing before educational associations, groups of social workers, medical men."[20]

Henry Herbert Goddard

Born in Vassalboro, Maine, Henry Herbert Goddard (1866–1957) received his master's degree from Harvard in 1889, taught for a year at the University of Southern California, then served for 6 years as a high school principal in

Ohio and Maine. He received his doctorate in 1899 from Clark University, following which he taught at the Pennsylvania State Teachers College at Westchester until 1906, with a brief 1-year respite for study in Germany. With the opening of the first research program at the Vineland Training School in 1906, Goddard was appointed director and developed the first psychological laboratory devoted exclusively to the study of mentally retarded individuals. In addition to his interest in the Binet-Simon intelligence scale, he was highly active in the development of tests for use with American military forces during World War I. He was also a prolific writer, producing such works as *The Kallikaks, Feeble-Mindedness, The Criminal Imbecile,* and *School Training of Defective Children.* In 1918, Goddard assumed responsibility for the State Bureau of Juvenile Research for Ohio, publishing several books in this area, including *The Psychology of the Normal and Subnormal, Human Efficiency and Levels of Intelligence,* and *Juvenile Delinquency.* From 1922 until his retirement in 1938, he was professor of clinical psychology at Ohio State

University, where he again published several books, one dealing with multiple personalities and another with the education of gifted children.

Lewis Madison Terman

While Goddard had a tremendous impact on testing in terms of mental retardation, Lewis Terman (1877–1956) had the greater impact on the measurement of intelligence per se. Born in rural Indiana, he received his early education in a one-room schoolhouse. Following a 2-year normal school (an early educational college) education, Terman taught in a country school prior to completing his Bachelor's Degree. Following receipt of that degree, he served as a high school principal for 3 years and entered Indiana University, where he received his Master's Degree in 1903, and his Doctorate Degree from Clark University in 1905. Subsequently, Terman served as a high school principal in San Bernardino, California, for a year; then taught for 4 years at the Los Angeles State Normal School. Terman became head of Stanford's department of psychology in 1910, a position he held for 20 years. During this period, he became a major influence in psychology and mental testing.

In 1916, Terman published a revision of Binet's intelligence scale, the Stanford-Binet Test of Intelligence, which became the most popular test of intelligence throughout the country. The great success of this test encouraged Terman and his colleague, Maud A. Merrill, to revise the Stanford-Binet in 1937.

Terman introduced the intelligence quotient, originally conceived by the German William Stern in 1914, to the standard operational interpretation of intelligence tests. Using the IQ, he provided a new classification system in 1916 that is still cited:

> Above 140, near genius or genius.
> 120–140, very superior intelligence.
> 110–120, superior intelligence.
> 90–110, normal or average intelligence.
> 80–90, dullness, rarely classifiable as feeble-mindedness.
> 50–70, morons.
> 20 or 25–50, imbeciles.
> Below 20 or 25, idiots.[21]

Henry Herbert Goddard.

Lewis Madison Terman.

In addition to his interest in testing and mentally retarded individuals, Terman conducted one of the most unique studies of gifted people on record. In 1921, he tested 1,500 children with an average age of 11 and IQs above 140 and followed their development, experiences, and careers well into adulthood. The results of this study were published in a series of four volumes entitled, *Genetic Studies of Genius*. At the time of his death, he was working on the fifth volume, representing one of the longest studies of gifted individuals, or of any group of persons.

Fred Kuhlmann

The other highly active person in intelligence testing among mentally retarded persons was Fred Kuhlmann (1876–1941) of the Research Department at Fairbault, Minnesota. He conducted a significant number of studies using the Binet test and introduced his own condensed and slightly modified version of the 1908 scale in 1911.

By 1911, Kuhlmann reached the conclusion that ''the tests really offer an instrument that

enables us to measure the intellectual development of children of the ages ranging from 3–12 years; but the method is practical, convenient, and rapid.'' He was, however, quite conservative when discussing the constancy of results; ''classification according to mental age is valid only for the time being. A child that is an imbecile to-day may be feeble-minded only as he grows older, or he may remain an imbecile. The prognosis is reserved.''[22]

Of these early scientists, Goddard studied a wide range of children and adults with varying exceptional needs and inevitably found that mental retardation was the underlying problem, with all its negative social ramifications. This was true whether he was performing one of his genealogical studies, estimating mental retardation among immigrants, or examining those receiving some form of special education.

One cannot escape the impression that Goddard, in all his enthusiasm, social concern, and misguided but well entrenched notions about heredity, had one primary goal in mind: to seek out and identify those who were mentally re-

Fred Kuhlmann.

tarded rather than to view intelligence testing as an aid to better education and programming. Goodenough's criticism that his "crusading zeal often blinded him to sources of error in his work" was not without justification.[23]

Terman, in contrast, hoped that intelligence testing would give rise to a productive, beneficial differential psychology—one that would be of value in appropriate educational programming and vocational guidance. The ultimate goal was to assist each person, regardless of intelligence, to realize a satisfying life consistent with the tenets of the mental hygiene movement.

One can readily perceive that the early leaders in the field of testing differed appreciably in their basic concepts and perhaps their intentions. These differences would be manifested in several other critical areas. While Goddard was relentless in his proclamation that "feeble-minded children are trainable but not improvable in intellectual capacity," others were not so convinced.[24] "A child might be feeble-minded at first and become normal later," wrote Kuhlmann.[25]

Further, unlike Goddard, Kuhlmann did not ignore social-cultural implications: "The dividing line between feeble-mindedness and the normal is more difficult to determine. It is probably not fixed. An individual is normal when he can take care of himself, when he can get sufficient remunerative work to meet his personal needs, and when his intelligence does not rank him below the average of the society in which his parents live."[26]

Intelligence tests, then as today, possessed one serious drawback: they failed to provide a clear distinction between the upper limits of mild mental retardation and normalcy. Thus, while Goddard had little reservation about classifying an individual, child or adult, as mentally retarded, others again were more conservative and sought substantial supportive data, though most were not as elaborate as Fernald, who wrote:

The diagnosis of ordinary cases of idiocy and imbecility is a simple matter. Even the high-grade cases occurring in childhood present few difficul-

ties. The upper levels of the so-called moron grade as seen in late childhood, and adolescence, are often most perplexing and difficult. An accurate and incontestible diagnosis of one of these borderline cases can be satisfactorily made only after a thorough physical examination of the patient, knowledge of the family history, personal history especially the story of his infancy and early childhood, school history and records, social and moral reactions, sexual habits, emotional stability, associates, interests, and the fullest inquiry as to his general information and practical knowledge. Appropriate psychological investigation by formal tests is especially indicated in these doubtful cases. The recent literature of the subject abounds in most elaborate and voluminous syllabi for routine examination and record, but a simple record of significant positive and negative findings is the most practical for diagnostic use. More than one examination is often required. It may be necessary to place the patient in a selected environment where his behavior and reactions may be carefully watched by a competent observer for a period of weeks or months before a final diagnosis and prognosis can be safely made.[27]

Fernald reviewed the matter in principle, William Healy in practice: "Two . . . children are of a rag picker. Parents do not know their ages. Were seen in their environment. One becomes a lawyer by change of environment. In a case of this kind, one hesitates about making a final diagnosis. One wonders if the individual is not suffering from a general mental disability due to the physical condition. It is necessary to put together these physical conditions in order to get a fair diagnosis."[28]

In contrast to Goddard, Terman and Knollin were concerned most about the final decision: "If a child is rated as feeble-minded, although dull, has nevertheless a degree of intelligence which will enable him to live a fairly normal social and industrious life, the mistaken diagnosis may result in depriving such a child of the very opportunities necessary for his fullest development."[29] Nevertheless, Terman believed intelligence tests possessed a tremendous potential for identifying "higher grade defectives," which would "bring tens of thousands of these high-grade defectives under the surveillance and protection of society . . . curtailing the reproduction of feeble-mindedness and in the elimination of an enormous amount of crime, pauperism, and industrial inefficiency."[30]

At the same time, Terman felt that the intelligence tests would be somewhat of a blessing to mentally retarded persons: "When we have learned the lessons which intelligence tests have to teach, we shall no longer blame mentally defective workmen for their industrial inefficiency, punish weak-minded children because of their inability to learn, or imprison and hang mentally defective criminals because they lack the intelligence to appreciate the ordinary codes of social conduct."[31]

In spite of the fact that many public school systems adopted the Binet test of intelligence by 1912 and employed at least one "Binet examiner," the tests were not without their critics. In addition to his previous observations concerning the efficacy of the Binet tests, Fernald believed that many of the items, especially those relating to vocabulary and abstract concepts were beyond the experiences of the poor.

Others agreed with Fernald. In 1913, Squire complained that the Binet test involved both knowledge and innate ability and was significantly influenced by language.[32] Several years earlier, Ayres contended that the test depended too much on environmental experiences and the child's ability to use words fluently, read and write, repeat words and numbers, solve puzzle tests, and define abstract terms.[33]

Berry, in 1913, observed that tests at the various ages were not of equal difficulty.[34] At the same time, Doll contended that the test was inaccurate beyond age 10; more importantly, he challenged the rationale underlying the test construction practices. He recommended that, in the future, three aspects vital to proper intelligence test development be taken into consideration: a definite knowledge or clear hypothesis of the psychology of the various age levels, a careful selection of those mental functions essential or contributory to intelligence, and objectivity in item selection.[35]

As early as 1913, Goddard reported that there was little, if any, significant change in the intellectual performances of 346 "children" of both sexes, of mental ages 1 to 12, and physical ages of 5 to 40, after three annual testings on the Binet scale. He concluded it was highly probable that intelligence as measured was constant.[36] Terman originally reported similar results. Subsequently, most professionals accepted the premise that one's IQ held constant. Terman was particularly short sighted in this area, especially as he clearly understood that performance of the gifted or normal person could readily be adversely influenced by "poverty, social neglect, physical defects, or educational maladjustments."[37]

Other tests of intelligence soon made their way into the examiner's arsenal. In 1915, the Australian S. D. Porteus introduced to Americans his test of mazes, believing that mentally retarded persons were discriminated against when using Binet scales because of shyness, a lack of confidence, and speech difficulties.[38] Thus was introduced the first fundamentally "culture-free" test. Similarly, in 1916, Doll issued a new set of norms for estimating intelligence through speed of performance on a form board, a device which had its origins with Seguin.

PREVALENCE

In 1915, Kuhlmann introduced to professionals in the field of mental retardation the distribution of IQs according to the normal curve, indicating that 1 percent of the total population would be mentally retarded with a ratio of idiot to imbecile to moron of 1:3:12. The 1-percent-of-the-total-population estimate was cited for many years.

ETIOLOGY

The list of clinical conditions associated with mental retardation continued to grow: Fröhlich's syndrome (adiposogenital dystrophy), 1900; Corpeuter's craniosynostosis, 1901; Apert's syndrome (acrocephaly-syndactyly), 1906; Von Reuss's disease (hepatolenticular degeneration), 1912; Crouzon's disease (familial craniosynostosis), 1912; Niemann-Pick's disease (abnormal lipid metabolism),

1914; and Krabbe's disease (globoid cell leukodystrophy), 1916. The exact genetic nature of these disorders and their biochemical components were not well understood.

Several texts, both of which were relatively ignored at the time, clearly pointed to the future. In 1909, the English physician A. Garrod published *Inborn Errors of Metabolism,* in which he advanced the theory that genetic abnormalities produced mental retardation and other disorders by blocking specific steps in the body's chemical reactions sequences.[39] This work received little attention until the 1940s, when biochemical disorders became better defined. Similarly, the English physician Eugene Talbot, professor of stomatology, released his "study of degenerative evolution" in 1911. He cautioned the expectant mother against the consumption of such toxic agents as alcohol, tobacco, coffee, and narcotic drugs, especially opiates, which, at that time, were frequently prescribed. He also recognized the hazards of infectious diseases and such metallic substances as lead and mercury upon the intellectual development of children.[40]

The debate over alcohol continued unabated. While many felt that alcohol was deleterious and should be avoided, others still argued that since the consumption of alcohol was so common, there should be many more mentally retarded births.

Infectious diseases, especially whooping cough and scarlet fever, were associated with mental retardation, as were meningitis and encephalitis of varying causes. Maternal and child malnutrition were also duly noted. In essence, with the exception of the more rare chromosomal and genetic disorders, most general causes of mental retardation were recognized.

Of particular interest to many physicians, both within and without the field, was the recently discovered endrocrine disorder associated with cretinism. Based on that relationship, a number of medical persons began to explore the impact of thyroid, adrenal, thymus, and pituitary glandular dysfunctions on both physical and mental development. Some hoped to cure mental retardation through "organotherapy." For years an ad appeared in the *American Journal of Mental Deficiency* promoting a blend of anterior pituitary, thymus, and thyroid substances that reportedly had produced "some brilliant results."[41] This "shotgun" approach to glandular therapy with mental retardation, regardless of known or unknown etiology, remained popular into the 1930s.

The relationship between mental illness and mental retardation continued to be explored with the growing recognition that mentally retarded persons could become severely emotionally disturbed. Borrowing from Kraepelin, Bleuler, in 1911, identified this condition as "pfropfschizophrenia," which was defined as "dementia praecox . . . grafted upon weakmindedness which had existed from childhood without focal phenomena."[42] Though the notion that mentally retarded individuals could become mentally ill was widely accepted, the tongue-twisting label was not.

Heredity

The misconception of heredity and its role in mental retardation is aptly illustrated by Barr's analysis of 3,050 cases published in 1904. Barr carefully distinguished between causes acting before birth, at birth, and after birth. Under each category, he listed a number of etiological factors, such as syphilis (prenatal), premature and difficult labor (perinatal), and meningitis and accidents (postnatal). In spite of this analysis, however, Barr attributed most of these cases and their etiological components directly to heredity: "By all, the hereditary causes, whether acting singly or in combination are found to be most pronounced and these again are distinctly accentuated in the condition of mothers during gestation, and in the heredities of imbecility and of phthisis. Furthermore the influence of some congenital causes is frequently traceable in many of the accidental and developmental causes attributed."[43] This broad concept of heredity with all its underlying misconceptions was commonly held by most authorities. "Heredity" continued to include what one would currently consider to be within the realm of genetics and related biochemical disorders; prenatal, natal and postnatal injuries; as well as social learning. Naturally, under such circumstances, heredity would prove devastating to mentally retarded persons: "We have surely found evidence in support of the theory," wrote Barr in 1904, "that the transmission of imbecility is at once the most insidious and the most aggressive of degenerative forces; attacking alike the physical, mental, and moral nature, enfeebling the judgment and the will, while exaggerating the sexual impulses and the perpetuation of an evil growth, a growth too often parasitic; ready to unite with any neurosis it may encounter, and from its very sluggishness and inertia refusing to be shaken off; laying latent it must be, but sure to reappear . . . through a century to the fourth or fifth generation."[44]

As a natural consequence of these misguided notions of heredity, the major burden of responsibility fell upon the very unsure shoulders of feebleminded women:

> Feeble-minded women are almost invariably immoral, and if at large usually become carriers of venereal disease or give birth to children who are as defective as themselves. The feeble-minded woman who marries is twice as prolific as the normal woman.[45]

> There is no class of persons in our whole population who, unit for unit, are so dangerous or so expensive to the state. This excepts no class, not even the violently insane. They are much more dangerous and expensive than the ordinary insane or the ordinary feeble-minded or the ordinary male criminal. Why is this? They are dangerous because being irresponsible wholly or in part they become the prey of the lower class of vile men and are the most fertile source for the spread of all forms of venereal disease. They have not the sense or the understanding to avoid disease or any care as to its spread. They are most expensive to the state because they are the most fruitful source of disease and mentally defective children who are apt to become state charges.[46]

Three areas of inquiry lent support and impetus to such judgments: 1) a series of genealogical investigations, the most famous of which was Goddard's study of the Kallikaks, pub-

lished in 1912, 2) the rediscovery of Mendel's law of heredity by DeVries and his associates at the turn of the century, and 3) studies among defective delinquents.

The Kallikaks This study had its beginning with the admission of Deborah Kallikak, an 8-year-old girl born in an almshouse, to the training school at Vineland. Kallikak was a fictitious name derived from two Greek words: *kalos,* meaning pleasing or attractive, and *kakos,* meaning evil.[47]

Goddard called upon his field workers to gain information concerning Deborah's ancestors. They were able to trace her lineage back to her great-great-great-grandfather, Martin, Sr., who, as a soldier during the Revolutionary War, had a misguided adventure with a "feebleminded girl" whom he met in one of the local drinking establishments. This relationship resulted in the birth of an illegitimate son, Martin Kallikak, Jr., from whom came 408 direct descendants, 143 of whom Goddard had "conclusive proof were feeble-minded"; 36 of whom were illegitimate; 33, sexually immoral persons, mostly prostitutes; 24, confirmed alcoholics; 3, epileptic; 82, died in infancy; 3, criminals; and 8, kept houses of ill fame. Only 46 were found to be "normal."

Following the Revolutionary War, Martin Kallikak, Sr., who was of normal intelligence and from a "good" family, married a woman with equal credentials, and from this union descended in direct line 496 people, none of whom was mentally defective and only one, insane. Only three, according to Goddard, were in any sense degenerate, two being alcoholics and one sexually immoral. The descendants included doctors, judges, educators, trainers, landowners, and, in short, respectable citizens who were "prominent in every phase of social life." There were no epileptics, no illegitimate children, no immoral women, and no criminals. Thus, Goddard concluded:

> The Kallikak family presents a natural experiment in heredity. A young man of good family becomes through two different women the ancestor of two lines of descendants,—the one characterized by thoroughly good, respectable, normal

citizenship, with almost no exception; the other being equally characterized by mental defect in every generation. This defect was transmitted through the father in the first generation. In later generations, more defect was brought in from other families through marriage. In the last generation it was transmitted through the mother, so that we have here all combinations of transmission, which again proves the truly hereditary character of the defect.

We find on the good side of the family prominent people in all walks of life and nearly all of the 496 descendants owners of land or proprietors. On the bad side we find paupers, criminals, prostitutes, drunkards, and examples of all forms of social pest with which modern society is burdened.

From this we conclude that feeble-mindedness is largely responsible for these social sores.

Feeble-mindedness is hereditary and transmitted as surely as any other character. We cannot successfully cope with those conditions until we recognize feeble-mindedness and its hereditary nature, recognize it early, and take care of it.[48]

Most authorities of the day hailed Goddard's report as "epic-making."[49] A few, such as J. (John) E. (Edward) Wallace Wallin, simply rejected the entire approach: "Many hereditary charts are based on the sheerest guesswork, on data gathered by persons quite lacking in scientific discrimination and quite unskilled in the art of hereditary, psychological, or medical diagnosis. . . . I shall in no way concern myself with passing out the confusing, blundering, slipshod, inaccurate, unscientific ways in which many . . . of the published hereditary charts have been worked up and interpreted."[50]

In reality, the field workers' data-gathering skills would be unacceptable today. Goddard described their approach: "After some experience, the field-worker becomes expert in inferring the condition of those persons who are not seen, from the similarity of the language used in describing them to that used in describing persons whom she [Katherine E. Kite] has seen."[51] Katherine Kite herself noted that much of her information was gathered from hearsay and secondary sources: "There is an immense amount of information to be gotten from county records and especially from family Bibles. Some of my most interesting histo-

ries have really been based on the records I have been able to get out of old family Bibles."[52]

Years later, Goddard's study was rejected by all but a few as invalid, since there was no way of knowing or even estimating the intelligence of Deborah's ancestors. As Goodenough observed in 1949, "The assistants whom he employed to secure his genealogical records had relatively little training but were fired with Goddard's enthusiasm. That they may sometimes have tended to find mental defect where mental defect was to be expected was perhaps inevitable under the circumstances, but no one can doubt the sincerity of their attempts to get at the facts."[53] While many of Goddard's attitudes and positions changed over the years, as late as 1942 he still staunchly defended his Kallikak study and its approach.[54]

Deborah Kallikak   What of Deborah Kallikak herself? Born on February 11, 1899, Deborah was an attractive young lady of 22 at the time of the study. Those who worked closely with her described her as

cheerful, inclined to be quarrelsome, very active and restless, very affectionate, willing, and tries; is quick and excitable, fairly good-tempered. Learns a new occupation quickly, but requires a half-hour or twenty-four repetitions to learn four lines. Retains well what she has once learned. Needs close supervision. Is bold towards strangers, kind towards animals. Can run an electric sewing machine, cook, and do practically everything about the house. Has no notable defect. She is quick and observing, has a good memory, writes fairly, does excellent work in wood-carving and kindergarten [where she is an assistant], is excellent in imitation. Is a poor reader and poor at numbers. Does fine basketry and gardening. Spelling is poor; music is excellent; sewing excellent; excellent in entertainment work. Very fond of children and good in helping care for them. Has a good sense of order and cleanliness. Is sometimes very stubborn and obstinate. Is not always truthful and has been known to steal, although does not have a reputation for this. Is proud of her clothes. Likes pretty dresses and likes to help in other cottages, even to temporarily taking charge of the group.[55]

To Goddard, however, she was "a typical illustration of the mentality of the high-grade, evil-minded person, the moron, the delin-

Deborah Kallikak.

lenient justice-of-the-peace but Deborah per force remained in our custody."[57] A later attempt at community placement also failed for similar, healthy reasons. Upon her return "in sack cloth and ashes," Deborah noted, "It isn't as if I'd done anything really wrong. It was only nature."[58]

At 49 years of age, she was described as a "healthy, vigorous middle-aged female . . . energetic, capable, industrious . . . well trained and respectful. What shatters her chance of even mediocre success is the fact that her emotions are too easily influenced and her egoism cannot be influenced at all."[59] By this time, she had become resigned to her fate: "I guess after all I am where I belong. . . . I don't like this feeble-minded part, but anyhow I am not idiotic like some of the poor things you see around here. Folks say to me, 'Why don't you try to get out?' Well, I've been out and you know it wasn't so good. I'm famous, I know, but I guess there's a lot of people in the outside world who don't care whether I'm famous or not. Here everybody who *is* anybody, knows all about me and what I can do. With the wonderful friends that I got and the work I like so much, this place is my home."[60]

Deborah Kallikak died at the age of 79 on June 18, 1978. Described as a "wonderful lady," her later years were painful as a result of severe arthritis. Though she engaged in many community activities, such as visiting friends and employees, she remained in the institutional setting. In later years, she was offered one more opportunity to move into the community but rejected such a proposal, primarily because of her constant need for medical attention.[61]

Goddard's Kallikak study was not singular, and both the nature and techniques of his efforts, as well as their interpretation, received considerable support from other investigators, especially Arthur Estabrook and Charles Davenport.

In 1912, Estabrook followed up Dugdale's original Juke study. Of 2,094 subjects who were of Juke blood and 726 who married into the Juke family, 366 were paupers, 171 were criminals, and 10 had been murdered. In school, 62

quent, the kind of girl or woman who fills our reformatories. They are wayward, they get into all sorts of trouble and difficulties, sexually and otherwise, and yet we have been accustomed to account for the defects on the basis of viciousness, environment, or ignorance. . . . There is nothing that she might not be led into, because she has no power of control, and all her instincts and appetites are in that direction that would lead to vice . . . a product of 'bad stock'."[56]

As an adult, Deborah became the favorite of key administrators and, in the judgment of some staff, developed a "haughty attitude." Being a normal, healthy young lady, Deborah engaged in heterosexual activities much to the chagrin of others. After meeting a new young male employee, "her skill with woodworking tools made it possible to alter her window screen and this fact, together with a moonlit campus and a convenient lover, set the stage for a romantic interlude. This had not progressed far when it was fortunately discovered. The young man was kindly dismissed by a did well, 288 did fairly, 458 were retarded 2 or more years, and 176 never attended school. School data for the rest of the family were unobtainable. There were 282 intemperate individuals and 277 harlots. Estabrook concluded, in part: 1) cousin-matings and defective germ-plasms were undesirable since they produce defective offspring irrespective of the parents' somatic make-up; 2) there was an hereditary factor in licentiousness; 3) pauperism was an indication of weakness, physical or mental; 4) all the Juke criminals were feebleminded, and the eradication of crime in defective stocks depends upon the elimination of mental deficiency.

Estabrook also contended that while environment may have a potentially positive effect, it could not overcome the impact of heredity. Consequently, "two practical solutions of this problem are apparent. One of these is the permanent custodial care of feeble-minded men and all feeble-minded women of childbearing age. The other is the sterilization of those whose germ-plasm contains the defects which society wishes to eliminate . . . sterilization of those carrying epilepsy, feeblemindedness, etc., is entirely practicable. . . . Contrary to public belief, sterilization would interfere with the real liberty of the individual less than custodial care."[62]

Over the next 15 years, a number of studies were reported on various families from poor, isolated areas with similar results. Included were the "Nams" by Estabrook, 1912; the "Hill Folk" by Davenport and Danielson, 1912; the "Dack" family by Finlayson, 1916; and the "Mongrol Virginians, the Win Tribe" by Estabrook and McDougle, 1926.[63]

In *Feeble-mindedness: Its Causes and Consequences,* published in 1920, Goddard reported on a hereditary study of 300 residents at Vineland and offered an interpretation based on Mendelian laws. He concluded that 164 (54 percent) of the residents were feebleminded due to direct hereditary causes; 34 (11.3 percent), probably hereditary; and 37 (12 percent), involved in "neuropathic ancestry," that is, family histories that showed relatives suffering various brain affections, such as pa-

ralysis, apoplexy, brain disease, and the like, epilepsy, insanity, blindness, deafness, and other neurotic conditions. Only 57 (19 percent) were considered accidental; and 8 (2.6 percent) could not be explained, their families were of normal intelligence. Goddard concluded, on the basis of his data, that at least 64.3 percent of the sample were probably the result of direct heredity factors and 12 percent were questionable. He also concluded that "feeble-mindedness is a unit character, and due either to the presence of something which acts as an inhibitor, or due to the absence of some stimulus which sends the normal brain on to further development. . . ." Thus, it "is perfectly clear that no feeble-minded person should ever be allowed to marry or to become a parent."[64]

Goddard's interpretation that mental retardation was transmitted as a "Mendelian recessive" was adopted by many in the eugenics movement. Even so, according to early calculations, neither segregation nor sterilization would eliminate feeblemindedness. In 1917, East, for example, used Goddard's theory and estimated that one American in 14 probably carried the trait in a recessive form and, although normal to all appearances, one-fourth of the offspring would be feebleminded if mating occurred with another carrier.[65] Punnet carried East's thinking and calculations one step further—assuming 10 percent of the American population to be carriers of the mental defect, if only those who were actually feebleminded were "dealt with," it would require more than 8,000 years to eliminate mental retardation.[66]

Heredity and the Defective Delinquent
The moral imbecile of yesterday became the "defective delinquent" of the day. As defined by Fernald in 1912, the defective delinquent was "one whose mentality is so imperfectly developed that he is unable to support himself honestly, and whose acts repeatedly conflict with established social and legal requirements."[67]

Advancements in mental testing soon resulted in the systematic evaluation of inmates in various reformatories and other correctional facilities, and the results were devastating for those considered mentally retarded. MacMurphy's extensive review of the literature resulted in the conclusion that most prostitutes were feebleminded because "mental defectives with little sense of decency, with no control of their passions, with no appreciation of the sacredness of the person and the higher references of life, become a center of evil in the community, and inevitably lower the moral tone."[68] Similarly, many criminals—men, women, boys, and girls, regardless of age or crime—were reportedly mentally retarded: "Perverts and venereal diseased are overwhelmingly mental defective, as in public drunkenness, and shoplifting and the picking of pockets are acts of the feeble-minded and one of the large proportions shown by statistics."[69] Of 120 delinquent girls at a girls' reformatory in eastern Pennsylvania, only 15 had normal mentality, Hill reported in 1914.[70]

Other studies indicated that the largest percentage of unmarried mothers were mentally retarded. In 1917, Jean Weidensall, associated with the Cincinnati General Hospital, reported that only 20 percent of the unmarried mothers studied could be considered of normal intelligence; 58 percent were feebleminded, of whom 40 to 45 percent were "almost without question so low-grade mentally as to make life under institutional care the only happy one for themselves and the most economical and the only safe arrangement for society."[71]

Terman, in 1916, explained why feebleminded youth revealed a proclivity toward delinquency:

> The answer may be stated in simple terms. Morality depends upon two things: (a) the ability to foresee and to weigh the possible consequences for self and others of different kinds of behavior; and (b) upon the willingness and capacity to exercise self-restraint. That there are many intelligent criminals is due to the fact that (a) may exist without (b). On the other hand, (b) presupposes (a). In other words, not all criminals are feebleminded, but all feeble-minded are at least potential criminals. That every feeble-minded woman is a potential prostitute would hardly be disputed by any one. Moral judgment, like business judgment, social judgment, or any other kind of higher thought process, is a function of intelligence.

> Morality cannot flower and fruit if intelligence remains infantile.[72]

The more knowledgeable William Healy, director of the Juvenile Psychopathic Institute of Chicago and later of the Judge Baker Foundation, disagreed: "With regard to the environment, nobody can doubt for a minute that the social situation in which a mental defective of the higher grade belongs by birth or upbringing, is part and parcel of his story and bears upon the problem of how he will turn out as far as conduct is concerned. Indeed, environment is the largest part of the story."[73]

By 1920, a number of persons working closely with mentally retarded individuals in their natural environments, and thus being more sensitive to the influence of societal experiences, began to change general opinions concerning mental retardation, criminality, and heredity. For example, Frederick Farnell, neurologist to the public schools of Providence, Rhode Island, in describing the behavior of a neglected mentally retarded boy, concluded, "heredity can hardly be said to have been the cause of this trouble."[74] Guy Fernald, psychiatrist in a penal system wrote that behavior, not any intelligence deficiency, should be the focal point of modification.[75] Similarly, Anderson, of the Municipal Court of Boston, contended that "surely no one would be so unwise as to claim that within the constitutional makeup of these individuals could be found the sole explanation of their differences in behavior."[76] These attitudes were to play an important part in modifying the role of institutions and in encouraging community placement.

Dr. Southard, who worked closely with Fernald at Waverly, finally admonished his professional colleagues in 1918 to stop using the term heredity in its broadest, generic sense:

> I feel there is an extraordinarily high percentage of cases of feeble-mindedness of a non-hereditary nature. I am, of course, here using the term *hereditary* as distinct from the word *congenital*. A great many of the conditions underlying brain disorder in the feeble-minded are congenital but not hereditary in the modern sense of the term. I think that in our work in propagandas among the laity, and even among the educated laity, we

ought to make very clear to every audience what we mean by the term *hereditary*. The whole balance of social work in its largest sense upon feeble-mindedness may be altered if we allow the educated laity to think that by *hereditary* we sometimes mean *congenital*.[77]

SOCIAL CONTROL AND PREVENTION

Throughout most of this period, the professional community armed with scientific data from hereditary studies, pursued most aggressively such restrictive measures as controlled marriage, sterilization, and segregation through institutionalization. The American Breeders' Association in 1913 best summarized the sentiments of many. This organization suggested that the "following classes must generally be considered as socially unfit and their supply should if possible be eliminated from the human stock if we would maintain or raise the level of quality essential to the progress of the nation and our race: (1) the feeble-minded, (2) paupers, (3) criminaloids, (4) epileptics, (5) the insane, (6) the constitutionally weak, (7) those predisposed to specific diseases, (8) the congenitally deformed, and (9) those having defective sense organs."[78]

The Association also explored possible approaches to realizing race improvement, taking into consideration life segregation, sterilization, restrictive marriage laws and customs, systems of matings purporting to remove defective traits, polygamy, and euthanasia. Of these approaches, the Breeders' Association, respecting current social mores, suggested that only the first two would prove acceptable and effective. Some states did attempt to exercise control over marriage, however.

RESTRICTIVE MARRIAGE

The need for controlled marriage was urged by a number of professionals. T. Diller, clinical professor of neurology at the University of Pittsburgh, argued, as did many, that man should observe the same careful selection in his breeding habits as he did with his plants and animals: "There is a very widespread notion

that the marriage between two persons is a matter of their affair and their affair only and that the next door neighbor should not in any way meddle in the matter. I believe none of us here [addressing the American Association on Mental Deficiency] would subscribe to this doctrine. We have a right not only to take an interest in the subject of marriage, but I believe it is our duty to do so."[79]

Eventually, 39 states passed laws prohibiting marriage among mentally retarded persons or establishing the grounds for annulment.[80] Prior to receiving a marriage license, each person had to declare that he or she had not been judged feebleminded: "On the back of every marriage certificate [in Michigan], there is an oath that must be taken. That is that the individual has not been treated for insanity or mental defectiveness, and, if previously treated, has been cured of gonorrhea or syphilis."[81] Though such laws were looked upon favorably, it was generally realized that they would be ineffective: "Restricted marriage laws are unavailing because the unfit reproduce their kind regardless of marriage laws," observed Hart in 1913.[82] Some professionals contended that mentally retarded and mentally ill persons would simply lie about their status (if, in fact, it had been diagnosed). Others were concerned about the sanctity of marriage and the family. As anticipated, such laws proved ineffective, as did, by and large, more complicated attempts at sterilization.

STERILIZATION

Nothing was discussed more frequently or fervently than sterilization during the first several decades of the twentieth century. Risley would "render innocuous" through surgical means a vast range of human beings who, regardless of intelligence or other personal attributes, would reflect any "form of mental alienation or disease" or whose lives were "peculiar and erratic." Though most professionals would not (and did not) support Risley's position, some did, nevertheless, sanction sterilization of mentally retarded persons. A few, such as Barr, Wilmarth, and Johnstone, were highly supportive of sterilization. Johnstone, for example, indicated that he believed in "steriliza-tion for the morons or dangerous types of feeble-minded."[83] Some, such as Matzinger, professor of psychiatry with the Medical Of-fices at the University of Buffalo, though en-tirely cognizant of the many etiological aspects associated with mental retardation, concluded that the only way to preclude the occurrence of mental retardation in subsequent generations would be through the *"absolute and certain prevention of descendants from the mentally defective. There is no alternative."*[84]

In general, however, neither the profes-sional community as a whole, political repre-sentatives, nor the public in general were en-thusiastic about sterilization. In 1913, for example, Murdoch indicated that while he was not opposed to sterilization, he thought the procedure would be "simply a drop in the bucket for supplying a remedy for the great social burden of the feeble-minded."[85] Rogers questioned the feasibility of sterilization in view of current knowledge: "I might say that I do not believe that sterilization laws will be as helpful as many anticipate. . . . I do not see how sterilization can be applied as a generally eugenic measure at the present time. Our knowledge at best, notwithstanding many star-tling contributions to the subject of late, is too limited as to the definite sources of mental deficiency, and a clear differentiation of nor-mal germ plasm, to permit any general classifi-cation of such a law."[86] Walter Fernald, E. Southard of the Boston State Hospital, and others, including Goddard, supported Rogers's position.

Political representatives were equally cau-tious. For example, Woodbridge N. Ferris, governor of Michigan, believed that profes-sional statements such as "If all states had these laws, four generations would eliminate nine-tenths of the crime, insanity and sick-ness" were simply "extravagant claims."[87]

In addition to reducing the occurrence of mental retardation in subsequent generations,

some support was given to sterilization for other reasons, including these:

1. Sterilized mentally retarded adults would be allowed to marry since they could not reproduce their kind.
2. Mentally retarded adults were not intellec-tually capable of providing a proper en-vironment and training for children.
3. Sterilization would control undesirable sexual behavior, which, in some in-stances, was apparently limited to masturbation.

Indiana was the first state to pass enabling legislation in the area of sterilization on March 9, 1907. By 1912, eight states had passed such legislation: Indiana, Connecticut, Wash-ington, California, Iowa, Nevada, New Jersey, and New York. These laws were not intended solely for the prevention of mental retardation. Of the eight states, five included rapists; all included confirmed criminals; six specifically made reference to idiots, imbeciles, and the feebleminded; four included the insane; and two included epileptics. Iowa had a more ex-pansive sterilization provision, which included habitual drunkards, drug fiends, syphilitics, and certain prostitutes and procurers. Accord-ing to Davies, between 1907 and 1958, 30 states recorded a total of 31,038 sterilized mentally retarded persons (10,990 males, 20,048 females).[88]

In some states, mentally retarded residents had no choice or voice in the matter, in others, they did. Consent to the operation on the part of the resident was considered "voluntary," which often involved a simple choice: be ster-ilized or remain in the institution.

To recapitulate, many in the professional community genuinely believed that heredity was the prime etiological factor associated with mental retardation, a condition which was the source of most social ills and which, through advancement in mental testing, was readily di-agnosable.* At the same time, control of mar-

*Southard offered one of the few tempered judgments of mental retardation: "Feeble-mindedness is no doubt a leading social problem, educational, moral, legal, economic in its ramifications [but] so bright are many of its prospects (compared, for example, with closely adjacent problems of insanity, nervous breakdown, crime, prostitution, drug addiction, business dishonesty, and Bolshevism)."[90]

riages was deemed impractical, if not impossible, and sterilization on a large scale was not generally accepted. Only one alternative remained—segregation through institutionalization:

> We must get away from the idea, and get the public away from the idea, that our institutions for the feeble-minded are institutions simply for the training of the feeble-minded children. The care of the feeble-minded is, as is the care of the insane, a problem for the state, not the city or county. The good to be accomplished by the segregation of an able-bodied feeble-minded woman is too remote to appeal to the shortsighted local guardian of the poor who is too interested in keeping down the tax rate in his district during his term of office and is too accessible to the family and friends of the one who should be segregated.[89]

The attitudes of these professionals must be taken within the context of the times. In other words, these sentiments were not simply those of a few given professionals; they reflected the prevalent thinking of the Progressive Era and its reform movements. As recently assessed by Rothman:

> Progressives' sense of paternalism enabled them to move in harsh and stringent ways against those that they believed to be irreformable and beyond rehabilitation—namely the recidivist, the defective, the mentally retarded, and the unworthy poor. . . . Accordingly, many Progressives accepted the eugenic arguments of the time and were eager to confine the retarded for life, particularly the borderline retarded who might pass as normals and so go on to propagate a race of defectives. Some Progressives were also ready to sterilize the retarded, to make that operation the prerequisite for release into the community.[91]

Not surprisingly, considering the attitudes of the day, states began to pass laws governing the behavior of mentally retarded persons. Over the years, nine states passed laws prohibiting the sale of alcohol to mentally retarded persons; one forbade the sale of firearms. Eighteen states refused mentally retarded persons the right to vote; six refused them the right to draw contracts; and nine refused them admission to the state national guard.[92]

All states eventually passed some form of protective law. To illustrate, 13 states passed specific laws prohibiting the mistreatment of mentally retarded persons, and four prohibited their public exhibition. A number of these laws were aimed at circuses and carnivals. The Barnum and Bailey circus always featured microcephalic adults advertised under various, publicly tantalizing labels. Between 1851 and 1901, for example, Maximo and Bartola—the "Bird-Headed Dwarfs"—were among the show's prime attractions. During the 1920s, Slitzie, a microcephalic adult billed as "Maggie, the Last of the Aztecs," was popular. Another long-standing feature of the Barnum and Bailey circus was Zip, the "Monkey Man," who allegedly had been captured by a party of adventurers in search of gorillas along the river Gambia. Dressed in a furry jumpsuit and allowed only to grunt in public, Zip was actually a mentally retarded boy of a poor American black family. While Barnum and Bailey's "Show of Life" raised some community concern and was partly instrumental in the passage of protective laws, the main offense was the hundreds of circuses and carnivals displaying preserved abnormal fetuses, which in the rather macabre language of the circus world were known as "pickled punks."[93]

SOCIAL CARE AND TREATMENT

As indicated, the early decades of the twentieth century were characterized by the most negative of attitudes toward the morality, abilities, and social responsibilities of persons deemed mentally retarded. Such attitudes naturally affected programming. Perhaps the observations of Walter Fernald throughout the period of 1900 to 1919 most accurately trace the predominant concepts concerning mentally retarded individuals and their place in a progressive, democratic society. Let us consider both the man and his ideas.

WALTER E. FERNALD

By the turn of the century, the once influential and powerful voice of Isaac Kerlin was silent, but his mantle and aura of authority passed to

Walter E. Fernald.

Walter Fernald. Born at Kittery, Maine, Fernald (1859–1924) was educated in the public schools and obtained his medical degree from the Medical School of Maine. After serving 5 years as assistant physician at the State Insane Hospital at Mendota, Wisconsin, he became the first resident superintendent of the Massachusetts School for the Feeble-Minded. There he devoted the rest of his life to the development of facilities and educational programs for mentally retarded persons.

Fernald's contributions to the field were many, both positive and negative. He always expressed his positions with conviction and frequently in forceful, hyperbolic terms. His early years were marked by strong, but very negative judgments on mentally retarded persons. In 1903, he observed:

> The brighter class of the feeble-minded with their weak will-power and deficient judgment are easily influenced for evil, and are prone to become vagrants, drunkards, and thieves. The modern scientific study of the deficient and delinquent classes as a whole has demonstrated that a large proportion of our criminals, inebriates and prostitutes are really congenital imbeciles, who have been allowed to grow up without any attempt being made to improve or discipline them. Society suffers the penalty of this neglect in an increase of pauperism and vice, and finally, at a great increased cost, is compelled to take charge of adult imbeciles in almshouses and hospitals; and of imbecile criminals in jails and prisons, generally for the remainder of their natural lives. As a matter of mere economy, it is now believed that it is better and cheaper for the community to assume the permanent care of this class before they have carried out a long career of expensive crime.[94]

In 1909, he wrote:

> Imbeciles are children even in adult life. They make friends quickly and are cheerful and voluble. They are boastful, ungenerous, ungrateful. Notwithstanding their stupidity they are cunning in attaining their own ends. . . . They are vain in dress. . . . They manifest unbound egotism. . . . They are prone to lie without reason. . . . They are inclined to steal. . . . They are morally insensible. . . . They seldom show embarrassment or shame when detected in wrong-doing. . . . Few imbeciles have been seen to blush. They show an early craving for tobacco and alcohol. They are proverbially lazy and fond of idleness. . . . Imbeciles of both sexes usually show active sexual propensities and perversions at an early age.[95]

In 1912, he added fuel to his fiery observations:

> The past few years have witnessed a striking awareness of professional and popular conscience of the widespread prevalence of feeble-mindedness and its influence as a source of wretchedness to the patient himself and to his family, and as a causative factor in the production of crime, prostitution, pauperism, illegitimacy, intemperance and other complex social diseases. . . . The feeble-minded are a parasitic, predatory class, never capable of self-support or of managing their own affairs. The great majority ultimately become public charges in some form. They cause unutterable sorrow at home and are a menace and a danger to a community.[96]

Unlike some of his colleagues, however, Fernald grew in his understanding of and appreciation for mentally retarded persons; and in later years, he put forth great effort to reverse publicly his earlier positions concerning their attributes. His alteration in concept and attitude also resulted in his introducing and/or supporting many innovative programs, including community placement. This change in attitude is well reflected in his 1918 statement: ". . . there are both bad feeble-minded and good feeble-minded, and that not all of the feeble-minded are criminalists and socialists and immoral and antisocial; we know they are not. We know that a lot of the feeble-minded are generous, faithful and pure-minded. I never lose an opportunity to repeat what I am saying now, that we have really slandered the feeble-minded. Some of the sweetest and most beautiful characters I have ever known have been feeble-minded people."[97]

By the time of his death on Thanksgiving Day, 1924, his school had become an international center for the training of workers in the field of mental retardation. He was much in demand as a lecturer and consultant and was very active in the American Association on Mental Deficiency and on the National Committee for Mental Hygiene.

He was also largely responsible for most of the progressive legislation passed in Massachusetts during his years at the state school, including laws:

1. requiring the census and registration of the feeble-minded in the State;
2. establishing Psychiatric clinics for the examination of retarded school children in the public schools;
3. permitting the parole of the feeble-minded from the State Schools;
4. legally recognizing the defective delinquents and making separate institutional provision for them;
5. requiring that an inquiry shall be made into the mental status of prisoners.[98]

In spite of his earlier positions, Fernald provided great impetus to the human treatment and education of mentally retarded persons. His personal warmth, charm, and dedication helped him convince the public as well as legislators to provide greater support to them in the home and community, as well as in the institution.

Fernald's comments on the abilities and social expectancies of mentally retarded people, as indicated, reflected a general professional consensus and trend. It should be noted again, however, that pre–World War I sentiments did not simply reflect personal biases but, rather, a position consistent with sophisticated research in the area of heredity.

RESIDENTIAL SERVICES

Negative attitudes toward mentally retarded persons had significant impact not only upon the rise in institutional populations but also as to their characteristics. As Bernstein noted in 1920, "Whereas ten years ago 80% of [admissions] were idiots and imbeciles and only 20% border-line cases or morons, now only 20% are of the idiot and imbecile class and 80% are morons or border-line cases."[99]

In 1917, of the 48 contiguous states, 31 had institutions for either mentally retarded or epileptic persons (regardless of intelligence), including 24 that served both populations; 10 for epileptic people only; 17 for mentally retarded individuals only; and 2 for mentally ill and epileptic residents.[100] Eventually, facilities for the epileptic admitted those mentally retarded. In 1900, 9,334 mentally retarded persons were in such residential facilities; by 1930, that number had grown to 68,035.[101]

While the number of mentally retarded persons admitted to institutions gradually increased, the majority requiring residential care were still in other facilities. Wilson, for example, hesitantly revealed in 1924 that for the District of Columbia, "over 200 people that are definitely feeble-minded, some of very tender years, are in our Hospital for the Insane."[102] Other states simply contracted with private facilities or neighboring states to provide for a few retarded persons.[103] A large number of mentally retarded persons were still served in various county-sponsored facilities.

Philosophy and Programs

Protective paternalism was the order of the day: "Nothing essential to your comfort and happiness that can be reasonably supplied you will be denied, but you must be placed where your conduct can be watched and controlled, as a wise parent watches and controls his immature child," announced Wilmarth in 1906.[104]

This revised role of institutions, from training of children to the prevention of mental retardation in subsequent generations by the segregating adults, was significant. As would be anticipated, much of this change was directed against women considered mentally retarded. States modified their laws, placing greater emphasis on admitting and retaining adult women in institutions. In 1901, for example, Indiana's 1889 admission law was amended to extend the age limit for admission from 16 in the case of women to 45. In the judgment of its sponsor, a "more worthy act could not have been enacted."[105] By 1919, institutions intended solely for women were established in New York, New Jersey, and Pennsylvania.

Like all other institutions, and in spite of the fact that the residents were women—"the greatest menace to society amongst any of the groups of mental defectives"—it was fully expected that they would operate a farm, being responsible for such tasks as tending chickens and rabbits, cow herding, milking, sheep herding, and the general planting and harvesting of crops.[106] While the largest percentage of young ladies were committed for various sexual offenses, many of which were undoubtedly quite minor, moral education emphasized religious training of one's choice and other similar activities. No curricular or counseling provisions were made concerning sex or related problems and responsibilities.

An increasing adult population once again raised the issue of the educational role of an institution. Some superintendents placed such a low priority on education that in 1913 Fernald complained, "We have lost the confidence of parents; the confidence of the parents of prospective patients; and also lost the confidence of the legislators who noticed the deterioration of patients."[107] Fernald was referring to not only inadequacy of basic care for many residents but also the fact that many institutions had virtually abandoned their educational programs.

He and others strongly supported education: "I believe in our work and think that every feeble-minded child should have all the education of which he is capable."[108] Cobb of

Syracuse, New York, agreed: "I am heartily in favor of the idea of educating the feeble-minded of all grades."[109] Similarly, Rogers of Fairbault, Minnesota, urged the training of the feeble-minded all along the line. The fundamental happiness of the whole institution community is centered about the training department and the interest it fosters. . . ."[110] Goddard, however, again expressed reservation: "If a child has mentality of six or seven or eight, and we know his mental development has stopped, is there use whatever of sending him into the school department, unless he is too small to go to work and we only wish to entertain him?"[111]

As regards education in a residential facility, it is difficult to understand the reasoning of those who preferred not to promote education in view of the youngsters they were serving. Assuming a modicum of editing by the classroom teacher, the linguistic performance of some residents was astounding, as illustrated by the sad epistle by one of Barr's residents written in 1902:

MY DEAR FATHER:

I wish you would leave me come home for my birthday which is not far off. It comes on the 25th of September, which is Thursday. There is one question I wish to ask you and it is this: if I ask you to take me home, you say you haven't the money and if I run away why you seem to have it to bring me back, and that is what puzzles me. I only wish I could spend just one month with you, I would be more than satisfied, and you know I have been here exactly 9 years and haven't been home in a decent way yet, and I guess I never will. If you can't give me a little change, I will have to make it myself, I will never show my face near home, and you can depend upon it. From

Your unthought of Son
"H.F.W."[112]

Barr, like many of his colleagues at the turn of the century, strongly advocated the separation of sexes under all circumstances, including the classroom: "The separation of the sexes is another problem which experience is slowly defining. At Elwyn, teachers are a unit in declaring there is nothing gained in co-education, even inconvenience, while nerve strain in disciplining is greatly increased, and a re-arrangement of classes according to sex rather than grade is already being advisable."[113]

Adults continued to work long, long hours. Even adolescents attending school quite frequently performed several hours of work before the school day and returned to work in the evening. Work activities remained basically the same as in earlier years. Women participated in resident care of younger residents, cooking, housekeeping, sewing, and laundry work; men engaged in a variety of farm tasks, yard work, and maintenance. Some of the boys and men also worked for local farmers and engaged in such money-saving projects for the state as reforesting. The importance of resident labor to the basic operation of the public residential facility cannot be underestimated. It was not uncommon for institutions prior to World War I to have an overall staff-resident ratio of 1:6 or greater (as compared with 1:1 today). In essence, most of the vital operational functions of the facility were performed by residents. Employees served primarily as supervisors of resident workers rather than providers of direct service.

Such practices reinforced the institutional model developed during the later years of the nineteenth century, that is, the colony plan with its heavy reliance on utilization of resident labor serving a heterogeneous population. This does not mean, however, that there were no significant changes occurring in the residential setting or that new ideas were not being generated. A few genuinely progressive administrators grew with their experiences, envisioned new roles for residential facilities, and began to explore the desirability of community placement programs.

In 1903, Fernald introduced his colleagues to the concept of the farm colony or farm group as it became known. In brief, in 1901 Fernald transferred 50 boys to a farm located 61 miles from the main institution at Waverly. The farm was staffed with a matron, two women cooks, two female attendants, and three men as farm workers. At the time of his report, the "boys" were still devoting most of their long days of work to putting the farm in shape. A second colony to accommodate 180 "boys" was start-

ed shortly after. Through this program, mentally retarded men remained productive while living in an environment separate from the large institution, one which allowed for greater independence and freedom. Both "brighter" and "low-grade" men participated. Like many of Fernald's ideas, this project was emulated by several other progressive leaders. One of its strongest and most successful proponents was Charles Bernstein of New York.

Charles Bernstein and the Revised Colony Concept

Lesser known today but remarkably sensitive and innovative for his time, Charles Bernstein (1872–1942) was born in Carlisle, New York. Orphaned at the age of 9 when his widowed mother died of measles, Bernstein was raised in a strict German Protestant home by his educated bachelor uncle, where, as a result, he developed a strong interest in learning and a great sympathy for children. As a young man he wrote, "If ever I have the care of children, I shall be fair to them and let kindness rule my acts."[114]

Charles Bernstein.

At an early age, Bernstein was afflicted with a very severe case of eczema, one unresponsive to medical treatment. In order to receive more sophisticated care, he went to Albany and lived with Dr. Griffin, from whom he developed an intense interest in medicine. Bernstein actively pursued this interest, receiving his medical degree in 1894. He immediately accepted a position as a medical intern at the Rome State School, where in 1902 he was appointed acting superintendent. In 1904, at the age of 31, he was duly appointed to the latter position.

Throughout his career, Bernstein repetitively expressed the opinion that institutional environments were inappropriate and had a markedly adverse effect on development and behavior: "The State should set aside a certain amount for the foundation of homes for the subnormal; they need a different line of treatment or training . . . if we are going to put these children in an abnormal environment from the time of birth, they will not be saved."[115] After Bernstein had experience with community programs, he reconfirmed his belief in the adaptability of behavior and the importance of environment.

Many of these cases having never lived in a normal or reasonable home in which to learn normal home and family life, and many others having lived as children in great congregate institutions where little or no manual and individual training, and especially no normal family domestic training was available, and having thus become institutionalized, the only fair treatment for these doubtful cases, after giving them such training, is to give them one or more favorable trials in a normal, well-selected family and thus furnish an opportunity to round out such domestic training and experience; for does not every normal child develop through experience and right habit-forming opportunities. During the past ten years I have seen many boys and girls thus rehabilitated, and the fact that a few fail on the first trial, or repeatedly, is no sure criterion that our judgment of the case was fallible, for I have many times seen these very same cases of failure almost immediately succeed when placed in another environment, and from then on make good.[116]

The need for rehabilitation in the community was but one of three basic principles of Bernstein's philosophy. He also strongly advocated the development of the individual through per-sonalized programs. No one method of treatment or training was deemed appropriate for all mentally retarded individuals.

While he did not establish the first community colony, Bernstein promoted the idea to a degree well beyond that which even its originators may have intended. In 1917, Bernstein reviewed not only the marked success of his five farm colonies for men but also his unique colony program for "girls." The nature of both program and client was well described in his newspaper announcement:

Rome, N.Y., Oct. 7, 1914

A working girls' home has been established at 209 West Thomas Street, telephone number 172-J, where girls are available for domestic work, sewing, etc., by the day, week, or month. The girls going out from this place to work are capable of doing all kinds of domestic work except special cooking. They are only able to do common cooking.

Their service may be secured by telephone. The rate is $.50 per day, and their services will be available for employment at any time on short notice. Settlement for services will be paid direct to the manager of the home. Girls will be regularly rendered weekly for such services.

These girls are not markedly defectives, but are girls who have been orphans or have never known a normal home, and when late in life they have gone out into the world, they have been unable to get along because of lack of proper home training and normal worldly experiences, as a result of which they were sent to this Asylum for study, care, and training, and we are sending them out to work, after having been thoroughly trained and tested here to see if they can get in touch with the world under normal conditions, and thus learn to be self-sustaining and possibly have their entire freedom.[117]

Bernstein rented a house in the community which became both the girls' home and their social center. During the reporting year, 67 girls had passed through the program and 42 (63 percent) had remained in the community. Bernstein was enthusiastic about the progress these young ladies made, believing that the community program not only rendered them self-sustaining but also saved them from "lives of institutional servitude." His efforts were not without their problems, however: "To be sure, we did experience in the beginning attempts to discourage the project, such as a series of

Group home.

anonymous post cards sent to the women who were employing the girls, stating that they should be ashamed to employ scab labor. . . ."[118]

By 1935, he had created 52 such local homes or colonies serving both children and adults. He even planned a community facility for "custodial women with IQs of 11–30."

Though obviously a warm and sympathetic person who showed concern for both residents and employees, Bernstein could be obdurate and persistent. More than one governor complained about his raising "hell among the boys in the legislature."[119]

There is little doubt that Bernstein's attitudes and concepts were among the most humane and progressive of his time. His community colonies of yesteryear were remarkably similar to many alternative living settings of today.

By 1920, approximately half the public institutions in the United States had initiated a colony program. The proliferation of such programs, following the leadership of Bernstein and Fernald, greatly expanded alternative placement possibilities. Contrary to popular opinion, institutions from their very inception had active placement programs; however, they relied primarily on independent living or being returned to the home. In 1910, for example, 1,009 residents were discharged: 55 to themselves, 864 to friends or relatives, and 90, unknown.[120]

Also contrary to popular opinion, those discharged included the more severely affected. In 1916, Kuhlmann reported that of six institutions studied, there was a 5 percent turnover rate per year. Over 5 years, 11 percent of the idiots were discharged, 19 percent of the imbeciles, and 36 percent of the morons.[121] These facilities, however, had no restriction or retention rules. In all too many instances when a child was committed to an institution it was safe to conclude that he had "come to stay."[122]

In addition to the innovations involving new colony programs, several facilities initiated a series of community-oriented services. Fernald, for example, reported on an outpatient clinic held in connection with his state facility at Waverly, which had been established as early as 1891. Between 1891 and 1920, over 6,000 mentally retarded individuals had been referred for evaluation, diagnosis, and consultation. Chronological ages of outpatients ranged from less than 1 year to over 25, with the majority falling between 10 and 14 years of age. Each case was studied according to 10 "fields and zones of inquiry," which included: 1) physical examination, 2) family history, 3) personal and developmental history, 4) school record, 5) school examination, 6) general information, 7) economic history, 8) social history, 9) moral history, and 10) psychological evaluation. As observed previously, Fernald never accepted intelligence test scores as either the sole or major diagnostic factor in mental retardation.

Of the thousands of cases that had been diagnosed as feebleminded at the clinic, Fernald noted, "the majority have not subsequently applied for admission and are not known to have seriously misbehaved"; and by 1920, "we are advising more patients under home care than are now being cared for in the institution itself."[123] In 1920, Woodhill reported on this particular program, indicating that in response to frequent requests by the public school systems, the outpatient program at the institution moved into the community and provided monthly medical clinics in different parts of the state. For the period 1915 to 1920, 1,155 school children were examined. Different advice was given for different levels of retardation, and while the idiots were not considered appropriate for school, they were not automatically referred for institutional placement. Special educational programming was considered appropriate for both the moderately and mildly retarded. The clinic usually did not suggest that anyone be excluded from a public school program unless he or she had an IQ below 20 or 25. If then, many youngsters were recommended for supportive home care. Subsequently, of the 783 cases diagnosed as mentally retarded, only 220 were considered appropriate for residential services and only 102 of these were ever admitted.[124]

In addition to the few facilities that developed such services, Johnstone at Vineland, New Jersey, established a statewide central point of referral, whose "distinctive work is publicity and propaganda and it desires to make widely known the best that is now being done in every state." The central point of referral also provided a roster of agencies that provided services for mentally retarded persons.[125]

A number of reasons underlay these significant changes in attitudes toward residential services and their growing support of community programs. First, there simply was not enough money or other resources to provide residential programming for all mentally retarded persons as advocated at the turn of the century. This fact resulted in the sentiment that, for children and adolescents, institutions should serve only those who "could not be properly cared for in their homes."[126]

Second, many parents and relatives did not want their mentally retarded offspring placed in an institution: "If adequate institution provision were available today, they would not be feasible [since many] parents or friends are unable or unwilling to see the necessity for such segregation."[127] Many families did not appreciate the professional notion that a great societal good would be served by segregating their son and daughter, brother or sister. As Wilmarth lamented, "I once wrote to the sister of one of our wards who had been an illegitimate mother five times before the age of twenty-seven years, and asked if the public safety did not demand that we watch over the sister. She replied and asked what I supposed she cared for the public."[128]

Third, many, if not most, institutions failed to provide the environment and services needed by the residents and expected by the parents. Exposés and scandals became common press. Most institutions were overcrowded, understaffed, underprogrammed, and underfinanced. Also, as Bernstein attested, all too many relied on severe physical means of discipline.

Fourth, public schools began to respond favorably to serving mentally retarded persons within their domain, and a number of mental health clinics and universities, in addition to institutions, offered at least the beginnings of community support programs.

Fifth, and perhaps of greatest consequence, mentally retarded persons themselves demonstrated the ability to meet the demands of an open society. Studies involving both post-institutional and post-school activities clearly documented their success. Significant, at least in terms of its impact upon other superintendents, was the study reported by Fernald. In 1916, he surveyed former residents of Waverly, Massachusetts, who had been discharged between 1890 and 1914. The results not only surprised the investigator but, combined with other reports of the day, destroyed the absoluteness of institutionalization.

Fernald noted that only 1,537 individuals had been discharged during the 25-year period of the study, most during the latter years. His explanation was simple:

The relatively small number of discharges for so long a period, with an average number present ranging from 640 in 1890 to 1660 in 1914, shows that the policy of long-continued segregation was consistently followed during the entire period. We honestly believe that nearly all of these people should remain in the institution indefinitely. Some were allowed to go because they seemed to have no vicious tendencies, and their friends were intelligent and able to look out for them, but the majority were dismissed under protest. Not a few of the males took matters into their own hands, and ran away.[129]

Of the 1,537 former residents, 279 could not be located, 175 were out of state, and 437 had been transferred to other institutions. Of the remaining 646 individuals, 470 were males and 176, females. In short, Fernald found that 250 (60 percent) of the men were doing well in the community, as were 52 (36 percent) of the 143 surviving women. Though this success rate would be considered low by current standards in a society with many support services, Fernald's results were a surprise to many. He concluded that "the survey shows that there are bad defectives and good defectives. It also shows that even some apparently bad do 'settle down.' And it shows much justice in the plea of the well-behaved adult defective to be given a

'trial outside' for apparently a few defectives do not need or deserve life-long segregation. It is most important that the limited facilities for segregation should be used for the many who can be protected in no other way."[130]

Though Fernald did not publish his findings until 1919, he shared the results and his conclusions with persons attending the annual convention of the American Association on Mental Deficiency in 1917. At this same meeting, Elizabeth Farrell reported the very positive results of her ongoing study of the post-school performance of special class students, and Bernstein described in very favorable terms the success of his off-grounds programs.

Sixth, the rigid doctrine of heredity and crime, as previously discussed, was seriously—and successfully—challenged by a number of persons of various professional persuasions and responsibilities. The studies by Fernald and Farrell offered further proof that many mentally retarded individuals were not disruptive in the community.

Seventh, there was a changing attitude toward the roles of institutionalized programs in other sectors of the social service delivery section. Criminologists and penologists advanced the notion of parole, and orphanages were considered inappropriate, at least for normal children. Institutional leaders were familiar with these trends.

Finally, many mentally retarded men served their country well during World War I.

In essence, research, professional experience with mentally retarded persons in the community, a changing social consciousness, and the clarification and restricted use of the term *heredity* significantly and positively affected many attitudes and the future course of programming for mentally retarded persons.

Problems and Issues

One of the major problems confronting institutions at that time, and well into the future, involved the appropriate placement of the defective delinquent. Considerable controversy surrounded this issue, with a number of alternative approaches being advocated. Those closest to the institutional scene were not anxious to have the delinquent, at least the more serious offender, committed to their facilities. This is well documented by the position advocated by a subcommittee of the American Association on Mental Deficiency in 1919: "It is the unanimous opinion of this committee that the class of defective delinquents who have criminal tendencies is not properly placed in an institution for the feeble-minded, and should have special provision for its custody and care."[131]

Persons representing the penal system were equally adamant that the defective delinquent did not belong in an industrial school or penitentiary, for several reasons. Some believed the penal system failed to offer appropriate treatment or training: "It is clearly more economical and undoubtedly more humane—to provide proper hospital and other treatment suited to the needs of these individuals than to go on locking them up in jails. . . ."[132] Others objected to the placement of defective delinquents in the penal system because of the high rate of recidivism, which, in turn, reflected badly on the new parole system.

The primary recommendation advanced by both groups was that special treatment facilities be established for the defective delinquent.[133] Not unexpectedly, such proposals were rejected by various legislative bodies, primarily because of associated costs. The next best alternative as recommended by a number of authorities was to set aside a building or an area within either the institution or reformatory intended to serve the defective delinquent.

Guy Fernald, one of the most knowledgeable persons in the field of delinquency and mental retardation advocated three solutions:

1. Legal provision for the commitment of defective delinquents by the court.
2. Provision of a suitable environment or institution to which to commit.
3. Differentiation of the defective from among other offenders by psychiatrical authority competent to advise the court.[134]

In the final analysis, however, the commitment of the defective delinquent remained in the hands of the court and the varying attitudes and predisposition of judges. Regrettably,

many adhered to Guy Fernald's recommendation that defective delinquents' stay should "be indefinite . . . they must show that they are reformed before they may be tried out for parole."[135] As a result, many mentally retarded persons were committed for lifelong incarceration in an institution for minor misdemeanors.

In 1915, Illinois passed the first commitment law to take into consideration this particular problem. The law was drafted by the State Charities Commission assisted by judges of the county, municipal and circuit courts in the county of Cook, social workers throughout the state, and the legal department of Northwestern University. In passing this law, Illinois became the only state at that time to operate exclusively by a commitment law that provided that if "it is unsafe and dangerous to the welfare of the community for him [the mentally retarded person] to be at large," any relative, guardian, or reputable citizen of the county could petition for his placement in a residential facility. Section 20 of the law also provided that any feebleminded person committing a crime could, at the discretion of the court, be placed in one of the institutions. Subsequently, a large number of "feebleminded criminals" were committed to institutions, much to the chagrin of persons working in such facilities.[136] This law was extensively applied by some judges during the first 2 years; 1,201 persons were committed—double the admission rate for the preceding 2 years. Furthermore, the law had the effect, in essence, of placing no restriction on admissions, and thus the entire character of the state institutions changed substantially. Under the new law, a number of infants and children were committed; the notion of "dangerious to oneself or to others" put a very broad placement prerogative at the disposal of the judge.

Another issue of the day, which has persisted into the present, concerned the appropriate and desirable size of a residential facility. Again, there was considerable controversy and debate on this particular issue. Despite those few progressive individuals who were looking at alternatives to a central institution, the institution remained the primary vehicle for residential services. The recommended number of residents reflected one's priorities: residents or costs. Thus, Little maintained that 500 was a desirable size, so one would know each of the residents. E. R. Johnstone believed 750 should be maximum for several reasons: 1) size would be economical and 2) "if the institution is not very large, we get good classes."[137] Johnstone also contended that 750 should be maximum in order to retain a family atmosphere. Others, such as Wilmarth of Wisconsin, advocated for a bed capacity of 1,000; Murdoch believed a state colony should be planned for 2,000 to 3,000; and Smith of Illinois placed no limit on the size except that which the superintendent could properly organize and administer.[138] Those who advocated for large institutions often noted that the colony plan had added efficiency to such an operation. Clearly, the question was one not of small versus large institutions but, rather, the degree of largeness that would be most acceptable.

With the increase in size and number of residents served, institutions rapidly encountered a host of problems, ranging from inadequate financial resources to the unavailability of quality staff. Political patronage was common and troublesome. The informal relationship between administration and staff associated with smaller facilities was lost; administration became highly structured and often rigid. To help guide employee performance, many institutions developed statements of expectancies or creeds, most of which placed priority on loyalty to the institution and its administration.

In the final analysis, the then often cited value of institutions would today represent its greatest condemnation—dependence and sameness:

> The way in which the feeble-minded, even in the same age-level groups, vary from each other is a matter of considerable social, educational, economic and even legal import. Perhaps these differences are not nearly so clear in institutions, into which, of course, are sorted the unsuccessful defectives, and wherein the well-recognized nature of institutional life there is a tendency for inmates to drop their variances.[139]

COMMUNITY SERVICES

The initial twenty years of this century witnessed the development of a number of community services for mentally retarded persons. Of greatest importance was the establishment and expansion of special educational opportunities for mentally retarded students throughout the country. These experiences plus growing support from other community agencies resulted in less demand for institutional programs.

Special Education

By 1900, special education was fairly well accepted, at least in principle, by most metropolitan school systems, and the growth of "ungraded" classes was rather substantial. New York, for example, established its first ungraded class in 1900; by 1906, there were 14 classes; by 1910, 103 classes; by 1912, 131 classes.[140] By 1922, 133 cities in 23 states had enrollments of 23,252 pupils in special education classes of all types.[141]

As early as 1911, New Jersey passed the first state law requiring mandatory special education of mentally retarded children. All municipalities having as many as 15 children who were 3 or more years retarded in school were to provide special classes for their instruction. Between 1915 and 1922, a number of other states followed suit, including California, Connecticut, Illinois, Louisiana, Massachusetts, Minnesota, Missouri, New York, Oregon, Pennsylvania, Utah, Wisconsin, and Wyoming. Like many such laws, however, it was implemented in a fragmentary manner.[142]

In 1915, Minnesota provided state aid in the amount of $100 for each child enrolled in a special class, and in 1919, Pennsylvania passed legislation enabling the local school districts to work collaboratively in meeting the needs of developmentally disabled children. By the mid-1920s, special education had clearly become a state responsibility, legislatively and operationally.

During this time, there were no accurate national estimates of the number of students considered eligible for special educational programs. It was most difficult to obtain any precise statement, since the purposes of special education, eligibility criteria, and diagnostic measures used varied widely. In 1914, as a result of his study of the New York school population, Goddard estimated that 2 percent of school-age children were feeble-minded. Thus, for that city's school system, he estimated that 50,000 children would fall into that class, an "army bound to be more or less a burden on society."[143] Many educational planners adopted the 2 or 3 percent estimate.

Purposes and Goals The basic philosophy underlying special programs for mentally retarded students changed during the first two decades of the century. In the beginning, as indicated, special programs for mentally retarded students were initiated primarily to remove the most difficult or trying from the regular classroom setting. Emphasis was not placed on training mentally retarded individuals to become self-sustaining citizens in an open society for the remainder of their lives. Rather, many in educational circles continued to believe that following termination of formal school experiences, most mentally retarded individuals would end up in institutions, as they should. In 1916, Ada Fitts, a highly respected supervisor of special classes in Boston, wrote, "Most will agree that the ideal condition would be for many of the mentally defective to go from the school directly to the institution, and thus safeguard the public from inefficiency, unemployment, pauperism, vagrancy, degeneracy, and all the other social consequences of feeble-mindedness."[144]

It is quite obvious that early educators held beliefs and opinions similar to those of institutional administrators and others. When it became obvious that institutions would not be built for all persons considered mentally retarded, Lincoln of the Boston school system noted that "this being the case, it seems . . . that the next best thing is being done in the way of raising the moral tone of children, and making them more capable in their family life. They might forget how much 8 and 3 make, but they will never forget their manners, nor their sewing and darning, and they will never again

be the helpless loads they once were to their families. A few will earn small wages in shops; some will be valuable at home. Probably very few will marry, if we had a law for the custodial care of the adult feeble-minded woman, a clear danger would be removed."[145]

Though attitudes of special education administrators and teachers were to change, it remained very difficult for many to reject the notion that the public school system prepared people for institutional living. As late as 1920, Ada Fitts complained, "a grave handicap for Special Classes is the tendency in the minds of school authorities to regard these Classes as bridges leading to institutions and filling them with low grade unimprovable cases, or with delinquents."[146]

Regardless of philosophy, however, placement in a special class was deemed a most serious decision. "Mainstreaming" was definitely preferred in some school systems. In 1903, Lincoln was adamant in his opinion that special classes were "*not* meant for those who, however dull, can be reached by regular classwork skillfully administered."[147] Many teachers and administrators worked diligently to see some of their students returned to the regular class. Goddard disagreed with this position: "A child once feeble-minded is never made normal."[148] In spite of some teachers' concern for the return of feebleminded students to the regular class, many educators and psychologists tended not to believe in the educability of intelligence. This can be readily understood when such outstanding psychologists as Edward Thorndike and Rudolph Pinter firmly maintained that intelligence was uninfluenced by environment. Both held the position that "all sorts of mental traits as well as that complex trait called general intelligence, are inherited in the same way as purely physical traits. The potency of environment is not nearly so great as is commonly supposed."[149] Even in later years when the impact of heredity had decreased and it was realized that the behavioral/moral characteristics of feebleminded children were subject to modification through experience, mental retardation per se remained in the minds of most an irreversible condition.

As noted, special class placement was considered a most serious matter. Therefore, such a decision was rarely left to the sole judgment of the classroom teacher and/or the administrator. Most schools, at least as a matter of policy, required a more extensive evaluation. Walsh, for example, desired a report by the school principal and social worker, as well as a comprehensive clinical study of the child's physical, psychological, and pedagogical status.[150] Additionally, in most school systems, parental wishes were taken into consideration. In Boston, for example, no parent was "obliged against his will to send his child to these classes."[151]

In reality, many allegedly mentally retarded children were placed in special classes without the benefit of the thorough evaluation so often recommended. Anderson, for example, reported that large school systems simply did not have access to enough trained psychologists, and that, in essence, lists of youngsters 3 or more years educationally retarded were compiled; from these lists, principals would identify those youngsters to attend special classes.[152] As Anderson noted in later years, "the selection of children for special instruction was not far from being on a basis of rejection."[153] (It should be noted that the 3-year performance/chronological age difference was consistent with Binet's 1907 recommendations.)

Student Characteristics and Eligibility
The composition of special classes was uniquely different during the first 20 years of special class history than it was following World War I. In the beginning, classes of five to 15 mentally retarded students varied widely in terms of ages, physical handicaps, and degrees of mental retardation. Of the first 15 children enrolled in Boston's special class, "two had had rickets, six convulsions, one epilepsy, three were seriously deaf, four had difficulty with ordinary movements of walking . . . ten spoke with defective articulation, several had deformed palates, and only three had good teeth."[154] In addition to reflecting upon the general health status of these students, Lincoln's statement indicates that early classes were not intended solely or even primarily for

the mildly retarded. Goddard described the school population in the special classes of New York City as including "imbeciles of Mongolian types, microcephalic idiots, hydrocephalic cases, cretins, a large number of middle and high-grade imbeciles, and also a large number of morons. . . ."[155] The exclusion of the moderately and severely mentally retarded students from special classes was not to occur until 1915, when the intelligence quotient became a primary guidepost.

As has been historically true with special classes, most of the students were male: Farrell reported a 2:1 ratio of boys to girls. Her explanation of this phenomenon was quite simple: boys were more "troublesome."[156]

Most of the children who entered the special classes were from severe poverty areas. This was aptly illustrated by Anderson, who discussed the need for teachers to bring in special clothing and to provide baths for the children since their parents lacked adequate facilities: "There is no hot water at all, no cold water except that connected with the sink in the dark hallway, no soap or towels; conditions are such that it would be difficult for people of good intelligence to keep clean, much more those of weak intellect or worse. When one has visited these homes, one wonders how the children come to school from such homes as clean as they do. While such conditions seem absolutely hopeless, they can be met with surprising measures of success by working through the children in the school to the home."[157]

By 1920, the schools were much more discriminating in terms of the populations considered appropriate for attendance in a public school setting and enrollment in a special class. Those who believed that the public school served as a bridge between home and institution tended to exclude the mildly retarded population from the special class, emphasizing the more moderately and severely mentally retarded. Cleveland's classes, for example, were intended for "children of the imbecile type; in fact, we are taking no high grade morons into our classes."[158] This practice gave rise to Ada Fitts's concern that under such a philosophy "there is great danger of limiting special classes to children of too low intelligence quotient. It is far better to err in sending a misfit with one too high than one too low."[159]

On the other hand, Mary McDowell, who was director of the "feeble-minded schools" in Kenosha, Wisconsin, indicated that by 1920 they were employing the IQ test and rejecting any students with an IQ less than 40 in their school programs. Chicago's special classes only admitted mildly retarded students. The rationale for excluding the moderately retarded student was provided by Schmidt of the Chicago school system:

> Now if the imbecile is going to live in his home he is forming habits in reference to that home and in that way the school, I think, can do much less for him than the intelligent parent can do. When the imbecile comes to me for examination, I am in the habit of saying that they in the home can do more for the child as they are always going to live in the home. If he learns to wipe dishes and do little errands to help his mother occasionally that is the best kind of training he can have. A school training would not transfer over to the trainee in many instances.[160]

Gradually, the minimum IQ level would creep up to 50.

Curriculum and the School Day The first special class set a general pattern of programming that was to remain basically unaltered for the next 60 years: the first half of the day was devoted to the three R's and the latter half to such nonacademic areas as manual training or domestic arts, physical education, music, and art. The entire issue of academic subjects was suspect: "Nearly all the experienced teachers and the principals," wrote Goddard in 1914 about the New York city school system, "are agreed that bookwork is largely wasted upon these children but they feel compelled to carry it on because it is in the tradition of the system, and because the parents insist that their children should be taught to read and write."[161] Goddard lent his professional weight to this negative position: "With regard to the three R's *they are almost entirely out of place with children who are mentally defective.*"[162]

Fortunately, many special class teachers did not heed this advice, even though progress in

this area was notably difficult to realize, as indicated by a 1903 progress report on the first 15 special education students in Boston: "They had been admirably taught, and yet, at the average age of nearly 12 none can now do first-grade primary work efficiently and at the normal rate of speed, and none are in any single study much beyond the attainments of that grade, except in manual work."[163]

The emphasis was clearly on manual training and domestic arts, partly because "the working hands make strong the working brain," partly because such training had a potential for future occupational pursuits, and partly because of the youngsters' difficulty in acquiring academic skills.[164] Physical education also was a highly prized curricular area for a variety of reasons, ranging from "there is no brain stimulus except that which comes through the muscle" to its importance in developing "attention, continuity, orderliness, and restraint."[165]

Most early special educators were concerned almost exclusively with curriculum. There is little indication of the methods employed with the exception that great reliance was placed on concrete experience and games. Most teachers probably used an eclectic approach, employing regular educational techniques (especially kindergarten), Montessori's ideas, and Seguin's concepts.

There was a tendency among most school systems not only to follow the 50:50 ratio of academics to nonacademics but also to have a slightly shorter school day. In Boston, for example, the typical day for the special class child was 9:00 to 12:00, 2 hours shorter than for normal youngsters. There was some feeling that these youngsters could neither tolerate nor particularly benefit from a full school day.

Witmer again was the exception. His summer schools represented the most unique and sophisticated educational offerings available for retarded children. The program, though limited in length, reflected individual diagnosis and programming as well as an interdisciplinary approach: "The daily program included opening exercises, the morning talk to all, paper language, written language, numbers, relaxation, manual work, reading, gymnasium and pool, drawing, sense training, games, physical work, folk dancing, and articulation. Other topics included quiet work, specialized corrective procedures, and story dramatization. Specific diagnostic procedures and individualized treatment programs were offered, and as much attention was paid to rest and nutrition as to academic acquisitions."[166] The class was divided into three groups with a teacher-student ratio of 1:6.

Efficacy of the Special Class   One of the earliest reported follow-up studies was by Lincoln in 1909. It indicated that perhaps special education was not accomplishing much for most students:

> In all, 264 pupils appear to have been taught; 24 of these were sent to Waverley; 5 died, 15 were removed to private schools, 36 re-entered our regular public schools, 97 are still enrolled in the special classes, and 87 have been dismissed as having reached the age-limit of sixteen, or on account of illness, removal, etc. Of the 36 sent back to regular school work, probably one-half are satisfactory pupils, mostly in the lower grades (first to fourth) and receiving promotion in the usual way. Not enough time has passed to determine their capacity for higher grade work. Some have been placed in ungraded or "coaching" classes, merely because their age disqualified them for primary grades, and have done well there. Others have been so placed because the pride of the parents forbade the children remaining in a "dummy class"; such cases are apt to do nothing but sit through the term. Of the 87 dismissed, about 17 are known to be earning wages from a very trifling amount up to $3.50 per week. None are independent, but some might be called self-supporting under direction. Nearly the same number of girls are useful at home, much as girls of their age usually are. About 19 or 20 are known as a menace to society through vicious or criminal tendencies.[167]

Soon, however, it was demonstrated that special education programs were proving highly effective for two reasons: 1) prolonged attendance in school and 2) successful post-school adjustment and achievement. In a day when many youngsters dropped out of school before age 14, Fitts, Farrell, and Boehme all reported that many special class adolescents stayed beyond the regulation school age.

As briefly mentioned before, in 1915, Farrell published a follow-up study of 350 former special class students from the New York City school system. These results challenged the negative allegations of those such as Goddard who contended that following school, mentally retarded persons "are generally on the street, in the juvenile court, or are sent to some institution."[168]

In order to implement her study, Farrell had teachers and settlement workers gather information concerning former students by visiting their home, their employer, or by interviewing the parent at school. Of the 350 former students who left classes at 16 years of age, 92 percent attended school until their sixteenth birthday (which, as indicated, was quite an accomplishment), and only 4 percent had been placed in an institution for the feebleminded (less than 1 percent being girls). Only 1 percent of the boys were placed in a penal institution. Of greatest consequence was that 54.8 percent of the former students were employed for wages, 8.8 percent were employable but temporarily out of work at the time of the investigation, 24.6 percent were cared for at home and many of these at home were considered to be of economic value. Though employment tended to cluster around trades, factories, and stores, job diversity was quite remarkable.[169]

Other studies tended to support the findings of Farrell's efforts but were not nearly as well documented. Nevertheless, collectively they led to a new importance and expanded role of special education.

There were two reasons underlying the early successes in post-school experiences among mentally retarded persons. First, several of the larger school systems established what was known as "after-care work" programs. As described by Ada Fitts,

> When a boy or girl reaches the age when he or she may legally leave school, all assistance desired is given in finding suitable employment. This teacher guides them to lines of work for which they are adapted—and as far as possible steers them away from undesirable unemployment and blind alleys. She is known to many employees of unskilled labor who take these Special Class pupils with full understanding of their limitations. She keeps

track of them when they change employment and they come repeatedly for guidance and advice. She becomes acquainted with the families of these boys and girls and knows their home conditions. . . . Probably no other phase of special class work is of more importance than this social and after-care work.[170]

Second, some school systems permitted the mentally retarded student to remain in the school well beyond the legal age. In view of these positive experiences, it is not surprising that many educators asked for extended opportunities for mentally retarded persons.

In essence, both local community and state were being called upon with increasing frequency to assume a direct responsibility for the mentally retarded adult. Also, the emphasis was shifting to noninstitutional programming.

Special Class vs. Segregated Schools Arguments concerning special classes versus special segregated schools continued for the same reasons discussed previously. While most educators preferred special classes in the regular school to facilitate social interaction, others supported the special, segregated school. Creswell of Grand Rapids, Michigan, was concerned that the youngster would be "unhappy, when he is continually forced to bear the slights of the normal child."[171] Similarly, Anderson supported the segregated school, contending that the "children can be better graded, the work can be better organized and systematized, and more can be accomplished in special schools for defectives."[172]

Teacher Recruitment and Training With the development of special classes, one of the most critical problems confronting early administrators was locating educators well qualified for the task. Most authorities, even Goddard, believed that mentally retarded students required the assistance of an excellent educator: "Every employer of teachers knows the difference between a good teacher and a poor one, and one of the former; but nowhere in the whole educational system is this difference so important as in the case of teachers of defectives. Nowhere are good teachers so valuable and nowhere is the poor teacher such an utter failure and capable of doing much

harm."[173] As usual, there was the exception: "It is a question whether a dull, slow, conscientious, and well-trained teacher is not far better for dull and feeble-minded students than a bright, mentally quick teacher."[174]

Witmer was most demanding of his teachers: "The teacher must know each child as an individual. She must consult physicians in order that they may assist in her work through the medical treatment of the physical causes of retardation. She must either visit the homes of her children or she must have a social worker who will make such visits to report to her. The employment of discipline, to take only one example, must meet the individual's needs. Whether severe or lax discipline is called for will depend upon the kind of treatment to which the child is subjected at home. If the claim is made by teachers of special classes that they have not the time to visit in the homes, this simply means that they have not the time to do their work properly. The teacher, however, is not a social visitor primarily. She is primarily a psychologist working in a practical field, applying psychological principles day by day to the mental development of each child. Clinical psychology combines information gathered from many different scientific sources, and applies this information to the understanding and treatment of each child's individual needs."[175]

The common practice was to recruit teachers from among those with training in either kindergarten (preferred) or primary education. Some experience in a residential setting was also desired. The Boston school system, for example, during the first several years of operation sought teachers with some experience at Barre or at Mrs. Seguin's school; some of the teachers were also sent to Elwyn to study for a period of 3 months. In 1902, the Vineland Training School announced the first formal 6-week summer school training program for public school teachers.[176] Thus was established the precedence for the training of special teachers that was to endure for a half century. Many elementary school teachers who ultimately assumed positions in special classes spent at least one summer acquiring theoretical and practical educational and recreational experiences with mentally retarded persons in a residential setting. Vineland's early effort was rapidly emulated by others, and the summer school training of teachers became a major objective of many residential facilities throughout the country.

Witmer's training program was again unique for its day, setting forth both formal experiences and institutional exposure. Two or three summers were deemed necessary to obtain a well-rounded course of preparation in the kind of individual psychology required for teaching backward children. Fifteen courses in psychology were offered at the summer school of 1911, each occupying at least 1 hour a day for the 6 weeks of the session. These courses included a wide range of studies including educational psychology, anatomy, physiology, hygiene, physical education, mental and physical defects, social and health aspects of school work, special education programs, and tests and measurements.

Witmer's program was well received. Enrollment increased from 84 educator students in 1910 to 221 in 1911.

By 1909, some of the larger cities had introduced special examinations and offered licensure in the area of mental retardation. New York, for example, required educators interested in special education to complete an 8-hour examination successfully. The examination included four major areas of inquiry: 1) Principles (e.g., "Name the physiological functions the development of which throws light on the probable mental condition of a child. Show how this knowledge may be practically used by a teacher"), 2) Practical Tests (e.g., "Indicate the relation between intuition and mental power. Illustrate"), 3) Methods of Teaching (e.g., "Describe the kind of construction work that should be given to the choreic child"), and 4) Principles of Education (e.g., "Describe in detail a method of testing the power of imagination in defective pupils, stating the materials used. Of what specific use to a teacher is such testing?"). According to Goddard, however, these examinations were not particularly effective in selecting good teachers: "We have found certified teachers in these classes who are no way fitted for the work. On the other hand, we have found people who are teaching as substitutes, having failed the examination, who nevertheless are doing excellent work."[177]

In the final analysis, the first 20 years of this century witnessed some very dramatic changes in at least the role and purpose of special education, and certainly the results of these early experiences played a significant part in altering public attitudes. While many mentally retarded youngsters, or those considered to be mentally retarded, benefited from such programs, not all developmentally disabled youngsters were so fortunate. The problem of youngsters with epilepsy remained acute. Many school systems refused to provide educational experiences for them in the school setting, for example, the "Cleveland public schools have assumed the responsibility for two classes of the socially incompetent, the epileptics and the feeble-minded. It is admitted that at least one of these classes, the epileptic presents so unsatisfactory a pedagogical problem as to warrant elimination. The medical and educational treatment, which these cases require, makes them proper subjects for an institution only."[178]

Other Community Services

While educational and residential programs were the two leading service vehicles for mentally retarded persons, other community agencies and professional groups became increasingly sensitive to this problem and a few offered assistance. As discussed previously, mentally retarded juvenile delinquents were being seen by mental health clinics or special, court-appointed psychiatrists. Granted, the number of persons assisted was relatively small; nevertheless, such services were available.

The fledgling field of pediatrics also began to assume a major role. Though many physicians had dedicated their professional lives to children throughout the course of medical history, pediatrics as a medical entity had its inception at the turn of the century, being concerned primarily with nutrition and the infant. This initial interest soon broadened to encompass early home programming and parenting. Thus, McCready, a "paedologist," attempted to aid mentally retarded infants through a variety of treatments, including drugs, nutritional diets, and water massage. Recognizing that none of these was a panacea for the problem of mental retardation or even of appreciable succor, he nevertheless strongly urged working with mentally retarded youngsters in the home.[179] The public health nurse also became increasingly involved with home services.

The Call for Comprehensive Services

By 1919, most authorities in the field of mental retardation and other agencies concerned about the welfare, care, and training of persons so affected knew that it was time to develop a comprehensive array of services. Without it, the needs of mentally retarded persons would remain unmet, especially within the community setting. The most definitive early proposal outlining community services was provided by Fernald. In prefacing his comments concerning the need for community-based programming, he emphasized that mentally retarded persons did not constitute a single homogeneous group: "The idiot, imbecile, and moron present different needs and dangers. Each of these groups has different troubles, according to age and sex. Rural, sparsely-settled communities, with homogeneous racial population, have conditions pertaining to the defective which differ from those of urban industrial centers, with cosmopolitan racial complications."[180]

According to Fernald, therefore, a comprehensive service system should include:

1. Early identification and registration of mentally retarded persons—"The keynote of a practical program for the management of mental defectiveness is to be found in effect, which seems to have been proved, that those defectives whose defect is recognized while they were young children and have received proper care and training during childhood are, as a rule, not especially troublesome after

they have been safely guided through the period of early adolescence."[181]

2. Visitation of every mentally retarded person in the home.

3. Home support programs and training manuals for parents.

4. A knowledgeable person in mental retardation in each locality of size because every mentally retarded person is entitled to health and mental examinations and care.

5. In large centers, there should be a cadre of special examiners and/or mental health clinics. Travelling mental health clinics should be readily available in rural areas, all sponsored by state government.

6. Legal provisions and protections for mentally retarded persons.

7. Specialized educational opportunities should be provided since mentally retarded children were entitled "even more than a normal child" to education according to his needs and capabilities.

8. Post-school follow-up or after-care assistance in health.

9. Outpatient clinics through institutions.

To this listing can be added the suggestions of others of the day:

10. Alternative residential opportunities as proposed by Bernstein: foster homes for children and group homes for adolescents and adults.

11. Genetic counseling—"The physician has knowledge of family histories and tendencies. He has access to family councils. His advice in individual cases is eagerly sought and generally followed. He has exclusive opportunity to teach and inculcate certain accepted principles of practical eugenics . . . the well informed physician has the pleasant privilege of allaying the fears of those who misinterpret and magnify the possibilities of morbid heredity in their own families."[182]

12. Research into the causes and treatment of mental retardation.[183]

13. A continuing education program for mentally retarded persons beyond the legal school age of 14 or 16.[184]

14. A national documentation service.[185]

As summarized by Fernald, "we must recognize his condition while he is a child, then protect him from evil influences, train and educate him according to his capacity, make him industrially efficient, teach him to acquire correct habits of living, and, when he has reached adult life, continue to give him the friendly help and guidance he needs. These advantages should be accessible to every feeble-minded person in this state."[186]

Naturally, any effective program would require a well-trained cadre of professionals working collaboratively—"psychiatrists, psychologists, teachers, school authorities, normal schools, parents, social workers, institutional officials, parole officers, court officials, prison officials, and so forth. There would be a centralized formulation of plans and methods, but most of the real work would be done in the local community."[187] Everyone called for a massive program of public information.

While cooperation at the state level was deemed essential, early promoters of community services still viewed implementation as a local responsibility. The state was requested to cooperate and facilitate, not to rule or regulate. Similarly, though national interest was sought, direct federal participation was not. Johnstone best expressed the prevalent attitude: "If the larger work of extension is to be successful it must be done in the spirit of unselfish cooperation—giving only when asked, going only when wanted, aiding only when assistance is needed, withdrawing when its presence is not desired. Law, regulation, or force cannot accomplish what an unofficial body can do. The work must be founded upon friendship and good will."[188]

THE "GREAT WAR" AND THE MENTALLY RETARDED ADULT

The period under review ended with World War I, the advent of which presented the professional community with another topic for debate: the ability of mentally retarded persons to serve in the armed forces. While this was of major concern during the war, the problem had been studied rather extensively in Germany around the turn of the century. Schaeffer, for example, in his 1906 study, *Der Moralische Schwachsinn,* found five major problems with mental defectives serving in the army:

1. They were the object of mistreatment at the hands of other soldiers.
2. They were repeatedly in conflict with discipline and military law.
3. They were notoriously intolerant of alcohol, and when under its influence frequently commit military crimes.
4. They were emotionally unstable and irritable. Especially were they characterized by unreasonable outbreaks of temper and of assaults upon their superiors.
5. They frequently committed suicide.[189]

Military personnel of the German army recommended the rejection of mentally retarded persons.

In 1917, the Surgeon General of the United States Army released a document entitled "To the Psychiatrist and Neurologist Assigned to Special Duty in the Military Camps of the United States Government," which outlined who should be considered ineligible for admission into the armed services. Among the six neurological and psychiatric problems was "Mental Deficiency, Category V." In this instance, the psychiatrist was cautioned to "look for defect in general information with reference to native environment, ability to learn, to reason, to calculate, to plan, to construct, to compare weights, sizes, and so forth; defect in judgment, foresight, language, output of effort, suggestibility, stigma of degeneration, muscle incoordination."[190]

Early efforts to screen and eliminate such candidates produced a variety of statistics. In 1918, Hastings reported that in New York, of the 12,000 men rejected for psychiatric reasons, 30 percent, or 4,000, were considered mentally retarded. As of May 1, 1919, of 72,297 cases of nervous and mental diseases discovered among troops in the country, 22,374 were considered to involve mental deficiency.[191] After the war, the provost marshal general issued a report that a little over 5.5 percent of registrants rejected or discharged from the army were mentally defective.[192]

A large number of mentally retarded persons, however, did serve in the military during World War I and did so admirably, often in specialized work battalions. As in World War II, quite often the physical examination left much to be desired: "I was recently told by a psychologist in the service of the government," reported Bliss in 1919, "that the high grade moron was often accepted by the final examining board, because of his good appearance physically, even though the psychologist had rejected him. The moron's glib answers to questions, and his good looks generally, often deceive people who do not know the defective."[193]

At the end of the war, Army Regulation #65 specified that "a feeble-minded individual who has the intelligence of a child of eight years may be accepted to service in the Army."[194] This position was not well received by the professional community, which felt that while some men "did mighty well and were good fighters and were killed," a large number did "badly."[195] In response to the army regulation, members of the American Association on Mental Deficiency at their 1919 annual business meeting unanimously approved the following resolution, which was forwarded to the Secretary of War, the Adjutant General, and the Surgeon General of the Army: ". . . said regulation [should] be altered so as to direct that feeble-mindedness (mental defect) shall be one of the conditions which shall disqualify an applicant for admission to the Army."[196]

Not only did some feebleminded men present problems, so did some feebleminded women who,

enamored by the glamour of the uniform, thrilled with the ideal of bravery and romance which these soldiers presented, hung around the camps seeking the acquaintance, friendship and association of the soldiers. . . . The government has very properly recognized the menace of leaving these women in and around the camps, taken them into custody and in a good many cases has had them cared for in the various state institutions for the feeble-minded, providing not only safety and decent lives for them, but also safety to young and thoughtless men in our armies from the ravages of diseases that uncontrolled, are far more dangerous and deadly, because more lasting, than the bullets of the enemy, or the dreadful exposure and hardships so often necessary in the life of a soldier.[197]

A sad commentary to World War I was that some mentally retarded men left an institution, joined the services, did well, and upon coming home were readmitted. Community alternatives were unavailable.

Yet, taking all things into consideration, one can conclude that the period of 1900 to 1920 was most remarkable. Attitudes toward mentally retarded persons changed dramatically, from the idea that such individuals were inherently amoral and incorrigible, requiring lifelong institutionalization to the belief that education and community support would result in productive citizens. Direct services for mentally retarded persons and their families, however, were at best fragmentary and not universally proffered. Nevertheless, communities were more alert and sensitive to the value and unique problems of such youngsters and adults and began to develop a variety of appropriate services. State governments also paid greater heed to mentally retarded persons; that not all their decisions were necessarily wise or consistent with human needs diminishes neither their interest nor their activity.

Chapter

7

"Normalcy," Depression, and the New Deal

(1920–1939)

To some political historians, the 1920s were similar to the 1950s in that the decade following the end of a war was marked by public apathy and complacency. Only three issues were of national concern: immigration, prohibition, and crime. In essence, the 1920s were not noted for social reforms in any respect, since, in the judgment of historian Ernest May, most "Americans in the early twenties felt that the progressive years had accomplished all the reforms the country needed—indeed, perhaps more than needed. To the average man—and the average politician—there were no issues left to fight."[1]

Though there were no political heroes during the 1920s, the American public suffered no loss of people with whom to identify or exciting moments. The car was king of the day and its makers admired by many: Henry Ford, the Studebaker brothers, Walter Chrysler, and William Crapo Durant, who created General Motors. Paralleling the rise of the Ku Klux Klan was the expansive religious revival typified by such individuals as Billy Sunday and Sister Aimee. Hemingway and Fitzgerald redirected American literature as did Grant Wood painting and George Gershwin music. There were movies, speakeasies, and baseball: Valentino, Capone, and Babe Ruth, and the hero of heroes, Charles Lindbergh.

On October 24, 1929, the stock market plummeted and the United States was rapidly ushered into a period of great depression and great reform. From the moment Franklin D. Roosevelt was inaugurated on March 4, 1933, the country underwent a dramatic and permanent change in its perspective as to the responsibilities of government. While President Hoover relied upon private corporations and charitable organizations to respond to the needs of people in distress, Roosevelt, though inherently conservative, envisaged a new role for government. In 1938, he declared: "Government has a final responsibility for the well-being of its citizenship. If private and cooperative endeavor fails to provide work for willing hands and relief for the unfortunate, those suffering hardship from no fault of their own have a right to call upon government for aid; and a government worthy of its name must make fitting response."[2]

Between 1933 and 1938, the federal government exercised its latent legislative muscle in passing a series of acts that would affect the majority of American people: the Agricultural Adjustment Act, the National Industry Recovery Act, the Public Works Administration, the Reconstruction Finance Corporation, the Securities and Exchange Commission, the Civilian Conservation Corps, the Labor Relations Act, and the Fair Labor Standards Act of 1938, which formally abolished child labor, set a national minimum wage of 40 cents an hour, and established the 40-hour work week with time-and-a-half for overtime. By 1934, the federal government was spending millions to assist the 12 to 16 million Americans who were out of work; one of every six American citizens was receiving some form of public assistance.

Of greatest importance in terms of long-range implications for mentally retarded persons and their families was the passage of the Social Security Act in 1935. This act, in a single effort, created a national system of old-age insurance; established a federal-state program for unemployment insurance; provided federal aid to states on a matching basis for the care of dependent mothers and children, the crippled, and the blind; and supported public health services.

UNDERSTANDING OF MENTAL RETARDATION

According to Leo Kanner, the period 1920 to 1940 represented the "great lull."[3] In other words, the thinking and programming of the past decade were, in his judgment, to persist until World War II. The evidence does not entirely support that assessment, however. Many changes were occurring, new ideas were generated, and mental retardation as a phenomenon continued to grow in complexity.

Perhaps the most significant change was one of attitude among the field's leaders. Both Fernald and Goddard dramatically renounced their former positions.

In 1924, Fernald delivered his famous speech about the "Legend of the Feeble-Minded":

A composite portrait of a mythical person, embodying all the bad qualities of many defectives,

appeared as the hero of what I like to call the "Legend of the Feeble-Minded." This legend conveyed the impression that the feeble-minded were almost all of the highly hereditary class; they were almost invariably immoral, most of the women bore illegitimate children; nearly all were antisocial, vicious and criminal; they were all idle and shiftless and seldom supported themselves; they were highly dangerous people roaming up and down the earth seeking whom they might destroy.[4]

Fernald firmly denied this concept of mentally retarded persons, and acknowledged "that feeble-mindedness is not an entity, to be dealt with in a routine way, but is an infinitely complex problem. . . . No two defectives are exactly alike. What is good for one may be bad for another. An individual defective may be expressed or described only by an equation—his intelligence, plus his body, plus his family, plus his training, plus his personality traits, plus his morals, etc. No routine procedure will meet the needs of this highly differentiated group."[5]

Like other progressive medical superintendents, Fernald came to the realization that mental retardation, especially at higher levels of functioning, was not predominantly a medical problem but, rather, one of education and economics: "The problem of the moron is largely economic. The idle defective has no money, feels inferior and does his worst. The defective who works all day at good wages seldom makes trouble. The industrially trained defective can always get work."[6]

Fernald's declarations probably surprised no one, since, as we have already seen, he had been advocating many of these concepts for a number of years. His stature in the field, however, lent credence and support to a new era of positivism. In contrast, Goddard's complete turn-about in 1928 must have startled at least some of his audience: "The problem of the moron is a problem of education and training," he explained. "As for myself, I think I have gone over to the enemy with only one reservation. This may surprise you, but frankly when I see what has been made out of the moron by a system of education, which as a rule is only *half right,* I have no difficulty in concluding that when we get an education that is entirely right there will be no morons who cannot manage themselves and their affairs and compete in the struggle for existence." Further, he charged that it was time to "change several of our time honored concepts—first of all, feeblemindedness (the moron) is *not incurable;* secondly, the feebleminded do not generally need to be segregated in institutions. . . ."[7]

Few persons had so radically altered their very strong points of view in so little time, but leaders such as Fernald and Goddard always deserve the honors and recognition they receive. They both profited immensely from their experiences, approached mental retardation with uncertainty and question, and were most willing to express professionally and publicly their altered perspectives and directions.

Such changes in attitude were due primarily to three sets of experiences. First, and perhaps most significant, as institutions expanded their services into the communities and as communities developed more programs, all concerned were introduced to a new population of mentally retarded individuals: those who were not delinquent, who were well adjusted to their home and community, and whose parents were both capable and dedicated. This was certainly the case with Fernald, for he readily acknowledged that the experiences of his traveling clinic gave him an entirely different perspective as to the characteristics of mentally retarded individuals, their families, and the settings from which they came. As he explained:

> The "legend of the feeble-minded" was based on a study of the only known large groups of defectives of that period and they were those who *had* got into trouble and *were* in institutions, who *were* largely of the hereditary class and *had* behaved badly and *were* shiftless and lazy. As a group they were the neglected and untrained and uncared for defectives. It was entirely logical to assume that all defectives had similar history and tendencies. The legend ignored the defectives from good homes with no troublesome traits of character and behavior. It would be equally logical to describe an iceberg without reference to the 87% of bulk invisible below the surface of the sea.[8]

Second, continued reports of successful parole or community placement programs of institutions were influential. Not only were former residents successfully functioning within the community, other studies revealed that mental retardation was not a primary cause of poverty. Only 25.7 percent of families on relief in New York City, reported Haines in 1925, were diagnosed as feebleminded (including parents and/or children with IQs less than 70).[9] A few years later, Foley reported that few of the adults placed from the Rome State School into various areas of New York were on relief: only 5 percent of the males and 7 percent of the females needed such assistance.[10] Interestingly, in spite of the depressed economic conditions of the time, many trained mentally retarded persons found gainful employment.[11]

Third, the failure of intelligence testing, as will be discussed, demonstrated that many factors other than heredity were involved with intellectual performance.

Other influences also changed attitudes and judgments. The courts' insistence on viewing mental retardation in terms of social behavior was important. While many in the professional community classified mental retardation in terms of intellectual performance, the courts still emphasized social conduct. Professionals who entered the field of mental retardation from either counseling or corrections tended to highlight the social interpretation. The 1920s also gave rise to the mental hygiene movement in the United States with its emphasis on emotional and social development.

DEFINITION AND CLASSIFICATION

No major change in the tripartite concept of mental retardation occurred during this period. Edgar Doll, for example, observed in his presidential address to the 1936 annual meeting of the American Association on Mental Deficiency that at least three critical elements must exist before a person can be recognized as feebleminded, namely, "(1) social inadequacy, (2) due to low intelligence, (3) which has been developmentally arrested."[12] What did change, however, was the growing emphasis on the social and developmental aspects of mental retardation as opposed to its statistical interpretation. Doll further proposed that "idiocy, imbecility, and moronity shall not be defined in mental age terms, but in social terms."[13]

In view of growing attention to the social dimensions of mental retardation in concept, a short-lived attempt was made to distinguish between mental retardation according to social adequacy. Thus, the White House Conference on the Handicapped Child in 1930 used the term "mental deficiency" to refer to retarded intelligence and social competence and "feeblemindedness" to refer to retarded intelligence and social incompetence. Though "mental deficiency" would replace "feeblemindedness" as a generic label during the 1940s, the social competence dichotomy was not widely adopted.[14] Similarly, some authorities, such as Doll, wanted the moron considered separately from the imbecile and idiot since the latter conditions were definitely physical in origin.[15] This division, though commonly used in Europe, was rejected in this country.

ASSESSMENT OF INTELLIGENCE

Persons interested in the testing movement were confronted with many challenges during the 1920s. First was a widespread dissatisfaction with the current state of the art, second was the impact of the mental hygiene movement, and third was the changing concept of mental retardation.

As regards the first point, research continued to indicate that the Binet intelligence scale, including revised versions, was unable to provide the fine distinction between mild degrees of mental retardation and normality. Adding to the confusion was the question of the appropriate cutoff point for determining mild retardation. Experience during World War I with group tests frightened most psychological examiners and others concerned with mental retardation; using a mental age of 11 resulted in 24.1 percent of the white participants being potentially classifiable as feebleminded.[16] Raising that mental age cutoff point to 13 would, as Goddard observed in 1928, result in approximately 50 percent of the population being considered mentally retarded.[17] No one

wished to even imply that that many individuals could conceivably be feebleminded, let alone be classified as such. Ultimately, the acceptable mental age fluctuated from 9 to 11, with widely different statistical results. Similarly, when the IQ became more generally applied, interpretations for mild degrees of mental retardation varied from between 50 and 60 to between 75 and 80. In the final analysis, even the most ardent advocates of mental tests did not want the percentage of mentally retarded persons to deviate significantly from approximately 2 or 3 percent of the population.

The value of the Binet test in terms of practical utilization was also questioned, particularly by educators who contended that the information was "only approximately correct as all mental defectives of the same mental age are not capable of doing the same grade of school work."[18] This resulted in the rapid generation of scaled educational tests.

The reliability of repetitive measurement, or the constancy of the IQ, also came under serious challenge from a wide range of sources. As early as 1919, Terman warned that his research indicated that significant changes in IQ scores were not unusual. Specifically, he found that about one out of six children's IQ changed as much as 10 points, and one out of 50 by 20 points or more.[19] Terman's results were verified by a number of persons working directly with mentally retarded individuals, including Hoakley and Vanuxem.[20]

Another difficulty facing mental testers was the assumption that one's mental development, as measured, would cease by age 16. Research by Raymond, Woodall, Wladkowsky, and others soon dispelled this notion.[21]

Persons working in mental health clinics and other such settings sensitive to the impact of the mental hygiene or child development movement were indignant over the constant emphasis placed on intelligence per se. Mental hygienists attacked intelligence tests rather harshly. Potter, for example, implored that intelligence be placed in perspective, and that "human efficiency depends upon the adjustment to three groups of factors, namely, in their order of importance, instincts, emotions, and intelligence." Instincts and emotions included such aspects as "energy, ambition, competition, altruism, love, friendship, longing, cravings, hope, and so on."[22] Not only would these various factors influence ultimate functioning as a human being in a social setting, they would also impinge upon test performance. Others, such as Twitmyer, contended that motivational and aptitude testing were of prime import.[23]

Such questions and disagreements did not, however, prove discouraging but actually stimulated a great flurry of activity in the field of testing. To many psychologists, the answer rested with multiple testing. Thus, a wide range of tests were developed, including the National Intelligence Test; nonverbal tests, such as Porteus' Maze Test and Healy Picture Completion Test; Goodenough Draw a Man Test; aptitude tests, such as Seashore's Musical Talent Test; a variety of personality tests; and Gessell's infant developmental scales. The Binet scale was again revised in 1937; in 1939, David Wechsler introduced the Wechsler-Bellevue Test. Eventually, the Wechsler scales, both adult and children's forms, were used as much, if not more, than the Stanford-Binet. By 1939, Hildreth could identify 4,279 articles and studies on mental testing.[24]

In 1924, Doll offered a penetrating analysis of the state of the testing art that remained valid throughout this period:

1. There is at present considerable uncertainty as to the age at which the development of general intelligence ceases.
2. We are not agreed as to what is the average mental age of unselected adults.
3. We are not agreed as to how this problem is complicated by differences in nationality and color, and whether such differential mental age averages as were established by the Army studies should be employed in differential diagnosis.
4. We are not agreed as to the methods of calculating and of interpreting intelligence quotients although perhaps no single scientific term is now more glibly and less intelligently used among school people and clinical psychologists, than this much-abused device.
5. We are much confused as to the statistical

devices to be employed in the standardization of tests and the interpretation thereof.
6. The significance of unequal standing in a succession of tests, is not at present subject to exact interpretation.
7. Recent work has indicated the great importance of differentiating individuals as to types of ability, as well as levels, and we are beginning to understand that special talent may socially offset special disability or even general disability.
8. The role of the emotions in relation to the social significance of intelligence is still a matter of opinion rather than knowledge. These uncertainties need not prevent us from continuing our practical service, but should certainly encourage us to proceed cautiously and with due respect for the rapid progress which is being made in the academic field.[25]

In spite of all concerns about testing, however, to the average professional, their validity was immutable. According to Goodenough, "mental ages and IQs obtained from half a dozen different group tests were joyfully computed and entered on children's permanent record cards by teachers and school principals with as much assurance as their grandfathers had placed in the skull maps drawn up by their favorite phrenologist. The decade of the twenties was the heyday of the testing movement, the age of innocence when an IQ was an IQ and few ventured to doubt its omnipotence."[26]

A few persons, such as Kuhlmann, Porteus, and Doll, however, desired a different form of assessment, one consistent with the sociolegal concept of mental retardation. Thus arose the interest in the measurement of adaptive behavior.[27]

Researchers at the Vineland School, especially Edgar Doll, were the undisputed leaders in this area of assessing human behavior. It should be noted, however, that earlier test developers were not insensitive to social adaptability. In 1910, Binet and Simon related their levels of retardation to a table of traits distinguishing between idiot, imbecile, and moron. For example, among the tasks that idiots could perform were prehension and walking; imbeciles could eat alone, dress, and make a bed; and morons could comb hair, garden, iron, and cook.[28]

Similarly, in 1914, Goddard translated his levels of mental retardation in terms of industrial capacity which, in essence, identified the relationship between mental age and adaptive behavior in the work setting. While the idiot, at best, had no industrial potential, the imbecile could perform tasks of duration, such as washing dishes; and the highest level moron could use machinery, tend animals, and did not require supervision for routine work.[29]

Various researchers at the Vineland Training School had been concerned with the development of social measures of intelligence for a number of years. For example, Porteus in 1921 introduced a social rating scale for defectives, intended to identify a series of personality traits and characteristics among feebleminded defectives. Results of his social rating scale indicated that mildly retarded persons were characterized by a lack of planning capacity, suggestibility, irresolution, impulsiveness, excitability, obtrusiveness, and moodiness.[30]

In addition, during the 1920s, the Vineland Laboratory implemented a series of job-analysis studies which, in turn, related to the notion of adaptive behavior, adjustment, and social group relationships. In 1929, Doll devised a score card for evaluating changes and behavior of hospitalized mental patients prior to, during, and following psychiatric care. This scale again dealt with such personal aspects as appearance and anger.[31]

In 1936, Edgar Doll introduced his Vineland Social Maturity Scale. This 117-item scale measured an individual's abilities and growth in terms of everyday situations. It would be the primary measurement of adaptive behavior for the next several decades.

Behavioral research studies, excluding those related to mental testing, were few and far between; but the exceptions were most interesting. In 1927, Harry Baker reported an extensive study of characteristic differences between "bright" and "dull" students.[32] During the 1930s, the research section of the Training School at Vineland made a concerted effort to study the behavior and learning characteristics of severely retarded youngsters, those within the age range of 7 to 12 years with a mental age

of less than 3.3 years. Several problem-solving situations were investigated, and severely retarded children were found to have unusual learning styles and personality characteristics, both of which, combined with limited language, influenced learning behavior. A supplemental series of studies established that such youngsters could be conditioned to make simple discriminations and that incentives played an important role.[33] Interestingly, Doll, who was then director of the research section, anticipated the future when he observed, "the experimental study of idiocy reveals hitherto unsuspected capacities for adaptive learning when the things to be learned and the modes of learning them are conceived along lines of anthropoid training rather than along lines of infant training."[34] Thirty years later, the field of mental retardation would discover (or rediscover) operant conditioning procedures based primarily on animal research.

The second series of reports were by Alfred Strauss and his colleagues, including Heinz Werner and Newell Kephart. These studies dealt with the learning characteristics of mentally retarded youngsters, divided according to endogenous and exogenous. They indicated that exogenous (brain-injured) youngsters tended to show certain characteristics, such as distractibility and perseveration, which adversely affected learning. Within a period of approximately 10 years, these early efforts would evolve into a theory, which, as will be seen, would have a significant impact upon the education and training of both mentally retarded and normal youngsters.

PREVALENCE

The estimated prevalence of mental retardation in the population varied from .5 percent to over 3 percent, depending upon the age of the individual. Though the federal government no longer conducted national studies in this area, other agencies did, including the Indiana Committee on Mental Defectives. In 1922, the Committee, having surveyed all "places where feeble-minded naturally gathered, such as river and creek bottoms and houseboats and the rugged unproductive areas," reported that only 1.65 percent of the population was feeble-minded. Of the 44,000 identified mentally retarded persons, however, 18,000 (41 percent) were considered in need of institutional care, a substantially high estimate for the day.[35] In contrast, Ecob estimated, based on his research, that .5 percent of the total population in New York probably would be considered to be mentally retarded.[36]

Studies of various school populations tended to be relatively consistent, denoting that approximately 3 percent of school-age children and adolescents were mentally retarded. In 1922, Estabrook, for example, found 116 feebleminded youngsters in the total school population of 3,500.[37]

ETIOLOGY

Both knowledge (and suspicion) of various etiological influences associated with mental retardation advanced during this period. New disorders and syndromes were identified, including sulphatide lipidosis by Witte, 1921; Greig's disease (hypertelorism), 1924; the syndrome of Rud (infantilism and congenital ichthyosis), 1927; Cornelia de Lange's syndrome (microcephaly, abnormal face and limbs), 1933; phenylketonuria by Fölling, 1934; Turner's syndrome (gonadal dysgenesis), 1938; and toxoplasmosis, a parasitic infection, by Wolf, Cowen, and Paige, 1939.[38]

Much attention was devoted to syphilis, especially after the introduction of the Wassermann test. Results were mixed and confusing, with institutions reporting as high as 19 percent of the population being so infected.[39] Repetitive studies finally determined that the general incidence of syphilis among mentally retarded persons, at least those in institutional settings, ranged from 3 to 5 percent, which was approximately the same for the general population.[40] Thus, while it was generally believed that syphilis could produce mental retardation, no one would predict the frequency with which it occurred.

Much attention was also devoted to endocrinal disorders. Nearly every condition of un-diagnosed mental retardation was associated with one glandular disorder or the other, usually without specificity. As with any new discovery, the reported incidence of glandular disorders among mentally retarded persons was initially quite high. In 1924, for example, Potter stated that 74 percent of 100 mental defectives autopsied showed glandular changes.[41] In 1935, Jackson reported that of 3,548 mentally retarded pupils in the Detroit public schools, 712 had some endocrine disorder, 281 being hypothyroid. While he did not wish to state the relationship between such disorders and mental retardation, he was justifiably concerned about treating the condition in order to avoid the development of goiters.[42]

A number of additional causes were associated with mental retardation, including toxemia of pregnancy, vitamin B deficiencies, acute respiratory infections, subdural hematomas, and suffication from smoke.[43] In 1929, Murphy reported on microcephaly following maternal pelvic irradiation.[44] The list of potential causes of mental retardation was rapidly becoming inexhaustible.

New diagnostic techniques appeared, including Dandy's encephalography in 1918 and Hans Berger's electroencephalogram in 1929.[45] The latter resulted in many brain wave studies of mentally retarded persons and became a popular tool for estimating the occurrence of brain injury.

Of greater consequence, however, was the discovery in 1926 that enzymes were proteins, which ultimately led to the discovery of the pathways of metabolism at each step by specific enzymes. Thus, by 1939, the very capable George Jervis of the Medical Research Department at Letchworth Village in New York described the biochemical nature of phenylketonuria, then known as oligophrenia phenylpyruvic amentia; accordingly, the "amino-acid is not completely oxidized, a block occurring at the stage of phenylpyruvic acid. The unoxidized acid is therefore excreted in the urine."[46] By 1940, biochemical disorders involving the lipids, carbohydrates, and amino acids were identified, but far from understood.

Once again, the question of heat, cold, and the effects of weather on mental retardation was raised. Mills studied the intelligence of people born at different times of the year and concluded that "feeble-minded individuals tend more to be conceived during the less stimulating months of mid-summer and fall, when the conception rate of the mentally superior . . . is lowest."[47]

Down's syndrome, or Mongolism, began to receive the attention that had been devoted to cretinism in years past. Alleged causes of this syndrome were many, including chance, "alcoholic conception," syphilitic heredity, degenerative ancestry, remnants of a Mongolian race scattered throughout Europe, maternal emotional disturbance during pregnancy, physical illness, maternal hyperthyroidism, and short birth intervals.[48] During the 1930s, a growing number of researchers, such as England's Lionel Penrose and America's M. Kuenzel, commented upon the advanced maternal age of mothers.[49] A number of medical persons viewed Down's syndrome as being related to some form of biochemical or glandular disorder, including the pituitary gland, the adrenal gland, and, of course, the thyroid gland.[50] Not surprisingly, many Down's syndrome youngsters received some form of glandular therapy. As early as 1924, Davenport suggested that Down's syndrome was the result of a chromosomal disorder that affected the "chemico-physical processes," which adversely affected the subsequent proper development of the endocrine functions.[51] His hypothesis would not be verified for another 30 years.

The many advances in the field were reflected in the medical classification recommended by the Committee on Nomenclature of the American Association on Mental Deficiency in 1932. The seven categories included: 1) diseases due to prenatal influences, 2) diseases due to infection, 3) diseases due to trauma, 4) diseases due to convulsive disorders, 5) diseases due to or consisting of static mechanical abnormality (hydrocephalus), 6) diseases due to disturbances of metabolism, growth, or nutrition, and 7) new growth (e.g., tuberous sclerosis).[52]

Heredity

During these 20 years, the issue of the role of heredity in mental retardation was in the state of continual flux and transition, partly because of altering attitudes among professionals toward mentally retarded persons and partly because of advances in scientific knowledge. It must be remembered, however, that the question of heredity and mental retardation was not an interest exclusive to persons working in the field. It was of marked concern to individuals and groups anxious about race betterment and the quality of American intelligence. The professional community, as will be seen, modified its positions much more quickly than did eugenics-minded persons.

The question of heredity, race betterment, and immigration was of both national and international concern during the 1920s. Subsequently, there was an outpouring of related studies and sociopolitical tracts, most of which were racially unfavorable. A number of quasi-scientific studies using army test data were conducted shortly after World War I, all of which tended to blame an alleged deterioration of intelligence and mental functioning in the United States to immigration practices. One of the most frequently cited documents was Carl Brigham's A Study of American Intelligence, published in 1923. In the introductory comments, Robert M. Yerkes, chairman of the Research Information Service for the National Research Council, noted, "It behooves us to consider their reliability [the results of Brigham's study] and their meaning, no one of us as a citizen can afford to ignore the menace of race deterioration or the evident relations of immigration on national progress and welfare."[53] Brigham re-evaluated the data on over 100,000 American whites and blacks as well as foreign persons who took Alpha army test A or B. In brief, he concluded that the nature of American intelligence was decreasing by the rapidly increasing number of non-Nordic immigrants, especially those from Greece, Italy, Spain,

Portugal, Turkey, Ireland, and Wales. American blacks were the least desirable of all. His prognostication was rather dismal: "If all immigration were stopped now, the decline of American intelligence would still be inevitable. This is the problem which must be met and our manner of meeting it will determine the future course of our natural life."[54] The "inevitable" decline would result from the intermingling of various immigrants as well as intermarriages between blacks and whites.

Brigham's results and interpretations were supported by other researchers of the day, even those who studied children. Morrison and Cornell, for example, reported that "the median scores for the Italian group are markedly lower than for children of the same age from native American parentage." Although these results were qualified—"How much of this apparent inferiority was due to lower mental endowment and how much to language difficulties cannot be determined by this study"— the data were frequently cited; the qualification was not.[55]

While most professionals in the field set aside such genealogical studies as those of the Kallikaks, the Jukes, and the Nams, these studies still received considerable national exposure and were frequently quoted by persons in support of sterilization, deportation, and stronger immigration controls. Both the genealogical studies and supporters of the race betterment movement were ferociously attacked by the famed defender Clarence Darrow—not from the standpoint of law but from that of an outraged humanist. In 1925, he asked:

Is there, then, any mystery about the Juke family? What is all the shouting about, anyhow? Why do the eugenists dodge the perfectly obvious facts to bolster up their case for tinkering with the human race? The Jukes' story is the story of any number of other families environed as they were. Living in a sterile country, surrounded by poverty, condemned by conditions which have always been common to certain localities, they developed a manner of living and acquired a reputation which as social heritages were passed on from generation to generation. A few members of the family were sent to prison. As the record shows, they found it difficult to get work in the small commu-

nity where they lived. They lacked education where there were no schools nor any adequate opportunity to learn. It is the story of the squalid section of every isolated, sterile, rural community and of every poverty-stricken city district. This has been abundantly proven, if proof were necessary, in the growing improvement of the family. . . . The history of the Jukes family is largely that of all pioneers, of all workers, of the great mass which make up the warp and woof of every country. Their history is the "short and simple annals of the poor." Some men may preach hell-fire sermons, or make speeches in the Senate and the court room. Others do rough work of the world. Which are the most important in the scheme of life, assuming that there is any scheme of life?[56]

"I, for one," he wrote a year later, "am alarmed at the conceit and sureness of the advocates of this new dream. I shudder at their ruthlessness in meddling with life. I resent their egoistic and stern righteousness. I shrink from their judgment of their fellows. Every one who passes judgment necessarily assumes that he is right. It seems to me that man can bring comfort and happiness out of life only by tolerance, kindness and sympathy, all of which seem to find no place in the eugenists' creed. The whole programme means the absolute violation of what men instinctively feel to be inherent rights."[57]

Studies among mentally retarded persons, however, took new directions during the 1920s and 1930s. Ancestral pedigree studies, such as the Jukes, were abandoned and a number of more direct, but equally suspect investigations were conducted comparing children's intelligence with that of their allegedly mentally retarded parents.

Atkinson, in his 1927 investigation of infants of incarcerated delinquent females, reported mentally retarded teen-age mothers produced five mentally retarded infants, five of borderline intelligence, and two who were "inferior." Of five mothers with normal intelligence, one child was judged mentally retarded, another of borderline intelligence, one "inferior," and three average.[58] Mary Vanuxem, however, studied the children of delinquent females at the Laurelton State Village and discovered that of 213 children, four times as many had IQs above rather than below that of their mothers. Since most of the women were "quite pretty," Vanuxem suggested that they had attracted relatively normal men.[59] These results were supported by Woodall's study of 119 surviving children of 192 mothers who were residents at the Walter E. Fernald State School. In brief, the "average mental level of the children was superior to that of their mothers."[60] Each of these studies was interpreted in terms of heredity, never in terms of environment, nor of their possible interrelationship.

In 1939, however, Skeels and Dye reported their classic investigation conducted through the University of Iowa that clearly demonstrated the effects of environment on measured intelligence. Briefly, the authors communicated the results of a 3-year study with equated groups of children subjected to different degrees and kinds of environmental stimulation. One group was kept in a barren, unstimulating orphanage environment, while the others were afforded the rich stimulation of an excellent preschool program. Those children in the impoverished environment lost on the average 16 IQ points, while those in the enriched environment gained an average of 5 points. The extreme individual loss was 43 points; the extreme gain was approximately 60 points.[61]

In essence, during this period, the notion of heredity changed significantly. The estimated incidence of mental retardation that was related to such factors decreased from nearly 100 percent at the turn of the century to approximately 30 percent by the early 1930s.[62]

MENTAL RETARDATION
AND MENTAL ILLNESS

Psychiatry and the mental hygiene movement as a whole began to examine the occurrence of mental illness among mentally retarded persons with hopes of both clarifying questions of etiology and identifying appropriate resources for treatment. There was little agreement among authorities with regard to these issues or whether, in fact, mentally retarded persons

were susceptible to mental illness. Berley, for example, claimed the moron was more prone to psychosis than was a normal person, while Bartemeier contended that "the reason we find relatively few insane defectives is that their relatively simpler nervous system renders them less sensitive to disturbing influences than in the normal individual."[63] To confuse the issue, Myerson believed that "if feeble-mindedness is entangled in a genetic way with psychosis, clinical investigation of the phenomena has no practical value."[64]

In spite of such debates, staff from both institutions for mentally retarded and mentally ill persons reported residents who were mentally retarded and mentally ill. Vanuxem found 8 percent of the female residents at Laurelton were emotionally disturbed, while Hunsicker reported that 158 of 5,000 new admissions to the Allentown State Hospital involved psychosis with mental deficiency or mental deficiency, schizophrenic basis.[65]

As to cause, however, there remained no common consensus; while no one specified a consistent, direct hereditary factor, Greene believed that the difference between so-called functional psychosis and mental deficiency was one of degree only and that both conditions had a common pathogenetic origin in children that could be eugenic, environmental, or both.[66] Other psychiatrists, such as Potter, emphasized the environment: "How much heredity plays a part in the various types of adjustment is an unsettled question; but personally, I am willing to believe that it is more a matter of parental example and environmental influences rather than parental chromosomes and hereditary characteristics."[67]

Means for effectively treating and/or coping with severe mental illness among mentally retarded persons were not discussed, short of arguing whether the affected should be programmed in an institution for mentally retarded persons or in a mental hospital. Neither side felt that they were appropriate.

Problems that could produce emotional difficulties among mentally retarded persons were described at length by professionals associated with the mental hygiene and child guidance movements. Considerable concern was expressed about the effects of being labeled "dumb," about repetitive failure, and about the increasingly poor outlook for job placement.[68]

To combat or prevent potential dangers to mental health, parents and professionals were given such advice as:

1. The mentally retarded person must be made to face up to reality, especially as regards intellectual and occupational limitations.
2. The mentally retarded should not be allowed to daydream too much.
3. The mentally retarded should pursue successful abilities and interests since "no one can be inferior in *everything!*"
4. The mentally retarded should be encouraged to become self-assertive.
5. Of extreme importance, the mentally retarded child should develop "habits of obedience and discipline which will help avoid adolescent concerns and problems."[69]

Athletics, play, exercises, and participation in various social, youth-oriented organizations were all encouraged. Most authorities, however, realized that it would be extremely difficult, if not impossible, for the mentally retarded person to avoid feelings of inadequacy. Though some of the suggestions appear naive by current standards and expectancies, they signaled an increasing sensitivity to the personal development of mentally retarded individuals.

THE MENTALLY RETARDED OFFENDER

The juvenile delinquent and adult offender continued to be of significant interest to persons in the field of mental retardation, corrections, and jurisprudence during the 1920s and 1930s. In 1926, the American Prison Association defined the term *defective delinquent* as

an offender, who, because of mental subnormality, at times coupled with mental instability, is not amenable to the ordinary custody and training of the average correctional institution and whose presence therein is detrimental to both the type of individual herein described and to the proper development of the methods of rehabilitation of other groups of delinquents. Further, the defective delinquent, because of his limited intelligence and suggestibility, requires prolonged and careful training, preferably in a special institution to develop habits of industry and obedience.[70]

This concept did not receive extensive support by those in the field of either mental retardation or jurisprudence. First, the definition was somewhat self-serving; second, it failed to discriminate between subgroups of mentally retarded offenders, which was considered essential.

To rectify this failure, the mentally retarded offender was often classified into two groups: 1) the *defective delinquent,* "the mental defective, who through lack of proper early training or through bad association and environment forms criminal habits" and 2) the *delinquent defective,* who is "one in whom the intelligence deficiency is the outstanding characteristic."[71] Defective delinquents were usually mildly mentally retarded individuals with acquired (and often thought to be intentional) criminal habits. They were believed to constitute a major social threat. In contrast, delinquent defectives were more severely mentally retarded individuals whose conflicts with the law were "purely accidental, being due primarily to their mental defect," or a result of "undesirable associates," or associated with serious "personality defects."[72] As a group, delinquent defectives were not considered a social threat.

Though there were markedly different opinions concerning the origins of antisocial behavior and their relationship to mental retardation, heredity was no longer considered a prime factor. The emphasis had switched to parenting, early experiences, individual stress, and inability to cope. Montaque's 1930 analysis and conclusion that 30 percent of mentally retarded criminals were of hereditary origin was the exception.[73] A few persons, such as Doll, attributed some dimensions of "instability" resulting in criminal behavior to a variety of physical factors, including toxemia from focal infections, congenital syphilis, epilepsy, and endocrine disorders.[74] In this, he was alone.

Most agreed that the primary precipitating factors in the development of delinquency and other forms of criminal behavior among mentally retarded persons reflected an inappropriate environment. In fact, nearly every aspect of an impoverished setting was identified by someone, including immorality in the family, alcoholic parents, child abuse, parental emotional problems, parental criminal activity and example, poverty itself, illiteracy, inadequate physical homes and neighborhoods, and poor physical health.[75]

Herman Adler, the famed criminologist and director of the Institute for Juvenile Research in Illinois, studied the problem from both a theoretical and statistical perspective and made several significant observations. From a theoretical point of view, he contended:

> Too great a discrepancy between what one imagines one is or should be considered to be and what the world actually considers one to be will lead to a condition of strain; and just as in other fields of nature, where there is too great a difference in the height or potential between two participants in an equilibrium, the equilibrium will be re-established more or less violently.
>
> In my opinion, these strains and stresses are among the most important factors at the bottom of delinquency. . . . The one important point, however, which cannot be too greatly emphasized in all this is that from the point of view of treatment there is much to encourage us. While it is perfectly true that the inherited characteristics are probably not to be changed, and that for instance the intelligence quotient is probably in most cases a fixed quantity; nevertheless, the delinquency and crime represents the result of so complex a series of relationships that we are unjustified in saying that treatment can be of no avail. The marvelous works that have been achieved in the treatment of the feeble-minded are evidence enough that the behavior may be controlled, even where the intelligence is very low. . . .[76]

Several years later, following an extensive study of delinquency and crime involving 5,404 prison cases, Adler concluded: "So far as intelligence is concerned, as determined by tests, the prison population in Illinois is a fair sample of the community from which the prisoners came. Therefore, so far as our observation goes, and it is corroborated by findings elsewhere, there is no correlation between crime and intelligence."[77]

In spite of many changing attitudes, few were willing to accept Adler's conclusions in their entirety. Most concurred with Eleanor Glueck's interpretations based on the results of her study of 500 delinquent mentally retarded juvenile males. While there were similarities between environmental conditions surrounding delinquents of "lower and higher intelligence," such situations were aggravated with the appearance of mental retardation and differences between the two groups "definitely flow from the mental deficiency in their families."[78] Therefore, "mental deficiency though not a direct cause of delinquency is a complicating factor of great potency, the presence of which in addition to other causative influences severely breaks down the individual's resistance to anti-social behavior."[79] Also, "there is a far higher proportion of children of lower intelligence among delinquent groups than in the general population of children; the likelihood of delinquency among children of lower intelligence is greater than among those of higher intelligence; the families of young delinquents of lower intelligence are even less able than those of higher intelligence to participate constructively in any program for the supervision and treatment of such children."[80]

A number of researchers reported that defective delinquents were common among incarcerated populations. Though Sutherland's review of 350 studies reported a significant decrease in the number of juvenile delinquents judged to be mentally retarded from a median of 50 percent for 1910 to 1915 to a median of 20 percent for 1925 to 1928,[81] individual studies continued to show a significant discrepancy in such percentages, which ranged from 13 to 40 percent.[82]

The relative percentage, however, was much lower for adult mentally retarded offenders. For example, a 1929 study conducted in New Jersey reported that 30 percent of the youngsters in boys' homes were considered mentally retarded; 15 percent in reformatories; but only 8 percent in state prisons.[83]

The nature of crimes committed by mentally retarded persons varied considerably, ranging from parking violations to first-degree murder. Jacoby's 1923 report of 309 mentally retarded individuals (IQ 65 or less), examined in the

Psychopathic Clinic of the Recorders Court for Detroit, Michigan, listed 43 different offenses committed by mentally retarded persons. Of these, the most serious involved disturbing the peace (79 offenders), drunkenness (50), and grand larceny (21). Fifteen males were accused of nonsupport, and one female of murder. With the exception of armed robbery and drunkenness among men, the percentage of mentally retarded persons committing crimes in the various categories exceeded that of a comparable normal population.[84] In spite of such reports, all realized that one could not continue to discuss delinquency or criminal behavior among mentally retarded persons while considered a homogeneous group.

SOCIAL CONTROL AND PREVENTION

While many in the professional community were beginning to view mental retardation in a positive light, the public in general and their political representatives in particular were less convinced. Few citizens would have taken umbrage with the mayor of Boston's representative who greeted the membership of the American Association on Mental Deficiency in 1921 with the observation that he hoped that those who were not in attendance would "through the medium of the press, become more intimately acquainted with the problem of the feeble-minded, which at present is choking up our courts, filling our pauper institutions, clogging our schools and our industrial life."[85] Immigration, sterilization, and institutionalization remained popular topics of both discussion and action.

IMMIGRATION

As a result of such studies as have been cited and a growing antipathy toward immigrants for a variety of reasons, especially those from Ireland and Italy, Congress passed the Immigration Act of 1924, which expanded its definition of undesirables and set quotas. Every immigrant was required to state whether or not he was a member "of each class of individuals

excluded from admission to the United States," which, according to Section 26, included aliens "afflicted with idiocy, insanity, imbecility, feeble-mindedness, epilepsy, constitutional psychopathic inferiority, chronic alcoholism, tuberculosis in any form, or a loathsome or dangerous contagious disease. . . ."[86]

The federal government also increased its efforts to enforce these regulations, including the identification and deportation of mentally retarded persons, a task which proved somewhat difficult. Though the more severely mentally retarded persons with multiple handicapping conditions or obvious clinical features were readily identifiable, mild degrees of mental retardation proved more elusive. First, the definition of mental retardation was "broad and elastic," according to Laurence Kolb of the U.S. Public Health Service:

> Under the regulations governing mental inspection of aliens, a feeble-minded person is identified as "one who has a mental defect, congenital or acquired in early life, and whose common knowledge, retentiveness of memory, reasoning power, learning capacity, and general mental reactions are severely and distinctly below that exhibited by the average race living under a similar environment.[87]

This definition avoided both an arbitrary measure and a purely social criterion, thus leaving the final decision to the judgment of the examiners. Much to the chagrin of persons who viewed deportation as a eugenics technique, some of the examiners, "including many physicians, apparently held the view that persons able to work and collect wages, or to sweep out the house and dress the baby, could not be feeble-minded [and] there was sincere opposition to the deportation of aliens who could do such things."[88]

The problem was further exacerbated, according to Kolb, by the fact that there was an insufficient number of examiners and no reliable measure of intelligence to identify mental retardation within acceptable limits of legal and moral responsibility. During the peak years of immigration, for example, more than 5,000 persons passed through Ellis Island in one day, with two physicians examining each alien as he or she passed by; one physician passed upon the person's mentality and the other upon physical status. It was not difficult to realize that under this system anyone without manifest signs of abnormality remained unnoticed and unchallenged. Nevertheless, the certification rate of unacceptable mental conditions increased. In 1904, one alien in every 5,300 was deported because of mental retardation; by 1915, one in every 720; and by 1927, one in every 234.[89]

In addition to enacting more strict procedures, the government also increased its fine on steamship companies from $250 to $1,000 for each mentally retarded or mentally ill person brought to this country. This also had its effect.

In spite of such practices, however, many persons considered mildly mentally retarded were admitted to the United States, and some were institutionalized. In 1926, Laughlin surveyed American institutions, discovered that of 48,567 residents, 1,932 were foreign born, and complained, "Our laws for a long time have forbidden the entrance of feeble-minded persons into the United States. Here we have 1,932 such persons. This is *prima facie* evidence that practically all of these come through in violation of the law, because feeble-mindedness, generally, is a thing which can not come from causes arising since admission to the United States. . . ."[90]

The renewed emphasis on deportation affected not only those turned away at Ellis Island but also those who were already in this country and in institutions. By 1926, at least 30 mentally retarded persons from institutions had been deported.[91] In 1928, the American Association on Mental Deficiency registered its support of deportation.[92]

During the 1930s, the country was faced with the overwhelming problems of the Depression, and national attention was diverted from immigration. Nevertheless, and in spite of altering attitudes, immigration, as we shall see, continued to be a sensitive issue for many years.

STERILIZATION

Massive segregation of mentally retarded persons in institutions was no longer deemed feasible, and marriage laws were unenforceable. Therefore, the only remaining sure solution to prevention was through sterilization, a practice which was to be advocated by some for years to come, for two reasons. A few persons continued to recommend this measure purely for purposes of preventing the transmission of defect; most, however, urged it because feeble-minded persons could not provide appropriate parenting experiences for their children.

In addition to the old arguments concerning heredity, advances in medicine and allied sciences raised new concerns. As indicated by H. S. Jennings, for example, recent progress in endocrinology as well as anticipated progress in this area could result in an increase of genetic abnormalities. Thus, while treatment might be successful in genetically associated biochemical disorders, and the person maintained at a normal or near normal level of functioning, the basic genetic abnormality would not be affected. Individuals previously unable to propagate would now be in a position to spread the disorder. Thus, "so fast as we can discover individuals that bear seriously defective genes—whether themselves personally defective or not—so rapidly must those individuals be brought to cease propagation."[93]

While a few institutional administrators remained among the most concerned about sterilization, even they were more constrained. They no longer advocated sterilization for all or even most mentally retarded persons. Like others, they supported the notion of "selective sterilization." Unfortunately, "selective sterilization" usually referred to any mildly mentally retarded person considered eligible for community placement.

As indicated, there was a growing sentiment during the 1930s that sterilization should almost become an automatic process with mildly retarded persons simply because they would be unfit parents. "The feeble-minded parent is not only a biologically poor parent, he is also an environmentally and educationally poor parent," wrote Doll in 1929.[94]

Perhaps the most rigid position was advanced by Selling and Finn in 1936. They suggested that health clinics coordinate all mental retardation activities, and, as part of their program, "all defectives would be sterilized after the onset of puberty in such a way as to maintain a proper endocrine balance. The goal is to maintain as many defectives well adjusted in the community as possible."[95]

Yet, a growing number of leaders in the field were opposed to sterilization, among them the recently liberalized Goddard:

In the community these morons will marry and have children. And why not? When nine-tenths of the mentally 10 year old people are marrying why should the other tenth be denied? Moreover if moronity is only a problem of education and the right kind of education can make out of them happy and useful hewers of wood and drawers of water, what more do we want?[96]

While some superintendents were quite hesitant to place young women in the community without sterilization, Charles Bernstein and his staff looked at the situation from a remarkably different perspective. Following a description of one of Rome State School's placement programs for girls and young ladies, there ensued an interesting discussion involving Bernstein, Inez Stebbins, supervisor of the parole program, and other members in the audience at an American Association on Mental Deficiency annual convention. Although, unfortunately, the dialogue is too lengthy to report in its entirety, several exchanges illustrate the general posture of Bernstein's staff and their belief that undesirable sexual activities were to be precluded by example, training, and experiences rather than sterilization:

DR. MC PHERSON (to Miss Stebbins): Perhaps you can get them into normal intercourse with those of the opposite sex, what do you have in mind is going to come of that?

MISS STEBBINS: I think that some of the girls, as a matter of fact, many of the girls whom we place on parole in this way, have just as much right to their lives as most of the rest of us.

DR. MC PHERSON: Have they any right to get married?

MISS STEBBINS: They become excellent housekeepers. They have learned in these excellent homes which we have provided, how to bring up children. They have just as much ability as many of the maids have, store clerks, some telephone operators, etc., who are out in the world earning their own living and taking care of themselves and never coming to the institution. Why not? We have caught only the few sands of the seashore. Why limit them just because they happen to have been sent to us?

DR. MC PHERSON: May I ask—have you no sense of responsibility towards the girl that has been committed to you? You are not responsible for the telephone operators and the maids that have not been committed to you. Did you ever see a feeble-minded girl that was able to bring up a child properly?

MISS STEBBINS: Many of them. I would like to show you some of them.[97]

Many superintendents felt that, in essence, sterilization was of little overall significance and presented many problems since, in the words of McNairy, "Little hope can be had of reducing the number, were these methods [sterilization] universely adopted, because of the great difficulty in differentiation of the moron, the borderline and the retarded in development."[98] Though a number of sterilizations were performed as indicated previously, the vast majority of mentally retarded persons, whether in the community or in the institution, did not undergo this indignity. Neither they, their parents, many professionals, nor the public as a whole supported sterilization.

Further, the constitutionality of sterilization was questioned. By 1926, 23 states had enacted related laws; however, some of them were declared unconstitutional, including those of Indiana, Nevada, New Jersey, and New York. In contrast, those of Michigan and Virginia were declared constitutional. Only the Supreme Court could resolve such differences; in 1927, it heard the Virginia case of *Buck* v. *Bell*. This case, which drew national attention, involved Carrie Buck, an 18-year-old feeble-minded white woman who had been committed to the State Colony for Epileptics and Feeble-minded of Virginia. She was both a daughter of a feebleminded mother in the same institution and a mother of an illegitimate feebleminded child. The Supreme Court's decision, presented by Justice Holmes, read, in part:

> We have seen more than once that the public welfare may call upon the best citizens for their lives. It would be strange if it could not call upon those who already sap the strength of the State for these lesser sacrifices, often not felt to be such by those concerned, in order to prevent our being swamped with incompetents. It is better for all the world, if instead of waiting to execute degenerative offspring for crime, or to let them starve for their imbecility, society can prevent those who are manifestly unfit from continuing their kind. The principle that sustains compulsory vaccination is broad enough to cover the cutting of the Fallopian tubes. . . . three generations of imbeciles are enough![99]

SOCIAL CARE AND TREATMENT

The early 1920s saw familiar names continue to advocate familiar positions but with greater fervor and urgency. Bernstein persisted in his judgment "what many of our social misfits and mentally alienated subjects need is not lock-ups and custodial institutions or even hospitals, except the latter temporarily for purposes of classification and treatment when acutely ill, but rather changes of environment."[100] Murdoch again implored superintendents and others to "make our commitment examinations more rigid, separate our institutional and non-institutional cases more carefully, provide proper education for many of the morons outside the institution and see to it that they are never committed."[101] State and local governments were increasingly requested to provide an array of services for mentally retarded persons in the community.

RESIDENTIAL SERVICES

The role of institutions in serving mentally retarded persons during the 1920s and 1930s revealed the diversity of thinking and purpose that would persist for years. Some authorities continued to view the institution as a primary

vehicle for accommodating mentally retarded persons of "defective stock" for whom "permanent custodial care must be provided, unless they are to be sterilized."[102] Those who held this position (and there were many) honestly believed that this was in the best interest of the feebleminded:

> Life in an institution is ideal for one of defective stock. Here he has wise supervision, suitable occupation, plenty of healthy and moral recreation, good food, proper clothing, prompt medical attention, the companionship of his peers and such preparation for the life to come as he is able to comprehend.
> Outside an institution even the harmless subnormal finds but little of real life. Some get along apparently well and happily. Most of them are more or less conscious of their inferiority. The busy world has no time or patience with them. They lost jobs, become tramps, follow the first red flag and become the prey of the evil minded.
> Inside, they have a real place in a simple environment. They even get on the stage (the only stage in the world that is safe for a subnormal girl). They show off their simple accomplishments to a simple audience. They are appreciated instead of being belittled. They, who outside must always be the followers, the drudges, the abused, become on the inside the leaders, and in this leadership they hold up their heads and walk erect.
> Outside, those who go to regular school drag behind their mates. They are the big hulking bodies in seats meant for little children. They take three or four times their share of the time of the teacher. Even then they learn habits of idleness because with thirty other children the teacher still must neglect them. They practice and teach immorality. When at last the patience of the teacher is exhausted or when the school law so ordains they are turned out to become the drifters, and the delinquents.[103]

Others, such as Bernstein, as previously noted, were less enthusiastic about the appropriateness and effectiveness of residential programming. As regards mildly mentally retarded persons, this was the growing sentiment of the field.

In the final analysis, however, and in spite of varying philosophical postures, institutions continued to serve a population of individuals whose needs could not or were not met in the community, regardless of level of retardation. It was not uncommon to find the mentally retarded population divided into four classes, similar in nature to those set forth by Kerlin in the late nineteenth century:

1. Those whose families were financially able to satisfy their needs
2. Those whose families could cope most adequately with the appearance of mental retardation
3. Those whose families, for varying internal reasons, could not cope with the offspring and who had "a right to be relieved of such a burden"
4. Those whose behavior, personal or social, presented such problems that maintenance at home or in the community was inadvisable[104]

Of these four groupings, the last two were considered appropriate for institutionalization. Level of mental retardation per se was not a direct consideration; rather, the emphasis was almost exclusively on the financially limited family's ability to meet the needs of their mentally retarded offspring.

An additional reason for institutionalization during the 1920s and 1930s was related to education. Special education classes were offered primarily in large cities. As mentally retarded persons demonstrated the ability to benefit from such programs, parents in more rural areas occasionally requested institutionalization of their offspring primarily for educational purposes.

The proper size of an institution continued to be set at between 1,000 and 3,000 residents, with reasons reflective of bygone thinking. Less than 1,000 residents was considered uneconomical and over 3,000 was too large and "likely to get in a rut."[105]

Waiting lists were long, and overcrowding, even by the then existing standards, was almost universal. For example, in 1935, Pennsylvania reported that 2,827 persons were awaiting admission; Massachusetts, approximately 3,000.[106] Waiting lists during the Depression jumped by 100 percent in Maryland.[107] Institutions in Indiana were overcrowded by 40 percent, and Polk School in Pennsylvania by 84 percent.[108]

The idea that institutions should provide a homelike environment was abandoned in the interests of economy and ease of resident management. According to Wallace, dormitories should accommodate 105 pupils and combine "economy of construction with efficiency of management."[109] Wallace also offered two fundamental principles in planning an institution: "Don't have a dark corner or a dark closet in it," and "Plan it so that the person doing the work will never have to take two steps where one would do." All equipment and fixtures were to be standard (and the same), and all light switches were to be placed outside the room, 6 feet high, making it "inconvenient for the children to meddle with them."[110] McNairy's recommendations that "dormitories should be located from back forward, for idiots, imbeciles, and morons" was widely adopted. Dehumanizing physical conditions were rapidly becoming one of the outstanding characteristics of institutions.[111]

Most institutions implemented what has become known as the "medical model," in which nearly all programs, including nursing, recreation, and social work were under the supervision of a medical clinical director. Psychologists and educators could make assignments with "the cooperation of the medical department." This approach, in the judgment of many, resulted in an over-concern with physical health and safety, thus treating mental retardation as an illness.

Institutional programs also remained closed to outside scrutiny. Marjorie Lenz of the Erie County Probation Department of Buffalo, New York, complained of this practice and others: "We need more community knowledge of the constructive resources in our training schools. For instance, the wards for imbeciles and idiots should be closed even to officials of Courts, but less secrecy as to the program for the higher-grade child and [there needs to be] more discrimination in the schools' treatment of responsible parents, relatives or workers."[112]

Change, however, was occurring. Most administrators of multipurpose facilities now realized that programming for morons should be limited not only in terms of numbers but also in terms of length of stay. Most also recognized the need to provide for at least the custodial care needs of the more severely affected.

As regards mildly mentally retarded persons, many institutional superintendents, as well as others, were constantly bringing to the attention of both their professional colleagues and the public in general that "many morons, if trained and not neglected, will be found to be capable of community life."[113] Mary Wolfe addressed this issue quite firmly:

The institutions should accept the responsibility of impressing upon the public the facts that the major portion of mental defectives are adjusting and must adjust in the community, and that it is neither possible nor necessary to place this whole group in institutions, that social agencies must study their cases more carefully and learn to differentiate between those defectives who need temporary assistance in adjusting in the community and those that need institution care, that the public schools must become increasingly responsible for the proper education and training of this group and the community for their better care and protection.[114]

Regardless of such pronouncements, however, the institution's leadership role in the field was not diminished. Many persons, representing both the institution and the community, fully expected the institution to be "the pivot of a well balanced state program for the care of the feeble-minded," to continue to serve as educational and scientific centers, be responsible for the development of various community activities, to develop clinics in the community, and to provide the supervision required to maintain individuals in the community.[115]

During the 1930s, the question of racial balance and characteristics was beginning to be studied in institutions serving large metropolitan areas. In 1931, for example, Stowell reported a comparative study of certain mental defects found among institutionalized whites and blacks from the District of Columbia. First, a disproportionate number of black children (49 percent of the total institution population of 355) had been committed by the Board of Public Welfare. Second, black children's intellectual performances, though mildly retarded, were superior to those of white residents, a result which was in opposition to most IQ studies. Stowell's explanation of these results was rather unique in that it emphasized socioeconomic factors:

It is quite evident from the foregoing conclusions that the general findings at the District Training School are far different from those found elsewhere. We have a colored population that is of higher mentality than the white. This may be explained partly by the fact that the group is not a fair sampling of the feebleminded children in the District. White people tend to take more care of their mentally afflicted than do the colored; they give them more attention and supervision, and take more frequent advantage of the public facilities, (such as the Child Guidance Clinics, Health Centers, etc.) which aid them in gaining a better understanding of their children. Their economic circumstances permit them to keep them in the home for a longer period of time, and it is occasionally evident that even though the children become very burdensome or are so low grade that they are not easily cared for, the families are loathe to give them up. When in difficulty and brought into contact with the Courts the white children are given the benefit of aid and counsel and are afterwards protected to a greater extent against becoming further nuisances. The colored children however come from families in which the economic circumstances are such that they do not receive proper supervision and attention for as long a period of time. They are not given the care received by the white children and also because of the lower economic level of the colored population, they need not stray far from the normal path of Negro standards of living to get into trouble and be apprehended by the Court. Petty crimes bring them into contact with the law and the families are not then able to give them the protection and supervision to keep them out of Institutions. Another result of the lack of proper care is that the children do not receive needed medical attention and therefore many of them die in early infancy.[116]

In the South, separate facilities for blacks and whites were maintained. As explained by Benjamin Whitten, "In connection with this matter, we may state what is recognized as an obvious fact by everyone—viz., the status of the colored race is rather well defined. Tradition, custom, political determination, as well as other economic and social practices, have set apart the colored people from the whites. It is considered as sound social philosophy and factual social psychology that this accepted demarcation and fairly definite separation gives the Negro certain advantages, and at the same time, it assures the whites their sense of superiority and authority."[117]

Philosophy and Programs

As more institutions opened in various sections of the country, philosophies of programming tended to vary according to the general purpose of the institution and the attitude or positions of the superintendent. Those who advocated strongly for parole or community placement established training and work experience programs aimed in that direction. Those who did not favor parole, or at least for the relatively young person, concentrated their efforts on training capable institutional helpers.

Most institutions offered educational programs for mildly retarded youngsters; however, as discovered by Elise Martens in one of the earliest federally sponsored surveys of educational services in institutions, the quality of that education was often suspect. While, for example, the maximum teacher-student ratio in the public schools was 1:30, it was not uncommon to find a 1:70 ratio in an institution. Further, many of the teachers were unqualified. Not surprisingly, Martins recommended that educational programs be placed under the jurisdiction of state departments of education.[118]

Some superintendents continued to view education with reservation: "Give every child in our institution everything he *ought* to know and *can make use of* when he becomes an adult in body. No more than this, but no less than this," wrote E. R. Johnstone in 1924.[119] Others persisted in the view that the institution's primary obligation was "to provide and maintain a comfortable and happy home" rather than train for independence and placement.[120]

In spite of such sentiments, innovative ideas were being tried. Wolfe and Vanuxem introduced a system of self-government in their facility for feebleminded women of childbearing age.[121] E. R. Johnstone introduced task analysis to both academic and manual arts.

Brown urged expanded social training for residents, including a thorough familiarity with the topic of sex.[122]

A few others, such as E. L. Johnstone at Woodbine, New Jersey, and G. Veith at the Letchworth Village in Thielles, New York, attempted educational programs with more severely affected youngsters with remarkable results. Veith offered a program to 57 girls, "various types of high grade idiots and low grade imbeciles" who could neither dress nor undress. The only admission criteria were that each girl had to be able to walk to and from her classroom and have use of one hand. After 30 months, the residents had ceased soiling, could dress themselves, and had become productive. Though their IQs had not changed, their adaptive behavior showed remarkable improvement:

> With training they become better social beings. They have become producers, supplying many of the worthwhile articles needed by others they have actually come to realize that they are not utterly useless but a part of the genuine life of the little community in which they are living. They are more interested in their play and surroundings, and have manifested a kindlier feeling to their companions. Not only has their personal appearance been markedly improved by sex habits and the wetting and soiling of the clothing have likewise been eliminated to a large degree.[123]

E. L. Johnstone instituted a three-phase program for severely retarded residents: classes for 1) the development and coordination of motor and physiological functions, 2) classes for teaching diversional and recreational activities, and 3) handwork classes. The median chronological age of the population was 18 and the median mental age was 2 years, 2 months. All residents apparently participated. The program as described was exceptional, providing for the total development of such youngsters in a pleasant, stimulating living environment. Adaptive equipment was individually designed to facilitate the acquisition of self-help skills. Anyone working with the more severely affected would do well to read Johnstone's 1938 report.[124]

Such programs, however, were a rarity. Most severely mentally retarded youngsters remained neglected in back wards, invisible to programmers or visitors.

In 1923, a special treatment facility for mentally retarded offenders was established. This facility, the State Institution for Defective Delinquents in Napanoch, New York, received considerable attention during the 1920s and 1930s. In design it was a prison; and though intended to serve 400 juvenile mentally retarded male offenders, for many years its population was, as Ellis said, "something of a hodgepodge."[125]

Napanoch's basic program for defective delinquents emphasized 1) removal of physical defects, 2) academic and industrial training, 3) a sequence of most to least secure placements—cell housing to congregate dormitory to cubicle dormitory housing to farm house and colony housing, and 4) "judicious" parole and adequate parole supervison.[126] Habit training and discipline were also critical. By 1929, Napanoch, like other correctional programs, had adapted a military approach. Massachusetts' colony program for defective delinquents followed an almost identical pattern without the call for a prison environment.[127]

Both Massachusetts and New York rated their respective specialized programs highly:

1. The establishment of the institutions for defective delinquents has tremendously simplified the problem in the schools for the feebleminded. It has given them the opportunity to get rid of the very troublesome and dangerous, though small, minority of disciplinary cases.
2. It has simplified as well the problem of reformation in the reformatories, and the proportion of feebleminded inmates upon whom any program of reformation has little effect has been greatly reduced in these institutions.
3. The courts have been relieved of the hopeless task of attempting to prescribe for the confirmed recidivist.[128]

Parole, in most cases, existed solely at the discretion of the facility's administrator. For the defective delinquent in a mental retardation facility, release was highly contingent on predicted ability to adjust to society. In reality, the defective delinquent could be held indefinitely, regardless of original offense. In some states,

such as Illinois, a mentally retarded person committed to a correctional facility could serve his term, at the end of which the warden could "file a petition on those cases with a low intelligence quotient and a commissioner may commit him to an institution for the feebleminded."[129]

At least one superintendent required that any parolee be sterilized: "On account of the double handicap of this type, defective and delinquent, we insist on sterilizing them before they leave the institution. . . . In fact, in recent years this is one of the earliest steps taken in treatment."[130] The same administrator did not release female offenders, regardless of offense, until at least age 35.

Not surprisingly, the select few who were paroled were successful. To illustrate, Battery and Thayer of Napanoch reported a 73.6 percent success rate. Needless to say, the prospects for mentally retarded offenders were quite bleak, and there is little question that their basic rights were held in abeyance.[131]

There was a wide range of opinions and practices as regards community placement. At the end of the continuum were administrators like Charles Bernstein who encouraged early discharge of both boys and girls, including the moderately retarded; on the other end were those who did not support any placement program. In between were those like McPherson of the Belchertown State School, Massachusetts, who preferred not to place women until after menopause.[132]

In 1922, Hoakley reported that of 37 responding institutions, only 21 (57 percent) had any form of parole program. A subsequent study by the Committee on Research of the American Association on Mental Deficiency 15 years later indicated that not much gain had been made. Of the responding institutions, over 50 percent had less than 10 percent of their residents on parole, 87 percent had not placed any residents in a boarding home, 84 percent had no residents in a colony, and only 23 percent had residents in training for community placement.[133] In terms of conditions that favored community placement, the Committee on Research reported favorable home conditions (25.0 percent), good behavior in the institution (20.5 percent), emotional stability (18.1 percent), intelligence rating (13.3 percent), and employability (12.2 percent).[134]

Other follow-up studies tended to support the key elements of a good or at least receptive home and employability. In 1938, Frankel reported that of 1,258 persons first admitted during 1930 to 1932, 324 (23 percent) had been discharged after an average stay of 34 months. Of these, 168 lived with their parents, 46 with relatives, 54 in their employer's home, 29 were married and in their own homes, and the remainder were either in the army or in the Civilian Conservation Corps (CCC). Supervision and support were readily available.[135]

Owing to the selective nature of discharge programs, the overall success rate exceeded the 90 percent level.[136] Interestingly, many of those discharged found jobs, even during the Depression. Those who supported community placements were pleased with the results. One even noted that "we have restored to nearly two hundred boys and girls a large measure of their constitutional rights: Life, Liberty, and the pursuit of Happiness."[137]

The CCC deserves special note. This federal program, approved by Congress in 1933 and terminated in 1944, provided employment opportunities for many young men in the area of conservation. Though federal regulations declared that "no one-time institutional resident shall be accepted," hundreds of mildly retarded men from institutions across the country participated most successfully.[138] The CCC provided not only an exceptional employment opportunity for mildly retarded residents, but also it increased their visibility as stable, contributing members of society.

Problems and Issues

The question of coeducational versus single-sex residential facilities remained an item of debate, with most favoring bisexual facilities because of normalization. Mary Wolfe argued against that notion: "I would like to challenge the statement that the life in a bi-sex institution is normal. This may be true while the inmates are children, but unfortunately children grow up, and just as soon as they reach a certain age, there are safe-guards erected between the two sexes, so that practically the same situation exists as in a one-sex institution. Beyond a certain limit, connection between the two sexes cannot be permitted in a two-sex institution after the children are grown."[139] She also struck a feminist note:

> With regard to the matter of staff, perhaps women have no right to be ambitious, but they have their ambitions as well as men, and it makes a difference as to the type of woman you are going to get to form your staff, whether a woman physician, for instance, is going to be put aside in her own little niche and see younger men, who come on the staff after she does, push past her and right on up to a superintendency and she stay right where she began. That happens over and over again in our bi-sex institutions. I claim that I can attract at Laurelton, where we have a one-sex institution, a higher and better type of medical woman than can be attracted under those circumstances, because I can say to a woman, "You have your chance to move right up without being placed in any kind of unfair competition with the men of the medical staff.[140]

A major problem confronting most institutions was the recruitment and retention of qualified personnel. Turnover rates of 200 percent per year were not uncommon, with the result that "we have fallen far short of being able to organize this dissimilarity of personalities to function socially and efficiently as we wish."[141] Long hours, few days off, inadequate pay, and the absence of any fringe benefits were hardly conducive to either recruitment or retention; consequently, many superintendents fought for the 8-hour work day, pay increases, improved living conditions (most employees lived on the grounds), and fringe benefits.

Even C. S. Little, superintendent of Letchworth Village, New York, well known for his strong positions and stronger words, advocated for such improvements since he obviously desired to attract a different type of employee:

> The present day employee, en masse, has absolutely no interest in anything except time off and pay day. The women are largely made up of two types; the feeble, senile, or neurasthenic woman who has worn out her usefulness everywhere else

and who seeks the institution as an asylum where she can always find an audience to listen to her tales of pain, disease and crime; the other type is the short-haired girl, usually of a low intelligence rating, who comes for no other purpose than to stay a few weeks, make the acquaintance of the taxicab drivers in the vicinity and to leave as soon as her stock of finery is replenished. The male employee is . . . sometimes a thug, often a thief, and always determined to get a living without work.[142]

State bureaucracies grew rapidly during the 1920s and 1930s, much to the chagrin of many—if not all—superintendents. While most recognized the need for some centralized structure, few directors disagreed with Watkins's analysis that the state agency's "proper functioning depends entirely, and in the last analysis on personnel, which for the most part, are inadequately trained, politically appointed and, clothed with a little brief authority, they oftentimes lose sight of the bigger and more fundamental things in institutional administration. . . . Under the guise of big business, economy and efficiency, many centralization schemes have been foisted upon the public which have tended merely to increase its payroll, to retard progress and to fail to render the service needed and expected."[143]

Civil service was also attacked rather frequently since most superintendents felt it protected the less than adequate employee. In the truculent words of Little, "It is a law designed to protect the inefficient and to land them in places to which their own ability would have never brought them."[144]

These were extremely difficult times for persons desiring to improve the quality of residential living. Economic conditions, overcrowding, long waiting lists, unresponsive governments, often accompanied by negative attitudes resulted in producing those dehumanizing conditions that would not begin to be resolved until the 1970s.

COMMUNITY SERVICES

Through the professional and legislative efforts of Fernald, Massachusetts remained in the forefront of progressive thought and actions. Specifically, the aims and accomplishments of

the state in relationship to the feebleminded included:

1. The early recognition of the needs of a feeble-minded child.
2. The right of the feeble-minded child to receive a suitable education.
3. The establishment of school mental clinics, the work of the traveling clinics, special classes, and vocational training.
4. Community placement.[145]

Institutions, in theory if not in practice, were to play a limited role: "Home care with special class training should take preference wherever possible over institutional care," admonished Stanley Davies in 1925. Further, he wrote:

1. There is no substitute for good, average home care, and the love and individual attention which the child receives in the normal relationship between parent and child.
2. The institution at best is an artificial environment.
3. Services can be provided cheaper at home.[146]

Ecob's 1924 study, previously cited, clearly illustrates the positive thinking of the day. Of the 412 morons studied, 18 percent were considered employable; 42 percent, useful at home; 17 percent, harmless; 16 percent, troublesome; and only 7 percent, an actual menace. Similarly, in a study of 415 imbeciles and idiots, 18 percent were employable, 11 percent were useful at home, 26 percent were harmless, 37 percent were troublesome, and only 8 percent constituted any form of menace. Ecob concluded that approximately 7 percent of the mentally retarded population was either antisocial or presented some form of socially related problem. This held true, regardless of degree of retardation, for, as indicated, "the degree of defect is not the determining factor in selecting for institutions. Many a low-grade idiot is receiving excellent home care."[147]

In July, 1929, President Hoover sent out a call for a conference to study the health status and well-being of children in the United States. The conference, which was held on November 19 to 22, 1930, concentrated on four major areas: 1) medical services, 2) public health administration, 3) education and training, and 4) the handicapped. One of the subcommittees dealt specifically with problems involving mental deficiency. Members of the subcommittee included many familiar names: Anderson, Baker, Bernstein, Davies, Dayton, Doll, Goddard, Haines, Kuhlmann, Potter, Sandy, Smith, Wallace, Watkins, Wylie, and E. R. Johnstone, chairman.

Their report was prefaced with the first Bill of Rights for the Handicapped Child. Accordingly, the handicapped child had a right:

1. To as vigorous a body as human skill can give him.
2. To an education so adapted to his handicap that he can be economically independent and have the chance for the fullest life of which he is capable.
3. To be brought up and educated by those who understand the nature of the burden he has to bear and who consider it a privilege to help him beat it.
4. To grow up in a world which does not set him apart, which looks at him, not with scorn or pity or ridicule—but which welcomes him, exactly as it welcomes every child, which offers him identical privileges and identical responsibilities.
5. To a life on which his handicap casts no shadow, but which is full day by day with those things which make it worth while, with comradeship, love, work, play, laughter, and tears—a life in which these things bring continually increasing growth, richness, release of energies, joy in achievement.[148]

The subcommittee advanced its concept of "a desirable program" that included 1) identification and registration, 2) early diagnosis, 3) therapeutic prevention, including special classes and modified curricula, institutional care and training, and colonization and parole, 4) community supervision, vocational training follow-up, and supervision of home conditions and parental training, 5) sterilization, and 6) research. The subcommittee's position with regard to sterilization represented a broad program to prevent reproduction among most mildly retarded persons. Finally, the subcommittee recommended that there should exist a strong state agency to provide for the direction and control of the more general aspects of the work of local agencies. In essence, the subcommittee's report was conservative and somewhat disappointing.

It should be noted that advances in community services were not evident throughout the country. Home training, special classes, colonies, community supervision, and other such programs tended to be available only in the northeastern states of size, midwestern states of size, and California. Services in the southern, southwestern, or western states were extremely limited, if available at all. Rural services, regardless of state, were also few in number.

Further, and regardless of state, homes for dependent children, county poor farms, and almshouses continued to be used rather extensively. In 1929, Doll estimated that twice as many mentally retarded persons in need of residential care were tended in such facilities as were in state institutions.[149] In 1936, he again observed that many mentally retarded persons were still in almshouses.[150] Nor, as evidenced by Harry Evans's extensive study, *The American Poor Farm and its Inmates,* published in 1926, had conditions improved one iota from the days of Dorothea Dix. Wrote Evans:

The poor farm is our human dumping ground into which go our derelicts of every description. Living in this mess of insanity and depravity, this prison place for criminals and the insane, are several thousand children and respectable, intelligent old folks, whose only offense is that they are poor. . . . Many of the intelligent, already weakened in body and morale, break mentally under the strain. Daily association with the idiotic and the feeble-minded, many of whom are incapable of caring for their bodies and are filthy beyond belief, is enough to drive a healthy person insane. Officials estimated that some 75 percent of the inmates of almshouses were feebleminded. It was common for feebleminded women and girls to be made pregnant by other inmates or by attendants.[151]

Specifically:

Sandusky, Ohio: "An imbecile woman's only bed is an old box filled with straw and a dirty quilt. She was very unkempt, barefooted, covered with flies. Concrete, filthy floors. A disgraceful place."[152]

North Carolina: "For several years an uncontrollable blind man lay on a pallet with one end of a chain around his ankle and the other stapled to the floor."[153]

Tioga County, New York: "Everybody lives together—the blind, the feeble-minded, the intelligent, the children, the epileptic, the contaminated, the noisy,—and the flies and vermin."[154]

These conditions would persist until World War II.

Bidding out practices, which continued throughout the 1920s, were also condemned by Evans, who rightly assessed them as sheer exploitation. From his comments it would appear that the feebleminded were particularly sought by contractors: "Perhaps there are a few feeble-minded huskies among the forty paupers who can moil and toil in the fields. Perhaps there are a few strong feeble-minded women who can wash dishes and scrub. There will be profit from their labor."[155]

Not only were feebleminded paupers good workers, but they neither understood their rights nor possessed the knowledge and skills needed to arrange their terms of employment. As Evans noted, this form of slavery continued to exist because mentally retarded paupers could neither protest nor fight for their rights: "If these unfortunates had the capacity to organize, the capacity and opportunity to speak, to print, to vote, their conditions would be relieved. Because they are mute, they are neglected."[156]

Institutional-type programs, including orphanages, special schools, and residential facilities, began to lose favor for both philosophical and political-financial reasons. Adoption became the favored approach for dependent children during these two decades, but again mentally retarded youngsters were excluded from such consideration. Social agencies in Pennsylvania, for example, were cautioned to "protect adopting families from unwittingly taking children whose heredity casts doubts about their ability to attain the mental and moral caliber necessary to meet the standards of life in the adopting home."[157] In Utah, adoption of a child who was "afflicted with feeble-mindedness, epilepsy, insanity, or a venereal infection as a result of conditions existing prior to the adoption" could be vacated.[158]

Justification of such policies was contained in the Annual Report of the Massachusetts Department of Public Welfare for the year ending November 30, 1935: "Experience has proven to organizations engaged in this work over a period of years that few well-planned adoptions have resulted in disappointment. It is readily understood that a child of good parentage and of average mental ability, when placed in a home of ordinary people, will grow up to be a credit to his family. But, when the child or parents, either one of whom was lacking in mental, physical, and moral background, is placed in the home of a couple likewise lacking in the same qualities, the chances of success are small."[159]

The effects of the Depression were devastating not only to the millions of unemployed citizens but also to those who relied on public funding for special services and programs. Nearly every aspect of special programming for mentally retarded students was affected; special education in small cities was "greatly hampered" by the lack of adequate funds, and institutional construction and improvements stopped.[160] Also, financial destitution of families reduced the number of mentally retarded persons discharged from residential facilities and increased the number returned or admitted.[161]

Some relief was offered with the passage of the Social Security Act of 1935. More than half of the 48 states included mentally retarded and other handicapped children in their eligibility criteria for Social Security benefits.[162] The 1930s nevertheless remained extremely lean years.

In spite of (or because of) the Depression, two new, interrelated approaches were adopted to meet the needs of mentally retarded individuals: family care, modeled after the program started hundreds of years previous in Gheel, Belgium, and foster/boarding homes for children and adults. Both were to prove successful.

The family care program was initiated by Charles Vaux, superintendent of the Newark (New Jersey) State School. As a member of a special committee of the New York State Department of Mental Hygiene to investigate home and community possibilities, Vaux was exposed to family care programs in Europe and decided to emulate those efforts in the United States. Selected was the small community of Walworth, population 300, located 17 miles from the school. Some villagers, otherwise unemployed, or marginally employed, were more than willing to participate in the program even though the board and room reimbursement rate was only $4 per week. Between January, 1933, and September of the same year, 32 adults (CA 33–65) were placed with 14 families. At that point, Vaux ran out of funds to expand the program.[163]

Adults selected were those who, in the judgment of the staff and the clinical director, could benefit from such a program but who, at the same time, did not require extensive care. This does not mean, however, that participating adults were mildly retarded or free from presenting problems. The IQ range of those placed was 19 to 84 with a mean of 50; one of the adults was blind, two were paralytic, one was epileptic, one was severely crippled, and one was psychotic.

Blindness presented no severe problem, the frequency of epileptic episodes reduced significantly, and the behavior of the disturbed resident improved remarkably. By 1936, the program included 103 former residents living in 49 homes, including school-age youngsters 5 to 15 years of age and with an IQ range of 54 to 85 with a mean of 62.[164]

Vaux summarized his experiences by concluding that the residents "can enjoy a happier, more normal kind of life with more liberty; the majority of families will take a greater personal interest in the welfare of the patient than their contract implies; that many patients will improve and some sufficiently to raise their economic status; that schools in neighboring villages will accept our younger patients without question; that many children of school age will attain a good social adaptation; and that the total average per capita cost is less than for institutional residents."[165] Regrettably, the program soon lost its prime motivator. On July 22, 1939, Vaux fell down a flight of stairs at the school, suffered severe injuries, and died the following day. His program, however, continued.

Other boarding home programs were also successful. In 1938, for example, Myra Kuenzel reported on the activities of the Children's Home of Cincinnati, Ohio, which had placed and was supervising homes for probated feebleminded children and adults of all ages

and degrees of deficiency.[166] Thus, by 1940, families and various home settings were being used in lieu of institutional placement.

Special Education

During the two decades under consideration, special education, or the recognition of the mentally retarded student as an individual with differing educational needs, was fully established. Like institutional services several generations earlier, special education was considered no longer an experiment but an integral part of the educational scene, as evidenced by the comments of the U.S. Commissioner of Education in 1937:

> Clearly, special education for physically and mentally handicapped children has passed the experimental stage. Its value has been unquestionably established. When school administrators in communities of all sizes recognize and meet the problem of making adequate adjustment for every child who is handicapped or who is gifted, whether that adjustment be in special classes or through special arrangements in regular classes, then and then only will exceptional children come into the education birth right which is theirs.[167]

Parents, professionals, and institutional personnel all urged the expansion of special educational opportunities, and in spite of the Depression, special classes continued to be developed, primarily in urban areas. By 1930, 16 states had passed mandatory or permissive legislation relative to special education (these were Alabama, California, Connecticut, Illinois, Kansas, Louisiana, Massachusetts, Minnesota, Missouri, New Jersey, New York, Oregon, Pennsylvania, Washington, Wisconsin, and Wyoming). In 1929, there were 46,625 children in 2,552 special classes for mentally retarded persons in 266 cities.[168] By 1934, 84,458 mentally retarded students were enrolled in special classes sponsored by 427 cities.[169] While the number of students enrolled increased substantially, it still represented a small portion of those in need.

The Council for Exceptional Children
The heightened recognition of mentally retarded and other exceptional children, concomitant with expanding educational opportunities, soon raised the need for special educators to form an association to facilitate

communication and to promote the interests of their students. The summer of 1922 witnessed the formation of the Council for Exceptional Children, which, from that day forth, would play an immeasurably important role in advancing educational opportunities for not only mentally retarded students but other disabled youngsters, as well.

During that summer, Elizabeth E. Farrell taught several courses for the Teachers College of Columbia University. One of her students was Henrietta A. Johnson, who, according to another founding member, LaVinia Warner, provided the spark that ignited the development of the council. Johnson met with other supervisors who also indicated a willingness to support such an effort. The supervisors, in turn, presented their proposal to Farrell, assuming that she would take an active and aggressive role in promoting such an association, and indeed she did.[170] On August 10, 1922, an evening dinner meeting was held in a local New York City hotel and the organization was officially founded. Though there is some confusion as to who actually attended the initial meeting, the following list of 11 participants was thoroughly researched by Harley Z. Wooden:

1. Jennie L. Ball, superintendent, School for Backward Girls, M. E. Mission, Aligarh, India
2. Jessie B. Doring, teacher of ungraded classes, New York City
3. Elizabeth E. Farrell, inspector of ungraded classes, New York City
4. Helen Hayes Harman, director of education, Children's Hospital, Pandall's Island, New York City
5. Henrietta A. Johnson, supervisor of vocational guidance and special classes, Oakland, California
6. Maud Keator, senior supervisor of special education, State Department of Education, Hartford, Connecticut
7. Estella McCafferty, principal, Jackson Opportunity School, Kansas City, Missouri
8. Imogene Palen, teacher of lipreading, Toronto, Ontario, Canada, schools

9. Alice H. Smith, supervisor of special classes, Stoneham, Massachusetts
10. Alice C. Smithick, conductor of psychological tests, Montclair, New Jersey
11. M. LaVinia Warner, director, Department of Special Education, Ohio University, Athens, Ohio[171]

Elizabeth Farrell assumed responsibility for serving as the council's first president, a role she filled most successfully for 4 years. The council held its first convention in Cleveland, Ohio, on February 26 and 27, 1923.

The International Council for the Education of Exceptional children, as the organization was originally called, initiated its first publication in 1928, "Newsletter of the International Council for Exceptional Children," which continued until 1932. In 1933, the organization shortened its title to the International Council for Exceptional Children; a year later, it entered into agreement with Wooden to publish a new journal entitled *International Council for Exceptional Children Review*, later renamed the *Journal of Exceptional Children* and currently called *Exceptional Children*. In 1958, the association again changed its title to The Council for Exceptional Children.

Elizabeth E. Farrell   Elizabeth E. Farrell (1870–1932) not only played a key role in the foundation and development of the council, she was one of the foremost leaders in the development of programs for mentally retarded persons in the United States. Starting as a regular class teacher prior to the turn of the century, she soon became interested in mentally retarded persons and in 1906 was appointed "Inspector of Ungraded Classes" for New York City. Not only did she advance the cause of special education, she was highly sensitive to the totality of human functioning and was among the first to insist upon a multidisciplinary approach to meeting the needs of such youngsters. In this, she undoubtedly was influenced by the thinking of Witmer.

In addition to her supervisory responsibilities, she taught at the University of Pennsylvania, New York University, and the Columbia Teachers College, and she initiated the *Ungraded* magazine for special education. As

Elizabeth E. Farrell.

eighty to ninety percent of the children who, because of inferior intelligence combined with emotional instability accentuated by adverse home conditions, are likely to become a menace to society. And this can be done before the children have actually become violators of the law. In other words, we could select from our special classes the children who stand most in need of institutional treatment while yet young enough for the institution to do something with them. On the other hand, there does not seem to be much doubt but what many children sent to institutions for the feeble-minded and now paroled might have remained at home and been educated in the public schools provided they had been put into the special class from the beginning of their school life.[173]

Quite often mentally retarded students were bound to remain in their special class for the duration of their formal educational experiences. School systems that tended to view special class placement circumspectly, however, also appeared to be most flexible. Nevertheless, few permitted the student to make the decision, as apparently did the Battle Creek (Michigan) Public Schools:

The mentally deficient or borderline child can have the opportunity of being in a group with the curriculum devised to meet his needs but . . . his placement in this group depends upon his own choice. In actual practice a mentally deficient or border-line child rarely chooses to be in one of the groups with a more complicated curriculum, but some of the brighter children do choose the curriculum specifically devised for the mentally deficient children. In the junior high school it is quite possible for a shop class, which is an elective, to contain superior as well as deficient children. In practice, no child is retained in the closely supervised small group after he can make an adjustment in any of the other groups, which automatically means that any child who becomes aware of the mentally deficient group as being different is automatically transferred out, so that it is fair to say that there are no special classes as commonly conceived, that every child is in a group by choice, and if other children cast reflections upon his placement he always has the opportunity of supporting his own choice of placement or requesting change.[174]

early as 1928, she urged the establishment of classes throughout the system for children with IQs less than 50 and, at the same time, sought to develop trade schools for older mentally retarded girls and boys. As described by a close colleague, she was not only intelligent but possessed a "forceful personality, full of deep emotion and driving determination."[172]

Student Characteristics and Eligibility
Students placed in special classes varied widely, depending on opportunity and attitudes toward special education. As evidenced by enrollment data, many communities (and some states) provided no special educational opportunities. This was particularly true in the more rural areas of the country.

Some schools approached special class placement cautiously; others did not. Street and Fuller, for example, argued:

By continuing to select from the first grade those pupils who are failing in their work and stand lowest in intelligence and by putting them into special classes where they are taught by experienced teachers who have had special training in the teaching and study of exceptional children, I believe that it will be possible for us to pick out

By the mid-1920s, many, but by no means all, school systems began to exclude mentally retarded children, especially those with IQs of less than 50. As explained by Gladys Ide, director of special education for Philadelphia:

The Philadelphia School System does not try to take care of all of the feebleminded children which are to be found in the City. Many of these children would be physically incapable of attending school and more of them are not able to care for their bodily needs sufficiently well to make it possible to permit their placement in school. . . . That is, they could not compete socially with children on the playground and in the classroom nor could they profit by class instruction enough to warrant the extra burden their presence in the school produced.[175]

In one year alone, 1937, 300 students were excluded from Pennsylvania schools.[176] As indicated, this was a common practice across the country.

Parents appealing such decisions found the courts still supportive of the school board: "The power of the school committee to exclude children from school is very broad and is to be exercised for the best interests of all the people" (*Committee* v. *Johnson,* 1941).[177]

New legal directions, however, were beginning to appear. In 1936, the Iowa Supreme Court supported special education, maintaining that the local school board had the right over the parents' objections to place a mentally retarded child in a special class in another school district, stating, "In failing to cause the child to attend the special class, or some private school, or to attend comparable private instruction, and that since no claim as to mental or physical unfitness was made, the parents could be held criminally negligent for neglect of duty under the compulsory attendance laws."[178] The Ohio court challenged the use of the IQ test for purposes of excluding mentally retarded youngsters from school and required the approval of any exclusions by the state Department of Education.[179]

Larger cities that excluded trainable children from public school participation often attempted to provide home instruction through either their educational or social welfare agencies. Parents were taught to cope with their child and were provided with home training manuals.

Interestingly, while some school systems were refusing to establish programs for the more seriously affected mentally retarded youngsters, others were making a concerted effort to serve multiply handicapped children. By 1939, for example, New York City had established three classes for the latter: two were for "retarded and crippled children with impaired vision, and one is for those with deafness in addition to the mental handicap."[180]

Purposes and Goals   As more and more attention was devoted to mentally retarded students and an increasing number of school systems attempted to establish successful programs, divergent opinions naturally arose. Three primary schools of thought, subject to considerable variation, were evident. First, there was the more conservative approach, which emphasized productive citizenship, habit training, and happiness: "Our aim in the education of the special class child is to make him a law abiding member of society and to enable him to become wholly or partially self-supporting through engaging in unskilled labor. The folly of attempting to make skilled laborers out of this type of individual, when twenty percent of the normal population gainfully employed are engaged in unskilled labor, is self evident."[181]

Adherents of this philosophy placed great emphasis on such tenets as finishing what is undertaken, learning to work, and "putting forth one's best effort" to "build up specific, useful, usable habits in each child according to his needs," for "specific habits are what the mentally deficient child must have."[182] E. R. Johnstone's primary principle—"Happiness first, all else follows"—was adopted by many of this school.[183]

Educators advocating these positions also took a conservative posture with regard to the abilities of mentally retarded persons—thus, for example, C. Berry of the Detroit public schools stressed: "the fact that the mental defective learns more slowly and forgets more quickly than the average person means that he should be taught only what he needs to know and only when he needs to know it."[184]

The infectious "happiness first" concept even spread to the normal school. C. Elliott, director of special education for the Michigan State Normal College, observed: " 'Happiness first, all else follows' is full of first class pedagogy. It is indeed certain that unless the child is made happy in his work, he will accomplish little. The inhibitions to mental and emotional reaction induced by the lack of the normal joys of childhood are obvious in the life of any child so deprived, and especially in the lives of those unfortunate ones who have never been able to keep pace with their fellows. Happiness then could well be accepted as the first goal of the special class."[185]

Second was the "progressive" school of thought. As explained by one adherent, Florence N. Beaman of the Little Red School House in New York City, the child's social and emotional growth were of prime import. In other words, "the teacher has to know that the retarded child's satisfactions (like hers) lie in the relatively simple understanding of immediate life situations:

1. An ease and a joy in social relations with contemporaries.
2. A familiarity and security in his own environment so that he can prepare his own food, care for his own clothes, and make his own dwelling livable.
3. The ability to work in an occupation commensurate with his own abilities.
4. The disposition to keep physically fit.[186]

Thus, the goals and curriculum should respond to three questions:

1. What are the needs of the children in this group in relation to the community in which they live, not only from a factual viewpoint, but also physical, social, emotional, and occupational growth?
2. What levels of capacity and of understanding are to be satisfied?
3. What real situations exist which can stimulate and can help to solve the foregoing needs?[187]

The third group comprised those individuals who were not easily stampeded into the prevalent notion of segregation and the irreversibility of mental retardation. Such educators viewed programs for mentally retarded persons at multiple levels and, at the same time, made every effort to provide those experiences that would enable the mentally retarded student to return to the regular classroom. J. E. Wallace

Wallin, for one, viewed special education in terms of its "special aid and attention, individual instruction, or differentiated training."[188] He advocated what would be viewed today as three levels of special education classes. In contrast with the then current practices of many school systems, Wallin encouraged the establishment of classes for trainable youngsters (IQs approximately 30 or 35 to 50), special classes for the mildly retarded who could not return to the regular class and compete in that setting, and classes for mildly mentally retarded persons or those with severe educational lags who could be programmed in special classes with the full intent of returning to the regular classroom. He found that this multiple approach resulted in 42 percent of special class youngsters being returned to their regular classrooms.[189]

Educators of this school believed, as did Wallin, that "children transferred to the special classes should not be assigned for the reasons that they are feeble-minded socially and industrially considered, nor should it be assumed that they are feeble-minded although most of them or all of them may prove to be so, they should be assigned solely because their mental and educational potentials are so limited that they cannot do satisfactory work in all of the regular branches of the curriculum beyond the primary grades (or the beginning of the third grade)."[190] In brief, they did not believe that special classes should exist for students who simply appeared to be feeble-minded on the basis of some intelligence test or statistical parameter.

While representatives from each of these schools of thought emphasized citizenship, productivity, and a self-fulfilling life to the fullest degree possible, differences in priorities were evident. The overall model, however, that guided the development of special education in the late 1930s resulted from the first conference sponsored by a federal agency on the special education of mentally retarded individuals. This 3-day conference was held in October, 1934 and was supported by the Section on Exceptional Children and Youth of the U.S. Office of Education. Under the guidance of Elise H. Martens, chief of the section, the conference produced a statement outlining the general objectives of special education based on the youngster's needs:

> The basic educational objectives applicable to the mentally deficient child, which should determine the type and degree of curriculum adjustment that must be made, involved the four principles of (1) educating each child *in keeping with his capacities, limitations, and interests;* (2) education with each child *for achievement on his own level,* without attempting to force him into activities beyond his abilities; (3) educating each child *for some participation in the world's work* and also *for participation in those social and cultural values which are within his reach;* and (4) educating each child *with full consideration of the best interests of all children.*[191]

Curriculum As one might well imagine, the various philosophies and attitudes concerning the role and objectives of special education would, in turn, be reflected in curricular provisions. The conservative school, which perhaps reflected the most negative attitude toward mentally retarded youth, persistently emphasized their limitations; provided the least amount of education necessary; encouraged habit training in manners, social conduct, health and health care; limited academic experiences; and placed a priority on manual training and happiness.[192]

Persons assuming the "progressive" posture highlighted social experiences as well as individual needs and interests. Manual training and the development of skills essential to independent or semi-independent living as adults were also integral parts of the curriculum.

Those approaching a more flexible approach emphasized remedial skills for those youngsters deemed capable of returning to the regular class. Those who gave little educational evidence of such progress pursued a curriculum intended for academic preparation as well as sociopersonal adjustment.

The broad-based yet practical curricular guidelines developed at the conference sponsored by the U.S. Office of Education were applied frequently. Academic instruction emphasized age-appropriate skills needed by the student to function within his community:

reading emphasized street names, highway and traffic signs, food names, prices, newspaper ads, and the like. In addition, manual experiences were deemed important, as were health habits and physical development, group participation, art, physical activities, social studies, mental hygiene, and character education.

Though the curricular suggestions introduced many activities that would not have been considered by more conservative groups, too much significance was attached to mental age. It was assumed that a mentally retarded student's interests and activities corresponded directly with mental age. This restrictive concept resulted in the undesirable practice of retaining special class adolescents in the elementary school environment.[193]

In addition to the guidelines prepared by the U.S. Office of Education, a number of textbooks appeared during this period. Most notable among these were those by J. E. Wallace Wallin, 1924; Annie Inskeep, 1926; William Featherstone, 1932; and Christine Ingram, 1935.[194]

Regardless of philosophy or intent, one thing was certain: the special education program was always assigned the worst classroom or location possible. Ada Fitts lashed out at the attitudes underlying this practice, asking, "Shall we be satisfied with school authorities who simply segregate the backward child, treat him as an outcast, give him an untrained teacher, make no attempt to understand him or his problem?"[195]

Methodology Basic approaches to special education again varied with the particular school of thought. The more conservative concept of mental retardation as well as the role of special education was well reflected in the writings of Berry:

> Since the mentally retarded child is weakest in judgment and reasoning, as much use as possible should be made of the substitutes for these higher mental processes, viz., imitation, habit, and memory. Like the normal individual, he desired to do the things his companions are doing. He may not always understand why they do things in a certain way and it is not always necessary that he should for we are not training him to be a leader but a follower. Much time has been wasted and

marked injustice done to the mentally retarded child in attempting to get him to live up to the standard of conduct higher than that of the group to which he belongs . . . it is enough . . . if we can get him to imitate successfully the conduct of his own group . . . only through imitation can he find satisfaction in the social life of those with whom he must live.[196]

This certainly did not offer the most promising outlook for mentally retarded people.

Those who supported this school of thought were somewhat prone to offer tidbits of advice:

We must say exactly what we mean if we wish to be properly understood.
Scolding and fault finding takes away energy from the recipient.
Praise increases energy.
Enlarged ego, commonly called swelled head, usually means that a child really believes it can do something it has never yet accomplished. Give it a chance.
The tone of your voice gives pain or comfort.
All the world craves a sympathetic listener.[197]

Also:

They *do* fatigue easily.
In most instances they are a class apart from the virile, energetic, ambitious citizen.
They are not capable of self-direction.
You must accept from the subnormal worker only that he shall do the task immediately before him.[198]

The conservatives also tended to view special education as something to be accomplished within the confines of the classroom setting. In contrast, progressives promoted community interaction-type activities. Those who advocated the most flexible approach to special education were also more eclectic in methodology. Not only did they utilize elementary school methods and incorporate many of the remedial techniques outlined by such instructional experts as Kirk and Monroe in reading and Fernald in arithmetic, but they employed many of the varied ideas developed by the progressives and those in the mental hygiene movement.[199]

Though special educational methods had moved away from those methods traditionally used in schools, many of the modifications were based on pragmatic experience rather than on any learning theory. Thus, some of the cardinal principles were:

1. Select something that will have interest and that has possibilities of development.
2. Start at a point where the children will be able to do the work.
3. Make it have a definite application to their present and future needs.[200]

Out of experience also grew the unit or project approach. It was enthusiastically described by Elise Martens in 1935:

Perhaps the peak of the discussion of the conference was reached when it was developed that all of this content material, to serve its greatest purpose, must be integrated into what is educationally known as a *"unit of experience."* Teaching a spelling lesson or a reading lesson or even making a wooden box loses its significance as a medium of helping the child to adjust himself to life situations unless that process in itself is vividly related to those life situations. Unless it is a part of the whole experience in which the *child is participating* as a member of the group, it becomes only an isolated element of learning that has no meaning to him. A class project in cooperative living, built around the child's need for shelter or food or some other phase of his natural experience, can give all the opportunity in the world for teaching numbers, spelling, reading, social responsibility, manual skills, and even the arts and sciences. Far better to give drill in connection with a living project in which the child is vitally and enthusiastically interested and for which he needs certain knowledge and skills than to place it in its own tight compartment utterly apart from anything that really matters to him.[201]

Though Elizabeth Kelly introduced an audience of mental retardation professionals to some of Piaget's concepts in 1938, his theory would not receive serious attention in the United States for another 30 years.[202] One European influence was felt, however, and that was the contributions of the Belgian physician and educator, Ovide Decroly.

Ovide Decroly Ovide Decroly (1871–1932) studied medicine at the University of Ghent and in Berlin. As a result of his early hospital work in Brussels, he came into contact with many mentally retarded youngsters. Based on his experiences, he concluded that the best treatment for such children was through education; consequently, he established a special school for the "retarded and abnormal" in Brussels in 1901. A few years later, believing his techniques would be equally appropriate with normal youngsters, Decroly turned his attention in that direction. Though he was highly successful and published frequently, his work was not widely recognized in the United States until Alice Descourdes, his translator, published her text, *The Education of Mentally Defective Children,* in 1928. [203]

According to Descourdes, Decroly centered his program on the child, his activities, and his environment, which included family, community, and the world in general. Teaching involved five fundamental principles. First, and reminiscent of Rousseau's *Emilé,* "The fundamental principle, on which all concerned with defective children are agreed, and which cannot be too much insisted on, is the utilization of the *natural activity* of the pupil. The child must *do* things, with his body, his hands, and his brains." Second, "particular importance must be attached to *perceptual knowledge and sensory training,* with considerable recognition of

Ovid Decroly.

the techniques developed by Seguin. Third, activities presented "must have a high degree of *correlation* or concentration." In other words, different subjects should group themselves around a single central theme. The fourth principle was *individualization.* The last principle was as much social as pedagogical: "*the utilitarian character of the teaching.* We must look to the immediate utilization in actual life of the ideas acquired in the course of our teaching. It is essential for the child to acquire as quickly as possible the means of earning his living, and with that object, we must discover and develop his capabilities and utilize what mental powers he possesses, without wasting of it, by directing all of his teaching towards a practical end."[204]

Decroly and Descourdes outlined a large number of games which could be utilized in both academic and nonacademic areas. Games served to cultivate a child's spontaneous attention, lead him to self-activity, and, at the same time, provided a measure of progress for both child and teacher. Decroly and Descourdes used games much in the same manner as Montessori with one important difference: a natural, rather than a formal, structured setting was provided. The ideas Decroly proposed set a new tone for special education, and in the judgment of Kirk and Johnson, he was "one of the more modern educators of mentally defective children."[205]

Efficacy of the Special Class Research during this period continued to confirm the success of special education programs. The most frequently cited study was that by Baller in 1936. He found that 206 former special class students as adults were doing as well as an equal number of control subjects in such areas as marriage and divorce, respect for the law, and employment. He concluded: "The results of this study of the present social status of a group of mentally deficient subjects seems to justify the conclusion that, taken together, they have fared better in the task of providing livings for themselves and getting along with their fellow men and the early prognosis indicated they might. That it is possible for many of them to remain law-abiding and useful citizens is suggested by the altogether satisfactory present status of a considerable number of the group."[206]

Teacher Training   As indicated previously, 16 states had, by 1930, passed legislation authorizing special education. Of these, 10 also set forth legal requirements for teacher certification, which, in most instances, was limited to an elementary degree plus supplemental training.[207] In general, most teachers held a 1- or 2-year degree in regular education and attained certification by enrolling in several summer school programs conducted at an institution for mentally retarded persons.

Normal schools, colleges, and universities began to recognize the mentally retarded student. By 1930, 45 teachers colleges and normal schools in 22 states as well as 54 colleges and universities in 30 states and the District of Columbia were at least offering an introductory course on the exceptional child. A few colleges, however, had established special education departments: Summer Normal School at Yale (Connecticut); The State Normal School, Salem (Massachusetts); State Normal College, Ypsilanti (Michigan); The State Normal and Training School, Oswego (New York); The State Teachers' College, Milwaukee (Wisconsin); and Miami University, Oxford (Ohio).[208] Most of these schools continued to rely heavily on institutional summer programs.

By 1930, however, many school supervisors, including Farrell and Berry, were calling for a full 4-year degree program, the first two years of which would be devoted to elementary education, the last two to special education. Further, they desired the teacher to have 2 years elementary experience before specializing. In this way, the special educator would understand the normal child and set realistic expectancies for the mentally retarded child. Many also wanted their teachers to gain special training in the public schools rather than in institutional settings.

Teacher expectancies expanded substantially; in the opinion of Elizabeth Kelly, teachers of mentally retarded students should:

1. Endeavor to know the family and environmental background of the child so as to be able to guide his emotional and social development.
2. Become acquainted with the mental and physical growth of the individual—note his limitations and do not expect him to work beyond them.
3. Scientifically use psychological and statistical results together with other adequate gauges so as to program for growth, especially emotional and social.
4. Become aware of the knowledge and skills necessary to guide the mentally retarded, for all mental levels, in an educational program.
5. Become cognizant, together with the family and community of the social as well as the mental capacities of the individual—and the part he has to play in the community with such potentialities.
6. Use *constructively* the agencies that the school system may offer (visiting teachers—psychologist) in an effort to help solve his problems.
7. Ever look onward and upward unflinchingly, holding to the progressive viewpoint and carrying on toward a democratic educational goal without fear and against all odds.[209]

The role obviously required new knowledge as well as a modicum of research skills.

The 1920s and 1930s saw many gains and heightened hopes. Mentally retarded persons were viewed in a new, positive light, professionals examined both their assumptions and their tools, universities and colleges began to acknowledge the exceptional child, and reliance on institutions began to shift to reliance on the community, and communities were responding. So it was in Germany also, until the advent of Adolph Hitler and his political party, which once again demonstrated the fragility of humanitarianism.

THE NAZI EXPERIENCE

"Race betterment" realized its most irrational but powerful proponent in Adolph Hitler, who, in *Mein Kampf*, published in 1924, set forth his ideology of the folk state that ultimately resulted in the death of millions:

> The folkish state must make up for what everyone else today has neglected in this field. *It must set race in the center of all life. It must take care to keep it pure. It must declare the child to be the most precious treasure of the people. It must see*

to it that only the healthy beget children; that there is only one disgrace; despite one's own sickness and deficiencies, to bring children into the world, and one highest honor: to renounce doing so. And conversely it must be considered reprehensible: to withhold healthy children from the nation. Here the state must act as the guardian of a millennial future in the face of which the wishes and the selfishness of the individual must appear as nothing and submit. It must put the most modern medical means in the service of this knowledge. It must declare unfit for propagation all who are in any way visibly sick or who have inherited a disease and can therefore pass it on, and put this into actual practice. Conversely, it must take care that the fertility of the healthy woman is not limited by the financial irresponsibility of a state regime which turns the blessing of children into a curse for the parents. It must put an end to that lazy, nay criminal, indifference with which the social premises for a fecund family are treated today, and must instead feel itself to be the highest guardian of this most precious blessing of a people. Its concern belongs more to the child than to the adult.

Those who are physically and mentally unhealthy and unworthy must not perpetuate their suffering in the body of their children. In this the folkish state must perform the most gigantic educational task. And some day this will seem to be a greater deed than the most victorious wars of our present bourgeois era. By education it must teach the individual that it is no disgrace to dishonor one's misfortune by one's own egotism in burdening innocent creatures with it; that by comparison it bespeaks a nobility of highest idealism and the most admirable humanity if the innocently sick, renouncing a child of his own, bestows his love and tenderness upon a poor, unknown young scion of his own nationality, who with his health promises to become some day a powerful member of a powerful community. And in this educational work the state must perform the purely intellectual complement of its practical activity. It must act in this sense without regard to understanding or lack of understanding, approval or disapproval.

A prevention of the faculty and opportunity to procreate on the part of the physically degenerate and mentally sick, over a period of only six hundred years, would not only free humanity from an immeasurable misfortune, but would lead to a recovery which today seems scarcely considerable.[210]

Implementation of Hitler's pure race policy began on September 1, 1939, with his brief note to Reichsleiter Bouhler and Dr. Brandt stating that they were "authorized to extend

the responsibilities of physicians still to be named in such a manner that patients whose illness, according to the most critical application of human judgement, is incurable, can be granted release by euthanasia."[211]

In the beginning, mentally retarded and mentally ill persons in institutions were starved to death. Within a month, however, *Aktion T4*, a more organized program, was initiated. It called for the identification of all patients with schizophrenia, epilepsy, encephalitis, and a number of other diseases. This resulted in the systematic gassing of 70,000 mentally retarded and mentally ill persons.[212] As described by one witness, Bert Honolka:

. . . It was the strawberry season. This is in June or July [presumably of 1940]. I was part of the staff that accompanied a transport of patients. Usually, we wore civilian clothes. Before the transport started, I was told to put on a physician's white coat, however, so that as far as the patients were concerned, I would appear to be a doctor or a doctor's helper. The members of the transport were told that they were going to be moved. But they were not told where. The transport went to the city of Brandenburg, to the old prison downtown, parts of which had been rebuilt into a crematory, since the prison was empty. During the trip, we had to be careful to see that the busses' white curtains were drawn. On the way, between Berlin and Brandenburg, we stopped in Werder, and everyone got a basket of strawberries, and then we delivered the people to Brandenburg.

We went in with these people. We stayed around, for the SS guards told us, "Why don't you have a look at the show." The people were sorted, out, the men in one group, the women in another.

Everyone had to undress completely. The reason they were given was that before being moved to another building, they would have to take a bath and be deloused. All patients had to open their mouths, and an automatic four digit stamp was pressed against their chests. By looking at the numbers, the staff later knew who had gold teeth. In order not to alarm the sick people, physicians gave them a superficial examination. They then were taken into the shower room. When the intended number of people were inside, the door was locked. At the ceiling, there were installations in the shape of showerheads through which the gas was admitted into the room.

I think that 50 people entered for such a gassing. There were a few young girls among them, and we said to ourselves, "Boy, what a shame."

There was only a single door to the room, and you could see through the peephole exactly when all were dead.

About 15 or 20 minutes later, the gas was let out of the room, since it was clear from looking through the peephole that no one was alive any more. Next, by use of the stamped numerals, it was ascertained who the people were who, as the examination had shown, had gold teeth. The dead had their gold teeth broken out. . . .[213]

Hitler ordered this program stopped on August 23, 1941, in response to the public outcry and legal action of Clemens Count Galen, Bishop of Munster in Westphalia. It continued, however, but more subtly and discreetly—many mentally retarded patients continued to be destroyed via injection. At the same time, *Aktion 14F13* was implemented, resulting in the extermination of approximately 20,000 more mentally retarded, mentally ill, and other "physically or socially undesirable" persons in concentration camps. This program included Jewish persons, who previously had not been "considered worthy of euthanasia."[214] Thus began the holocaust.

Chapter

8

CONFLICT AND CHANGE

(1940–1959)

B Y 1940, HALF THE WESTERN WORLD was at war. Germany, which had already consumed much of central Europe, was striking at Britain and would soon launch its might against its ally, Russia. On December 7, 1941, Japan attacked an unalert Pearl Harbor, committing the United States to the war. During the next 3 years, 8 months, and 26 days, 15 million American men and women served the nation's armed services throughout the world, 405,000 of whom did not return.[1]

On August 6, 1945, a single plane dropped a single bomb on Hiroshima; 8 days later Germany surrendered, followed by Japan on September 2. The country's joyous victory celebration did not diminish a lingering sadness over the unexpected death of its longest-serving president, Franklin D. Roosevelt, on April 12.

The war was won, but peace was not: the Cold War and the Berlin air lift, 1948; the Korean "police action," 1950–1953; and a commitment to Southeastern Asia, 1954.

Following World War II, an expanded federal government retained an interest in the economic health and well-being of the country providing farm price support; long-term, low-interest GI loans; and continued minimum wages. In 1946, the Congress welcomed three new members to its rank: John F. Kennedy, Richard M. Nixon, and Lyndon B. Johnson.

Jackie Robinson joined the Dodgers baseball team in 1945, signalling a major advance in racial relations in America. The Supreme Court's decision in *Brown* v. *Board of Education* (1954) that "separate facilities are inherently unequal" set forth new directions in the educational provisions of opportunities for minority youth on a constitutional basis.

These two decades, initially motivated by the needs of war, saw a renaissance in science—miracle drugs, nuclear fission and fusion, radioisotopes, the laser beam, the Salk vaccine, microelectronics, and, of course, television. During the 1950s, the United States was especially prosperous, producing half of the world's oil, half of its automobiles, and 40 percent of its industrial output.[2] All in all, it was a time of basic prosperity with a promising, though occasionally frightening future.

UNDERSTANDING OF MENTAL RETARDATION

Many advances were made in understanding mental retardation and mentally retarded persons during this period, based on knowledge gained from many different experiences and fields of professional endeavor. Mental retardation gradually emerged from the fringe of concern and the interest of a few to become a highly visible social responsibility, drawing attention from a wide range of professional and political groups. While, to some degree, this represented a progressive extension of the precepts and trends already noted during the previous decades, World War II greatly accelerated recognition and treatment.

MENTALLY RETARDED PERSONS AND WORLD WAR II

World War II saw a country united in a common cause as it had never been before or after. Everyone—including mentally retarded people—were expected to contribute wholeheartedly to the war effort. Unlike World War I, professional groups no longer claimed that mentally retarded citizens should not serve their country.

The greatest sacrifices were, of course, made by the tens of thousands of mentally retarded men and women who entered the military service, fighting in all theaters of the war. In many respects, experiences with this war were similar to those of World War I. Though local selective service agencies were urged by the National Selective Service System to "reject those registrants whose conditions are such as positively indicate physical and mental breakdown, or failure to adjust themselves to responsibility or military service after being inducted,"[3] an induction rate of 10,000 persons per day resulted in a "greatly hastened process."[4] Thus, the initial rejection rate was relatively low, that is, 11.8 percent for reasons of mental deficiency, of which, however, only 4.2 percent were actually classified as moron, imbecile, or idiot.[5] From the beginning of selective service to the end of the war, 716,000 individuals between ages 18 and 37 were rejected on grounds of mental deficiency.[6]

Following induction, those recruits who displayed academic or intellectual deficiencies were reevaluated and, in many cases, offered supplemental training. Only a small number of those inductees were ultimately discharged; most responded well to the additional training.[7] The Army's position was explained by Major Donald E. Baier of the Adjutant General's Office:

The Army is doing its best to identify and classify men of marginal ability who are subject to selective service; to accept for military service all of those who can learn to do any Army job for which they are suited; to give special training beyond that required by the bulk of recruits; to control their number in any unit for their own and their comrades' protection; and to discharge only those who fail completely to reach minimum standards of proficiency. The Army is doing its utmost to preserve for those of marginal ability the privilege of contributing their share to the successful prosecution of the war in which we are all engaged.[8]

A mental age of 8 was found adequate for the Army, 10 for the Navy.[9]

According to a number of follow-up studies of mentally retarded persons in the service, primarily former institutional residents, most performed adequately. Haskell and Strauss, for example, reported that of 100 former residents, 51 percent were in the Army, 19 percent in the Navy or Merchant Marines, 4 percent in the Marine Corps, 7 percent in the Air Force, and 7 percent in the medical corps. The young men ranged in IQ from 50 to 80 plus. Of the 84 members of the original group that could be located, 88 percent had done well and 31 percent had been promoted at least once.[10] Whitney and MacIntyre also reported that 86 percent of their 72 boys from Elwyn remained on active duty.[11] A more extensive study by Weaver in 1946 based on 8,000 mentally retarded military personnel found that 56 percent of males and 62 percent of females with IQs less than 75 rendered acceptable service. Each of these success rates greatly exceeded Doll's prediction that only 10 percent of mentally retarded persons would have the "toughness" required for military life.[12]

Primary reasons for failure in military service were behavioral rather than intellectual. While 35.3 percent of the men from the Sonoma State Home (California), for example, were discharged because of unsatisfactory conduct, such as desertion, absence without leave, or court-martial, only 19.6 percent were rejected for inadequate intellectual functioning. In essence, military success and adaptability were reflective of personal traits and characteristics rather than measured intelligence or educational achievement.[13] This again raised the question among many professionals as to the value of intelligence testing and its application, at least to the military situation. As articulated by Hubbel in 1945,

> In view of the differences of opinion with regard to the adaptability of mental defectives in the Armed Forces, particularly those who have a low IQ, the following brief case history may be of interest.
>
> B. W., born July 30, 1915; admitted to Newark State School, Newark, New York, March 10, 1932; diagnosis, imbecile, IQ 48; paroled for employment February 15, 1941; escaped from employment May 11, 1941. Following his escape, he joined the Army and was in Hawaii during the bombing of Pearl Harbor.
>
> He recently visited the institution attired in the uniform of the U.S. Army with the rank of Private First Class. He appeared to be happy, contented and in excellent physical condition. He spontaneously stated that the Army has done a great deal for him. He has served in four campaigns in the Pacific and wore a badge indicating combat service and had received a Presidential Citation. He related that some time ago he was promoted to the rank of sergeant, but was demoted for insubordination. However, he was never absent without leave, sent money regularly to his mother and purchased bonds. He admitted that during combat, he was quite scared, particularly when on one occasion he accidentally stumbled in the woods and a bullet whizzed by where he had previously stood.
>
> Three of our boys have been promoted to sergeants, several have been made corporals, and one is a seaman, first class.
>
> It is quite apparent that in the selection of inductees for Army training, too much reliance can not be placed upon the psychometric test.[14]

Not only did many mentally retarded young men and women fulfill their military obligations most respectfully, but others became highly efficient industrial workers, often to the pleasant surprise of their mentors: "Many educators both in institutions for the subnormals and in the public school field, have been amazed and delighted at the way in which the trained subnormal boy and girl has fitted into society during the war years."[15]

Manpower shortages combined with a state of national emergency opened doors of occupational opportunity previously closed to mentally retarded persons. Coakley clearly demonstrated the difference. Prior to World War II, only two of her 20 wards had been steadily employed. During the war, all 20, with IQs ranging from 40 to 75, were engaged in industry, performing critical tasks and receiving appropriate remuneration. Included were five machine operators in ordnance plants, a truck inspector, a winch assembler, a fuse assembler, a shell sprayer, and a bullet assembler.[16]

For those who could not or did not find work in a defense plant, many other occupational opportunities were available for both moderately and mildly retarded individuals:

> Those with an IQ of 36 to 49 consisted of fruit workers, ranch workers, putting covers over clothing at dry cleaners, railroad track man (IQ 39—formerly IQ 36), kitchen help (hotels), seed company, etc.
>
> Those with an IQ of 50 to 80 and above were fruit workers, ranch workers, hospital workers, truck assistants, bottle sorters, glass packers, shipyard workers, flangers, welders, scalers, apprentices, electricians, sheet metal workers, bus boys, dish washers, cooks (railway diners), cannery, filling cigarette vending machines, stock girls, longshoremen, merchant marine, etc., seventeen of these cases were epileptics.[17]

Those who could not leave the institution also contributed in many ways, including farming and gathering increased crops, canning, assisting with scrap salvage, repairing toys and clothes, participating in air-raid duty, and conserving rationed materials and goods.[18]

These circumstances changed dramatically after the end of the war; returning veterans naturally held priority. This time Doll's prediction held true: "the mental defective who may be occupationally and socially successful today as a result of the critical shortage of civilian manpower would presumably quickly be shuffled back to poverty and dependency when the war is over."[19]

DEFINITION AND CLASSIFICATION

The nature of mental retardation and its definition continued to be debated throughout the 1940s and 1950s. As mental retardation became increasingly important to many sociolegal decisions and as identification (and labeling) became increasingly critical with the advent of expanded educational and vocational opportunities, the problem became exponentially more complex; no one felt completely comfortable with either its definition or its assessment.

For persons responsible for planning, implementing, and financing related programs, the situation was particularly vexing. Again, it was a problem not of recognizing the moderately or more severely affected, but, rather, the critical separation of the mildly retarded from the normal population; or, who should get special services and who should not.

In 1941, Yepsen, participating in a symposium, observed that definitions fell into one or more of the following three groups:

1. Those which use as criteria the inability to learn common acts.
2. Those in which the observed community or social behavior is deficient.
3. Those in which reference is made to the individual's relationship to, or place in, a larger group, using statistical procedures and quotients in order to form such judgments.

He was quick to note the deficits of each: learning can be adversely affected by many influences other than low intelligence; "social incompetence is the result of mental deficiency—or one of a variety of other causes"; and intelligence tests lacked the validity required. As regards the latter:

Many still fail to recognize the fallibility of the intelligence quotient as a diagnostic instrument. Unfortunately the intelligence quotient is the sole diagnostic technique in many clinics and has a place in the statutes of at least one state. It is a concept which is readily understood by even the most uninformed layman but it is a dangerous concept when it is used without regard to other factors. If the consequences were not so serious it would be ludicrous, as in the case of two individuals whose quotients are but one point apart and are, therefore, mentally deficient and normal. The test used, the user of the test, the conditions under which it is used, the age of the person examined, the chances of error in the calculation of life age, test age, and the quotient itself,—these factors are infrequently thoroughly understood by the persons using the quotient method of diagnosis.[20]

Kuhlmann, who participated in the same symposium, argued that too many dimensions had been added to the notion of mental deficiency, such as social conduct. To him, mental deficiency was "a mental condition resulting from a subnormal rate of development of some or all mental functions."[21] His basic point was that mental retardation had various meanings and subtleties, depending on the professional interests involved. Psychologists could not, in his judgment, provide a functional definition to meet the needs of sociologists, educators, physicians, and others with special professional needs.

The third, and most successful, panel member in promoting a new concept of mental retardation was Edgar Doll. He held that there were six criteria essential to an adequate concept and definition of mental retardation: 1) social incompetence, 2) due to mental subnormality, 3) which has been developmentally arrested, 4) which obtains at maturity, 5) is of constitutional origin, and 6) is essentially incurable. In essence, he took an approach diametrically opposed to Kuhlmann: his definition was inclusive rather than exclusive; he believed that the problem was not one of concept but one of criteria refinement, description, measurement, and "what precise degrees indicate mental deficiency."[22]

Though Doll's definition was cited frequently and social aspects received increasing attention, many professionals remained troubled by the two interrelated dimensions of "constitutional origin" and "incurability." Contemporary environmental studies tended to refute such assumptions.

In 1942, for example, Skeels provided follow-up data concerning the development of the orphanage children originally described in 1939. After 2 years, those residents transferred to the more stimulating environment of the Glenwood State School revealed an average IQ gain of .5 points in contrast to the control group remaining in the orphanage, which had an average loss of 26.2 points. Eleven of the 13 youngsters in the experimental group "attained normal or above average intelligence and were placed in adoptive homes." Skeels concluded: "A change from marked mental retardation to normal intelligence in children of preschool age is possible in the absence of organic disease or clinical deficiency by providing a more adequate psychological prescription."[23] These results were not disputed, nor were similar findings by Spitz in 1945, Levy in 1947, or Pasmanick in 1946.[24] In essence, cultural studies clearly indicated that mental retardation could result from the absence of adequate stimulation and appropriate learning experiences and that intellectual performance could be enhanced under suitable conditions.

In addition, research continued to demonstrate that the IQ as a unitary measure of intelligence was relatively unstable.[25] Blacks were discriminated against since "inferior social and cultural factors constituted the environment of Negro children."[26] Finally, the very concept of intelligence became more complex. No longer a matter of a few perceptual discriminations—vocabulary items, comparisons, and retention—through investigations by such talented persons as J. P. Guilford, intelligence now represented a matrix configuration of fundaments, classes, relations, patterns, problems, and implications about figural, structural, and conceptual content.[27] Nothing remains simple.

In brief, growing experiences arising from expanded special educational programs, more sophisticated assessment devices and assessors, as well as culturally related research gave rise to the identification of a large number of persons whose IQs were within the mild range of mental retardation statistically determined, who emanated from poverty areas, and whose parents or other siblings were or appeared to be mentally retarded, but for whom there was no known physiological basis for reduced or modified intellectual functioning. These youngsters were variously labeled as "subcultural," pseudo-feebleminded, Binet students, intellectually retarded or subnormal, or of the "garden variety."[28] "Endogenous" and "familial" (in contrast to "exogenous," "brain injured," and "neurophrenic") were also commonly applied. This recognition did

not, however, resolve the controversy surrounding "incurability."

Doll and Sarason, both prominent leaders in this area, maintained that mental retardation per se was incurable and that those mentally retarded persons without demonstrable physical etiology from subcultural areas should not be labeled mentally retarded. In fact, no one should be so labeled until adulthood. According to Doll, the "question of curability is reducable to (1) mistaken terminology, (2) uncertain diagnosis, and (3) optimistic influence."[29] Their common position was predicated on two concerns. First, Doll, like most professionals in the field, was highly sensitive to the effects of labeling: "The label of feeblemindedness constitutes a definite disparagement of individual prestige. It leads to feelings of pity if not ostracism. It constitutes a barrier to an auspicious marriage. It suggests the advisability of institutional commitment. It may lead to sterilization, permanent confinement or other social discrimination."[30] Second, "true" mental retardation as opposed to "pseudo" or functional mental retardation implied different educational or treatment approaches.

The conceptual situation became increasingly convoluted. Mental retardation was labeled *mental deficiency, feeblemindedness, mental subnormality, mental handicap,* and *oligophrenia.* These rubrics, in turn, were applied both generically and specifically. Occasionally, some authorities, especially those favoring the British or social competence school, continued to view mental retardation as intellectual subnormality with social adequacy and feeblemindedness as intellectual subnormality without social adequacy.[31] Others simply applied all terms synonymously.

The environmental aspect also added to the confusion. To some professionals, environment included both physical and sociopsychological experiences; others concentrated almost exclusively on the latter. The insertion of "subcultural" introduced the adscititious problem of definition and concept: What constituted a subcultural environment? What elements or influences distinguished between the many youngsters from such setttings who were not considered mentally retarded as opposed to those who were?

In response to this situation, the American Association on Mental Deficiency in 1952 established a committee to formulate a definition and nomenclature of mental retardation. This was a rather dilatory response to Yepsen's request in 1941 that the Association assume this responsibility in hopes of "cleaning up many of the problems from the social, educational, legal, and research point of view and, in the end, benefit the individual and society."[32]

In 1959, committee's proposals were approved by the Association's membership and, with minor modifications, were widely distributed in 1961. The proposed definition was nationally accepted, even though it was not without its critics:

MENTAL RETARDATION REFERS TO SUBAVERAGE GENERAL INTELLECTUAL FUNCTIONING WHICH ORIGINATES IN THE DEVELOPMENTAL PERIOD AND IS ASSOCIATED WITH IMPAIRMENT IN ADAPTIVE BEHAVIOR.

Subaverage general intellectual functioning referred to performance greater than one standard deviation below the population mean of the age group involved on measures of general intellectual functioning, thus adjusting for variances among different tests of intelligence. The developmental period extended from birth to approximately 16 years of age. The criterion of impairment in adaptive behavior constituted the unique and essential feature of this definition. As Heber observed in 1962, the critical factor in this concept of mental retardation was inclusion of the dual criteria of reduced intellectual functioning and impaired social adaptation. Impaired adaptive behavior would be reflected in 1) maturation, or the rate at which an individual develops his basic motor and self-care skills, 2) learning, or the ability with which an individual gains knowledge from his experiences, and/or 3) social adjustment, or the ability with which the individual is capable of independently sustaining himself in a manner consistent with the standards and requirements of his society. The need to consider both measured intelligence and adaptive behavior was

emphasized. Thus, a person with an IQ of 75 or 80 who revealed no significant impairment in adaptive behavior was not to be judged mentally retarded.[33]

A comparison between the components of this definition and Doll's six criteria reveals several significant differences. The Association's terminology did not include the criterion that mental retardation be of constitutional (physical) origin; nor did it assume mental retardation to be essentially incurable.

The triparite division of mental retardation—moron, imbecile, and idiot—was abandoned in favor of a five-part structure based on the number of standard deviations from the mean. New terminology was introduced to avoid the negativism that had become associated with earlier classifications. The five levels and IQ ranges based on Stanford-Binet norms were:

Borderline (IQ 83–67)
Mild (IQ 66–50)
Moderate (IQ 49–33)
Severe (IQ 32–16)
Profound (IQ 16)

As noted, the new concept promulgated by the American Association on Mental Deficiency placed priority on adaptive behavior in determining mental retardation. In 1955, Sloan and Birch proposed a schema for each level of mental retardation, profound to mild, outlining proficiencies in terms of maturation and development, training and education, and social and vocational adequacy.[34]

The problem associated with adaptive behavior rested with measurement. While Doll's Vineland Social Maturity Scale was helpful in scaling developmental adaptive behaviors for youngsters, no similar device existed for older persons that took into consideration the multifarious aspects associated with successful living as an adult. Thus, intent was not matched by psychometric technology.

ASSESSMENT OF INTELLIGENCE

Testing problems associated with standardized intelligence tests during the preceding 2 decades did not diminish enthusiasm for this area of diagnosis or study. New verbal tests appeared and much time was devoted to inter- and intratest correlational studies. Subtests were analyzed in detail to increase precision and in the hopes of distinguishing between endogenous and exogenous youngsters.[35] Much effort was also devoted to developing short-form versions, for reasons of efficiency and economy.[36]

To offset criticism that intelligence tests were too verbal, newer instruments, such as the Wechsler-Bellevue Scale for Adults and the Wechsler Scale for Children, included both verbal and performance sections. Since the performance items still required verbal instructions, some professionals argued that they were not true tests of performance. "Pure" performance tests, such as the Leiter International Performance Scale, and Raven's Progressive Matrices, were developed. Though such tests were considered closer to desirable measures of performance, they were not used extensively with mentally retarded persons.[37]

Several "culture-free" tests—the Davis-Eells Games and the Cattell Culture Free Test—were devised but found to be non-discriminating, yielding results equal to or less favorable than those obtained by mentally retarded persons on standardized intelligence tests.[38] Gellerman and Hays introduced an interesting approach to the culture question.[39] Rather than reduce the number of cultural items, they loaded the test with them, which, in turn, did discriminate between different groups. Their technique, however, was not pursued.

In essence, and in spite of the creativity and talent that went into test design and evaluation, no substantial advances were made. That fine distinction between normality and mild mental retardation remained as elusive as ever.

Though persons experienced in developing tests and assessing their effectiveness became increasingly sensitive to their advantages and limitations, front-line practitioners did not. In 1960, Garrison expressed his concern that measures of mental ability had been "assigned more predictive value than they were designed to provide or than can be supported by research."[40] The IQ had assumed much more authority than it deserved. Consequently, many professionals responsible for children were confronted with the task of diminishing the "confusion, distortion, or oversimplification" assigned to the intelligence test.[41] "Stop 'IQ-ing' children," pleaded T. E. Newland, a noted educational psychologist.[42]

In addition to standardized tests of intelligence and culture-free tests, a new area of behavioral assessment received attention during the 1950s: projective techniques. During the 1940s and 1950s, Freudian and neo-Freudian theories and concepts held sway in many professional quarters, including those concerned with mentally retarded persons. Thus, such terms as "flat affect," "ego strength," "repressed feelings," and "oral fixation" appeared in the literature with increasing frequency.

Projective techniques, most of which were developed during this period, proved especially interesting vehicles for studying intellectual and personality characteristics of mentally retarded people. The most famous was the Rorschach test, consisting of 10 ink-blot cards and developed originally in Germany. Dr. Rorschach included 10 "morons" and "imbeciles" in his original sample and found their responses to be of "poor quality, stereotyped interest content, a predominance of human and animal detail, and an egocentric extratensive experience type."[43] From these data, Rorschach concluded that the test distinguished between normal and mentally retarded persons. Arbitman, as well as several European investigators, however, did not find that their mentally retarded subjects responded in a manner consistent with Rorschach's experiences.[44] Thus, as regards intelligence, no norms were ever agreed upon.

H. A. Murray's Thematic Apperception Test—a set of 20 pictures—was also used in an effort to explore the intellectual functionings of mentally retarded subjects. Again, the responses reflected a "naiveté of material and dearth of energy."[45] The World Test yielded similar results: mentally retarded children constructed "empty worlds."[46] Machover studied characteristics of human-figure drawings among mentally retarded persons and discovered a "sort of undifferentiated mass of stimulation with little discrimination of detail."[47]

Despite such results, these tests failed to offer a more refined means of assessing intelligence. Nevertheless, they unequivocally revealed that mentally retarded persons had "personalities" and feelings and were subject to emotional disorders. Unfortunately, changing theories of personality development, combined with difficulties in establishing validating evidence in support of projective techniques, led to the demise of this area of inquiry.

LEARNING RESEARCH

One of the most remarkable developments during this time involved the proliferation of research studies into nearly every behavioral aspect of mental retardation. In 1948, McPherson could locate only 14 studies of learning among mentally retarded persons. This soon changed; the 1950s were years of unparalleled research activity, much of which was supported through federal grants.[48]

In 1952, the Institute for Research on Exceptional Children was established at the University of Illinois, Urbana, under the direction of Samuel A. Kirk. This interagency, multiply funded institute aimed at both research and doctoral training in special education.[49] In 1954, the George Peabody College for Teachers received a grant of $122,880, plus supplemental support, for promising students to pursue graduate training in psychology and mental retardation. This major training/research center was directed by Nicholas Hobbs and Lloyd Dunn.[50] In 1953, the Association for Retarded Citizens laid the foundations for its research programs; in 1955, the American Association on Mental Deficiency received a 3-year federal grant of $232,000 to implement their Project on Technical Planning on Mental Retardation,

headed by Herschel N. Nisonger.[51] In 1958, the Southern Regional Education Board formed a panel on mental retardation, headed by William Hurder, to "direct attack on some of the training and research problems of the field."[52] In brief, the day of a few behavioral studies being generated by a few institutional research programs was over. Universities and various professional associations throughout the country began to examine the behavioral development of mentally retarded children, youth, and adults.

The range of learning studies was extensive, including rote memory, discrimination sets, motor proficiency, attending behavior, manual dexterity, concept formation, reaction time, transfer of training, tactual perception, learning sets, incentive levels, localization, probability, and word learning. Many of these studies were comparative in nature, attempting to ascertain whether or not gifted, average, and mentally retarded persons had different learning characteristics. None was found, at least consistently.

Achievement motivation, self-concept, and motivational support also were investigated. Many of these studies involved basic learning theories, such as classical conditioning, Hull's systematic behavior theory, Rotter's social learning theory, Lewin's field theory, Osgood's communication model, and Piaget's developmental theory. In addition, and in terms of long-term implications, operant conditioning and the effects of various reinforcement procedures were extensively explored.

The flurry of research activity during this period was, however, episodic, lacking what Stolurow termed a "second level of effort."[53] Many represented doctoral dissertations by young men and women who, following graduation, did not pursue their research interests. As summarized by Nicholas Hobbs in 1959, "Looking backward at behavioral research and mental retardation, there is little to be excited about. Looking forward, from this time of renewed interest in acquiring basic understanding of the process involved, there is ground for real optimism."[54]

PREVALENCE

The estimated number of mentally retarded persons continued to fluctuate, due primarily to the criteria used. For example, the Onondaga County (New York) Census in 1955 included under mental retardation "all children under 18 years of age and residents of Onondaga County on March 1, 1953, identified as definitely mentally retarded, or suspected of mental retardation on the basis of developmental history, poor academic performance, IQ score, or social adaptation when contrasted with their age peers."[55] Not surprisingly, this yielded a prevalence rate of mental retardation of 7.6 for youngsters 11 years of age to 8.2 for youngsters 14 years of age. In contrast, when more specific criteria were applied, such as group data with students with IQs less than 65, the prevalence rates dropped significantly. Thus, Weiner found that among the Hawaii school children, the prevalence of mental retardation varied between 2.3 and 3.1 percent.[56] Lemkau and associates in their survey of the Baltimore area found that 3.2 percent of school children and 1.2 percent of adults were mentally retarded.[57] By the end of the period under consideration, however, the general figures included in the President's Panel on Mental Retardation report had already been commonly adopted: approximately 3 percent of the population *at some time* during their life probably would be diagnosed as mentally retarded, of which 2.6 percent would fall within the mild range, 0.3 percent in the moderate range, and 0.1 percent in the severe and profound range.[58]

The Panel fully anticipated that their estimates would be subject to considerable fluctuation not only with age but with socioeconomic status. This was amply demonstrated by the study of Chicago's special education students conducted by Mullen and Nee in 1952.[59] Mildly mentally retarded or educable students tended to cluster in lower socioeconomic areas, while more severely retarded (and excluded) children tended to be distributed equitably throughout the city, with an actual higher prevalence among middle and upper class areas.

Similarly, 50 percent of the special education students in Detroit were from depressed economic areas.[60]

ETIOLOGY

During this 20-year period, medical science again made remarkable advances. New and increasingly complex etiological factors were associated with mental retardation.

In 1941, the Australian ophthalmologist Norman Gregg brought to the world's attention the devastating effects of viral infection upon the fetus, even when such infection might go unnoticed by the mother.[61] His study, which followed an epidemic of the German measles, not only revealed the multiple handicaps resulting from infection—congenital cataracts, heart disease, deafness, and mental retardation—but also dispelled the long-held notion that "the fetus was, with few exceptions such as syphilis relatively invulnerable to the usual infectious agents producing illness in the mother."[62]

Blood incompatibility also became associated with mental retardation. In 1940, Landsteiner and Wiener identified the Rh, or Rhesus factor; and by 1943, its role in stillbirths and mental retardation was clearly established.[63] In a few years, A and B iso-immunization were added to the list of incompatible mother-child blood groups.[64]

New syndromes, often of a biochemical nature, were described, including: Lowe's syndrome (oculocerebrorenal), 1952; Maple syrup urine disease (ketoaciduria) by Menkes, Hirsh, and Craig, 1954; Hartnip's disease (tryptophan abnormality) by Baron, Dent, Harris, and Hart, 1956; Prader-Willi syndrome (adiposohypogenitilism), 1956; familial leuco-dystrophy by Degar, 1957; argininosuccinic aciduria by Allen Cusworth, Dent, and Wilson, 1958; and cystathioninuria by Harris, 1959.[65] One no longer addressed biochemical disorders under the rubric of "glandular"; rather, one spoke of lipids, carbohydrates, amino acids, and polysaccharides.

Until the 1950s, the etiology of Down's syndrome remained a common topic of medical debate. Suspected causes remained numerous, including syphilis, parental alcoholism, abnormal smallness of the amniotic sac, and contraceptive chemical agents.[66] Even fluoride in water was momentarily suspect.[67]

Clements Benda, the highly respected physician and director of the Wallace Research Laboratory at Wrentham, Massachusetts, and instructor in neuropathology at Harvard, maintained that Down's syndrome was not hereditary in origin. His research, as well as that of others, into maternal age and previous medical histories, led him to hypothesize that Down's syndrome was a result of a maternal endocrinal imbalance. He held out the hope that some day one would be able to diagnose Mongolism in utero in time to effect corrective therapy.[68] Benda was by no means alone in his reasoning. Many believed that the frequent occurrence of Mongolism among older women precluded heredity. A few researchers, such as England's Lionel Penrose, however, contended that some hereditary dimension had to be involved.[69]

The etiology of Down's syndrome and other previously identified syndromes were to be explained in part during the 1950s by a series of major medical advances—advances which opened new vistas for scientific research. First, improved techniques for the examination of human chromosomes by Hsu and Pomerat in 1953 led to the discovery by Tijo and Levan in 1956 that the normal number of human somatic cells was 46 instead of 48 as previously supposed.[70] In 1959, Lejeune, Gautier, and Turpin reported that Down's syndrome youngsters had 47 chromosomes.[71] In the same year, Jacobs and Strong discovered that Klinefelter's syndrome involved an extra sex chromosome, and Ford and associates identified the XO chromosome complement in Turner's syndrome.[72]

Second, Nobel prize winners James Watson and Francis Crick of Cambridge University developed a model of the molecular structure and manner of replication of the deoxyribonucleic acid (DNA) in 1953.[73] Though DNA was first identified by Oswald Avery in 1944, the Watson-Crick model significantly advanced molecular genetics. In 1956,

Kornberg discovered the pathway leading to the biosynthesis of DNA. Marianne Grunberg-Manago and Severo Ochoa of New York University synthesized a number of simplified models of ribonucleic acid (RNA), the code-transporting mechanism. Thus began the exciting and challenging era of biochemical genetics.

Despite such discoveries, most mentally retarded persons remained etiologically undiagnosed and were frequently listed as "undifferentiated." As summarized by George Tarjan, one of the field's most outstanding physicians and contributors, in 1959, "A primary causative agent—be it a trauma, a virus, a gene, any other noxa, or a simple combination of these—has been identified in only a few types of mental deficiencies. In most forms we can neither ascertain all the etiological factors, nor quantify their importance."[74]

Medical advances were made not only in regard to identification of probable causes of mental retardation but also in prevention and treatment. Penicillin, which was discovered in 1929 but not available to the public until after World War II, was administered successfully to infants with congenital syphilis and other bacterial infections, reducing the risk of intellectual damage. In the early 1950s, streptomycin, a more potent antibiotic, was marketed. These two drugs, plus the many others to be developed, played a most significant role in increasing the life expectancy of severely, profoundly, and moderately retarded youngsters, who are particularly susceptible to respiratory infection.

Surgery was used to treat nonobstructive hydrocephalus and subdural hematomas.[75] In 1947, the Swedish surgeon Torkildsen reported on the first shunt procedure (ventriculocisternostomy) with hydrocephalic persons. New biochemical treatments for epilepsy were proving increasingly effective, and at long last, many persons so afflicted found relief and acceptance.

This news, however, was not received well by all in the medical community. Walter C. Alvarez, whose medical advice columns appeared regularly in many newspapers and popular periodicals throughout the country, was notably concerned; he wrote: "One must wonder how much longer the comparatively few persons able to earn more money than they need for their own or family support can support the millions unable to earn. Modern medicine is keeping alive those who will never 'pull their weight in the board.'"[76]

MENTAL RETARDATION, MENTAL ILLNESS, AND JUVENILE DELINQUENCY

As evidenced in the discussion concerning assessment, the growing tendency was to view mild mental retardation as an environmental problem. This does not mean, however, that mental retardation was considered solely a psychological phenomenon. The extremes of the argument were that at one end of the spectrum, mental deficiency remained an incurable condition of "physical or constitutional defect" and, at the other, "emotional disturbances, inferior cultural milieu, and some standard economics were mainly responsible for the existence of the moron." Representing the former position, Goldstein contended that 40 to 50 percent of mental retardation was basically hereditary; the remaining 50 to 60 percent was due to glandular imbalance, birth injury, or other physical causes, such as concussion or syphilis. Undesirable lower socioeconomic environments were responsible to the degree that they gave rise to greater exposure to disease and physical dangers, inadequate nutrition, and, in general, poor physical health and care.

In spite of such differences, however, few argued that mental retardation either precluded emotional disturbance or automatically predicted antisocial behavior. In this regard, environment, in terms of human experiences, was critical. Thus, even persons maintaining the organic-involvement position of Goldstein noted that "mental deficiency is manifested in a variety of personality patterns" and "mental deficiency does not necessarily result in delinquency. . . ."[77] Neuer, assuming a more psychiatrically oriented approach, wrote:

If the environment does not offer affection and compensating rewards, and cannot provide substituting and socially acceptable opportunities for sex energy outlets, then the child will revolt. Its impulses will rebel against the tribulating frustration and against the very persons who execute the law of the family, the social group and society.

The child will resort to fight or flight according to the constitutional setup of its endocrine, and autonomous nervous system. It might become destructive and antisocial, or it might withdraw from society altogether. A child filled with persistent hate or constant fear cannot learn. It becomes irresponsive to all stimulation necessary for the normal development of intelligence, which is an integration of the adaptive, language, and interpersonal behavior.[78]

That emotional disturbance could result in repressed functioning sufficient to simulate mental retardation was demonstrated by a number of studies. The most unique discovery in this area, however, was by Leo Kanner, director of the Children's Psychiatry Services at Johns Hopkins Hospital and a person with a longstanding interest in mental retardation.

In 1943, he reported a new category of mental illness among children which often simulated mental retardation: infantile autism. After having seen and studied 39 such children, he wrote:

Most of these children were brought primarily with the assumption that they were severely feebleminded or with the question of auditory impairment. Psychometric tests yielded indeed very low quotients, and often absent or inadequate responses to sounds gave good reason for the suspicion of deafness. But careful examination showed that the children's cognitive potentialities were only masked by the basic disorder. In all instances it could be established that hearing as such was not defective.

The common denominator in all these patients is a disability to relate themselves in the ordinary way to people and situations from the beginning of life. Their parents referred to them as always having been "self-sufficient," "like in a shell," "happiest when left alone," "acting as if people weren't there," "giving the impression of silent wisdom." The case histories indicate invariably the presence from the start of extreme autistic aloneness which, whenever possible, shuts out anything that comes to the child from the outside. Almost every mother recalled her astonishment at the child's failure to assume the usual anticipatory posture preparatory to being picked up. This kind of adjustment occurs universally at four months of age.

Nearly two-thirds of the children acquired the ability to speak, while the others remained mute. But language, even when present, did not, over a period of years, serve to convey meaning to others. Naming presented no difficulty; even long and unusual words were retained with remarkable facility. An excellent rote memory for poems, songs, lists of presidents, and the like made the parents at first think of the children proudly as child prodigies. . . .

The child's behavior is governed by an anxiously obsessive desire for the maintenance of sameness that nobody but the child himself may disrupt on rare occasions. Changes of routine, of furniture arrangement, of a pattern, of the order in which everyday acts are carried out can drive him to despair. . . .

Every one of the children has a good relation to objects; he is interested in them; he can play with them happily for hours. He can be fond of them, or get angry at them if, for instance, he cannot fit them into a certain space. . . .

The children's relation to people is altogether different. Every one of them upon entering the office immediately went after blocks, toys, or other objects without paying the least attention to the persons present. It would be wrong to say that they were not aware of the presence of persons. But the people, as long as they left the child alone, figured in about the same manner as did the desk, the bookshelf, or the filing cabinet. . . .

Even though most of these children were at one time or another looked upon as feebleminded, they are all unquestionably endowed with good cognitive potentialities.[79]

This discovery had a significant impact on both psychiatry and mental retardation. It documented the fact that very young children and infants could become emotionally disturbed and further highlighted the need for the very careful examination of youngsters suspected to be mentally retarded.

In the final analysis, it was generally agreed that mentally retarded persons had widely diverse personalities, could become emotionally disturbed, and that emotional disturbance among normal individuals could result in functional retardation, even of relatively severe degrees. In response, various forms of psychotherapy were attempted. Results of the few studies reported were quite mixed. Chase reported that 94 percent of his institutional group showed improved behavior following therapy; Fisher and Wolfson indicated that eight of their 12 aggressive females' behaviors were significantly modified following use of Slavon's Activity-Interview Therapy; and Snyder and Sechrest reported that directive therapy in a group setting helped improve routine housekeeping duties and the like.[80] In contrast, using nondirective techniques, Vail could only note that "those patients who attended the fewest number of sessions had shown the greatest improvement."[81] Similarly, Ringleheim and Polatsek found analytic, nondirective counseling to be of little value, as did Subotnik and Callahan using play therapy with eight mentally retarded boys.[82] This area was not pursued with a "second effort," much to Sarason's disappointment: "The hopeless attitude which is expressed today regarding the defective individual's amenability to psychotherapy seems also to be a result of diagnostic labels. Once an individual is diagnosed as mentally deficient, it is generally assumed that the psychotherapeutic procedures applicable to the normal person are not feasible with him. . . ." and he was "surprised that more systematic research has not been carried out and the results of available studies have not influenced current practices to any noticeable degree."[83] In spite of Sarason's concern, as indicated, psychotherapy was not aggressively pursued.

Perhaps one reason for the limited attention to psychotherapy involved the wave of enthusiasm for newly discovered chemical substances. Many had high hopes that advances in psychopharmacology would do much to improve both behavior and intellectual functioning. Chief among these early substances were the mild tranquilizers chlorpromazine and reserpine.

Early clinical reports indicated significant improvement in behavior. Wolfson, for example, reported that among his subjects, the tranquilizing substance (serpasil) had been sufficiently effective to reduce the need for camisoles by 64 percent and other restraints by 66 percent.[84] More scientific studies involving control groups did not support such findings, however. Intellectual functioning did not improve, nor was aggressive, hyperactive behavior or anxiety appreciably modified.[85] Similarly, the amphetamine sulfates were found to be ineffective.[86]

Side effects, however, even under low dosage conditions, were evident, ranging from drowsiness to seizures. Not surprisingly, Wardell and his colleagues concluded their research analysis with the warning, "These drugs have serious potentially fatal side effects and should be used only with caution and under close supervision."[87] Unfortunately, regardless of the research evidence and Wardell's warning, tranquilizers were used freely and often indiscriminately, especially in residential situations. Increased control of under-programmed residents all too often was the goal.

Though intended to improve intellectual functioning rather than modify behavior, glutamic acid (an amino acid derivative) received considerable attention during the late 1940s and early 1950s. In 1944, Zimmerman and Rosa conducted several experiments involving the administration of glutamic acid to white rats. Following treatment, the animals ran a maze faster with fewer errors.[88] Stimulated by these results and their implications for human learning, Albert and associates were first to study the drug's effect with mentally retarded persons 6 to 26 years of age with IQs ranging from 22 to 73. They recorded increases in IQs of 5 to 17 points.[89]

Within a matter of several years, Zimmerman and his co-workers reported a series of studies all showing significant gains in measured IQ.[90] In 1950, Quinn and Durling followed up with a study of 31 residents at the Wrentham State School (Massachusetts) and again reported favorable, though mixed, results, concluding that "large numbers of children in institutions above the Idiot level would be benefitted by the administration of moderate amounts of glutamic acid."[91]

To the public, a miracle drug—a sure cure for mental retardation—had been found. To the scientific community, these early results simply justified further research. As is so often the case, early enthusiasm was soon replaced with pessimism. Over the next several years, studies

by McCulloch, Loeb and Tuddenham, Kurland and Gilgash, and others diminished any hopes that a new "brain food" had been discovered.[92] Other therapies were tried, yielded mixed or poor results, and were soon abandoned, including electric shock, lobotomy, and various vitamin therapies.[93]

As regards juvenile delinquency, it was generally accepted that antisocial behavior was acquired. To illustrate, Town wrote: "Although these feeble-minded fresh from the protection of the schools have no innate flair for evil, the drift of the street life carries them to the courts."[94] Similarly, E. L. Johnstone stated: "It is obvious that no appreciable amount of delinquency or crime is due chiefly to mental deficiency as such. Nevertheless, the latter is often contributory."[95]

Incidence studies among the delinquent population continued to indicate that approximately 8 percent was mentally retarded.[96] In contrast to earlier studies, Hartman reported that recidivism was more common among the more intelligent than among the mentally retarded; however, mildly retarded persons tended to be disproportionately represented among first offenders.[97] Thus, attitudes toward and understanding of delinquency among mentally retarded persons remained approximately the same as in the 2 preceding decades.

SOCIAL CONTROL AND PREVENTION

By 1940, most states had abandoned the notions of restricted marriage, sterilization, and institutionalization as a primary means of controlling future generations of mentally retarded persons. The increasing number of mentally retarded persons identified, the proliferation of special programs, revised expectancies concerning the stability of IQ scores and heredity, and lack of public and legislative support rendered such efforts impracticable. There was also growing opposition to sterilization as a substitute for the adequate supervision of young adult mentally retarded men and women in the community.

There were, however, the exceptions,

which, regardless of intent, violated the basic human and constitutional rights of this group of citizens. Two such programs were the sterilization and parole system of F. O. Butler, medical director and superintendent of the Sonoma State Home, California, and the social control practices of South Dakota.

Butler, who firmly believed that sterilization was essential to successful community adjustment, consistently practiced what he preached. From 1919, a year after he became superintendent, through 1943, 4,310 residents—2,445 females and 1,865 males—were sterilized. These included males with IQs up to 122 and females with IQs up to 114.[98] Sterilization was, in fact, "a standard procedure for patients about to be paroled who are still in their reproductive period."[99] They included boys and girls 11 years of age. Special concern was expressed about women so that they would not have to "go through the stress of pregnancy."[100] Butler's control of the situation was absolute:

> Paroled girls are permitted to date, and to carry on courtships, with the approval and under the supervision of the social worker. Disreputable suitors are discouraged whenever possible.
>
> It is well known to the patients that no marriage is legal without the Medical Superintendent's approval; therefore, the suitors are usually presented for inspection. When the prospective groom is interviewed, the meaning of sterilization is explained to him. Factors which determine whether or not a marriage is to be approved include the physical, marital, and occupational status of the prospective groom, and whether his interest in the girl is sincere or for purposes of exploitation.[101]

No state attacked the problem of social control with more fervor than South Dakota under the direction of F. V. Willhite, physician and superintendent of the State School and Home for the Feeble-Minded. During the 1930s, South Dakota passed a Control Law that provided for the "identification, registration, adjudication, prevention of marriage and supervision in the community, of all the feeble-minded in the state. . . ."[102] Implementation of this legislation required a state-level agency to administer the program, a legal determination of

mental retardation, and county supervision. Legal determination in this case involved the judgment of a lay board that relied primarily on intelligence test data.

Once determined as mentally retarded, the individual's name, together with a relatively complete picture of his life history, was recorded on a central registry. Registered names, in turn, were sent to the State Clerk(s) of Courts who were responsible for issuing marriage licenses. If an individual's name were on the list, licensure was denied. If the person crossed a state line to get married, "corrective treatment" was in order: institutionalization and/or sterilization.[103]

Implementation of this program encountered considerable resistance, including the "failure of teachers to recognize and report retarded individuals; opposition to the program by school superintendents, teachers, and school boards, who fear unfavorable reaction on the part of parents and public, and finally, a lack of understanding on the part of officials, educators, legislators and the general public of the magnitude of mental deficiency."[104]

Adjudication came no easier. Many of the adjudicators were hesitant to label the mildly affected as mentally retarded and, as Willhite complained, there was also a "collection of minor objections such as politics, religion, sympathy for the relatives, and sometimes personal relationships."[105] After 8 years of effort, Willhite reported that 30 percent of the state's mentally retarded population had been registered, and every effort was being made to control their right to "marry and reproduce their kind, and in so doing, create an ever-increasing number of defectives for the next generation to care for."[106]

Private organizations, such as Birthright, Inc., which started in 1943, maintained the posture that sterilization was appropriate and that "procreation was not a right to be unrestrictively exercised but that it was a responsibility to be assumed by those capable of producing normal offspring and of giving them necessary care."[107] Not only was Mrs. Olden, spokesperson for the organization, interested in the welfare of the child, she was also concerned about the relatively new social security program: "Since Social Security has been made an obligation of government, met by granting huge sums and subsidies, it is essential that we control the quality of life which is to be made secure."[108] "Racial deterioration" was duly noted.

Olden was not alone in her concern for the future of the intelligence of the national population. As late as 1945, Whitney again raised the question of immigration, inasmuch as the percentage of mentally retarded persons committed to institutions had increased substantially—from 46.7 per 100,000 population in 1923 to 77.9 in 1941:

> First, we have admitted to this country and to our institutions a proportionately large number of mental defectives from abroad. Secondly, we have admitted into this country a relatively large number of mentally defective producing stock. Without casting reflections on racial or national immigration but simply to show what available statistics seem to imply this study indicates that relatively few mental defectives or individuals of mentally defective stock are Scandinavian, French, Spanish, Welsh, Scotch, German, or English.
>
> On the other hand a relatively large number come from the following groups: Negro, Italian, Hebrew, Irish, Polish, Russian, and S. E. Europeans.
>
> This study is too incomplete to offer us an answer to the problem of increased mental deficiency yet the trends indicated seem to be of importance. A thorough screening by the immigration authorities would eliminate, not only the mental defectives, but those of mental defective or psychopathic stock who will be clamoring for admission now that World War II is at an end.[109]

The impact of the Jewish extermination combined with the outstanding performance of various racial groups in the country's service during World War II put an end to such discussions. Concerns undoubtedly lingered, but they were no longer a matter of public utterance.

SOCIAL CARE AND TREATMENT

Though institutions continued to be built and an increasing number of mentally retarded persons were admitted, the major focus was on the development of community services. Persons participating in the 1940 White House Conference on Children in a Democracy noted critical failures in programming for mentally retarded persons, reemphasizing community services: "Successive studies have brought out the fact that earlier emphasis upon identifying and labelling mental deficiency, upon setting up rigid classifications (especially those of numerical intelligence quotients), upon isolating and institutionalizing persons so classified, was being pushed beyond limits that were scientifically sound or socially useful . . . appropriate education and suitable employment in the community are frequently the best treatment for persons with such limitations."[110]

COMMUNITY SERVICES

Many communities, especially in metropolitan areas and populous states, were responding. A wide range of diagnostic clinics were established: speech, hearing, orthopedic, child guidance, and mental health.[111] Such programs, supported by public and/or private funds, appeared in universities, hospitals, schools, welfare agencies, and institutions.[112] Home care programs also expanded under welfare, educational, parental, and institutional auspices.[113] Sheltered workshops, such as Goodwill Industries, began to offer special training and work opportunities for some mentally retarded adults.[114] The YMCA/YWCA, neighborhood houses, and other generic recreation programs welcomed a few adult mentally retarded persons into their midst.[115]

The expansion of community services was evident in many respects. By 1960, there were 173 sheltered workshops in 35 states and the District of Columbia; there were 124 day-care centers; there were 64 residential camps in 29 states and 89 day camps in 28 states; and 83 special mental retardation clinics had been established in 41 states and the District of Columbia.[116]

In spite of such advances, however, many services for mentally retarded persons were unavailable. For example, child guidance clinics, which were established shortly after World War I, were intended to serve "those children obviously maladjusted because of constitutional defects (feeblemindedness or organic disease resulting in personality problems) and normal children whose personalities had become twisted and warped through their efforts to adjust to an abnormal environment."[117] By the 1940s, however, they served almost exclusively normal youngsters with personal difficulties. G. S. Stevenson, medical director of the National Association of Mental Health, explained in 1952, "Behavior problems of normal children were mistakenly believed to be more intriguing, and as a result have come to preoccupy us to the exclusion of the mental defective. . . ."[118]

Initial surveys of community services discovered that mentally retarded persons represented a large population with highly diversified needs that were not being met. Herschel Nisonger, in one of the first attempts at comprehensively evaluating a state's program, found many inadequacies, including lack of trained personnel, gaps in programs, duplication of services, lack of coordination, and a severe absence of public understanding.[119]

A major change during this period involved the concept of the "responsible community." Prior to World War II, local communities were primarily, if not often exclusively, responsible for meeting the needs of mentally retarded and other disadvantaged people. Following World War II, much authority shifted to the state, and the federal government also became increasingly involved. Most state institutions, for example, came under state-level authority, as did special education.

As noted, the federal government began to show greater interest in mentally retarded persons, often spurred to action by the Association for Retarded Citizens. Highlights of its activities included:

1943—the Industrial Rehabilitation Act of 1920 was amended to create the Office of Vocational Rehabilitation, intended to serve both mentally and physically disabled persons.

1946—the National Mental Health Act established the National Institute of Mental Health, which devoted funds to both training and research in mental retardation.

1950—the National Institute of Neurological and Communicative Disorders and Strokes was created, which sponsored a major perinatal research project.

1954—the Cooperative Research and Education Act was passed, which for several years provided research funds for mental retardation.

1956—the National Institute of Mental Health earmarked $250,000 for mental retardation research.

1957—the Department of Health, Education, and Welfare made federal funds available to promote and support specialized diagnostic clinics for mentally retarded persons.

1957—the Social Security Act of 1935 was amended to include a disability clause to provide retirement income to survivors in case of death or disability, which also authorized payments to "adult disabled children."

1958—the first categorical piece of legislation specifically devoted to mental retardation was passed: P.L. 85-926 authorized federal funds to universities for training of mental retardation specialists.

By today's standards, such federal contributions were relatively modest. Yet, they established the precedence and framework for the unparalleled explosion of federal activity during the 1970s.

The Association for Retarded Citizens of the United States

Beginning in the early 1930s, a few parent groups began to form throughout the country. The first such group was the Cuyahoga County (Ohio) Council for the Retarded Child in 1933. This council operated and financed the first parent-supported community class for the "gravely" retarded.[120] In 1936, the Washington Association for Retarded Children organized, followed in a few years by the Welfare League for Retarded Children, New York. By 1950, 88 such local groups with a total membership of 19,300 persons had been established in 19 states.[121]

According to Woodhull Hay, first secretary of the Association for Retarded Citizens, there were seven reasons underlying parent efforts to form local groups:

1. Evidence that institutions were limited in what they could do for children;
2. Increased awareness that regular public school programs were unsuited for such children;
3. The need to disseminate knowledge and information concerning mental retardation;
4. The need to challenge the validity of the finality in the words, "Nothing can be done for your child";
5. The desire of parents to learn what more could be done for these children and to pursue projects in their behalf;
6. The need to strengthen the growing conviction that the responsibility is social, i.e., money should be provided for building a fuller life for the mentally handicapped; and
7. The realization that it was not enough spiritually just to care for one's own child.[122]

To this listing, one can readily add that parents were markedly concerned about poor institutional programs, the exclusion of mentally retarded children from public school programs, and professional mismanagement.

Parents of mentally retarded youngsters had an opportunity to gather together and discuss their mutual problems at the annual meetings of the American Association on Mental Deficiency in 1947, 1949, and 1950. During the last one, the parents seriously considered the development of a national parent association and scheduled their first convention for Minneapolis in September, 1950. Ninety persons registered at that convention, of which 42 were delegates from 23 organizations in the states of California, Connecticut, Illinois, Massachusetts, Michigan, Minnesota, Missouri, New Jersey, New York, Ohio, Texas, Vermont, Washington, and Wisconsin.[123] Subsequently, "Parents and Friends of Mentally Retarded Children" was created with the overall goal of promoting "the general welfare of the mentally retarded of all ages everywhere: at home, in the community, in institutions, and in public, private, and religious groups."[124] Their first major publication, a national newspaper

entitled "Children Limited" served as a most adequate means for communicating with the various groups and interested parents and professionals throughout the country. Known for years as the National Association for Retarded Citizens, in 1980 it assumed the title "Association for Retarded Citizens of the United States."

The formative years of the Association were not always easy. According to Edith Stern, local interest and splinter groups made it difficult to develop a sense of national oneness.[125] In spite of initial difficulties, the Association expanded rapidly, reaching a membership of over 250,000 by 1970, and was highly effective in promoting a wide range of programs, from prevention to comprehensive community services. In 1967, the Youth ARC was formed. It also grew rapidly; within 10 years, over 25,000 young volunteers between the ages of 13 and 25 were active participants.

In addition to providing support and guidance among themselves and in promoting legislation and other activities to stimulate the development of appropriate programming, many local groups directly sponsored some sort of project, frequently to aid the trainable child living at home. In 1955, the Association conducted a survey and found that an estimated 1,015 community services directly benefiting mentally retarded persons and their families were operated by ARC's 412 member units. In addition, 405 services were available, which were stimulated by local units. Services most frequently operated by local units included classes for trainable children (221), classes for educable children (124), nursery school classes (94), recreation or social group (86), counseling and guidance programs for parents (79), parent education classes or courses (78), summer day camps (55), sheltered workshops (49), and special clinics (33).[126]

A number of parent groups were formed to meet the needs of institutionalized persons. In the early days, as indicated by Margaret Richards, the purpose of such organizations "was to bring something of ourselves to [the institution] and to promote the welfare of patients there by giving of our time, interest, and money."[127] After a few years' experience plus a growing confidence in their organization, locally and nationally, parents began to state their expectations in straightforward terms: better physical environment, more appropriate medical and dental care, treatment, therapy and training for the multiply handicapped child, and a greater concern about the happiness and life-style of the residents.[128] A new and powerful voice was being heard.

Next to obtaining services for their youngsters, the most overwhelming problem confronting parents was "professional neglect, rejection, and mishandling."[129] This was an age-old problem. Throughout the 1940s and early 1950s, professional literature and conduct reflected judgments and opinions that could only interfere with parent-professional relationships:

> The occurrence of mental retardation brings forth deep feelings of inadequacy.[130]
>
> Parents blame themselves for the condition and are intensely anxious.[131]
>
> Parents are confused, despairing, defensive, and angry—a "death wish . . . appears somewhere in the majority of interviews." Therefore, parents "resolve their emotional problems by excessive concern, over-protection, and over-indulgence."[132]
>
> Of 11 families, only one reflected an accepting attitude; three were rejecting; and seven were ambivalent, which was evident in "either overprotective, neglecting or overly strict handling of the child."[133]

Years later, Phil Roos, parent, psychologist, and former superintendent of an institution, recorded his early parental experiences and noted that being a knowledgeable professional did not diminish "the parent as patient" relationship:

> I had suddenly been demoted from the role of a professional to that of "the parent as patient"; the assumption by some professionals that parents of a retarded child are emotionally maladjusted and are prime candidates for counseling, psychotherapy, or tranquilizers. My attempts to point out the many indications of developmental delays and neurological disturbances were categorically dismissed as manifestations of my "emotional problems." I was witnessing another captivating professional reaction—the "deaf ear syndrome"; the attitude on the part of some professionals that parents are complete ignoramuses so that any conclusion they reach regarding their own child is categorically ignored. Later I found that suggestions I would make regarding my own child would be totally dismissed by some professionals, while these same suggestions made as a professional about other children would be cherished by my colleagues as professional pearls of wisdom.[134]

In brief, in the eyes of many professionals, parents were unable to cope with their grief, never matured beyond that point, and subsequently could not manage their youngsters appropriately. With such impressions, it is little wonder that professionals were neither secure nor comfortable in dealing with parents. All too often, the advice was confusing: "Send him to an institution." "Keep him at home." "Wait, he'll outgrow it." To compound the problem, professionals rarely had anything but advice to offer; programs were still few and far between.

James Gallagher, then assistant professor at the Institute for Research on Exceptional Children and a parent of a youngster suffering from severe bronchial asthma, was one of the few voices in the professional community who spoke out against the prevailing attitudes: "Most parents have genuine affection for their children despite some negative reservations that may often be revealed under stress. The parents can be, and should be, valuable assistants in the training program of many kinds of exceptional children. A professional person who can understand and accept the reasons for the attitudes of parents, and also understands his or her own emotional reactions to the child and the parents, will be able to provide a richer and more effective training program for the exceptional child."[135]

By the latter half of the 1950s, the professional community had become sensitive to the fact that parental adjustment and acceptance involved a series of stages. Rosen, for example, studied 36 mothers and found their progression was similar to Dewey's "Steps in Thinking": 1) awareness, 2) recognition, 3) seeking for the cause, 4) seeking for the solution, and 5) acceptance.[136] Other counselors, such as Howard Kelman, began to report about the many parents who had not experienced excessive difficulties with their retarded children: "Despite the fact that many of these children were severely retarded, they had been excellently trained and managed by their parents."[137]

Special Education

Of all services developed for mentally retarded persons during this period, none received greater attention than public education. It was in this arena that greatest gains were evident and the foundations for still greater change were laid.

Educational Goals and Programs for the Mildly Mentally Retarded   Goals for the educable mentally retarded were stated more definitively than in previous years. Underlying all goals, however, was the clear expectancy that such students were to be educated to participate fully and responsibly in society as individuals, as marriage partners, as parents, and as hard-working, law-abiding, taxpaying employees in the open labor market. As stated during the Midcentury White House Conference on Children and Youth, "The handicapped, when cared for and educated, represent, next to unemployed women, the largest reservoir of unused manpower upon which to draw."[138] Earlier successes with special education and the performance of mentally retarded persons during World War II fostered a high level of confidence and expectancy.

Educational goals for the mildly retarded, cited from the most popular text of the period, *Educating the Retarded,* by Professors Samuel Kirk and Orville Johnson included:

1. They should be educated to get along with their fellow men; i.e., they should develop social competency through numerous social experiences.
2. They should learn to participate in work for the purpose of earning their own living; i.e., they should develop occupational competence through efficient vocational guidance and training as a part of their school experience.
3. They should develop emotional security and

independence in the school and in the home through a good mental hygiene program.
4. They should develop habits of health and sanitation through a good program of health education.
5. They should learn the minimum essentials of the tool subjects, even though their academic limits are third to fifth grade.
6. They should learn to occupy themselves in wholesome leisure time activities through an educational program that teaches them to enjoy recreational and leisure time activities.
7. They should learn to become adequate members of a family and a home through an educational program that emphasizes home membership as a function of the curriculum.
8. They should learn to become adequate members of a community through a school program that emphasizes community participation.[139]

Programs or curricula intended to meet these goals stressed occupational adequacy, social competence, and personal adequacy. The relative priority of these goals again varied with educational philosophy. The conservative school of thought continued to emphasize academics and a "watered-down" regular curriculum; the liberal or "progressive" school stressed social competency. Most school systems, however, attempted to provide a balanced program of academic, social, and manual skills, frequently on the 50:50 time ratio discussed previously. General approaches used were similar to those developed during the 1930s: core topics, integrated units of instruction, practical applicants of acquired academic skills to daily living situations, and frequent outings in the community. Special educators familiar with John Dewey's educational principles naturally stressed meaningful experiences and activities. Variety abounded; as Birch observed, "A distinctly public school approach to mental deficiency cannot be claimed."[140]

Though much of what has just been presented seems quite similar to the educational discussion for the preceding 2 decades, new ideas were proposed and frequently implemented. The most significant of these was the greater division of special classes according to level and age. Thus, Kirk and Johnson discussed educational goals, curricula, and methodology according to five programmatic levels: pre-school, primary, intermediate, secondary, and post-school.[141]

Of these five levels, most attention was devoted to secondary programming. Among the many educational leaders in this area were Richard Hungerford, supervisor of special classes for the Detroit Public School System, and Elizabeth Kelly, supervisor of the Department of Special Education for the Newark, New Jersey, Public Schools.

According to Hungerford, "by 1935, it was apparent that the mentally retarded were losing out in the race for jobs [and] the true mentally defective was in danger of becoming a permanent welfare load—a condition expensive and socially dangerous for society as a whole and demoralizing for the defective himself."[142] The urgency for developing stronger secondary programs to ensure the occupational adequacy of mentally retarded persons was quite evident.

The primary goal of the secondary program was "life adjustment," or sociooccupational adequacy: "to develop the individual's capabilities and assist him in discovering his place in the economic society upon completion of his formal schooling."[143] According to Hungerford and Rosenzweig, occupational education represented the major change in special education during this period, a change which required:

1. Re-training of teachers to enable them to give guidance.
2. Preparation of job analyses for lower-level jobs.
3. Preparation of specialized teaching materials.
4. Giving intensified area training that is thoroughly adapted to the needs and abilities of the retarded.
5. Giving specialized job placement.
6. Giving continuous follow-up services.
7. Helping the public to understand and utilize the potentialities of the groups in varying degrees of employability.
8. Coordination of effort with parallel agencies.[144]

Beyond common consensus as to the need for secondary programs, there was little agreement as to who would be eligible and how the program should be designed and implemented. Some school systems devised a dual secondary program: classes in the regular high schools for the "superior" mentally retarded group (IQ range 60 or 70 and above), and special secondary schools or classes in the elementary schools for those with IQs less than 60 or 70.[145] Kelly envisioned a tri-level secondary program:

Level 1. For the most promising mentally retarded who have attained minimum academic, mechanical, and social standards, Senior Pre-Vocational School for Boys and Senior Pre-Vocational School for Girls.

Level 2. For the most promising mentally retarded boys and girls who have above average academic and mechanical ability and adequate social adjustment, Junior High School placement. After a two-year trial of fulfilling promise, these boys and girls may continue on to Senior High School. Of course, in both Junior and Senior High Schools, a special program is arranged for them, and a teacher versed in the philosophy of the subnormal will serve as their home teacher and their guide.

Level 3. For the least promising mentally retarded with achievement below the minimum standard, Junior Pre-Vocational School for Boys and Junior Pre-Vocational School for Girls.[146]

The Newark school system included the regular high school, special schools and, in some instances, classes in the elementary schools. Boston, on the other hand, relied on special centers for their adolescents. Detroit, in contrast, retained most of its adolescent groups at the intermediate or junior high school level.[147]

As regards vocational programming, there again were differences in opinion and practice. Some educators highlighted the sociopersonal aspects of human relationships and how to get along well in any occupational setting.[148] Others stressed detailed knowledge of and skills to specific jobs, such as becoming a filling station attendant. Most schools, however, sought a balance by augmenting occupational training with a basic curriculum core that included such areas as citizenship and interpersonal relationships.[149]

One of the benefits of the secondary program was the realization of Elizabeth Kelly's long-held position that the interests of adolescent mentally retarded individuals were more consistent with normal adolescents than with younger children. Subsequently, many secondary schools put forth serious efforts to integrate mentally retarded students into a variety of nonacademic high school activities, such as choir, band, and sports.

The federal government was also interested in the vocational training of mentally retarded persons. As indicated previously, the Industrial Rehabilitation Act of 1920 was amended to include mentally retarded persons in 1943, but little was done until 1950, when Salvadore Di Michael produced his monograph, *The Vocational Rehabilitation of the Mentally Retarded*.[150] Though the federal program lacked sufficient funds to rehabilitate more than a few hundred mentally retarded persons over the next several years, the book awakened a number of people to the urgency of the problem.

Secondary education, however, was not an exclusive interest; many special educators were equally concerned with the younger pupil. As noted by Kirk and Johnson in 1951, four options were available: ''(1) retain them in the first or second grades for two or three years since they had not learned to read; (2) exclude them from school; (3) institutionalize them if the parents and the institutions accept that procedure; or (4) admit them to special classes for mentally handicapped children when such an organization exists in a school system.''[151] The most common of these practices was the first, letting the younger child remain in the regular class setting until he had demonstrated repetitive failure and an inability to keep reasonable pace with his peer group. As will be recalled, 2 or 3 years' educational retardation was often one of the criteria used when considering special class placement. Not surprisingly, special educators objected to this practice since it meant that a mentally retarded youngster would be needlessly exposed to constant failure, which, in turn, would be deleterious to his personal development and sense of security and self-worth. Again, Kirk was among the foremost leaders in the development of programs for the preschool child, along with Ruth Melcher, Irene Stevens, and Gladys

Rhodes.[152] The curriculum developed for these youngsters centered around six areas:

1. Opportunities for self-help throughout the day in eating, dressing, and washing.
2. Opportunities to develop imagination and express ideas and feelings through free and constructive use of materials.
3. Opportunities to develop skill in using their bodies effectively.
4. Opportunities for social development through sharing ideas and materials as well as learning how to live together in a democratic manner.
5. Opportunities for self-expression in group situations.
6. Continual enlargement of actual school environment is provided for through the addition of pets, excursions about the neighborhood, and assisting in the kitchen.[153]

In addition to numerous innovations, many more mildly retarded students were served. National enrollment figures of 98,416 in 1940 rose to 109,000 in 1953 and to 361,000 in 1963.[154] Despite such gains, as late as 1963, only 20 percent of mildly retarded students were receiving special attention.[155]

One thing, however, remained constant: significantly more mildly mentally retarded boys than girls continued to be enrolled in special education, a fact which led Spalding and Kvaraceus to allege ''sexual discrimination'' in 1944. They claimed the situation ''may mean that girls are deprived of the opportunities presented in these high cost adjustment classes and that these classes are used for punitive purposes with questionable criteria as to placement.''[156]

Educational Goals and Programs for the Trainable Mentally Retarded A major event in the history of mental retardation occurred during the 1950s, when public schools accepted a clear educational responsibility for trainable mentally retarded students. This action signaled a greatly expanded societal role since it took into account that these individuals could not be expected to become self-supporting or to function as reasonably ''normal'' adults in the affairs of home, community, and country. The prevailing attitude until the 1950s was that the purpose of public schools was to prepare ''citizens to participate in civic matters and thus return something tangible or intangible to the state."[157] Now, however, trainable children were considered to "have the right to be trained to the maximum of their ability. . . ."[158] One of the strongest position statements put forth by the Association for Retarded Citizens during this decade was its "Education Bill of Rights for the Retarded Child" adopted on October 18, 1953. This bill proclaimed, in part: "Every child, including every retarded child, has the right to a program of education and training suited to his particular needs and carried forward in the environment most favorable for him, whether that be the community public school, the state residential school or his own home."[159]

The notion of training moderately retarded youngsters was not new; nor, as we have seen, were they being excluded from early special educational opportunities. Many moderately retarded youngsters are of Down's syndrome. It is highly probable, as discussed previously, that Seguin was at least aware of the Down's syndrome child, and Down himself, in 1866, noted, "the improvement which training effects in them is greatly in excess of what would be predicted if one did not know the characteristics of the type."[160]

For educational purposes, the definition of "trainable child" drafted by Wirtz and Guenther in 1957 was commonly cited:

A trainable individual is described as, that individual who, because of retarded mental development, would not profit from public school special classes for educable mentally handicapped, but who possesses potentialities for learning a) self-care, b) social adjustment in the home and neighborhood, and c) economic usefulness in the home, in a sheltered environment, or in the community under supervision.[161]

Most states passed legislation reflecting that concept, noting, however, that the child must be able to benefit from such experiences and be able to participate in the educational environment. Maryland's early statute illustrates such restrictions:

Whenever seven or more children, who are classified as severely mentally retarded on the basis of an individual psychological examination (approx-

imately 55 and below) and clinical findings, can be brought together, a special center may be organized

1. if such children are able to participate in group activities with profit to themselves and without injury to the group;
2. if such children are able to learn to care for their personal routines independently;
3. if such children are sufficiently controlled emotionally to respond to a teacher-pupil class relationship;
4. if such children have trainable motor skills;
5. if the school system has facilities adequate for their educational needs.[162]

As regards intelligence quotients, most professionals adhered to the recommendations of Goldstein that youngsters with IQs between 35 and 50 would do fairly well in the classroom, those with IQs between 25 and 35 would need supplemental support, and those with IQs approximately 25 or less would not benefit from formal school programming.[163] The commonly accepted prevalence of school-age trainable children in the United States was between 0.3 percent and 0.4 percent.[164]

Reasons why schools began to provide for trainable children are many. Moderately retarded people were living longer; there was a strong sense of the nuclear family, and many parents did not want to send their child to an institution, which often had a deplorable reputation; the position of the Association for Retarded Citizens; a broadening of public school responsibilities; the growing right of taxpayers to demand services for their children; and the redirection of educational policy-making from local school boards to state agencies. While each of these played their part, as one educator observed, "organized groups of militant parents of mentally retarded children have exerted much pressure on school systems and legislators to develop public day school programs for the severely retarded."[165] In 1951, California, Minnesota, and Wisconsin passed legislation providing for public school acceptance of the trainable youngsters. Six years later, 25 states recognized classes for trainable children; 12 by new legislation, 7 by administrative regulation, and 6 by administrative interpretation.[166]

Major objectives for "trainable" classes

were centered in physical health, self-help skills, stimulation of imagination and creative expression, social development, motor development, and intellectual development.[167] Extensive study of actual practices and curricular content conducted by the George Peabody College for Teachers at the end of the decade indicated that primary attention was being devoted to language development; motor development; sensory training; music, health, safety, and social studies; arithmetic; self-help, occupational education, and socialization; arts and crafts; dramatizations; science concepts; and practical arts. Language development, motor development, sensory training, and social skills were considered most important.[168]

By 1960, programs for trainable children were a way of life in most public school systems—even though early studies indicated that the youngsters' progress was no greater than that of those who remained at home.[169] Enrollment soared from approximately 5,000 students in 1953 to 30,000 in 1963.[170]

The introduction of trainable children into the school system soon raised the question of adult programming. Several studies conducted at that time revealed that upon completion of school, many trainable youngsters were institutionalized. Lorenz, for example, reported that 47 percent of trainable children enrolled in special classes for 5 years or more were institutionalized immediately upon leaving school.[171] There was a growing sentiment that this was a poor conclusion to special education. Thus, the need for developing post-school programs, especially sheltered workshops, received increasing attention.

Alfred Strauss and the Brain-Injured Child Some of the greatest, longest-standing contributions to special education for both mentally retarded and learning disabled children, especially in the area of methodology, were made during this period by Alfred Strauss (1897–1957). Born in Karlsruhe, Germany, Strauss received his medical degree from the University of Heidelberg in 1922. After further study in psychiatry, neurology, and special education, plus experience in private practice, he joined the staff of the university's Psychi-

Alfred Strauss.

atric and Neurological Clinic and, in addition, served as a child welfare consultant to the city of Heidelberg. With the rise of Hitler, Strauss left Germany in 1933, accepting a position as visiting professor with the University of Barcelona, Spain, where he helped establish several child guidance clinics. In 1937, he immigrated to the United States where he served as research psychiatrist and, later, as director of child care at the Wayne County Training School. In 1946, he resigned because of poor health but in 1947 opened his famous Cove School, in Racine, Wisconsin.

As indicated previously, both Doll and Strauss had been alert to some of the peculiar characteristics of brain-injured mentally retarded persons as early as the 1930s. Neither, however, was the first to identify this phenomenon. In 1877, Ireland observed that organically involved youngsters were more of a problem and less amenable to treatment and training than were other mentally retarded children.[172]

Strauss assiduously pursued this area of research, ultimately producing both a neurological theory to explain the unusual characteristics of brain-injured children and, in collaboration with others, devising various techniques appropriate to their instruction. In his most famous publication, *Psychopathology of the Brain-Injured Child,* coauthored with Laura Lehtinen and published in 1947, he offered the following definition:

> A brain-injured child is a child who before, during, or after birth has received an injury to or suffered an infection of the brain. As a result of such organic impairment, defects of the neuromotor system may be present or absent; however, such a child may show disturbances in perception, thinking, and emotional behavior, either separately or in combination. These disturbances prevent or impede a normal learning process.[173]

Neurologically, Strauss proposed that if the new portion of the brain, primarily the cerebral cortex, received even minimal damage during early development, more primitive behaviorisms would result as a consequence of the increased influence of the old brain. Though this relatively simple neurological theory failed to gain much attention, his discoveries concerning behavior and instruction did.

Perceptual disorders, according to Strauss, included the inability to distinguish between foreground and background, which, in turn, resulted in a high degree of distractibility and/or the overconcentration on very small details. Perseveration, the prolonged repetition of a response or behaviorism, was associated with perceptual disorders. As regards thinking disorders, brain-injured children frequently tended to classify objects according to color, imagination, minor details, and in more groups than normal youngsters. Their difficulty in realizing the scope of a problem quite often produced uncommon answers or forgetfulness. Behavioral disorders were reflected in excessive daydreaming, emotional instability, lack of inhibitions, impulsiveness, irritability, talkativeness, impaired attention, hyperactivity, aimlessness, confusion, and occasionally, hatefulness.

Strauss's educational approaches concentrated on "controlling the external, overstimulating environment and in educating the child to exercise voluntary control."[174] One of his major educational modifications was intended to decrease disinhibition, hyperactivity, and distractibility, which represented "exaggerated responsiveness to stimuli."[175] To this end, he eliminated all distracting stimuli from the classroom, covered the windows, and forbade teachers to wear jewelry. Carrels were also used. Various techniques were introduced to enhance attention and increase learning, including short assignments, outlining foreground objects, and requiring motor as well as verbal responses. In many instances, he adapted devices developed originally by Montessori and Seguin. These represent but a small sample of the various techniques developed by Strauss and his colleagues that are commonly used today in almost any learning setting where youngsters are having difficulty.

Special vs. Regular Class Placement
Though special classes were rapidly expanding throughout the country as the educational needs of mentally retarded persons became increasingly recognized, the debate over special versus regular class programming did not subside. On the contrary, it was a frequent issue, indicating considerable professional concern and uncertainty. No one felt entirely comfortable with segregating mentally retarded students, but realistically meeting total educational needs in the regular classroom seemed impossible.

Kirk summarized the situation in 1953 by calling attention to three prevailing points of view:

1. Special classes are necessary since the curriculum varies in kind or quality.
2. The regular class should be used since the curriculum does not vary significantly and since "a good teacher in any class adapts instruction to the level of learning of her children, that is all that is necessary for a special class program."
3. Both regular and special class arrangements should be used: "This point of view alleges that the curriculum of the special class is largely the regular curriculum similar to that for the normal child, but that

part of the curriculum and the teaching procedure is special, since the special aspects deal with methods and procedures adapted to the specific learning disabilities of the child which do not necessarily exist in the normal child."[176]

Others, who favored special classes did so for a variety of reasons, such as:

Schools are still too often institutions which require that the child must fit the curriculum rather than that the curriculum must fit the child.[177]

Obviously, pupils whose interest span is short cannot easily be taught successfully when intermingled with pupils whose interest span is four to six times longer. The grouping of subnormal pupils together facilitates adapting the instruction to their ability to concentrate as well as to their capacity for learning. Teachers of subnormal pupils have to be made aware of the psychological differences in learning of bright and dull pupils and must know how to adapt the educational program to fit the needs of the pupils.[178]

Segregation is attacked as being undemocratic because it labels pupils. It must be remembered, however, that if a subnormal pupil is left in a grade of 30 to 35 dull, average, and superior pupils, he will very likely be neglected a large part of the time because the teacher has neither the time nor the training to deal with him adequately. He will fail because he cannot possibly keep up with the others and then he will be labeled a failure. This is even more undemocratic than the worst segregation.[179]

The basic characteristic of mental deficiency is limitation—in adaptive power, in associative power, in learning speed; and this limitation is so great that it extends to the learning and practicing of the simple operations the average child picks up casually. [Therefore] no retardate is capable of getting enough from ordinary schooling to enable him to meet satisfactorily the demands of living. This is the distinguishing feature of mental deficiency. The mentally deficient require a different developmental program.[180]

Finally, Kirk, again, contended there were five positive attributes to special education: 1) modified or special academic materials, 2) clinical teaching procedures based on technical diagnosis, 3) systematic approaches, 4) individualized instruction, and 5) intensification of parent education.[181]

Those who advocated retaining mentally retarded students in the regular class did so for equally compelling reasons, often sociopersonal in nature:

Under plans of segregation pupils suffer from a feeling of inadequacy which comes from being singled out for special treatment. They are denied the opportunity of mingling with others of their age group and deprived of social experience that would be a stimulus to further development. The feeling of security gained from a sense of belonging is not achieved. . . . Education must concern itself more with what goes on in the mind of a child rather than with what goes on in a classroom. Modern educational philosophy assumes the right of every child to be educated according to his ability and social needs. It would seem right, therefore, that, with our knowledge of modern educational methods, a more scientific treatment than segregation be afforded all children within the school.[182]

Allan Chapman, psychiatrist and director of the Child Study Department of Minneapolis, outlined four "special-class hazards to mental health":

1. Stigmatization "that arises from the acknowledged and verified fact of intellectual weakness in the child"

2. The "practice of selecting children for retarded classes only after they have had long repeated failures both in daily work and at the time of promotion"

3. The "distinguishing marks that are applied only to children in retarded classes," such as no grade classification and different kinds of report cards

4. The "traumatic way in which children are introduced into the class," often implying that "the child is not worthy of a place with normal children"[183]

In 1953, Tenny wrote a paper unique for the day, treating mentally retarded persons as a minority group, in which he concluded that the "segregated nature of our special education programs have prevented the non-handicapped majority from intimate social contact with the handicapped in school and probably also discourages out-of-school contacts. Understanding and acceptance come about most readily through individual acquaintance; therefore segregation should be eliminated wherever possible."[184]

While the argument was not settled and special classes continued to develop, there was a concerted effort, at least among the field's leaders, to question special education and its practices. Should children still be failing in the regular classroom? Can we ever establish a basis for a child's education and social adjustment and prepare a program for him before, rather than after, he becomes a problem? Are academic skills still to be the yardstick of the total education and social growth of a child?[185]

All contended that greater caution needed to be exercised before placing any child in a special room. The special class was not intended to be a catch-all for troublesome children, and, as F. E. Lord complained in 1956, "Our special classes are far more heterogeneous than we would have hoped for," and they "still attract marginal children who don't belong there."[186]

Placement in the special class was no longer a simple matter of IQ and years of educational lag. More sensitive questions were posed:

1. Is this pupil's lack of educational aptitude one of special disability or general mental retardation?
2. Has this child been given every opportunity to adjust to the regular program? Has he been given as much help as was possible without sacrificing the educational opportunities of the other pupils?
3. To what extent are his home conditions contributing to his educational or mental retardation? Can these be remedied?
4. Has this child's past performance been in keeping with his abilities? If not, what factors in his environment were overlooked? Has the child's best interest been sacrificed to the desire to avoid conflict between the home and the school?
5. Will special room placement foster his general all-around social development?
6. Will placement at this time be more advantageous than at some time in the future?
7. How many more years will this child remain in school?
8. Have this child's interests been directed toward activities that are within the range of his limited ability?
9. Has an attempt been made to explain to the child, in terms that he is able to understand and appreciate, the desirability of special room placement?[187]

Much of the research of the day tended to support the advantages of special classes. First, the classic sociometric study reported by Johnson and Kirk in 1958 revealed that 69 percent of the retarded students were isolated or rejected by their normal peers in the regular classroom setting.[188] Second, most postschool studies continued to confirm the effectiveness of special classes. In 1953, Charles followed up the formerly special class students studied by Baller in 1935 and found a slightly higher success rate than previously reported: 83 percent were employable, 47.6 percent had held the same job for 3 to 20 years, and 78 percent had been married with a 21 percent divorce rate.[189] Kennedy surveyed 256 mildly retarded men and women, most of whom had been enrolled in a special class, and concluded, "Our study reveals that morons are socially adequate in that they are economically independent and self-supporting; and that they are not serious threateners of the safety of society, but are rather frequent breakers of conventional codes of behavior."[190] Abel reported that 55 percent of her adult female sample was capable of successful employment and that failure reflected on sociopersonal factors rather than innate ability.[191] Dinger found 83.2 percent of formal students to be employed, housewives, or in school. Of those working, 42 percent made more than their former teachers.[192] Porter and Milazzo also reported positive results.[193] In 1957, Saenger even reported a high rate of success in the community among the more severely affected.[194]

On the other hand, in 1960, Peterson and Smith found their mentally retarded subjects did not fare well following school:

1. Many mentally retarded subjects did not find jobs immediately upon leaving school.
2. Only slightly over half of the retarded subjects were currently employed.
3. The retarded subjects changed jobs frequently.
4. The retarded were not familiar with the services rendered by the Iowa Vocational Rehabilitation Division or employment agencies.
5. Most of the retarded subjects lived in substandard homes which were located in below average areas.

6. The retarded did not actively utilize recreational facilities of the community.
7. Many of the retarded subjects had numerous encounters with the law in which many serious offenses were committed.
8. Many of the retarded subjects appeared to have abused their credit.[195]

Differences in success were becoming evident. While Peterson and Smith held that appropriate specialized secondary educational programs would assist in ameliorating some of the problems encountered, a comparison of their results with those of Dinger and of Porter and Milazzo indicated that special class students in metropolitan cities were not as successful as were those in smaller communities.

Research studies of this nature would continue to be conducted, subject to a wide range of interpretation. None of these studies, however, took into consideration many of the variables that by current standards would be considered critical, and none was formulated to provide an answer to the most critical question of all: "Who benefits from special class placement as compared with those who benefit from regular class placement?"

The most controversial educational study of the day involved Bernadine Schmidt's doctoral dissertation, and rarely has a professional community descended upon a researcher with more fury or harshness. Briefly, the study involved 3 years of special training followed by 5 years of post-school evaluations. Subjects included 322 mentally retarded adolescents (254 experimental subjects, 68 control) in five special centers in Chicago. The programmatic goals included developing desirable personal behavior, improving the fundamental academic skills, developing the manipulative arch, improving work and study habits, learning occupational or related vocational information, and pre-employment experiences. The experimental approach was characterized by group planning, group experiences, in-school reproduction of situational experiences, and the use of creative and manipulative arts. All students participating in the study were reported to have IQs less than 70.

In 1946, Schmidt concluded on the basis of her data, that "59.7% of the total group were classifiable as low or high normal; only 7.2% were still feebleminded. . . . By the end of the study, the average adjustment of the total Experimental group was equal to that of the average adult, both according to standardized measures and their academic, vocational, and social activities."[196] The results received a great deal of attention in the public media—implying that mental retardation through appropriate educational programming was curable. This led to a number of critiques by such persons as Samuel Kirk, Florence Goodenough, and Lewis Terman.[197] Every aspect of her study was scrupulously examined, including initial testing, her role, accuracy of the data, the validity or appropriateness of tests utilized, and the adequacy of statistical treatments. In some way, each element was either questionable or suspect. Sarason concluded that her research represented "a good example of lack of theoretical and methodological rigor."[198] Of importance to Sarason was that Schmidt and most others failed to give due consideration to "social class background and the conditions of learning which they imply. Unless the remedial or training program takes account of social class differences, one cannot expect much from it."[199] While all aspects of the study mentioned may, in fact, have been questionable, her findings that the social, personal, and intellectual performance of culturally deprived youngsters could be improved through participative, simulation techniques were virtually ignored. Today, her study probably would be assessed more conservatively.

Teacher Training One of the greatest problems confronting school systems interested in initiating special education programs was recruiting qualified teachers, and more states were requiring certification. By 1953, 35 states and the District of Columbia had certification requirements that ranged from 12 hours in New York to 40 hours in Kansas. The average for the states was 22 semester hours or the equivalent of 1 full year.[200] The number of universities providing more than one or two courses did not keep pace with demand. In 1948, for example, Martens could draft only a tentative list of 23 teacher colleges that offered a sequence of courses in mental retardation.[201] By 1963, 25,000 teachers were in the field, regardless of qualifications, and this represented less than 30 percent of the estimated need. Even at that time, only 500 teachers were being graduated a year.[202] The manpower shortage in this area would remain until federal support programs became available in the mid-1950s and early 1960s.

RESIDENTIAL SERVICES

The role of institutions became increasingly suspect throughout this period, and the seeds of the 1970s, in terms of deinstitutionalization were firmly planted in increasingly fertile soil. The commonly held philosophical position at that time was that institutions should serve only severely and profoundly mentally retarded and antisocial or delinquent persons.[203] Even under these circumstances, however, only those children who could not be "properly cared for at home should be placed in an institution."[204] Many administrators, such as Engberg and Stevens, continued to urge not only extended support to communities but also direct assistance in promoting public knowledge and in coordinating community resources, at least for former residents.[205]

In practice, however, the clause "cannot be properly cared for at home" was more broadly interpreted by persons in the community than was often intended by institutional administrators, and institutional populations continued to increase exponentially until approximately 1970: 101,164 in 1940, 127,425 in 1950, 163,730 in 1960, and 186,743 in 1970.[206] Seventy-five percent of the institutions in the United States were built after 1950.[207]

Institutions were plagued by many problems during this period, starting with World War II. National priorities demanded men, materials, and financial resources, often stripping the residential facility of its limited manpower and leaving few dollars for expansion or improvement in spite of ever-increasing demands for service.

New admissions to institutions tended to be younger and more severely handicapped, a consequence of many factors.[208] There was a significant increase in the number of families in the United States from 1930 to 1940. While the population increased by only 7.2 percent, the number of families increased by 16 percent, with a corresponding increase in the number of births.[209] Advances in medical technology increased the survival rate of the distressed newly born, including moderately and more severely affected mentally retarded infants; and new medications were extending life by years for the more severely affected. During World War II, the absence of fathers often left management of physically affected youngsters too difficult for mothers; and, in many instances, mothers entered the labor market.[210] Then came the postwar baby boom.

The number of mentally retarded persons in institutions between 1934 and 1943 rose by 40 percent while the total population increased only 20 percent.[211] Admission rates in some states were astonishingly high. In Illinois, for example, the two institutions—Dixon and Lincoln—admitted an average of 92 persons a month during 1945 and 1946.[212] By 1948, the number of children in institutions for mentally retarded persons under 5 years of age had tripled.[213]

Much of this increased admission activity also can be attributed to the professional community. For the newly born mentally retarded infant and young child, all too many physicians advised, "It will be better if you never take the child home. You may become attached to it." Or, more directly, "Put him away."[214] Physicians knowledgeable about mental retardation tried to discourage this practice among their colleagues, pointing out that "early institutional placement of the mentally retarded child is too often ill-considered and unnecessary, and frequently has serious emotional consequences for the child and the family."[215] Their counsel, however, was heard by few and heeded by fewer.

Others in the professional community, however, were often equally unwise in urging institutionalization. York noted, "Commitments to institutions for the mentally defective come largely from urban centers. This undoubtedly is due to more intensive action on the part of social service agencies."[216] Social workers saw many advantages in institutions: "A good foster home has much to recommend it, but institutions can offer the following advantages; (a) a controlled or semi-controlled environment; (b) the experience of group living and interaction with other youngsters in the same setting; (c) the opportunity for diluted emotional relationships with the cottage parent; (d) greater permissiveness for acting-out or withdrawing in a group setting."[217] York might well have added the following to his comment (which was not intended to be derogatory) that special educators were often the catalysts in institutionalization. According to noted special educator and administrator Anna Engel:

> Every year the schools and social agencies register boys and girls for whom a prognosis for satisfactory adjustment is unfavorable. Many of the parents have been on relief year after year; some of them have been registered in the clinics as feeble-minded. Some are graduates of our special classes. Often the siblings in the family have come into conflict with the law. Some of them may already be in penal institutions. Investigation may disclose deplorable living conditions, undesirable standards and morals, and unsatisfactory supervision and control. Experience in other such cases has shown that there is little chance for boys and girls to develop into worthwhile men and women under such adverse conditions. Postponing institutionalization not only increases the difficulty and delays the ultimate adjustment, but it puts an unnecessary burden on society. Educators and social workers know the nature of the feeble-minded child. They know him to be weak in judgment and reasoning. They know that he is easily led and that he has poor emotional control. And when in addition, he is so emotionally unstable as to present serious school, family and neighborhood misconduct, there should be no delay in considering placement. The earlier that this is recognized, the better it will be for society and for the individual as well.[218]

Davies observed:

> While most of the children will be recommended for special training, doubtless many cases will be found either at the time of the first appearance before the school authorities, or after a trial in special classes, for whom institutional care is indicated. It is only through such study and selection on the part of the public school that mental defectives with marked anti-social proclivities can be institutionalized before troubles occur. Aside from the burdensome low-grade cases there are two principal conditions for the institutional care of mental defectives: (1) Continued serious delinquency, (2) undesirable home influences. As is all too well known, the former of these is all too frequently but a reflection of the latter.[219]

Waiting lists consequently grew and the quality of institutional life deteriorated, often to deplorable and inhuman conditions.* Overcrowding, by 30 to 40 percent, in facilities whose officially rated bed capacity rarely provided sufficient space in the first place was the rule rather than the exception.[222]

Staffing patterns, regardless of level of retardation, were totally inconsistent with the needs of the residents, and recruiting adequate numbers of qualified staff was nearly impossible. "Institutions," wrote Bertha Luckey, president of the American Association on Mental Deficiency in 1953, "are handicapped because of the lack of administrative leaders, doctors, teachers, psychologists, social workers, and a competent staff in all areas."[223] Working conditions, inadequate salaries, and isolated locations made recruitment and retention of professionals almost impossible.

Philosophy and Programs

Rows of beds, end to end, in colorless, drab wards typified most institutions. Nonambulatory, severely and profoundly retarded residents were housed in facilities originally intended for an ambulatory, mildly retarded population. Often they were not dressed beyond diapers (at best, in some facilities) and simply lay in bed all day. Adaptive equipment was a novelty.

Most direct care continued to be provided by more capable residents. As Doll readily ac-

---

*In 1940, New Jersey served 3,759 mentally retarded people in institutions; 1,032 awaited admission.[220] Over the next decade, the situation had not improved. Of 2,000 people seeking admission in California between 1952 and 1954, 1,082 were admitted and 781 were placed on a waiting list.[221]

knowledged, "We are all familiar with those relatively competent morons and even imbeciles on whom we rely for so much of our routine necessities. . . ."[224]

Treatment of the difficult-to-manage resident or those who could not be attended often relied on medication, camisoles, straitjackets, lock-ups, physical punishment, or tying to the bed.[225] Rare was the facility with staff whose training was adequate to provide required programming, even when the interest was evident. The problem of adequate programming for the aggressive, dangerous resident was not resolved. Some institutions added prison-type, maximum-security cell blocks to their physical plant.

In 1957, Kramer and his associates, based on an extensive examination of resident data for the Pacific State Hospital, expressed concern over the "high rate of mortality within the first few months following admission [among] severely retarded children with such diagnosis as Mongolism. . . ."[226] They also wondered if many adults potentially capable of community placement had not been simply "forgotten."[227]

In 1940, Ernest N. Roselle, superintendent of the Southbury Training School in Connecticut, identified the institution's role to provide custody, care, treatment, and training. The latter three aspects were considered educational in nature. In order to satisfy such educational obligations, he outlined a 12-point program:

1. Cottage or home training
2. General maintenance activities, many of which required training, e.g., general housekeeping, clothing repair, and care of the grounds
3. Farming and gardening
4. Production shops
5. Construction, repair, and utility operation
6. Recreation
7. Music
8. Physical education
9. Prekindergarten and kindergarten
10. Academic classes

11. Manual arts
12. Prevocational and vocational programming[228]

Training activities ranged from self-help skills to vocational placement. No institution even approached the realization of such a program as it affected the majority of residents. In fact, for many residents, especially the severely affected, programming often consisted of television and tranquilizers.

While programming in general was inadequate, pockets of gains were noted. First, many institutions during the 1950s began to offer some form of program for trainable youngsters, setting forth these objectives:

1. To teach the child to care for his daily physical needs;
2. To teach the child to live with other children;
3. To develop the child's capacities to the fullest so that he may more adequately carry on activities in his limited environment; and
4. To teach the child to play and be happy.[229]

Though there was no indication that such goals were intended to prepare people for community living, the widespread inclusion of trainable youngsters in the institution's educational program did constitute a major step forward.

A few institutions, such as the Training School at Vineland, New Jersey, continued experimental programs with the more severely affected, with promising results.[230] Similarly, the extended preacademic programs at Wayne County Training School were innovative and proved effective with "destructive, hyperactive, noisy, and irritable" boys.[231] Fried employed relaxation therapy and again reported quite favorable results.[232] The Pacific State Hospital initiated an adult education program that included extended academic instruction, prevocational experiences, and personal-social training.[233]

Some institutions, especially those guided by persons with an understanding of Freudian principles, began to look more positively at the psychosexual development of residents. This, in turn, resulted in a greater emphasis on coeducational activities and greater social-recreational interaction with the community.[234]

Occupational therapy became increasingly visible during this period. Intended for a broader-based group of residents than were enrolled in school, it supplied "work in crafts, needlework, weaving and beauty culture for girls, habit training, elementary crafts, painting and drawing, weaving, printing, metal work and carpentry for boys."[235] Since such programs usually were self-supporting, many residents spent years weaving rugs, hocking towels, or making ashtrays. Rarely were tasks changed, and rarely did residents profit materially from their productivity.

"Unlike occupational therapy, industrial therapy benefits not only the individual but the institution as well," wrote Beard in 1953.[236] In theory, industrial therapy was intended to provide a wide range of occupational experiences in preparation for discharge. In reality, residents continued to work long hours with little or no pay at their same job, year after year. In many facilities, an old practice had simply acquired a new label.

Professionals in disciplines other than education, occupational therapy, and vocational therapy began to write about their respective roles and activities, few of which, at that time, would substantially affect programming. Nurses were primarily concerned with "good housekeeping and maintenance"; psychologists with testing; social workers with collating social history data, counseling parents, and providing community placement follow-up.[237] Most served under departmentalized administrative structures, were cloistered in the administrative center, and rarely went near a resident building. While the interdisciplinary approach was introduced in some facilities, the practice frequently involved little else than "competition for patient time."[238] The unit system, transdisciplinary programming, as well as implementation of the developmental model were 20 years away. Nevertheless, the decision-making process gradually began to involve an ever-expanding circle of professionals.

Progressive administrators not only sought increased programming and staffing, but many also restated the desirability of relatively small facilities located in or at least near a community. Walker, for example, advocated not only community location but flexibility in construction and, like Roselle and so many others before him, would again champion an "atmosphere simulating a home life and one which fosters an atmosphere of hope rather than of institutionalization and/or despair." Institutions should not, he wrote, be conceived of in terms of "initial cheapness."[239] That, however, remained the political rule, and a number of obsolete, remote military installations, VA hospitals, and TB sanitoria became institutions for mentally retarded people following World War II.

Institutional Reform

By the 1950s, the need for institutional reform was righteously proclaimed from both within and without the institution. Administrators, practitioners, and parents were uniformly decrying current conditions and, in many instances, requesting change, especially in the quality of life and physical environment. Roselle, a leading reformer among administrators, once again set forth the notion of the resident's right to live in a more normal environment:

> We must, in advocating and projecting these institutions, insist again and again that children have certain special and inalienable rights, because they are children, to live in homes and communities which approach as nearly as possible the desirable standards of normal homes and communities. Society does not possess the moral right to confine these children during this formative period of their lives to institutional plants in conditions so foreign to the normal needs and interests of childhood as to stunt and warp permanently their growth and development and thereby handicap them still further in taking their rightful place in society. There is no excuse, in our opinion, and this includes the item of cost, for perpetuating in new institutional plants for children or in major additions to old ones the traditional forbidding, unhomelike, large, more or less congregate type of unit which has earned for itself in the aggregate the term "institutional" with its unfortunate implications.[240]

Though Roselle believed that an institution should be laid out like "a community or subdivision of a small city," his reform measures, in actuality, still fell far short of today's expectations. For example, he advocated two-story "cottages" to accommodate 24 to 50 mildly mentally retarded persons and single-story units for up to 90 severely and profoundly mentally retarded residents. Such proposals, however, were markedly ahead of their time, when most groups, including the Association for Retarded Citizens, were pleading for institutions to accommodate no more than 1,500 residents.[241]

The deepening crisis in institutional programming brought about by these influences raised the urgent need to establish standards not only to guide the development and assessment of residential programs but also to offer the administrator some objective basis upon which to approach the legislature for sorely needed positions and funds. As early as 1942, the American Association on Mental Deficiency began to explore this area, primarily in terms of staffing levels. In 1944, the Association's Committee on Standards and Policy issued its recommended staffing patterns based on two sizes of institutions: 1,200 beds and 2,000 beds.[242] The Committee's report represented a compromise, since little agreement could be reached concerning the ideal institutional size. Opinions about the proper number of beds continued to vary: from 500 to 2,880 beds. The Committee, however, did agree in preferring "detached houses to a large congregate building. Recommendations for size range from 50 children in a dormitory to 72. At present, only two members are so bold as to recommend the relatively small number of 50 patients to the dormitory."[243] In 1949, the committee revised the staffing standards to provide for additional personnel. The aide-resident ratio, for example, increased from 1:10 to 1:8.9.

In 1953, the American Association on Mental Deficiency presented a new set of "Standards for Public Training Schools" that approached the subject from a set of programmatic and administrative principles rather than numerically defined staffing patterns. In addition to some very fundamental principles of service to be rendered by the

institution as a whole, each of its respective service areas were similarly defined, ranging from medical services to the farm. Staffing was covered by the broad requirement of "an adequate number of efficient personnel, competent in their respective duties and conforming to proper physical, mental, educational, and character standards for the duties they are to perform, and under competent supervision."[244]

Blain soon called for the accreditation of mental retardation facilities, and likewise, as recorded by the Association's Committee on Administration in 1954, "Parents and particularly those organized in associations are very deeply concerned in this matter [i.e., rating of institutions]. They desire that something be done as soon as practical and thoroughly."[245]

In 1959, the Association launched a major effort to undertake a study of standards and published an extensive set of them in 1964, including reference to management services, admission and release, institutional programming, personnel, training and staff development, physical plant, and records, reporting, and research. After several trial years with these standards, the need for formal accreditation became increasingly obvious, and by 1971, the entire effort evolved into the Accreditation Council for Facilities for the Mentally Retarded, a multi-agency supported program.[246] Its standards were in turn later adopted almost in their entirety by the federal government when it established regulations governing federal funding of institutional programs.

Deinstitutionalization

While deinstitutionalization as a national goal was not realized until the 1970s, as a concept it was highly visible by 1950. Though no one advocated closing all institutions, their primary purpose was "to rehabilitate as many as possible for community placement," including the delinquent.[247]

As early as 1940, Hackbusch from Pennsylvania had stated, "I do not believe that the techniques for working with mental defectives are so esoteric that they cannot be part of the community educational system or of the community agency."[248] Approximately 10 years later, Hilding Bengs, mental health commissioner of Pennsylvania, was among the first to place institutions in the perspective of a single community service:

This alternative which seems obvious is the strengthening of community relationships to the point that institutional service may be generally considered only complementary to local services and only an episode in the total design of living. For an institution at best is a poor substitute for the private home and its free community. It must perforce sacrifice individualization in the best interests of the group. In public facilities a various degree of overcrowding is traditional. It can only be a different world where basic security may be assured at all times but where those intangibles of personal relationships are not sustained. Therefore, if an institution is a substitute and not a complement, let it be so for only those who in the last analysis do not need and cannot profit from a home and community. Also let the institution be a temporary substitute in default of the natural home. In this way the institution becomes a part of the community and is directly related to society and not apart from it.[249]

Again, there was a call for "due process of law," this time by Hackbusch in 1950, especially as it related to admission practices:

Commitment to an institution for any reason whatsoever should not be made without due process of law, or an orderly legal procedure. This holds true for the mental defective as well as for any other person. Placement in an institution for mental defectives is a serious matter and should be made only after measures have been taken to prevent unnecessary and unjust institutionalization. Legal commitment procedures should be designed to protect the civil rights of the individual and to give him the security and protection of state guardianship. These procedures should, as far as possible, be uniform throughout the nation and should provide the safeguards of careful diagnosis by thorough study, not merely an I.Q., and certification by qualified persons in the field of medicine and psychology.[250]

To implement a massive program of deinstitutionalization at that time, however, was impossible. First, most institutions lacked the ability to provide the environment and training essential to prepare people for community placement. As a frustrated Roselle observed,

The institutions in which the members of this association [AAMD] are most deeply interested care for and train the deviates in our social structure. These deviates constitute by common consent the most difficult, if not the most challenging, sector of our population to care for, train, and salvage so far as possible for useful, purposeful living. Society demands that we shall meet this responsibility well. We are expected to prepare and to return as many of our charges as possible to their homes and communities for effective living and to do so as expeditiously and as thoroughly as possible, and it is increasingly costly if we do not do so. With this responsibility placed squarely upon us, we have a right to demand of society that it shall supply us with adequate plants to house adequate programs to meet this responsibility. To expect us to meet the needs of this group of our population, having such difficult needs in care and training, with mediocre plants and programs is indeed inviting worse than mediocre results. And such is, unfortunately, the results we and our public so often see.[251]

Economic circumstances had changed with the advent of World War II, and having foster children or adults in the home was no longer financially attractive or desirable. As Weingold observed in 1957, the foster family program that had been developed in New York state had diminished rather substantially by 1941: of 47 original homes for men, only 26 were still operational; of 46 homes for women, only 22 were operational. Only 7 percent of those on institutional registers were in community placement programs.[252]

Facilities interested in promoting deinstitutionalization and family care were confronted by a number of problems, including a changing resident population, from mildly mentally retarded to more severely multiply handicapped persons. To illustrate, between 1945 and 1960, the percentage of mildly retarded persons admitted to residential facilities decreased from 43.7 to 29.2.

In 1953, when the Pacific Colony State Hospital initiated its community care program, placement personnel met with two problems: community resistance and the fact that potential foster parents only wanted to serve younger children and those with no obvious developmental anomalies or physical handicapping conditions. Nor were foster parents willing to accept such a responsibility for a nominal fee.[253]

Parents also objected for a variety of reasons:

1. I like Pacific Colony, the patient is happy there, he has friends on the ward, he needs medical supervision which only the institution can give.
2. Prior to commitment he was in private or County boarding homes and these were highly unsatisfactory.
3. The outside world is cruel to the handicapped, whereas the institution understands and is kind.
4. The proposed home is operated by a family of unacceptable racial or religious grouping.
5. The patient might escape from the home and be killed.
6. We waited a long time to advance up the waiting list, and now just as we have fully accepted the child's being there for life, you raise the whole question all over again.[254]

Another factor affecting placements was a change in farming practices and the shift of population from rural to urban centers. Many institutions preferred to place residents in rural areas for a variety of reasons, ranging from protection (i.e., to avoid "criticism" and "ridicule") to "isolation" and "the large gardens furnished a liberal supply of fresh vegetables at nominal costs."[255] An increasingly mechanized society involving fewer farmers made it more difficult to make such placements. Despite the growing number of studies that continued to affirm quite clearly that mentally retarded persons could live in the community, residents who were not basically self-sustaining were not likely to be discharged.[256]

Taking all things into consideration—overcrowding, inadequate programming, unresponsive legislators, unsatisfactory staff, high turnover rates, bad press, inadequate community services, and increasing parental pressure—it is little wonder that one superintendent noted that his job required "the hide of a rhinoceros, the constitution of an ox, a natural liking of people, and a willingness to sacrifice one's life and his family to his calling"; he died of a bleeding ulcer.

All in all, the 1940s and 1950s were a very mixed period. Once again, mentally retarded men and women demonstrated both a willingness and an ability to serve their country. Many died, many were maimed. Few knowledgeable persons still held the old prejudices associated with heredity and crime; yet, an increasingly complex urban society often found little time for mentally retarded persons, especially the adults. Special education classes for the mildly mentally retarded grew in number, and, perhaps most important of all, trainable children were accepted into the public schools. Institutions also grew in number and in size, often bursting at the seams. Unable to recruit and retain adequate personnel, they frequently failed to provide the very rudiments of humane care. While institutional reform and deinstitutionalization were in the air, alternative living environments were less available. Nevertheless, these two decades laid the foundation for the 1960s and the 1970s. When occasional support was available, many mentally retarded persons were able to remain in the community. The federal government expanded its interest in this area, and the Supreme Court began to examine the question of civil rights. Special education not only opened its doors to moderately mentally retarded people but also began to examine some of its traditional approaches. Institutional programs were severely criticized and challenged.

Chapter

9

EPILOGUE

H ISTORIES OF THIS NATURE rarely include recent events whose full impact cannot be appreciated. Yet, one would be remiss in ignoring the many remarkable advances realized over the past 20 years.

HIGHLIGHTS OF THE 1960s AND 1970s

These years were among the nation's most tumultuous. The 1960s witnessed some of the greatest scientific achievements in the history of this country, especially in the area of aerospace technology. The glory of such accomplishments, however, was far overshadowed by the Vietnam War and the assassinations of John F. Kennedy, Robert Kennedy, and Martin Luther King, Jr. The 1970s were politically troubled years. Throughout both decades, however, two forceful trends were evident, both of which were of tremendous importance to mentally retarded citizens: expanded recognition of human and civil rights and substantially increased federal funding of human services and programs.

During these two decades, mentally retarded persons came out of the shadows and into the light. Heredity and serious physical insult were considered to account for only 10 to 15 percent of mental retardation; most mental retardation

was attributed to a broad array of cultural experiences—or an absence thereof. Increased sensitivity was apparent, and greater opportunity became the watchword of community action.

On January 20, 1961, John F. Kennedy became the 35th president of the United States. One of his many humanitarian interests, due perhaps to his experience as a brother of a mentally retarded sister, was to improve the quality of life for both mentally retarded and mentally ill persons.* In order to meet the needs of the former, he appointed a special President's Panel on Mental Retardation on October 11, 1961, prefacing their charge with the following:

> Both wisdom and humanity dictate a deep interest in the physically handicapped, the mentally ill, and the mentally retarded. Yet, although we have made considerable progress in the treatment of physical handicaps, although we have attacked on a broad front the problems of mental illness, although we have made great strides in the battle against disease, we as a nation have too long postponed an intensive search for solutions to the problems of the mentally retarded. That failure should be corrected.[1]

The 26-member panel, chaired by Leonard Mayo, and its six task forces included the best minds from nearly every field that had an influence upon mental retardation. The Panel's

---

*John F. Kennedy may not have been the only president with a mentally retarded sister. Page Smith, in *The Shaping of America*, noted that Thomas Jefferson's sister, Elizabeth, "was apparently mentally retarded."[2]

247

final report of 1962 presented 112 recommendations under eight headings:

Research in the causes of retardation and in methods of care, rehabilitation, and learning.

Preventive health measures including (a) a greatly strengthened program of maternal and infant care directed first at the centers of population where prematurity and rate of "damaged" children are high; (b) protection against such known hazards to pregnancy as radiation and harmful drugs; and (c) extended diagnostic and screening services.

Strengthened educational programs generally, and extensive and enriched programs of special education in public and private schools closely coordinated with vocational guidance, vocational rehabilitation, and specific training preparation for employment; education for the adult mentally retarded, and workshops geared to their needs.

More comprehensive and improved clinical and social services.

Improved methods and facilities for care, with emphasis on the home and the development of a wide range of local and community facilities.

A new legal, as well as social, concept of the retarded, including protection of their civil rights; life guardianship provisions when needed; an enlightened attitude on the part of the law and the courts; and clarification of the theory of responsibility in criminal acts.

Helping overcome the serious problems of manpower as they affect the field of science and every type of service, through extended support, and increased opportunities for students to observe and learn the nature of mental retardation.

Programs of education and information to increase public awareness of the problem of mental retardation.[3]

In addition to strongly emphasizing research and prevention, the report recommended that services constitute a comprehensive, community-centered continuum with a fixed point of referral; and that with federal assistance, the states and local communities bear the principal responsibility for financing and improving facilities for mentally retarded persons.

COMMUNITY SERVICES

Of significance to community programming, the President's Panel developed an array of direct services for mentally retarded persons, taking into consideration a wide range of special needs as well as life stages. The plan called upon nearly every agency, private and public, generic and specialized, to render services to mentally retarded persons and their families (see Table 2).

While in many respects the Panel's recommendations were illuminating and provided a stepping stone for the future, close examination reveals that most of the ideas and services suggested were identical to those proposed by Walter Fernald, Charles Bernstein, and others decades earlier.

Following review of the Panel's report and recommendations, President Kennedy addressed the Congress of the United States on February 5, 1963, clearly outlining the challenge:

We as a Nation have long neglected the mentally ill and the mentally retarded. This neglect must end, if our Nation is to live up to its own standards of compassion and dignity and achieve the maximum use of its manpower.

This tradition of neglect must be replaced by forceful and far-reaching programs carried out at all levels of government, by private individuals and by State and local agencies in every part of the Union.

We must act—

to bestow the full benefits of our society on those who suffer from mental disabilities;

to prevent the occurrence of mental illness and mental retardation wherever and whenever possible;

to provide for early diagnosis and continuous and comprehensive care, in the community, of those suffering from these disorders;

to stimulate improvements in the level of care given the mentally disabled in our State and private institutions, and to reorient those programs to a community-centered approach;

to reduce, over a number of years, and by hundreds of thousands, the persons confined to these institutions;

to retain in and return to the community the mentally ill and mentally retarded, and there to restore and revitalize their lives through better health programs and strengthened educational and rehabilitation services; and

to reinforce the will and capacity of our communities to meet these problems, in order that the communities, in turn, can reinforce the will and capacity of individuals and individual families.

We must promote—to the best of our ability and by all possible and appropriate means—the mental and physical health of all our citizens.[4]

Table 2. Array of direct services for the retarded*

Life stage	Components of special need						
	Physical & mental health	Shelter nurture protection	Intellectual development	Social development	Recreation	Work	Economic security
Infant	Specialized medical follow-up Special diets, drugs or surgery Home nursing	Residential nursery Child welfare services	Sensory stimulation	Home training Environmental enrichment			
Toddler	Correction of physical defects Physical therapy	Foster care Trained baby sitter	Nursery school				
Child	Psychiatric care Dental care	Homemaker service Day care Short stay home	Classes for slow learners Special classes—educable Special classes—trainable Religious education Boarding school	Scouting Work-school programs Speech training	Playground programs Swimming Day camps Residential camps		"Disabled child's" benefits
Youth	Psychotherapy		Occupational training	Youth groups Social clubs			Health insurance
Young adult	Facilities for retarded in conflict	Half-way house Guardianship of person Long-term residential care	Vocational counseling—Personal adjustment training	Marriage counseling	Bowling	Selective job placement Sheltered employment Total disability assistance Sheltered workshops	Guardianship of property Life annuity or trust
Adult		Group homes Boarding homes	Evening school	Social supervision Evening recreation			
Older adult	Medical attention to chronic conditions					Old age assistance	OASI benefits

*Not included are diagnostic and evaluation services, or services to the family; the array is set forth in an irregular pattern in order to represent the overlapping areas of need and the interdigitation of services. Duration of services along the life span has not been indicated here.
Source: President's Panel on Mental Retardation, 1962. p. 76.

Congress responded positively. Over the next 20 years, it passed 116 acts or amendments thereof that provided support for mentally retarded persons and their families in the areas of education, employment, health, housing, income maintenance, nutrition, rights, social services (including social security benefits), transportation, and vocational rehabilitation.[5] By 1976, 11 major federal agencies administered 135 special funding programs, often with more spirit than cooperation.[6] By 1980, the federal government was spending an estimated $4 billion per year on mental retardation. During the 1980–81 fiscal year 852,000 mentally retarded children received special education services, 165,500 mentally retarded persons received vocational rehabilitation services, and 640,000 mentally retarded persons received some form of support or assistance through Social Security legislation, including approximately 130,000 mentally retarded persons in public institutions.[7]

Added to the tremendous incentive provided by a dedicated president was the growing international recognition of the rights of mentally retarded persons. Nearly all professional organizations and agencies posited a statement of rights, but none was as significant as the "Declaration of General and Special Rights of the Mentally Retarded." This statement, originally drafted by the International League of Societies for the Mentally Handicapped in 1968, was adopted by the United Nations General Assembly in 1971. The seven articles of the declaration decreed:

Article I
The mentally retarded person has the same basic rights as other citizens of the same country and same age.
Article II
The mentally retarded person has a right to proper medical care and physical restoration and to such education, training, habilitation, and guidance as will enable him to develop his ability and potential to the fullest possible extent, no matter how severe his degree of disability. No mentally handicapped person should be deprived of such services by reason of the costs involved.
Article III
The mentally retarded person has a right to

economic security and to a decent standard of living. He has a right to productive work or to other meaningful occupation.
Article IV
The mentally retarded person has a right to live with his own family or with foster parents, to participate in all aspects of community life, and to be provided with appropriate leisure time activities. If care in an institution becomes necessary, it should be in surroundings and other circumstances as close to normal living as possible.
Article V
The mentally retarded person has a right to a qualified guardian when this is required to protect his personal well-being and interest. No person rendering direct services to the mentally retarded should also serve as his guardian.
Article VI
The mentally retarded person has a right to protection from exploitation, abuse and degrading treatment. If accused, he has a right to a fair trial with full recognition being given to his degree of responsibility.
Article VII
Some mentally retarded persons may be unable, due to the severity of their handicap, to exercise for themselves all of their rights in a meaningful way. For others, modification of some or all of these rights is appropriate. The procedure used for modification or denial of rights must contain proper legal safeguards against every form of abuse, must be based on an evaluation of the social capability of the mentally retarded person by qualified experts, and must be subject to periodic reviews and to the right of appeal to higher authorities.[8]

The declaration was widely adopted in the United States, as well as other countries, providing a platform for further reform and program development.

New and dynamic principles were also promulgated that significantly influenced programming in all sectors. First was the concept of the developmental model, which, according to the International League of Societies for the Mentally Handicapped, was predicated on the belief that all "retarded children and adults are considered capable of growth, learning, and development. Each individual has potential for some progress, no matter how severely impaired he might be. The basic goal of programming for retarded individuals consists of maximizing their human qualities."[9]

Second was the normalization principle, which again was defined by the International League as "a sound basis for programming which, by paralleling the normal patterns of the culture and drawing the retarded into the mainstream of society, aims at maximizing his human qualities, as defined by his particular culture. Retarded children and adults should, therefore, be helped to live as normal a life as possible. The structuring of routines, the form of life, and the nature of the physical environment should approximate the normal cultural pattern as much as possible."[10]

This principle, first developed in the Scandinavian countries, was transmitted to the United States primarily through the efforts of N. E. Bank-Mikkelson and Bengt Nirje. In 1969, Nirje referred to the concept of normalization as "making available to the mentally retarded patterns and conditions of everyday life which are as close as possible to the norms and patterns of the mainstream of society." Further,

1. Normalization means a normal rhythm of the day for the retarded.
2. Normalization implies a normal routine of life, i.e., not always structured.
3. Normalization means to experience the normal rhythm of the year with holidays and family days of personal significance.
4. Normalization means an opportunity to undergo normal developmental experiences of the life cycle, i.e., experiences and opportunities should be consistent with the appropriate life cycle whenever possible; adjustments and special provisions should be made for the mentally retarded adult and elderly.
5. Normalization means that the choices, wishes and desires of the mentally retarded themselves have to be taken into consideration as frequently as possible and respected.
6. Normalization means living in a bisexual world.
7. Normalization means normal economic standards for the mentally retarded.
8. Normalization means that the standards of the physical facility should be the same as those regularly applied in society to the same kind of facilities for ordinary citizens.[11]

Taken in their totality, these concepts implied that each mentally retarded person should live in the mainstream of society, if at all possible, and that any environment in which the individual resides should provide as normal a way of life as the individual is capable of handling effectively. Also, every effort must be made to assist the mentally retarded person, regardless of degree of retardation, to attain his maximum level of independence.

Special Education

Special education programs underwent significant change. Many of the issues that had been discussed over the years acquired new meanings, new preferences, and new priorities. In 1962, G. Orville Johnson reexamined a number of post-school follow-up studies and found it "paradoxical that mentally handicapped children having teachers especially trained, having more money (per capita) spent on their education, and being enrolled in classes with fewer children and a program designed to provide for their unique needs, should be accomplishing the objectives of their education at the same or at a lower level than similar mentally handicapped children who have not had these advantages and have been forced to remain in the regular grades." Johnson did not propose the elimination of special classes but wondered if the learning experiences offered "were meaningful with purpose and value."[12] Four years later, Lloyd Dunn reviewed the literature and published a position paper that severely questioned both the efficacy of special classes for mildly mentally retarded persons and their widespread use.[13] Special classes were also challenged by other experts seriously concerned about practices of labeling and classifying individuals as mentally retarded, believing that such practices not only damaged a youngster's self-perception but also created a baseline for self-fulfilling prophecies.[14] These factors and a growing national rights movement fostered a renewed interest in "mainstreaming" the mentally retarded person not only within the school environment but within society as a whole.

It was in the educational setting that the third branch of government—the judicial, or federal courts—first took a renewed interest in vigorously pursuing the rights of mentally retarded persons. The two landmark cases involved Pennsylvania and Washington, D.C. In 1971, a three-judge Federal District Court panel upheld a consent agreement between the Pennsylvania Association for Retarded Children and the Commonwealth of Pennsylvania, guaranteeing every mentally retarded child in the state the right to a free public education. This decision was supported and expanded in *Mills* v. *Board of Education* (1972). The latter judgment contended that no child in Washington, D.C. could be denied a public education because of mental, behavioral, physical, or emotional handicaps or deficiencies.[15]

The strongest position as regards the right to education for every mentally retarded child came forth in PL 94-142, the Education for All Handicapped Children Act of 1975. This federal legislation clearly mandated educational systems to provide a free and appropriate education for all mentally retarded youngsters up to 21 years of age. Advanced medical treatment, a prolonged life expectancy, and advancements in instructional techniques, based primarily on the principles of behavior modification, made this a realistic goal for even the most severely affected.

RESIDENTIAL SERVICES

As indicated before, both the number of institutions and the number of their residents expanded exponentially beginning in the 1950s. The resident population of state-administered institutions alone grew from 125,375 to 189,549 between 1950 and 1970.[16] Few institutions had the financial, personnel, or physical resources to meet the needs of residents, and the quality of life continued to deteriorate in many facilities. Klebanoff, then a state-level administrator, succinctly summarized the situation for many institutions: "Officials who solemnly declare the financial inability to provide increased facilities will plead for admission of a worthy case. As the worthy cases spill over into the corridors, the already inadequate personnel-to-resident ratios become impossible and there is little the staff can do except to fold laundry and keep a fire watch."[17]

In 1966, Burton Blatt and Fred Kaplan published a poignant photographic essay on the life of mentally retarded persons in residential settings. *Christmas in Purgatory* visually illustrated the inadequacies and dehumanizing conditions found in many institutions.[18] In 1972, Geraldo Rivera brought this problem to national attention through his televised exposé of the Willowbrook State School, New York. The early 1970s also witnessed the advent of capable, dedicated advocates, such as Gunnar Dybwad and Wolf Wolfensberger, the latter of whom wrote, "I can see no reason why small, specialized living units (mostly hostels) cannot accommodate all of the persons now in institutions."[19]

During the 1970s, the federal courts took a major interest in institutions, declaring many of their conditions and procedures unconstitutional. The first such case, which related to the right to treatment, was *Wyatt* v. *Stickney*. This landmark class action suit was brought against the Alabama Department of Mental Hygiene in 1970 by the guardian of Ricky Wyatt. In 1972, Judge Johnson of the District Court of the United States for the Middle District of Alabama, North Division, declared the constitutional rights of the mentally retarded residents were being violated. His decree included a 20-page appendix that defined minimum treatment standards for the state school to meet. The court created an independent monitoring committee to ensure implementation of its judgments.[20]

A second area of concern involved due process. In this instance, the *Lessard* v. *Schmidt* decision of 1972 declared Wisconsin's state statutes to be unconstitutional, since existing procedures failed to guarantee rights of due process. In other words, anyone deemed in need of residential treatment had the right to a trial, at which time his interests would be represented, witnesses could be called, and the need for institutionalization could be challenged.[21]

Finally, "involuntary servitude" came under review. For many years, as we have seen, residents spent hours meeting the operational needs of the institution. In 1973, a class action suit (*Souder* v. *Brennan*) was brought against the U.S. Department of Labor to compel it to enforce provisions of the Fair Labor Standards Act of 1966 relative to resident workers and residential facilities for both mentally ill and mentally retarded persons. The court held that the minimum wage, overtime, and other provisions of the Fair Labor Standards Act applied to developmentally disabled persons residing and working in a residential facility. Although this decision was subsequently overturned, the precedent was established that residents were no longer to provide free labor.

The need for institutional reform was evident. Not only had the courts declared that certain standards and procedures must be met, but the American Association on Mental Deficiency developed institutional standards and encouraged the establishment of the Accreditation Council for Services for Mentally Retarded and other Developmentally Disabled Persons, an independent agency.[23]

The *tour de force* of institutional reform, however, was the inclusion of institutions for mentally retarded persons under the 1971 amendments to Title 19 (Medicaid) of the Social Security Act. Not only did the regulations include many of the Accreditation Council's standards, but also the federal government provided critical financial support necessary to ensure their implementation.

Deinstitutionalization was sought as fervently as institutional reform. In order to accomplish this goal, not only did institutions have to make a concerted effort to increase the independence of their mentally retarded residents, preparing them for community placement, but communities, in turn, had to develop the broad array of services essential to maintaining mentally retarded people in the mainstream of society. Deinstitutionalization became a primary objective of the 1970s when President Nixon set a national goal of reducing institutional populations by 30 percent before the turn of the century. Success in this area is reflected in that between 1970 and 1979, the number of residents in state-administered institutions decreased by 50,139 persons, though the country's population continued to increase.[24]

In spite of these gains, the appropriateness of institutions as a treatment modality neverthe-less was questioned in federal court. In 1978, Judge Broderick, in *Halderman* v. *Pennhurst State School and Hospital, et al.*, challenged the very existence of institutions, since, in his judgment, they represented a "monumental example of the unconstitutionality with respect to the habilitation of the retarded. As such it must be expeditiously replaced with appropriate community-based mental retardation programs and facilities designed to meet the individual needs of each class member."[25] Though this decision was not upheld by the Supreme Court in 1981 (*Pennhurst State School* v. *Halderman*), support of the deinstitutionalization movement has not diminished.[26]

Two other noteworthy events occurred during this period. First was the Joseph P. Kennedy, Jr., Foundation Awards. This foundation, established in 1946 to foster programs of care, training, and treatment of mentally retarded persons and to promote research, presented its first set of awards for outstanding work in the field in December 6, 1962. The first recipients were:

1. The National Association for Retarded Children "for its outstanding role in awakening the nation to the problems of mental retardation and for proving, through a diversity of means that the retarded can be helped"

2. Samuel A. Kirk, director of the Institute for Research on Exceptional Children at the University of Illinois, for his untiring efforts pertaining to the early education of retarded children

3. Ivar Asbjorn Fölling, retired chief of the University Hospital Clinical Laboratory at Oslo, Norway, "for bringing on the new awareness of inborn errors of metabolism through his discovery of phenylketonuria"

4. Murray L. Barr, head of the Department of Microscopic Anatomy of the University of Ontario, for his discovery of sex chromatin

5. Joe Hin Tijo, a Dutch-Indonesian visiting scientist of the National Institutes of Health in Bethesda, Maryland, for his discovery of the exact number of chromosomes in man

6. Jerome Lejeune, director of the Department of Genetics at the University of Paris, for his discovery of chromosomal abnormalities associated with mongolism

Second was the establishment of the International Association for the Scientific Study of Mental Deficiency in 1964. The first president of this international organization, which meets every 3 years in various parts of the world, was Harvey A. Stevens, a well-known adminstrator from the United States and later a recipient of a Joseph P. Kennedy, Jr., Foundation Award.

No other 20-year period we have discussed saw as many humanitarian changes as did the 1960s and 1970s: rights, mainstreaming, advocacy, individual plans, interdisciplinary teams, normalization, developmental models, and deinstitutionalization; local, state, and federal support from each of government's three branches—executive, legislative, and judicial. Much was accomplished, and countless mentally retarded persons benefited from opportunities never before available. Yet, the gains and changes that time have wrought can be credited to no single person or group. They belong to a society whose attitudes, sense of responsibility, and human commitment have slowly but consistently grown over the past several hundred years.

Closing Comments

We have completed a rather extensive journey through time and have encountered a few of those people and events that have influenced the history of mental retardation. While no elaborate theories have been proposed to account for many of these changes, the course of this history does seem to teach three lessons about the fluidity of philosophies, the fallibility of research or its interpretation, and the dangers of professionalism.

First, as we have repeatedly seen, attitudes about mentally retarded persons, their place in the community, and society's responsibilities toward them have frequently and dramatically changed. Hopefully, the fine, humane, so-cially sensitive ideas presently being promulgated will remain in effect; yet, they will require constant affirmation by all dedicated persons. Nothing in the nature of man alone assures perpetual progress.

Second, as was well illustrated between 1900 and approximately 1915, inadequate research or erroneous interpretations greatly influenced both attitudes and programs. Scientists, Stephen J. Gould recently noted, "tend to behave in a conservative way by providing 'objectivity' for what society at large wants to hear."[27] Researchers in our field have not been and are not immune to such pressures. Subsequently, each of us must approach research and new theories circumspectly.

Finally, in many instances, mentally retarded persons have been treated in a manner that seemed to meet the needs of the professional community rather than themselves. Trilling once observed that "some paradox in our nature leads us, once we have made our fellow men the object of our enlightened interest, to go on to make them the objects of our pity, then our wisdom, ultimately of our coercion."[28] Historical evidence as it relates to the treatment of mentally retarded persons substantiates Trilling's observation. Once the professional community had adopted a philosophy or position, mentally retarded persons were often shaped to conform to those levels of professional expectancy. Thus, each of us must be constantly alert and sensitive to the rights of mentally retarded persons and should remember that the professional's role is to assist when necessary, never to command.

Certainly, the past warns that future progress for mentally retarded persons is never assured. If current philosophies and support systems are maintained and expanded, then the future is indeed most promising. One could look toward additional growth in all areas, including the correction of current practices that still restrict life-styles, impede community participation, and adversely affect social integration. Yet, all such advances will remain contingent upon society's respect for the inherent dignity of all people. In turn, society is simply you and me; no more, no less. The degree to which we serve, or enable others to serve, mentally retarded and other disabled persons is the degree to which we serve both ourselves and our country. In the words of a former president, "The manner in which our Nation cares for its citizens and conserves its manpower resources is more than an index of its concern for the less fortunate. It is a key to its future."[29]

SUPPLEMENTAL
READINGS

Listed below are a few articles and books on the history of mental retardation, most of which should be readily available in any university library.

General Historical Overviews of Mental Retardation:

Barr, M. *Mental illness and social policy: The American experience.* Philadelphia: P. Blakiston's Son, 1904.

Crissey, M. Mental retardation: Past, present, and future. *American Psychologist,* 1975, *30,* 800–808.

Davies, S. *The mentally retarded in society.* New York: Columbia University, 1959.

Doll, E. A historical survey of research and management of mental retardation in the United States. In: E. Trapp & P. Himelstein (eds.), *Readings on the exceptional child.* New York: Appleton-Century-Crofts, 1962.

Doll, E. (ed.). Historical review of mental retardation: 1800–1965. *American Journal of Mental Deficiency,* 1967, *72,* 165–189.

Haskell, R. Mental deficiency over a hundred years; a brief historical sketch of trends in this field. *American Journal of Psychiatry,* 1944, *100*(6), 107–118.

Kanner, L. *A history of the care and study of the mentally retarded.* Springfield, IL: Charles C Thomas, 1964.

Kirk, S., & Johnson, G. *Educating the retarded child.* Cambridge, MA: Houghton Mifflin, 1951. Pp. 69–114.

Kuhlmann, F. One hundred years of special care and training. *American Journal of Mental Deficiency,* 1940, *45,* 8–24.

Nowrey, J. A brief synopsis of mental deficiency. *American Journal of Mental Deficiency,* 1945, *49,* 319–357.

President's Committee on Mental Retardation. *Mental retardation past and present.* Washington, DC: U.S. Government Printing Office, 1977.

Raymond, C. Retrospect and prospect in mental deficiency. *American Journal of Mental Deficiency,* 1944, *49,* 8–18.

Rosen, J., Clark, G., & Kivitz, M. (eds.). *The history of mental retardation (collected papers)* (2 vols.). Baltimore: University Park Press, 1976.

Rosen, J., Clark, G., & Kivitz, M. The development of the program for the mentally defective in Massachusetts for the past one hundred years (1848–1948). *American Journal of Mental Deficiency,* 1948, *53,* 80–91.

Sloan, W., & Stevens, H. *A century of concern: A history of the American Association on Mental Deficiency 1876–1976.* Washington, DC: American Association on Mental Deficiency, 1976.

Wallin, J. *Education of mentally handicapped children.* New York: Harper, 1955. Pp. 1–39.

Whitney, E. The historical approach to the subject of mental retardation. *American Journal of Mental Deficiency,* 1949, *53,* 419–424.

Whitney, E. Mental deficiency in the 1880s and 1940s. *American Journal of Mental Deficiency,* 1950, *54,* 151–154.

Institutions for Mentally Retarded Persons:

White, W., & Wolfensberger, W. The evaluation of dehumanization in our institutions. *Mental Retardation,* 1969, *7*(3), 5–9.

Wolfensberger, W. The origin and nature of our institutional models. In: W. Wolfensberger & R. Kugel (eds.), *Changing patterns in residential services for the mentally retarded.* Washington, DC: President's Committee on Mental Retardation, 1969.

Wolfensberger, W. *The origin and nature of our institutional models.* Syracuse, NY: Center on Human Policy, 1974.

The Law:

Brakel, S., & Rock, R. *The mentally disabled and the law.* Chicago: University of Chicago Press, 1971.

Burgdorf, R. (ed.). *The legal rights of handicapped persons: Cases, materials, and text.* Baltimore: Paul H. Brookes Publishing Co., 1980.

Medicine:

Menolascino, F., & Egger, M. *Medical dimensions of mental retardation*. Lincoln, NE: University of Nebraska Press, 1978.

Whitney, E. Historical review of medicine and mental deficiency. *Journal of Psycho-Asthenics,* 1938, *43*(1), 64–71.

Mental Testing:

Goodenough, F. *Mental testing*. New York: Rinehart, 1949.

Sattler, J. *Assessment of children's intelligence and special abilities*. Rockleigh, NJ: Allyn & Bacon, 1982. Pp. 28–46, 96–112.

Professional Organizations:

Elkin, E. Historical perspectives. In: *A National Forum on Residential Services*, pp. 5–12. Arlington, TX: National Association for Retarded Citizens, 1977.

Hay, W. Associations for parents of mental retardates. New York: *Encyclopedia Americana*, 1952.

Lord, F. (ed.). A history of The Council for Exceptional Children. *Exceptional Children*, 1980–81, *47*, 37–55; 213–223; 285–296; 435–452; 527–562.

Milligan, G. History of the American Association on Mental Deficiency. *American Journal of Mental Deficiency*, 1961, *66*, 357–369.

Sloan, W., & Stevens, H. *A century of concern: A history of the American Association on Mental Deficiency 1876–1976*. Washington, DC: American Association on Mental Deficiency, 1976.

Special Education:

Jordan, J. (ed.). *Exceptional child education at the Bicentennial: A parade of progress*. Reston, VA: The Council for Exceptional Children, 1976.

Whitney, E. The E.T.C. of the mentally retarded. *American Journal of Mental Deficiency*, 1954, *59*, 13–25.

Special People and Events:

Doll, E. The American movement in mental deficiency: An apostrophe to the memory of a noble American (Samuel Gridley Howe). *American Journal of Mental Deficiency*, 1945, *49*, 358–363.

Lane, H. *The wild boy of Aveyron*. Cambridge, MA: Harvard University Press, 1976.

Pichot, P. French pioneers in the field of mental deficiency. *American Journal of Mental Deficiency*, 1948, *53*, 128–137.

Talbot, M. Edouard Seguin. *American Journal of Mental Deficiency*, 1962, *72*, 184–189.

Talbot, M. *Edouard Seguin: A study of an educational approach to the treatment of mentally defective children*. New York: Columbia University, 1964.

Whitney, E. Some stalwarts of the past. *American Journal of Mental Deficiency*, 1952, *57*, 345–360.

REFERENCE NOTES

Introduction

1. Schlesinger, 1963, p. 493.

Chapter 1

1. Lissner, 1959, p. 21.
2. Marti-Ibañez, 1959, p. 17.
3. Sagan, 1977.
4. Durant, 1935, p. 50.
5. Sumnar, 1906.
6. Leakey & Lewin, 1977, 1978.
7. Solecki, 1971, pp. 195–196.
8. Harms, 1976.
9. Kanner, 1949, p. 7.
10. Redfield, 1947.
11. Fletcher; in Dunton, 1944.
12. Harper, 1904, p. 7.
13. Abt, 1965, p. 21.
14. Fiedler, 1978, pp. 20–21.
15. Abt, 1965, p. 21.
16. Durant, 1935, p. 124.
17. Hamilton, 1930, pp. 23–24.
18. Abt, 1965, p. 12.
19. Durant, 1935, p. 204.
20. Bryan, 1930.
21. Ebbell, 1937, p. 117.
22. Ebbell, 1937, p. 118.
23. Haggard, 1934, p. 36.
24. Harms, 1976.
25. Casson, 1965, p. 57.
26. Douglas, 1962, p. 720.
27. Bowra, 1957, p. 5.
28. Durant, 1939, p. 50.
29. Plato, 1928, pp. 412–413.
30. Aristotle (undated), p. 315.
31. Payne, 1916, p. 5.
32. Durant, 1939, p. 81.
33. In Hamilton, 1930, p. 173.
34. Durant, 1939, p. 568.
35. Deutsch, 1949, p. 9.
36. Durant, 1944, p. 308.
37. Marti-Ibañez, 1959, p. 66.
38. Marks, 1817, pp. 25–26.
39. Chadwick & Mann, 1950, p. 204.
40. Chadwick & Mann, 1950, p. 90.
41. Marti-Ibañez, 1959, p. 65.
42. Chadwick & Mann, 1950, p. 51.
43. Chadwick & Mann, 1950, p. 193.
44. In Zilboorg, 1941, p. 39.
45. Chadwick & Mann, 1950, p. 2.
46. Durant, 1944, p. 422.
47. Payne, 1916, pp. 98–99.
48. Payne, 1916, pp. 243–244.
49. Payne, 1916, p. 243.
50. Kanner, 1964, pp. 5–6.
51. Marti-Ibañez, 1959, p. 92.
52. Zilboorg, 1941, p. 91.
53. Zilboorg, 1941, p. 91.
54. Zilboorg, 1941, p. 64.
55. Zilboorg, 1941, p. 20.
56. Zilboorg, 1941, p. 85.
57. Abt, 1965, p. 42.
58. Durant, 1944, p. 334.
59. Abt, 1965; Haggard, 1934.
60. Hadas, 1965, p. 166.
61. Payne, 1916, p. 213.
62. Durant, 1944, p. 360.
63. Lissner, 1957, p. 156.
64. Durant, 1950, p. 164.
65. Durant, 1950, pp. 183–184.

Chapter 2

1. Thomas, 1979, p. 47.
2. Durant, 1950, p. 433.
3. In Sherrard, 1966, p. 116.
4. In Tuchman, 1978, p. 207.
5. Durant, 1961, p. 48.
6. Shah, 1966, p. 10.
7. Klein, 1970.
8. In Grunner, 1930, pp. 509–510.
9. In Ruhräh, 1925, pp. 84–85.
10. In Ruhräh, 1925, p. 39.
11. In Ruhräh, 1925, p. 86.
12. Galdston, 1950, p. 206.
13. Haggard, 1934, p. 209.
14. Galdston, 1950, p. 110.
15. Galdston, 1950, p. 111.
16. Platter, 1614, pp. 35–36.
17. Platter, 1614, p. 36.
18. Tuke, 1882, p. 8.
19. Tuke, 1882, p. 8; in Deutsch, 1944, p. 13.
20. In Ruhräh, 1925, p. 166.
21. Tuke, 1882, pp. 20–21.
22. Tuke, 1882, p. 4.
23. Tuke, 1882, p. 31.
24. In Ireland, 1877, p. 336.
25. In Abt, 1965, pp. 57–58.
26. Durant, 1950, p. 820.
27. Gail, 1968.
28. In Alexander & Selesnick, 1966, p. 68.
29. In Deutsch, 1944, pp. 22–23.
30. In Zilboorg, 1941, p. 258.
31. In Deutsch, 1944, p. 21.
32. Dahmus, 1968, pp. 314–315.
33. Luther, 1652, p. 387.
34. Burdett, 1891, pp. 93.
35. Burdett, 1891, pp. 93–94.
36. Durant & Durant, 1967.
37. Tuke, 1882.
38. Kanner, 1964, p. 6; Theil, 1957.
39. Hibbert, 1975, pp. 225–226.
40. Fielder, 1978.
41. Henry, 1941.
42. In Wilson, 1975, p. 244.
43. Carty & Breault, 1967, p. 283.
44. A village, 1848, p. 222.
45. A village, 1848, p. 221.
46. Burdett, 1891.
47. Pollack, 1938.
48. Fields, 1974.
49. Wallin, 1955, p. 2.
50. Henry, 1941, p. 563.
51. Henry, 1941, p. 564.
52. Gail, 1968, p. 16.
53. In Tuke, 1882.

54. In Henry, 1941, pp. 259–260.
55. Tuke, 1882, p. 43.
56. Murray, 1974.
57. In Tuke, 1882, p. 287.
58. Hilliard & Kirman, 1965, p. 3.
59. Ireland, 1877.
60. In Pintner, 1923, p. 6.
61. Cowie, 1960, p. 42.
62. Krüsi, 1875, p. 16.
63. Marti-Ibañez, 1959, p. 222.
64. Giordani, 1961.
65. In Ruhräh, 1925, p. 266.
66. In Ruhräh, 1925, p. 287.
67. In Ruhräh, 1925, p. 335.
68. In Ruhräh, 1925, pp. 357–358.
69. In Ruhräh, 1925, p. 370.
70. In Kretchmer, 1964, p. 1.
71. In Ruhräh, 1925, p. 422.
72. Pinel, 1806, p. 165.
73. Pinel, 1806, p. 169.
74. Pinel, 1806, pp. 202–203.
75. Bacon (1914).
76. Murphy, 1949, p. 29.
77. Doll, 1962, p. 23.
78. Rousseau, 1762, pp. 28, 32.
79. Rousseau, 1762, p. 21.
80. In Tuke, 1882, p. 21.
81. Pintner, 1923, p. 7.
82. Abt, 1965, p. 71.
83. Abt, 1965, p. 81.
84. Gay, 1966, p. 116.
85. Gay, 1966, p. 118.
86. Giordani, 1961, pp. 76–77.
87. Tuke, 1882, p. 100.
88. Henry, 1941.
89. Tuke, 1882, p. 44.
90. Pinel, 1806, pp. 202–203.
91. Giordani, 1961, p. 1.
92. In Hamilton, 1978, p. 10.
93. Ireland, 1877, p. 292.
94. Haggard, 1934.
95. In Zilboorg, 1941, p. 319.
96. In Zilboorg, 1941, pp. 326–327.
97. In Manceron, 1977, p. 431.
98. In Manceron, 1977, p. 432.
99. In Zilboorg, 1941, p. 322.
100. Freedman et al., 1972, p. 9.
101. Deutsch, 1949.
102. Carlson & Dain, 1960.
103. In Zilboorg, 1941, p. 572.
104. Tuke, 1882, p. 131.
105. In Tuke, 1882, p. 132.
106. In Tuke, 1882, p. 101.
107. In Eby, 1952, p. 441.
108. Eby, 1952, pp. 432–433.
109. De Guimps, 1895, p. 6.
110. Froebel, 1889, p. 498.
111. In Eby, 1952, pp. 514–555.
112. Seguin, 1866, p. 54.

Chapter 3

1. Trevelyan, 1952, p. 135.
2. Trevelyan, 1952, p. 135.
3. In Haggard, 1934, p. 337.
4. Burchell, 1966, p. 73.
5. Murphy, 1949, p. 107.
6. Little, 1862, p. 302.
7. Heilman & Valenstein, 1979; Klein, 1970.
8. Shafer, 1974.
9. Boring, 1929, p. 5.
10. In Lane, 1976, p. 171.
11. Ireland, 1887, p. 28.
12. Esquirol, 1845, p. 448.
13. Esquirol, 1845, p. 467.
14. Esquirol, 1845, p. 417.
15. Seguin, 1846, p. 107.
16. Sequin, 1846, pp. 39–40.
17. Seguin, 1866, p. 189.
18. Seguin, 1866, pp. 69–70.
19. Seguin, 1866, p. 66.
20. Seguin, 1866, 1867, pp. 74–75, 81.
21. Down, 1867.
22. Penrose & Smith, 1966.
23. Wilbur, 1877, p. 33.
24. Down, 1887, p. 90.
25. Down, 1887, p. 297.
26. Down, 1887, p. 298.
27. Down, 1887, pp. 88–89.
28. Kanner, 1964.
29. Ireland, 1877, pp. 1, 282.
30. Ireland, 1877, p. 2.
31. Ireland, 1877, pp. 79, 203.
32. Ireland, 1877, p. 57.
33. Ireland, 1877, pp. 98–99.
34. Ireland, 1877, p. 204.
35. Ireland, 1877, pp. 232–235.
36. Ireland, 1877, p. 25.
37. Ireland, 1877, p. 28.
38. Ireland, 1877, p. 28.
39. Bourneville, 1901.
40. Dorland's; 1974, p. 393.
41. Pichot, 1948.
42. Duncan & Millard, 1866, p. 12.
43. West, 1868, p. 223.
44. West, 1868, p. 228.
45. West, 1868, p. 228.
46. West, 1868, p. 228.
47. Ireland, 1877.
48. Notices, 1847, p. 79.
49. Ireland, 1877, p. 170.
50. Esquirol, 1838.
51. In Pintner, 1923, p. 18.
52. Peterson, 1925.
53. Peterson, 1925.
54. Peterson, 1925.
55. Tuke, 1882, p. 182.
56. Dickens (1907), pp. 4–5.
57. Payne, 1916, p. 342.
58. In Ireland, 1877, p. 345.
59. In Hilliard & Kirman, 1965, p. 3.
60. In Hilliard & Kirman, 1965, p. 3.
61. Ireland, 1877, p. 340.
62. Ireland, 1877, p. 339.
63. Down, 1887, p. 29.
64. Ray, 1871, p. 343.
65. Ray, 1871, p. 121.
66. Ray, 1831, p. 72.
67. Wolfgang, 1961.
68. In Burdett, 1891, p. 61.
69. Esquirol, 1845, p. 62.
70. Brockett, 1881, p. 13.
71. Saint-Simon, 1825, p. 1.
72. Manceron, 1977, p. 479.
73. Brockett, 1881, p. 21.
74. In Wilbur, 1881, p. 29.
75. Seguin, 1866, p. 243.
76. Seguin, 1866, p. 273.
77. Seguin, 1866, p. 75.
78. Kanner, 1964, p. 17.
79. Millard, 1886, p. 393.
80. In Kanner, 1964, p. 25.
81. Ireland, 1877, pp. 192–193.
82. Down, 1887, pp. 2–3.
83. In Kanner, 1964, p. 28.
84. Kanner, 1964.
85. In Kanner, 1964, pp. 30–31.
86. In Ireland, 1877, p. 330.
87. Ireland, 1877.
88. Brown, 1882.
89. Tuke, 1882.
90. Brown, 1882, p. 231.
91. Brown, 1882, p. 330.
92. In Lane, 1976, pp. 40–41.
93. In Lane, 1976, pp. 41–42.
94. Lane, 1976, p. 69.
95. Esquirol, 1845, p. 485.
96. Ireland, 1877, p. 393.
97. Itard, 1806, p. xiii.
98. Itard, 1806, pp. 28–29.
99. Lane, 1976, p. 167.
100. Itard, 1806, pp. 100–101.
101. Itard, 1806, p. 53.
102. Seguin, 1866, pp. 83–84.
103. Talbot, 1964, p. 45.
104. Seguin, 1866, pp. 217–218.
105. Seguin, 1866, pp. 64–65.
106. Seguin, 1866, pp. 344–345.
107. Seguin, 1866, p. 345.
108. Report of the Royal Academy of Science, 1843. In: Rosen et al., 1976, pp. 107–110.
109. Walk, 1964.
110. Down, 1887, pp. 130–132.
111. Down, 1887, p. 139.
112. Ireland, 1877, p. 316.
113. Ireland, 1877, p. 304.
114. Ireland, 1877, p. 324.
115. Bucknill, 1873, p. 17.
116. Duncan & Millard, 1866, p. 63.
117. Kanner, 1964.
118. Maennel, 1909, p. 3.
119. Kanner, 1964.
120. Maennel, 1909, p. 71.
121. Maennel, 1909, p. 26.
122. Maennel, 1909, p. 27.
123. Maennel, 1909, pp. 104, 161.
124. Fernald, 1904, p. 31.

125. Maennel, 1909, pp. 134–136.
126. Maennel, 1909.
127. Notes and Abstracts, 1897.
128. Standing, 1962, p. 28.
129. Standing, 1962, p. 29.
130. Montessori, 1963a, p. 129.
131. Montessori, 1963b, p. 3.
132. Montessori, 1963a, p. 249.
133. Kilpatrick, 1914, p. 35.
134. Dewey & Dewey, 1915, pp. 157–158.

Chapter 4

1. In Wesep, 1960, p. 126.
2. In Woodward, 1937, p. 19.
3. Rothman & Rothman, 1975, p. 23.
4. In Eliot, 1938, pp. 67–68.
5. In Butts & Cremin, 1953, p. 67.
6. In Abbott, 1938, p. 216.
7. In Demos, 1970, p. 102.
8. Rothman & Rothman, 1975, p. 27.
9. Rothman & Rothman, 1975, p. 29.
10. Handlin & Handlin, 1971, p. 101.
11. Erikson, 1966, p. 145.
12. In Erikson, 1966, p. 145.
13. Witchcraft, 1848, p. 248.
14. Hofstadter, 1971b, p. 47.
15. Handlin & Handlin, 1971, p. 31.
16. Deutsch, 1949; Richards, 1935.
17. Tuke, 1882.
18. Kosimar, 1942.
19. In Friedman, 1973, p. 77.
20. Deutsch, 1949, p. 116.
21. In Deutsch, 1949, p. 52.
22. In Deutsch, 1949, p. 46.
23. Estabrook, 1928, p. 59.
24. In Deutsch, 1949, p. 61.
25. In Deutsch, 1949, p. 69.
26. In Deutsch, 1949, p. 70.
27. Hawke, 1971.
28. Hawke, 1971, p. ix.
29. In Hawke, 1971, pp. 376–377.
30. Frazer, 1974, p. 29.
31. Burdett, 1891.
32. Rush, 1812, p. 291.
33. Rush, 1812, p. 291.
34. In Frazer, 1974, p. 31.
35. Garraty, 1966, p. 217.
36. Garraty, 1966.
37. Eggert, 1972.
38. Frazier, 1971, p. 205.
39. Friedman, 1973, p. 189.
40. Deutsch, 1949.
41. Dix, 1848, p. 23.
42. Friedman, 1973.
43. In Deutsch, 1949, p. 120.
44. In Deutsch, 1949, pp. 129–130.

45. Dix, 1843, p. 9.
46. Dix, 1845, p. 51.
47. In Deutsch, 1949, p. 130.
48. Dickens, undated, p. 403.
49. Asylums and schools, 1847, pp. 77–78.
50. Meltzer, 1964, p. 224.
51. In Richards, 1935, pp. 74–75.
52. Mainwaring, 1980, p. 199.
53. Richards, 1935, p. 175.
54. *Report made to the legislature,* 1848.
55. In Richards, 1935, pp. 173–174.
56. Richards, 1935, p. 174.
57. Howe, 1849, p. 374.
58. In Richards, 1935, p. 175.
59. Haynes, 1935, p. 213.
60. Meltzer, 1964, p. 161.
61. Association of Medical Superintendents, 1848, p. 19.
62. Baker, 1930, p. 35.
63. Baker, 1930, p. 325.
64. In Deutsch, 1937, p. 178.
65. Dix, 1843, p. 1.
66. Wilson, 1975, p. 127.
67. Dix, 1846b, p. 4.
68. Dix, 1846a, pp. 3–4.
69. Dix, 1847, p. 5.
70. Dix, 1848, p. 3.
71. In Wilson, 1975, p. 246.
72. In Wilson, 1975, p. 276.
73. In Deutsch, 1949, p. 185.

Chapter 5

1. In Garraty, 1966, p. 517.
2. In Garraty, 1966, p. 516.
3. Garraty, 1966.
4. Smith, 1981, p. 739.
5. Garraty, 1966, p. 484.
6. Brodinsky, 1976.
7. In Handlin & Handlin, 1971, p. 110.
8. Beach, 1895, p. 573.
9. Kerlin, 1877, p. 20.
10. Kerlin, 1885, p. 5.
11. Kerlin, 1887, p. 37.
12. Rogers, 1892, p. 318.
13. In Kerlin, 1886, p. 2.
14. Johnson, 1897.
15. Kerlin, 1885, p. 11.
16. Wilbur, 1882, p. 190.
17. Johnson, 1897.
18. U.S. Department of the Interior, 1895.
19. Kerlin, 1884, pp. 4–5.
20. Kerlin, 1886, pp. 9–10.
21. Fish, 1892; Greene, 1886.
22. Greene, 1886.
23. Shuttleworth, 1886.
24. Wilbur, 1877, p. 33.
25. Wilmarth, 1889.
26. Keen, 1892, p. 345.
27. Keen, 1892.
28. Rogers, 1898, p. 95.

29. Kerlin, 1882, p. 207.
30. Sweringen, 1894, p. 490.
31. Rogers, 1889; Wilson, 1892.
32. Kerlin, 1887, p. 94.
33. Estabrook, 1916, p. vi.
34. Dugdale, 1877, p. 14.
35. Dugdale, 1910, pp. 65–66.
36. Dugdale, 1910, p. iii.
37. Wilbur, 1882, p. 192.
38. Broomall, 1889, p. 38.
39. Blake, 1892, p. 314.
40. Halmstead, 1892; Hrdlicka, 1898; Rogers, 1897.
41. Hrdlicka, 1898; Johnson, 1897; LeGalley, 1897; Springer, 1896; Wylie, 1899.
42. Mott, 1891, p. 36.
43. Osborne, 1894, p. 393.
44. Osborne, 1894, p. 393.
45. *U.S. statutes at large,* 1889–1891, p. 1084.
46. Osborne, 1894, p. 392.
47. In Osborne, 1894, p. 391.
48. Rogers, 1889, pp. 76–77.
49. Barr, 1895, p. 531.
50. Brown, 1877, p. 28.
51. Brown, 1877, p. 28.
52. Medical Statistics, 1875.
53. Seguin, 1866, pp. 454–456.
54. Ray, 1871, p. 87.
55. *Hays* v. *The Commonwealth,* 1896; *Pettigrew* v. *Texas,* 1882; *State* v. *Richards,* 1873; *Wood* v. *Dulaney,* 1852.
56. In Ashman, 1889, p. 24.
57. Ohio Board of State Charities, 1870, p. 28.
58. Board of Public Charities of the State of Illinois, 1873, p. 190.
59. Letchworth, 1875, pp. 233–234.
60. U.S. Department of Commerce, 1914.
61. Stewart; in Status of the Work, 1894, p. 73.
62. Meeting of superintendents, 1876, pp. 4–5.
63. Meeting of superintendents, 1876, p. 6.
64. Brown, 1886, pp. 294–295.
65. Seguin, 1866, p. 389.
66. In Brown, 1898, pp. 1–2.
67. Wilbur, 1852, pp. 16–17.
68. In Status of the Work, 1879, p. 96.
69. Williams, 1886, p. 416.
70. In Howe, 1850, p. 28.
71. Richards, 1884, p. 19.
72. Williams, 1886, p. 418.
73. Fish, 1894, p. 493.
74. Osborne, 1892, p. 386.
75. In Murdoch, 1925, pp. 146–147.
76. Kerlin, 1880.

77. Kerlin, 1891, pp. 24, 28.
78. Salisbury, 1892, p. 225.
79. Powell, 1882, p. 268.
80. Stewart, 1882, p. 236.
81. Howe, 1856, p. 13.
82. Knight, 1886, p. 17.
83. Knight, 1889, p. 52.
84. In Fish, 1894, p. 217.
85. Salisbury, 1892, p. 232.
86. In Scheerenberger, 1976a, p. 4.
87. Powell, 1886, p. 339.
88. Kerlin, 1885, p. 16.
89. Brown, 1898, p. 10.
90. Osborne, 1894, p. 397.
91. Mott, 1891, p. 36.
92. Johnson, 1897, p. 98.
93. Butler, 1883, p. 152.
94. Fernald, 1892, p. 457.
95. Johnson, 1897, p. 34.
96. Stewart, 1882, p. 270.
97. Wilbur, 1879, p. 96.
98. Fernald; in Osborne, 1892, p. 181.
99. Osborne, 1892, p. 182.
100. In Fish, 1894, p. 212.
101. Knight; in Osborne, 1894, p. 211.
102. Kerlin, 1892, p. 282.
103. Fish, 1889, p. 47.
104. Fish, 1892, p. 203.
105. Shuttleworth, 1886.
106. Brown, 1886.
107. Fish, 1882.
108. Wilmarth, 1889.
109. Down, 1887, pp. 114–115.
110. Carson, 1891, pp. 14–15.
111. Knight, 1895, p. 561.
112. In Fish, 1892, pp. 208–209.
113. Kerlin, 1877, p. 23.
114. Wilmarth, 1900, p. 57.
115. Johnson, 1900, p. 97.
116. Howe; in President's Committee, 1977, p. 5.
117. Kerlin, 1885, p. 17.
118. In Abbott, 1938, p. 38.
119. Abbott, 1938, p. 70.
120. In Abbott, 1938, pp. 42–43.
121. Laws of the state of Illinois, 1879, pp. 309, 312.
122. In Abbott, 1938, p. 138.
123. Abbott, 1938, p. 147.
124. Esten, 1900.
125. Steinbach, 1918, p. 104.
126. Esten, 1900, p. 13.
127. Farrell, 1908, p. 91.
128. Esten, 1900, p. 14.
129. Lawrence, 1900, p. 100.
130. Ward v. Flood, 1874.
131. In Zedler, 1953, p. 186.
132. Esten, 1900, pp. 10–12.
133. Johnson, 1897, p. 112.
134. Gulick, 1900, p. 10, 16.
135. Johnson, G.E., 1897, pp. 111–112.
136. Wallin, 1924.

137. Esten, 1900, p. 11.
138. Fernberger, 1931, p. 13.
139. Fernberger, 1931, p. 4.
140. Brotemarkle, 1931, pp. xix–xx.
141. Fernberger, 1931, p. 12.
142. Tulchin, 1957, p. 200.
143. In Milburn, 1908, pp. 70–71.
144. Lawrence, 1900, p. 100.
145. Esten, 1900, pp. 14–15.
146. Esten, 1900, p. 15.
147. Farrell, 1908, p. 94.

Chapter 6

1. May, 1964a.
2. Garraty, 1966, pp. 647–648.
3. May, 1964a, p. 52.
4. May, 1964a, p. 76.
5. President's Committee, 1977, p. 87.
6. U.S. Department of Commerce, 1914.
7. Committee on Classification, 1910, p. 61.
8. Barr, 1904, p. 90.
9. Kelly, 1903; Norsworthy, 1906, 1907.
10. Report of Committee on Psychological Research, 1901.
11. Binet & Simon, 1907, p. 3.
12. Binet, 1899.
13. Binet & Simon, 1910.
14. Peterson, 1925.
15. Binet & Simon, 1907, pp. 74–75.
16. Binet & Simon, 1907, p. 76.
17. Binet, 1909, p. 141.
18. Binet & Simon, 1909, p. 143.
19. Binet, 1907, p. 150.
20. Goodenough, 1949, p. 53.
21. Terman, 1916, p. 79.
22. Kuhlmann, 1911, pp. 91, 92.
23. Goodenough, 1949, p. 53.
24. Goddard, 1913b, p. 126.
25. Kuhlmann, 1913, p. 143.
26. Kuhlmann, 1911, p. 92.
27. Fernald, 1913, pp. 79–80.
28. Healy, 1913, p. 112.
29. Terman & Knollin, 1915, pp. 3–4.
30. Terman, 1916, p. 6.
31. Terman, 1916, p. 12.
32. Squire, 1913.
33. Ayres, 1911.
34. Berry, 1913.
35. Doll, 1913.
36. Goddard, 1913.
37. Terman, 1919, p. 12.
38. Porteus, 1915.
39. Garrod, 1909.
40. Talbot, 1911.
41. Journal of Psycho-Asthenics, 1921.
42. Bleuler, 1950, p. 1.
43. Barr, 1904, p. 123.

44. Barr, 1904, p. 102.
45. Fernald, 1912a, p. 91.
46. Bullard, 1909, p. 15.
47. Kanner, 1964.
48. Goddard, 1912, pp. 116–117.
49. Rogers, 1912, p. 84.
50. Wallin; In Kuhlmann, 1914, pp. 169–170.
51. Goddard, 1912, p. 15.
52. Kite, 1912, p. 147.
53. Goodenough, 1949, p. 54.
54. Goddard, 1942.
55. Goddard, 1912, pp. 7–8.
56. Goddard, 1912, pp. 11–12.
57. Reeves, 1938, p. 196.
58. Reeves, 1938, p. 197.
59. Reeves, 1938, p. 199.
60. Reeves, 1938, pp. 199–200.
61. Schultz, 1979.
62. Estabrook, 1916, p. 85.
63. Danielson & Davenport, 1912; Davenport, 1912; Estabrook & McDougle, 1926; Finlayson, 1916.
64. Goddard, 1920, pp. 547, 565.
65. East, 1917.
66. Punnet, 1917.
67. Fernald, W., 1912, p. 523.
68. MacMurphy, 1916, p. 62.
69. Parsons, 1918, p. 167.
70. Hill, 1914.
71. Weidensall, 1917, p. 293.
72. Terman, 1916, p. 11.
73. Healy, 1919, p. 70.
74. Farnell, 1912, p. 164.
75. G. Fernald, 1918, p. 85.
76. Anderson, 1918, p. 121.
77. Southard, 1918, p. 49.
78. Van Wagenen, 1914, pp. 186–187.
79. Diller, 1911, p. 24.
80. Best, 1965.
81. Vaughn, 1913, p. 135.
82. Hart; in Murdoch, 1913, pp. 37–38.
83. Murdoch, 1913, p. 40.
84. Matzinger, 1918, p. 20.
85. Murdoch, 1913.
86. Rogers; in Murdoch, 1913, pp. 43–44.
87. Ferris, 1913, p. 71.
88. Davies, 1959.
89. Murdoch, 1913, pp. 34–35.
90. Southard, 1919, p. 111.
91. Gaylin et al., 1978, pp. 81–82.
92. Best, 1965.
93. Fiedler, 1978, p. 18.
94. Fernald, 1903a, pp. 34–35.
95. Fernald, 1909, pp. 17–18.
96. Fernald, 1912, p. 88.
97. Fernald; in Bernstein, 1918, p. 98.
98. Wallace, 1925, p. 121.
99. Bernstein, 1920, p. 1.

100. Fernald, 1917.
101. U.S. Department of Commerce, 1923, 1934.
102. Wilson, 1924, p. 278.
103. Fernald, 1917.
104. Wilmarth, 1906, p. 205.
105. Concerning, 1901.
106. Vanuxem, 1925, p. 3.
107. Minutes, 1913, p. 58.
108. Minutes, 1913, pp. 60–61.
109. Murdoch, 1913, p. 41.
110. Minutes, 1913, p. 55.
111. Minutes, 1913, p. 55.
112. Barr, 1904, p. 334.
113. Barr, 1902, p. 7.
114. Riggs, 1936, p. 10.
115. Minutes, 1916, pp. 101, 110.
116. Bernstein, 1917, pp. 160–161.
117. Bernstein, 1917, pp. 156–157.
118. Bernstein, 1920, p. 17.
119. Riggs, 1936, p. 117.
120. U.S. Department of Commerce, 1914.
121. Kuhlmann, 1916.
122. Douglass, 1914, p. 135.
123. Fernald, 1920, pp. 83, 87.
124. Woodhill, 1920.
125. E. R. Johnstone, 1914.
126. Murdoch, 1913, p. 38.
127. Fernald, 1912b, p. 94.
128. Wilmarth, 1906, p. 265.
129. Fernald, 1919b, pp. 25–26.
130. Fernald, 1919b, p. 31.
131. Business Section, 1919, p. 156.
132. Anderson, 1916, p. 82.
133. Emerick, 1917; Murdoch, 1913.
134. Fernald, 1919c, p. 61.
135. G. Fernald, 1919, p. 62.
136. Leonard, 1918.
137. Murdoch, 1913, p. 42.
138. Murdoch, 1913.
139. Healy, 1918.
140. Goddard, 1914a.
141. Schleier, 1931.
142. President's Committee, 1977.
143. Goddard, 1914a, p. 51.
144. Fitts, 1916, p. 80.
145. Lincoln, 1903, p. 90.
146. Fitts, 1920, p. 120.
147. Lincoln, 1903, p. 86.
148. Goddard, 1914a, p. xvii.
149. Pintner, 1923, p. 395.
150. Walsh, 1914, pp. 59–60.
151. Lincoln, 1903, p. 86.
152. Anderson, 1917.
153. Anderson, 1940, p. 54.
154. Lincoln, 1903, pp. 84–85.
155. Goddard, 1914a, p. 4.
156. Farrell, 1915.
157. Anderson, 1917, p. 19.
158. Steinbach; in Wilmarth, 1919, p. 21.
159. Fitts, 1920, p. 120.

160. Schmidt; in Wilmarth, 1919, p. 21.
161. Goddard, 1914a, p. 9.
162. Goddard, 1914a, p. 10.
163. Lincoln, 1903, p. 84.
164. Rogers; in Lincoln, 1903, p. 90.
165. Jacob, 1905, p. 98; Lincoln, 1903, p. 88.
166. Witmer, 1911, pp. 13–14.
167. Lincoln, 1910, p. 90.
168. Farrell, 1914, p. 12.
169. Farrell, 1915.
170. Fitts, 1920, p. 122.
171. Creswell, 1914, p. 69.
172. Anderson, 1917, p. 83.
173. Goddard, 1914a, p. 26.
174. Peterson, 1925, p. 25.
175. Witmer, 1911, pp. 266–267.
176. E. R. Johnstone, 1914.
177. Goddard, 1914a, p. 25.
178. Mitchell, 1916, p. 110.
179. McCready, 1918.
180. Fernald, 1919b, p. 115.
181. Fernald, 1919b, p. 117.
182. Fernald, 1912b, pp. 98–99.
183. Schlapp, 1915, p. 177.
184. Wilmarth, 1919.
185. E. R. Johnstone, 1914.
186. Fernald, 1919a, p. 24.
187. Fernald, 1919b, p. 22.
188. E. R. Johnstone, 1914, p. 15.
189. In The experience of the German Army, 1911.
190. Notes, 1917, p. 18.
191. Hastings, 1918.
192. Fernald, 1919a, p. 63.
193. Bliss, 1919, p. 13.
194. Business Section, 1919, p. 168.
195. Jones; in Wilmarth, 1919, p. 20.
196. Business Section, 1919, p. 168.
197. Bliss, 1919, pp. 12–13.

Chapter 7

1. May, 1964b, p. 3.
2. Leuchtenburg, 1964a, p. 37.
3. Kanner, 1964.
4. Fernald, 1924, p. 211.
5. Fernald, 1924, pp. 217–218.
6. Fernald, 1924, p. 215.
7. Goddard, 1928, pp. 222, 224–225.
8. Fernald, 1924, p. 212.
9. Haines, 1925, p. 137.
10. Foley, 1929.
11. Smith, 1923, p. 143.
12. Doll, 1936, p. 35.
13. Doll, 1936, p. 38.
14. Ellis, 1933.
15. Doll, 1936.
16. Woodall, 1929.
17. Goddard, 1928.

18. Moran, 1921, p. 127.
19. Terman, 1919.
20. Hoakley, 1932.
21. Raymond, 1927; Wladkowsky, 1938; Woodall, 1931.
22. Potter, 1922, p. 22.
23. Twitmyer, 1927.
24. Hildreth, 1939.
25. Doll, 1924, pp. 305–306.
26. Goodenough, 1949, p. 68.
27. Doll, 1927; Kuhlmann, 1920; Porteus, 1921.
28. Binet & Simon, 1910, p. 353.
29. Goddard, 1914.
30. Porteus, 1921.
31. Doll, 1953, pp. 30–33.
32. Baker, 1927.
33. Aldrich, 1931.
34. Doll, 1936b, pp. 42–43.
35. Estabrook, 1922, p. 14.
36. Ecob, 1924.
37. Estabrook, 1922.
38. Crothers, 1938.
39. Robinson, 1923.
40. Myerson, 1930.
41. Potter, 1924.
42. Jackson, 1935.
43. Crothers, 1938.
44. Murphy, 1925.
45. Davis, 1939.
46. Jervis, 1939, p. 13.
47. Mills, 1937, p. 18.
48. Bean, 1925; Davenport & Allen, 1925; Myers, 1938.
49. Penrose; in Kuenzel, 1929.
50. Vas; in Myerson, 1926; Timme, 1928.
51. Davenport, 1924.
52. Report of Committee on Nomenclature, 1932.
53. Brigham, 1923, p. viii.
54. Brigham, 1923, p. 210.
55. Morrison & Cornell, 1923, p. 185.
56. Darrow, 1925, p. 157.
57. Darrow, 1926, p. 135.
58. Atkinson, 1927.
59. Vanuxem, 1931.
60. Woodall, 1932, p. 350.
61. Skeels & Dye, 1939.
62. Doll, 1934; Penrose, 1934.
63. Bartemeier, 1925 p. 315; Berley, 1915.
64. Myerson, 1928, p. 110.
65. Hunsicker, 1938; Vanuxem, 1935.
66. Greene, 1930.
67. Potter, 1922, pp. 27–28.
68. Lowrey, 1928.
69. Pratt, 1926, p. 240–241.
70. Battery & Thayer, 1929, pp. 69–70.
71. Thayer, 1925, pp. 38–39.
72. Smith, 1924, p. 335.
73. Montaque, 1930.

74. Doll, 1921.
75. Glueck, 1935; Montaque, 1930; Willey, 1929.
76. Adler, 1922, pp. 54–56.
77. Adler, 1922, p. 56.
78. Glueck, 1935, p. 285.
79. Glueck, 1935, pp. 285–286.
80. Glueck, 1935, p. 289.
81. Sutherland, 1931.
82. Willey, 1929.
83. Doll, 1929, pp. 164–165.
84. Jacoby, 1923.
85. Address, 1921, p. 21.
86. *U.S. statutes at large,* 1925.
87. Kolb, 1928, pp. 196–197.
88. Kolb, 1928, pp. 192–193.
89. Kolb, 1928.
90. Laughlin, 1926, p. 218.
91. Laughlin, 1926.
92. Executive session, 1928.
93. Jennings, 1927, p. 237.
94. Doll, 1929, p. 163.
95. Selling & Finn, 1936, p. 274.
96. Goddard, 1928, p. 255.
97. Stebbins, 1931, pp. 69–70.
98. McNairy, 1923, p. 28.
99. *Buck* v. *Bell,* 1927.
100. Bernstein, 1921, p. 44.
101. Murdoch; in Bernstein, 1921, p. 59.
102. E. R. Johnstone, 1924, p. 51.
103. E. R. Johnstone, 1924, pp. 51–52.
104. Smith, 1922, p. 59.
105. Brown, 1925, p. 347.
106. Hackbusch, 1935; Raymond; in Matthew, 1932.
107. Keatings; in Matthews, 1932.
108. McGonagle, in Matthews, 1932; Watkins, 1928.
109. Wallace, 1924, p. 265.
110. Wallace, 1924, pp. 264–269.
111. McNairy, 1924, p. 271.
112. Lenz, 1939, p. 205.
113. Sandy, 1926, p. 162.
114. Wolfe, 1936, p. 135.
115. Fernald, 1924, p. 19.
116. Stowell, 1931, pp. 280–281.
117. Whitten, 1937, pp. 36–37.
118. Martens, 1935.
119. E. R. Johnstone, 1924, p. 283.
120. Biggs, 1923, p. 121.
121. Vanuxem, 1922.
122. Brown, 1923; E. R. Johnstone, 1929.
123. Veith, 1927.
124. E. L. Johnstone, 1938.
125. Ellis; in Battery & Thayer, 1929, p. 80.
126. Thayer, 1925, p. 38.
127. Bates, 1928.
128. Bates, 1928, p. 14.
129. Sukov, 1939, p. 184.
130. Butler, 1929, pp. 53–54.
131. Battery & Thayer, 1929.

132. News and Notes, 1938, p. 210.
133. Report of the chairman, 1937, pp. 198–199.
134. Report of the chairman, 1937, p. 200.
135. Frankel, 1938.
136. Hoakley, 1922; Little & Johnson, 1932; Matthews, 1921.
137. Cobb, 1923, p. 148.
138. Haskell & Strauss, 1943, p. 7; Willson, 1944.
139. Wolfe; in Moeder, 1932, p. 52.
140. Wolfe, in Moeder, 1932.
141. McNairy, 1924, p. 273.
142. Little, 1923, p. 60.
143. Watkins, 1932, pp. 459–460.
144. Little, 1923, p. 61.
145. Kline, 1924, p. 39.
146. Davies, 1925, p. 213.
147. Ecob, 1924, p. 21.
148. E. R. Johnstone, 1931, p. 340.
149. Doll, 1929.
150. Doll, 1936b.
151. Evans, 1926, p. 1.
152. Evans, 1926, p. 13.
153. Evans, 1926, p. 66.
154. Evans, 1926, p. 64.
155. Evans, 1926, p. 16.
156. Evans, 1926, p. 29.
157. Report to the General Assembly meeting, 1929, p. 117.
158. *Revised statutes of Utah,*1933.
159. Annual report of the Massachusetts Department of Public Welfare, 1935.
160. Baker, 1937; Watkins, 1932.
161. Moeder, 1932.
162. Hanna, 1938.
163. Vaux, 1935.
164. Vaux, 1936.
165. Vaux, 1936, pp. 87–88.
166. Kuenzel, 1938.
167. Baker, 1937, p. 152.
168. Scheier, 1931.
169. Report of Committee on Statistics, 1945, p. 345.
170. Warner, 1942.
171. Wooden, 1980.
172. Phillips, 1935, p. 73.
173. Berry, 1923, p. 135.
174. Street & Fuller, 1935, pp. 191–192.
175. Ide, 1932, p. 412.
176. Newland, 1939.
177. *Committee* v. *Johnson,* 1941.
178. *State* v. *Ghrist,* 1936.
179. *Board of Education of Cleveland Heights* v. *State ex. rel. Goldman,* 1933.
180. Barger, 1939, p. 199.
181. Berry, 1923, p. 133.
182. Taylor, 1921, pp. 30–31; Taylor, 1924, p. 164.

183. E. R. Johnstone, 1924, p. 54.
184. Berry, 1930.
185. Elliot, 1928.
186. Beaman, 1938, p. 87.
187. Beaman, 1938.
188. Wallin, 1924.
189. Wallin, 1924, p. 176.
190. Wallin, 1924, p. 181.
191. Martens, 1935.
192. Berry, 1936.
193. Martens, 1935.
194. Featherstone, 1932; Ingram, 1935; Inskeep, 1926; Wallin, 1924.
195. Fitts, 1921, p. 17.
196. Berry, 1936, pp. 116–117.
197. E. R. Johnstone, 1924, p. 54.
198. E. R. Johnstone, 1924, pp. 50–51.
199. Grace Fernald, 1943; Kirk, 1940; Monroe, 1937.
200. Galbraith, 1925, p. 160.
201. Martens, 1935, pp. 40–41.
202. Kelly, 1938.
203. Descourdes, 1928.
204. Descourdes, 1928, pp. 54–55.
205. Kirk & Johnson, 1951, p. 82.
206. Baller, 1936, pp. 238–239.
207. Scheier, 1931.
208. Scheier, 1931.
209. Kelly, 1938, p. 97.
210. Hitler, 1924, pp. 403–404.
211. Remak, 1969, pp. 133–134.
212. Grunberger, 1971, p. 451.
213. Remak, 1969, pp. 137–138.
214. Remak, 1969, p. 141.

Chapter 8

1. Leuchtenberg, 1964b.
2. Smith, 1981.
3. Frankel, 1944, p. 68.
4. Menninger, 1943, p. 55.
5. Frankel, 1944.
6. Ginzberg & Bray, 1953, p. 41.
7. Wittson et al., 1943.
8. Baier, 1943, p. 66.
9. Hunt et al., 1944.
10. Haskell & Strauss, 1943.
11. Whitney & MacIntyre, 1944.
12. Weaver, 1946.
13. Whitney & MacIntyre, 1944.
14. Hubbel, 1945, pp. 136–137.
15. Yepsen, 1945, p. 29.
16. Coakley, 1945.
17. Butler, 1945a, p. 298.
18. Bassett, 1944, p. 78.
19. Doll, 1944, p. 66.
20. Yepsen, 1941, pp. 202–203.
21. Kuhlmann, 1941, p. 213.
22. Doll, 1941, p. 215.
23. Skeels, 1942, pp. 349–350.
24. Levy, 1947; Pasmanick, 1946; Spitz, 1945.
25. Dearborn & Rothney, 1941; Honzik et al., 1948.

26. Malzberg, 1943.
27. Guilford, 1956.
28. Doll, 1947a, 1961; Sarason, 1959.
29. Doll, 1947b, p. 423.
30. Doll, 1941, p. 214.
31. Doll, 1947b, p. 421.
32. Yepsen, 1941, p. 205.
33. Heber, 1961.
34. Sloan & Birch, 1955.
35. Baroff, 1959; Beck & Lam, 1955; Bijou, 1942.
36. Finley & Thompson, 1958.
37. Alper, 1958; Shotwell, 1945.
38. Bensberg & Sloan, 1955; Papania et al., 1955.
39. Gellerman & Hays, 1951.
40. Garrison, 1960, p. 510.
41. Newland, 1952, p. 51.
42. Newland, 1952.
43. Molish, 1958, p. 283.
44. Arbitman, 1953.
45. Masserman & Balken, 1938.
46. Buhler et al., 1951.
47. Molish, 1958, p. 283.
48. McPherson, 1948.
49. Stolurow, 1958.
50. Bulletin, 1954.
51. Milligan, 1961.
52. Hurder, 1959, p. 754.
53. Stolurow, 1959, p. 332.
54. Hobbs, 1959, p. 239.
55. New York Department of Mental Hygiene, 1955, p. 87.
56. Weiner; in Kirk & Bateman, 1964.
57. Lemkau et al., 1942.
58. President's Panel on Mental Retardation, 1962.
59. Mullen & Nee, 1952.
60. Engel, 1940, p. 304.
61. Gregg, 1941.
62. Yannet, 1953, p. 449.
63. Landsteiner & Wiener, 1940.
64. Yannet & Leiberman, 1945.
65. Craft, 1979; Menolascino & Egger, 1978.
66. Jervis, 1942.
67. Berry, 1957.
68. Benda, 1946.
69. Penrose, 1951.
70. Hsu & Pomerat, 1953; Tijo & Levan, 1956.
71. Lejeune et al., 1959.
72. Ford et al., 1959; Jacobs & Strong, 1959.
73. Watson & Crick, 1953.
74. Tarjan, 1959.
75. Putnam, 1953.
76. In Tarjan, 1958.
77. Goldstein, 1948, pp. 210–211.
78. Neuer, 1947.
79. Kanner, 1948, pp. 717–720.
80. Chase, 1953; Fisher & Wolf-son, 1953; Snyder & Sechrest, 1959.
81. Vail, 1955, p. 151.
82. Ringleheim & Polatsek, 1957; Subotnik & Callahan, 1959.
83. Sarason, 1959, p. 224.
84. Wolfson, 1957.
85. Craft, 1957; Ison, 1957; Mitchell, 1959; Pallister & Stevens, 1957; Rosenblum et al., 1957.
86. Craft, 1959; Cutler et al., 1940.
87. Wardell et al., 1958, p. 343.
88. Zimmerman & Rosa, 1944.
89. Albert et al., 1946.
90. Zimmerman et al., 1946, 1947, 1949.
91. Quinn & Durling, 1950.
92. Kurland & Gilgash, 1953; Loeb & Tuddenham, 1950; McCulloch, 1950.
93. Angus, 1949; Campbell, 1953; Stevenson & Strauss, 1943; Stimson, 1959; Strom et al., 1947.
94. Town, 1941, p. 457.
95. E. L. Johnstone, 1942.
96. Yepsen, 1941; Willoughby, 1945.
97. Price & Halperin, 1940.
98. Butler, 1945b, p. 509.
99. Kaplan, 1944, p. 381.
100. Butler, 1945b, p. 513.
101. Kaplan, 1944, p. 381.
102. Willhite, 1942, p. 405.
103. Willhite, 1940, p. 406.
104. Willhite, 1940, p. 147.
105. Willhite, 1940, p. 148.
106. Willhite, 1942, p. 404.
107. Olden, 1945, p. 118.
108. Olden, 1945, p. 119.
109. Whitney, 1945, pp. 221–222.
110. President's Committee, 1977, p. 29.
111. Birch, 1953.
112. Birch, 1953; Wortis, 1954.
113. Dudley, 1956.
114. Jacobs & Shern, 1956.
115. McBride et al., 1953.
116. Wallin, 1962.
117. Thom, 1942, pp. 189–190.
118. Stevenson, 1952, pp. 719–720.
119. Nisonger, 1948.
120. Wallin, 1962, p. 88.
121. Hay; in NARC, 1954.
122. Hay, 1952a,b.
123. NARC, 1954, p. 1.
124. Elkin, 1976, p. 7.
125. Stern, 1951.
126. Rigler, 1956.
127. Richards, 1953, p. 57.
128. Robbins, 1957.
129. Roos, 1978, p. 26.
130. Coughlin, 1947.
131. Sheimo, 1951.
132. Smith, 1952, pp. 809–810.
133. Grebler, 1951, p. 482.
134. Roos, 1978, p. 15.
135. Gallagher, 1956, p. 294.
136. Rosen, 1955.
137. Kelman, 1956, p. 62.
138. Mackie, 1951, p. 130.
139. Kirk & Johnson, 1951, p. 118.
140. Birch, 1953, p. 572.
141. Kirk & Johnson, 1951.
142. Hungerford, 1941, p. 102.
143. Syden, 1962, p. 331.
144. Hungerford & Rosenzweig, 1944, p. 212.
145. Symposium, 1942, p. 81.
146. Kelly, 1943, p. 81.
147. Symposium, 1942.
148. Michal-Smith, 1951.
149. Hungerford, 1941.
150. Di Michael, 1950.
151. Kirk & Johnson, 1951, p. 135.
152. Kirk & Stevens, 1943; Melcher, 1939; Rhodes, 1943.
153. Kirk, 1950, pp. 308–309.
154. Mackie, 1965; Report of Committee on Statistics, 1945.
155. Mayo, 1963.
156. Spalding & Kvaraceus, 1944, p. 44.
157. The trainables, 1959, p. 12.
158. Goldberg, 1959, p. 12.
159. NARC, 1954.
160. Down, 1866, p. 262.
161. Wirtz & Guenther, 1957, p. 171.
162. Goldberg, 1957, p. 148.
163. Goldstein, 1956.
164. Goldberg, 1957.
165. Rothstein, 1953, p. 171.
166. Goldberg, 1957.
167. Boggs, 1954, p. 363.
168. Hudson, 1960.
169. Cain & Levine, 1961; Dunn & Hottel, 1958.
170. Mackie, 1965.
171. Lorenz, 1953.
172. Ireland, 1877.
173. Strauss & Lehtinen, 1947, p. 4.
174. Strauss & Lehtinen, 1947, p. 131.
175. Strauss & Lehtinen, 1947, p. 130.
176. Kirk, 1953, p. 138.
177. Yepsen, 1945, p. 291.
178. Cowen, 1940, p. 52.
179. Cowen, 1940, p. 71.
180. Hungerford et al., 1949, pp. 550–552.
181. Kirk, 1953.
182. Segregation, 1946, p. 240.
183. Challman, 1941, pp. 42–44.
184. Tenny, 1953, p. 264.

185. Segregation, 1946, p. 240.
186. Lord, 1956, pp. 321–322.
187. Rautman, 1944, pp. 100–101.
188. Johnson & Kirk, 1950.
189. Charles, 1953.
190. Kennedy, 1948, p. 97.
191. Abel, 1940.
192. Dinger, 1961.
193. Porter & Milazzo, 1958.
194. Saenger, 1957.
195. Peterson & Smith, 1960, p. 406.
196. Schmidt, 1946, pp. 117–118.
197. Kirk, 1948; A critique, 1949.
198. Sarason, 1951, p. 246.
199. Sarason, 1951, p. 246.
200. Rothstein, 1954.
201. Martens, 1950.
202. Mayo, 1963.
203. Sloan & Birch, 1955.
204. Storrs, 1950, p. 181.
205. Engberg, 1952; Stevens, 1956.
206. U.S. Department of Commerce, 1975.
207. In Ellis, 1978.
208. Goldstein, 1959; Sabagh & Windle, 1960.
209. Reed, 1946.
210. Pense, 1947.
211. Whitney & Caron, 1947.
212. Belinson, 1946.
213. Jolly, 1953.
214. Jolly, 1953, p. 633.
215. Slobody & Scanlon, 1959, p. 974.
216. York, 1942, p. 539.
217. Lerner, 1952, p. 105.
218. Engel, 1940, p. 306.
219. In Engel, 1940, p. 307.
220. Frankel, 1940, p. 10.
221. Tarjan & Forbes, 1955.
222. Pense, 1947; Weingold, 1957.
223. Luckey, 1953, p. 215.

224. Doll, 1944, p. 65.
225. Weingold, 1957.
226. Kramer et al., 1957, p. 494.
227. Kramer et al., 1957, p. 495.
228. Roselle, 1940.
229. Roewer, 1952, p. 553.
230. Deacon, 1952.
231. Patterson, 1943, p. 230.
232. Fried, 1941.
233. Freeman et al., 1956.
234. Harris & Kinney, 1947; Walker, 1948.
235. Dilcer, 1942, p. 203.
236. Beard, 1953, p. 547.
237. Berger & Waters, 1956; Kassler, 1957, p. 598.
238. Price, 1953, p. 87.
239. Walker, 1953a, p. 231.
240. Roselle, 1954, p. 597.
241. Elkin, 1976; Weingold, 1957.
242. Report of the Committee on Standards and Policy, 1944.
243. Report of the Committee on Standards and Policy, 1944, p. 315.
244. Walker, 1953b, p. 361.
245. Blain, 1952, p. 523.
246. Scheerenberger, 1976b.
247. Storrs, 1950; Walker, 1952.
248. Hackbusch, 1940, p. 297.
249. Bengs, 1953, pp. 385–386.
250. Hackbusch, 1950, p. 257.
251. Roselle, 1954, p. 598.
252. Weingold, 1957.
253. Benson, 1953, p. 722.
254. Benson, 1953, p. 723.
255. Krishef, 1959, p. 865; Wearne, 1941, p. 594.
256. Bijou et al., 1943; Harold, 1955; Kinder et al., 1941; Krishef, 1959; Wearne, 1941; Wolfson, 1956.

Epilogue

1. President's Panel, 1962, p. 196.
2. Smith, 1980, p. 576.
3. President's Panel, 1962, pp. 14–15.
4. Kennedy, 1963.
5. U.S. Department of Education, 1980.
6. Comptroller General of the United States, 1976.
7. Some facts, 1981.
8. United Nations, 1971.
9. International League, 1971, p. 2.
10. International League, 1971, p. 2.
11. Nirje, 1969.
12. Johnson, 1962.
13. Dunn, 1968.
14. Hobbs, 1975.
15. *Mills* v. *The Board of Education*, 1972.
16. Scheerenberger, 1978.
17. Klebanoff, 1964.
18. Blatt & Kaplan, 1966.
19. Wolfensberger, 1971, p. 32.
20. *Wyatt* v. *Stickney*, 1972.
21. *Lessard* v. *Schmidt*, 1972.
22. *Souder* v. *Brennan*, 1973.
23. Joint Commission on Accreditation of Hospitals, 1971.
24. Scheerenberger, 1980.
25. *Halderman* v. *Pennhurst State School and Hospital et al.*, 1978.
26. *Pennhurst State School and Hospital* v. *Halderman*, 1981.
27. Gould, 1977, p. 277.
28. In Gaylin et al., 1978, p. 72.
29. Kennedy; in President's Panel, 1962, p. 196.

BIBLIOGRAPHICAL
GUIDE TO
REFERENCE NOTES

Abbott, G. *The child and the state*, Vol. II. Chicago: University of Chicago Press, 1938.

Abel, T. A study of a group of subnormal girls successfully adjusted in industry and the community. *American Journal of Mental Deficiency*, 1940, *45*, 66–72.

Abt, I. *History of pediatrics*. Philadelphia: W. B. Saunders, 1965.

Address of welcome. *Journal of Psycho-Asthenics*, 1921, *26*, 11–16.

Adler, A. A behavioristic study of delinquency. *Journal of Psycho-Asthenics*, 1922, *27*, 39–56.

Albert, K., & Warden, C. The level of performance in the white rat. *Science*, 1944, *100*, 476.

Albert, K., Hoch, P., & Waelsch, H. Preliminary report on the effect of glutamic acid administration in mentally retarded subjects. *Journal of Nervous and Mental Diseases*, 1946, *104*, 263–274.

Aldrich, C. Experimental studies of idiot behavior. *Journal of Psycho-Asthenics*, 1931, *36*, 282–293.

Alexander, F., & Selesnick, S. *The history of psychiatry*. New York: Harper & Row, 1966.

Alper, A. A comparison of the Wechsler Intelligence Scale for Children and the Arthur Adaptation of Leiter International Performance Scale with Mental Defectives. *American Journal of Mental Deficiency*, 1958, *63*, 312–316.

Anderson, M. *Education of defectives in the public schools*. New York: World Book, 1917.

Anderson, M. Selection and classification of mentally retarded. *Phi Delta Kappan*, 1940, *23*, 54–56.

Anderson, V. Feeble-mindedness as seen in court. *Journal of Psycho-Asthenics*, 1916, *21*, 82–87.

Anderson, V. Studies in personality among feeble-minded delinquents seen in court. *Journal of Psycho-Asthenics*, 1918, *23*, 117–142.

Angus, L. Prefrontal lobotomy as a method of therapy in a special school. *American Journal of Mental Deficiency*, 1949, *53*, 470–476.

Annual report of the Massachusetts Department of Public Welfare, Boston, 1935.

Arbitman, H. Rorschach determinants in mentally defective and normal subjects. *The Training School Bulletin*, 1953, *50*, 143–151.

Aristotle. [*Politics*] (B. Jawett, trans.). New York: Carleton House, undated.

Ashman, W. The medico-legal study of idiocy. *Proceedings of the Association of Medical Officers of American Institutions for Idiotic and Feebleminded Persons*, 1889, 17–31.

Association of Medical Superintendents of American Institutions for the Insane. *American Journal of Insanity*, 1848, *5*, 19.

Asylums and schools for idiots. *American Journal of Insanity*, 1847, *4*, 76–79.

Atkinson, M. A study of infants of feebleminded delinquent females. *Journal of Psycho-Asthenics*, 1927, *31*, 110–128.

Ayres, L. The Binet-Simon measuring scale for intelligence. Some criticism and suggestions. *Psychological Clinic*, 1911, *5*, 187–196.

Babbitt, I. *Rousseau and romanticism*. Boston: Houghton Mifflin, 1928.

Bacon, R. *Roger Bacon essays*. New York: Russell, 1914.

Baier, D. The marginally useful soldier. *American Journal of Mental Deficiency*, 1932, *48*, 62–66.

Baker, B. Administrative policies, past and present. *Journal of Psycho-Asthenics*, 1937, *42*, 149–159.

Baker, C. Dorothea Dix. In: A. Johnson & D. Malone, (eds.), *Dictionary of American biography*, Vol. III, pp. 323–325. New York: Charles Scribner's, 1930.

Baker, H. *Characteristic differences in bright and dull pupils*. Bloomington, IL: Public School Publishing Company, 1927.

Baller, W. A study of the present social status of a group of adults, who, when they were in elementary schools, were classified as mentally deficient. *Genetic Psychology Monographs*, 1936, *18*(3), 165–244.

Baller, W., & Schalock, H. Conditioned response treatment of enuesis. *Exceptional Children*, 1956, *22*, 233–236, 247–248.

Barger, W. Where the New York State Program for the care of mental defectives fails to meet the needs of the schools. *Journal of Psycho-Asthenics*, 1939, *44*, 198–202.

Baroff, G. Bender-Gestalt visuo-motor function in mental deficiency. *American Journal of Mental Deficiency*, 1956, *60*, 753–760.

Barr, M. Moral paranoia. *Proceedings of the Association of Medical Officers of American Institutions for Idiotic and Feebleminded Persons*, 1895, 522–531.

Barr, M. The imperative call for our present to our future. *Journal of Psycho-Asthenics*, 1902, *7*, 5–8.

Barr, M. *Mental illness and social policy: The American experience*. Philadelphia: P. Blakiston's Son, 1904. (a)

Barr, M. Classification of mental defectives. *Journal of Psycho-Asthenics*, 1904, *9*, 29–38. (b)

Bartemeier, L. Psychosis in the feebleminded. *Journal of Psycho-Asthenics*, 1925, *30*, 314–324.

Bassett, D. New Jersey institutions for mentally deficient. Their contributions and place in the war effort. *American Journal of Mental Deficiency*, 1944, *49*, 75–79.

Bates, S. Practical problems of the defective delinquent. *Journal of Psycho-Asthenics*, 1928, *33*, 110–114.

Battery, P., & Thayer, W. The defective delinquent. *Journal of Psycho-Asthenics*, 1929, *34*, 69–81.

Beach, F. Types of idiocy and imbecility. *Proceedings of the Association of Medical Officers of American Institutions for Idiotic and Feebleminded Persons*, 1895, 573–586.

Beaman, F. Progressive education for the mentally retarded child. *Journal of Psycho-Asthenics*, 1938, *43*, 86–89.

Bean, R. Some anatomical characteristics of the mongoloid, a hypomorph white type. *Journal of Psycho-Asthenics*, 1925, *30*, 293–303.

Beard, R. Industrial therapy with mental defectives. *American Journal of Mental Deficiency*, 1953, *57*, 547–553.

Beck, H., & Lam, R. Use of the WISC in predicting organicity. *Journal of Clinical Psychology*, 1955, *11*, 154–158.

Belinson, L. The organization of a rehabilitation program for the mentally deficient. *American Journal of Mental Deficiency*, 1946, *51*, 102–110.

Benda, C. Ten years research in mental deficiency. *American Journal of Mental Deficiency*, 1946, *51*, 170–185.

Bengs, H. Mental deficiency: An orientation. *American Journal of Mental Deficiency*, 1953, *57*, 384–389.

Bensberg, G., & Sloan, W. The use of the Cattell Culture Free Test with mental defectives. *American Journal of Mental Deficiency*, 1955, *59*, 499–503.

Benson, F. Problems faced by an institution in placing mentally deficient patients in family care. *American Journal on Mental Deficiency*, 1953, *57*, 719–726.

Berger, A., & Waters, T. The psychologist's concept of his function in institutions for the mentally retarded. *American Journal of Mental Deficiency*, 1956, *60*, 823–826.

Berley, H. The psychosis of the high imbecile. *American Journal of Insanity*, 1915, *75*, 15–19.

Bernstein, C. Self-sustaining feeble-minded. *Journal of Psycho-Asthenics*, 1917, *22*, 150–161.

Bernstein, C. Rehabilitation of the mentally defective. *Journal of Psycho-Asthenics*, 1918, *23*, 92–103.

Bernstein, C. Colony and extra-institutional care for the feebleminded. *Mental Hygiene*, 1920, *4*, 1–29.

Bernstein, C. Colony care for isolation defective and dependent cases. *Journal of Psycho-Asthenics*, 1921, *26*, 43–59.

Berry, C. Some limitations of the Binet-Simon Test of Intelligence. *Transactions*, 1913, *5*, 649–654.

Berry, C. The mentally retarded child in the public schools. *Journal of Psycho-Asthenics*, 1923, *28*, 129–136.

Berry, C. The aims and methods of education as applied to mental defectives. *Journal of Psycho-Asthenics*, 1930, *35*, 68–72.

Berry, C. Public school education of mentally retarded children. *Journal of Psycho-Asthenics*, 1936, *41*, 111–130.

Berry, W. A study of the incidence of mongolism in relation to the flouride content of water. *American Journal of Mental Deficiency*, 1957, *62*, 634–636.

Best, H. *Public provisions for the mentally retarded in the United States*. New York: Crowell, 1965.

Biggs, B. A conception of the superintendent's responsibilities. *Journal of Psycho-Asthenics*, 1923, *28*, 119–123.

Bijou, S. The psychometric pattern approach as an aid to clinical analysis. *American Journal of Mental Deficiency*, 1942, *46*, 354–362.

Bijou, S., Ainsworth, M., & Stockey, M. The social adjustment of mentally retarded girls paroled from the Wayne County Training School. *American Journal of Mental Deficiency*, 1943, *47*, 422–428.

Binet, A. Attention et adaptation. *L'Anneé Psychologique*, 1899, *6*, 284–404.

Binet, A. *Les idées modernes sur les enfants*, Paris: E. Flammarion, 1909.

Binet, A., & Simon, T. Application des méthodes nouvelles au diagnostic du niveau intellectual chez des enfants normaux et anormaux d'hospice et d'école primaire. *L'Anneé Psychologique*, 1905, *11*, 245–366. (a)

Binet, A., & Simon, T. Méthodes nouvelles pour le diagnostic du niveau intellectual des anormaux. *L'Anneé Psychologique*, 1905, *11*, 191–244. (b)

Binet, A., & Simon, T. [*Mentally defective children*] (W. B. Drummond, trans.). London: E. Arnold, 1907.

Binet, A., & Simon, T. L'arriération. *L'Anneé Psychologique*, 1910, *16*, 49–360.

Birch, J. Patterns of clinical services for exceptional children. *Exceptional Children*, 1953, *19*, 214–222.

Blain, D. Values of institutional standards. *American Journal of Mental Deficiency*, 1952, *56*, 519–523.

Blake, L. Some practical and speculative views derived from six months' experience at Elwyn. *Proceedings of the Association of Medical Officers of American Institutions for Idiotic and Feebleminded Persons*, 1892, 313–317.

Blatt, B., & Kaplan, I. *Christmas in purgatory*. Boston: Allyn and Bacon, 1966.

Bleuler, E. [*Dementia praecox or the group of schizophrenics*] (J. Zinkin, trans.). New York: International Universities Press, 1950.

Bliss, G. Mental defectives and the war. *Journal of Psycho-Asthenics*, 1919, *24*, 11–17.

Board of Education of Cleveland Heights v. *State ex. rel. Goldman*, 191 N.W. 914, 47 Ohio, App. 417 (1933).

Board of Public Charities of the State of Illinois. *Second biennial report, 1872*. Springfield, IL: State Printer, 1873.

Body of Liberties (1641). In: C. Eliot (ed.), *American historical documents*, pp. 66–84. New York: Collier, 1938.

Boggs, E. Day classes for severely retarded children. *American Journal of Mental Deficiency*, 1954, *58*, 357–370.

Boring, E. *A history of experimental psychology*. New York: Century, 1929.

Bourneville, D. Scléreuse tubereuse des convulsion cérébrales. *Archives of Neurology*, 1880, *1*, 91, 391.

Bowra, C. *The Greek experience*. New York: World, 1957.

Brigham, C. *A study of American intelligence*. Princeton: Princeton University Press, 1923.

Brockett, L. In memory of Eduoard Seguin. *Proceedings of the Association of American Institutions for Idiotic and Feebleminded Persons*, 1881, 9–23.

Brodinsky, B. Twelve major events that shaped America's schools. *Phi Delta Kappan*, 1976, *58*(1), 68–77.

Broomall, J. The helpless child. *Proceedings of the Association of Medical Officers of American Institutions for Idiotic and Feebleminded Persons*, 1889, 38–41.

Brotemarkle, R. (ed.). *Clinical psychology*. Philadelphia: University of Pennsylvania Press, 1931.

Brown v. *Board of Education*, 347 U.S. Supreme Court 485 (1954).

Brown, C. Prevention of mental disease. *Proceedings of the Association of Medical Officers of American Institutions for Idiotic and Feebleminded Persons*, 1877, 25–35.

Brown, C. A visit to four English institutions. *Proceedings of the Association of Medical Officers of American Institutions for Idiotic and Feebleminded Persons*, 1882, 226–235.

Brown, G. In memory—Hervey B. Wilbur. *Proceedings of the Association of Medical Officers of American Institutions for Idiotic and Feebleminded Persons*, 1886, 291–295.

Brown, G. President's annual address. *Journal of Psycho-Asthenics*, 1898, *3*, 1–11.

Brown, S. The year's progress in New York State in the care of mental defectives. *Journal of Psycho-Asthenics*, 1923, *28*, 198–203.

Brown, S. State administrative problems in the care of mental defectives. *Journal of Psycho-Asthenics*, 1925, *30*, 346–355.

Bryan, C. *The Papyrus Ebers*. New York: D. Appleton, 1930.

Buck v. *Bell*, 274 U.S. 200, 47 S. Ct. 584 (1927).

Bucknill, J. Idiocy. *Journal of Mental Science*, July, 1873.

Buhler, C., Lumry, G., & Carol, H. "World Test" standardization studies. *Journal of Child Psychiatry*, 1951, *2*, 2–69.

Bullard, W. The high-grade mental defectives. *Journal of Psycho-Asthenics*, 1909, *14*, 14–15.

Bulletin: Peabody college gets grant for study of mental retardation. *Exceptional Children*, 1954, *21*, 2.

Burchell, S. *Age of progress*. New York: Time, 1966.

Burdett, H. *Hospitals and asylums of the world*. London: J. & A. Churchill, 1891.

Business Section. *Journal of Psycho-Asthenics*, 1919, *24*, 156–169.

Butler, A. Editorial: Does the education of the feeble-minded pay? *Proceedings of the Association of Medical Officers of American Institutions for Idiotic and Feeble-minded Persons*, 1883, 152.

Butler, F. Care and treatment of the defective delinquent. *Journal of Psycho-Asthenics*, 1929, *34*, 52–61.

Butler, F. Mental defectives in military service and wartime industries. *American Journal of Mental Deficiency*, 1945, *50*, 296–300. (a)

Butler, F. A quarter of a century's experience in sterilization of mental defectives in California. *American Journal of Mental Deficiency*, 1945, *50*, 508–513. (b)

Butts, R., & Cremin, L. *A history of education in American culture*. New York: Holt, Rinehart & Winston, 1953.

Cain, L., & Levine, S. A study of the effects of community and institutional school classes for trainable mentally retarded children. *Exceptional Children*, 1961, *28*, 217–220.

Campbell, J. Electric shock treatment in mental deficiency. *American Journal of Mental Deficiency*, 1953, *58*, 112–113.

Carlson, E., & Dain, N. The psychotherapy that was moral treatment. *American Journal of Psychiatry*, 1960, *117*, 519–524.

Carson, D. President's address. *Proceedings of the Association of Medical Officers of American Institutions for Idiotic and Feebleminded Persons*, 1891, 14–15.

Carty, R., & Breault, G. Geel: A comprehensive community mental health program. *Perspectives in Psychiatric Care*, 1967, *5*, 281–285.

Casson, L. *Ancient Egypt*. New York: Time, 1965.

Cattell, J. Mental tests and measurements. *Mind*, 1890, *15*, 373–379.

Chadwick, J., & Mann, W. *The medical works of Hippocrates*. Oxford: Blackwell Scientific Publications, 1950.

Challman, A. Mental health in special classes. *Journal of Exceptional Children*, 1941, *8*, 42–49.

Charles, D. Ability and accomplishments of persons earlier judged mentally deficient. *Genetic Psychology Monographs*, 1953, *47*, 3–71.

Chase, M. The practical application of psychotherapy in an institution for the mentally deficient. *American Journal of Mental Deficiency*, 1953, *58*, 337–341.

Coakley, F. Study of feeble-minded wards employed in war industries. *American Journal of Mental Deficiency*, 1945, *50*, 301–306.

Cobb, O. Parole of mental defectives. *Journal of Psycho-Asthenics*, 1923, *28*, 145–148.

Combe, G. *Constitution of man*. New York: Fowlers and Wells, 1851.

Committee on Classification of Feeble-minded. *Journal of Psycho-Asthenics*, 1910, *15*, 61–67.

Committee v. *Johnson*, 35 N.E. 2nd 801, 309, Mass. 476 (1941).

Comptroller General of the United States. *Returning the mentally disabled to the community*. Washington, DC: General Accounting Office, 1976.

Concerning recent legislation. *Journal of Psycho-Asthenics*, 1901, *7*, 83–85.

Condillac, E. [*An essay on the origin of human knowledge*]

(T. Nugent, trans.). London: Lamb, 1746. (Reprinted by Scholar's Facsimiles & Reprints, Gainesville, FL, 1971.)

Coughlin, E. Parental attitudes toward handicapped children. *Child,* 1947, *1,* 11–16.

Cowen, P. Education for mentally handicapped. *Phi Delta Kappan,* 1940, *23,* 51–53.

Cowie, L. *Seventeenth century Europe.* New York: Frederick Ungar, 1960.

Craft, M. Tranquilizers in mental deficiency: Chlorpromazine. *Journal of Mental Deficiency Research,* 1957, 91–95.

Craft, M. Mental disorder in the defective: The use of tranquilizers. *American Journal of Mental Deficiency,* 1959, *64,* 63–71.

Craft, M. *Tredgold's Mental Retardation* (12th ed.). London: Balliere Tindall, 1979.

Creswell, C. Special school versus special classes. *Journal of Psycho-Asthenics,* 1914, *19,* 67–74.

A critique of the evaluation of the study by Bernadine G. Schmidt entitled: "Changes in Personal, Social, and Intellectual Behavior of Children Originally Classified as Feebleminded." *Exceptional Children,* 1949, *15,* 225–234.

Crothers, B. Birth injuries and the illnesses of infancy in the etiology of mental deficiency. *Journal of Psycho-Asthenics,* 1938, *43,* 32–37.

Cutler, M., Little, J., & Strauss, A. The effect of benzadrine on mentally deficient children. *American Journal of Mental Deficiency,* 1940, *45,* 59–65.

Dahmus, J. *The Middle Ages.* Garden City, NY: Doubleday, 1968.

Danielson, F., & Davenport, C. *The hill folk.* Cold Harbor, NY: Eugenics Record Office, 1912.

Darrow, C. The Edwards and the Jukes. *American Mercury,* 1925, *6,* 147–157.

Darrow, C. The eugenics cult. *American Mercury,* 1926, *8,* 129–137.

Darwin, C. *The origin of species.* A Facsimile of the First Edition. Cambridge, MA: Harvard University Press, 1975.

Davenport, C. *The Nams.* Cold Harbor, NY: Eugenics Record Office, 1912.

Davenport, C. Influence of endocrines on heredity. *Journal of Psycho-Asthenics,* 1924, *29,* 132–147.

Davenport, C., & Allen, G. Family studies on mongoloid dwarfs. *Journal of Psycho-Asthenics,* 1925, *30,* 266–286.

Davies, S. The institution in relation to the school system. *Journal of Psycho-Asthenics,* 1925, *30,* 210–226.

Davies, S. *The mentally retarded in society.* New York: Columbia University, 1959.

Davis, D. Encephalography—The method and its use in mental deficiency. *Journal of Psycho-Asthenics,* 1939, *44,* 72–78.

Deacon, K. An experiment in the cottage training of low-grade defectives. *American Journal of Mental Deficiency,* 1952, *47,* 195–202.

Dearborn, W., & Rothney, J. *Predicting the child's development.* Cambridge, MA: Harvard University Press, 1941.

DeGuimps, R. [*Pestalozzi: His life and work*] (J. Russell, trans.). New York: Appleton-Century-Crofts, 1895.

Demos, J. *A little commonwealth.* New York: Oxford University Press, 1970.

Descourdes, A. [*The education of mentally defective children*] (E. Row, trans.). New York: D.C. Heath, 1928.

Deutsch, A. *The mentally ill in America* (2nd ed.). New York: Columbia University Press, 1949.

Dewey, J., & Dewey, E. *Schools of tomorrow.* New York: E. P. Dutton, 1915.

Dickens, C. American Notes. In: *Collected works of Charles Dickens,* pp. 337–521. New York: Greystone Press, undated.

Dickens, C. *Oliver Twist.* New York: Dutton, 1907.

Dilcer, D. What occupational therapy can do for the mentally defective. *American Journal of Mental Deficiency,* 1942, *47,* 203–208.

Diller, T. Some practical problems relating to the feebleminded. *Journal of Psycho-Asthenics,* 1911, *16,* 20–25.

DiMichael, S. *Vocational rehabilitation of mentally retarded.* Washington, DC: U.S. Government Printing Office, 1950.

Dinger, J. Post-school adjustment of former educable retarded pupils. *Exceptional Children,* 1961, *27,* 353–360.

Dix, D. *Memorial to the legislature of Massachusetts.* Boston: Munroe and Francis, 1843.

Dix, D. *Memorial soliciting a state hospital for the insane submitted to the legislature of Pennsylvania, February 3, 1845.* Harrisburg, PA: J.M.G. Lescue, 1845.

Dix, D. *A review of the present condition of the State Penitentiary of Kentucky with brief notices and remarks upon the jails and poor-houses.* Frankfort, KY: A. G. Hodges, 1846. (a)

Dix, D. *Memorial soliciting an appropriation for the State Hospital for the Insane at Lexington; and also urging the necessity for establishing a new hospital in the Green River Country.* Frankfort, KY: A. G. Hodges, 1846. (b)

Dix, D. *Memorial soliciting enlarged and improved accommodations for the insane of the state of Tennessee by the establishment of a new hospital.* Nashville, TN: B. R. M'Kennie, 1847.

Dix, D. *Memorial soliciting a state hospital for the protection and cure of the insane submitted to the General Assembly of North Carolina.* Raleigh, NC: Seaton Gales, 1848.

Doll, E. Suggestions on the extension of the Binet-Simon Measuring Scale. *Transactions,* 1913, *5,* 665–669.

Doll, E. Form board speeds as diagnostic age tests. *Journal of Psycho-Asthenics,* 1916, *20,* 55–62.

Doll, E. Classification of defective delinquents. *Journal of Psycho-Asthenics,* 1921, *26,* 91–100.

Doll, E. Capabilities of low-grade feeble-minded. *Training School Bulletin,* 1924, *21,* 65–77.

Doll, E. Borderline diagnosis. *Journal of Psycho-Asthenics,* 1927, *32,* 45–59.

Doll, E. Community control of the feebleminded. *Journal of Psycho-Asthenics,* 1929, *34,* 161–175.

Doll, E. Annual report from the Department of Research. New Jersey: Training School at Vineland, 1934, *31,* 112–123.

Doll, E. *The Vineland Social Maturity Scale.* Publication of the Training School at Vineland, Department of Research, Series 1936, No. 3, April 1936. (a)

Doll, E. Current thoughts on mental deficiency. *Journal of Psycho-Asthenics,* 1936, *41,* 33–49. (b)

Doll, E. The essentials of an inclusive concept of mental deficiency. *American Journal of Mental Deficiency,* 1941, *46,* 214–219.

Doll, E. Mental defectives and the war. *American Journal of Mental Deficiency*, 1944, *49*, 64–66.

Doll, E. Feeble-mindedness versus intellectual retardation. *American Journal of Mental Deficiency*, 1947, *51*, 456–459. (a)

Doll, E. Is mental deficiency curable? *American Journal of Mental Deficiency*, 1947, *51*, 420–428. (b)

Doll, E. Mental deficiency vs. neurophrenia. *American Journal of Mental Deficiency*, 1953, *57*, 477–480.

Doll, E. *The measurement of social competence*. Minneapolis: Educational Test Bureau, 1953.

Doll, E. Trends and problems in the education of the mentally retarded, 1800–1940. *American Journal of Mental Deficiency*, 1962, *72*, 175–183.

Dorland's illustrated medical dictionary. Philadelphia: W. B. Saunders, 1974.

Douglas, J. (ed.). *The new Bible dictionary*. Grand Rapids, MI: Wm. B. Erdmans, 1962.

Douglass, M. Special lines of work and results sought. *Journal of Psycho-Asthenics*, 1914, *19*, 135–149.

Down, J. Observations on an ethnic classification of idiots. *Rep. Obs. London Hospital*, 1866, *3*, 259–262.

Down, J. Observations on an ethnic classification of idiots. *Journal of Mental Science*, 1867, *13*, 121–123.

Down, J. *Mental affections of children and youth*. London: J. & A. Churchill, 1887.

Dugdale, R. *The Jukes: A study in crime, pauperism, disease, and heredity*. New York: G. P. Putnam, 1877. (Reprinted by Arno Press, 1970).

Dugdale, R. *The Jukes: A study of crime, pauperism, disease, and heredity*. New York: G. P. Putnam, 1910.

Duncan, P., & Millard, W. *A manual for the classification, training, and education of the feeble-minded, imbecile, and idiotic*. London: Longmans, Green, 1866.

Dunn, L. Special education for the mildly retarded—Is much of it justifiable? *Exceptional Children*, 1968, *35*, 5–22.

Dunn, L., & Hottel, J. *The effectiveness of special day class training programs for severely mentally retarded (trainable) children*. Nashville, TN: George Peabody College for Teachers, 1958.

Dunton, W. The second half-century of the journal. *American Psychiatric Association: One Hundred Years*, 1944, 41–60.

Durant, W. *Our Oriental heritage*. New York: Simon and Schuster, 1935.

Durant, W. *The life in Greece*. New York: Simon and Schuster, 1939.

Durant, W. *Caesar and Christ*. New York: Simon and Schuster, 1944.

Durant, W. *The age of faith*. New York: Simon and Schuster, 1950.

Durant, W. *The age of reason begins*. New York: Simon and Schuster, 1961.

Durant, W., & Durant, A. *Rousseau and revolution*. New York: Simon and Schuster, 1967.

East, E. Hidden feeblemindedness. *Journal of Heredity*, 1917, *8*, 215–217.

Ebbell, B. (trans.). *The Papyrus Ebers*. London: Oxford University Press, 1937.

Eby, F. *The development of modern education*. Englewood Cliffs, NJ: Prentice-Hall, 1952.

Ecob, K. New York state's accomplishments and immediate aims in extra institutional care of mental defectives. *Journal of Psycho-Asthenics*, 1924, *29*, 20–31.

Eggert, G. Fight for the 8-hour day. *American History*, 1972, *7*, 36–44.

Eliot, C. (ed.). *American historical documents*. New York: Collier, 1938.

Elkin, E. Historical perspectives. In: *A national forum on residential services*, pp. 5–12. Arlington, TX: National Association for Retarded Citizens, 1977.

Elliot, C. The training of teachers for the feebleminded. *Journal of Psycho-Asthenics*, 1928, *33*, 166–176.

Ellis, W. *The handicapped child: Report of the Committee on Physically and Mentally Handicapped of the White House Conference on Child Health and Protection*. New York: Century, 1933.

Emerick, E. Progress in the care of the feeble-minded in Ohio. *Journal of Psycho-Asthenics*, 1917, *22*, 73–79.

Engberg, E. The institution's role in public education. *American Journal of Mental Deficiency*, 1952, *57*, 4–8.

Engel, A. When should the school refer the mental defective to the specialized agency or institution? *American Journal of Mental Deficiency*, 1940, *45*, 304–309.

Erikson, K. *Wayward Puritans: A study in the sociology of defiance*. New York: John Wiley & Sons, 1966.

Esquirol, J. E., *Des maladies mentales, considérées sous les rapports médiceux, hygiéniques, et médico-légaux, 1772–1840*. Paris: Baillière, 1838.

Esquirol, J. E. *Mental maladies: A treatise on insanity*. Facsimile of the English Edition of 1845. New York: Hafner, 1965.

Estabrook, A. *The Jukes in 1915*. Washington, DC: Carnegie Institute of Washington, 1916.

Estabrook, A. The work of the Indiana Committee on Mental Defectives. *Journal of Psycho-Asthenics*, 1922, *27*, 12–17.

Estabrook, A. The pauper idiot pension in Kentucky. *Journal of Psycho-Asthenics*, 1928, *33*, 59–61.

Estabrook, A., & McDougle, I. *Mongrel Virginians: The Win tribe*. Washington, DC: Carnegie Institute, 1926.

Esten, R. Backward children in the public schools. *Journal of Psycho-Asthenics*, 1900, *5*, 10–16.

Evans, H. *The American poorfarm and its inmates*. Des Moines: The Loyal Order of Moose, 1926.

Executive Session. *Journal of Psycho-Asthenics*, 1928, *33*, 264.

The experience of the German army with the defectives and the feeble-minded. *Journal of Psycho-Asthenics*, 1911, *16*, 68–76.

Farnell, F. A consideration of feeble-mindedness. *Journal of Psycho-Asthenics*, 1912, *16*, 160–172.

Farrell, E. Special classes in the New York City schools. *Journal of Psycho-Asthenics*, 1908, *13*, 91–96.

Farrell, E. The place of the school in the problem of mental deficiency. *Transactions*, 1914, *3*, 435–443.

Farrell, E. A preliminary report on the careers of three hundred fifty children who have left ungraded classes. *Journal of Psycho-Asthenics*, 1915, *20*, 20–26.

Featherstone, W. *The curriculum of the special class*. New York: Teachers College, Columbia University, 1932.

Fernald, G. The defective delinquent class differentiating tests. *American Journal of Insanity*, 1912, *72*, 523–594.

Fernald, G. The defective delinquent since the war. *Journal of Psycho-Asthenics*, 1919, *24*, 55–64.

Fernald, G. Curative treatment vs. punitive for defective delinquents. *Journal of Psycho-Asthenics*, 1920, *25*, 161–167.

Fernald, Grace. *Remedial techniques in basic school subjects.* New York: McGraw-Hill, 1943.

Fernald, W. Some of the methods employed in the care and training of feeble-minded children of the lower grades. *Proceedings of the Association of Medical Officers of American Institutions for Idiotic and Feebleminded Persons,* 1892, 450–457.

Fernald, W. Mentally defective children in the public schools. *Journal of Psycho-Asthenics,* 1903, *8,* 25–35. (a)

Fernald, W. Farm colony in Massachusetts. *Journal of Psycho-Asthenics,* 1903, *7,* 74–80. (b)

Fernald, W. Mentally defective children in the public schools. *Journal of Psycho-Asthenics,* 1904, *8,* 25–35.

Fernald, W. The imbecile with criminal instincts. *Journal of Psycho-Asthenics,* 1909, *14,* 16–38.

Fernald, W. The burden of feeble-mindedness. *Journal of Psycho-Asthenics,* 1912, *17,* 87–111.

Fernald, W. The diagnosis of the higher grades of mental defect. *Journal of Psycho-Asthenics,* 1913, *18,* 73–84.

Fernald, W. The growth of provision for the feeble-minded in the United States. *Mental Hygiene,* 1917, *1,* 34–59.

Fernald, W. After-care study of the patients discharged from Waverley for a period of twenty-five years. *Ungraded,* 1919, *5,* 25–31. (a)

Fernald, W. State programs for the care of the mentally defective. *Journal of Psycho-Asthenics,* 1919, *24,* 114–122. (b)

Fernald, W. An out-patient clinic in connection with a state institution for the feeble-minded. *Journal of Psycho-Asthenics,* 1920, *20,* 81–89.

Fernald, W. The diagnosis of the higher grades of mental defect. *Ungraded,* 1922, *7,* 126–130.

Fernald, W. Thirty years' progress in the care of the feeble-minded. *Journal of Psycho-Asthenics,* 1924, *29,* 206–219.

Fernberger, S. History of the psychological clinic. In: R. Brotemarkle (ed.), *Clinical psychology,* pp. 10–37. Philadelphia: University of Philadelphia Press, 1931.

Ferris, W. Governor's address. *Journal of Psycho-Asthenics,* 1913, *18,* 67–72.

Fiedler, L. *Freaks.* New York: Simon and Schuster, 1978.

Fields, S. Asylum on the front porch. *Innovations,* 1974, *1,* 15–16.

Finlayson, A. *The Dack family: A study in hereditary lack of emotional control.* Cold Harbor, NY: Eugenics Record Office, 1916.

Finley, C., & Thompson, J. An abbreviated Wechsler Intelligence Scale for children for use with educable mentally retarded. *American Journal of Mental Deficiency,* 1958, *63,* 373–480.

Fish, W. The medical treatment of idiots and imbeciles. *Proceedings of the Association of Medical Officers of American Institutions for Idiotic and Feebleminded Persons,* 1882, 215–225.

Fish, W. Institution discipline. *Proceedings of the Association of Medical Officers of American Institutions for Idiotic and Feebleminded Persons,* 1889, 45–48.

Fish, W. Custodial care of adult idiots. *Proceedings of the Association of Medical Officers of American Institutions for Idiotic and Feebleminded Persons,* 1892, 203–218.

Fish, W. Custodial care of adult idiots. *Proceedings of the Association of Medical Officers of American Institutions for Idiotic and Feebleminded Persons,* 1894, 217.

Fisher. L.. & Wolfson, I. Group therapy of mental defectives. *American Journal of Mental Deficiency,* 1953, *57,* 463–476.

Fitts, A. How to fill the gap between the special classes and institutions. *Journal of Psycho-Asthenics,* 1916, *20,* 78–87.

Fitts, A. The value of special classes for the mentally defective pupils in the public schools. *Journal of Psycho-Asthenics,* 1920, *25,* 115–123.

Foley, R. A study of the patients discharged from the Rome State School for the twenty year period ending December 31, 1924. *Journal of Psycho-Asthenics,* 1929, *34,* 190–207.

Ford, C., Jones, K., Miller, O., Mittwoch, U., Penrose, L., Ridler, M., & Shapiro, A. The chromosomes in a patient showing both mongolism and the Klinefelter syndrome. *Lancet,* 1959, *1,* 711–713.

Frankel, E. The 1400 who entered New Jersey institutions for the mentally deficient. *Journal of Psycho-Asthenics,* 1938, *43,* 186–200.

Frankel, E. The development of the program for the mentally deficient in New Jersey: A statistical review. *American Journal of Mental Deficiency,* 1940, *45,* 110–118.

Frankel, E. Incidence of previous institutional care among selective service registrants—The New Jersey experience of 100,000 men. *American Journal of Mental Deficiency,* 1944, *49,* 68–74.

Frazer, J. America's "Turbulent Spirit" Dr. Benjamin Rush. *American History,* 1974, *9(7),* 20–31.

Frazier, T. (ed.). *Underside of American history.* New York: Harcourt Brace Jovanovich, 1971.

Freedman, A., Kaplan, H., & Sadock, B. *Modern synopsis of comprehensive textbook of psychiatry.* Baltimore: Williams & Wilkins, 1972.

Freeman, D., Ott, W., & Dinsmore, M. School program for mentally retarded adults. *American Journal on Mental Deficiency,* 1956, *61,* 94–104.

Fried, R. Ten years of relaxation and self-direction at Bailey Hall and a description of new methods in training of children. *American Journal of Mental Deficiency,* 1941, *45,* 459–463.

Friedman, L. *A history of American law.* New York: Simon and Schuster, 1973.

Froebel, F. *[Autobiography]* (E. Michaelis & H. K. Moore, trans.). Syracuse, NY: C. W. Bardeen, 1889.

Gail, M. *Life in the Renaissance.* New York: Random House, 1968.

Galbraith, L. Group activity in a special class. *Journal of Psycho-Asthenics,* 1925, *30,* 156–161.

Galdston, I. The psychiatry of Paracelsus. *Bulletin of the History of Medicine,* 1950, *24,* 205–218.

Gallagher, J. Rejecting parents. *Exceptional Children,* 1956, *22,* 273–276, 294.

Garraty, J. *The American nation.* New York: Harper & Row, 1966.

Garrison, I. Developing potential of exceptional children. *Exceptional Children,* 1960, *26,* 510.

Garrod, A. *Inborn errors of metabolism.* London: Oxford University Press, 1909.

Gay, P. *Age of enlightenment.* New York: Time, 1966.

Gaylin, W., Glasser, I., Marcus, S., & Rothman, D. *Doing good.* New York: Pantheon Books, 1978.

Gellerman, S., & Hays, W. A proposed correction for the confounded effects of cultural variation in intelligence quotients. *American Journal of Mental Deficiency,* 1951, *56,* 177–179.

Ginsberg, E., & Bray, D. *The uneducated*. New York: Columbia University Press, 1953.

Giordani, I. *St. Vincent de Paul*. Milwaukee: Bruce, 1961.

Glueck, E. Mental retardation and juvenile delinquency. *Journal of Psycho-Asthenics*, 1935, *40*, 267–290.

Goddard, H. *The Kallikak family: A study in the heredity of feeblemindedness*. New York: Macmillan, 1912.

Goddard, H. The improvability of feeble-minded children. *Journal of Psycho-Asthenics*, 1913, *17*, 121–131.

Goddard, H. *School training of defective children*. New York: World Book, 1914. (a)

Goddard, H. A brief report on two cases of criminal imbecility. *Journal of Psycho-Asthenics*, 1914, *19*, 31–35. (b)

Goddard, H. *Feeble-mindedness: Its causes and consequences*. New York: Macmillan, 1920.

Goddard, H. Feeblemindedness: A question of definition. *Journal of Psycho-Asthenics*, 1928, *33*, 219–227.

Goddard, H. In defense of the Kallikak study. *Science*, 1942, *95*, 574–576.

Goldberg, I. Current status of education and training in the United States for trainable mentally retarded children. *Exceptional Children*, 1957, *24*, 146–154.

Goldberg, I. The school's responsibility for "trainable" mentally retarded children. *Phi Delta Kappan*, 1959, *40*, 373–376.

Goldstein, H. Lower limits of eligibility for classes for trainable children. *Exceptional Children*, 1956, *22*, 226–227.

Goldstein, H. Population trends in U.S. public institutions for the mentally deficient. *American Journal of Mental Deficiency*, 1959, *63*, 599–604.

Goldstein, I. Implications of mental deficiency. *American Journal of Mental Deficiency*, 1948, *53*, 207–226.

Goodenough, F. *Mental testing*. New York: Rinehart, 1949.

Gould, S. *Ever since Darwin*. New York: Norton, 1977.

Grebler, A. Parental attitudes toward mentally retarded children. *American Journal of Mental Deficiency*, 1951, *56*, 475–483.

Greene, H. A case of pre-natal shock impression. *Proceedings of the Association of Medical Officers of American Institutions for Idiotic and Feebleminded Persons*, 1886, 345–349.

Greene, R. Psychoses and mental deficiencies, comparisons, and relationship. *Journal of Psycho-Asthenics*, 1930, *35*, 128–147.

Gregg, N. Congenital cataract following German measles. *Ophthalmological Society of Australia Transactions*, 1941, *3*, 35.

Grunberger, R. *The 12-year Reich*. New York: Holt, Rinehart, & Winston, 1971.

Grunner, O. *A treatise on the canon of medicine of Avicenna*. London: Luzac, 1930.

Guilford, J. The structure of intellect. *Psychological Bulletin*, 1956, *53*, 267–293.

Gulick, L. Rationale of the gymnastic treatment of the feeble-minded. *Journal of Psycho-Asthenics*, 1900, *4*, 113–122.

Hackbusch, F. 270 patients on the waiting list. *Journal of Psycho-Asthenics*, 1935, *40*, 319–335.

Hackbusch, F. When should the general social agency or the school refer the mentally defective client to an agency specializing in work with defectives? *American Journal of Mental Deficiency*, 1940, *45*, 296–303.

Hackbusch, F. Commitment procedures. *American Journal of Mental Deficiency*, 1950, *54*, 257–259.

Hadas, M. *The twelve tables*. New York: Columbia University, 1965.

Haggard, H. *The doctor in history*. New Haven: Yale University Press, 1934.

Haines, T. Mental defect and poverty. *Journal of Psycho-Asthenics*, 1925, *30*, 136–145.

Haines, T. Mental deficiency among public school children in the United States. *Journal of Psycho-Asthenics*, 1931, *36*, 31–38.

Halderman v. *Pennhurst State School and Hospital*, 466 F. Supp. 1295, U.S. Third Circuit Court of Appeals (1978).

Halmstead, T. Adenoids and their relation to feeble-minded children. *Proceedings of the Association of Medical Officers of American Institutions for Idiotic and Feebleminded Persons*, 1892, 286–292.

Hamilton, E. *The Greek way*. New York: W. W. Norton, 1930.

Hamilton, M. (ed.). *Fish's outline of psychiatry*. Chicago: Year Book Medical Publishers, 1978.

Handlin, O., & Handlin, M. *Facing life: Youth and the family in American history*. Boston: Little, Brown & Co., 1971.

Hanna, A. Some observations on extramural care of mentally deficient children. *Journal of Psycho-Asthenics*, 1938, *43*, 115–121.

Harms, E. The historic aspect of child psychiatry. In: R. Jenkins & E. Harms (eds.), *Understanding disturbed children*. Seattle: Special Child Publications, 1976, 10–24.

Harold, E. Employment of patients discharged from the St. Louis State Training School. *American Journal of Mental Deficiency*, 1955, *60*, 397–402.

Harper, R. *The code of Hammurabi*. Chicago: University of Chicago Press, 1904.

Harris, M. *Cannibals and kings: The origins of cultures*. New York: Random House, 1977.

Haskell, R., & Strauss, A. One hundred institutionalized mental defectives in the armed forces. *American Journal of Mental Deficiency*, 1943, *48*, 67–71.

Hastings, G. Registration of the feeble-minded. *Journal of Psycho-Asthenics*, 1918, *22*, 136–149.

Hawke, D. *Benjamin Rush*. New York: Bobbs-Merrill, 1971.

Hay, W. *Association for parents of mental retardates*. Arlington, TX: National Association for Retarded Citizens, Vol. 2, 1952. (a)

Hay, W. Associations for parents of mental retardates. New York: Encyclopedia Americana, Vol. 2, 1952. (b).

Haynes, G. Charles Sumner. In: D. Malone (ed.), *Dictionary of American biography*, Vol. IX. New York: Charles Scribner, 1935, 208–214.

Hays v. *The Commonwealth*, 98 Ky. 593, 33 S.W. 1104 (1896).

Healy, W. Some types of mental defectives. *Journal of Psycho-Asthenics*, 1913, *18*, 111–114.

Healy, W. Normalities of the feeble-minded. *Journal of Psycho-Asthenics*, 1918, *23*, 175–186.

Healy, W. The diagnosis of feeble-mindedness in relation to social prognosis, especially delinquency. *Journal of Psycho-Asthenics*, 1919, *24*, 69–74.

Heber, R. *A manual on terminology and classification in mental retardation* (2nd ed.). Monograph Supplement to the *American Journal of Mental Deficiency*, 1961.

Heilman, K., & Valenstein, E. (eds.). *Clinical neuropsychology.* Cambridge, MA: Oxford University Press, 1979.

Henry, W. Mental hospitals. In: G. Zilboorg, *A history of medical psychology,* pp. 558–589. New York: W. W. Norton, 1941.

Hibbert, C. *The house of medics.* New York: William Morrow, 1975.

Hildreth, G. *Bibliography of mental tests and rating scales* (2nd ed.). New York: Psychological Corporation, 1939.

Hill, H. The work at Sleighton Farm. *Journal of Psycho-Asthenics,* 1914, *18,* 230–232.

Hilliard, L., & Kirman, B. *Mental deficiency* (2nd ed.). Boston: Little, Brown, & Co., 1965.

Hitler, A. *Mein Kampf* (R. Manheim, trans.). Boston: Houghton Mifflin, 1943.

Hoakley, Z. Extra-institutional care for the feeble-minded. *Journal of Psycho-Asthenics,* 1922, *27,* 117–137.

Hoakley, Z. The variability of intelligence quotients. *Journal of Psycho-Asthenics,* 1932, *37,* 144–146.

Hobbs, N. Research in mental retardation: Prospects and strategies. *American Journal of Mental Deficiency,* 1959, *64,* 229–239.

Hobbs, N. *Issues in the classification of children* (2 vols). San Francisco: Jossey-Bass, 1975.

Hofstadter, R. The coming of the Americans. *American History,* 1971, *6*(6), 4–11.

Honzik, M., MacFarlene, J., & Allen, L. The stability of mental test performance between two and eighteen years. *Journal of Experimental Education,* 1948, *17,* 309–324.

Howe, S. *Report of Commission to Inquire into the Conditions of Idiots of the Commonwealth of Massachusetts.* Boston: Senate Document No. 51, 1848.

Howe, S. The condition and capacities of the idiots in Massachusetts. Reproduced in: *American Journal of Insanity,* 1849, *5,* 374–375.

Howe, S. *Report to Massachusetts Senate.* Boston: Senate Document No. 38, 1850.

Howe, S. *Eighth annual report.* Boston: Massachusetts School for Idiotic Children, 1856.

Hrdlicka, A. Anthropological studies. *Journal of Psycho-Asthenics,* 1898, *3,* 47–75, 99–136.

Hsu, T., & Pomerat, C. Mammalian chromosomes *in vitro.* II. A method for spreading the chromosomes of cells in tissue culture. *Journal of Heredity,* 1953, *44,* 23–29.

Hubbel, H. Mental defectives in the armed forces. *American Journal of Mental Deficiency,* 1945, *50,* 136–137.

Hudson, M. Lesson areas for the trainable child. *Exceptional Children,* 1960, *27,* 224–229.

Hungerford, R. The Detroit plan for occupational education of the mentally retarded. *American Journal of Mental Deficiency,* 1941, *46,* 102–108.

Hungerford, R., & DeProspo, C. *Realistic guidance in special education.* New York: The Association for New York City Teachers of Special Education, 1949.

Hungerford, R., & Rosenzweig, L. Development of special education for the retarded. *Exceptional Children,* 1944, *10,* 210–213.

Hunsicker, H. Symptomatology of psychosis with mental deficiency. *Journal of Psycho-Asthenics,* 1938, *43,* 51–56.

Hunt, W., Wittson, C., & Jackson, M. Selection of naval personnel with special reference to mental deficiency.

American Journal of Mental Deficiency, 1944, *48,* 245–252.

Hurder, W. Report of the Southern Regional Education Board. *American Journal of Mental Deficiency,* 1959, *63,* 754–755.

Ide, G. Aspects of special education for the handicapped child. *Journal of Psycho-Asthenics,* 1932, *37,* 412–419.

Idiots. *American Journal of Insanity,* 1849, *5,* 373–375.

Ingram, C. *Education of the slow-learning child.* Yonkers, NY: World Book, 1935.

Inskeep, A. *Teaching dull and retarded children.* New York: Macmillan, 1926.

International League of Societies for the Mentally Handicapped. Report of Frankfurt Conference. *The Record,* 1971, June, 2.

Ireland, W. *On idiocy and imbecility.* London: J. & A. Churchill, 1877.

Ison, M. The effect of thorazine on Wechsler scores. *American Journal of Mental Deficiency,* 1957, *62,* 543–547.

Itard, J. *The wild boy of Aveyron* (1806) (G. Humphrey & M. Humphrey, trans.). New York: Appleton-Century-Crofts, 1962.

Jackson, A. The relation of hypothyroidism and mental deficiency. *Journal of Psycho-Asthenics,* 1935, *40,* 92–95.

Jacob, A. Systematic physical training for the mentally defective. *Journal of Psycho-Asthenics,* 1905, *9,* 98–112.

Jacobs, A., & Sherman, C. Training facilities for severely physically and mentally handicapped. *American Journal of Mental Deficiency,* 1956, *60,* 721–728.

Jacobs, J. Experiments in prehension. *Mind,* 1887, *12,* 75–79.

Jacobs, P., Baikie, A., Court-Brown, W., & Strong, J. The somatic chromosomes in mongolism. *Lancet,* 1959, *1,* 710.

Jacoby, A. Mental defects as seen in criminal courts. *Journal of Psycho-Asthenics,* 1923, *28,* 66–82.

Jennings, H. Health progress and race progress: Are they incompatible? *Journal of Psycho-Asthenics,* 1927, *32,* 232–242.

Jervis, G. A contribution to the study of the influence of heredity on mental deficiency. *Journal of Psycho-Asthenics,* 1939, *44,* 13–24.

Jervis, G. Recent progress in the study of mental deficiency—Mongolism. *American Journal of Mental Deficiency,* 1942, *46,* 467–481.

Johnson, A. The self-supporting imbecile. *Proceedings of the Association of Medical Officers of American Institutions for Idiotic and Feebleminded Persons,* 1900, *4,* 91–100.

Johnson, G.E. What we do, and how we do it. *Journal of Psycho-Asthenics,* 1897, *2,* 98–105.

Johnson, G.O. Special education for the mentally handicapped—A paradox. *Exceptional Children,* 1962, *8,* 62–69.

Johnson, G.O., & Kirk, S. Are mentally handicapped children segregated in the regular grades? *Journal of Exceptional Children,* 1950, *17,* 65–68, 87–88.

Johnstone, E. L. Training activities for mental defectives of the lower mental grades. *Journal of Psycho-Asthenics,* 1938, *43,* 109–115.

Johnstone, E. L. The relation of mental deficiency to delinquency. *Federal Probation,* 1942, April–June, pp. 27–28.

Johnstone, E. R. The extension of the care of the feeble-minded. *Journal of Psycho-Asthenics*, 1914, *19*, 3–18.

Johnstone, E. R. Social objectives for subnormals. *Training School Bulletin*, 1924, *21*, 49–57.

Johnstone, E. R. Address of the president. *Journal of Psycho-Asthenics*, 1929, *34*, 177–190.

Johnstone, E. R. Report of the Committee on Mental Deficiency of the White House Conference. *Journal of Psycho-Asthenics*, 1931, *36*, 339–350.

Joint Commission on Accreditation of Hospitals. *Standards for residential facilities for the mentally retarded*. Chicago: Joint Commission on Accreditation of Hospitals, 1971.

Jolly, D. When should the seriously retarded infant be institutionalized? *American Journal of Mental Deficiency*, 1953, *57*, 632–636.

Kanner, L. *Child psychiatry*. Springfield, IL: Charles C Thomas, 1948.

Kanner, L. *A miniature textbook of feeblemindedness*. New York: Child Care Publications, 1949.

Kanner, L. *A history of the care and study of the mentally retarded*. Springfield, IL: Charles C Thomas, 1964.

Kaplan, O. Marriage of mental defectives. *American Journal of Mental Deficiency*, 1944, *48*, 379–384.

Kassler, R. Professional nursing personnel and their functions. *American Journal of Mental Deficiency*, 1957, *62*, 597–600.

Keen, W. Linear craniotomy for the relief of idiotic conditions. *Proceedings of the Association of Medical Officers of American Institutions for Idiotic and Feeble-minded Persons*, 1892, 344–353.

Kelly, E. Maturity as a factor in the education of the mentally deficient. *Journal of Psycho-Asthenics*, 1938, *43*, 91–97.

Kelly, E. Organization of special classes to fit the needs of different ability groupings. *American Journal of Mental Deficiency*, 1943, *48*, 80–86.

Kelly, R. Psychophysical tests of normal and abnormal children. *Psychological Review*, 1903, *10*, 345–352.

Kelman, H. Individualizing the social integration of the mentally retarded child. *American Journal of Mental Deficiency*, 1956, *61*, 860–864.

Kennedy, J. F. *Message from the President of the United States*. Washington, DC: House of Representatives (88th Congress), Document number 58, 1963.

Kennedy, R. *The social adjustment of morons in a Connecticut city*. Hartford: Mansfield-Southbury Training Schools, 1948.

Kerlin, I. The organization of establishments for the idiotic and imbecile classes. *Proceedings of the Association of Medical Officers of American Institutions for Idiotic and Feebleminded Persons*, 1877, 19–35.

Kerlin, I. *The mind unveiled*. Philadelphia: U. Hunt, 1880.

Kerlin, I. The epileptic change and its appearance among feeble-minded children. *Proceedings of the Association of Medical Officers of American Institutions for Idiotic and Feebleminded Persons*, 1882, 202–211.

Kerlin, I. Provisions for imbeciles. Report of the Committee on Provisions for Idiotic and Feeble-minded Persons. *Proceedings of the Association of Medical Officers of American Institutions for Idiotic and Feebleminded Persons*, 1886, 1–17.

Kerlin, I. Provisions for imbeciles. Report of the Committee on Provisions for Idiotic and Feeble-minded Persons. *Proceedings of the Association of Medical Officers of*

American Institutions for Idiotic and Feebleminded Persons, 1886, 1–17.

Kerlin, I. Moral imbecility. *Proceedings of the Association of Medical Officers of American Institutions for Idiotic and Feebleminded Persons*, 1887, 32–37.

Kerlin, I. *Manual of Elwyn: 1863–1891*. Philadelphia: Lippincott, 1891.

Kerlin, I. President's annual address. *Proceedings of the Association of Medical Officers of American Institutions for Idiotic and Feebleminded Persons*, 1892, 274–285.

Kilpatrick, W. *The Montessori system examined*. Boston: Houghton Mifflin, 1914.

Kinder, E., Chase, A., & Buck, E. Data secured during a follow-up study of girls discharged from supervised parole from Letchworth Village. *American Journal of Mental Deficiency*, 1941, *45*, 572–578.

Kirk, S. *Teaching reading to slow-learning children*. New York: Houghton Mifflin, 1940.

Kirk, S. An evaluation of the study by Bernadine G. Schmidt entitled: "Changes in Personal, Social, and Intellectual Behavior of Children Originally Classified as Feebleminded." *Psychological Bulletin*, 1948, *45*, 321–333.

Kirk, S. A project for pre-school mentally handicapped children. *American Journal of Mental Deficiency*, 1950, *54*, 305–310.

Kirk, S. What is special about special education: The child who is mentally handicapped. *Exceptional Children*, 1953, *19*, 138–142.

Kirk, S., & Johnson, G. *Educating the retarded child*. Cambridge, MA: Houghton Mifflin, 1951.

Kirk, S., & Stevens, I. A pre-academic curriculum for slow-learning children. *American Journal of Mental Deficiency*, 1943, *47*, 396–405.

Kite, E. Mental defect as found by the field-worker. *Journal of Psycho-Asthenics*, 1912, *17*, 145–154.

Klebanoff, L. Out of mind—out of sight. *Journal of Education*, 1964, *147*, 82–86.

Klein, D. *A history of scientific psychology*. New York: Basic Books, 1970.

Kline, G. Accomplishments and immediate aims in Massachusetts in community care of the feeble-minded. *Journal of Psycho-Asthenics*, 1924, *29*, 32–40.

Knight, G. The state's duty towards epileptics. *Proceedings of the Association of Medical Officers of American Institutions for Idiotic and Feebleminded Persons*, 1886, 11–18.

Knight, G. President's address. *Proceedings of the Association of Medical Officers of American Institutions for Idiotic and Feebleminded Persons*, 1889, 51–53.

Knight, G. The feeble-minded. *Proceedings of the Association of Medical Officers of American Institutions for Idiotic and Feebleminded Persons*, 1895, 559–563.

Kolb, L. Mentally defective aliens as related to immigration. *Journal of Psycho-Asthenics*, 1928, *33*, 191–203.

Komisar, L. *Down and out in the USA*. New York: Franklin Watts, 1973.

Kramer, M., Person, P., Tarjan, G., Morgan, R., & Wright, S. A method for determination of probabilities of stay, release, and death, for patients admitted to a hospital for the mentally deficient. *American Journal of Mental Deficiency*, 1957, *62*, 481–495.

Kretchmer, N. Birth defects. *Perspectives in Biology and Medicine*, 1964, *8*, 1–6.

Krishef, C. The influence of rural-urban environment upon the adjustment of discharges from the Owatonna State

School. *American Journal of Mental Deficiency,* 1959, *63,* 860–865.

Krüsi, H. *Pestalozzi: His life, work, and influence.* New York: American Book, 1875.

Kuenzel, M. A survey of Mongolian traits. *Journal of Psycho-Asthenics,* 1929, *34,* 149–160.

Kuenzel, M. The training of the mentally deficient in foster families. *Journal of Psycho-Asthenics,* 1938, *43,* 135–139.

Kuhlmann, F. Binet and Simon's system for measuring intelligence of children. *Journal of Psycho-Asthenics,* 1911, *15,* 76–92.

Kuhlmann, F. Degree of mental deficiency in children as expressed by the relation of age to mental age. *Journal of Psycho-Asthenics,* 1913, *17,* 132–144.

Kuhlmann, F. Dr. Wallin's reply to my review of his "Mental Health of the School Child." *Journal of Psycho-Asthenics,* 1914, *19,* 154–170.

Kuhlmann, F. What constitutes feeble-mindedness? *Journal of Psycho-Asthenics,* 1915, *19,* 214–236.

Kuhlmann, F. Part played by the state institutions in the care of the feeble-minded. *Journal of Psycho-Asthenics,* 1916, *21,* 3–24.

Kuhlmann, F. The results of mental re-examinations of the feeble-minded. *Journal of Psycho-Asthenics,* 1920, *25,* 147–160.

Kuhlmann, F. Definition of mental deficiency. *American Journal of Mental Deficiency,* 1941, *46,* 206–213.

Kurland, A., & Gilgash, C. A study of the effect of glutamic acid on delinquent adult male mental defectives. *American Journal of Mental Deficiency,* 1953, *57,* 669–680.

Landsteiner, K., & Wiener, A. An agglutinable factor in human blood recognized by immune sera for rhesus blood. *Proceedings of the Society for Experimental Biology and Medicine,* 1940, *43,* 223.

Lane, H. *The wild boy of Aveyron.* Cambridge, MA: Harvard University Press, 1976.

Laughlin, H. The eugenical sterilization of the feeble-minded. *Journal of Psycho-Asthenics,* 1926, *31,* 210–218.

Lawrence, C. Principles of education for the feeble-minded. *Journal of Psycho-Asthenics,* 1900, *4,* 100–108.

Laws of the state of Illinois, 1879.

Leakey, R., & Lewin, R. *Origins.* New York: E. P. Dutton, 1977.

Leakey, R., & Lewin, R. *People of the lake.* New York: Doubleday, 1978.

LeGalley, M. Teeth and jaws of the feeble-minded. *Journal of Psycho-Asthenics,* 1897, *2,* 55–60.

Lejeune, J., Gautier, M., & Turpin, R. Les chromosomes humains en culture de tissues. *Comptes rendus hebdomadaires des seances de l'Academie des Sciences* (Paris), 1959, *248,* 602.

Lemkau, P., Tietze, C., & Cooper, M. Mental-hygiene problems in an urban district. *Mental Hygiene,* 1942, *26,* 274–278.

Lenz, M. Where does the program for feebleminded fail to meet the needs of the court. *Journal of Psycho-Asthenics,* 1939, *44,* 203–205.

Leonard, T. General synopsis of the commitment law in Illinois and three years' experience with it. *Journal of Psycho-Asthenics,* 1918, *23,* 169–174.

Lerner, S. The diagnostic basis for institutional care for children. *Social Casework,* 1952, *33,* 105–110.

Lessard v. *Schmidt.* Civil Action No. 71-C-602, U.S. District Court, Eastern District of Wisconsin (1972).

Letchworth, W. Pauper and destitute children in the state of New York. In: State Board of Charities, *Eighth annual report.* Albany: State Printer, 1875.

Leuchtenburg, W. *New Deal and global war.* New York: Time, 1964. (a)

Leuchtenburg, W. *The great age of change.* New York: Time, 1964. (b)

Levy, R. Effects of institutional versus boarding home care on a group of infants. *Journal of Personality,* 1947, *15,* 233–241.

Lincoln, D. Special classes for feeble-minded children in the Boston Public Schools. *Journal of Psycho-Asthenics,* 1903, *7,* 83–93.

Lincoln, D. Special classes for mentally defective children in the Boston Public Schools. *Journal of Psycho-Asthenics,* 1910, *14,* 89–92.

Lissner, I. *The living past.* New York: G. P. Putnam's Sons, 1957.

Little, A., & Johnson, B. A study of the social and economic adjustments of one hundred thirteen discharged parolees from Laconia State School. *Journal of Psycho-Asthenics,* 1932, *37,* 233–251.

Little, C. Random remarks on state institutions. *Journal of Psycho-Asthenics,* 1923, *28,* 59–65.

Little, W. On the influence of abnormal parturition, difficult labors, premature birth, and asphyxia neonatorum, on the mental and physical condition of the child, especially in relation to deformities. *Obstetrical Transactions,* 1862, *3,* 293–346.

Loeb, H., & Tuddenham, R. Does glutamic acid influence mental functions? *Pediatrics,* 1950, *6,* 72–77.

Lord, F. A realistic look at special classes. *Exceptional Children,* 1956, *22,* 321–325, 342.

Lorenz, M. A follow-up study of eighty-four beta class pupils. In: M. Reynolds, R. Ellis, & J. Kiland (eds.), *A study of public school children with severe mental retardation.* St. Paul, MN: State Department of Education, 1953.

Lowrey, L. The relationship of feeblemindedness to behavior disorders. *Journal of Psycho-Asthenics,* 1928, *33,* 96–100.

Luckey, B. The time has come. *American Journal of Mental Deficiency,* 1953, *58,* 215–223.

Luther, M. *Colloquia Mensalia.* London: William Du-Gard, 1652.

McCready, E. The treatment of mental defectives through physical and medical measures. *Journal of Psycho-Asthenics,* 1918, *23,* 43–47.

McCulloch, T. The effect of glutamic-acid feeding on cognitive abilities of institutionalized mental defectives. *American Journal of Mental Deficiency,* 1950, *55,* 117–122.

Mackie, R. The Midcentury White House Conference and Exceptional Children. *Exceptional Children,* 1951, *17,* 129–131, 168.

Mackie, R. Spotlighting advances in special education. *Exceptional Children,* 1965, *31,* 77–81.

MacMurphy, H. The relation of feeble-mindedness to other social problems. *Journal of Psycho-Asthenics,* 1916, *21,* 58–63.

McNairy, C. President's conception of our task. *Journal of Psycho-Asthenics,* 1923, *28,* 94–99.

McNairy, C. Some phases of construction, organization,

and administration of an institution for the feebleminded in the south. *Journal of Psycho-Asthenics*, 1924, *29*, 271–275.

McPherson, M. A survey of experimental studies of learning in individuals who achieve subnormal ratings on standardized psychometric measures. *American Journal of Mental Deficiency*, 1948, *52*, 232–254.

Maennel, B. [*Auxiliary education*] (E. Sylvester, trans.). New York: Doubleday, 1909.

Mainwaring, M. Phrenology—Why not to take each other at face value. *Smithsonian*, 1980, *11*(8), 193–212.

Malzberg, B. The racial distribution of mental defectives in New York State. *American Journal of Mental Deficiency*, 1943, *47*, 326–333.

Manceron, C. [*Twilight of the old order*] (P. Wolf, trans.). New York: Alfred A. Knopf, 1977.

Marks, E. *The aphorisms of Hippocrates*. New York: Collins, 1817.

Martens, E. A conference on curriculum for mentally retarded children. *Journal of Psycho-Asthenics*, 1935, *40*, 35–37.

Martens, E. Some problems concerned with educational programs in residential schools. *Journal of Psycho-Asthenics*, 1938, *43*, 128–134.

Martens, E. Preparation of teachers for mentally deficient children. *American Journal of Mental Deficiency*, 1950, *54*, 449–455.

Marti-Ibañez, F. *The epic of medicine*. New York: Clarkson N. Potter, 1959.

Masserman, J., & Balken, E. The psycho-analytic and psychiatric significance of fantasy. *Psychoanalytic Review*, 1939, *26*, 343–379, 535–549.

Matthews, M. One hundred institutionally trained male defectives in the community under supervision. *Journal of Psycho-Asthenics*, 1921, *26*, 60–70.

Matthews, M. Mansfield's waiting lists: Active and closed. *Journal of Psycho-Asthenics*, 1932, *37*, 223–232.

Matzinger, H. The prevention of mental defect. *Journal of Psycho-Asthenics*, 1918, *23*, 11–21.

May, E. *The Progressive Era*. New York: Time, 1964. (a)

May, E. *War, boom and bust*. New York: Time, 1964. (b)

Mayo, L. Philosophy and recommendations of the President's Panel on Mental Retardation relating to education, vocational rehabilitation, and training. *Exceptional Children*, 1963, *29*, 425–430.

Medical statistics of the provost marshall general's bureau, Vol. 2. Washington, DC: War Department, 1875.

Meeting of superintendents. *Proceedings of the Association of Medical Officers of American Institutions for Idiotic and Feebleminded Persons*, 1876, 4–6.

Melcher, R. A program of prolonged pre-academic training for the young mentally handicapped child. *Journal of Psycho-Asthenics*, 1939, *44*, 202–215.

Meltzer, M. *A light in the dark: The life of Samuel Gridley Howe*. New York: Thomas Y. Crowell, 1964.

Menninger, W. The problem of the mentally retarded and the army. *American Journal of Mental Deficiency*, 1943, *48*, 55–61.

Menolascino, F., & Egger, M. *Medical dimensions of mental retardation*. Lincoln: University of Nebraska Press, 1978.

Michal-Smith, H. Personality training in vocational education for the retarded child. *Exceptional Children*, 1951, *17*, 108–110.

Milburn, R. Problems of feeble-mindedness. *Journal of Psycho-Asthenics*, 1908, *13*, 51–73.

Millard, M. Letter from M. Millard. *Proceedings of the Association of Medical Officers of American Institutions for Idiotic and Feebleminded Persons*, 1886, 392–394.

Milligan, G. History of the American Association on Mental Deficiency. *American Journal of Mental Deficiency*, 1961, *66*, 357–369.

Mills v. *The Board of Education*, Civil Action No. 1939-71, U.S. District Court of the District of Columbia (1972).

Mills, C. Seasonal influences in the production and manifestation of mental disease. *Journal of Psycho-Asthenics*, 1937, *42*, 125–129.

Minutes. *Journal of Psycho-Asthenics*, 1913, *18*, 51, 54–61.

Minutes. *Journal of Psycho-Asthenics*, 1916, *21*, 94–112.

Mitchell, A., Hargis, C., McCarry, F., & Powers, C. Effects of prochlorperazine therapy on educability in disturbed mentally retarded adolescents. *American Journal of Mental Deficiency*, 1959, *64*, 57–62.

Mitchell, D. *Schools and classes for exceptional children*. Cleveland: The Survey Committee of the Cleveland Foundation, 1916.

Moeder, L. The problem of mental deficiency in Pennsylvania. *Journal of Psycho-Asthenics*, 1932, *37*, 33–58.

Molish, H. Contributions of projective tests to problems of psychological diagnosis in mental deficiency. *American Journal of Mental Deficiency*, 1958, *63*, 282–293.

Monroe, M. *Remedial reading*. New York: Houghton Mifflin, 1937.

Montaque, H. The causes of delinquency in mentally defective boys. *Journal of Psycho-Asthenics*, 1930, *35*, 104–114.

Montessori, M. *The secret of childhood*. Calcutta: Orient Longmons, 1963. (a)

Montessori, M. *Education for a new world*. Wheaton, IL: Theosophical Press, 1963. (b)

Moran, M. School tests for school grading and measures of intelligence. *Journal of Psycho-Asthenics*, 1921, *26*, 127–138.

Morrison, J., & Cornell, W. Report on Westchester findings. *Journal of Psycho-Asthenics*, 1923, *28*, 171–191.

Mott, R. Remarks of Hon. R. A. Mott. *Proceedings of the Association of Medical Officers of American Institutions for Idiotic and Feebleminded Persons*, 1891, 35–37.

Mullen, F. & Nee, M. Distribution of mental retardation in an urban school population. *American Journal of Mental Deficiency*, 1952, *56*, 777–790.

Murdoch, J. State care for the feeble-minded. *Journal of Psycho-Asthenics*, 1913, *18*, 34–45.

Murdoch, J. The relation of mental deficiency to morals, religion, and ethics. *Journal of Psycho-Asthenics*, 1925, *30*, 146–153.

Murphy, D. Maternal pelvic irradiation as a cause of microcephaly. *Journal of Psycho-Asthenics*, 1929, *34*, 208–210.

Murphy, G. *Historical introduction to modern psychology*. New York: Harcourt, Brace and Company, 1949.

Murray, J. *The kings and queens of England*. New York: Charles Scribner's Sons, 1974.

Murray, M. Needs of parents of mentally retarded children. *American Journal of Mental Deficiency*, 1959, *63*, 1078–1088.

Myers, C. An application of the control group method to

the problem of etiology of mongolism. *Journal of Psycho-Asthenics*, 1938, *43*, 142–149.

Myerson, A. Schizophrenia: The hereditary relationship of feeblemindedness and schizophrenia. *Association for Research in Nervous and Mental Diseases*, 1928, 100–104.

Myerson, A. The pathological and biological basis of mental deficiency. *Journal of Psycho-Asthenics*, 1930, *35*, 203–226.

National Association for Retarded Children (NARC). *Blueprint for a crusade*. Arlington, TX: National Association for Retarded Citizens, 1954.

National Association for Retarded Citizens (NARC). Educational bill of rights for the retarded child. *American Journal of Mental Deficiency*, 1954, *58*, 516.

Neuer, H. Prevention of mental deficiency. *American Journal of Mental Deficiency*, 1947, *50*, 721–729.

New York Department of Mental Hygiene. *Technical report of the mental health unit*. Syracuse: Syracuse University Press, 1955.

Newland, T. A study of uneducable children excluded from Pennsylvania Public Schools. *Journal of Psycho-Asthenics*, 1939, *44*, 187–196.

Newland, T. Are exceptional children assessed or tested? *Exceptional Children*, 1952, *19*, 51–55.

News and Notes. *Journal of Psycho-Asthenics*, 1938, *43*, 210.

Nirje, B. A Scandinavian visitor looks at U.S institutions. In: W. Wolfensberger, & R. Kugel (eds), *Changing patterns in residential services for the mentally retarded*, pp. 51–58. Washington, DC: President's Committee on Mental Retardation, 1969.

Nisonger, H. Ohio's program for mentally deficient children. *American Journal of Mental Deficiency*, 1948, *53*, 103–108.

Norsworthy, N. The psychology of mentally deficient children. *Archives of Psychology*, no. 1, 1906.

Norsworthy, N. Suggestions concerning the psychology of mentally deficient children. *Journal of Psycho-Asthenics*, 1907, *12*, 3–17.

Notes. *Journal of Psycho-Asthenics*, 1917, *22*, 18.

Notes and Abstracts. *Journal of Psycho-Asthenics*, 1897, *2*, 88.

Notices of Books, Essays and Articles on Insanity. *American Journal of Insanity*, 1847, *4*, 79–80.

Ohio Board of State Charities. *Third annual report*. Columbus, OH: State Printers, 1870.

Olden, M. Birthright, Inc.—Its roots, fruits, and objectives. *American Journal of Mental Deficiency*, 1945, *50*, 115–120.

Osborne, A. The founding of a great institution and some of its problems. *Proceedings of the Association of Medical Officers of American Institutions for Idiotic and Feebleminded Persons*, 1892, 173–185.

Osborne, A. President's annual address. *Proceedings of the Association of Medical Officers of American Institutions for Idiotic and Feebleminded Persons*, 1894, 386–399.

Pallister, P., & Stevens, R. Effects of serpasil in small dosage on behavior, intelligence, and physiology. *American Journal of Mental Deficiency*, 1957, *62*, 267–274.

Papania, N., Rosenblum, S., & Keller, J. Responses of lower social class, high-grade mentally handicapped boys to a "culture fair" test of intelligence—The Davis-

Eells Games. *American Journal of Mental Deficiency*, 1955, *59*, 493–498.

Paré, A. *Monstres et prodiges* (1573). In: C. Gregory (ed.), *Animaux, monstres et prodiges*. Paris: Le Club Francais du Livre, 1954.

Parsons, H. Mental defect as a bar to reformation. *Journal of Psycho-Asthenics*, 1918, *23*, 163–168.

Pasmanick, B. A comparative study of the behavioral development of negro infants. *Journal of Genetic Psychology*, 1946, *69*, 3–44.

Patterson, R. Organization of a residence unit for pre-academic training of mentally deficient children. *American Journal of Mental Deficiency*, 1943, *48*, 174–178.

Payne, G. *The child in human progress*. New York: G. P. Putnam's Sons, 1916.

Penrose, L. A contribution to the genetic study of mental deficiency. *British Medical Journal*, 1934, *1*, 10.

Penrose, L. Maternal age in familial mongolism. *Journal of Mental Sciences*, 1951, *97*, 737–747.

Penrose, L., & Smith, G. *Down's anomaly*. London: J. & A. Churchill, 1966.

Pennhurst State School and Hospital v. Halderman, Civil Action Nos. 79-1404, 79-1408, 79-1414, 79-1415, 79-1489, U.S. Third Circuit Court of Appeals (1981).

Pense, A. The problem of the preschool mentally deficient child. *American Journal of Mental Deficiency*, 1947, *52*, 168–171.

Peterson, J. *Early conceptions and tests of intelligence*. Chicago: World Book, 1925.

Peterson, L., & Smith, L. A comparison of the post-school adjustment of educable mentally retarded adults with that of adults of normal intelligence. *Exceptional Children*, 1960, *26*, 404–408.

Pettigrew v. Texas, 12 Tex. App. 225 (1882).

Phillips, H. Elizabeth E. Farrell. *Exceptional Children*, 1935, *1*, 73–76.

Pichot, P. French pioneers in the field of mental deficiency. *American Journal of Mental Deficiency*, 1948, *53*, 128–137.

Pinel, P. *A treatise on insanity*. Facsimile of the London 1806 edition (D. D. Davis, trans.). New York: Hafner, 1962.

Pintner, R. *Intelligence testing: Methods and results*. New York: Henry Holt, 1923.

Plato's Republic. New York: Carlton, 1928.

Platter, F. *Observationum in hominis affectibus*. Basel, Switzerland: Ludovici, Koenig, 1614.

Pollack, H. A visit to a French family-care colony. *Journal of Psycho-Asthenics*, 1938, *43*, 40–46.

Porter, R., & Milazzo, T. A comparison of mentally retarded adults who attended a special class with those who attended regular school classes. *Exceptional Children*, 1958, *24*, 410–412, 420.

Porteus, S. Mental test for feeble-minded: A new series. *Journal of Psycho-Asthenics*, 1915, *19*, 200–213.

Porteus, S. A social rating scale for defectives. *Journal of Psycho-Asthenics*, 1921, *26*, 117–126.

Potter, H. The relation of personality to the mental defective with a method for its evaluation. *Journal of Psycho-Asthenics*, 1922, *27*, 27–38.

Potter, H. Clinical types of endocrine dysfunctions in mental defectives. *Journal of Psycho-Asthenics*, 1924, *29*, 90–97.

Powell, F. Status of the work—Iowa. *Proceedings of the*

Association of Medical Officers of American Institutions for Idiotic and Feebleminded Persons, 1882, 267–268.

Powell, F. President's address. Proceedings of the Association of Medical Officers of American Institutions for Idiotic and Feebleminded Persons, 1886, 386–391.

Pratt, G. Mental hygiene as applied to the feeble-minded. Journal of Psycho-Asthenics, 1926, 31, 236–244.

President's Committee on Mental Retardation. Mental retardation past and present. Washington, DC: U.S. Government Printing Office, 1977.

President's Panel on Mental Retardation. A proposed program for national action to combat mental retardation. Washington, DC: Superintendent of Documents, 1962.

Price, B., & Halperin, S. Sterilization laws—Bane or banner of eugenics and public welfare? American Journal of Mental Deficiency, 1940, 45, 134–144.

Price, M. The team approach to cottage problems. American Journal of Mental Deficiency, 1953, 58, 82–87.

Punnet, R. Eliminating feeblemindedness. Journal of Heredity, 1917, 8, 464–465.

Putnam, T. The surgical treatment of infantile hydrocephalus. California Medicine, 1953, 78, 29–32.

Quinn, K., & Durling, D. Twelve months' study of glutamic acid therapy in different clinical types in an institution for the mentally deficient. American Journal of Mental Deficiency, 1950, 54, 321–332.

Rautman, A. Special class placement. Journal of Exceptional Children, 1944, 10, 99–102.

Ray, I. A treatise on the medical jurisprudence of insanity. Boston: Little, Brown, 1831.

Ray, I. A treatise on the medical jurisprudence of insanity. Boston: Little, Brown, 1871.

Raymond, C. Intellectual development in morons beyond the chronological age of sixteen years. Journal of Psycho-Asthenics, 1927, 32, 243–248.

Redfield, R. The folk society. American Journal of Sociology, 1947, 52, 293–308.

Reed, V. You are one of these. Nation's Business, June, 1946.

Reeves, H. The later years of a noted mental defective. Journal of Psycho-Asthenics, 1938, 43, 194–200.

Remak, J. (ed.). The Nazi years. Englewood Cliffs, NJ: Prentice-Hall, 1969.

Report made to the legislature of Massachusetts on idiocy. Boston: Collidge and Wiley, 1848.

Report of Committee on Nomenclature. Journal of Psycho-Asthenics, 1932, 37, 483–485.

Report of Committee on Psychological Research. Journal of Psycho-Asthenics, 1901, 7, 21–26.

Report of Committee on Statistics, November, 1945. American Journal of Mental Deficiency, 1945, 50, 345–347.

Report of the chairman, Research Committee. Journal of Psycho-Asthenics, 1937, 42, 188–222.

Report of the Committee on Standards and Policy. American Journal of Mental Deficiency, 1944, 48. 315–317.

Report of the Royal Academy of Science (French), 1843: A description of Seguin's school in Paris. Reprinted in: M. Rosen, G. Clark, & M. Kivitz (eds.), The history of mental retardation (Collected Papers), Vol. 1, pp. 107–111. Baltimore: University Park Press, 1976.

Report to the General Assembly meeting, State of Pennsylvania, 1929, 117.

Revised statutes of Utah, 1933, Title XIV, Chap. 4.

Rhoades, G. The non-academic part of our program for the mentally retarded. Exceptional Children, 1943, 9, 107–111.

Richards, J. The education of the feeble-minded. Proceedings of the Association of Medical Officers of American Institutions for Idiotic and Feebleminded Persons, 1884, 18–29.

Richards, L. Samuel Gridley Howe. New York: Appleton-Century-Crofts, 1935.

Richards, M. The retarded child in a state school and the problems he presents from a parent's viewpoint. American Journal of Mental Deficiency, 1953, 58, 56–59.

Riggs, J. Hello, doctor: A brief biography of Charles Bernstein, M.D. New York: Roycroft, 1936.

Rigler, N. Nationwide survey of unit services. American Journal of Mental Deficiency, 1956, 61, 432.

Ringelheim, D., & Polatsek, I. Group psychotherapy with a mentally deficient group, a preliminary study. American Journal of Mental Deficiency, 1957, 60, 157–162.

Robbins, M. What parents expect the institution to do for their children. American Journal of Mental Deficiency, 1957, 61, 672–674.

Robinson, D. Interrelationship of venereal disease and feeble-mindedness. Journal of Psycho-Asthenics, 1923, 28, 149–161.

Roewer, W. A program for the trainable mentally deficient child. American Journal of Mental Deficiency, 1952, 56, 551–559.

Rogers, A. Status of the work—Minnesota. Proceedings of the Association of Medical Officers of American Institutions for Idiotic and Feebleminded Persons, 1889, 72–77.

Rogers, A. President's address. Proceedings of the Association of Medical Officers of American Institutions for Idiotic and Feebleminded Persons, 1891, 28–34.

Rogers, A. Report of five cases of mental and moral aberration among the feeble-minded at the Minnesota school for feeble-minded. Proceedings of the Association of Medical Officers of American Institutions for Idiotic and Feebleminded Persons, 1892, 318–325.

Rogers, A. Futility of surgical treatment. Journal of Psycho-Asthenics, 1898, 3, 93–95.

Rogers, A. Book review of The Kallikak family. Journal of Psycho-Asthenics, 1912, 17, 83–84.

Roos, P. Parents of mentally retarded children—misunderstood and mistreated. In: A. Turnbull & H. Turnbull, (eds.), Parents speak out, pp. 12–27. Columbus, OH: Charles E. Merrill, 1978.

Roselle, E. Educational personnel. American Journal of Mental Deficiency, 1940, 45, 171–175.

Roselle, E. Some principles and philosophy in the planning and development of institutional plants with particular reference to visitation for the mentally retarded. American Journal of Mental Deficiency, 1954, 58, 595–624.

Rosen, L. Selected aspects in the development of the mother's understanding of her mentally retarded child. American Journal of Mental Deficiency, 1955, 59, 522–528.

Rosen, M., Clark, G., & Kivitz, M. (eds.). The history of mental retardation (collected papers), Vol. 1. Baltimore: University Park Press, 1976.

Rosenblum, S., Callahan, R., Buoniconto, P., Graham, B., & Deatrick, R. The effects of tranquilizing medication (reserpine) on behavior and test performance of maladjusted, high-grade retarded children. American Journal of Mental Deficiency, 1957, 62, 663–671.

Rothman, D., & Rothman, S. (eds.). *Sources of the American social tradition.* New York: Basic Books, 1975.

Rothstein, J. California's program for the severely retarded child. *Exceptional Children,* 1953, *19,* 171–173.

Rothstein, J. Certification requirements for teachers of the mentally retarded. *Exceptional Children,* 1954, *20,* 312, 314, 316–320.

Rousseau, J. *Emilé* (B. Foxley, trans.). New York: E. P. Dutton, 1911.

Ruhräh, J. *Pediatrics of the past.* New York: Paul B. Hoeber, 1925.

Rush, B. *Medical inquiries and observations upon the diseases of the mind.* Facsimile of the Philadelphia 1812 Edition. New York: Hafner, 1962.

Sabagh, G., & Windle, C. Recent trends in institutionalization rates of mental defectives in the United States. *American Journal of Mental Deficiency,* 1960, *64,* 618–624.

Saenger, G. *The adjustment of severely retarded adults in the community.* Albany, NY: State Interdepartmental Health Resources Board, 1957.

Sagan, C. *The dragons of Eden: Speculations on the evolution of human intelligence.* New York: Random House, 1977.

Saint-Simon, C. *Nouveau christianisme.* Paris: Bassange, 1825.

Salisbury, A. The education of the feeble-minded. *Proceedings of the Association of Medical Officers of American Institutions for Idiotic and Feebleminded Persons,* 1892, 219–234.

Sandy, W. Community responsibility and mental deficiency. *Journal of Psycho-Asthenics,* 1926, *31,* 189–194.

Sarason, S. Mental subnormality and the behavioral sciences. *Exceptional Children,* 1951, *17,* 243–247.

Sarason, S. *Psychological problems in mental deficiency* (3rd ed.). New York: Harper & Row, 1959.

Scheerenberger, R. *A pictorial history of residential services in Wisconsin.* Madison: American Association on Mental Deficiency—Wisconsin Chapter, 1976. (a)

Scheerenberger, R. *Deinstitutionalization and institutional reform.* Springfield, IL: Charles C Thomas, 1976. (b)

Scheerenberger, R. Public residential services for the mentally retarded. In: N. Ellis, (ed.), *International review of research in mental retardation,* Vol. 9, pp. 187–208. New York: Academic Press, 1978.

Scheerenberger, R. *Public residential services for the mentally retarded, 1979.* Madison, WI: National Association of Superintendents of Public Residential Facilities for the Mentally Retarded, 1980.

Scheier, L. *Problems in the training of certain special-class teachers.* New York: Columbia University, 1931.

Schlapp, A. Recent progress in dealing with feeble-minded and mentally defective dependent children. *Journal of Psycho-Asthenics,* 1915, *19,* 175–187.

Schlesinger, A. The historian and history. *Foreign Affairs,* 1963, *41,* 491–497.

Schmidt, B. Changes in personal, social, and intellectual behavior of children originally classified as feeble-minded. *Psychological Monographs,* 1946, *281,* (Whole No.).

Schultz, H., director, Vineland State School. Personal communication, April 5, 1979.

Segregation versus non-segregation of exceptional children. *Exceptional Children,* 1946, *12,* 235–240.

Seguin, E. *Traitment moral, hygiéne, et éducation des idiots et des autres enfants arriérés.* Paris: J. B. Baillière, 1846.

Seguin, E. *Jacob Rodrigues Pereire: Sur sa vie et ses travaux.* Paris: J. B. Baillière, 1847.

Seguin, E. *Idiocy and its treatment by the physiological method.* New York: William Wood, 1866.

Selling, L., & Finn, H. A projected administrative scheme for the care of mentally retarded individuals. *Journal of Psycho-Asthenics,* 1936, *41,* 268–277.

Shafer, E. Phrenology's golden years. *American History,* 1974, *8*(10), 36–43.

Shah, M. *The general principles of Avicenna's Canon of Medicine.* Karachi, Pakistan: Naveed Clinic, 1966.

Sheimo, S. Helping parents of mentally defective children. *American Journal of Mental Deficiency,* 1951, *56,* 42–47.

Sherrard, P. *Byzantium.* New York: Time, 1966.

Shotwell, A. Arthur performance ratings of Mexican and American high-grade mental defectives. *American Journal of Mental Deficiency,* 1945, *49,* 445–449.

Shuttleworth, G. The health and physical development of idiots as compared with mentally sound children of the same age. *Proceedings of the Association of Medical Officers of American Institutions for Idiotic and Feeble-minded Persons,* 1886, 315–322.

Skeels, H. A study of the effects of differential stimulation on mentally retarded children: A follow-up report. *American Journal of Mental Deficiency,* 1942, *46,* 340–350.

Skeels, H. & Dye, H. A study of the effects of differential stimulation on mentally retarded children. *Journal of Psycho-Asthenics,* 1939, *44,* 114–136.

Sloan, W., & Birch, J. A rationale for degrees of retardation. *American Journal of Mental Deficiency,* 1955, *60,* 258–264.

Slobody, L., & Scanlan, J. Consequences of early institutionalization in mental retardation. *American Journal of Mental Deficiency,* 1959, *63,* 971–974.

Smith, E. Emotional factors as revealed in the intake process with parents of defective children. *American Journal of Mental Deficiency,* 1952, *56,* 806–812.

Smith, G. Practical consideration of the problems of mental deficiency as seen in a neuro-psychiatric dispensary. *Journal of Psycho-Asthenics,* 1922, *27,* 57–74.

Smith, G. Comments on the relationship of mental defects to the problems of delinquency and crime. *Journal of Psycho-Asthenics,* 1924, *29,* 325–344.

Smith, P. *The shaping of America.* New York: McGraw-Hill, 1980.

Smith, P. *The nation comes of age.* New York: McGraw-Hill, 1981.

Snyder, R., & Sechrest, L. Directive group therapy with defective delinquents. *American Journal of Mental Deficiency,* 1959, *64,* 117–123.

Solecki, R. *Shanidar.* New York: Alfred A. Knopf, 1971.

Some facts: Millions are retarded. *Images,* 1981, *2*(3), 4.

Souder v. *Brennan,* Civil Action No. 482-73, U.S. District Court for the District of Columbia (1973).

Southard, E. Remarks on the progress of the Waverley researcher in the pathology of the feeble-minded. *Journal of Psycho-Asthenics,* 1918, *23,* 48–59.

Southard, E. An attempt at an orderly grouping of the

feeble-minded (hypophrenias) for clinical diagnosis. *Journal of Psycho-Asthenics,* 1919, *24,* 99–113.

Spalding, W., & Kvaraceus, W. Sex discrimination in special class placement. *Exceptional Children,* 1944, *11,* 42–44.

Spitz, R. Hospitalism. *Psychoanalytic Study of the Child,* 1945, *1,* 53–74.

Springer, A. Attention. *Journal of Psycho-Asthenics,* 1896, *1,* 85–88.

Squire, C. Some requirements of graded mental tests. *Transactions,* 1913, *5,* 645–648.

Standing, E. *Maria Montessori.* New York: New American Libraries, 1962.

State v. *Ghrist,* 222 Iowa 1096, 270 N.W. 376 (1936).

State v. *Richards,* 39 Conn. 590, (1873).

Status of the work before the people and the legislature. *Proceedings of the Association of Medical Officers of American Institutions for Idiotic and Feebleminded Persons,* 1879, 96.

Status of the work before the people and the legislature. *Proceedings of the Association of Medical Officers of American Institutions for Idiotic and Feebleminded Persons,* 1894, 71.

Stebbins, I. An evaluation of homes for parole placement of mental defectives. *Journal of Psycho-Asthenics,* 1931, *36,* 50–70.

Steinbach, C. Report of the special class department, Cleveland, Ohio. *Journal of Psycho-Asthenics,* 1918, *23,* 104–109.

Stern, E. Problems of organizing parent groups. *American Journal of Mental Deficiency,* 1951, *56,* 11–17.

Stevens, H. The residential school's contribution to the coordination of services for the mentally retarded. *American Journal of Mental Deficiency,* 1956, *61,* 20–23.

Stevenson, G. A community program for the mentally retarded. *American Journal of Mental Deficiency,* 1952, *56,* 719–726.

Stevenson, I., & Strauss, A. The effects of an enriched Vitamin B_2 (Riboflavin) diet on a group of mentally defective children with retardation in physical growth. *American Journal of Mental Deficiency,* 1943, *48* 153–156.

Stewart, J. The industrial department of the Kentucky institution for the education and training of feeble-minded children. *Proceedings of the Association of Medical Officers of American Institutions for Idiotic and Feebleminded Persons,* 1882, 236–239.

Stimson, C. The treatment of cerebral palsy in mentally retarded patients using high-frequency low voltage, electric current. *American Journal of Mental Deficiency,* 1959, *64,* 73–80.

Stolurow, L. The Institute for Research on Exceptional Children. *Exceptional Children,* 1958, *24,* 429–434.

Stolurow, L. Requirements for research on learning in mental deficiency. *American Journal of Mental Deficiency,* 1959, *64,* 323–332.

Storrs, H. Place of the institution in state programs for the care and supervision of the mentally deficient. *American Journal of Mental Deficiency,* 1950, *54,* 178–181.

Stowell, G. Comparative study of certain mental defects found in institutionalized whites and negroes in the District Training School. *Journal of Psycho-Asthenics,* 1931, *36,* 267–281.

Strauss, A., & Lehtinen, L. *Psychopathology of the brain-injured child.* New York: Grune & Straton, 1947.

Street, R., & Fuller, M. Community responsibility for the care of the mentally deficient child. *Journal of Psycho-Asthenics,* 1935, *40,* 190–194.

Strom, O., Last, S., Brody, M., & Knight, C. Prefrontal leukotomy; Results in 30 cases of mental disorder with observations on surgical technique. *Journal of Mental Science,* 1947, *89,* 165–169.

Subotnik, L., & Callahan, R. A pilot study in short-term play therapy with institutionalized educable mentally retarded boys. *American Journal of Mental Deficiency,* 1959, *63,* 730–735.

Sukov, M. Contribution to the concept of mental deficiency. *Journal of Psycho-Asthenics,* 1939, *44,* 184–188.

Sumnar, W. *Folkways.* New York: Ginn, 1906.

Sutherland, E. Mental deficiency and crime. In: K. Young (ed.), *Social attitudes.* New York: Henry Holt, 1931.

Sweringen, B. Comments in minutes of Fort Wayne meeting. *Proceedings of the Association of Medical Officers of American Institutions for Idiotic and Feebleminded Persons,* 1894, 490–491.

Syden, M. Preparation for work: An aspect of the secondary school's curriculum for mentally retarded youth. *Exceptional Children,* 1962, *28,* 325–332.

Symposium: Educational provisions for mentally deficient adolescents. *American Journal of Mental Deficiency,* 1942, *47,* 79–95.

Talbot, E. *Developmental pathology.* Boston: Gorham Press, 1911.

Talbot, M. *Edouard Seguin: A study of an educational approach to the treatment of mentally defective children.* New York: Columbia University, 1964.

Tarjan, G. Medicine is changing. *American Journal of Mental Deficiency,* 1959, *63,* 1001–1004.

Tarjan, G., & Forbes, L. A preadmission and diagnostic service for the mentally deficient: A report on 2000 cases. *American Journal of Mental Deficiency,* 1955, *60,* 340–345.

Taylor, G. Education and training of the feeble-minded. *Journal of Psycho-Asthenics,* 1921, *26,* 24–31.

Taylor, G. The course of study for mental defectives. *Journal of Psycho-Asthenics,* 1924, *29,* 166–182.

Tenny, J. The minority status of the handicapped. *Exceptional Children,* 1953, *20,* 260–264.

Terman, L. *The measurement of intelligence.* Cambridge, MA: Riverside Press, 1916.

Terman, L. *The intelligence of school children.* New York: Houghton Mifflin, 1919.

Terman, L., & Knollin, H. Some problems relating to the detection of borderline cases of mental deficiency. *Journal of Psycho-Asthenics,* 1915, *20,* 3–9.

Thayer, W. Institutional training of the defective delinquent. *Journal of Psycho-Asthenics,* 1925, *30,* 38–46.

Theil, R. *And there was light.* New York: Alfred A. Knopf, 1957.

Thom, D. The contribution and progress of the child guidance movement. *American Journal of Mental Deficiency,* 1942, *47,* 189–194.

Thomas, H. *A history of the world.* New York: Harper & Row, 1979.

Tijo, J., & Levan, A. The chromosome number of man. *Hereditas,* 1956, *42,* 1–6.

Timme, W. Mongolism and its treatment. *Journal of Psycho-Asthenics,* 1928, *33,* 89–95.

Town, C. The feeble-minded—A community problem. *American Journal of Mental Deficiency*, 1941, *45*, 449–458.

The trainables . . . Are they the public school's responsibility? *Children Limited*, 1959, *8*, February, 12.

Trevelyan, G. *History of England*, Vol. III. Garden City, NY: Doubleday, 1952.

Tuchman, B. *A distant mirror*. New York: Alfred A. Knopf, 1978.

Tuke, D. *History of the insane in the British Isles*. Facsimile of the 1882 edition. Amsterdam: E. J. Bonset, 1968.

Tulchin, S. In memoriam: Lightner Witmer, Ph.D. *American Journal of Orthopsychiatry*, 1957, *27*, 200–201.

Twitmyer, E. The psychologist's approach to the problem of mental deficiency. *Journal of Psycho-Asthenics*, 1927, *32*, 31–40.

United Nations. *Declaration of general and special rights of the mentally retarded*, New York: United Nations Building, 1971.

U.S. Department of Commerce. *Insane and feebleminded in institutions, 1910*. Washington, DC: U.S. Government Printing Office, 1914.

U.S. Department of Commerce. *Mental defectives and epileptics in state institutions, 1929–1932*. Washington, DC: U.S. Government Printing Office, 1934.

U.S. Department of Commerce. Bureau of the Census. *Feebleminded and epileptic in institutions*. Washington, DC: U.S. Government Printing Office, 1923.

U.S. Department of Commerce. *Historical statistics of the United States: Colonial times to 1970*. Washington, DC: U.S. Government Printing Office, 1975.

U.S. Department of Education. *Summary of existing legislation relating to the handicapped*. Washington, DC: U.S. Government Printing Office, 1980.

U.S. Department of the Interior. *Report on the insane, feeble-minded, deaf and dumb, and blind (Eleventh Census: 1890)*. Washington, DC: U.S. Government Printing Office, 1895.

U.S. statutes at large, 51st Congress, 1889–1891, *26*, 1084.

U.S. statutes at large, 68th Congress. Washington, DC: U.S. Government Printing Office, 1925.

Vail, D. An unsuccessful experiment in group therapy. *American Journal of Mental Deficiency*, 1955, *60*, 122–132.

Van Wagenen, B. Surgical sterilization as a eugenic measure. *Journal of Psycho-Asthenics*, 1914, *18*, 185–196.

Vanuxem, M. Self-government as applied to feeble-minded women. *Journal of Psycho-Asthenics*, 1922, *27*, 18–26.

Vanuxem, M. *Education of feebleminded women*. New York: Teachers College, Columbia University, 1925.

Vanuxem, M. A preliminary study of children of women admitted to the Laurelton State Village. *Journal of Psycho-Asthenics*, 1931, *36*, 310–329.

Vanuxem, M. The prevalence of mental disease among mental defectives. *Journal of Psycho-Asthenics*, 1935, *40*, 242–252.

Vaughn, V. Race betterment. *Journal of Psycho-Asthenics*, 1913, *18*, 128–138.

Vaux, C. Family care of mental defectives. *Journal of Psycho-Asthenics*, 1935, *40*, 168–169.

Vaux, C. Family care. *Journal of Psycho-Asthenics*, 1936, *41*, 82–88.

Veith, G. Training the idiot and imbecile. *Journal of Psycho-Asthenics*, 1927, *32*, 148–168.

A village of lunatics. *American Journal of Insanity*, 1848, *4*, 217–222.

Walk, A. The pre-history of child psychiatry. *British Journal of Psychiatry*, 1964, *110*, 754–767.

Walker, G. Some psycho-sexual considerations of institutionalized mental defectives. *American Journal of Mental Deficiency*, 1948, *53*, 312–317.

Walker, G. Standards for public training schools. *American Journal of Mental Deficiency*, 1952, *57*, 43–49.

Walker, G. The role of the superintendent in construction. *American Journal of Mental Deficiency*, 1953, *58*, 230–235. (a)

Walker, G. Standards for public training schools. *American Journal of Mental Deficiency*, 1953, *57*, 361–372.(b)

Wallace, G. Plan and construction of an institution for feeble-minded. *Journal of Psycho-Asthenics*, 1924, *29*, 256–270.

Wallace, G. In memoriam: Walter E. Fernald. *Journal of Psycho-Asthenics*, 1925, *30*, 16–23.

Wallin, J. Classification of mentally deficient and retarded children for instruction. *Journal of Psycho-Asthenics*, 1924, *29*, 166–182.

Wallin, J. *Education of mentally handicapped children*. New York: Harper, 1955.

Wallin, J. New frontiers in the social perspective of the mentally retarded. *Training School Bulletin*, 1962, *59*, 89–104.

Walsh, E. Ungraded class work in New York City. *Journal of Psycho-Asthenics*, 1914, *19*, 59–66.

Ward v. Flood, 48 Cal. 36, 17 Amer. Rep. 405 (1874).

Wardell, D., Rubin, H., & Ross, R. The use of reserpine and chlorpromazine in disturbed mentally deficient patients. *American Journal of Mental Deficiency*, 1958, *63*, 330–344.

Warner, M. Early history of the International Council for Exceptional Children. *Journal of Exceptional Children*, 1942, *8*, 244–268.

Watkins, H. Administration in institutions of over two thousand. *Journal of Psycho-Asthenics*, 1928, *33*, 235–254.

Watkins, H. Presidential address. *Journal of Psycho-Asthenics*, 1932, *37*, 456–466.

Watson, J., & Crick, F. A structure for deoxyribonucleic acid. *Nature* (London), 1953, *171*, 737–738.

Wearne, R. The adjustment of family care children in Wassaic State School. *American Journal of Mental Deficiency*, 1941, *45*, 594–597.

Weaver, T. The incidence of maladjustment among mental defectives in military environment. *American Journal of Mental Deficiency*, 1946, *51*, 238–246.

Weidensall, J. The mentality of the unmarried mother. *National Conference of Social Work*, 1917, *44*, 287–294.

Weiner, B. Hawaii's public school program for mentally retarded children. Summarized in S. Kirk & B. Bateman, *10 years of research at the Institute for Research on Exceptional Children*. Urbana: University of Illinois, 1964.

Weingold, J. A plan for state and community action. *American Journal of Mental Deficiency*, 1957, *62*, 14–25.

Wesep, H. *Seven sages*. New York: Longmans, Green, 1960.

West, C. *Diseases of infancy and childhood*. Philadelphia: Henry C. Lea, 1868.

Whitney, E. Our horizons. *American Journal of Mental Deficiency*, 1945, *50*, 54–58.

Whitney, E., & Caron, R. A brief analysis of recent statistics on mental deficiency. *American Journal of Mental Deficiency*, 1947, *51*, 713–720.

Whitney, E., & MacIntyre, E. War record of Elwyn boys. *American Journal of Mental Deficiency*, 1944, *49*, 80–85.

Whitten, B. Address of the president. *Journal of Psycho-Asthenics*, 1937, *42*, 33–43.

Wilbur, H. *First annual report of the trustees of the New York State Asylum for Idiots to the legislature of state*. Albany, NY: State Printers, 1852.

Wilbur, H. The classification of idiocy. *Proceedings of the Association of Medical Officers of American Institutions for Idiotic and Feebleminded Persons*, 1877, 29–35.

Wilbur, H. Instinct not predominant in idiocy. *Proceedings of the Association of Medical Officers of American Institutions for Idiotic and Feebleminded Persons*, 1880, 135–144.

Wilbur, H. Some of the abnormal characteristics of idiocy and the methods adopted in obviating them. *Proceedings of the Association of Medical Officers of American Institutions for Idiotic and Feebleminded Persons*, 1882, 190–201.

Willey, G. The mental handicap of delinquents. *Journal of Psycho-Asthenics*, 1929, *34*, 82–99.

Willhite, F. A program for the control of the mentally deficient. *American Journal of Mental Deficiency*, 1940, *45*, 145–151.

Willhite, F. Program for the social control of the mentally deficient. *American Journal of Mental Deficiency*, 1942, *46*, 404–408.

Williams, T., & Richards, J. *Proceedings of the Association of Medical Officers of American Institutions for Idiotic and Feebleminded Persons*, 1886, 413–422.

Willoughby, R. Rhode Island's experiment in registration. *American Journal of Mental Deficiency*, 1945, *50*, 121–125.

Willson, G. The Civilian Conservation Corps as an adjustment outlet for boys trained in state institutions for the mentally deficient. *American Journal of Mental Deficiency*, 1944, *46*, 124–128.

Wilmarth, A. Mongolian idiocy. *Proceedings of the Association of Medical Officers of American Institutions for Idiotic and Feebleminded Persons*, 1889, 57–61.

Wilmarth, A. Institution construction and organization. *Journal of Psycho-Asthenics*, 1900, *5*, 57–62.

Wilmarth, A. To whom may the term, feeble-minded, be applied? *Journal of Psycho-Asthenics*, 1906, *10*, 203–205.

Wilmarth, A. Influenza in an institution for the feeble-minded. *Journal of Psycho-Asthenics*, 1919, *24*, 18–29.

Wilson, D. *Stranger and traveler*. Boston: Little, Brown, 1975.

Wilson, G. Presentation of plan for an institution for the feeble-minded in the District of Columbia. *Journal of Psycho-Asthenics*, 1924, *29*, 276–280.

Wilson, W. Some notes on the treatment of epilepsy. *Proceedings of the Association of Medical Officers of American Institutions for Idiotic and Feebleminded Persons*, 1892, 304–312.

Wirtz, M., & Guenther, R. The incidence of trainable mentally handicapped children. *Exceptional Children*, 1957, *23*, 171–172, 175.

Witchcraft and insanity. *American Journal of Insanity*, 1849, *3*, 246–261.

Witmer, L. *The special class for backward children*. Philadelphia: The Psychological Clinic Press, 1911.

Wittson, C., Harris, H., & Hunt, W. Evaluation of the brief psychiatric interview. *Journal of Psychology*, 1943, *16*, 107–114.

Wladkowsky, E. A preliminary study of mental growth after the age of fourteen years in an institution for mental defectives. *Journal of Psycho-Asthenics*, 1938, *43*, 181–187.

Wolf, T. An individual who made a difference. *American Psychologist*, 1961, *16*, 245–248.

Wolfe, M. The extra-mural responsibility of the institution. *Journal of Psycho-Asthenics*, 1936, *41*, 131–136.

Wolfensberger, W. Will there always be an institution? I. The impact of epidemiological trends. *Mental Retardation*, 1971, *9*(5), 14–20.

Wolfgang, M. Pioneers in criminology: Cesare Lombroso (1835–1909). *Journal of Criminal Law, Criminology, and Police Science*, 1961, *52*, 361–391.

Wolfson, I. Clinical experience with serpasil and thorazine in treatment of disturbed behavior of mentally retarded. *American Journal of Mental Deficiency*, 1957, *62*, 276–283.

Wood v. Dulaney, 23 Miss. 410 (1852).

Woodall, C. The Army Alpha test to mental defectives. *Journal of Psycho-Asthenics*, 1929, *34*, 82–99.

Woodall, C. Analysis of I.Q. variability. *Journal of Psycho-Asthenics*, 1931, *36*, 247–266.

Woodall, C. The children of mentally defective and mentally retarded mothers. *Journal of Psycho-Asthenics*, 1932, *37*, 328–358.

Wooden, H. Founding of the council. *Exceptional Children*, 1980, *47*, 47–55.

Woodhill, E. Public school clinics in connection with a state school for the feeble-minded. *Journal of Psycho-Asthenics*, 1920, *25*, 94–103.

Woodward, W. *A new American history*. New York: The Literary Guild, 1937.

Wortis, J. Towards the establishment of special clinics for retarded children: Experiences and suggestions. *American Journal of Mental Deficiency*, 1954, *58*, 472–478.

Wyatt v. Stickney, Civil Action No. 3195-N, U.S. District Court, Middle District of Alabama, North Division (1972).

Wylie, A. Investigation concerning the weight and height of feeble-minded children. *Journal of Psycho-Asthenics*, 1899, *4*, 47–57.

Yannet, H. The progress of medical research in the field of mental deficiency. *American Journal of Mental Deficiency*, 1953, *57*, 447–452.

Yannet, H., & Lieberman, R. A and B iso-immunization as a possible factor in the etiology of mental retardation. *American Journal of Mental Deficiency*, 1945, *50*, 242–244.

Yepsen, L. Defining mental deficiency. *American Journal of Mental Deficiency*, 1941, *46*, 200–205.

Yepsen, L. Post-War problems in guidance of the mentally subnormal. *American Journal of Mental Deficiency*, 1945, *50*, 291–295.

York, R. Sub-marginals—Agricultural, economic and mental. *American Journal of Mental Deficiency,* 1942, *46,* 538–541.

Zedler, E. Public opinion and public education for the exceptional child, court decisions, 1873–1950. *Exceptional Children,* 1953, *19,* 187–188.

Zilboorg, G. *A history of medical psychology.* New York: W. W. Norton, 1941.

Zimmerman, F., & Rosa, S. Effect of glutamic acid and other amino-acids in maze learning in the white rat. *Archives of Neurology and Psychiatry,* 1944, *51,* 446–451.

Zimmerman, F., Burgemeister, B., & Putnam, T. Effect of glutamic acid functioning in children and in adolescents. *Archives of Neurology and Psychiatry,* 1946, *56,* 489–506.

Zimmerman, F., Burgemeister, B., & Putnam, T. A group study of the effect of glutamic acid upon mental functioning in children and in adolescents. *Psychosomatic Medicine,* 1947, *9,* 175–183.

Zimmerman, F., Burgemeister, B., & Putnam, T. The effect of glutamic acid upon the mental and physical growth of mongols. *American Journal of Psychiatry,* 1949, *105,* 275–287.

INDEX

19th century category, 66
Lunatic Asylum Act of 1853, 66
Luther, Martin, 27
  attitude toward mentally retarded, 32–33

McCafferty, Estella, 202
McCready, E., 173

McCulloch, T., 225
McDougle, I., 152
McDowell, Mary, 169
Machover, 220
MacIntyre, E., 214
MacMurphy, H., 153
McNairy, C., 191, 193
McNaughton case (1843), 67
McPherson, M., 191, 196, 220
Maennel, B., 84
Magendie, Francois, 52
Maimonides, 28
Maine, 143, 144, 157
Mainstreaming, 58, 167, 254
Maison Royale des Aliéné de Charenton, 54
Malaria
  considered cause of cretinism, 57
  in 17th century and 18th century Europe, 37
Malleus Maleficarum, 32
Malnutrition, associated with mental retardation, 148
Malpighi, Marcello, 38
Manceron, C., 69
Mann, Horace, 99, 103, 104, 105, 110, 121
Mansur Hospital, Cairo, 34
Manual arts, in curriculum for mentally retarded students, 169, 195, 206, 231, 242
Manual communication, 50
Manual dexterity, studies of, 220
Manual for the Classification, Training, and Education of the Feeble-Minded, Imbecile, and Idiotic, 62
Maple syrup urine disease, 221
Marfan's disease, 52
Marriage, of mentally retarded persons
  annullments of, in 19th century, 66
  court's positions toward, in mid 19th century, 118
  restrictions on, 113, 117, 154, 190, 225, 226
Martens, Elise, 195, 206, 207, 239
Marti-Ibanez, 14
Maryland, 106, 193, 234
Massachusetts, 91, 92, 93, 100, 101, 102, 103–104, 106, 110, 123, 125, 129, 131, 158, 166, 193, 196, 198, 201, 209, 229
Massachusetts Department of Public Welfare, 200
Massachusetts General Court, 92
Massachusetts School for Idiots and Feeble-Minded Youth, 104
Massachusetts School for the Feeble-Minded, 157
Mather, Cotton, 93
Matzinger, H., 155
May, Ernest, 177
Mayflower, 91
Mayo, Leonard, 247
Measles, 30
Medford (Massachusetts residential facility), 100
Media, Pennsylvania, 119, 121
Medicaid, 253

Medical Inquiries and Observations Upon the Diseases of the Mind, 98
"Medical model," in institutions, 193
Medical papyri, from ancient Egypt, 10
Medical practitioners
  in ancient Egypt, 9
  in ancient Greece, 14
  in ancient Rome, 16, 17
  in Mesopotamia, 7
  see also Physicians
Medical School of Maine, 157
Medici, house of, 33
Medicine
  advances in
    in 19th century, 51–52, 53, 58, 61
    in 17th and 18th centuries, 38–40, 45
    in 20th century, 147–148, 183–184, 221–222, 240, 252
  in ancient Egypt, 9–10
  in ancient Greece, 14
  in ancient Rome, 16, 17–19, 25
  in Mesopotamia/Babylonia, 7, 8
  in Middle Ages and Renaissance, 26, 27, 30–31
  military, 96
Medicine man, 4
"Medico-Pedagogical Institute" model, 62
Mein Kampf, 209
Melcher, Ruth, 233
Memory, 139, 140
  in curriculum for mentally retarded students, 71, 79, 206
  studies of, 64, 116, 220
  tests of, 64
Mendel, Gregor Johann, 51–52, 149
Mendelian laws, 152
Menes, King, 8
Meningitis, 148
  related to idiocy, by Bourneville, 61
  treatment of, described by Avicenna, 28
Meningo-encephalitis, 61
Menkes, 221
Mental Affections of Children and Youth, 56
Mental age, factor in educational programming, 206
"Mental deficiency," label of, 217
  introduction of, 180
Mental handicap, label of, 217
Mental health clinics, 173
Mental hospitals
  in colonial America, 96, 97
  in 19th century, 65, 67–68, 99, 105, 106
  organization of, Pinel's contributions to, 46
  in 17th century, 43
  in 20th century, 138, 143, 186
Mental hygiene movement, 138, 146, 179, 180, 186, 207
Mental illness
  and mental retardation, understanding of relationship, 87, 148, 186–187
  understanding of
    in ancient Greece, 14
    in ancient Rome, 18
    Esquirol, 54
    Locke, 41
    in 19th century, 52, 63
    Pinel's categories, 40
    Rush, 98